Botswana
& Namibia

Matthew D Firestone

Adam Karlin

ETOSHA NATIONAL PARK (p264)
One of Africa's most unusual national parks, where herds of wildlife congregate against a ghostly bleached-white backdrop

SKELETON COAST (p304)
An eerie seascape of billowing fog clouds and dew-wet dunes

DAMARALAND (p292)
An ancient basalt landscape, riven by ephemeral river valleys and harbouring hundreds of rock engravings

SWAKOPMUND (p311)
Sun, sea and sandboarding – indulge all your adventure whims in seaside Swakopmund

SOSSUSVLEI & SESRIEM (p335)
Trek the towering red dunes of Sossusvlei or ride out on horseback in the Sesriem canyon

FISH RIVER CANYON (p358)
One of Africa's most awe-inspiring sights

ANGOLA

KAOKOVELD

OWAMBO REGION

KAVANGO REGION

DAMARALAND

OTJOZONDJUPA

NAMIBIA

WINDHOEK

ATLANTIC OCEAN

Tropic of Capricorn

DIAMOND AREA 1 & SPERRGEBIET NATIONAL PARK (Restricted Access)

RICHTERSVELD NP

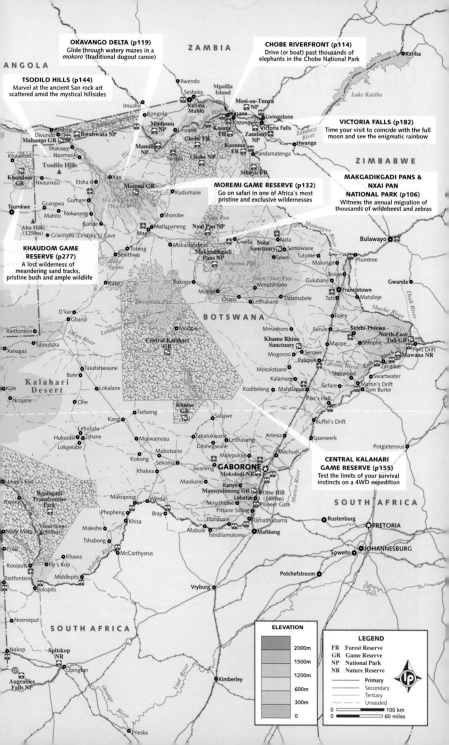

OKAVANGO DELTA (p119)
Glide through watery mazes in a *mokoro* (traditional dugout canoe)

CHOBE RIVERFRONT (p114)
Drive (or boat) past thousands of elephants in the Chobe National Park

TSODILO HILLS (p144)
Marvel at the ancient San rock art scattered amid the mystical hillsides

VICTORIA FALLS (p182)
Time your visit to coincide with the full moon and see the enigmatic rainbow

MAKGADIKGADI PANS & NXAI PAN NATIONAL PARK (p106)
Witness the annual migration of thousands of wildebeest and zebras

MOREMI GAME RESERVE (p132)
Go on safari in one of Africa's most pristine and exclusive wildernesses

KHAUDOM GAME RESERVE (p277)
A lost wilderness of meandering sand tracks, pristine bush and ample wildlife

CENTRAL KALAHARI GAME RESERVE (p155)
Test the limits of your survival instincts on a 4WD expedition

ZAMBIA

ANGOLA

ZIMBABWE

BOTSWANA

SOUTH AFRICA

SOUTH AFRICA

Kalahari Desert

ELEVATION

2000m
1500m
1200m
600m
300m
0

LEGEND

FR   Forest Reserve
GR   Game Reserve
NP   National Park
NR   Nature Reserve

Primary
Secondary
Tertiary
Unsealed

0 ——— 100 km
0 ——— 60 miles

On the Road

MATTHEW D FIRESTONE Coordinating Author
This picture was taken just before a somewhat less than graceful landing on the edge of the Namib Desert just outside Swakopmund. As I quickly learned, jumping out of the plane (p319) and pulling the cord is the easy part, but landing on your legs – and not sorely on your bum – takes a bit of practice.

ADAM KARLIN Just waiting for that damn elephant to come… Here I am in Moremi Game Reserve (p132). There are a lot of elephants here, for the record. But at least I didn't get charged by one, which is exactly what happened to me in Nxai Pan National Park. Getting charged by elephants, in unequivocal terms, sucks.

For full author biographies see p406.

Botswana & Namibia Highlights

Botswana and Namibia are Africa's little-known tourist destinations but are worthwhile destinations in their own right, each offering diverse landscapes ripe for intrepid exploration. Both contain huge stretches of emptiness and quintessential African landscape – from dust-red desert to the thundering Victoria Falls. This is a place where you are able to indulge in adrenaline-soaked activities such as sandboarding and also visit some of Africa's pristine national parks to avail yourself of unrivalled opportunities for wildlife watching. For backpackers seeking travel cred to cashed-up tourists wanting the ultimate luxury experience, Botswana and Namibia should undoubtedly be elevated to the top of their travel lists. Visit www.lonelyplanet.com/botswana and www.lonelyplanet.com/namibia for more destination information.

MANFRED GOTTSCHALK

① SCORCHED EARTH

Alone in the middle of Sossusvlei (p335), you get the sense of what a day at the beach must be like in hell. Sand permeates everything, from your eyes and ears to your shoes and rucksack, and the only water in sight is the few drops left at the bottom of your canteen. Climbing up the nearest dune, you survey the seemingly endless swath of nothingness that surrounds you, and admit that the world can at times be a cruel and unforgiving place.

Matthew D Firestone, Lonely Planet Author

DEUTSCHLAND IN THE DESERT

Namibia is a country that defies African stereotypes, and this is perhaps nowhere more true than in the historic colonial town of Lüderitz (p348). Straddling the icy South Atlantic and the blazing hot Namib Desert is this bizarre mini-Deutschland that is seemingly stuck in a time warp. After washing down a plate of sausages with an authentic Weiss beer, you'll survey the Teutonic architecture of the town, and check the map again while shaking your head in disbelief.

**Matthew D Firestone,
Lonely Planet Author**

3

2

SEE WHERE ART WAS INVENTED

We are a young race, but nothing brings you back to the eldest roots of humanity like gaping at the rock paintings (p144) of the San that dot the Tsodilo Hills and the Tuli Block. In those ghostly handprints and shapeshifting shamans and phantom hunts you detect something: the first attempts of mankind to record what is. The first sparks of imagination. The beginning of interpretation, and creativity for creativity's sake.

Adam Karlin, Lonely Planet Author

4

GOING ON SAFARI AT DAY BREAK

The alarm clock shakes you out of your sleeping bag just minutes before the sun breaks free of the horizon, but as you lace up your leather boots and clean the dew from your binoculars, the thrill of the safari quickly sharpens your senses. The big cats are prowling in the morning light, and out here on the edge of the Etosha Pan (p264), you can have a front-row seat to the life-and-death drama of Mother Nature.

Matthew D Firestone, Lonely Planet Author

RICHARD I'ANSON

GAME DRIVING NO-NOS ON NXAI PAN

Be careful driving around the Nxai Pan (p109). They're so beautiful you forget at times what side track you've disappeared down, and then, if you're an idiot like myself – bam. There's an elephant, startled and about to charge. Now the question is: go back the way you came, into dangerous elephant territory? Or continue into unknown sections of the park? This, friends, is African adventure, and its dangers are not to be underestimated.

**Adam Karlin,
Lonely Planet Author**

6

5 THE MIGHTY SPRAY

When you stand before Victoria Falls (p182), the clichés abound, for this is the mighty *Mosi-oa-Tunya* or the 'the Smoke that Thunders'. Unfortunately, visiting the falls during the peak of the heaviest rainy season in decades results in an entirely different experience. Wrapped in layers of plastic, clutching my water-logged camera with a kung-fu action grip, I am pelted by sheets of mist and gusts of spray that pay fitting tribute to the fury of the falls.

Matthew D Firestone, Lonely Planet Author

7 STARING ACROSS THE BIG EMPTY

There's nothing quite like driving across the salt pans of the Makgadikgadi (p103) – the endless expanses of white are so incredibly vast and empty they shrink your sense of self and expand it to the endless horizon all at once. It's a reminder that man has yet to control the world, because I can't imagine the harshness of this world ever being anything close to tamed.

Adam Karlin, Lonely Planet Author

ADRIAN BAILEY

THE ZEN OF THE OKAVANGO

Slipping into the Okavango Delta on a *mokoro* (dugout canoe; p124) isn't just relaxing – it can almost make you comatose, and there are times you just want to doze off. Not because the land is boring – because that sweet ripple of boat on reeds is as soothing as a lullaby in the crib. But then you note the animals all about, and it's as if the marriage of land and water reminds you of the connections that keep the entire natural world in bala – bleck! Sorry, another midge flew into my mouth.

**Adam Karlin,
Lonely Planet Author**

8

OLD-SCHOOL ADVENTURING WITH BUSH PILOTS

Remember those bits in the Indiana Jones movies where the hero got in a plane and a red line tracked his movements across the globe? That's the old-school sense of adventure you get from flying in a single-engine Cessna over Botswana's game reserves. Shake hands with that pilot in the button-down shirt tucked into short shorts and get ready to soar vintage-style, Dr Jones.

Adam Karlin, Lonely Planet Author

9

TOM COCKREM

ADRIAN BAILEY

10 **BUSH DRIVING**

Driving through the Kaokoveld (p298), even with a fully loaded 4WD and a support convoy behind you, is not for the faint of heart. White knuckles clench the steering wheel for dear life as you precariously manoeuvre your vehicle through bush tracks that stretch across a primeval landscape. The fuel needle seems to noticeably plunge as you accelerate through a sandy patch, though fortunately you've brought along a few extra jerry cans for the journey.

Matthew D Firestone, Lonely Planet Author

Contents

Regional Map Contents

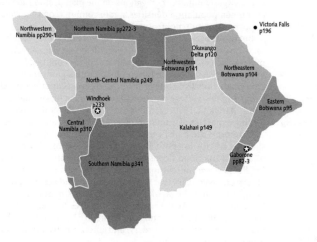

Destination Botswana & Namibia

Botswana and Namibia are two of Africa's hidden gems, and very much remain frontier realms for intrepid travellers to discover. Here you will find the oldest rust-red desert in the world, quintessential African landscapes teeming with wildlife, preternaturally blue skies stretching above vast open horizons, and silent spaces where emptiness and desolation can quickly become overwhelming. And, unlike more well-trafficked African destinations, tourism in Botswana and Namibia is not the jaded experience of vans packed to the brim with camera-toting tourists, but rather an adrenaline-soaked, hair-raising affair of off-road bush driving amid some of the wildest parks on the continent.

Together, these two countries offer extremes of environment and diversity of landscape, the total sum of which is like nothing else in Africa. From the sun-baked salt pans of the Makgadikgadi super-lake, and the rolling sea of red dunes stretching across the Namib, to the emerald-green waterways of the Okavango Delta, and the stark desolation of the rocky beaches lining the Skeleton Coast, Botswana and Namibia together comprise one of the most ecologically diverse corners of Africa. This defining geography fosters one of the largest animal congregations on the planet, alongside one of the lowest human population densities, a rare combination that yields unequalled opportunities for wildlife watching.

But this is barely half the picture, for Botswana and Namibia are also two of Africa's model nations, no longer fledgling democracies, but modern mineral-rich economies at the vanguard of the continent's future. Four decades of progressive leadership combined with significant mining investment have made Botswana one of the powerhouse economies of Africa. Despite being Africa's youngest nation, having only achieved independence from South Africa in 1990, Namibia isn't too far behind as one of the world's leading exporters of uranium, silver and other semi-precious metals.

Diamonds are a girl's best friend, a fact that has generated enormous sums of wealth for both Botswana and Namibia. Owing to large tracts of alluvial diamond deposits, both governments in partnership with the De Beers diamond company have capitalised on their mineral wealth. However, given fears that the region's diamond seams may run out in the decades to come, the rapidly developing tourism industry is becoming ever more important. As the world turns its eyes to South Africa in 2010 for the continent's first ever hosting of the FIFA World Cup, the hope is that football fans will cross borders, and inject a hefty bit of tourism revenue into neighbouring countries.

To date, the Botswana government has been able to afford a sensitive policy of 'high cost-low volume tourism', and as a result has retained some of Africa's largest tracts of wilderness. However, as economic pressures increase, it remains to be seen how the future of the industry will be managed, especially in regards to the mounting environmental problems facing threatened areas such as the Okavango Delta. For more than twenty years now, local interests have sought to dam up the flowing lifeline of the delta, though the pursuit of irrigated farmland could come at a heavy price.

Namibia too has had its share of environmental roadblocks over the years, most notably the government's failed attempts at damming up Epupa Falls

FAST FACTS

Population:
Botswana 1.64 million;
Namibia 2.1 million

Area:
Botswana 582,000 sq km;
Namibia 825,000 sq km

Country code:
Botswana ☎ 267;
Namibia ☎ 264

Capital:
Botswana Gaborone;
Namibia Windhoek

Languages:
Botswana English,
Ttswana;
Namibia English,
Afrikaans, German,
Owambo, Kavango,
Herero, Khoikhoi (Nama/
Damara), San dialects

Money:
Botswana pula (P);
Namibia Namibian
dollar (N$)

Phrases:
Botswana *Dumela?*
(How are you?),
dankie (thank you);
Namibia *Howzit?*
(How are you?)

Famous for:
Botswana Okavango
Delta, Chobe National
Park, the Kalahari;
Namibia Namib Desert,
Kalahari, Etosha Pan

in the heart of the Himba homelands. However, the country has benefited greatly from the presence of the US Agency for International Development Aid (Usaid), which has long supported Namibia's network of community-based conservancies. A recent audit showed that Namibia's 30-plus registered conservancies earned more than US$2 million, compared with just US$100,000 in 1995. The hope is that as more of these conservancies begin to make real money, struggling local communities can finally become self-sufficient.

Unfortunately, good relations are vital to the success of the South African Development Community (SADC), and not everyone is being a good neighbour these days. The political and economic instability in Zimbabwe is negatively impacting every regional issue from tourism to trade, and the fallout is hitting Botswana especially hard. Illegal immigration has spiralled out of control along Zimbabwe's porous border, and rising crime rates and local resentment over competition for limited jobs has turned Botswana into Mugabe's staunchest African critic. Conversely, during San Nujoma's tenure as Namibian president, he sided with Zimbabwe and President Mbeki in South Africa on virtually every issue.

'more than 50% of the country depends on the agricultural industry for their livelihood'

For current Namibian President Hifikepunye Pohamba, Nujoma's hand-picked successor, stepping up the expropriation of white-owned farms in an attempt to narrow the economic divide has been a priority. However, many argue that Namibia's problems do not lie in the redistribution of farming land. As a desert country, more than 50% of the country depends on the agricultural industry for their livelihood, yet it remains the least profitable area of Namibia's largely mining-based economy. It has also been argued that the government's efforts would be better spent investing in manufacturing and light industry, though shortages of skilled workers and qualified personnel make progress in these areas slow going, and the pending energy crisis looms large on the economic horizon.

While Botswana and Namibia both have had their fair share of challenges, the single biggest problem facing sub-Saharan Africa is the catastrophic impact of HIV/AIDS, which threatens to undermine the progress the region has made in the post-colonial era. No longer just a health issue, but an economic obstacle as well, the infection strikes at those in their most productive years, while tackling the virus effectively puts a huge strain on government resources. In response to the epidemic, it has been argued by regional leaders that additional foreign investment is necessary to enable governments to step up public health education and to improve medical infrastructure.

Although Namibia is rated as a middle-income country, and is therefore not eligible for certain financial aid or debt relief, this image is badly skewed as most of the wealth remains in the hands of only 5% of the population. In fact, the majority of its sparse population lives in dire poverty on less than US$2 per day, and corruption is an unfortunate feature of the political landscape. HIV/AIDS is rapidly cutting a swath through the population.

In Botswana, the government does not take HIV/AIDS lightly, and in 2002 it became the first country in the world to offer antiretroviral treatment free of charge to its citizens. In addition, the government has thrown its weight behind educational programs, and speaks frequently and publicly on the threat infection poses to the general wellbeing of the country. In the country's mission statement, Vision 2016, the government has pledged to halt the further transmission of HIV/AIDS by 2016. It's a lofty goal perhaps, but Botswana's progressive policies have helped to temper the public denial of disease that marked the tenure of South African President Mbeki.

In the years ahead, it will be the young generations of Botswana and Namibia that must rise to the challenge of maintaining their countries' continued economic growth and social development. Already Botswana and Namibia are some of the most predominantly urban societies in the world, and providing vocational and professional jobs is one of the highest priorities on the political agenda. The future will also continue to test the resilience of both Botswana's and Namibia's national unity, a vitally important component of the peace that has typified both countries since independence.

Getting Started

With a human population of less than two million, most of it concentrated along the far eastern border, vast tracts of landlocked Botswana are occupied by wildlife alone. At the best of times, the country truly seems to stretch for millions of miles, unfurling its natural blessings of endless vistas and vast open spaces with every bend of the road.

See Botswana Climate Charts (p161) for more information.

Not to be outdone by its neighbour, Namibia is a land of extremes, defined by desolate landscapes and shaped by a harsh climate. The country is also home to some of the world's grandest national parks, ranging from the desert plains of the Namib-Naukluft, to the game-rich salt flats of Etosha.

Romantic and unspoiled Botswana and Namibia may be, but you'll need plenty of time and a little bit of cash to fully enjoy them. Got both? You'll be rewarded with some of the most spectacular wildlife viewing this life has to offer. Fortunately, even if you're lacking one or the other, you can easily customise your trip to focus on just a few of the highlights that define these truly world-class travel destinations. For most travellers to Namibia, pre-planning involves reserving a rental car and booking your first couple of nights accommodation in advance.

WHEN TO GO
Botswana

One of the best times to visit is undoubtedly springtime (September to October), when the migrant bird species start appearing, and the country's thorny flora is in full bloom. Weatherwise, September/October happens to be the hottest and most humid time of the year in most of the country.

The flooding of the Okavango Delta from late December through to March (Botswana's summer time) is a time of plenty, although it's one of the worst times to travel. Prolonged rains can render 4WD tracks impassable, and may

---

DON'T LEAVE HOME WITHOUT...

- valid travel insurance (p164 and p371).
- driving licence and car documents if driving, along with appropriate car insurance (p175 and p382).
- sunglasses, sun block and a hat.
- a good tent, warm sleeping bag, air mattress and torch (flashlight) if you're planning on doing your own camping.
- a water bottle, purification tablets and a medical kit (p387).
- insect repellent and anti-malarial tablets (p390).
- sturdy walking boots for trekking and sandals or flip-flops.
- binoculars and a camera with a long lens.
- a long-sleeved jacket or fleece for cold desert nights.
- a Leatherman-style multipurpose tool and a compass.
- a universal washbasin plug and an adaptor for electrical appliances.
- a bathing suit for safari lodge swimming pools.
- GPS (with instructions!) if you're planning a 4WD expedition.
- a few extra memory cards for the digital camera.

DO-IT-YOURSELF SAFARI

Travelling independently in Africa is always a challenge, but it's an experience that often makes up a large part of the adventure. First things first, you'll need to consider the variables of the weather – heavy rains and long, dry summers have a big impact on driving conditions and, more importantly, on what animals you'll see and where.

Independent 'self-drive' tours are possible in both Botswana and Namibia (see p32), although these are cheaper and more popular in Namibia where any good travel agency can advise on itineraries and sleeping options. Throughout this book we have provided GPS coordinates to help with navigating remote and inaccessible areas.

For more information on travelling in Africa, pick up a copy of Lonely Planet's *Read This First: Africa*. Also see the Top Tens boxed text on opposite for some more DIY ideas.

---

also force the closure of parts of the Chobe National Park and Moremi Game Reserve. Some lodges operating in and around the Okavango, Moremi and Chobe also shut up shop from December to February.

By autumn (March and April), the flood waters have reached the upper delta. Days are clear, dry and sunny, but nights are cold. This is a great time for viewing wildlife as the animals rarely wander far from water sources. As autumn waxes into winter (May to August), the flood waters pass along the delta, usually reaching Maun some time towards the end of June. In the Kalahari, temperatures below freezing are normal at night time, especially in July and August.

One final thing to keep in mind are the busy school holiday periods: about two weeks in April, one month around July and September and two months in December/January.

Namibia

Namibia's desert hinterland is dry and arid, although generally, the mountainous Central Plateau (including Windhoek) is a bit cooler than the rest of the country. With 300 days of sunshine a year, there isn't really a 'best' time to visit Namibia. Having said that, the dry season from May to October is a good time for viewing wildlife. During these months you can expect clear, sunny days averaging around 25°C and cold desert nights. However, between June and August, the coastal towns of Swakopmund and Walvis Bay are subject to warm east winds, which often create miserable sandstorm conditions.

See Namibia Climate Charts (p367) for more information.

There are two rainy seasons in Namibia, the 'little rains' from October to December and the main rainy period from January to April. The latter is characterised by brief showers and occasional thunderstorms. January temperatures in Windhoek can soar up to 40°C, and from December to March, Namib-Naukluft Park and Etosha National Park become very hot, which means that some of the long hiking trails are closed.

In the north, rainfall steadily increases, reaching its maximum of over 600mm per year along the Okavango River, which enjoys a subtropical climate. From January to March, the northeastern rivers of the Caprivi Strip may flood, making some roads either impassable or hard to negotiate.

School holidays are another busy period, and places such as Swakopmund are booked solid over Christmas and Easter.

COSTS & MONEY
Botswana

Travelling around Botswana isn't cheap due to the government's 'high cost-low volume' policy. The absolute cheapest way to get around the country is by using public transport, eating locally, camping and arranging a couple of local tours into the wildlife reserves. On this basis, you could get by on about US$30 to US$50 per day. The cheapest safaris, on the other hand, are around US$100 to US$150 per person per day (sharing).

For most independent travellers aiming to travel on a midrange budget, your single biggest expense will be the hire of a vehicle. A 4WD will set you back around US$100 to US$150 per day, with a tank of petrol costing roughly US$40 to US$60. Add to this a sprinkling of midrange hotels, restaurant meals and camp entrance fees (US$30 per person per day), and you'll probably be looking at a daily budget more like US$200 to US$250.

For about US$250 to US$400 per person, you could book yourself on a pretty good organised safari. Travelling in low season (October to June) and sharing the cost of vehicle hire with other travellers are two ways of reducing some of the costs.

At the top end of the scale, you'll probably be booking yourself on an all-inclusive mobile or fly-in safari. At this level, you're getting the very best that Africa has to offer, and it will set you back at least US$400 per person per night. For true high rollers, there is virtually no upper limit to the price and glamour of tour packages available in safari-chic Botswana.

Namibia

It's easier to get around Namibia on a restricted budget. If you're camping or staying in backpacker hostels, cooking your own meals, and hitching or using local minibuses, you could get by on as little as US$20 to US$40 per day.

A plausible midrange budget, which would include car hire and B&B, or double accommodation in a mixture of hotels, rest camps and lodges, would be around US$75 to US$125. In the upper range, accommodation at hotels, meals in restaurants, escorted tours and possibly fly-in safaris will cost upwards of US$300 per person per day. In this case, it may be better to prebook a fly-drive or organised tour overseas.

To reach the most interesting parts of Namibia, you'll have to take an organised tour or hire a vehicle. Car hire may be expensive for budget travellers, but if you can muster a group of four people and share costs, you can squeak by on an additional US$20 to US$50 per day – that's assuming a daily average of around 200km in a 2WD/4WD vehicle with the least expensive agency, including petrol, tax and insurance. The plus side of a 4WD is that many vehicles are equipped with camping gear.

TRAVELLING RESPONSIBLY

For a detailed discussion of environmental issues affecting Botswana and Namibia, see p75 and p228, respectively.

TRAVEL LITERATURE

To track down hard-to-find books try the following online bookstores: www.amazon.com, www.stanfords.co.uk, www.thetravelbookshop.co.uk and www.africabookcentre.com.

Africa: A Biography of the Continent (John Reader) Any understanding of modern Botswana and Namibia will be greatly enhanced by reading Reader's well-regarded continental tome. A sweeping and highly readable overview of the continent covering history, environment and anthropology, it is absolutely crammed with well-researched detail, which helps to dispel many a stereotype.

Cry of the Kalahari (Mark and Delia Owens) An absorbing adventure story of two young American zoologists who set off for the Kalahari with little more than a change of clothes. What results is a seven-year sojourn, and a unique insight into the amazing animals of the Kalahari.

Histories of Namibia: Living Through the Liberation Struggle (told to Colin Leys and Susan Brown) A fascinating insight into the horrific and sometimes hilarious experiences of Namibian activists who engaged wholeheartedly in the bitter war for independence.

BOTSWANA HOW MUCH?

One day *mokoro* trip P500

Ostrich egg shell bracelet P35

Stalk of sugar cane P35

Foreign newspaper P10-15

Night in a budget hotel P175

NAMIBIA HOW MUCH?

Dune surfing N$180

1L bottle water N$2

Bottled beer N$6

Snack N$5

Foreign newspaper N$12

Night in a budget hotel N$90

TOP 10

NAMIBIA BOTSWANA
Gaborone

COMMUNITY & CONSERVATION PROJECTS

1 **AfriCat** (www.africat.org) Helps to ensure the continued survival of Namiba's big cats; stop by their guest farm in Otjiwarongo (p255) for an up-close encounter.

2 **Birdlife International** or **Birdlife Botswana** (www.birdlife.org or www.birdlifebotswana .org.bw) Your membership dues help preserve Botswana's diverse avian life, and you'll be able to tap into the knowledge of an avid birding community.

3 **Children in the Wilderness** (www .childreninthewilderness.com) A charity that can use your donation to help host vulnerable children for week-long wilderness retreats.

4 **Conservation International** (www.con servation.org) One of the world's most respected conservation organisations, CI is committed to protecting the planet's most vulnerable spaces.

5 **Integrated Rural Development and Nature Conservation** (www.irdnc.org.na) A well-established NPO that links wildlife

conservation to rural development and democratic initiatives.

6 **Kalahari Conservation Society** (www.kcs .org.bw) Become a member and help protect the Kalahari and all of its inhabitants, from man to mongoose.

7 **Khama Rhino Sanctuary** (www.khamarhino sanctuary.com) A small but vitally important sanctuary, Khama protects the last remaining rhinos in Botswana.

8 **Raleigh International** (www.raleighinter national.org) One of the leaders in providing overseas volunteer projects for people on gap years or career breaks.

9 **Save the Rhino** (www.savetherhino.org) A wonderful charity worth your support, Save the Rhino is leading the fight in preserving one of Africa's most endangered animals.

10 **Working Group for Indigenous Minorities of Southern Africa** (WIMSA; www.san.org .za) A community-based organisation that advocates on behalf of San communities across the region.

DO-IT-YOURSELF IDEAS

1 Drive yourself through **Etosha National Park** (p264).

2 Go overland from the Chobe Riverfront to **Maun** (p114).

3 Book your own *mokoro* (dugout canoe) trip (sans tour operator) in the **Okavango Panhandle** (p137).

4 Do some serious spelunking in **Gcwihaba (Drotsky's) Cave** (p142).

5 Put your GPS skills to the test in the **Kaokoveld** (p298).

6 Explore the **Makgadikgadi Pans** (p103) without a guide (not for the faint of heart).

7 Climb to the top of the **Spitzkoppe** (p292) or the **Brandberg** (p293).

8 Hike from one end of **Fish River Canyon** (p358) to the other.

9 Find the hottest new bars and clubs in **Windhoek** (p244).

10 Hike through the dunes near **Swakopmund** (p316) – bring lots of water!

ANIMALS TO WATCH OUT FOR

1 White rhinos and black rhinos

2 Lions

3 Leopards

4 Cheetahs

5 Spotted and striped hyenas

6 Desert elephants

7 Ostriches

8 Cape fur seals

9 African buffalo

10 Warthogs

The Healing Land: A Kalahari Journey (Rupert Isaacson) A moving account of Isaacson's personal journey of discovery and the unfolding tragedy of the displaced San. Most of all, it highlights the confusion and corruption of a people who have lost what is most meaningful to them, their *n!oresi* (literally 'lands where one's heart is').

The Lost World of the Kalahari (Laurens van der Post) An anthropological classic depicting in almost mystical terms the traditional lifestyles of the San. The author's quest for an understanding of the San's religion and folklore is continued in his subsequent works, *Heart of the Hunter* and *The Voice of Thunder*.

The No.1 Ladies Detective Agency Collection (Alexander McCall Smith) Set in Mma Ramotswe's beloved Botswana, these gentle detective stories are a refreshing change to how life in Africa is usually portrayed. McCall Smith captures his characters and their traditional codes of behaviour effortlessly.

Other suggestions:

Born of the Sun: A Namibian Novel (Joseph Diescho and Celeste Wallin)
Botswana: The Road to Independence (Peter Fawcus and Alan Tilbury)
Nervous Conditions (Tsitsi Dangarembga)
On the Run (Kapoche Victor)
Rivers of Blood, Rivers of Gold: Europe's Conflict with Tribal Peoples (Mark Cocker)
Place of Reeds (Caitlin Davies)
Serowe: Village of the Rain Wind (Bessie Head)
Sheltering Desert (Henno Martin)
The Purple Violet of Oshaantu (Neshani Andreas)
The Lion Children (Angus, Maisie and Travers McNeice)
Whatever You Do, Don't Run (Peter Allison)

INTERNET RESOURCES

There's no better place to start your web explorations than the **Lonely Planet website** (www.lonelyplanet.com), with up-to-date news and the Thorn Tree forum, where you can post questions.

All Africa (www.allafrica.com) A gateway to all things African, this website posts around 1000 articles a day, collated from over 125 different news organisations.

The Botswana Gazette (www.gazettebw.com) Website of Botswana's leading independent newspaper.

Government of Botswana (www.gov.bw) Official government site with current news and links to businesses and government departments.

Namibian Tourism Board (www.namibiatourism.com.na) A good-looking, user-friendly site providing a wide range of general travel information on Namibia.

The Namibian (www.namibian.com.na) For up-to-date news, log on to Namibia's main English-language newspaper.

Itineraries
CLASSIC ROUTES

BEST OF BOTSWANA & VICTORIA FALLS

Two to Three Weeks / Maun to Victoria Falls

Starting in **Maun** (p120), the classic staging point for all Botswanan safaris, you can stock up on supplies before heading out to the **Okavango Delta** (p119), either by *mokoro* (dugout canoe) or charter plane. If you're pinching your pennies, there's no shortage of budget camping trips to choose from, though it's certainly worth stretching your budget to allow for a few nights in one of the safari-chic tented camps in the wildlife-rich **Moremi Game Reserve** (p132).

The next stage of your bush travel is a 4WD expedition through **Chobe National Park** (p109), with stops at **Savuti** (p116), **Linyanti Marshes** (p117) and the **Chobe Riverfront** (p114). Whether you travel by private vehicle or tour bus, the overland route through Chobe is one of the country's most spectacular and wildlife-rich journeys.

After another supply stop in the border town of **Kasane** (p109), it's time to cross the border into either Zimbabwe or Zambia to visit the world-famous **Victoria Falls** (p182). Whether you base yourself in **Livingstone, Zambia** (p186) or **Victoria Falls, Zimbabwe** (p194), it's worth exploring life on both sides of the Zambezi River. And of course, if you've got a bit of cash burning a hole in your pocket, there's no shortage of pulse-raising **activities** (p183) to help you get a quick adrenaline fix.

For the majority of the trip, you will have to be completely self-sufficient and fully confident in your navigation and survival skills. For the less adventurous, tour operators in Maun are happy to help you organise a custom safari.

BEST OF NAMIBIA   Three to Four Weeks / Windhoek to Noordoewer

Before striking off into the desert, spend a couple of days getting your bearings in the lovely capital of **Windhoek** (p231), which still bears architectural traces of its German colonial history. Ideally, with a rental car loaded with plenty of supplies and a few friends, make a beeline north for **Etosha National Park** (p264), one of the finest safari parks on the continent.

Although you're going to have to backtrack, you can quickly bypass Windhoek en route to seaside **Swakopmund** (p311), where you can take your holiday up a notch in a flurry of exciting activities including dune boarding and quad-biking. Back on the main road south, keep the heart beating during a scramble up the massive barchan dunefields of **Sossusvlei** (p336) and/or a trek through **Sesriem Canyon** (p336).

Continuing the canyon theme, head south for **Fish River Canyon** (p358), a geological wonder of monumental proportions that is one of Africa's hidden highlights. From Fish River Canyon, detour west to marvel at the German anachronism that is **Lüderitz** (p348). Nearby, you can stop off at the diamond-mining ghost town of **Kolmanskop** (p355), and explore the overwhelming emptiness of the **Sperrgebiet**, (p354), Namibia's newest national park.

Finish things off in **Noordoewer** (p362), which sits astride the Orange River, and is the jumping off point for white-water rafting through some wild canyon country. Alternatively, head across the South African border to cosmopolitan Cape Town, which you can enjoy for a week or a weekend before setting off on the next adventure.

This enormous itinerary meanders more than 2500km, from dusty bushveld to dramatic canyons. It combines a good dose of culture with death-defying activities, and all of it is accessible with a 2WD vehicle. There are also decent, if slow, public transport links.

ROADS LESS TRAVELLED

SECRETS OF THE KALAHARI

Two to Three Weeks /
Kgalagadi Transfrontier Park to Tsodilo Hills

If you're looking to leave the khaki-clad tourist crowds behind, this off-the-beaten-track option in Botswana takes you straight through the heart of the Kalahari. If starting in Johannesburg, head north for the border where you can cross at Bokspits to enter the enormous **Kgalagadi Transfrontier Park** (p152). The park is one of the only spots in the Kalahari where you can see shifting sand dunes, though the undisputed highlight is its pristine wilderness and low tourist volume.

From here, head east towards Gaborone, and then loop back on yourself to enter the southern gates of the utterly wild **Khutse Game Reserve** (p154). From here, traverse north through some exciting 4WD territory into the adjoining **Central Kalahari Game Reserve** (p155), where you can navigate one of the continent's most prominent topographical features. Before leaving, spend a night or two in **Deception (Letiahau) Valley** (p157), renowned for its rare brown hyenas.

Heading north, you'll pass through **D'kar** (p150), where you can pick up some beautiful San crafts. Then press on for the remote **Gcwihaba (Drotsky's) Cave** (p142), renowned for its 10m-long stalagmites and stalactites, as well as Commerson's leaf-nosed bats. Finally, at the furthermost tip of the country, you'll come to the mystical **Tsodilo Hills** (p144), which are a treasure chest of painted rock art, and continue to be revered by local communities.

This route is only accessible by 4WD vehicle. Throughout the trip, you will have to be completely self-sufficient and fully confident in your navigation and survival skills. For the less adventurous, tour operators in Maun can help you organise a custom safari.

CAPRIVI TO KAOKOVELD

Many places in Namibia give you a vague sense that you've reached the end of the earth, but some of the destinations in this itinerary really are other-worldly. Getting to them, too, presents a major challenge that definitely requires determination as well as a fair bit of cash.

To do this trip as a continuous journey, you're best off starting from **Kasane** (p109) in Botswana. From here, you can charter a plane or boat to **Mpalila Island** (p282), a luxuriously remote retreat stranded in the middle of the Zambezi. From here, head into Namibia's **Caprivi Strip** (p278), and visit the mini-Okavango of the **Mamili National Park** (p283) before plunging into the untamed wilderness that is **Khaudom Game Reserve** (p277).

From Khaudom the road will take you south through **Grootfontein** (p259), from where it's worth making a short detour to the **Waterberg Plateau Park** (p256). The park is famous as a haven of endangered species like sables, roans and white and black rhinos, some of which you may be lucky enough to spot along one of the well-marked hiking trails.

North of Grootfontein the road takes you into Namibia's cultural heartland, the Owambo region, from where you can access the remote and mysterious **Kaokoveld** (p298), homeland to the Himba and one of the most inaccessible areas of the country.

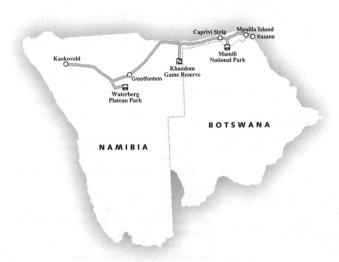

This is not an itinerary for the faint-hearted. You'll need either a plane or a boat to get to Mpalila Island, where you'll have to be booked into one of the lodges. Other than that you'll need a 4WD, and you can just about forget public transport.

TAILORED TRIPS

WILDLIFE HIGHLIGHTS

Top of everyone's list has to be the amazingly varied protected areas in Botswana and Namibia, which represent some of the continent's most pristine environments, and contain a bewildering array of bird and animal life.

For classic images of wildlife herds and predators, head straight for **Etosha National Park** (p264), or cross the border into Botswana and be spoilt for choice between the **Moremi Game Reserve** (p132), **Savuti** (p116) or **Chobe National Park** (p109). All of these parks protect an absolute abundance of animal life that is sheltered and protected by classic African safari country.

Birding enthusiasts should head straight for the **Okavango Delta** (p119) when it is in full flush in September and October. Similarly, **Mamili National Park** (p283) in northeast Namibia is a lush riverine environment full of hippos, buffaloes and birds.

For a more off-the-beaten-track experience head for the **Makgadikgadi & Nxai Pans National Park** (p106), which sees some of the largest wildlife migrations in Africa. Or seek out Deception (Letiahau) Valley in the **Central Kalahari Game Reserve** (p155) and the **Khama Rhino Sanctuary** (p96) in eastern Botswana for specialty sightings of brown hyenas and white rhinos, respectively.

ADRENALINE JUNKIE

Namibia and Botswana provide a picture-perfect backdrop for some nerve-racking activities. The two activity capitals of the region are undoubtedly Namibia's **Swakopmund** (p311) and, in the far east and across the eastern border, the dramatic arena of **Victoria Falls** (p183). In the former you can indulge in sandboarding, quadbiking, camel and horse riding and even skydiving. At the latter, go microlighting over the falls, white-water rafting, or do one of the most spectacular bungee jumps in the world, straight off the Victoria Falls railway bridge.

If that all seems a bit too extreme, opt for some straightforward trekking. **Fish River Canyon National Park** (p358), Africa's equivalent of the Grand Canyon, is hard to beat. There are also fantastic treks into the **Tsodilo Hills** (p144) in Botswana to view San rock art, or down the ephemeral river valleys of **Damaraland** (p292) in northern Namibia.

For trekking with a different spin, try some rhino tracking at **Palmwag** (p297), accompany a San guide into the salty deserts of the **Makgadikgadi Pans** (p103), or

join one of the bird-watching trails from camps in the **Okavango Delta** (p130), where you can even take scenic flights over the watery green wonderland.

There aren't many opportunities for rock climbers despite the fantastic rocky arena of Namibia, but you can summit the stunning **Spitzkoppe** (p292) if you're equipped for a technical scramble to the top. Skilled equestrians can also gallop through **Sesriem Canyon** (p336) and/or **Tuli Block** (p100), either of which brings the thrill of the safari to horseback.

DESERT TO DELTA

One of the joys of travelling overland between Namibia and Botswana is the startling contrast between a pure desert environment and some lush and verdant wetlands.

In Namibia, much of the beauty is in the detail. The **Namib-Naukluft Park** (p330) is an amphitheatre of sand where unique desert mammals and insects struggle to survive. Even more ghostly is the **Skeleton Coast National Park** (p307) in the far northwest of the country, advertising itself as the world's largest graveyard of shipwrecked vessels. And finally, the secret desert hinterland of the **Sperrgebiet** (p354), one of the most pristine desert ecosystems in the world, is open to the general public for the first time in the history of the country.

A stark contrast to the shifting sands, the **Okavango Delta** (p119) is awash with water between December and March, and is a veritable paradise of birds, animals, insects and fish. Other watery havens are the remote **Linyanti Marshes** (p117), the swampy environs of **Savuti** (p116) and Namibia's mini-Okavango, **Mamili National Park** (p283). Together, these vitally important aquatic ecosystems harbour some of the highest concentrations of bird and animal life in Africa.

And of course, in this far northeastern corner of Botswana, it's a mere hop, skip and jump across the border to gaze at one of the most majestic natural wonders of the world, the smoke that thunders, namely **Victoria Falls** (p182).

OFF-ROADING

If you're fortunate enough to have a sturdy and well-outfitted rental vehicle, as well as a significant amount of 4WD experience in extreme environments, off-roading in Botswana and Namibia will truly test your limits. Before you leave the road, it is important to stress that back country driving in this part of the world is more of an expedition than a casual detour – you will have to be completely self-sufficient, and it's recommended that you travel with at least one other vehicle.

If the notion of exploring 12,000 sq km of disorientating saltpans is your idea of an adventure, then calibrate your GPS and head straight to the **Makgadikgadi Pans** (p103). For a true sense of the breadth and scope of the Kalahari, be sure to explore the **Central Kalahari Game Reserve** (p155), the continent's largest protected area. Or, navigate the apricot-coloured dune fields and the camelthorn-dotted grasslands of the **Kgalagadi Transfrontier Park** (p152).

On the Namibian side of the fence, head to the northwestern corner of the country to journey through the **Kaokoveld** (p298), a rugged terrain of desert mountains that is crisscrossed by slowly vanishing sandy tracks. Alternatively, brave the treacherous fog-covered and sand-blown salt roads of the famous **Skeleton Coast** (p304), one of the world's most inhospitable stretches of coastline.

National Parks & Reserves

Since David Livingstone made his epic journeys into the African interior, Europe has been enthralled by the idea of Africa's untamed wilderness. For many this image of Africa – giant skies and wildlife-packed plains – is the 'authentic Africa' of dreams, an enviable place of space and freedom where man and animal live in a complex, symbiotic relationship. But, as with most dreams, this experience of untouched wilderness is elusive, especially given that the realities of modern Africa are increasingly urban, and the effect of large-scale tourism erodes that very experience of escape.

Still, almost nowhere in Africa is this sense of wilderness more attainable than in Botswana's spectacular national parks, and Namibia's dramatic and sparsely populated open spaces. In taking the painful lessons of other African countries to heart, and insisting on a low volume-high cost tourism policy, Botswana has so far managed to preserve a uniquely 'wild' wilderness. Next door, Namibia's unusually harsh climate and stark environment have perversely acted to preserve many of its unique desert-adapted species.

VISITING THE NATIONAL PARKS IN BOTSWANA

Botswana is serious about preserving its wildlife, and has long pursued a far-sighted policy of sustainable tourism that is aimed at preserving the country's pristine natural environment. Budget travellers may feel excluded by some of the prohibitive costs, but the money you pay on entering the national parks goes a long way in both contributing to the development of local communities and bolstering conservation strategies.

As a result, most national parks in Botswana boast four of the Big Five – buffalo, elephant, leopard and lion. In **Chobe National Park** (p109) alone the elephant population has swelled to 60,000, and in **Moremi Game Reserve** (p132), there survives one of the few healthy wild dog populations in Africa. Because the Okavango Delta and Chobe River provide an incongruous water supply in a semi-arid environment, nearly all Southern African mammal species are present in the Moremi Game Reserve, parts of the Chobe National Park and the Linyanti Marshes. In the **Makgadikgadi & Nxai Pans National Park** (p106), herds of wildebeest, zebra and other hoofed mammals migrate between their winter range on the Makgadikgadi plains and the summer lushness of the Nxai Pan region.

In total, about 17% of Botswana is designated as national park or reserve, while another 20% is vaguely defined as 'wildlife management areas' (WMA), hence an impressive amount of the country is protected. Most of the parks in Botswana are characterised by vast open spaces with a few private safari concessions, next to no infrastructure and very limited amenities. Exceptions include the Chobe National Park and Moremi Game Reserve, which both have relatively larger volumes of travellers visiting each year.

The Department of Wildlife & National Parks (DWNP)

All public national parks and reserves in Botswana are run by the **DWNP** (Map pp82-3; ☎ 318 0774; dwnp@gov.bw; Government Enclave, Khama Cres, Gaborone; 7.30am-12.45pm & 1.45-4.30pm Mon-Fri), which is also responsible for the Botswana section of the **Kgalagadi Transfrontier Park** (p152). Because this park is jointly run by the DWNP and its South African counterpart, the opening hours,

NATIONAL PARK FEES PER DAY IN BOTSWANA

Infants and children up to the age of seven are entitled to free entry into the national parks.

	Citizens	Residents	Foreigners	Safari Participants
adult	P10	P30	P120	P70
child (8-17)	P5	P15	P60	P35
camping	P5	P20	P30	
vehicles <3500kg		P10		P50

camping costs and entry fees are different compared with the rest of the DWNP parks (see above).

The gates for each DWNP park are open from 6am to 6.30pm (1 April to 30 September) and from 5.30am to 7pm (1 October to 31 March). It is vital that all visitors be out of the park, or settled into their campsite, outside of these hours. Driving after dark is strictly forbidden.

BOOKING
Reservations for any campsite can be made up to 12 months in advance at the **DWNP** (Map pp82-3; ☎ 318 0774) office in Gaborone. You can also book through the **Maun DWNP office** (Map p122; ☎ 686 1265; Boseja, Maun), beside the police station. Chobe National Park bookings are also available at the **Kasane DWNP office** (Map p112; ☎ 625 0235).

Be advised that you can no longer pay for your permits at park gates anymore. Also, all reservations, cancellations and extensions must be made at the Gaborone or Maun DWNP offices in person, or by or email or letter – not over the telephone.

Payment in either Botswanan pula or by credit card must be received within one month or you forfeit the booking. In either case, the DWNP will send you, by fax, letter or email, a receipt with a reference number on it that you must keep and quote if you need to change your reservation.

Once you have booked it is difficult to change anything, so make sure to plan your trip well and allow enough time to get there and look around. A refund (less a 10% administration charge) is only possible with more than 30 days' notice.

It is worth double-checking these regulations with the DWNP because conditions change.

To reserve a campsite, you need to tell the DWNP:
- The name of the preferred campsite(s) within the park, in order of preference.
- The number of nights required, and the date of your arrival to and departure from the park and campsite.
- The number of adults and children camping.
- The vehicle's number plates and also the country in which the vehicle is registered.
- Proof of your status if you are not paying 'foreigner' rates.

CAMPING
The DWNP runs several reasonably comfortable campsites with braai (barbecue) areas, showers (usually cold) and sit-down flush toilets in the Moremi Game Reserve and Chobe National Park. The camping areas in other DWNP parks and reserves, though, are usually fairly basic (ie cleared spots in the dust with a pit latrine nearby). The good news is that these campsites are almost always superbly located and surrounded by wildlife.

BEST OF BOTSWANA

Park	Features	Activities	Best time
Central Kalahari Game Reserve p155	52,800 sq km; one of the largest protected areas in the world; semi-arid grassland	wildlife-viewing; walking; visiting San villages	Sep-Oct
Chobe National Park p109	11,700 sq km; mosaic of grassland & woodland; high elephant population	wildlife-viewing; bird-watching; fishing	year-round
Kgalagadi Transfrontier Park p152	38,000 sq km; straddles the South African border; semi-arid grassland	wildlife-viewing; bird-watching	Dec-May
Khutse Game Reserve p154	2590 sq km; adjoins Central Kalahari Game Reserve, same features	wildlife-viewing; walking; visiting San villages	Sep-Oct
Makgadikgadi & Nxai Pans NPs p106	7300 sq km; largest saltpans in the world; migratory zebra & wildebeest; flamingos	wildlife-watching; trekking with San; quad biking	Mar-Jul
Mokolodi Nature Reserve p92	30 sq km; close to capital; variety of plains game including white rhinos	wildlife-watching; walking	Apr-Nov
Moremi Game Reserve p132	3800 sq km; grassland, floodplains & swamps; huge wildlife density	wildlife-viewing; walking; scenic flights; boating	Aug-Dec
Tuli Game Reserve p100	collection of private reserves; unique rock formations	wildlife-viewing; horseback riding; walking; night drives	May-Sep

Camping areas are usually small (often with only two or three places to pitch a tent), limited in number and popular, so booking ahead as far as possible is strongly recommended. It is very important to remember that you will not be allowed into any park run by the DWNP without a reservation for a DWNP campsite.

Campsite reservations are normally only kept until 5.30pm – by which time you should be set up at the campsite anyway.

VISITING THE NATIONAL PARKS IN NAMIBIA

Despite its harsh climate, Namibia has some of the world's grandest national parks, ranging from the world-famous, wildlife-rich **Etosha National Park** (p264) to the immense **Namib-Naukluft Park** (p330), which protects vast dunefields, desert plains, wild mountains and unique flora. There are also the smaller reserves of the Caprivi region, the renowned Skeleton Coast and the awe-inspiring **Fish River Canyon National Park** (p358), which ranks among Africa's most spectacular natural wonders.

Around 15% of Namibia is designated as national park or conservancy. Access to most wildlife parks is limited to closed vehicles only. A 2WD is sufficient for most parks, but for **Mamili National Park** (p283), **Khaudom Game Reserve** (p277) and parts of **Bwabwata National Park** (p278), you need a sturdy 4WD with high clearance.

Entry permits (N$80 per person and N$10 per vehicle per day) are available on arrival at park entrances, but campsites and resorts must be booked in advance.

Namibia Wildlife Resorts (NWR)

The semiprivate **Namibia Wildlife Resorts** (NWR; www.nwr.com.na) manages a large number of rest camps, campsites and resorts within the national parks. You can book them through NWR's main office in Windhoek (Map p236; ☎ 285 7200; www.nwr.com.na; Erkrath Building, Independence Ave). If prebooking is impossible (eg if you're pulling into a national park area on a whim), there's a good chance you'll find something available on the spot, but have a contingency plan in case things don't work out. This is not advised for Etosha or Sossusvlei, which are perennially busy.

BOOKING

When booking a campsite or resort with NWR, fees must be paid by credit card before the booking will be confirmed. Note that camping fees are good for up to four people; each additional person up to eight people will be charged extra.

To reserve a campsite, you need to tell the NWR:

- Your passport number.
- The name of the preferred campsite/resort within the park, in order of preference.
- The date of your arrival to and departure from the park.
- The number of adults and children (including ages) camping.
- The vehicle's number plates and also the country in which the vehicle is registered.
- Proof of your status if you are not paying 'foreigner' rates.

Prebooking is always advised. Bookings may be made up to 12 months in advance. Note that pets aren't permitted in any wildlife-oriented park.

CAMPING & RESORTS

On average, campsites cost from N$50 for an undeveloped wilderness site to up to N$200 for the rest camps in Etosha, which feature pools, shops, restaurants, kiosks and well-maintained ablutions blocks with hot water. These rates are good for one person, though you generally need to pay a bit more for your vehicle and any additional campers.

NWR also offers a range of other possibilities targeted at upmarket travellers. For example, Etosha National Park hosts luxury chalets that range from N$900 to N$1600 per person, and are stacked with modern amenities including air-con and satellite TV. These properties are also attractively perched around watering holes, which offers world-class game viewing from the comfort of your own private balcony.

Finally, NWR recently opened the ultra-exclusive Onkoshi Camp in Etosha, which is situated on a remote saltpan that is well removed from tourist traffic, and defined by five-star opulence and total intimacy. The privilege of staying here for a night will set you back thousands and thousands of Namibian dollars, but the experience is unparalleled. Note that since chalets and other private accommodation options are very popular, they should be booked – well in advance – through the main office in Windhoek.

National parks' accommodation may be occupied from noon on the day of arrival to 10am on the day of departure. During school holidays,

BEST OF NAMIBIA

Park	Features	Activities	Best time
Etosha National Park p264	22,275 sq km; semi-arid savannah surrounding saltpan; 114 mammal species	wildlife-viewing; bird-watching; night drives	May-Sep
Fish River Canyon National Park p358	161km long; Africa's longest canyon; hot springs; rock strata of multiple colours	hiking; bathing	May-Nov
Khaudom Game Reserve p277	3840 sq km; bushveld landscape crossed by fossilised river valleys	wildlife-viewing; hiking; 4WD exploration	Jun-Oct
Mamili National Park p283	320 sq km; mini-Okavango; 430 bird species; canoe trails through park	wildlife-viewing; bird-watching; canoe trips	Sep-Apr
Mudumu National Park p282	850 sq km; lush riverine environment; 400 bird species	wildlife-watching; bird-watching; guided trails	May-Sep
Namib-Naukluft Park p330	50,000 sq km; Namibia's largest protected area; rare Hartmann's zebras	wildlife-watching; walking	year-round
Skeleton Coast National Park p307	20,000 sq km; wild, foggy wilderness; desert-adapted animals	wildlife-viewing; walking; fly-in safaris	year-round
Waterberg Plateau Park p256	400 sq km; table mountain; refuge for black and white rhinos and rare antelopes	wildlife-viewing; rhino tracking; hiking	May-Sep

visitors are limited to three nights at each camp in Etosha National Park and Namib-Naukluft Park, and 10 nights at all other camps. Pets aren't permitted in any of the rest camps.

Hiking

Hiking is limited and highly regulated in Namibian national parks – advance booking is essential. Several long-distance routes are available in various locales including Waterberg Plateau four-day hike, Naukluft eight-day hike, Ugab River and the five-day Fish River Canyon hike. The Naukluft and Daan Viljoen hikes are limited to groups of three to 12 people; the Waterberg unguided hike is open to three to 10 people; the Ugab and Waterberg guided hikes accommodate groups of three to eight people; and the Fish River hike allows groups of three to 40 people.

Conservancies & Private Game Reserves

A new concept in Namibia is the conservancy, an amalgamation of private farms or an area of communal land where farmers and/or local residents agree to combine resources for the benefit of wildlife. The most widely known organisation is the **Namibia Community Based Tourism Trust** (NACOBTA; ☎ 061-250558; www.nacobta.com.na), which oversees a large number of community-run campsites. At any of these locations, you can set up camp for the night for around N$50 per person, and participate in a wide range of activities including bush walks, village tours and guided hikes. Nearly 100,000 people currently live within the more than 30 registered conservancies in Namibia.

Another sort of protected area is the private game reserve, of which there are now more than 180 in Namibia. The largest of these, by far, are the 200,000-hectare **NamibRand Nature Reserve** (p339), adjoining the Namib-Naukluft Park, and the 102,000-hectare **Gondwana Cañon Park** (p361), bordering Fish River Canyon Park. In both, concessionaires provide accommodation and activities for visitors. Most of the smaller game reserves are either private game farms or hunting farms, which sustain endemic animal species rather than livestock.

SAFARIS

The unique landscapes of Namibia and Botswana make for a special safari experience. The typical image of khaki-clad tourists bush-whacking through the scrub is just one tiny aspect of an experience that can incorporate anything from ballooning over the undulating dunes of the Namib, to scooting along the lush channels of the Okavango in a traditional *mokoro* (dugout canoe). Horse-riding, trekking, birding, fishing, night-drives and camel safaris are all on the agenda as the typical safari transforms itself into a highly sophisticated experience that reconnects with that vital sense of adventure.

FLY-IN SAFARIS

If the world is your oyster, then the sheer sexiness of taking off in a little six-seater aircraft to nip across to the next remote safari camp or interior-designed lodge is a must. It also means you'll be able to maximise your time and cover a selection of parks and reserves to give yourself an idea of the fantastic variety of landscapes on offer.

The biggest temptation will be to cram too much into your itinerary, leaving you rushing from place to place. Be advised, it's always better to give yourself at least three days in each camp or lodge in order to really avail yourself of the various activities on offer.

While a fly-in safari is never cheap, they are all-inclusive and what you pay should cover the cost of your flight transfers as well as meals, drinks and activities in each camp. Obviously, this all takes some planning and the earlier you can book a fly-in safari the better – many operators advise on at least six to eight months notice if you want to pick and choose where you stay.

Fly-in safaris are particularly popular, and sometimes a necessity, in the Delta region of Botswana. Given the country's profile as a top-end safari destination, many tour operators specialise in fly-in safaris or include a fly-in element in their itineraries. A fly-in safari with the concessionaire, Wilderness Safaris (see p50), is also the only way to reach the remote northern area of the Skeleton Coast.

MOBILE SAFARIS

Most visitors to Botswana and Namibia will experience some sort of organised mobile safari – ranging from an all-hands-on-deck 'participation safari', where you might be expected to chip in with camp chores and supply your own sleeping bag and drinks, all the way up to top-class, privately guided trips.

As trips at the lower end of the budget scale can vary enormously in quality it pays to canvass opinion for good local operators. (This can be done on Lonely Planet's Thorn Tree forum, http://thorntree.lonelyplanet.com, or by chatting to other travellers on the ground.) Failing this, don't hesitate to ask lots of questions of your tour operator and make your priorities and budget clear from the start.

Maun (p120) is Botswana's mobile safari HQ, whilst most safaris in Namibia will need to be booked out of Windhoek (p231). For those booking through overseas tour operators, try and give as much notice as possible, especially if you want to travel in the high season (see p15). This will give you a better chance of booking the camps and lodges of your choice.

OVERLAND SAFARIS

Given the costs and complex logistics of arranging a big safari, many budget travellers opt for a ride on an overland expedition, run by specialists like **Africa in Focus** (www.africa-in-focus.com) and **Dragoman** (www.dragoman.com). Most of these expeditions are multicountry affairs with Namibia and Botswana featuring as part of a longer itinerary starting in either Cape Town (South Africa) or Nairobi (Kenya) and covering a combination of countries including Namibia, Botswana, Zimbabwe, Zambia, Malawi and Tanzania.

The subject of overlanding often raises passionate debate among travellers. For some the massive trucks and concentrated numbers of travellers herded together are everything that's wrong with travel. They take exception to the practice of rumbling into tiny villages to 'gawk' at the locals and then roaring off to party hard in hostels and bush camps throughout the host countries. Often the dynamics of travelling in such large groups (15 to 20 people at least) creates a surprising insularity resulting in a rather reduced experience of the countries you're travelling through.

For others, the overland truck presents an excellent way to get around on a budget and see a variety of parks and reserves whilst meeting up with people from different walks of life. Whatever your view, bear in mind that you're unlikely to get the best out of any particular African country by racing through on such inflexible itineraries.

The classic overland route through Namibia and Botswana takes in Fish River Canyon, Sossusvlei, Etosha National Park, Swakopmund, the Skeleton Coast, the Caprivi Strip, the Okavango Delta, Chobe National Park and on to Victoria Falls in Zimbabwe.

SELF-DRIVE SAFARIS

It's possible to arrange an entire safari from scratch if you hire your own vehicle. This has several advantages over an organised safari, primarily total independence and being able to choose your travelling companions. However, as far as costs go, it's generally true to say that organising your own safari will cost nearly as much as going on a cheap organised safari. Also bear in mind that you'll need to make all your campsite bookings (and pay for them) in advance, which means that you'll need to stick to your itinerary.

Apart from the cost, vehicle breakdowns, accidents, security, weather conditions and local knowledge are also major issues. It's not just about hiring a 4WD, but having the confidence to travel through some pretty rough terrain and handle anything it throws at you. However, if all this doesn't put you off then it can be a great adventure.

(Continued on page 49)

WILDLIFE & HABITAT David Lukas

At first glance this region may not seem very attractive to wildlife – Botswana is interminably flat and mostly covered in sand, while Namibia is one of the starkest and driest places on Earth. However, it is here that huge numbers of wildlife still wander their ancestral routes on a scale scarcely seen elsewhere in Africa. In fact Botswana and Namibia both offer superb wildlife-viewing opportunities, particularly in the north where the Chobe and Okavango Rivers create one of the world's premiere wetland ecosystems rife with massive concentrations of elephants and water buffaloes, along with wild dogs, lions and leopards.

Cats

In terms of behaviour, the six cats found in Botswana and Namibia are little more than souped-up housecats; it's just that they may weigh half as much as a horse, or jet along as fast as a speeding car. With their excellent vision and keen hearing, cats are superb hunters. And some of the most stunning scenes in Africa are the images of big cats making their kills. If you happen across one of these events, you won't easily forget the energy and ferocity of these life-and-death struggles.

1 Leopard
Weight 30-60kg (female), 40-90kg (male); length 170-300cm More common than you realise, the leopard relies on expert camouflage to stay hidden. During the day you might only spot one reclining in a tree after it twitches its tail, but at night there is no mistaking their bone-chilling groans that sound like wood being sawn at high volume.

2 Lion
Weight 120-150kg (female), 150-225kg (male); length 210-275cm (female), 240-350cm (male) Those lions sprawled out lazily in the shade are actually Africa's most feared predators. Equipped with teeth that tear effortlessly through bone and tendon they can take down an animal as large as a bull giraffe. Each group of adults (a pride) is based around generations of females that do all the hunting; swaggering males fight amongst themselves and eat what the females catch.

3 Caracal
Weight 8-19kg; length 80-120cm The caracal is a gorgeous tawny cat with extremely long, pointy ears. This African version of the northern lynx has jacked up hind legs like a feline dragster. These beanpole kickers enable this slender cat to make vertical leaps of 3m and swat birds out of the air.

4 Cheetah
Weight 40-60kg; length 200-220cm Less cat than greyhound, the cheetah is a world-class sprinter. Although it reaches 112km/h, the cheetah runs out of steam after 300m and must cool down for 30 minutes before hunting again. This speed comes at another cost – the cheetah is so well adapted for running that it lacks the strength and teeth to defend its food or cubs from attack by other large predators.

5 Black-Footed Cat
Weight 1-2kg; length 40-60cm More kitten than cat, this pint-sized predator is one of the smallest cats in the world. Though only 25cm high, this nocturnal cat is a fearsome hunter that can leap six times its height and must eat a prey item every hour.

6 Wildcat
Weight 3-6.5kg; length 65-100cm If you see what looks like a tabby wandering along fields and forest edges you may be seeing a wildcat, the direct ancestor of our domesticated housecats. Occurring wherever there are abundant mice and rats, the wildcat is readily found on the outskirts of villages where it can be best identified by its unmarked rufous ears and longish legs.

Primates

While East Africa is the evolutionary cradle of primate diversity, giving rise to over 30 species of monkeys, apes, and prosimians (the 'primitive' ancestors of modern primates), the southern portion of Africa is such a relative newcomer on the scene that Botswana and Namibia are home to a mere three species. Of these, only the Chacma baboon is common and widespread, but they are so fascinating to watch that they make up for the absence of other primates.

❶ Vervet Monkey

Weight 4-8kg; length 90-140cm These locally common monkeys spend a lot of time on the ground, but always in close proximity to trees where they can escape from their many predators. For this reason they are largely restricted to the well-wooded areas of northern Botswana and Namibia. Each troop of vervets is composed of females that defend a home range passed down from generation to generation, while males fight each other for bragging rights and access to females. If you think their appearance too drab, check out the extraordinary blue and scarlet colours of their sexual organs when they get excited.

❷ Lesser Galago

Weight 100-250g; length 40cm Galagos belong to a group of prosimians that have changed little in 60 million years. Best known for their frequent bawling cries (hence the common name 'bushbaby'), the lesser galago is a creature of the night, with incredible night vision and a habit of marking their territories with urine posts. They are phenomenally agile and acrobatic, making 5m-long leaps between trees and even leaping into the air to catch flying prey. In Botswana and Namibia they are only found in lush forested woodlands along the rivers of the north.

❸ Chacma Baboon

Weight 12-30kg (female), 25-45kg (male); length 100-200cm Common enough to be overlooked once you've seen a few, Chacma baboons are worth watching because they have exceedingly complex social dynamics. See if you can spot signs of friendship, deception, or deal-making within a troop. Their very long muzzles and bare faces are an adaptation for making emphatic facial signals at each other, and you're likely to see a lot of exaggerated expressions if you spend any time watching these baboons.

Cud-Chewing Mammals

Africa is arguably most famous for its astounding variety of ungulates – hoofed mammals that include everything from buffaloes to giraffes and rhinos. Many of these animals live in groups to protect themselves from the continent's formidable predators, with herds once numbering in the hundreds of thousands. The subgroup of ungulates that ruminate (chew their cud) and have horns are called bovines. Among this family, the antelopes are particularly numerous, with over a dozen species in Botswana and Namibia.

① African Buffalo

Weight 250-850kg; length 220-420cm Imagine a cow on steroids, then add a particularly fearsome set of curling horns, and you get the massive African buffalo. Thank goodness they're usually docile, because an angry or injured buffalo is an extremely dangerous animal.

② Hartebeest

Weight 120-220kg; length 190-285cm Yes the long face of the hartebeest is an odd sight, but it allows this short-necked antelope to reach down and graze while still looking up for predators. Commonly seen on open plains, the red-tinged hartebeest is easily recognised by its set of strangely twisted horns.

③ Gemsbok

Weight 180-240kg; length 230cm With straight towering 1m-long horns and boldly patterned face, this elegant desert antelope can survive for months on the scant water it derives from the plants it eats. Other adaptations include being able to survive temperatures that would kill other animals, and having a lowered metabolism so they don't have to eat much food.

④ Impala

Weight 40-80kg; length 150-200cm Gregarious and having a prodigious capacity to reproduce, impalas can reach great numbers very quickly, effectively outstripping predators' ability to eat them all. Females gather in huge clans while roaring males compete furiously for rights to mate. If they get scattered they use high kicks to disperse odours that help them find each other. Visit Namibia's Etosha National Park (p264) to see the unique black-faced impala.

⑤ Klipspringer

Weight 8-18kg; length 80-125cm Bug-eyed and perpetually walking on its tippy-toes, the tiny klipspringer finds safety on steep rocky outcrops in the mountains of central Namibia. Here, pairs establish permanent territories and communicate with each other by whistling and leaving scents produced by a dark gland in front of their eye.

⑥ Springbok

Weight 20-40kg (female), 30-60kg (male); length 135-175cm Lacking the vast grasslands of East Africa, Botswana and Namibia are home to only a handful of gazelle-like antelopes, including the lithe little springbok. This nomadic antelope uses its uniquely narrowed face to selectively reach the most nutritious grass shoots.

⑦ Wildebeest

Weight 140-290kg; length 230-340cm Famous for the vast herds that traverse the Serengeti, the wildebeest of northern Botswana are instead rather sedentary creatures, moving only when conditions fluctuate seasonally. Because they favour expansive views, wildebeest are in turn easily viewed themselves.

Hoofed Mammals

A full stable of Africa's mega-charismatic animals can be found in this group of ungulates. Other than the giraffe, these ungulates are not ruminants and can be seen over a much broader range of habitats than bovines. They have been at home in Africa for millions of years and are among the most successful mammals to have ever wandered the continent. Without human intervention, Africa would be ruled by elephants, zebras, hippos and warthogs.

❶ Black Rhinoceros
Weight 700-1400kg; length 350-450cm Pity the rhinoceros for having a horn that is worth more than gold. Once widespread and abundant south of the Sahara, the rhino has been poached to the brink of extinction. Unfortunately, females may only give birth every five years. The best viewing location in all of Africa might be at Etosha National Park's Okaukuejo waterhole (p268).

❷ Mountain Zebra
Weight 230-380kg; length 260-300cm The unique mountain zebras of central Namibia differ from their savannah relatives in having unstriped bellies and rusty muzzles. Although each zebra is as distinctly marked as a fingerprint, scientists still aren't sure what function these patterns serve. Do they help zebras recognise each other?

❸ African Elephant
Weight 2200-3500kg (female), 4000-6300kg (male); height 2.4-3.4m (female), 3-4m (male) Elephants are phenomenally abundant at Chobe National Park (p109), where up to 55,000 congregate in the lush wetlands. Even more interesting are the unique desert-loving elephants of Namibia, and no one, not even a human or lion, stands around to argue when a towering bull elephant stands guard over a precious waterhole. Commonly referred to as 'the king of beasts', elephant society is actually ruled by a lineage of elder females.

❹ Hippopotamus
Weight 510-3200kg; length 320-400cm The hippopotamus is one strange creature. Designed like a floating beanbag with tiny legs, the 3000kg hippo spends its time in or very near water chowing down on aquatic plants. Placid? No way! Hippos have tremendous ferocity and strength when provoked.

❺ Rock Dassie
Weight 1.8-5.5kg; length 40-60cm It doesn't seem like it, but those funny tailless squirrels you see lounging on rocky outcrops of central Namibia are an ancient cousin to the elephant. You won't see some of the features that dassies (known elsewhere in Africa as hyraxes) share with their larger kin, but look for tiny tusks when one yawns.

❻ Warthog
Weight 45-75kg (female), 60-150kg (male); length 140-200cm Despite their fearsome appearance and sinister tusks, only the big males are safe from lions, cheetahs, and hyenas. To protect themselves when attacked, warthogs run for burrows and back in while slashing wildly with their tusks.

❼ Giraffe
Weight 450-1200kg (female), 1800-2000kg (male); height 3.5-5.2m The 5m-tall giraffe does such a good job with upward activity – reaching up to grab high branches, towering above the competition – that stretching down to get a simple drink of water is difficult. Though they stroll along casually, they can outrun any predator.

1

Carnivores

It is a sign of Africa's ecological richness that the continent supports a re-markable variety of predators. In addition to six types of cats, Botswana and Namibia are home to a couple dozen other carnivores ranging from slinky mongooses to highly social hunting dogs. All are linked in having 'carnassial' (slicing) teeth, but visitors may be more interested in witnessing the superb hunting prowess of these highly efficient hunters. When it comes to predators expect the unexpected and you'll return home with a lifetime of memories!

❶ Bat-Eared Fox

Weight 3-5kg; length 70-100cm This delightful tawny animal has huge ears that it swivels in all directions to pick up the sounds of subterranean food items like termites that it unearths with bursts of frantic digging. Monogamous pairs of these highly social foxes will often mingle with other pairs and families when hunting for food.

❷ Spotted Hyena

Weight 40-90kg; length 125-215cm The spotted hyena is one of South Africa's most unusual animals. Living in packs ruled by females that grow penis-like sexual organs, these savage fighters use their bone-crushing jaws to disembowel terrified prey on the run or to do battle with lions. The sight of maniacally giggling hyenas at a kill, piling on top of each other in their eagerness to devour hide, bone, and internal organs, is unsettling.

❸ Meerkat

Weight 0.5-1kg; length 50cm The area's several species of mongoose may be best represented by the delightfully named meerkat (also known as a suricate). When not wrestling and playing, energetic and highly social meerkats spend much of their time standing up with looks of perpetual surprise. If threatened they all spit and jump up and down together.

❹ Cape Fur Seal

Weight 80kg (females), 350kg (males); length 120-200cm Over 2 million fur seals can be found along the coastlines of South Africa, with several giant breeding colonies located on Namibia's remote Skeleton Coast (p304). Not a particularly social creature but forced to gather in dense numbers as protection against marauding brown hyenas, these colonies are turbulent, noisy and exciting to watch.

❺ Hunting Dog

Weight 20-35kg; length 100-150cm Fabulously and uniquely patterned so that individuals recognise each other, hunting dogs run in packs of 20 to 60 that ruthlessly chase down antelopes and other animals. Organised in complex hierarchies maintained by rules of conduct, these highly social canids are incredibly efficient hunters. At the same time, disease and persecution has pushed them into near extinction and they now rank as one of Africa's foremost must-see animals. Look for them at Botswana's Moremi Game Reserve (p132).

1

Birds of Prey

Botswana and Namibia are home to about 70 species of hawks, eagles, vultures and owls, meaning that you are likely to see an incredible variety of birds of prey here. Look for them perching on trees, soaring high overhead, or gathered around a carcass; though the scolding cries of small birds harassing one of these feared hunters may be your first clue to their presence.

5

❶ African Fish Eagle
Length 75cm Given its name, it's not surprising that you'll see the African fish eagle hunting for fish around water. With a wingspan over 2m this replica of the American bald eagle presents an imposing appearance, but it is most familiar for its loud ringing vocalisations that have become known as 'the voice of Africa'.

❷ Secretary Bird
Length 100cm In a region flush with unique birds, the secretary bird literally stands head and shoulders above the masses. With the body of an eagle and the legs of a crane, the secretary bird towers 1.3m-tall and walks up to 20km a day in search of vipers, cobras and other snakes that it kills with lightning speed and agility. This idiosyncratic, grey-bodied raptor is commonly seen striding across the savannah.

❸ Pale Chanting Goshawk
Length 55cm Small clusters of these slim grey raptors with stunning red beaks and legs are often seen perched low on bushes or fallen trees. Look closely because they are probably following some other small hunter like a honey badger and hoping to snap up anything that escapes the badger's notice.

❹ Bateleur
Length 60cm The bateleur is an attractive serpent-eagle with a funny name. French for 'tightrope-walker', the name refers to its distinctive low-flying aerial acrobatics. In flight, look for this eagle's white wings and odd tailless appearance; close up look for the bold colour pattern and scarlet face.

❺ Lappet-Faced Vulture
Length 115cm Six of Southern Africa's eight vultures can be seen mingling with lions, hyenas and jackals around carcasses in Botswana and Namibia. Here through sheer numbers they compete, often successfully, for scraps of flesh and bone. It's not a pretty sight when gore-encrusted vultures take over a carcass that no other scavenger wants, but it's the way nature works. The monstrous lappet-faced vulture, a giant among vultures, gets its fill before other vultures move in.

Birds

Come to Botswana and Namibia prepared to see an astounding number of birds in every shape and colour imaginable. If you're not already paying attention to every bird you see, you may find them an energising and pleasant diversion after a couple days of staring at sleeping lions.

① Lesser Flamingo
Length 100cm Coloured deep rose-pink and gathering by the hundreds of thousands on shimmering salt lakes, the lesser flamingo creates some of the most dramatic wildlife spectacles found in Africa, especially when they all fly at once or perform synchronised courtship displays.

② Lilac-Breasted Roller
Length 40cm Nearly everyone on safari gets to know the gorgeously coloured lilac-breasted roller. Related to kingfishers, rollers get their name from the tendency to 'roll' from side to side in flight as a way of showing off their iridescent blues, purples and greens.

③ Cape Gannet
Length 85cm It's hard to beat the spectacular mayhem at a gannet breeding colony. When not gathering in vast numbers to nest on offshore islands, these crisply marked seabirds congregate by the thousands to catch fish with high-speed dives into the waves.

④ Ostrich
Length 200-270cm If you think the ostrich looks prehistoric, you aren't far off. Standing 2.7m and weighing upwards of 130kg, these ancient flightless birds escape predators by running away at 70km/h or lying flat on the ground to resemble a pile of dirt. Most that you see in Southern Africa are from feral stock, but genuinely wild ostriches are still found in the Kalahari.

⑤ Jackass Penguin
Length 60cm Yes, they are silly looking but jackass penguins are actually named for their donkeylike calls, part of the ecstatic courtship displays given by the males. Found along the Namibian coast and on offshore islands, some penguin colonies are ridiculously tame.

⑥ Hamerkop
Length 60cm The hamerkop is a stork relative with an oddly crested, cartoonish, woodpecker-like head. Nicknamed the 'hammerhead', it is frequently observed hunting frogs and fish at the water's edge. Look for its massive 2m-wide nests in nearby trees.

⑦ Ground Hornbill
Length 90cm Looking somewhat like a turkey, the ground hornbill spends its time on the ground in search of insects, frogs, reptiles, and small mammals that it kills with fierce stabs with its large powerful bill. Check out the bare fluorescent red skin on their heads.

⑧ Namaqua Sandgrouse
Length 25cm Looking like stocky painted pigeons, these hardy desert birds fly up to 20km a day to reach waterholes, where they line up in great numbers to drink at the water's edge. Males soak their breast feathers and fly back to the nest so their chicks can drink too.

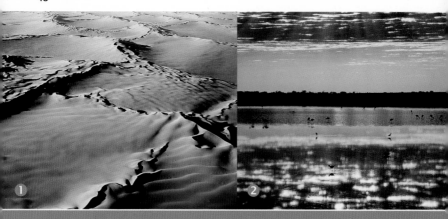

Habitats

Because every animal occupies a specific type of habitat it is worth learning how to recognise the region's most common habitats in order to enhance your wildlife-viewing experience. Fortunately for visitors, the habitats of Botswana and Namibia are pretty simple to learn.

1 Semiarid & Arid Desert

Much of Botswana and Namibia is covered by some type of sandy or rocky desert ecosystem. Deserts are distinguished by their levels of rainfall, with arid deserts rarely seeing more than 50mm of rain a year and semiarid deserts averaging 125 to 250mm of rain. Lack of water limits larger animals such as zebras, lions, and elephants to waterholes, but when it rains this habitat explodes with plant and animal life. During the dry season many plants shed their leaves to conserve water and grazing animals move on in search of food and water.

2 Wetlands

Given the extreme aridity of Botswana and Namibia it almost comes as a surprise that one of the world's greatest inland river deltas occurs in this region, along with some of Africa's most significant marsh and wetland habitats. Each year, the Okavango River rages across Namibia and floods some 16,000 sq km of northern Botswana creating one of the grandest explosions of life on the planet, with everything from elephants to hippos to red lechwes (a unique aquatic antelope) occurring by the thousands.

3 Savannah & Grassland

Savannah is *the* classic African landscape – broad rolling grasslands dotted with acacia trees and filled with abundant animals – unfortunately Botswana and Namibia are so dry and sandy that grasslands and savannah occur only in scattered patches. This habitat is home to herds of zebras and antelope, in addition to fast-sprinting predators like cheetahs.

(Continued from page 32)

Your greatest priority will be finding a properly equipped 4WD (see p179 and p384), including all the necessary tools you might need in case of a breakdown. A happy compromise might be to hire a vehicle from a reputable company such as **Safari Drive** (☎ 44-1488-685055; www.safaridrive.com) or **Sunvil Africa** (☎ 44-20-82329777; www.sunvil.co.uk), who hire out fully equipped Land Rovers and offer a top-notch support service with bases in Maun, Kasane, Victoria Falls and Windhoek.

Another South African outfit you might consider is **Britz** (see p175), which also has offices in Australia and New Zealand. While it doesn't have an office in either Botswana or Namibia and doesn't offer any in-country backup, it does rent out the most fantastically equipped 'safari 4WD', which comes complete with roof tent, stove and fridge.

Note: If you're planning a self-drive safari in northeastern Namibia or northern Botswana, you'll need to watch out for the wet season (December to March) when some tracks become completely submerged and driving is particularly risky.

You can find pretty much all the camping essentials you need in the supermarket chain, Pick & Pay, which has outlets throughout Botswana and Namibia. It stocks everything from tents and sleeping bags to cooking equipment and fire lighters. For specialist items like GPS, you'll need to bring your own – although in Botswana you'll find some specialist shops in Maun.

LOCAL TOUR OPERATORS

Typically most visitors to Botswana and Namibia will book a safari with a specialist tour operator and many local operators do the bulk of their business this way. The recommendations below provide an overview of some of the best operators in Botswana and Namibia. Other agencies are listed throughout the guide.

Audi Camp Safaris (☎ 686 0599; www.safaris-botswana.com) Specialises in budget mobile and *mokoro* trips. Safaris are practically all-inclusive but you have to bring your own sleeping bags and drinks. It also runs the friendly, no-frills Audi Camp (p126).

Capricorn Safaris (☎ 686 1165; www.capricornsafaris.com) One of the largest operators in Botswana with affiliations in Kenya and Tanzania. Focus on luxury tented safaris in all the main national parks. Note: groups can be quite large.

Desert & Delta Safaris (☎ 686 1234; www.desertdelta.co.za) A top-notch tour operator with luxury camps and lodges located in Moremi, Chobe, Savuti and the Okavango Delta. You can expect a uniformly high standard of service.

Kaie Tours (☎ 397 3388; www.kaietours.com) A Gaborone-based tour operator specialising in well-priced art and craft tours, hiking trails, overnight stays with local families and camping safaris in the Kalahari with San guides.

Kwando Safaris (☎ 686 1449; www.kwando.co.za) One of the largest operators in Botswana offering safaris exclusively in private concessions rather than national parks, which means they are able to operate off-road and offer night drives.

Masson Safaris (☎ 686 2442; www.massonsafaris.com) A family-run outfit based in Botswana with over 20 years experience in running mobile safaris. It also tailor-makes itineraries for children.

Sanctuary Lodges (☎ 27-11 781 1497; www.sanctuarylodges.com) Owned by Geoffrey Kent, the owner of Abercrombie & Kent, Botswana's Sanctuary Lodges has the same high standards and ubiquitous 'luxury' decor of the A&K brand.

Ulinda Safari Trails (☎ 680 0244; www.ulinda.com) Run by professional hunter Jane Bettaney. Her extensive experience in the bush and natural passion for animals (she's also an experienced wildlife photographer) makes her an exceptional guide.

UP CLOSE & PERSONAL

The threat of attack by wild animals is rare, but compliance with a number of guidelines will further diminish the chances of an unwelcome encounter. The five most dangerous animals are the Big Five: lion, leopard, buffalo, elephant and rhinoceros.

■ Always sleep inside a tent and be sure to zip it up completely. If you hear a large animal outside, lie still even if it brushes against the tent.

■ Never pitch a tent in an open area along a riverbank as this is probably a hippo run.

■ When camping, don't keep fresh fruit – especially oranges – in your tent, because they can attract elephants.

■ If you encounter a lone buffalo, a lion (especially a lioness) or an elephant that detects your presence back away slowly and quietly.

■ Do not run away from a lion. If you respond like a prey species, the lion will react accordingly.

■ Elephant cows with calves should be avoided, and do not approach any elephant with visible injuries.

■ When travelling in a boat watch for signs of hippos and steer well away from them.

■ When a hippo feels threatened, it heads for water – don't be in its way!

■ Visitors should take care not to swim in rivers or waterholes where crocs or hippos are present. Always use extreme caution when tramping along any river or shoreline.

■ Be aware that hyenas are also potentially dangerous, although they're normally just after your food.

Wild Attractions Expeditions & Safaris (☎ 686 0300; www.africansecrets.net) This safari company runs out of Island Safari Lodge. Very big on bird-watching and *mokoro* trips for which it uses local polers.

Wilderness Safaris (☎ 27-11 807 1800; www.wilderness-safaris.com) Wilderness Safaris manages an impressive array of luxury camps and lodges in Namibia, Botswana, Zimbabwe and further afield, and supports a number of commendable conservation and community projects.

Wild Dog & Crazy Kudu Safaris (☎ 222636; www.wilddog-safaris.com) This popular backpacker-orientated tour operator runs a variety of expeditions throughout Namibia.

Botswana

DOUG MCKINLAY

Botswana History

Botswana's history is much more than a footnote to the histories of neighbouring giants South Africa, Zimbabwe and Angola. The vast Kalahari thirst lands, which cover some 80% of the country, and the miraculous, green-fingered delta have been central to the historical and cultural geography of the region for thousands of years. What's more, the country's history is a source of African inspiration. As elsewhere on the continent, its empires have risen and fallen, conquered and been oppressed, but throughout the historical narrative the Batswana have subtly engineered their political destiny to help their country emerge as one of the most stable and forward-looking on the continent.

FIRST FOOTPRINTS

To understand Botswana one must look at its extraordinary timeline. Here, history extends back through the millennia to the earliest rumblings of humanity on the planet, when humans took their first footsteps on the savannahs of Southern and eastern Africa. Developing rudimentary tools, these people hunted and gathered across the abundant plains, moving seasonally over grassland and scrub in and around the extensive wetlands that once covered the north of the country.

By the middle Stone Age, which lasted until 20,000 years ago, the Boskop, the primary human group in Southern Africa, had progressed into an organised hunting and gathering society. They are thought to be the ancestors of the modern-day San (see p63).

Archaeological evidence and rock art found in the Tsodilo Hills (see p144) place these hunter-gatherers in shelters and caves throughout the region from around 17,000 BC. The tempura paintings that gave expression to the natural world in which they lived attest to their increasing level of sophistication. Slowly, clumsy stone tools gave way to bone, wood and eventually iron implements. Better tools meant more efficient hunting, which allowed time for further innovation, personal adornment and artistic pursuits such as the emerging craft of pottery.

Such progress prompted many of these hunter-gatherers to adopt a pastoral lifestyle – sowing crops and grazing livestock on the exposed pastures of the Okavango Delta and the Makgadikgadi lakes. Some migrated west into central Namibia, and by 70 BC some had even reached the Cape of Good Hope.

SETTLEMENT

Following the fragmented trail of ancient pottery, archaeologists and anthropologists have been able to piece together the complex, criss-crossing

Although mainly a school textbook, *History of Botswana* by T Tlou and A Campbell is the most readable account of Botswana's history from the Stone Age to the late 1990s.

Common rock-art themes include the roles of men and women, hunting scenes and natural medicine. The latter includes examples of trance dancing and spiritual healing using the San life force, known as *nxum*.

TIMELINE

17,000 BC	380–20 BC	AD 420
Evidence of Khoisan settlement at a site in the Tsodilo Hills (Depression Shelter) dates from this period; some rock paintings from this era are still in evidence today.	At this time, Stone Age farming techniques begin to filter into Botswana. Along the upper Zambezi River watershed, Stone Age tools begin to evolve into Iron Age tools.	The remnants of beehive-shaped houses made of grass matting, occupied by Iron Age farmers, date from this period. The main location of these ruins is in the area around Molepolole.

migration of different tribal groups into Southern Africa. From AD 200 to 500, Bantu-speaking farmers started to appear on the southern landscape from the north and east. To begin with, relations between the San and Khoikhoi appear to have been cordial, and the groups mixed freely, traded and intermarried.

After all, there was much to learn from each other. The farmers brought with them new political systems and superior agricultural and metalworking skills. At the Tswapong hills near Palapye there's evidence of an early iron-smelting furnace that dates back to AD 190. One of the earliest and most powerful Bantu groups to settle in the region was the Sotho-Tswana, who consisted of three distinct entities: the Northern Basotho (or Pedi), who settled in the Transvaal of South Africa; the Southern Basotho of Lesotho; and the Western Basotho (or Batswana), who migrated north into Botswana.

By about AD 600, Zhizo newcomers from Zimbabwe had spread along the northern edges of the Kalahari and around Sowa (Sua) Pan, and they introduced more advanced skills in mining, livestock farming and pottery. By about 1000, another wave of Zhizo (called the Toutswe) arrived and settled near Palapye.

The Toutswe were prosperous cattle herders, with large kraals (cattle enclosures), a capital city and a string of hilltop villages. They also hunted westwards into the Kalahari and traded eastwards towards the Limpopo River. But, despite their apparent strength and wealth, somewhere between 1250 and 1300 the Toutswe were conquered by their gold-rich neighbours, the Mapungubwe. They in turn were absorbed into the growing sphere of influence of Great Zimbabwe, one of Africa's most legendary ancient kingdoms. Between the 13th and 15th centuries, Great Zimbabwe incorporated many chiefdoms of northeastern Botswana, and the region was still part of Zimbabwe-based dynasties, notably the Torwa and Rozwi, several hundred years later.

> Botswana's three main mines – Orapa, Letlhakane and Jwaneng – produce 22% of the world's gem-quality diamonds.

The only other significant migrations into Botswana were those of the Herero in the late 19th century. Faced with German aggression in Namibia, they fled eastwards, settling in the north-western extremes of Botswana (see the boxed text, p206).

RISE OF THE TSWANA

Perhaps the most significant development in Botswana's long history was the evolution of the three main branches of the Tswana tribe during the 14th century. It's a typical tale of family discord, where three brothers – Kwena, Ngwaketse and Ngwato – broke away from their father, Chief Malope, to establish their own followings in Molepolole, Kanye and Serowe respectively. Realistically, these fractures probably occurred in response to drought and expanding populations eager to strike out in search of new pastures and arable land.

600–1300	1200–1400	1300–1500
Around Serowe a thriving farming culture emerges, dominated by rulers living on Toutswe hill. These peoples trade to the east with the Limpopo people, as evidenced by the use of shells as currency.	The Sotho emerge as a major power in what is now the modern day South African Transvaal. Their power expands in all directions, including north into what is now Botswana.	The new state of Great Zimbabwe incorporates many chiefdoms in northeastern Botswana and flourishes through the gold trade. The lucrative gold routes will be dominated by Zimbabwe from the 13th to 15th centuries.

The Ngwato clan split further in the late 18th century following a quarrel between Chief Khama I and his brother Tawana, who subsequently left Serowe and established his chiefdom in the area around Maun. The four major present-day Batswana groups – the Batawana, Bakwena, Bangwaketse and Bangwato (see p62) – trace their ancestry to these splits.

THE DIFAQANE

As people fanned out across Southern Africa, marking out their territories of trade and commerce, the peaceful fragmentation of the past became increasingly difficult. By the 1700s villages were no longer small, open affairs but fortified settlements situated on strategic, defensive hilltops. This mood of aggression was exacerbated by the increasing trade in ivory, cattle and slaves, which prompted raids and counter-raids between powerful tribes eager to gain control over these lucrative resources.

The most prominent aggressor was the Zulu warlord Shaka, the new chief of the Zulu confederation. From his base in Natal he launched a series of ruthless campaigns aimed at forcibly amalgamating or destroying all tribes and settlements in his way. By 1830, the Bakwena and Bangwato areas had been overrun and survivors had started the *difaqane* (literally 'the scattering' or exodus). In his wake came his equally ruthless Ndebele general, Mzilikazi, who continued to send raiding parties into the villages of Botswana and forced villagers to flee as far as Ghanzi and Tshane in the heart of the Kalahari. His troops also defeated the Bangwaketse, who fled into the desert, finally settling near Letlhakeng.

The Tswana states of Ngwaketse, Kwena and Ngwato were only reconstituted in the 1840s after the ravages of the *difaqane* had passed. Realising from their experience that their divided nation was vulnerable to attack, they began to regroup under the aegis of King Segkoma I.

These new states were then organised into wards under their own chiefs, who then paid tribute (based on labour and cattle) to the king. They were also highly competitive, vying with each other for the increasing trade in ivory and ostrich feathers being carried down new roads to the Cape Colony in the south. Those roads also brought Christian missionaries into Botswana for the first time and enabled the Boer trekkers to begin their migrations further north.

THE BOERS & THE BRITISH

While Mzilikazi was wreaking havoc on the Batswana and missionaries were busy trying to convert the survivors to Christianity, the Boers were feeling pressured by their British neighbours in the cape. So in 1836, around 20,000 Boers set out on the Great Trek across the Vaal River into Batswana and Zulu territory and proceeded to set up their own free state ruling the Transvaal – a move ratified by the British in the Sand River Convention of 1852. Effectively,

The prime mover behind the missionary effort during the early 19th century was the uncompromising Robert Moffat, who was responsible for the first translation of the Bible into Tswana.

Enjoy the drama of discovery in David Livingstone's *Missionary Travels*, a bestseller when it was published and still going strong. Janet Wagner Parsons' biography *The Livingstones at Kolobeng* is another good read.

from 1450	1500–1600	early 1700s
The Kingdom of Butua, which is based near Bulawayo in modern Zimbabwe, controls trade in salt and hunting dogs around the area of the Makgadikgadi Pans.	The main Tswana dynasties from central Sotho break up and establish their own followings at Molepolole, Kanye and Serowe, precipitating the modern divisions of the current Sotho language groups.	Yeyi farmers and fishermen migrate into the Okavango Delta, mixing with local Khoi and San people. Population migrations move from the upper Chobe down through the Okavango throughout the 18th century.

this placed the Batswana under the rule of the so-called new South African Republic, and a period of rebellion and heavy-handed oppression ensued. Following heavy human and territorial losses, the Batswana chiefs petitioned the British government for protection from the Boers.

But Britain had its hands full in Southern Africa and was in no hurry to take on and support a country of uncertain profitability. Instead, it offered to act as arbitrator in the dispute. By 1877, however, animosity against the Boers had escalated to such a dangerous level that the British conceded and annexed the Transvaal – thereby starting the first Boer War. The war continued until the Pretoria Convention of 1881, when the British withdrew from the Transvaal in exchange for Boer allegiance to the British Crown.

With the British out of their way, the Boers once again looked northwards into Batswana territory. In 1882 the Boers managed to subdue the towns of Taung and Mafikeng and proclaimed them the republics of Stellaland and Goshen. They might have gone much further had it not been for the annexation of South West Africa (modern-day Namibia) by the Germans in the 1890s.

With the potential threat of a German-Boer alliance across the Kalahari, which would put paid to their dreams of expansion into mineral-rich Rhodesia (Zimbabwe), the British started to look seriously at the Batswana petitions for protection. In 1885 they proclaimed a protectorate over their Tswana allies, known as the British Crown Colony of Bechuanaland.

Building of a Nation: A History of Botswana from 1800 to 1910 by J Ramsay, B Morton and T Mgadla provides perhaps the best account of colonial history.

CECIL JOHN RHODES

British expansion in Southern Africa came in the form of a private venture under the auspices of the British South Africa Company (BSAC), owned by millionaire businessman Cecil John Rhodes.

By 1889 Rhodes already had a hand in the diamond-mining industry in Kimberley (South Africa), and he was convinced that other African countries had similar mineral deposits just waiting to be exploited. He aimed to do this through the land concessions that companies could obtain privately in order to colonise new land for the crown. The system was easily exploited by Rhodes, who fraudulently obtained large tracts of land from local chiefs by passing off contracts as treaties. The British turned a blind eye, as they eventually hoped to transfer the entire Bechuanaland protectorate to the BSAC and relieve themselves of the expense of colonial administration.

Realising the implications of Rhodes' aspirations, three Batswana chiefs – Bathoen, Khama III and Sebele – accompanied by a sympathetic missionary, WC Willoughby, sailed to England to appeal directly to the British parliament for continued government control of Bechuanaland. Instead of taking action, the colonial minister, Joseph Chamberlain, advised them to contact Rhodes directly and work things out among themselves.

Seretse Khama: 1921–1980 by N Parsons, W Henderson and T Tlou is the definitive biography of the great man who became the country's first president.

1700–50	1800–40	early 1800s
The Ngwaketse chiefdom is founded in southeast Botswana in 1700. By 1750, the state has expanded into a powerful military force, and controls the copper mines of Kanye.	Aggressive Zulu and Ndebele raiders attack Batswana villages; the *difaqane* (forced migration) sees people scattering across the land and leads to some of the largest human migrations in Southern African history.	New roads being built from the South African Cape Colony in the south bring both Boer (Afrikaner) farmers and Christian missionaries. King Sechele (1829–92) of the Kwena is baptised by David Livingstone.

Naturally, Rhodes was immovable, so the delegation approached the London Missionary Society (LMS), who in turn took the matter to the British public. Fearing that the BSAC would allow alcohol in Bechuanaland, the LMS and other Christian groups backed the devoutly Christian Khama and his entourage. The British public in general felt that the Crown should be administering the empire, rather than the controversial Rhodes. Public pressure rose to such a level that the government was forced to concede to the chiefs. Chamberlain agreed to continue British administration of Bechuanaland, ceding only a small strip of the south-east (now known as the Tuli Block) to the BSAC for the construction of a railway line to Rhodesia.

COLONIAL YEARS

By 1899 Britain had decided it was time to consolidate the Southern African states, and it declared war on the Transvaal. The Boers were overcome in 1902, and in 1910 the Union of South Africa was created.

By selling cattle, draught oxen and grain to the Europeans streaming north in search of farming land and minerals, Bechuanaland enjoyed an initial degree of economic independence. However, the construction of a railway through Bechuanaland to Rhodesia and a serious outbreak of foot-and-mouth disease in the 1890s destroyed the transit trade. This new economic vulnerability, combined with a series of droughts and the need to raise cash to pay British taxes, sent many Batswana to South Africa to look for work on farms and in mines. Up to 25% of Botswana's male population was abroad at any one time. This accelerated the breakdown of traditional land-use patterns and eroded the chiefs' powers.

Set in a poor salt-mining town *Jamestown Blues* by Caitlin Davies explores the disparities between expatriate and local life through the eyes of a young Motswana girl.

The British government continued to regard the protectorate as a temporary expedient until it could be handed over to Rhodesia or the new Union of South Africa. Accordingly, investment and administrative development within the territory were kept to a bare minimum. Even when there were moves in the 1930s to reform administration or initiate agricultural and mining development, these were hotly disputed by leading Tswana chiefs, on the grounds that they would only enhance colonial control. So the territory remained divided into eight largely self-administering 'tribal' reserves and five white settler farm blocks, with the remainder classified as 'crown' (ie state) land. Similarly, the administrative capital, Mafikeng, which was situated outside the protectorate's border, in South Africa, remained where it was until 1964.

INDEPENDENCE

The extent to which the British subordinated Botswanan interests to those of South Africa during this period became clear in 1950. In a case that caused political controversy in Britain and across the empire, the British government banned Seretse Khama from the chieftainship of the Ngwato and exiled him for six years. This, as secret documents have since revealed,

1885	**1895**	**1950**
The German colony of South West Africa (now Namibia) could potentially stretch across the Kalahari and border the Boer republic of the Transvaal. The British respond by proclaiming a protectorate over their Tswana allies.	An attempt to hand Botswana over to Cecil Rhodes is thwarted by three Batswana chiefs appealing to London. The three chiefs are hailed as heroes, and their mission encourages a sense of Tswana nationalism.	The British government bars Seretse Khama from chieftainship of the Ngwato and exiles him for six years to placate the South African government, which objected to Khama's marriage to a British woman.

was in order to appease the South African government, which objected to Khama's marriage to a British woman at a time when racial segregation was enforced in South Africa.

This only increased growing political agitation, and throughout the 1950s and '60s Botswanan political parties started to surface and promote the idea of independence. Following the Sharpeville Massacre in 1960, South African refugees Motsamai Mpho, of the African National Congress (ANC), and Philip Matante, a Johannesburg preacher affiliated with the Pan-Africanist Congress, joined with KT Motsete, a teacher from Malawi, to form the Bechuanaland People's Party (BPP). Its immediate goal was independence.

In 1962 Seretse Khama and Kanye farmer Ketumile 'Quett' Masire formed the moderate Bechuanaland Democratic Party (BDP). The BDP formulated a schedule for independence, drawing on support from local chiefs such as Bathoen II of the Bangwaketse, and traditional Batswana. The BDP also called for the transfer of the capital into Botswana (ie from Mafikeng to Gaborone) and a new non-racial constitution.

The British gratefully accepted the BDP's peaceful plan for a transfer of power, and Khama was elected president when general elections were held in 1965. On 30 September 1966, the country – now called the Republic of Botswana – was granted full independence.

Seretse Khama wisely steered Botswana through its first 14 years of independence. He guaranteed continued freehold over land held by white ranchers and adopted a strictly neutral stance (at least until near the end of his presidency) towards South Africa and Rhodesia. The reason, of course, was Botswana's economic dependence on the giant to the south, but, that said, Khama refused to exchange ambassadors with South Africa and officially disapproved of apartheid in international circles.

MODERN POLITICS

Sir Seretse Khama died in 1980 (not long after Zimbabwean independence), but his Botswana Democratic Party (BDP), formerly the Bechuanaland Democratic Party, continues to command a substantial majority in the Botswana parliament. Sir Ketumile 'Quett' Masire, who succeeded Khama as president from 1980 to 1998, followed the path laid down by his predecessor and continued to cautiously follow pro-Western policies.

Over the last 40 years the BDP has managed the country's diamond windfall wisely. Diamond dollars have been ploughed into infrastructure, education and health. Private business has been allowed to grow and foreign investment has been welcomed. From 1966 to 2005, Botswana's economy grew faster than any other in the world.

Festus Mogae handed over the presidency to vice president Ian Khama (son of Sir Seretse Khama) on 1 April 2008, a move that generated some grumbles

Botswana: The Road to Independence by P Fawcus and A Tilbury is an erudite explanation of the country's more recent history written by two of Britain's most senior administrators during the protectorate period.

Transparency International (TI) has released its 2004 annual index of perceived corruption among public officials and politicians in 145 countries. Botswana is ranked as the least corrupt country in Africa.

1960	1965–66	1967–71
The Bechuanaland People's Party (BPP) is founded; the following year a legislative council is set up. The Bechuanaland Democratic Party (later Botswana Democratic Party, BDP) – led by Seretse Khama – is founded in 1962.	Bechuanaland becomes self-governing. One year later, independence is declared and the country becomes the Republic of Botswana, with Sir Seretse Khama as its first president.	For years, Botswana is financially dependent on Britain, but when diamonds are discovered in the area around Orapa, the planning and execution of economic development takes off.

WHAT NEXT?

In 1970 Botswana ranked as one of the world's poorest countries, with a shocking GDP per capita of less than US$200. Educational facilities were minimal, with less than 2% of the population having completed primary school and fewer than 100 students enrolled in university. In the entire country there was only one, 12km-long, paved road. It's hardly surprising, then, that the country played no role in regional or continental politics.

Then, in 1967, Botswana effectively won the jackpot with the discovery of diamonds at Orapa. Two other major mines followed at Letlhakane in 1977 and Jwaneng in 1982, making Botswana the world's leading producer of gem-quality stones. This catapulted the country from a poor, provincial backwater to a regional player of some substance able to form the Southern African Development Community (SADC), whose function is to coordinate the disparate economies of the region.

However, as its life span is estimated at only 35 years, the diamond boon has its dark side. The Botswana government faces a bleak future if it fails to find alternative revenue streams. It's a difficult dilemma for a government with a precarious economy that is desperately trying to diversify into manufacturing, light engineering, food processing and textiles. Tourism, too, is set to play a major role in the country's future, although the challenge will be to increase revenue without adversely affecting the environment and local communities.

With nearly 30% of the population still living below the poverty line and the growing popularity of the socialist Botswana National Front (BNF) and Botswana Congress Party (BCP), Botswana's future is less assured now than it has been at any time in the last 40 years.

as Khama was never elected as president. Since assuming power Khama has cracked down on drinking, demanding earlier curfews at bars (sometimes enforced, sometimes not). In addition, Khama, former commander of the Botswana Defence Force, has appointed military and law enforcement colleagues to government posts traditionally held by civilians. For example, a former police commandant was made director of BTV, the national TV channel, in 2009, which provoked some uproar from local journalists who said they were worried about government interference in news gathering. Khama was up for election at the time of writing, and it was widely expected he would win and keep the BDP in the country's driver's seat.

The official government website is www.gov .bw. Through it you can contact government ministries, read up on the constitution and budget, and keep abreast of any other Botswanan issues you care about.

With an ever-diminishing resource of diamonds, the country remains economically vulnerable (see the boxed text, above). Local media buzzes with articles that worry the economy has not yet diversified enough into other industries. Unemployment has been curbed and stands at a respectable 7.5% (down from perhaps 40% in 2004), but 30% of the population still lives below the poverty line. And the economy is in a precarious position: in 2009 Reuters reported the country's GDP shrank by 20.3% in the first quarter of the year. A young generation of educated Batswana, lured by the malls of Gaborone, are demanding greater opportunities away from traditional rural life, and the government has some huge responsibilities to live up to.

1974–90	2002	2008
Botswana becomes one of the frontline states seeking to bring majority rule to Zimbabwe, Namibia and South Africa. It also becomes a refuge for political exiles from South Africa.	Botswana becomes the only country in the world to offer antiretroviral drugs to its HIV-infected citizens free of charge. Nonetheless, the AIDS epidemic remains, by far, the nation's greatest public health issue.	Ian Khama, son of Botswana founding father Sir Seretse Khama, assumes the presidency of the nation.

Botswana Culture

THE NATIONAL PSYCHE

Proud, conservative, resourceful and respectful, the Batswana have an ingrained feeling of national identity and an impressive belief in their government and country. Their history – a series of clever manoeuvres that meant they avoided the worst aspects of colonisation – does them proud and lends them a confidence in themselves, their government and the future that is rare in post-colonial Africa. Admittedly this faith in government and progress has been facilitated by Botswana's incredible diamond wealth, which has allowed for significant investment in education, health and infrastructure.

Although there are some 26 tribal groups in Botswana, the fact that around 60% of the population claims Tswana heritage makes for a clear and stable majority. And since independence, the government has endeavoured to foster the national identity. Unlike those of Namibia, citizens of Botswana are known as Batswana regardless of their tribal affiliations and almost everyone communicates via the lingua franca of Tswana, a native language, rather than Afrikaans or English.

Education has also had a unifying effect on the population, and the government proudly claims that its commitment of over 30% of its budget to education is the highest per capita in the world. Visitors can't help but be impressed by the number and quality of schools throughout Botswana and the commitment by parents to educate their children. As a result, adult literacy is an impressive 74.4% (the average for the rest of sub-Saharan Africa is 58.5%) and most Batswana are well informed and politically engaged.

No people are without worries, though. The Batswana realise that the wealth of the diamond mines is a temporary thing, and they are not all optimistic at the pace of the diversification of the economy. And there are some who say the Batswana are not prudently investing their wealth, spending it instead on cars that are then driven to Gaborone's malls. Consumer versus traditional culture is hardly a uniquely Batswana phenomenon, but it is one that has seized the attention of the nation.

The news website www .afrol.com has a bunch of excellent articles on African culture and society. It's easy to search by country and the site holds a massive archive of past features.

LIFESTYLE

Traditional culture acts as a sort of societal glue. Respect for one's elders, firmly held religious beliefs, traditional gender roles and the tradition of the *kgotla* – a specially designated meeting place in each village where grievances can be aired – create a well-defined social structure with some stiff mores at its core. But despite some heavyweight social responsibilities the Batswana have an easy-going and unhurried approach to life, and the emotional framework of the extended family makes for an inclusive network. As the pace and demands of modern life increase, this support is becoming ever more vital as men and women migrate to cities to work in more lucrative jobs, usually leaving children behind to be cared for by other family members.

Historically, the Batswana are farmers and cattle herders. Cattle, and to a lesser extent goats and sheep, are still, in many ways, the measure of a man. Villages grew up around reliable water sources and developed into complex settlements with *kgosi* (chiefs) ultimately responsible for the affairs of the community.

Batswana village life is admirably organised. Each family is entitled to land, and traditional homesteads are social affairs, consisting of communal eating places and separate huts for sleeping, sometimes for several family

When visiting rural settlements, it's a good idea to announce your presence to the chief and ask permission before setting up camp. Women should dress modestly, especially in villages and in the presence of chiefs.

ETIQUETTE TIPS

Although there are a lot of rules of social etiquette within Batswana culture, foreigners are not expected to know or abide by most of them. Of course, you should maintain common sense – wearing shorts and T-shirts to church, for example, won't endear you to anyone. In general, you should always err on the side of modesty when interacting with locals. For instance, despite the way they dance at the club, Batswana traditional culture frowns on excessive public displays of affection between couples, married or not. Even public hand-holding is pretty rare. With that said, Batswana, who are used to riding in cramped kombis and growing up in rural villages, may not have the same sense of personal space you possess, and might think nothing of resting a hand on your leg on a crowded bus.

Because the national culture is so defined by hierarchy, it is not common for children to question or talk back to parents, or for underlings to contradict overlings As an aside, this is one reason the character Mma Ramotswe, from the *No. 1 Ladies Detective Agency* novels, rings a bit false. The regular questioning she engages in, while a nice narrative trope, simply cuts against the grain of preserving social order that is at the heart of Batswana culture. This is why justice has so often been investigated, and punishment determined, within the communal village venue of the *kgotla*.

Keep in mind a Motswana is a single citizen of the nation, while the people of the country refer to themselves as the Batswana in the plural. Their language is Tswana.

---

members. In each village the most important building is the *kgotla*, where social and judicial affairs are discussed and dealt with.

Even today as mud-brick architecture gives way to breeze blocks, and villages grow into busy towns and cities, most homes retain traditional features and life is still a very social affair. The atmosphere in family compounds is busy and convivial, although everything is done at a leisurely pace. Likewise, in shops and businesses people spend a huge amount of time greeting and agreeing with each other, and checking up on each other's welfare. It may be that this measured and sociable attitude has contributed to Botswana's prevailing atmosphere of peace in a largely troubled region.

As in Namibia, greetings are an important formality in Botswana and should not be overlooked. You tend to get better answers to your questions if you greet people with a friendly '*Dumela*', followed by a '*rra*' (for men) and '*mma*' for women. It is also important to emphasise that a two-hand handshake (ie your left hand on your elbow while you shake) is preferable to a Western-style handshake. Putting your left hand on your elbow is also important when money is changing hands. For more information about basic greetings, see the boxed text, p212.

> The entertainment page of www.thevoicebw.com is a great source of news and views about what's hot and what's not in the Batswana social scene.

ECONOMY

Botswana is a happy exception to the litany of poor economic performance that plagues so much of Africa. Its proven record of good governance and lack of corruption – it consistently ranks as the least, or one of the least corrupt countries in Africa, by Transparency International – has encouraged both international investment and a healthy degree of confidence among the local populace. This is despite the fact that most Batswana still live in rural areas and are dependent on crop and livestock farming, and only 0.7% of the land is arable.

The measure of success of most Batswana is cattle ownership; most of the beef harvested from the country's national herd is exported. But the country's main industry has been, from five years since independence till today, diamonds.

> If you want to learn some Tswana, the major indigenous language in Botswana, pick up *First Steps in Spoken Setswana* or the *Setswana-English Phrasebook*.

Botswana has been the largest producer of gem diamonds in the world since the early 1980s, and excavates nearly a quarter of the world's diamond supply. Jwaneng, the single-richest diamond mine in the world, has been operating since 1982. With the exception of the Lerala mine, opened in 2008, the country's diamond industry is run by Debswana, a joint venture between the Botswanan government and South African company De Beers. The government has spread this wealth throughout Botswana's small population fairly equitably, a model for resource management and wealth re-investment that has been the envy of the rest of Africa. Currently, Gaborone hosts the headquarters of the 14-nation Southern African Development Community (SADC).

But mineral resources alone does not a strong economy make, and the question of how the economy will evolve is a perennial one. Along with financial services, tourism has become one of the primary drivers of this diversification. Although Botswana does not possess the brand reputation or hotel infrastructure of Sub-Saharan tourism giants like Kenya and South Africa, its profile is increasing. Because so much land is un-arable and the population is so low, there are not as many issues over reserving large tracts of land for game reserves.

The average Motswana has a per capita income of $14,300. In Zimbabwe, that number is around $200; its $5200 in Namibia and $1400 in Zambia. Those numbers speak for themselves in terms of the quality of life of the Botswanan population. The issue of economic diversification is a clear and present one, but given the state of her neighbours, it's nice that Botswana's biggest economic question is over how to maintain her prosperity.

POPULATION

Botswana's population in 2009 was estimated at almost two million, a figure that takes into account the fact that Botswana has one of the highest rates of

EDUCATION: A RIGHT OR A PRIVILEGE?

The British almost entirely neglected the educational needs of the Batswana. By independence in 1966 there were only a few secondary schools in the country and literacy rates languished at 15%.

After independence, education became a buzzword, but how to fund such a costly exercise in a poor and underdeveloped country? Luckily for Botswana, diamonds came to the rescue and in the 1970s the government ploughed its new-found revenue into primary and secondary school education programs. By 1981 an amazing 84% of primary school–aged children were attending classes, and secondary and tertiary education were offered as well. Not satisfied with this stunning progress, the government abolished school fees in 1987 in an attempt to get even more children into schools.

But as Botswana's diamond deposits diminish, the government is faced with some unattractive economic choices: in January 2006 part-payment of school fees was reintroduced, amid much controversy. The new cost to parents is now around 5% of the total cost of each child's education over the year, a sum of P194 for secondary children and P452 (US$84) for those attending senior secondary school.

Despite these relatively modest sums, many people will be unable to meet the costs. The move was roundly condemned by opposition parties, who pointed out that almost a third of Batswana lived below the poverty line.

The then minister of education, Jacob Nkate, insisted that the reintroduction of school fees was an essential cost-cutting exercise in the face of falling revenues, although he was also keen to emphasise that Botswana remains committed to the concept of universal access envisaged in the country's development plans. For the time being the best compromise the government has on offer is a means test to exempt the poorest of the poor from paying the fees.

HIV infection in the world. Since the early 1990s the annual birth rate has dropped from 3.5% to about 2.3%, and for a period the annual population growth rate was estimated at a negative – minus 0.04% in 2006. This has since changed to a growth rate of 1.9%. Officially, life expectancy soared from 49 years at the time of independence (1966) to about 70 years by the mid-1990s. It's thought that without the scourge of AIDS, life expectancy in Botswana would now be around 74 years, on a par with the USA. Instead, today's figure is about 62 years, which is still a marked improvement on 33 years, the life expectancy around 2006. That increase is testament to the government's generally sound handling of antiretroviral drug distribution and commitment to condom distribution and sex education.

The adoption of a European-style central government and a capitalist economic system has resulted in the mass migration of people into urban areas in search of cash-yielding vocational and professional jobs. Botswana is now one of the world's most predominantly urban societies, with nearly 60% of the population living in urban centres, mostly in eastern Botswana. Like most African countries, Botswana has a youthful population: the median age is 21.7 years old.

PEOPLE OF BOTSWANA

All citizens of Botswana – regardless of colour, ancestry or tribal affiliation – are known as Batswana (plural) or Motswana (singular). In the lingua franca of Tswana, tribal groups are usually denoted by the prefix 'ba', which means 'the people of...'. Therefore, the Herero are known as Baherero, the Kgalagadi as Bakgalagadi, and so on. Botswana's eight major tribes are represented in the House of Chiefs, the country's second legislative body.

Batswana

Botswana means 'land of the Tswana' and about 60% of the country's population claims Tswana heritage. The origins of the Tswana are simple enough (see p53). As land-owning agriculturalists, the Tswana tribes have clearly defined areas of influence. The Bangwato are centred on the Serowe area, the Bakwena in and around Molepolole and the Bangwaketse near Kanye. A later split in the Bangwato resulted in a fourth group, the Batawana, who are concentrated near Maun in the northwest.

The greetings *'dumela rra'*, when speaking to men, and *'dumela mma'*, when speaking to women, are considered compliments and Batswana appreciate their liberal use.

Bakalanga

Botswana's second largest ethnic group is the Bakalanga, another powerful land-owning group whose members are thought to descend from the Rozwi empire – the culture responsible for building Great Zimbabwe. In the colonial reshuffle, the Bakalanga were split in two and now some 75% of them live in western Zimbabwe. In Botswana, they are based mainly, although not exclusively, around Francistown.

Herero

The Herero probably originated from eastern or central Africa and migrated across the Okavango River into northeastern Namibia in the early 16th century. In 1884 the Germans took possession of German South West Africa (Namibia) and systematically appropriated Herero grazing lands. The ensuing conflict between the Germans and the Herero was to last for years, only ending in a calculated act of genocide that saw the remaining members of the tribe flee across the border into Botswana (see the boxed text, p206).

The refugees settled among the Batawana and were initially subjugated but eventually regained their herds and independence. These days the Herero are among the wealthiest herders in Botswana.

Basubiya

The Basubiya, Wayeyi and Mbukushu are all riverine tribes scattered around the Chobe and Linyanti Rivers and across the Okavango Panhandle. Their histories and migrations are a textbook example of the ebb and flow of power and influence. For a long time, the Basubiya were the dominant force, pushing the Wayeyi away from the Chobe River and into the Okavango after a little spat over a lion skin, so tradition says. The Basubiya were agriculturists and as such proved easy prey for the growing Lozi empire (from modern Zambia), which in turned collapsed in 1865. They still live in the Chobe district.

Wayeyi (Bayei)

Originally from the same areas in Namibia and Angola as the Mbukushu, the Wayeyi moved south from the Chobe River into the Okavango Delta in the mid-18th century to avoid the growing conflict with the Basubiya. They established themselves around Lake Ngami and eventually dispersed into the Okavango Delta. At the same time the Bangwato (a Batswana offshoot) were pushing northwards and came into contact with the Wayeyi. Over time this relationship became a form of clientship, which many Wayeyi still feel resentful about today.

In 1948 and 1962 the Wayeyi made efforts to free themselves of Batswana rule, but neither attempt succeeded. In 1995, these efforts were renewed in a more concerted manner with the establishment of the Kamanakao Association, which aims to develop and protect Wayeyi culture and language. Following this, the Wayeyi decided to revive their chieftainship and on 24 April 1999 they elected Calvin Diile Kamanakao as Chief Kamanakao I and recommended him for inclusion in the House of Chiefs. The government rejected this proposal, so in 2001 the Wayeyi took the matter to the High Court, which passed judgment that chiefs elected by their own tribes should be admitted to the house. In 2008 Shikati Fish Matepe Ozoo was appointed to the House of Chiefs by former president Festus Mogae. In the meantime, the UNHCR has pointed out that most Wayeyi children cannot speak their ancestral tongue, one of the keys to maintaining a distinct ethnic identity.

For an insider's account of one of the most dramatic love stories and political scandals of its time, read Seretse and Ruth: Botswana's Love Story, *written by Wilf and Trish Mbanga.*

Mbukushu (or Hambukushu)

The Mbukushu, who now inhabit the Ngamiland area around the Okavango Delta, were originally refugees from the Caprivi Strip in northeastern Namibia. They were forced to flee south in the late 18th century after being dislodged by the forces of Chief Ngombela's Lozi empire. The Mbukushu carried on to southeastern Angola, just north of present-day Andara (Namibia). There, they encountered Portuguese and African traders, who began purchasing Mbukushu commoners from the tribal leadership to be used and resold as slaves. To escape, some Mbukushu headed back to the Okavango Panhandle, where they mixed and intermarried with the Batawana. Many remain in and around the villages of Shakawe and Sepopa.

San

Once the San roamed over most of the African continent. Certainly they were living in the Kalahari and Tsodilo Hills as far back as 30,000 years ago, as archaeological finds in the Kalahari have demonstrated. Some linguists even credit them with the invention of language. Unlike most other African countries, where the San have perished or disappeared through war and

For some cultural info on life in a Batswana village, get hold of a copy of Serowe: Village of the Rain and Wind *by Bessie Head.*

interbreeding, Botswana and Namibia retain the remnants of their San communities – barely 100,000 individuals in total, which may include many mixed San. Of these, around 60% live in Botswana (the !Kung, G//ana, G/wi and !xo being the largest groups) and 35% in Namibia (the Naro, !Xukwe, Hei//kom and Ju/hoansi), with the remainder scattered throughout South Africa, Angola, Zimbabwe and Zambia.

THE PAST
Traditionally the San were nomadic hunter-gatherers who travelled in small family bands (usually between around 25 and 35 people) within well-defined territories. They had no chiefs or hierarchy of leadership and decisions were reached by group consensus. With no animals, crops or possessions, the San were highly mobile. Everything that they needed for their daily existence they carried with them.

The term 'Basarwa,' used to describe the San, is considered pejorative. It literally means 'people of the sticks'.

Initially the San's social flexibility enabled them to evade conquest and control. But as other powerful tribes with big herds of livestock and farming ambitions moved into the area, inevitable disputes arose over the land. The San's wide-ranging, nomadic lifestyle (some territories extended over 1000 sq km) was utterly at odds with the settled world of the farmers and soon became a source of bitter conflict. This situation was rapidly accelerated by European colonists, who arrived in the area during the mid-17th century. The early Boers pursued an extermination campaign that lasted for 200 years and killed as many as 200,000 indigenous people. Such territorial disputes, combined with modern policies on wildlife conservation, have seen the San increasingly disenfranchised and dispossessed. What's more, in the modern world their disparate social structure has made it exceedingly difficult for them to organise pressure groups to defend their rights and land as other groups have done.

FIGHTING OVER THE CKGR
Today the San are largely impoverished. Many work on farms and cattle posts or live in squalid, handout-dependent and alcohol-plagued settlements centred on boreholes in western Botswana and northeastern Namibia as debate rages around them as to their 'place' in modern African society.

As late as 1910, the farmers around Grootfontein (Namibia) petitioned a local magistrate to let them class the San as *vogelvrei* (game) to be shot all year round.

Nearly all of Botswana's and Namibia's San were relocated from their ancestral lands to new government settlements such as New Xade in the central Kalahari. It's one of the biggest political hot potatoes for the current Botswanan government. In 2006 this resettlement program earned the government a reprimand from the UN's Committee on the Elimination of Racial Discrimination. The Botswanan government maintains that its relocation policies have the San's best interests at heart (see the section 'Relocation of Basarwa' on the government website, www.gov.bw). Development, education and modernisation are its buzzwords. The trouble is, many San actively rejected the government's version of modernisation if it meant giving up their ancestral lands and traditions.

A significant landmark was the ruling of South Africa's highest court in favour of the Richtersveld people (relatives of the San) of Northern Cape Province in 2003. For the first time, the court recognised that indigenous people have both communal land ownership and mineral rights over their territory. Such a ruling had important implications for countries such as Botswana, which operates under the same Roman-Dutch legal system.

The court case brought by the First People of the Kalahari (FPK) against the government's relocation policies was concluded in May 2006, and approximately 1000 San attached their names to the effort. During the proceedings many San tried to return home to the Central Kalahari Game Reserve

(CKGR), but most were forced off the grounds of the reserve. In December 2006 the high court ruled that the eviction of the San was 'unlawful and unconstitutional'. One justice went so far as to say that not allowing the San to hunt in their homeland 'was tantamount to condemning the residents of the CKGR to death by starvation'.

THE FUTURE
The outlook for the San is uncertain. One of Africa's greatest dilemmas in the 21st century is how to preserve old cultures and traditions while accepting and adapting to the new.

Historical precedents, like those of the Native Americans, the Innu of Canada and the Australian Aborigines, certainly don't encourage optimism. But the groundswell of protest generated by grassroots bodies such as the Southern African minorities organisation **WIMSA** (Working Group for Indigenous Minorities of Southern Africa; www.san.org.za) is gaining ever more international attention.

Tourism provides some measure of economic opportunity for the San, who are often employed in Ghanzi- and Kalahari-based lodges as game guides and trackers. But it is also argued that for this race to survive into the 21st century, they require not only self-sufficiency and international support but institutional support and recognition from within the Gaborone government.

> For a window on the life of the San, join local hunter !Nqate in Craig and Damon Foster's film *The Great Dance*, an inspiring collaborative project that involved the local community at every stage of the filming and editing.

RELIGION
As the scholarly Anglican priest John Mbiti said, 'Africans are notoriously religious', and Batswana society is imbued with spirituality, whether that be Christianity or local indigenous belief systems. For most Batswana religion is a vital part of life, substantiating human existence in the universe as well as providing a social framework.

Botswana's early tribal belief systems were primarily cults centred on ancestor worship. For the Batswana this meant the worship of Modimo, a supreme being who created the world and represented the ancestors. Other ethnic groups may have differing cosmologies, but the majority of belief systems revolve around the worship of an omnipotent power (for the San it is N!odima and for the Herero it is Ndjambi) and the enactment of rituals to appease the ancestors, who are believed to play an active role in everyday life.

By the 19th century Christian missionaries had begun to arrive and brought with them an entirely new set of ideas that dislodged many indigenous traditions and practices. They established the first schools and as a result the Christian message began to spread.

Today about 30% of Batswana adhere to the Christian faith (the majority are either Catholic or Anglican), while around 60% adhere to the practices of the African Religion, an indigenous religion that integrates Christian liturgy with the more ritualistic elements of traditional ancestor worship. It comprises a variety of churches (the Healing Church of Botswana, the Zionist Christian Church and the Apostolic Faith Mission) and is extremely popular in rural areas.

> Have no idea about the African Religion? Then log on to Chidi Isizoh's religious resource, www.afrikaworld.net/afrel, where you can plumb the depths of marriage, music and myth.

WOMEN IN BOTSWANA
In one of the most peaceful and admired countries in Africa, violence against women is shockingly prevalent. In a survey conducted by the **Women's International League for Peace and Freedom** (www.peacewomen.org), 86% of respondents rated violence against women as a community problem and 88% said it was on the increase. Over 60% saw severe beating as the most prevalent form of abuse; 47% identified rape. A third of respondents knew a woman who had fled her home due to violence.

Traditional culture is often cited as the 'excuse' for battering women, as traditional law permits men to 'chastise' their wives. Monica Tabengwa, director of Metlhaetsile Women's Information Centre, went on record saying, 'Most women expect to be battered and most men consider it their duty to batter'. Similarly, women married under traditional law (or in 'common property') are regarded as legal minors and require their husband's consent to buy or sell property and enter into legally binding contracts.

In addition, Botswana's current laws prohibit rape but do not recognise the concept of marital rape. The minimum sentence for rape is 10 years; the penalty increases to 15 years with corporal punishment if the offender is HIV positive, and to 20 years with corporal punishment if the offender knew they were HIV positive at the time of the rape.

Women married under traditional law are legal minors. According to the **Social Institutions and Gender Index** (http://genderindex.org), 'They need their husband's consent for access to property other than land, access to bank loans and any other legally binding contract'. As a result, 'increasingly, women in Botswana are exercising their right to marry out of common property [traditional marriage]'.

Girls are taught that it is culturally unacceptable for them to talk about anything to do with sex, whatever their rights may be on paper. Mothers, meanwhile, have been taught to guard family 'secrets' at all costs, which only allows any abuse to proliferate. Groups have also noted that there are instances of older men taking advantage of younger women by offering them economic support or academic 'help' in exchange for sexual favours. Peace Women estimates one in five students have been asked to have sex with their teachers, and of these half have accepted the proposition. A shocking 14% of these cases occur in primary schools.

In a speech on World AIDS Day in 2005, then-President Mogae cited economic imbalances, lack of empowerment and gender-based violence and inequality as some of the key contributing factors to the soaring rate of HIV in 15- to 19-year-old girls. He ended his speech by urging every Batswana 'to summon [their] deeper moral ethics and sense of responsibility to put a stop to this behaviour'.

ARTS

Botswana's earliest artists were the San, who painted the world they lived in on the rock walls of their shelters. They were also master craftsmen, producing tools, musical instruments and material crafts from wood, leather and ostrich eggshells. This fundamental artistic aesthetic in the most utilitarian pots, fabrics, baskets and tools is one of Botswana's (and Africa's) greatest artistic legacies. But the contemporary art scene in Botswana is not confined to the material arts; there are also immensely talented painters and sculptors producing some dynamic modern artwork.

Architecture

Traditional Batswana architecture is compact and beautiful, and blends well with the landscape. A typical village would have been a large, sprawling and densely populated affair, comprising hundreds of round mud-brick houses (*ntlo* or rondavel) topped with neat thatched roofs of *motshikiri* (thatching grass).

The mud bricks used for construction are ideally made from the concrete-like earth of the termite mound and then plastered with a mixture of soil and cow dung. Often, the exterior is then decorated with a paint made from a mixture of cow dung and different coloured soils. The paint is spread by hand using the unique *lekgapho* designs, which are lovely and quite fanciful.

Since 1998 Botswana has tumbled 35 places down the human development index compiled by the UN, which measures quality of life. In 2005 it was ranked at 131 out of a total of 177 countries.

To find out about Botswana's stance on controversial human-rights issues, log on to the website of the locally based advocacy organisation Ditshwanelo (www .ditshwanelo.org.bw).

AIDS: THE PLAGUE OF SUB-SAHARAN AFRICA

While sub-Saharan Africa is home to roughly 11% of the world's population, it currently accounts for almost 67% of all estimated global HIV cases. Twenty-four of the world's most affected countries are in Africa, and Botswana's HIV prevalence places it second among them. According to UNAIDS and the World Health Organization, nearly 24% of all Batswana are HIV positive, and women represent over half of those cases.

Botswana symbolises the tremendous challenge that HIV/AIDS poses to African development in the 21st century. It is blessed with sizeable diamond reserves that have fuelled rapid economic growth since independence and have raised incomes for thousands of its citizens to world-class standards. Yet more than 11,000 people die of HIV/AIDS here every year. In 2001, former president Festus Mogae lamented that, unless the epidemic was reversed, his country faced 'blank extinction'.

More worryingly, AIDS is making Africa, and Botswana, poorer by the day, as the virus tends to hit people in their most productive years. Researchers at ING Baring forecast that by 2010 the South African economy will be 17% smaller. They could be wrong, but there is no doubt that AIDS will make a lot of things worse before they get any better.

With all of that said, while the situation is not resolved by any means, Botswana has also taken some of the most admirable steps of any sub-Sahara African nation in reversing the damaging trends wrought by AIDS. In 2001, Botswana became the first African country to trial antiretroviral (ARV) drug therapy on a national scale, for which it earned international praise. And it is one of just a handful of countries worldwide that have committed to providing ARV treatment free to all of its HIV-positive citizens. In addition, it has committed itself to reversing the epidemic by 2016.

These policies are already bearing some fruit. Life expectancy, which was once an appalling 33 years, is up to almost 62. In a 2008 report UNAIDS estimated that the antiretroviral treatment program was covering 91,780 people, and transmission of the disease from mother to child was down from between 20% and 40% to between 4% and 6%. Across Gaborone, you see billboards asking passers-by: 'Who is in YOUR sexual network?'.

But issues remain. Anecdotally, workers in medical NGOs in Gaborone told us the prevalence of antiretrovirals has made some people less likely to practice safe sex. Traditional male circumcision, an integral part of Southern African culture, is also responsible for spreading the disease. And the continuing patterns of social migration between the countryside and the city are potentially exposing more Batswana to the epidemic.

To keep up with the effects of HIV/AIDS on sub-Saharan countries, log on to www.unaids.org, www.avert.org and www.who.int.

The thatch on the roofs is also an intricate business. Roof poles are taken from strong solid trees, lashed together with flexible branches and covered with tightly packed grass. When it's finished, the thatch is coated with oil and ash to discourage infestation by termites. Barring bad weather, a good thatching job can last five to 15 years and a rondavel can last 30 years or more.

These days, cement is the building material of choice, so the traditional home with its colourful designs may eventually die out. *Decorated Homes in Botswana,* by Sandy and Elinah Grant, is an attempt to capture just some of the wonderful examples of traditional architecture and promote the art of home decorating.

One interesting and accessible village where visitors can see traditional Botswanan architecture is Mochudi (p89), near Gaborone.

Traditional Arts & Crafts

Botswana is most famous for the basketry produced in the northwestern regions of the Okavango Delta by Wayeyi and Mbukushu women. Like most material arts in Africa they have a practical purpose, but their intricate construction and evocative designs – with names like Tears of the Giraffe or Flight of the Swallows – are anything but.

In the watery environs of the delta the baskets serve as watertight containers for grains and seeds. The weaving is so tight on some that they were also used as beer kegs. All the baskets are made from the leaf fibre of the real fan palm (*mokolane*) and colours are derived from soaking the fibres in natural plant dyes. The work is incredibly skilful and provides one of the most important sources of income for rural families.

The best place to purchase the work is the Shorobe Baskets Cooperative (p129) in Shorobe. While it is always better to buy craftwork in the area in which it is produced (you tend to get better prices and the proceeds go directly to the community in question) another good place to browse for high-quality crafts is Botswanacraft (p88) in Gaborone.

Also be on the lookout for traditional San crafts including ostrich-eggshell jewellery, which can be purchased from Contemporary San Art Gallery & Craft Shop (p151), a community-run cooperative in D'kar. If you're in the Gaborone area, it's also worth paying a visit to the renowned Oodi Weavers (see the boxed text, p91).

Dance

For information about Botswanan literature, music and dance, see the Arts & Culture Review in the *Mmegi* newspaper; the Lifestyle supplement in the *Botswana Guardian;* and Read, Listen & Watch in the *Botswana Gazette.*

In traditional tribal societies dance has an important symbolic role in expressing social values and marking the different stages of life. It is also a key component of traditional medicine and ancestor worship, where dance is a medium of communication with the spiritual realm. In a world without TV it's also a great excuse for a community knees-up.

The most well-documented dances in popular travel literature like *The Healing Land* (see p19) and films like *The Great Dance* are those of the San, whose traditional dances have many different meanings. They were a way to thank the gods for a successful hunt and plentiful rains, to cure the sick, and to celebrate a girl's transition into womanhood. Implements used in San dancing include decorated dancing sticks, fly whisks created from wildebeest tails, and dancing rattles, which are leather strings through cocoons full of tiny stones or broken ostrich eggshells.

One of the more interesting dances is the *ndazula* dance, a rain dance used to thank the gods for a plentiful harvest. Another is *borankana,* which originated in southern Botswana but is now enjoyed all over the country. It features in dance and music competitions and exhibitions and is practised by school groups across Botswana. *Borankana,* which is Tswana for 'traditional entertainment', includes the unique *setlhako* and *sephumuso* rhythms, which feature in music by artists such as Nick Nkosanah Ndaba.

Most visitors will encounter traditional dancing in the rather staged displays at top-end safari camps. A more genuine and less affected arena is the Maitisong Festival (see the boxed text, p85), Botswana's biggest arts festival, held at the end of March in Gaborone.

Literature

Born in Zimbabwe, Alexander McCall Smith has brought Batswana life to light in his popular detective series, beginning with *The No. 1 Ladies' Detective Agency,* which has recently become a TV series. Read more at www.mccallsmith.com.

The first work to be published in Tswana was the Holy Bible (completed by 1857), shortly followed by *The Pilgrim's Progress.* However, Botswana's first major work of fiction was *Mhudi* (1930), written by the pioneer Motswana writer Sol Plaatje. Plaatje, along with his contemporary, LD Raditladi, also translated the works of Shakespeare into Tswana, in addition to Raditladi's plays and love poetry.

But these are the exceptions and most 19th-century literature to come out of Botswana was adventurous travel literature like *The Lion Hunter of*

South Africa (1856) by Roualeyn Gordon Cumming – the archetype of the modern safari adventure. Likewise, David Livingstone's *Missionary Travels* was another bestseller and has rarely been out of print since its first publication in 1857.

Botswana's most famous modern literary figure was South African–born Bessie Head (1937–86), who fled apartheid in South Africa and settled in Sir Seretse Khama's village of Serowe. Her writings, many of which are set in Serowe, reflect the harshness and beauty of African village life and the physical attributes of Botswana itself. Her most widely read works include: *Serowe – Village of the Rain Wind, When Rain Clouds Gather, Maru, A Question of Power, The Cardinals, A Bewitched Crossroad* and *The Collector of Treasures,* which is an anthology of short stories.

Since the 1980s Tswana novel writing has had something of a revival with the publication in English of novels like Andrew Sesinyi's *Love on the Rocks* (1983) and Gaele Sobott-Mogwe's haunting collection of short stories, *Colour Me Blue* (1995), which blends fantasy and reality with the everyday grit of African life.

Other novels that lend insight into contemporary Batswana life are *Jamestown Blues* (1997) and *Place of Reeds* (2005) by Caitlin Davies, who was married to a Motswana and lived in Botswana for 12 years. The former, fictional, work tells of expatriate life as seen through the eyes of a young Motswana girl. More affecting, however, is Davies' story of her life as a Motswana wife and mother in *Place of Reeds*. Equally interesting are American Norman Rush's two books, a collection of short stories on expatriate life called *Whites* (1992) and his prize-winning novel *Mating* (1993), a comedy of manners featuring two Americans in 1980s Botswana.

Unity Dow, Botswana's first female high court judge, has also authored four books to date, all of them dealing with contemporary social issues in the country; we recommend *Far and Beyon'* (2002).

For a comprehensive library of African literature, including lots of hard-to-find studies and local fiction, try www.africabookcentre.com.

POETRY
Like many African cultures, Botswana has a rich oral tradition of poetry and much of Botswana's literary heritage, its ancient myths and poetry, is still unavailable in translation. One of the few books that are available is *Bayeyi & Hambukushu: Tales from the Okavango,* edited by Thomas J Larson, which is a primary source of oral poetry and stories from the Okavango Panhandle region.

Botswana's best-known poet is probably Barolong Seboni, who, in 1993, was poet in residence at the Scottish Poetry Library in Edinburgh. He has written several books of poems, including the short volume *Love Songs* (1994) and *Windsongs of the Kgalagadi* (1995), which details some of the Batswana traditions, myths and history that have been recited for centuries. He is now a senior lecturer in the English department of the University of Botswana and in 2004 he was one of the star performers at the eighth **Poetry Africa Festival** (www.cca.ukzn.ac.za).

More modern poetry tends to highlight current issues. For example, *The Silent Bomb* aimed to promote awareness of HIV/AIDS. It was written by AIDS activist Billy Mosedame (1968–2004), who himself succumbed to the virus in February 2004.

One of the few Batswana playwrights whose works have been performed in Botswana is Albert GTK Malikongwa; his work includes *The Smell of Cowdung* and *Chief Mengwe IV.*

Music
Music, like dance, is one of Africa's oldest traditions. It's a form of expression dating back thousands of years to the earliest San societies, where men gathered around their campfires playing their thumb pianos (*mbira*) accompanied by music bows.

Today, Botswana's music scene is as rich and varied as ever, with ancient and modern musical traditions fuelling a contemporary fusion scene of vibrant beauty. Is this diluting Batswana culture? Yes, but it also attracts new listeners, safeguarding a sound-world of extraordinary range and diversity.

Jazz, reggae, gospel and hip-hop are the most popular forms of modern music – almost nothing else features on Batswana radio or is played live in nightclubs and bars. Bojazz is the colloquial term for a form of music called Botswana jazz. It has been immortalised by Nick Nkosanah Ndaba, among others, who recently released *Dawn of Bojazz*, the first bojazz album to be produced in Botswana. Another popular artist is Ras Baxton, a Rastafarian who plays what he calls 'tswana reggae', but he, like many other Batswana artists, has to go to South Africa to make a living. Banjo Mosele is huge all around the nation, and we interview Bonjour Keipidile, perhaps the greatest living guitarist in Botswana, in our Okavango chapter (see the boxed text, p123).

Other strange fusion sounds are *gumba-gumba*, a modern blend of Zulu and Tswana music mixed with a dose of traditional jazz – the word comes from the township slang for 'party'. Alfredo Mos is the father of *rumba kwasa*, that African bum-gyrating jive that foreigners have so such trouble emulating. Hot on his heals is *kwasa kwasa* king Franco, one of the most successful artists in Botswana at the moment alongside the Wizards, Vee and Jeff Matheatau.

Wildly popular is Botswana's version of hip-hop, championed by the Wizards, who fuse the style with ragga and R&B. There's even a TV show *(Strictly Hip Hop)*, on Wednesday evenings, hosted by the inimitable Draztik and Slim, co-founders of the South African hip-hop label Unreleased Records. It's nearly always been the case that talented Batswana musicians have had to move to South Africa to make a living, but as of this writing there was still some decent talent here, including Kast, Scar, Vee and Stagga Don Dada. Kwaito music, the South African township fusion of hip-hop, house and all things that make booties shake, is also hugely popular.

One reliable measure of local talent is *My African Dream*, Botswana's version of *Pop Idol*. The show is faithfully watched across the country and, as these things are wont to do, has plucked at the musical dreams of many a Gaborone-bound Motswana youth.

Aside from this, jazz festivals are held every few weeks in the winter (dry season) in and around Gaborone, including Bojanala Waterfront at the picturesque Gaborone Dam (p92) and at the huge National Stadium (p84). These festivals are great fun, safe and cheap. Details are advertised in the English-language newspapers.

Compact discs and cassettes of traditional San music are available in D'kar (p150) and at Botswanacraft outlets in Gaborone (p88).

Get into the *rumba kwasa* groove by picking up the *Alfredo Mos* DVD. It features six videos of his concerts and recordings.

FOOD & DRINK
Staples & Specialties

Forming the centre of most Batswana meals nowadays is *mabele* (sorghum) or *bogobe* (porridge made from sorghum), but these staples are rapidly being replaced by imported maize mealies, sometimes known by the Afrikaans name *mealie pap*, or just plain *pap*. This provides the base for an array of meat and vegetable sauces like *seswaa* (shredded goat or lamb), *morogo* (wild spinach) or *leputshe* (wild pumpkin). For breakfast, you might be able to try *pathata* (sort of like an English muffin) or *megunya*, also known as fat cakes. These are little balls of fried dough that are kind of like doughnuts minus the hole and, depending on your taste, the flavour.

The more challenging environment of the Kalahari means that the San have an extraordinary pantry, including desert plants like *morama*, which produces leguminous pods that contain edible beans. There is also an immense tuber that contains large quantities of water. Other desert delectables include marula fruit, wild plums, berries, tsama melons, wild cucumbers and honey. There's also a type of edible fungus (grewia flava) related to the European truffle but now known to the marketing people as the 'Kalahari truffle'.

It's most unlikely that travellers will encounter any of these dishes, although some top-end safari lodges do make variations on some of the more conventional Batswana meat and vegetable recipes. Otherwise, you'll be dining on international fare, some of which is quite sumptuous considering the logistical problems of getting food in and out of remote locations. Many hotels offer buffets, and there's always a good selection of fruit and vegetables. In larger towns you'll even find a selection of Indian and Chinese restaurants.

Oh, and don't forget mopane worms. These fat suckers are pulled off mopane trees and fried into little delicacies – they're tasty and a good source of protein. You might be able to buy some from ladies selling them by the bag in the Main Mall in Gaborone; otherwise, they're pretty common up in Francistown.

Drinks

Decent locally made brews include Castle Lager (made under licence from the South African brewery), St Louis Special Light and Lion Lager; also available are the excellent Windhoek Lager (from Namibia) and Zambezi Lager (from Zimbabwe).

Traditional drinks are plentiful. Legal home brews include the common *bojalwa*, an inexpensive sprouted-sorghum beer that is brewed commercially as Chibuku. Another serious drink is made from fermented marula fruit. Light and non-intoxicating *mageu* is made from mealies or sorghum mash. Another is *madila*, a thickened sour milk that is used as a relish or drunk ('eaten' would be a more appropriate term) plain.

Mosukujane tea and lengane tea are used to treat headaches/nausea and arthritis respectively. They're a bit strong in flavour, but locals faithfully tout their remedial properties.

Botswana Environment

THE LAND

Around 100 million years ago the supercontinent Gondwanaland dramatically broke up. As the land mass ripped apart, the edges of the African continent rose up, forming the mountain ranges of Southern and Central Africa. Over the millennia, water and wind weathered these highlands, carrying the fine dust inland to the Kalahari Basin. At 2.5 million sq km it's the earth's largest unbroken tract of sand, stretching from northern South Africa to eastern Namibia and Angola, and to Zambia and Zimbabwe in the west.

At the centre of the basin sits Botswana, the geographic heart of sub-Saharan Africa, extending over 1100km from north to south and 960km from east to west, an area of 582,000 sq km that's equivalent in size to France. The country is entirely landlocked, and it is bordered to the south and southeast by South Africa, across the Limpopo and Molopo Rivers; to the northeast by Zimbabwe; and to the north and the west by Namibia.

Over 85% of the country, including the entire central and southwestern regions, is taken up by the Kalahari. The shifting sand dunes that compose a traditional desert are found only in the far southwest. Nearly all of the country is flat, characterised by scrub-covered savannah and a few lonely *kopjes* like Otse Hill (1489m). In the lower elevations of the northeast are the great salty deserts of the Makgadikgadi Pans, once a great super-lake and now the largest (about 12,000 sq km) complex of salt pans in the world.

But amid this vast thirst land Botswana harbours an environmental treasure, the spectacular Okavango Delta, which snakes into the country from Angola to form a watery paradise of 16,000 sq km of convoluted channels and islands. It is the world's largest inland delta and conservationists are keen to see it awarded World Heritage status. No less captivating are the smaller river systems of the Linyanti, Kwando and Selinda along the northern border with Namibia.

> Botswana has the largest network of national parks and private game reserves – along with the largest elephant population, the largest zebra migrations, the largest inland delta and the largest area of salt pans – in the world.

WILDLIFE

Botswana is a unique African destination: an unusual combination of desert and delta that draws an immense concentration of wildlife to its complex of wetlands in winter and dazzling array of birdlife during summer. It is also wild, pristine and expansive. Nearly 40% of the country is protected in some form or another, including almost the entire northern third of the land, and its national parks and reserves provide a safe haven for some 85 species of mammal and over 1075 species of bird.

For a rundown of all of Botswana's national parks, refer to the National Parks and Reserves chapter, p26.

Animals
MAMMALS

The opportunity of viewing a dazzling array of animals at home in some of Africa's most unspoilt environments is the main reason for visiting Botswana for most people. The Big Five (lion, leopard, elephant, buffalo and rhino) along with a huge variety of other less famous but equally impressive animals – antelopes, giraffes, zebras, wildebeest, red lechwe, puku and hippos – can be seen in abundance in Botswana's two main parks, Chobe National Park (p109) and Moremi Game Reserve (p132).

For more in-depth information about the wildlife found in Botswana, refer to p33 or pick up *Watching Wildlife Southern Africa*, published by Lonely

> The way to tell the difference between a 'mock charge' and a serious charge with an elephant is to look at the ears. During a mock charge the ears will be spread out and the elephant will be trumpeting loudly. In a serious charge the ears are folded back and the head is held down.

CONSERVATION ORGANISATIONS

Anyone with a genuine interest in a specific ecological issue is invited to contact one or more of the following organisations. These organisations do not, however, provide tourist information or offer organised tours (unless stated otherwise).

■ **BirdLife Botswana** (☎ Gaborone 319 0540; www.birdlifebotswana.org.bw) BirdLife International is actively involved in conservation projects, such as building observation posts, and organising bird-watching trips.

■ **Kalahari Conservation Society** (KCS; ☎ 397 4557; www.kcs.org.bw) A non-governmental organisation (NGO) formed by President Masire to conserve Botswana's wildlife. For more, see the boxed text, p155.

■ **Khama Rhino Sanctuary Trust** (☎ 463 0713; www.khamarhinosanctuary.com) Set up in response to Botswana's dwindling rhino populations, the sanctuary (see p96) aims not only to protect the reserves' rhinos but also to generate revenue for the local community and promote environmental education.

■ **Mokolodi International Volunteer Program** (☎ 316 1955; www.mokolodi.com) One of the few wildlife reserves in Botswana to offer volunteer positions working in the office or out in the field. Positions must be arranged in advance. For more, see p92.

■ **World Conservation Union** (IUCN; www.iucn.org) The IUCN (International Union for the Conservation of Nature and Natural Resources) is the world's largest conservation network, bringing together some 181 countries in a unique environmental partnership aimed at conserving the integrity and diversity of the world's environment. There is a branch in Botswana (☎ 397 1584; www.iucnbot.bw).

Planet. You'll also find special boxed texts throughout this guide with additional information on plants and animals as well as tips on how to get the best out of your wildlife viewing.

REPTILES

Botswana's dry lands are home to over 150 species of reptile. These include 72 species of snake, such as the poisonous Mozambique spitting cobra, Egyptian cobra and black mamba. Although about 80% of snakes in Botswana are not venomous, watch out for the deadly puff adder, much more frequently seen than the cobras and mamba. Tree snakes, known as boomslangs, are also common in the delta.

Lizards are everywhere; the largest are *leguaans* (water monitors), docile creatures that reach over 2m in length. Smaller versions, savannah *leguaans*, inhabit small hills and drier areas. Also present in large numbers are geckos, chameleons and rock-plated lizards.

Although Nile crocodiles are threatened elsewhere in Southern Africa, the Okavango Delta is full of them. You will hear rather than see them while gliding through the channels in a *mokoro* (traditional dugout canoe). Frogs of every imaginable shape, size and colour are more delightful; they jump from reeds to a *mokoro* and back again, and provide an echoing chorus throughout the delta at night.

The jaws and stomach of the spotted hyena are so strong that it can devour the whole carcass of a medium-sized antelope – bones, hoofs, horns and hide.

INSECTS & SPIDERS

Botswana boasts about 8000 species of insect and spider. The most colourful butterflies can be found along the Okavango Panhandle (the northwestern extension of the delta) and include African monarchs and citrus swallowtails. Other insects of note include stick insects, expertly camouflaged among the reeds of the Okavango Delta; large, scary but harmless button spiders; and

RESPONSIBLE TRAVEL

Tourism accounts for 12% of the GDP. On one hand it is a positive force – admission fees to Botswana's national parks and reserves are used to help protect the wildlife and environment, and tourism provides employment for thousands of people. The downside is that the creation of national parks and reserves at the expense of local communities gives rise to complex conflicts.

If you wish to minimise the negative impacts of your visit to Botswana and the region, please try the following:

■ Avoid hotels that waste water, for example on massive, manicured lawns.

■ Support local enterprises, for example stay at Batswana-owned hotels, employ local guides and buy souvenirs made in the country.

■ Ascertain if a tour operator is really 'ecofriendly' or just pretending to be.

■ Dress and act appropriately, and never give money or gifts to children. If you want to help, donate something to a recognised project, such as a school or hospital.

These guidelines are based on those issued by **Tourism Concern** (www.tourismconcern.org.uk). Other good organisations include **Action for Southern Africa** (www.actsa.org), **Tourism Futures** (www.tourism-futures.org) and **Planeta** (www.planeta.com). These organisations aim to preserve and protect local cultures and lands.

sac spiders, which look harmless but are poisonous (although rarely fatal) and live mainly in rural homes. The delta is also home to grasshoppers, mopane worms, locusts, and mosquitoes and tsetse flies in increasing and potentially dangerous numbers.

Scorpions are not uncommon in the Kalahari; although their sting is not fatal, it can be painful.

BIRDS

Botswana is not only a big wildlife country but also a birding paradise. Between September and March, when the delta is flush with water, you should be able to train the lenses of your binoculars on any number of Botswana's 550 species, including the delta's famous African skimmers, the endangered wattled crane, slaty egrets, African jacanas, bee-eaters, lilac-breasted rollers, pygmy geese and the shy Pel's fishing owl. You can still see many bird species in the dry season, when it's often easier to spot them around the few remaining water sources.

Most of Botswana's birding is concentrated in the north of the country around the Okavango Delta (see the boxed text, p136), the Chobe Riverfront (p114), the Nata Sanctuary (p103), the Tuli Block (p100) and the Limpopo River. However, another top spot is the Makgadikgadi and Nxai Pans National Park (p106), which are covered in a sea of pink flamingos, and other migratory birds, at certain times of the year.

Inevitably, the birdlife in Botswana is under threat from overgrazing, urban sprawl and insecticides that are used to tackle the scourge of tsetse flies that sometimes plagues the delta.

ENDANGERED SPECIES

To give yourself a fright, log on to the World Conservation Union's Red List of Threatened Species, www.redlist.org.

Thanks to the Okavango and Chobe Rivers, most Southern African species, including such rarities as puku, red lechwe, mountain reedbuck and sitatunga antelopes, are present in Moremi Game Reserve and Chobe National Park (particularly the remote Linyanti Marshes). Other endangered species in Botswana – but which are even more threatened elsewhere in Southern Africa – include wild dogs (also known as Cape hunting dogs), pangolins (anteaters) and aardvarks.

Endangered among our feathered friends are wattled cranes, African skimmers and Cape Griffon vultures, which are protected in the Mannyelanong Game Reserve (see p93) in Otse.

Generally, rhinos can only be seen in the Mokolodi Nature Reserve (p92) near Gaborone, and the Khama Rhino Sanctuary (p96) near Serowe. Rhinos have also now been reintroduced to the Moremi Game Reserve.

Plants

The Okavango Delta enjoys a riparian environment dominated by marsh grasses, water lilies, reeds and papyrus, and is dotted with well-vegetated islands thick with palms, acacias, leadwood and sausage trees. At the other extreme, the Kalahari is characterised by all sorts of savannah, including bush savannah with acacia thorn trees, grass savannah and arid shrub savannah in the southwest.

More than 2500 species of plant and 650 species of tree have been recorded in Botswana. The country's only deciduous mopane forests are in the north, where six forest reserves harbour stands of commercial timber, as well as both mongonga and marula trees. Also common around Botswana are camel-thorn trees, which some animals find tasty and which the San use for firewood and medicinal purposes; and motlopi trees, also called shepherd's tree, which have edible roots.

Common Wildflowers of the Okavango Delta and Trees & Shrubs of the Okavango Delta by Veronica Roodt have informative descriptions accompanied by useful paintings and drawings. Roodt has lived in Moremi for years.

ENVIRONMENTAL ISSUES

As a relatively large country with a very low population density, Botswana is one of Africa's most unpolluted and pristine regions. While Botswana doesn't suffer as greatly from the ecological problems experienced elsewhere in Africa, such as land degradation, deforestation and urban sprawl, some major ecological and conservation issues do continue to affect the country's magnificent deserts, wetlands and savannahs.

The Fence Dilemma

If you've been stopped at a veterinary checkpoint, or visited the eastern Okavango Delta, you'll be familiar with the country's 3000km of 1.5m-long 'buffalo fence', officially called the Veterinary Cordon Fence. It's not a single fence but a series of high-tensile steel-wire barriers that run cross-country through some of Botswana's wildest terrain. The fences were first erected in 1954 to segregate wild buffalo herds from domestic free-range cattle in order to thwart the spread of foot-and-mouth disease.

The main problem is that many fences prevent wild animals from migrating to water sources along age-old seasonal routes. While Botswana has set aside large areas for wildlife protection, these areas do not constitute independent ecosystems. As a result, Botswana's wildebeest population has declined by 99% over the past 20 years and all remaining buffaloes and zebras are stranded north of the fences. The worst disaster occurred in the drought of 1983, in which the Kuke Fence barred herds of wildebeests heading for the Okavango waters, resulting in the death of 65,000 animals.

The 80km-long Northern Buffalo Fence located north of the Okavango Delta has opened a vast expanse of wildlife-rich – but as yet unprotected – territory to cattle ranching. Safari operators wanted the fence set as far north as possible to protect the seasonally flooded Selinda Spillway; prospective cattle ranchers wanted it set as far south as possible, maximising new grazing lands; and local people didn't want it at all because they were concerned it would act as a barrier to them as well as to wildlife. The government sided with the ranchers and the fence opened up to 20% of the Okavango Delta to commercial ranching.

Richard Estes' excellent The Safari Companion is stuffed full of information on animal behaviours from mating and rearing of young to aggressive postures and territorial disputes.

To learn how to live with elephants, log on to www.livingwith elephants.org. This non-profit organisation has a commendable outreach program whereby local kids can learn about elephants by being in direct contact with them.

In 2003 the controversy started up again with the proposal of a new cordon fence around the Makgadikgadi Pans. When completed, the fence will extend for 480km and is intended to limit predator-livestock conflict along the Boteti River. However, on the completion of the western section of the fence the **Environmental Investigation Agency** (EIA; www.eia-international.org) found that the alignment failed to adhere to the suggestions of the DWNP's (Department of Wildlife and National Parks) Environmental Appraisal and as a result the majority of the Boteti River now lies outside the park, cutting off the animals within. The net effect was immediately felt: in early 2005 some 300 zebras died trying to reach the river. In addition, the cattle fence around the Okavango Delta has already been damaged by roving elephant herds.

With Botswana's beef-farming industry in the doldrums and the increasing importance of tourism to the country's economy, the Botswanan government will need to take time to reflect on the impact of the fences on the increasingly precious commodity of wildlife.

Dangers Threatening the Delta

Despite its status as a biodiversity hot spot and the largest Ramsar Wetland Site on the planet, the Okavango Delta has no international protection, despite the fact that many prominent conservationists think that it should be awarded World Heritage status. Unprotected as it is, there are a growing number of threats to its long-term existence and many environmentalists already consider it to be critically endangered.

For tips on how to build a fire, avoid uncomfortable situations with danger-ous animals and find something edible amid the scrub, dip into *An Explorer's Handbook* by Christina Dodwell.

Wetland ecosystems are among the most biologically productive in the world but are disappearing globally at an alarming rate partly due to climate change and partly due to mismanagement and unsustainable development. Already a survey team from the DWNP and BirdLife Botswana has concluded that the delta is shrinking. The Kubango River – originating in the highlands of Angola – carries less water and floods the delta for a shorter period of the year.

Other key threats include overgrazing, which is already resulting in accelerated land and soil degradation; commercial gill netting and illegal fire lighting; unplanned developments in Angola as post–civil war resettlement occurs; and pressure for new and increased abstraction of water for mining, domestic use, agriculture and tourism. Most worrying of these is the proposed extraction of water from the Okavango River to supply the growing needs of Namibia. One such proposal is the construction of a 1250km-long pipeline from the Okavango River to Namibia's capital, Windhoek, which first reared its head in 1997 and has grown and faltered in fits and starts since.

Conservation Interna-tional (www.conser vation.org) is an international organisa-tion heavily involved in projects in biodiversity hot spots, including the Okavango Delta.

In 1994 Botswana, Namibia and Angola signed the Okavango River Basin Commission (Okacom), aimed at coordinating the sustainable management of the delta's waters. Although the commission has high principles, the practicalities on the ground are far from simple and the process of moving towards a sustainable management plan and eventual treaty has been very slow. As Angola, the basin state where 95% of the water flow originates, settles into its first period of peace in some 30 years, it is hoped that the pace will accelerate. In 2003 a new initiative, entitled **Sharing Water** (www.n-h-i.org) was launched to facilitate a trans-boundary consensus.

Hunting

In mid-2001, the government initiated a complete ban on all hunting of lions and cheetahs due to concerns over the increasing gender imbalances in the populations of these two big cats. At the time local people were none too happy, saying that the ban would prevent them from protecting valuable livestock. Hunters, too, were metaphorically speaking up in arms, with one of the world's largest hunting organisations even enlisting the support of President George W Bush to lobby the Botswanan government to lift the ban.

Unfortunately for Botswana's big cats, the bank balances of rich Westerners and the influence of US presidents were even bigger and in 2005 limited lion hunting was once again on the cards in the Chobe and Kalahari regions. But President Ian Khama has never been convinced that the best way to save his country's cats is by letting them be blown away by wealthy hunters, and as of this writing, the government has stated its plans to stop hunting near game reserves and national parks. This decision in and of itself has faced opposition from hunters, and the future of hunting in Botswana remains undetermined.

If hunting does continue, expect it to be strictly regulated (and expensive; lion licenses were going for US$20,000 before Khama reined in the practice). Historically, all living and dead animals, as well as any sort of wildlife trophy, needed either a government permit or a receipt from a specially licensed shop before you could take it out of the country. This still includes all souvenirs such as ostrich eggs, feathers, carved bones and animal teeth.

If you ever indulged one of those *Born Free* fantasies, get hold of a copy of *The Lion Children* by Angus, Maisie and Travers McNeice, who really did grow up in the wild.

Poaching

Poaching is not common in Botswana due to its stable economy, which makes such a risky and illegal undertaking unnecessary and unattractive. Also, transporting hides and tusks overland from remote areas of Botswana to ports hundreds of kilometres away in other countries is well nigh impossible, especially considering Botswana's well-patrolled borders, which are monitored by the Botswana Defence Force (BDF).

Gaborone

Botswana's small capital often doesn't get a lot of love from its own residents, let alone tourists. Ask a Motswana who was born and raised in 'Gabs' where they're from, and they may well tell you the name of a family village or cattle post they've never seen. With that kind of civic boosterism, it's small wonder most travellers treat Gaborone as a waypoint and little more.

And let's be fair: you probably came to Botswana for the wildlife, not the nightlife. But nightlife is here in Gaborone, as well as, y'know, the pulse of the Botswanan nation. The capital may be a village that has grown too large, but it is the place – and this place exists everywhere in Africa – where a farmer moves to make his fortune, students train to lead their nation and the official course of the country is determined. A local Motswana may not see Gaborone as a traditional family 'home'. But she does see it as the place where her future, and that of her nation, is forged.

A relatively large expat scene, the upper crust of Batswana society and a surprisingly mixed population of black, white, Indian and mixed-race Africans – plus, increasingly, Chinese – makes Gaborone a spicier demographic stew than you might initially expect. Its malls, movies and restaurants are a good distraction from the dust and the delta, should you need one. And if you come here, you'll see how Gaborone's identity is continuously being created, much like the nation it governs.

HIGHLIGHTS

- Tracking elephants on the outskirts of the capital at the **Mokolodi Nature Reserve** (p92)
- Going on safari without ever leaving the city at the **Gaborone Game Reserve** (p81)
- Seeing modern African dance or medieval European theatre at **Maitisong Cultural Centre** (p87) cooperative in Oodi
- Buying local paintings at the **Thapong Visual Arts Centre** (p88)
- Visiting one of Botswana's best museums in the mud-walled village of **Mochudi** (p89)

- POPULATION: 186,007
- ELEVATION: 900M

HISTORY

Archaeological evidence suggests that the banks of the nearby Notwane River have been continuously occupied since at least the middle Stone Age. However, the first modern settlement, Moshaweng, was established in the late 1880s by Chief Gaborone of the Tlokwa clan. Early European explorers and missionaries named the settlement Gaborone's Village, which was then inevitably shortened to 'Gaborones' (interestingly enough, the 's' was not dropped until 1968).

In 1895 the South African diamond magnate Cecil Rhodes used Gaborone to launch the Jameson Raid, an unsuccessful rebellion against the Boers who controlled the gold mines near Johannesburg. Rhodes was forced to resign his post as prime minister of Cape Colony, and the raid served as the catalyst for the second Boer War (1899–1902).

In 1897 the railway between South Africa and Rhodesia (now Zimbabwe) passed 4km to the west of the village, and a tiny settlement known as Gaborone's Station soon appeared alongside the railway line. By 1966 the greater Gaborone area was home to fewer than 4000 inhabitants, though it was selected as the capital of independent Botswana due to its proximity to the railway line and its large water supply.

Although urban migration has characterised much of Gabs' recent history, economic turmoil in Zimbabwe has sparked a wave of illegal immigration to Botswana's capital. For more information on this controversial issue, see the boxed text, p80.

ORIENTATION

Gaborone sprawls to the point that outer neighbourhoods are called 'Phases' and 'Extensions' (romantic, eh?). It lacks a definitive town centre, so many shops, restaurants and offices are located in or near suburban malls and shopping centres, which form their own pulsing nodes throughout town. The Mall – also called the Main Mall – is the business heart of Gaborone and has a handful of shops, restaurants, banks and internet centres. Almost all government offices, and several embassies, are situated to the west of the Mall, in and around State House and Embassy Drs. There are also a number of shopping malls located outside the city centre; these are easily accessible by combi (minibus).

INFORMATION
Bookshops
Botshalo Books (Game City Mall) Recommended by expats for its good range of titles.
Botswana Book Centre (the Mall) Sells newspapers and magazines, guidebooks, wildlife guides, coffee-table books and novels.
Exclusive Books (Riverwalk Mall) This reader-recommended bookshop has a wide range of literature, non-fiction and travel books.
J&B Books (Broadhurst Mall) Located above Woolworths, this place sells new and second-hand novels in English.
Kingston's Bookshop (Broadhurst Mall) Has a huge array of novels, postcards, and books and maps about Botswana and the region.

Emergency
Ambulance (☎ 997)
Central Police Station (☎ 355 1161; Botswana Rd)
Fire department (☎ 998)
Police (☎ 999)

Internet Access
Many hotels are increasingly offering internet access, via either wi-fi or network cables.
Aim Internet (Botswana Rd; per hr US$3) Next to the Cresta President Hotel.
Sakeng Internet Access Point (the Mall; per hr US$3) In the Gaborone Hardware building.

Libraries
Alliance Française (☎ 355 3982; Embassy Dr; ⏰ 2-4.30pm Tue & Thu)
Botswana National Reference Library (☎ 358 0788; 3rd fl, Commerce House, Botswana Rd) Next to Debswana House, this is ideal for anyone doing research about Botswana and the region.
British Council (☎ 355 3603; the Mall; ⏰ Tue-Sun)
Gaborone Public Library (☎ 355 3664; Civic Centre, Independence Ave) Opposite the eastern end of the Mall.
University of Botswana (☎ 355 2450; Mobutu Dr) Contains plenty of books and periodicals dealing with national topics.
US Embassy Library (☎ 355 3982; Embassy Dr; ⏰ 2-4.30pm Tue & Thu)

Medical Services
Gaborone Hospital Dental Clinic (☎ 395 3777; Segoditshane Way) Part of the Gaborone Private Hospital.
Gaborone Private Hospital (☎ 300 1999; Segoditshane Way) For anything serious, head to this reasonably modern, but expensive, hospital, opposite Broadhurst Mall. The best facility in town.
Princess Marina Hospital (☎ 355 3221; Notwane Rd) Equipped to handle standard medical treatments

CROSSING BORDERS

Due to the political and economic instability that has swept through Zimbabwe in recent years, the volume of illegal migrants crossing into Botswana in search of work is on the rise. According to information from Botswana's Department of Immigration and the Council on Foreign Relations, the number of expatriated refugees from Zimbabwe once rose from 25,000 to 60,000 in a single year (2005–06). More recent numbers are difficult to come by, but the issue certainly hasn't gone away, and political unrest in Zimbabwe is usually followed by a spike in refugees crossing the border. That said, most refugees say in interviews that the lack of opportunities for stable employment is driving them abroad. Although most Batswana sympathise with the plight of Zimbabweans, and many will cheerfully describe them as 'hard-working' and 'clever,' a tension exists.

It is commonly argued that Botswana's economic activities rely heavily on migrant labour. For instance, at one point it was estimated that illegal aliens accounted for one in 15 residents of Francistown (p97), which is located near the Zimbabwean border and can be easily reached by immigrants. In Gaborone several economic sectors could not function without migrant labour, including public and private transport, domestic labour, agriculture, ranching and light industry. For an employer, the benefit of hiring migrants is that they are a cheap source of labour. Furthermore, most Zimbabweans are well educated and generally perform to their employers' satisfaction despite low wages.

However, the practice of hiring migrants contributes to unemployment, and many Batswana resent the increasing competition for jobs. Fear also plays a significant role in prejudice against migrant workers. Although Botswana is arguably the safest country in sub-Saharan Africa, crime rates are on the rise, and in newspapers and on the street Batswana are prone to blame Zimbabweans. But rising crime in Botswana is a complicated issue that cannot solely be attributed to Zimbabweans. Although illegal immigration is certainly a contributing factor, rising economic disparities are also to blame.

In a February 2009 article in the *Mmegi* newspaper, Zimbabwean immigrants claimed to have been sent home despite having time on their emergency travel documents, while others claimed to have been beaten by authorities. At the entrance to the District Immigration Office a small cottage industry of immigration 'consultants' has evolved, fast-talking promoters who claim to be able to shear through naturalisation red tape. Often, these claims are nothing more than cons.

Zimbabwe's volatility also threatens to damage Botswana's lucrative tourism sector. As recently as 2000, Zimbabwe was one of the most touristed destinations in Southern Africa. In particular, the town of Victoria Falls (p194) was among the most heavily trafficked destinations on the entire continent. As a result, Botswana used to benefit from Zimbabwean tourism, especially considering the former ease and reliability of transport between both countries. Today, however, tourism in Zimbabwe is virtually nonexistent, and there are fears that the country's collapse could deal a crushing blow to the tourism industry in neighbouring countries.

and emergencies but shouldn't be your first choice for treatment.

Money

Major branches of Standard Chartered and Barclays banks have foreign-exchange facilities and ATMs and offer cash advances. The few bureaux de change around the city offer quick service at better rates than the banks, but they charge up to 2.75% commission.
Barclays Bank (☎ 355 3411; Khama Cres)
Edcom Bureau de Change (☎ 361 1123) Near the train station.
Prosper Bureau de Change African Mall (☎ 360 0478); Broadhurst Mall (☎ 390 5358; Kagiso Centre)

SAA City Center (☎ 355 2021; Gaborone Hardware Bldg, the Mall) The American Express representative.
Standard Chartered Bank (☎ 355 2911; the Mall)
Western Union (☎ 367 1490; Gaborone Hardware Bldg, the Mall)

Post

In addition to the **Central Post Office** (the Mall), there is also a post office located across the road from Broadhurst Mall.

Tourist Information

Botswana Tourism Board (☎ 391 3111; www.botswanatourism.co.bw; Fairgrounds Office Park, Block B, Ground Floor; ☎ 7.30am-12.30pm & 1.45-4.30pm Mon-

Fri) Located in the Fairgrounds Office Park, a little ways south of the Main Mall, the tourism board has modernised and runs a very helpful operation these days. There is a tourism board kiosk in the lobby of the Cresta President Hotel (see p86).

Department of Wildlife & National Parks (DWNP; ☎ 318 0774; dwnp@gov.bw; Government Enclave, Khama Cres; ☒ reservations 7.30am-12.45pm & 1.45-4.30pm Mon-Fri) One of the two accommodation booking offices (the other is in Maun; see p121) for all national parks and reserves run by the DWNP.

Garcin Safaris (☎ 393 8190; www.garcinsafaris.com) If you've got a day or two to kill in Gabs, do yourself a favour and get in touch with resident and Gaborone expert Marilyn Garcin. She does great tours of the city, including a *No. 1 Ladies Detective Agency*–focused jaunt, and is a good contact for arranging onward travel into the rest of the country.

DANGERS & ANNOYANCES

For an African city, Gabs is safe, but it sure ain't Singapore. Crime happens here, especially of the opportunistic mugging sort. Take cabs at night, especially if you're a woman or on your own. Use drivers recommended by hotels and try to keep their phone numbers, as some people have been robbed in unmarked cabs. The Main Mall is fine to walk around in during the day. The Main Mall is the safest area to walk around after dark, but incidents can and do occur even here, and some areas always warrant a wide berth, such like Tsholofelo Park, just south of Gaborone Private Hospital. Try not to walk along public greenways, both a traffic hazard and a likely target for muggers (Gaborone locals don't tend to walk a lot, so these greenways are often a good place for muggers to find foreigners).

Traffic is becoming more of a problem as more Batswana buy cars and start driving, often for the first time in their lives. Be extremely careful on the road during the last weekend of the month, when everyone gets paid and many people get drunk and get behind the wheel – a very, very bad combination.

SIGHTS

There's more to do in Gaborone than the sprawl initially suggests. The juncture of motivated embassy staff, NGO types and ambitious Batswana makes for a fairly full calendar of events that focuses on cultural and arts-related activities. If you're hanging around for a bit, look for the **Gaborone Cowboys**, a (very) surreal subculture (cult?) of local men

who wear chains, chaps and cowboy hats, listen to heavy and death metal and ride around town on horseback.

Gaborone Game Reserve

This **reserve** (☎ 318 4492; per person/vehicle US$0.25/0.50; ☒ 6.30am-6.30pm) was established in 1988 by the Kalahari Conservation Society to give the Gaborone public an opportunity to view Botswana's wildlife in a natural and accessible location. Although the reserve is only 5 sq km, it's the third-busiest in the country and boasts wildebeests, elands, gemsboks, kudus, ostriches and warthogs. The birdlife, which includes kingfishers and hornbills, is particularly plentiful and easy to spot from observation areas. The reserve also has a few picnic sites, a game hide and a small visitor-education centre.

All roads in the reserve are accessible by 2WD; guided drives are not offered. The reserve is located about 1km east of Broadhurst Mall and can be accessed from Limpopo Dr.

Government Enclave

At the western end of the main mall is a gateway topped by a big Botswanan flag fronting a low-slung compound of plain brick buildings. Walk inside the grounds of this campus, note the doors with their entrances for speakers and chiefs and you realise this isn't an ambitious school, it's Botswana's **parliament**. There are no tours and you can't watch MP sessions, but you can casually walk through the heart of the main governing complex, which is pretty cool. Also, note around you all the big, ultramodern buildings squatting like spaceships about to launch into the Gaborone atmosphere. These are various ministry buildings, built with the monetary infusion of one of Africa's most stable economies.

National Museum, Monuments & Art Gallery

If you come with expectations reasonably lowered, you may enjoy this small but diverse **museum** (☎ 397 4616; 331 Independence Ave; admission free; ☒ 9am-6pm Tue-Fri, to 5pm Sat & Sun). It's a good way to kill an afternoon, anyway, especially if you're into taxidermy. For those not intrigued by stuffed wildlife, there are a number of exhibits on pre-colonial and colonial history as well as a permanent collection of traditional and modern African and European art. The ethnographic displays are probably the most

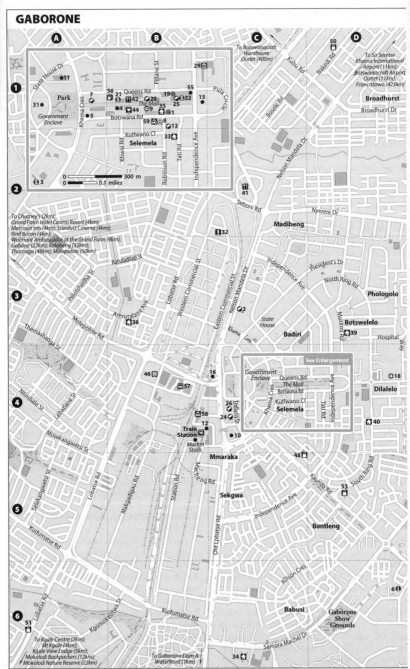

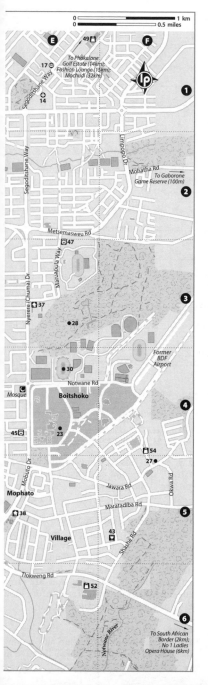

useful for anyone wanting to learn more about the demographic make-up of the country.

Diamond Trading Company

Here's where you come to, sort of, feel richer than Donald Trump on pay day. In this **building** (☎ 364 9000; Diamond Park) you'll learn pretty much everything there is to know and then some about Botswana's diamond industry. If you have time and aren't put off by red tape, you can muster a group and arrange a tour. If you're wondering: yeah, it's pretty awesome to hold several million dollars' worth of rocks in the palm of your hand.

Botanical Gardens

With a little love and a lot of work, these **gardens** (☎ 397 3860; 17991 Okwa Rd; admission free; ⏲ 7:30am-6pm) could be a great spot to visit in the future. Right now they're not much more than a cordoned-off area of the scrub that surrounds so much of Gaborone, inhabited by some admittedly cute monkeys. There are a few labelled trees and plants on site but, at the time of research, nothing in the way of a guide to the garden's attractions. Also on site is the attractive colonial hotel building (pretty much empty inside) where Rhodes helped plan the failed Jameson Raid in 1895.

Three Dikgosi (Chiefs) Monument

It's an interesting kind of history when your nationalist heroes are three guys who argued your country should *continue* to be a protectorate of Africa's biggest imperialist power, but welcome to Botswana. (It should be noted that, by helping to keep Botswana under the administration of the British Crown, the Batswana chiefs Bathoen, Khama II and Sebele prevented the country from coming under the control of Cecil Rhodes, who likely would have been a far more exploitative administrator.)

The chiefs are memorialised in imposing form at this large, badly placed (in the shadow of an office block) **monument** (☎ 367 4616; between Eastern and Western Commercial Sts; admission free; ⏲ 9am-6pm Tue-Fri, to 5pm Sat & Sun), which also includes panels featuring carvings of national virtues (including 'Botshabelo' (refuge), 'Bogaka' (heroism), 'Boitshoko' (Endurance), 'Maikarabelo' (global responsibility) and 'Boipuso' (Independence).

GABORONE

INFORMATION		
Aim Internet	**1**	B1
Alliance Française de		
Gaborone	(see 45)	
Angolan Embassy	**2**	C3
Barclays Bank Head		
Office	**3**	A2
Botshalo Books	(see 51)	
Botswana Book Centre	**4**	B1
Botswana National		
Reference Library	**5**	A1
Botswana Tourism Board	**6**	D6
British Council	(see 7)	
British High Commission	**7**	A1
Central Police Station	**8**	B1
Central Post Office	**9**	B1
Debswana House	**10**	C4
Department of Wildlife &		
National Parks	**11**	A1
Edcom Bureau de		
Change	**12**	B4
Exclusive Books	(see 52)	
French Embassy	**13**	B1
Gaborone Hospital		
Dental Clinic	(see 14)	
Gaborone Private		
Hospital	**14**	E1
Gaborone Public Library	**15**	B1
German Embassy	(see 49)	
Immigration Office	**16**	C4
J&B Books	(see 49)	
Kingston's Bookshop	(see 49)	
Namibian High		
Commission	(see 10)	
Post Office	**17**	E1
Princess Marina Hospital	**18**	D4
Prosper Bureau de		
Change	(see 49)	
Prosper Bureau de		
Change	(see 48)	
SAA City Center	(see 19)	
Sakeng Internet Access		
Point	**19**	B1
South African Embassy	**20**	B1
Standard Chartered ATM	**21**	B1

Standard Chartered		
Bank	**22**	B1
University of Botswana	**23**	E4
US Embassy	**24**	C4
US Embassy Library	(see 24)	
Western Union	(see 19)	
Zambian High		
Commission	**25**	B1
Zimbabwean High		
Commission	**26**	C4

SIGHTS & ACTIVITIES		
Botanical Gardens	**27**	F5
Diamond Trading		
Company	(see 10)	
Energym	(see 49)	
Gaborone Golf Course	**28**	E3
Maitisong Cultural		
Centre	(see 47)	
National Museum,		
Monuments & Art		
Gallery	**29**	B1
National Stadium	**30**	E4
Parliament	**31**	A1
Three Dikgosi		
Monument	**32**	C2

SLEEPING		
Brackendene Lodge	**33**	B2
Cresta Lodge	**34**	C6
Cresta President Hotel	**35**	B1
Ditshane Lodge	**36**	B3
Gaborone Sun Hotel &		
Casino	**37**	E3
Mondior Summit	**38**	E5
Motheo Apartments	**39**	D3
Tindi Lodge	**40**	D4

EATING		
25° East	(see 52)	
Bull & Bush Pub	**41**	C2
Equatorial Café	(see 52)	
Kgotla Restaurant &		
Coffee Shop	(see 49)	
King's Takeaway	**42**	B1

News Cafe	(see 38)	
Rodizio's	(see 52)	
Terrace Restaurant	(see 35)	

DRINKING		
Bull & Bush Pub	(see 41)	
Chatters Bar	(see 34)	
Linga Langa	(see 52)	
Lizzard Lounge	**43**	F5
Sportsmans Bar	**44**	B1

ENTERTAINMENT		
Alliance Française de		
Gaborone	**45**	E4
Capital Players	**46**	B4
Gaborone Sun Hotel &		
Casino	(see 37)	
Maitisong Cultural		
Centre	**47**	E4
New Capitol Cinema	(see 52)	
New Capitol Cinema	(see 51)	

SHOPPING		
African Mall	**48**	C5
Botswanacraft	(see 35)	
Broadhurst Mall	**49**	E1
Camphill Furniture	(see 35)	
Craft Workshop	**50**	D1
Game City Mall	**51**	A6
Jewel of Africa	(see 51)	
Kalahari Quilts	(see 50)	
Riverwalk Mall	**52**	E6
South Ring Mall	**53**	D5
Thapong Visual Arts		
Centre	**54**	F4

TRANSPORT		
Air Botswana	**55**	B1
Combi Stand	(see 58)	
Intercape Mainliner Bus		
Office	(see 56)	
Kudu Petrol Station	**56**	B1
Main Bus Terminal	**57**	B4
Taxi Stand	**58**	B4
Taxi Stand	**59**	B1

ACTIVITIES

The best source of information about what's going on is the *Botswana Advertiser,* which is published (free) each Friday. There's a bulletin board outside the National Museum that's also often pinned with info on what's going down over the week.

Golf

The best golf in the city is a little outside it, about 14km north in **Phakalane Golf Estate** (off Map pp82–3; ☎ 360 4000; Golf Dr, Phakalane), tucked into a somewhat out of place woodland-and-fancy-housing setting. Green fees for 18 holes are P140. **Gaborone Golf Course** is about 2km south of the city; temporary membership, which includes use of the swimming pool, bars and restaurants, costs US$10 per day. Green fees for nine/18 holes are an extra US$3/6, and equipment is available for hire at the pro shop.

Soccer

The **National Stadium** (☎ 392 3090; Notwane Rd; tickets from US$1) plays host to matches between teams in the country-wide Super League as well as the occasional international game. Matches start at 4pm on Saturday and Sunday and are usually advertised and publicised in the local English-language newspapers.

Gyms

You don't need a membership, just pop by **Energym** (☎ 316 1501; Broadhurst Mall) if you're in need of a workout. Rates vary.

FESTIVALS & EVENTS

The national holidays of **Sir Seretse Khama Day**, **President's Day** and **Botswana/Independence Day** (see p164) are always cause for celebration in the capital. Details about these events are advertised in local English-language newspapers and in the What's On column of the *Botswana Advertiser*. Gaborone also plays host to a number of local festivals and events.

Maitisong Festival (March/April) For more information, see the boxed text, below.

Traditional Dance Competition (late March)

Industry & Technology Fair (May) Held at the Gaborone Show Grounds.

International Trade Fair (August) Also held at the Gaborone Show Grounds.

SLEEPING

Gaborone primarily caters to domestic and business travellers, though there are a number of clean and friendly family-run lodges. If you have the cash to spare, there is a smattering of luxury hotels in Gabs.

If you don't have a private car, it's recommended that you either book your first night's accommodation before you arrive, or at least ring the hotel from the airport, bus or train station. Hotels are dotted all over the capital, so hiring a taxi to find a hotel with an available room is an expensive headache.

Budget

Mokolodi Backpackers (off Map pp82-3; ☎ 7411 1165; www.backpackers.co.bw; camping P75, dm/chalet P120/325; 🖵) If you're doing the budget thing, the self-drive thing or the overland thing, this is a good option, and the only real backpacker vibe around Gaborone. About 10km from the city, it has attractive chalets and good campsites, and the dorms aren't a bad deal either.

Tindi Lodge (☎ 395 3648; 487 South Ring Rd; r with/without bathroom P240/230) This friendly, family-run lodge is a little worn, but rooms are comfortable enough if you're looking to just crash for the night.

Brackendene Lodge (☎ 391 2886; Tati Rd; r from P290; 🕮 🖵) The Brackendene is one of the better-value hotels in town. Rooms are simple but large and kitted out with TVs and air-con, there's reliable internet in the lobby (supposedly moving into rooms, fingers crossed) and you're within walking distance of the Mall.

Ditshane Lodge (☎ 316 3737; 18576 Aresutalane Ave; s/d P300/350; 🕮 🐾) It may not be the most memorable stay of your trip, but Ditshane is an economic option for anyone in need of a good night's rest with basic fixings like TV and secure parking, and a little bit of thatch-chic.

Kgale View Lodge (off Map pp82-3; ☎ 312 1755; Phase 4, Plot 222258; r from P400) This locally recommended B&B has friendly service, cosy rooms and a generally welcoming atmosphere – it's the sort of place that books up fast with return customers, so call ahead.

Midrange & Top End

All places listed below offer rooms with bathroom, cable TV and air-con. Breakfast is not included in the price.

Metcourt Inn (off Map pp82-3; ☎ 391 2999, 363 7777; www.metcourt.com; s/d P465/535; 🕮) Located within the Grand Palm Hotel complex, this is a lovely little three-star option that will likely put you in mind of every business hotel you've ever stayed in, which can be a good thing after the bush.

Motheo Apartments (☎ 318 1587; motheo@info.bw; Moremi Rd, off Independence Ave; apt P396-786; 🕮 🖵 🐾) Has a good range of self-catering apartments that are a nice alternative to the big business-style blocks that characterise so many other Gaborone hotels. The properties come with internet, DSTV and other mod cons and are all self-catering.

MAITISONG FESTIVAL

Established in 1987, the Maitisong Festival is the largest performing-arts festival in Botswana and is held annually for seven days from mid-March to early April. The festival features an outdoor program of music, theatre, film and dance that takes place on several stages throughout the capital. There's also an indoor program, held in the **Maitisong Cultural Centre** (☎ 397 1809; Maruapula Way; 🕒 ticket office 8am-6pm Mon-Fri) and in the Memorable Order of Tin Hats (MOTH) Hall; highlights include some of the top performing artists from around Africa.

Programs to events are usually available in shopping malls and centres during the month leading up to the festival. Outdoor events are free; indoor events cost from P25 to P150. For P400 you can buy a ticket that provides access to everything on offer during the festival.

Cresta Lodge (☎ 397 5375; www.cresta-hospitality. com; Samora Machel Dr; r from P900; ✖ ♨) Located 2km outside the city centre, the attractively landscaped Cresta Lodge is a good choice if you're looking for a quiet night's rest in a three-star setting outside the urban sprawl.

Cresta President Hotel (☎ 395 3631; www.cresta -hospitality.co.bw; the Mall; r from P908; ✖ 🖳 ♨) The first luxury hotel in the city is located smack-dab in the middle of the Mall, which pretty much justifies the heavy price tag. It's modern, and service is helpful, and, while there're no surprises, that's a pleasant enough surprise in itself.

Gaborone Sun Hotel & Casino (☎ 355 1111; www.suninternational.com; Chuma Dr; d standard/luxury US$115/140; ✖ ♨) Once known for its high-brow atmosphere, the seemingly abandoned Gaborone Sun fails to compete with its up-market rivals. Still, it's not a bad choice, especially since guests can take advantage of the on-site restaurants, casino, swimming pool and golf course. The bar gets popular with expats in the evenings.

Walmont Ambassador at the Grand Palm (off Map pp82–3; ☎ 363 7777; www.walmont.com; Molepolole Rd; d from P1267; ✖ ♨) Located 4km west of the city centre, this resolutely modern and polished hotel is situated in a Las Vegas–inspired mini-city complete with restaurants, bars, a casino, a cinema and a spa. You'll pay to stay, but it's worth it for the pampering.

Mondior Summit (☎ 319 0600; www.mondior.com; cnr Mobuto Dr & Maratadiba Rd; s/d from P1312/1922; ✖ ♨) Probably the best hotel in town, the Mondior is chock-a-block with all the mod cons you need, plus Africa chic – think big, plush rooms in warm, rich monochromatic colour schemes. There's every service imaginable and a general sense of contemporary posh throughout.

EATING

If you're looking for cheap eats, Gabs enjoys a special love affair with African and Western fast food. There are also dozens of stalls near the bus station that sell plates of cheap traditional food (such as *mealie pap* and stew), as well as a few stands on the Mall during lunchtime.

If you're self-catering, there are well-stocked supermarkets in every mall and shopping centre, though unfortunately there isn't a large market in the city.

Budget

Equatorial Cafe (Riverwalk Mall; mains from P20) The best espressos in town are served here, along with fruit smoothies, falafel and gourmet sandwiches. It even has real bagels!

King's Takeaway (the Mall; meals P20-40) This local favourite serves up inexpensive burgers, chips and snacks to hungry office workers.

Kgotla Restaurant & Coffee Shop (Broadhurst Mall; meals US$4-6; ⏰ Tue–Sun) This deservedly popular expat hang-out above Woolworth's is renowned for its hearty breakfasts, vegetarian fare and coffee specialties.

Midrange & Top End

News Cafe (☎ 319 0600; cnr Mobuto Dr & Maratadiba Rd; mains P40-130) As trendy as Gabs gets, the News Cafe, in the Mondior Summit Hotel, has a continental European menu and a modernist vibe about it. The swish decor and design is all the rage with Gaborone's young and moneyed and expats longing for a bit of urban cool.

Bull & Bush Pub (☎ 397 5070; mains P45-80) This long-standing Gaborone institution is deservedly popular with expats, tourists and locals alike. Though there's something on the menu for everyone, the Bull & Bush is renowned for its thick steaks and cold beers. On any given night, the outdoor beer garden is buzzing with activity, and you can bet there's always some sporting event worth watching on the tube.

25° East (Riverwalk Mall; mains P45-120) This is a classy-looking Asian fusion joint that does very good Indian food, but we recommend passing on the Thai dishes. We know, we know – you see Thai food in Gaborone and get sorely tempted, but it's just not up to scratch here.

Chutneys (off Map pp82–3; ☎ 319 0545; mains P50-90; West Ring Rd) This gorgeous spot serves the best Indian food in Botswana, a good and varied collection of curries that are a brilliant break from *pap* and meat and more *pap*. The focus is on South Indian specialties, but there're all sorts of delicious mains pulled from around the sub-continent on the menu.

Terrace Restaurant (☎ 395 3631; the Mall; mains from P85) On the terrace of the Cresta President Hotel, this eclectic restaurant is a good spot for surveying the passing Mall scene below. Does very good chops and the like on its grill, or, if you're feeling colonial, enjoy some tea and watch life amble by.

Beef Baron (off Map pp82–3; ☎ 363 7777; Grand Palm resort; mains from P90) With a subtle name like 'beef baron', is there any wonder what's on offer here? Saw into one of those fat boys – widely regarded as the best steak in the city – and thank us later.

Rodizio's (Riverwalk Mall; set menu from P130) Part of a chain of Brazilian super meat houses/ samba parties, Rodizio's has a drill that may be familiar to you. Guys walk around with skewers of meat, and you hold up little flags indicating whether you want more or less. Gastrointestinal overload eventually occurs, but at least you die with a smile on your face and meat juice on your lips.

DRINKING

When money is made in Botswana it tends to come to Gabs, which means there's a fair few places here to let off some steam. Lots of them charge a P50 cover on weekends.

Bull & Bush Pub (☎ 397 5070) This popular restaurant is also the centre for expat night-life, where young Gaborone denizens go to behave badly – speaking of which, someone will probably be sick in the toilets on big nights. That said, the dance floor gets hot, the beer is cold and all in all this can be a hell of a fun place.

Chatters Bar (Samora Machel Dr; admission free) Located in Cresta Lodge, this classy bar features smooth, easy-listening live music most nights of the week. The bar is well stocked, though it's a bit pricey.

Fashion Lounge (off Map pp82–3; Phakalane) About 15km north of the city (all taxi drivers know where it is), this is Gabs' attempt at a sophisticated Manhattan martini bar. The effort is actually pulled off, but it does feel weird to be among all the *Sex and the City* wannabes so far from New York.

Lizzard Lounge (The Village) Very popular with local Batswana – those who play at being gangstas and, we've heard, real gangsters. Great for dancing, but it does get a little rough some nights.

Linga Langa (Riverwalk Mall) A vague cross between an American sports bar and British pub that gets pretty packed on weekend nights – it's a good place to start the evening.

Sportmans Bar (Botswana Rd) This friendly local watering hole is conveniently located on the Mall and has a couple of pool tables in case you're looking to do something other than get wasted.

ENTERTAINMENT

To find out what's going on in Gaborone and where, check the *Arts & Culture Review* lift-out in the *Mmegi/Reporter* newspaper, and the What's On section of the *Botswana Advertiser*.

As Gabs gets richer, nightclubs become more popular. They tend to be a cross between enormous disco ball funhouses and Southern African shebeens. Expect to pay around P50 cover on weekend nights.

Cinemas

Stardust Cinema (off Map pp82–3; ☎ 395 9271; Grand Palm Hotel Casino Resort, Molepolole Rd), and **New Capitol Cinema** (☎ 370 0111) at Riverwalk and Game City Malls all offer recent escapist Hollywood entertainment about every two hours between noon and 10.30pm daily.

Gaborone Film Society (☎ 392 5005) Screens classic films (mostly in English) every two weeks for members, but non-members are welcome. Contact the society for details, locations and prices, or check out the noticeboard at the National Museum.

Theatre

Alliance Française de Gaborone (☎ 397 3863; Mobutu Dr) The *alliance* occasionally sponsors shows and exhibitions featuring local and French art, music and film.

Maitisong Cultural Centre (☎ 397 1809; http:// maitisong.org; Maruapula Way; ☙ ticket office 8am-6pm Mon-Fri) Maitisong ('Place of Entertainment') puts on incredible shows in its large theatre, with events ranging from Shakespearean plays to Batswana music most weeks. Also home to the annual Maitisong Festival (see the boxed text, p85). You'd be remiss not to check this spot out if you're in Gabs for longer than a few days.

Capital Players (☎ 392 4511; Molepolole Rd) This local amateur troupe holds regular performances at the rather memorably named Memorable Order of Tin Hats (MOTH). (For the origins of the name, see http://www.first worldwar.com/features/moth.htm.)

No. 1 Ladies Opera House (off Map pp82–3; ☎ 316 5459) Located a few kilometres south of Gaborone, this collaboration between author Alexander McCall Smith and the local arts scene showcases Tswana singing, community theatre performances and, hopefully by the time you read this, full-scale opera shows. There's also a cute cafe that does good coffee and cakes.

Casinos

You must be at least 18 years old to gamble, and smart-casual dress is required to enter.

Gaborone Sun Hotel & Casino (☎ 361 6000; Chuma Dr)

Grand Palm Hotel Casino Resort (off Map pp82-3; ☎ 363 7777; Molepolole Rd)

SHOPPING

Gaborone is home to a number of Western-style malls that contain bars, restaurants, shops, supermarkets, takeaways, banks, office parks and petrol stations. The main malls are the African Mall, Broadhurst Mall, Riverwalk Mall, Game City Mall and South Ring Mall.

During the day, several stalls along the Mall sell reasonable carvings and tacky souvenirs at negotiable prices. But it's cheaper if you go straight to the source by visiting the nearby workshops in Oodi (see the boxed text, p91), Gabane (p91) and Thamaga (p91). If you don't have time to take a day trip, you can also get high-quality crafts (and fair prices) at the shops listed below.

Botswanacraft (off Map pp82-3; www.botswanacraft. bw) Airport (☎ 391 2209); Warehouse Outlet (☎ 392 2487) Botswana's largest craft emporium sells traditional souvenirs from all over the country including weavings from Oodi and pottery from Gabane and Thamaga. If your bargaining skills are deficient, fear not – prices are fixed. There's a good restaurant here if you're feeling peckish, and frequent cultural events are planned and performed. Also on site is Camphill Furniture (☎ 392 3038), which trades in homemade wooden furniture and a large selection of other local crafts.

Jewel of Africa (☎ 370 0216; jewel@global.bw; Game City Mall) This attractive shop offers an eclectic range of carvings, sketches, shawls and other assorted African knick-knacks. Although not everything is made in Botswana, prices here are reasonable (and fixed).

Craft Workshop (☎ 355 6364; 5648 Nakedi Rd, Broadhurst Industrial Estate) This small complex of shops sells crafts and souvenirs, and also plays host to a flea market on the morning of the last Sunday of each month. To get there take the 'Broadhurst Route 3' combi.

Thapong Visual Arts Centre (☎ 316 1771; the Village) A small gallery of modern and contemporary local work that should be a first stop for anyone interested in buying art that goes beyond the usual African wildlife stuff and wooden masks.

Kalahari Quilts (☎ 7261 6462; www.kalahariquilts. com; Broadhurst) These excellent local quilts are made by Batswana women and are a genuinely unique craft to take home. Each one bears an individual imprint, although all do a good job at capturing the primary-colour-heavy palette that is this country's sensory assault. There's a lot more than quilts around – baby slings, cushion covers and the like are all for sale.

GETTING THERE & AWAY

Air

From Sir Seretse Khama International Airport, located 14km from the centre, **Air Botswana** (☎ 395 2812; Botswana Insurance Company House, the Mall) operates scheduled domestic flights to and from Francistown (P682), Maun (P1057) and Kasane (P1057). The office also serves as an agent for other regional airlines.

For information about international flights to and from Gaborone, see p170.

Bus

Intercity buses and minibuses to Johannesburg (P80, seven hours), Francistown (P35, six hours), Selebi-Phikwe (P42, six hours), Ghanzi (P70, 11 hours), Lobatse (P10, 1½ hours), Mahalapye (P17, three hours), Palapye (P30, four hours) and Serowe (P32, five hours) depart from the main bus terminal. Please note that minibuses to Johannesburg drop you off in a very unsafe area near Park Station; try to have onward transport arranged *immediately* upon arrival. The main bus terminal also offers local services to Kanye (P10, two hours), Jwaneng (P28, three hours), Manyana (P6, 1½ hours), Mochudi (P7, one hour), Thamaga (P5, one hour) and Molepolole (P9, one hour).

To reach Maun or Kasane, change in Francistown. Buses operate according to roughly fixed schedules and minibuses leave when full.

The Intercape Mainliner to Johannesburg (US$25, 6½ hours) runs from the Shell petrol station beside the Mall. Tickets can be booked either through your accommodation or at the Intercape Mainliner Office. Mainliner buses are very popular and should be booked a week or so in advance. For more information, see p174.

Train

The day train departs for Francistown daily at 10am (club/economy class US$4/8,

6½ hours). The night train departs nightly at 9pm (1st-class sleeper/2nd-class sleeper/economy US$25/20/5, 8¼ hours). Coming from Francistown, the overnight service continues to Lobatse (US$1, 1½ hours) early in the morning, with only economy-class seats available from Gaborone. For current information, contact **Botswana Railways** (☎ 471 1375; www.botswanarailways.co.bw).

Hitching

To hitch north, catch the Broadhurst 4 minibus from any shopping centre along the main city loop (see below) and get off at the standard hitching spot at the northern end of town. There's no need to wave down a vehicle – anyone with space will stop for passengers. Plan on around P40 to Francistown, where you can look for onward lifts to Nata, Maun and Kasane. It's not advisable to try and hitch to South Africa – the way, as of research, was too dangerous to risk a ride with strangers.

See p180 for more about hitching in Botswana.

GETTING AROUND
To/From the Airport

Taxis rarely turn up at the airport; if you do find one, you'll pay around P70 to the centre. The only reliable transport between the airport and town is the courtesy minibuses operated by the top-end hotels for their guests. If there's space, non-guests may talk the driver into a lift.

Car

The following international car-rental companies have agencies (which may not be staffed after 5pm) at the airport:
Avis (☎ 391 3093)
Budget (☎ 390 2030)
Imperial (☎ 390 6676)

Combi

Packed white combis, recognisable by their blue number plates, circulate according to set routes and cost P2.70. They pick up and drop off only at designated lay-bys marked 'bus/taxi stop'. The main city loop passes all the main shopping centres except the new Riverwalk Mall and the Kgale Centre, which are on the Tlokweng and Kgale routes respectively. Combis can be hailed either along major roads or from the combi stand.

Taxi

Taxis, which can also be easily identified by their blue number plates, are surprisingly difficult to come by in Gabs. Very few cruise the streets looking for fares, and most are parked either in front of the train station or on Botswana Rd. If you manage to get hold of one, fares (negotiable) are generally P25 to P40 per trip around the city.

Taxi companies:
Final Bravo Cabs (☎ 312 1785)
Speedy Cabs (☎ 390 0070)

AROUND GABORONE

If the big-city sprawl is making you feel a bit claustrophobic, you can always choose from a number of interesting day trips into the surrounding countryside. Almost all can be visited via public transport or hired taxi, though you'll get around quicker if you have your own wheels. A few of the places listed also serve as nice city breaks if you're looking for a quiet night's rest.

NORTH OF GABORONE
Mochudi

As evidenced by ruined stone walls in the hills, the charming village of Mochudi was first settled in the 1500s by the Kwena, who are one of the three most prominent lineage groups of the Batswana. In 1871, however, the Kgatla settled here after being forced from their lands by north-trekking Boers. The Cape Dutch–style **Phuthadikobo Museum** (☎ 577 7238; www.phuthadikobomuseum. com; admission free; ☺ 8am-5pm Mon-Fri, 2-5pm Sat & Sun) details the history of the area with colourful displays on village life. After visiting the museum (donations are suggested), it's worth spending some time appreciating the traditional Batswana designs present in the town's mud-walled architecture. If you'd like to linger in Mochudi for a night, the easy-to-spot (it's bright pink) **Sedibelo Motel** (☎ 572 9327; Pilane-Mochudi Rd; d incl breakfast P150) has reasonably clean and comfortable rooms, and there's also an attached bar-restaurant.

Buses to Mochudi (P8, one hour) depart from Gaborone when full. By car, head to Pilane and turn east. After 6km, turn left at the T-junction and then right just before the hospital to reach the historic village centre.

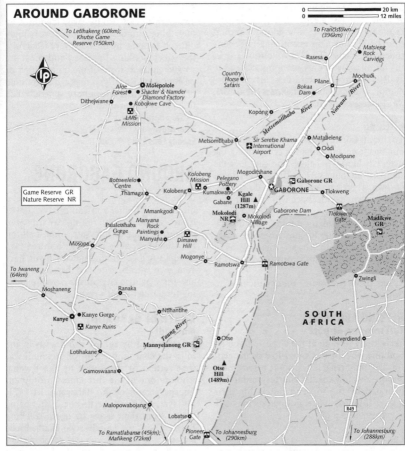

AROUND GABORONE

| 0 | 20 km |
| 0 | 12 miles |

To Letlhakeng (60km);
Khutse Game
Reserve (150km)

To Francistown
(396km)

Matsieng
Rock
Carvings

Rasesa

Country
Horse
Safaris

Mochudi

Aloe
Forest ● Molepolole
Shacter & Namder
Diamond Factory
Dithejwane ● Kobokwe Cave

Pilane

Bokaa
Dam

Kopong

LMS
Mission

Metsemotlhaba River

Norwane River

Metsomtlhaba

Sir Seretse Khama
International
Airport

Matabeleng

Oodi

Modipane

Mogoditshane

Kolobeng
Mission
Pelegano
Pottery
Kgale
Hill
(1287m)

Gaborone GR

GABORONE

Tlokweng

Botswelelo
Centre
Thamaga

Kolobeng
Kumakwane
Gabane

Gaborone Dam

Game Reserve GR
Nature Reserve NR

Mmankgodi

Mokolodi
NR
Mokolodi
Village

Tlokweng
Gate

Madikwe
GR

Manyana
Rock
Paintings
Palaletshaba
Gorge

Dimawe
Hill

Mosopa

Manyana

Mogonye

Ramotswa

Ramotswa Gate

To Jwaneng
(64km)

Moshaneng

Ranaka

Zwingli

Kanye ● Kanye Gorge

Ntlhantlhe

SOUTH
AFRICA

Kanye Ruins

Tuang River

Lotlhakane

Mannyelanong GR

Otse

Nietverdiend

Gamoswaana

Otse
Hill
(1489m)

Malopowabojang

Lobatse

R49

To Ramatlabama (45km);
Mafikeng (72km)

Pioneer
Gate

To Johannesburg
(290km)

To Johannesburg
(288km)

Bokaa Dam

Bokaa Dam is a popular spot for hiking and watching the sunset, though it can get a little crowded on the weekend. The 6km-long access road is passable by 2WD, and heads southwest near the turn-off to Mochudi at Pilane. Discreet, unofficial camping is permitted around the dam, but there is no campsite here.

Matsieng Rock Carvings

The Batswana regard this spot as one of the four 'creation sites'. According to legend, the footprint and rock carvings belonged to Matsieng, who marched out of a hole followed by wild and domestic animals. There is a small information board at the gate and,

on the other side of the fence from the car park, a tiny room with some explanations. The site lies at the end of a well-signposted 1km-long 2WD track that starts about 6km north of Pilane.

Kopong

Arne's Country Retreat (☎ 712 34567; arnes.retreat@ gmail.com; Lentsweletau Rd) is a friendly Swedish-run ranch specialising in horse riding, though it also offers cheap and tranquil accommodation. Camping costs US$5 per person, while double rooms with bathroom in the rustic guesthouse cost US$20. To get there, take the road from Gaborone towards Molepolole, then head to Kopong and follow the signs.

WEST OF GABORONE
Gabane

The ancient hilltop settlements around Gabane date from between AD 800 and 1200, and were built by the early Bangologa people, who once inhabited this area. A more contemporary attraction is **Pelegano Village** (☎ 394 7054; Gabane; ⏲ workshop 8am-4.30pm Mon-Fri, craft shop 7.30am-1pm Sat, 2-4pm Sun), established in 1982. This wonderful artisan complex is constantly trucking in local crafts and the like, such as hand-fired ceramics and wine bottles recycled into dinner glasses.

Gabane village is 12km southwest of Mogoditshane and 23km from central Gaborone. Pelegano Pottery is 900m along a dirt road that starts at the second turn-off along the road from Mogoditshane – look for the Pelegano signs. By public transport, take the bus towards Kanye from Gaborone (P10, 25 minutes) and walk the last bit to Pelegano Village.

Kolobeng Mission

From 1847 to 1852 this **mission** (admission free; ⏲ 8am-5pm) was the home of Dr David Livingstone (see the boxed text, p190). Unfortunately, the only remnants of the mission are the decaying floor of Livingstone's home and several graves, including that of his daughter Elizabeth. In addition, we've heard this out-of-the-way area is popular with criminals, so come in a group. The site is located just east of Kolobeng village and accessible by any bus to Kanye or Thamaga from Gaborone.

Manyana

Manyana is famous for its Zimbabwean-style **rock paintings**, which date back over 2000 years and feature paintings of three giraffes, an elephant and several antelopes. The site is located on the southern extreme of an 8m-high rock overhang about 500m north of the village. Because the site is hard to find, it's a good idea to hire a local from the village to act as a guide.

Before leaving the area, it's also worth visiting **Dimawe Hill**, an important historical site where several groups of warriors under Chief Sechele I halted the invading forces of the Boers from South Africa in 1852. The ruins are scattered around the granite hills, not far from the roadside about 5km before Manyana. Nothing is signposted, but it's a pleasant place to wander around.

The bus (P8, 1½ hours) from Gaborone stops at the T-junction at the end of the road in Manyana village.

Thamaga

The rural village of Thamaga is home to the **Botswelelo Centre** (☎ 599 9220; Molepolole Rd; tours P3; ⏲ 8am-5pm), which is also known as Thamaga Pottery. This non-profit community project was started by missionaries in the 1970s and now sells a wide range of creations for good prices. Tours must be booked in advance. Buses run frequently from the main bus terminal in Gaborone (P7, one hour).

Situated about 5km east of here, in Mmankgodi, is **Bahurutshe Cultural Lodge** (☎ 316 3737; www.bahurutsheculturallodge.com; camping/chalets P50/350), an innovative cultural village, chalet complex and camping ground where visitors can very easily access the traditional elements of Batswana music, dance and cuisine. The comfy chalets really do up the African hut thing, with cool stone, mud walls and

---

THE WEAVERS OF OODI

The village of Oodi is best known for the internationally acclaimed **Lentswe-la-Oodi Weavers** (☎ 310 2268; ⏲ 8am-4.30pm Mon-Fri, 10am-4.30pm Sat & Sun), a cooperative established in 1973 by Ulla and Peder Gowenius, two Swedes who hoped to provide an economic base for women from the villages of Oodi, Matebeleng and Modipane. At the workshop, wool is hand spun, then dyed using chemicals over an open fire (which creates over 600 colours) and finally woven into spontaneous patterns invented by individual artists. Most of the patterns depict African wildlife and aspects of rural life in Botswana, and are fairly priced considering the high quality of the work. The women can also weave customised pieces based on individual pictures, drawings or stories if requested.

By car, get on the highway from Gaborone towards Francistown, and take the turn-off for Oodi village. Follow signs for another 7.5km to the workshop. Any northbound bus from Gaborone can drop you off at the turn-off for Oodi, though you will have to walk or hitch the rest of the way.

rustic-smelling thatch enclosing you come the evening.

Molepolole

The name of this hillside village (pronounced *mo*-lay-po-*lo*-lay) means 'let him cancel it' and was apparently derived from the utterance of a *kgosi* (chief) in response to a spell placed upon the land where the village now stands. The village is also adjacent to a large and eerie **aloe forest**, which is full of indigenous marloth aloes and blooms spectacularly in September and October. According to legend, the Boers trekked into Molepolole in 1850 to punish Chief Sechele of the Bakwena for befriending David Livingstone. However, when they approached the village on a dark night, they mistook the aloes for ranks of Bakwena warriors and fled in fear.

The **Kgosi Sechele I Museum** (☎ 592 0917; Gaborone Rd; admission US$1; ☺ 9am-noon & 2-4pm Tue-Fri, 11am-4pm Sat), which is housed in the historic police station (built in 1902), features displays of traditional housing, plenty of paintings and photos of local history and some inevitable Livingstone memorabilia.

The **Old LMS Church**, built by the London Missionary Society (LMS), is 800m north of the town's hotel, and is now the Molepolole Congregational Church.

According to legend, **Kobokwe Cave** (also called Livingstone's Cave) was visited by Livingstone despite the warning by a Bakwena shaman that to do so would bring about a speedy death. The Scot's survival prompted Chief Sechele's conversion to Christianity. The cave is about 5km from Molepolole on the road to Thamaga.

About 1km south of Kobokwe Cave are the ruins of the **LMS Mission**, which operated from 1866 to 1884. West of the stream, below the ruin, is a high rock face from which the Bakwena apparently flung unauthorised witches and wizards.

If you need to stay here (there aren't a lot of options), try **Kodisa Lodge** (☎ 595 6835; r from P350), a pretty basic roadside sort of place that nonetheless offers very reasonably priced, comfy rooms with cleanliness if not character.

Buses regularly leave Gaborone for Molepolole (P9, 1½ hours).

Jwaneng

In 1978 the world's largest diamond deposit was discovered in Jwaneng. Today the mine,

run by Debswana, a partly government-owned mining company, produces around 10 million carats annually, and processes nearly 500,000 metric tonnes of rock per month. Security is so tight that, once a vehicle is allowed onto the mine site, it will never be allowed to leave.

Jwaneng is an open town, and non-Debswana employees may settle and establish businesses. **Mine tours** (per person P15) are possible by appointment with a week's notice through the **Debswana Public Relations Office** (☎ 588 4000) in Jwaneng.

Buses regularly leave from Gaborone (P35, three hours).

SOUTH OF GABORONE

Kgale Hill

Although the 'Sleeping Giant' (1287m) is located only a few hundred metres from the Gaborone sprawl, a quick two-hour hike to the top and back is perfect for clearing your head. There are three trails leading to the summit, all of which are well signposted. From the bus station, you can take any combi marked 'Kgale' or 'Lobatse' to the base of the hill. You may want to come here with a friend or two, as criminals are known to use Kgale Hill as a hideout.

Gaborone Dam

This dam along the Notwane River provides the city with fresh water, though it also serves as a popular recreational area. The dam offers ideal bird-watching amid the drowned trees and bushes, but swimming is not recommended (think crocodiles and bilharzia – see p391). The dam is home to the **Gaborone Yacht Club** (☎ 355 2241), which rents out canoes and windsurfers on weekends. Fishing is also popular from the edge of the dam. The dam is easily reached by following the Gaborone–Lobatse road.

Mokolodi Nature Reserve

This 3000-hectare private **reserve** (☎ 316 1955; www.mokolodi.com; ☺ 7.30am-6pm) was established in 1991 and is home to giraffes, elephants, zebras, baboons, warthogs, hippos, kudu, impala, waterbucks and klipspringers. The reserve also protects a few retired cheetahs, leopards, honey badgers, jackals and hyenas, as well as over 300 species of bird.

Mokolodi also operates a research facility, a breeding centre for rare and endangered species, a community-education centre and a sanctuary for orphaned, injured or confiscated birds and animals. It also accepts volunteers, though an application must be submitted prior to arrival, and a maintenance fee is levied according to the length of the program. See the website for more information.

It is important to note that the entire reserve often closes during the rainy season (December to March) – phone ahead before you visit at this time. Visitors are permitted to drive their own vehicles around the reserve (you will need a 4WD in the rainy season), though guided tours by 4WD or on foot are available. If you're self-driving, don't forget to pick up a map from the reception office so you don't get lost.

Park entry fees cost P65 per person per day. If you're not self-driving, two-hour day or night wildlife drives cost P120 per person. There are a number of other activities on offer, such as cheetah petting (P290), rhino tracking (P485) and horse safaris (P145).

Spending the night in the reserve is a refreshing alternative to staying in Gaborone. Though pricey, the **campsites** (P80 per person) at Mokolodi are secluded and well groomed, and feature braai (barbecue) pits, thatched bush showers (with steaming-hot water) and toilets. If you want to safari in style, there are also three-person **chalets** (per weekday/weekend day P420/560, 6 to 8 sleeper per day weekday/weekend day P560/765) situated in the middle of the reserve. Advance bookings are necessary. If you don't have a vehicle, staff can drive you to the campsite and accommodation areas for P10. At the time of research, the **Alexander McCall Smith Traditional Rest Camp**, a cluster of lovely African huts, had just opened in the reserve, but prices were not available yet and the camp had not begun accepting visitors. McCall Smith is supporting the camp.

The entrance to the reserve is located 12km south of Gaborone. By public transport, take a bus to Lobatse and get off at the signposted turn-off. From there, it's a 1.5km walk to the entrance.

Otse

The town of Otse (pronounced *oot*-see) is known for Otse Hill (1489m), Botswana's highest point, though the main attraction for travellers is the **Mannyelanong Game Reserve** (admission free; ⊙ daylight hr Sep, Oct & Feb-Apr). This reserve is the breeding centre for the endangered Cape Griffon vulture, which nests in the cliffs. (In case you were wondering, Mannyelanong means 'where vultures defecate' in Tswana.) The reserve was established in 1986 to arrest the alarming decline in vulture numbers here during the 1960s and 1970s. Loud noises can scare the birds and cause chicks and eggs to fall from the nests, so please mind the fences and be careful not to speak too loudly.

Otse village is located about 45km south of Gaborone. The Lobatse-bound bus can drop you outside the game reserve (which is obvious from the cliffs and fence).

Kanye

Built around the base of Kanye Hill, the capital of the Bangwaketse people is home to the **Kanye Gorge**, where the entire population of the town once hid during a Ndebele raid in the 1880s. An easy 1.5km walk along the cliff face from the eastern end of Kanye Gorge will take you to **Kanye Ruins**, the remains of an early-18th-century stone-walled village. Buses regularly travel between Gaborone and Kanye via Thamaga (P10, two hours). The bus station is 1.5km west of the main shopping centre.

Eastern Botswana

Eastern Botswana occupies a dual, almost contradictory identity within the make-up of the country. For the Batswana this relatively highly populated land may be the most important part of Botswana, where daily dramas play out to the tune of everyday Africa; for travellers, this is largely an ignored area, a place to be bypassed on the way to Maun, Kasane and the Kalahari.

That's the travellers' loss. This is, in many ways, the Batswana heartland, a land of scrub and seasonal rains that supports an agricultural ranch, field and stone landscape. In between cattle posts and farms are settlements that serve as population nodes for the Batswana, a race generally accustomed to wide open spaces and long blue skies. Those environmental elements are here, but they're padded by the towns, including Francistown, the second-largest settlement in the nation. You may need to pass this way if you're in need of an overland connection.

But you shouldn't think of Eastern Botswana, with its well-developed infrastructure, as just a depot for catching the next bus or a garage for servicing your 4WD. Besides interacting with Batswana culture at arguably its most accessible, there are a fair few private farms and reserves here that are good camping options for independent-minded travellers. The Tuli Block, a protuberance of ochre moonscape, bulges into Zimbabwe, dotted with herds of game, mourning jackals, the shadows of big cats and the archaeological traces of a former age. And the rhinos still roam here, in an innovative sanctuary named for one of the fathers of the nation.

HIGHLIGHTS

- Spotting some of the last remaining rhinos in Botswana at the **Khama Rhino Sanctuary** (p96)

- Admiring the diverse wildlife and rocky landscape of the private reserves in the **Tuli Game Reserve** (p100)

- Delving into Botswana's heritage at **Serowe** (p96), the former home of Sir Seretse Khama, Botswana's first president

- Checking out the urban vibe of **Francistown** (p97), Botswana's second-largest city

- Going off the beaten path in search of San cave paintings in the little-explored **Lepokole Hills** (p100)

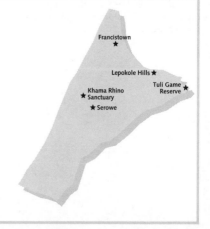

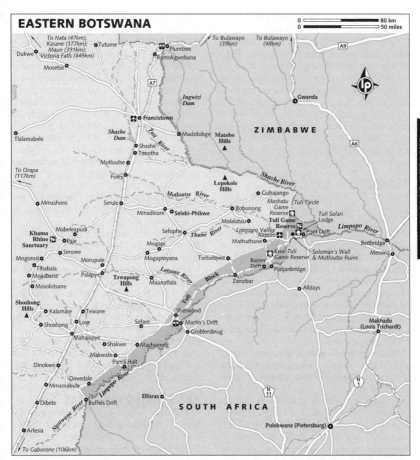

EASTERN BOTSWANA

0 ——— 80 km
0 ——— 50 miles

PALAPYE

Palapye's original name was 'Phalatswe', which means 'many impalas' in Sekgalagadi or 'large impala' in Tswana. To most Batswana, however, Palapye is known as the 'powerhouse of Botswana', due to the massive coal-burning power plant that was opened in nearby Morupule. Palapye's other claim to fame is that it's the birthplace of Festus Mogae, the country's former president. Unless they have a burning interest in coal, however, most travellers only stop in Palapye to break up the drive between Gaborone and Francistown.

About 20km southeast of Palapye, at the foot of the Tswapong Hills, are the ruins of the **Old Phalatswe Church**, which mark the former Bangwato capital of Phalatswe. After the Christian Bangwato chief Khama III and his people arrived from Shoshong in 1889, Phalatswe was transformed from a stretch of desert to a settlement of 30,000 people. The Gothic-style church was funded by the people and completed in 1892. When the Bangwato capital was moved to Serowe in 1902, Chief Khama sent a regiment to torch Phalatswe, but the church remained standing.

If you're craving air-con and cable TV, look no further than the **Cresta Botsalo Hotel** (☎ 492 0245; www.cresta-hospitality.com; Hwy A1; r incl breakfast P710;), one of the nicest establishments in the reliable Cresta chain. The attached Savuti Grille (P34 to P82) is a popular restaurant serving continental fare. The hotel is next to the Caltex petrol station, about 50m north of the junction along the highway.

Buses along the route between Gaborone (P25, four hours) and Francistown (P15, two hours) pass through Palapye and stop at the chaotic Engen Shopping Centre. From this shopping centre, shared taxis and combis (minibuses) also go to Serowe (P7, 30 minutes) and Orapa (P50, 4½ hours). If the trains are back up by the time you read this, those travelling between Gaborone and Francistown should stop at the railway station in central Palapye.

SEROWE

In 1902 Chief Khama III abandoned the Bangwato capital in Phalatswe and built Serowe on the ruins of an 11th-century village at the base of Thathaganyana Hill. Serowe was later immortalised by South African writer Bessie Head, who included the village in several of her works, including the renowned *Serowe – Village of the Rain Wind*. This book includes a chronicle of the Botswana Brigades Movement, which was established in 1965 at the Swaneng Hill Secondary School in Serowe and has since brought vocational education to many remote areas.

Although the modern town centre is drab and of little interest to travellers, it's worth visiting the **Khama III Memorial Museum** (☎ 463 0519; admission free; ◷ 8am-5pm Tue-Fri, 10am-4.30pm Sat), which was opened in 1985 and outlines the history of the Khama family. The museum includes the personal effects of Chief Khama III and his descendants as well as various artefacts illustrating Serowe's history. There are also exhibits on African insects and snakes, San culture and temporary art displays. The museum is about 800m from the central shopping area on the road towards Orapa. Donations are welcome.

Before leaving town, hike up to the top of Thathaganyana Hill where you'll find the **Royal Cemetery**, which contains the grave of Sir Seretse Khama, the founding father of modern Botswana (p56), and Khama III; the latter is marked by a bronze duiker (a small antelope), which is the Bangwato totem. Be advised that police consider this a sensitive area, so visitors need to seek permission (and possibly obtain a guide) from the police station in the barracks house. To reach the police station, follow the road opposite the Dennis petrol station until you reach the *kgotla* (traditionally constructed

Batswana community affairs hall), and the surrounding barracks; one of the buildings houses the police station.

The small but quaint **Tshwaragano Hotel** (☎ 463 0377; s/d P180/210) is built on the slopes of Thathaganyana Hill and boasts great views of the town. The attached bar-restaurant is usually the most hopping place in town, relatively speaking. Tshwaragano is located above the shopping area on the road to Orapa.

Another good option is the **Serowe Hotel** (☎ 463 0234; s/d P450/565), which is 2km southeast of town on the road to Palapye. Comfortable and well-furnished rooms ensure a quiet night's sleep, and the laid-back outdoor bar is a good bet for a nightcap. The popular restaurant serves English fare as well as a number of vegetarian meals.

Buses travel between Serowe and Gaborone (P25, four hours) about every hour. Alternatively, from Gabs catch a Francistown-bound bus, disembark at the turn-off to Serowe just north of Palapye, and catch a shared taxi or combi to Serowe. Combis and shared taxis also depart for Orapa (P50, four hours) when full; this combi route passes by the entrance to the Khama Rhino Sanctuary. Most buses, combis and taxis leave from a spot near Ellerines furniture shop in the central shopping area, while the mammoth bus station nearby remains empty.

KHAMA RHINO SANCTUARY

In response to declining rhinoceros populations in Botswana, the residents of Serowe banded together in 1989 to establish the 4300-hectare **Khama Rhino Sanctuary** (☎ 463 0713; www.khamarhinosanctuary.com; adult P33, vehicle under/over 5 tons P41/133; ◷ 8am-7pm; 🖭). Today the sanctuary protects the country's last remaining population of rhinos – 34 white and two black rhinos currently reside in Khama (with a baby black on the way as of this writing). The sanctuary is also home to wildebeests, impalas, ostriches, hyenas, leopards and over 230 species of bird.

The main roads within the sanctuary are normally accessible by 2WD in the dry season, though 4WD vehicles are necessary in the rainy season. However, all vehicles can reach the campsite and accommodation areas in any weather. The office at the entrance sells useful maps of the sanctuary as well as basic non-perishable foods, cold drinks and firewood.

No vehicle? Two-hour day/night wildlife drives cost P333 and can take up to four people. Nature walks (P133) and rhino-tracking excursions (P200), both one to two hours long, can also be arranged. You can also hire a guide to accompany your vehicle for P115.

Shady campsites (P53 per person) with braai (barbecue) pits are adjacent to clean toilets and (steaming hot) showers, while six-person dorms go for P293 per person. If you're looking to splurge for a night or two, rustic four-person chalets (P366 to P399 per night) and six-person A-frames (P512 to P800 per night) have basic kitchen facilities and private bathrooms. There's also a restaurant, bar and a swimming pool. If you don't have a vehicle, staff can drive you to the campsite and accommodation areas for a nominal charge.

The entrance gate to the sanctuary is about 26km northwest of Serowe along the road to Orapa (turn left at the unsigned T-junction about 5km northwest of Serowe). Khama is accessible by any bus or combi heading towards Orapa, and is not hard to reach by hitching.

MADIKWE GAME RESERVE

One of South Africa's most underappreciated wildlife reserves is only an hour from Gaborone, making Botswana's capital the closest urban base for exploring the wilderness wonderland that is **Madikwe Game Reserve** (☎ 27-21 424 1037; http://madikwe.safari.co.za; adult/child R50/20). There's Big Five wildlife viewing, red-sand and thorn-bush environs and plenty of lions.

Madikwe does not allow self-drive safaris or day visitors, which means you must stay at one of the park's 18 tourism lodges to play (we don't cover those lodges here, but see Lonely Planet's *South Africa* guide for more information). A Madikwe safari experience isn't cheap, but the old adage, 'you get what you pay for' rings true. With only trained park rangers (each lodge employs its own) allowed to drive inside the park, your chance of seeing wildlife is quite good.

Madikwe is in the northwest corner of South Africa, and is only 30km from Gaborone along the Tlokweng Rd, which becomes Rte 47/Rte 49 (the road is referred to by both numbers, which is a bit confusing) – all sealed highways. You will not be allowed through Madikwe's gates without a reservation, so an advance booking is mandatory. Make sure to arrange a pick-up from the gate with the lodge you've reserved at, as for obvious safety reasons you cannot simply walk through the reserve to reach it.

FRANCISTOWN
pop 115,000

In 1867 Southern Africa's first gold rush was ignited when German Karl Mauch discovered gold along the Tati River. Two years later, a group of Australian miners along with Englishman Daniel Francis arrived on the scene in search of their stake. Although Francis headed for the newly discovered Kimberley diamond fields in 1870, he returned 10 years later to negotiate local mining rights with the Ndebele king Lobengula and laid out the town that now bears his name.

Today, the second-largest city in Botswana is known more for its wholesale shopping than its mining history. Although there's nothing much in Francistown to interest travellers, it's a useful (and often necessary) stopover on the way to/from Kasane, Nata, Maun or Victoria Falls.

Information

If you're staying for more than a little bit, it's worth picking up a copy of the *Northern Advertiser* (P3) or *Metro* (P2), both published weekly. For a list of local attractions, pick up a copy of *Exploring Tati: Places of Historic and Other Interest In and Around Francistown* by Catrien van Waarden for P35 (available at the museum).

The Barclays and First National Banks along Blue Jacket St, among other banks, have ATMs and foreign-exchange facilities.

Butnet Internet (☎ 7167 7358; Rutherford St) The best-named internet cafe in Botswana.

Ebrahim Store (☎ 241 4762; Tainton Ave) The place to buy camping gear.

Nyangabgwe Hospital (☎ 211 1000, emergency 997)

Police station (☎ 241 2221, emergency 999; Haskins St)

Polina Laundromat (Blue Jacket St)

Post office (Blue Jacket St)

Sights

Housed in the 100-year-old Government Camp, the **Supa-Ngwao Museum** (☎ /fax 240 3088; snm@info.bw; off New Maun Rd; admission free; ☯ 8am-5pm Mon-Fri, 9am-5pm Sat) includes a prison and a police canteen. The museum contains interesting small displays about local and regional culture and history (*supa-ngwao* appropriately means 'to show culture' in Tswana). The museum also hosts temporary art exhibitions and occasional special events. The small shop

EASTERN BOTSWANA

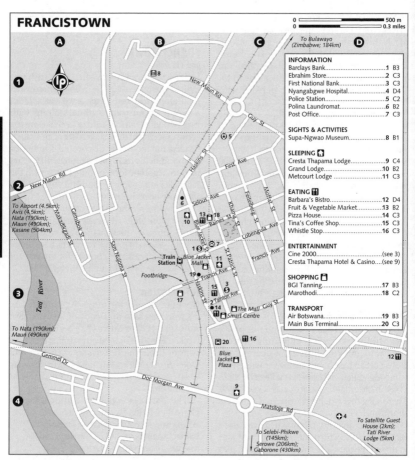

FRANCISTOWN

INFORMATION	
Barclays Bank	1 B3
Ebrahim Store	2 C3
First National Bank	3 C3
Nyangabgwe Hospital	4 D4
Police Station	5 C2
Polina Laundromat	6 B2
Post Office	7 C3

SIGHTS & ACTIVITIES	
Supa-Ngwao Museum	8 B1

SLEEPING	
Cresta Thapama Lodge	9 C4
Grand Lodge	10 B2
Metcourt Lodge	11 B3

EATING	
Barbara's Bistro	12 D4
Fruit & Vegetable Market	13 B2
Pizza House	14 C3
Tina's Coffee Shop	15 C3
Whistle Stop	16 C3

ENTERTAINMENT	
Cine 2000	(see 3)
Cresta Thapama Hotel & Casino	(see 9)

SHOPPING	
BGI Tanning	17 B3
Marothodi	18 C2

TRANSPORT	
Air Botswana	19 B3
Main Bus Terminal	20 C3

sells maps, books and locally made souvenirs, and acts as a tourist office. Donations are suggested.

Sleeping

Tati River Lodge (☎ 240 6000; www.trl.co.bw; camping per person P40, s/d from P540/629; ❄ ☐) On the riverbank, this is a pretty pleasant midmarket option that feels like an old-school country motel. It's popular with locals and strikes a decent balance between rustic and roadside.

Satellite Guest House (☎ 241 4665; s/d P200/250) This walled compound of motel-style units is uninspiring, though it's certainly cheap if you're counting every pula. Unfortunately, it's out in the suburbs (3.5km southeast of

the city centre) and can get noisy if there are a lot of guests.

Grand Lodge (☎ 241 2300; Blue Jacket St; s/d P250/300; ❄) This is an excellent choice if you want to stay in the city centre. Standard rooms become something special when you add aircon, cable TV, a fridge and a hotplate.

Metcourt Lodge (☎ 241 1100; Blue Jacket St; d P540; ❄) The Metcourt chain offers reliably comfy, solidly three-star accommodation across Botswana, and it doesn't disappoint in this regard in Francistown. The attached restaurant is good for a steak and a beer after long, dusty days.

Cresta Thapama Lodge (☎ 241 3872; www.cresta -hospitality.com; cnr Blue Jacket St & Doc Morgan Ave; s/d incl breakfast from P750; ❄ ☐) Francistown's most upmarket hotel boasts a four-star rating, though the overall ambience is a bit stuffy. But, if you're a fan of luxury and formality, you'll revel in the colonial-inspired rooms and can unwind in the casino or on the squash and tennis courts.

Eating
Self-caterers have a choice of several well-stocked supermarkets, as well as the fruit and vegetable market on the corner of Blue Jacket and Baines Sts.

Barbara's Bistro (Francistown Sports Club; meals from P30) Located in the eastern outskirts of town, this quaint, leafy spot is a good choice for inexpensive local specialties such as beef stew and *pap*.

Pizza House (Haskins St; pizzas from P28) If you're getting ready to head out to the wilds, savour every last bite of the wood-fired pizzas served here.

Tina's Coffee Shop (Blue Jacket St; meals P25-50) Whether you're here for a cuppa and cake or a heavy plate of chicken and rice, you'll enjoy the cosy atmosphere of this popular local shop.

Whistle Stop (Blue Jacket St; mains P25-50) Start your day right with a hearty breakfast from the Whistle Stop. Otherwise, if you're not an early riser, it also serves a good variety of grilled meat, fish, burgers and desserts.

Entertainment
To find out what's going on, check the noticeboard at the museum and the *What's On* column in the *Northern Advertiser*.

Cine 2000 (Blue Jacket St; US$2) If you need your Western-culture fix, this small cinema shows recent English-language films.

Cresta Thapama Hotel & Casino (Blue Jacket St) The bar attracts mostly business travellers, though there's a good selection of hard spirits here.

Shopping
BGI Tanning (☎ 241 9987) This small tannery, across the footbridge from the town centre, produces a variety of leather goods and sells locally made Shashe baskets, which have a good reputation for their quality and intricate design.

Marothodi (☎ 241 3646; Village Mall) Set up in 1978 as a cooperative for disadvantaged women, Marothodi produces exquisite (but pricey) fabrics and clothing featuring original motifs.

Getting There & Away
AIR
You can fly between Francistown and Gaborone with **Air Botswana** (☎ 241 2393; Francis Ave) for around P682.

BUS & COMBI
From the main bus terminal, located between the train line and Blue Jacket Plaza, buses and combis connect Francistown with Gaborone (P40, six hours), Maun (P60, five hours), Kasane (P65, seven hours), Nata (P25, two hours), Serowe (P23, 2½ hours), Selebi-Phikwe (P15, two hours) and Bulawayo, Zimbabwe (P30, two hours). Buses operate according to roughly fixed schedules and combis leave when full.

HITCHING
To go to Maun via Nata, take a taxi to the tree near the airport turn-off along New Maun Rd (everyone knows where it is). Heading south, wait at the Cresta Thapama roundabout or further south along the highway to Gaborone. For more about hitching in Botswana, see p180.

TRAIN
The overnight train to Gaborone (1st-/2nd-class sleeper US$25/20, economy US$5, 8¼ hours) leaves at 9pm, while the day train (club/economy class US$4/8, 6½ hours) leaves at 10am. The overnight service continues to Lobatse (US$1, 1½ hours) early in the morning.

Getting Around
As well as the ubiquitous combis, taxis cruise the streets and park at the bus station. A combi or shared taxi around town costs US$0.50.

Avis (☎ 241 3901) has an office at the airport, which is about 5.5km west of the town centre.

SELEBI-PHIKWE
pop 70,000

Following the discovery of copper, nickel and cobalt in 1967, the sleepy villages of Selebi and Phikwe were transformed into Botswana's third-largest city. Today, the mines currently produce 2.5 million tonnes of these metals per year. Although pleasant, Selebi-Phikwe (often called Phikwe) is little more than a stopover for travellers en route to northeastern Botswana from South Africa.

EASTERN BOTSWANA

Bosele Hotel & Casino (☎ 261 0675; Tshekedi Rd; s/d P600/750; ❄ ▩), conveniently located on the southeast corner of the mall, is a pleasant (but pricey) three-star hotel offering plush rooms surrounding a swimming pool and outdoor bar. If you want to go cheaper, try the bland **Travel Inn** (☎ 262 2999; travelinn@botsnet. bw; d P230-350; ❄ ▩).

From the central bus station, buses leave frequently to Gaborone (P45, six hours). Combis leave when full to Francistown (P15) and the South African border at Martin's Drift (P20).

LEPOKOLE HILLS

Don your Indiana Jones hat and get ready to explore one of the most exciting frontiers in archaeology. The Lepokole Hills, an extension of the Matobo Hills in Zimbabwe, are a Middle Earth–esque collection of dry ochre, granite pillars and castle *kopjes* (piles of rocks). They are also riddled with caves, gorges and overhangs decorated with paintings by the early San people, who retreated here from waves of Bantu and white migration. Scattered among the paintings are Stone Age tools, implements and accoutrement, very little of it properly excavated. We should hasten to add: taking home *any* archaeological finds is immoral and illegal. The hills are 25km north of Bobonong along a 4WD track. Permission to visit is required from the *kgosi* (chief) in Bobonong, and you might want to hire a local guide.

TULI GAME RESERVE

Tucked into the nation's right side pocket, the Tuli Block is a 10km- to 20km-wide swath of freehold farmland extending over 300km along the northern bank of the Limpopo River. The main attraction is the Tuli Game Reserve, a vast moonscape of muddy oranges and browns overlooked by deep blue sky. It's the sort of Dali-esque desert environment that puts one in mind of Arizona or Australia, yet the barren beauty belies a land rich in life. Elephants, hippos, kudu, wildebeests and impalas as well as small numbers of lions, cheetahs and leopards circle each other among rocks and *kopjes* scattered with artefacts from the Stone Age onwards; a well-supplied archaeologist would be in dusty heaven up here. More than 350 species of bird have also been recorded in the reserve.

Once owned by the British South Africa Company (BSAC), the land was ceded to white settlers after the railway route was shifted to the northwest. However, much of the land proved to be unsuitable for agriculture and has since been developed for tourism.

Information

One advantage of visiting the Tuli Game Reserve is that entrance is free. Night drives (not permitted in government-controlled parks and reserves) are also allowed, so visitors can often see nocturnal creatures, such as aardwolves, aardvarks and leopards. The disadvantage is that the Tuli Block is private land, so visitors are not allowed to venture off the main roads or camp outside the official campsites and lodges. Also, exploring this region without a private vehicle is virtually impossible. The best time to visit is from May to September, when animals are forced to congregate around permanent water sources.

Sights

The landscape in Tuli Block is defined by its unusual rock formations. The most famous feature is **Solomon's Wall**, a 30m-high dolerite dyke cut naturally through the landscape on either side of the riverbed. Nearby are the **Motloutse Ruins**, a Great Zimbabwe–era stone village that belonged to the kingdom of Mwene Mutapa. Both sights can be explored on foot, and are accessible from the road between Zanzibar and Pont Drift.

Sleeping

Kwa-Tuli Game Reserve (☎ 27-15 964 3895; www. kwatuli.co.za; camping per person R395) Set deep inside the block, Kwa-Tuli consists of two camps, Island and Koro. The former holds a series of luxury safari tents (for a middle-income price) perched on an island in the midst of the Limpopo River. Koro Camp is the headquarters of the non-profit Tuli Conservation Project. It's often filled with school groups, but phone ahead to see if your little ones can join the fun. Meanwhile, get some energy as the night goes on in the excellent bar or restaurant. Note that prices are in rand.

Tuli Safari Lodge (☎ 264 5303; www.tulilodge.com; camping from P55, tent camping incl full board & wildlife drives per person from P385, r incl full board & wildlife drives per person low/high season from P1135/1500; ❄ ▩) This lodge is set in a riverine oasis and surrounded by red rock country that teems with wildlife. Because it offers a range of accommodation to suit most budgets, it often feels more relaxed and less formal than other exclusive private reserves in the country. Be sure to have a drink at the outdoor bar built around the base of a 500-year-old Nyala tree. Reservations are strongly recommended. The game reserve is just beyond the Pont Drift border post.

Mashatu Game Reserve (☎ in South Africa 27-11 442 2267; www.mashatu.com; luxury tent/chalet incl full board & wildlife drives per person US$250/375; 🔀 🔉) One of the largest private wildlife reserves in Southern Africa is renowned for its big cats and frighteningly large elephant population (current estimates are well over 1000). The main camp is one of Botswana's most exclusive resorts and is home to the Gin Trap, a dugout bar that overlooks a floodlit watering hole. Although it's certainly worth the splurge, those with lighter wallets can still indulge in luxury at the tent camp, which features luxury linen tents complete with private showers and bathrooms. Only prebooked guests are allowed on the reserve. Rates include transfer from the Limpopo Valley Airfield or the Pont Drift border post. The game reserve is also just beyond the Pont Drift border post.

Getting There & Away

Mashatu and Tuli support a scheduled flight between Johannesburg, Kasane and the Limpopo Valley Airport, which is usually booked as part of a package with either of the reserves.

Most roads in Tuli Block are negotiable by 2WD, though it can get rough in places over creek beds, which occasionally flood during the rainy season. From Sherwood, a graded gravel road runs parallel to the South African border and provides access to the various lodges. The lodges can also be accessed from the west via the paved road from Bobonong.

If you're coming from South Africa, note that the border crossing at Pont Drift usually requires a 4WD, and can be closed when the river is too high. If you've prebooked your accommodation, you can leave your vehicle with the border police and then get a transfer by vehicle (if dry) or by cableway (if the river is flooded) to your lodge.

EASTERN BOTSWANA

Northeastern Botswana

For the tourist, Botswana is a land of waters and the barren lack thereof, and nowhere else does this contradiction of ecologies exist in such proximity as in the northeast. On the one side are the Chobe River, the Linyanti Marshes and their shared wet prairie: tall reeds cut by graze lines and grasslands, pulsing with some of the best wildlife concentrations in Southern Africa. Here, life and water dance a perennial duet, and the end result is a rich, velvet landscape where you're practically guaranteed good animal spotting.

On the other side is the Makgadikgadi, the largest network of salt pans in the world, a place where the lack of water leaves a similarly powerful, if also entirely different, impression. Yellow lions, honey-coloured impalas and dusty elephants mottle into the scrub and thorn brush, but even this spare, sparse flora eventually disappears into a long, unbroken sheet of shimmer, a space that encompasses a nothingness as large as Switzerland. The great salt pans are long, low and white, curtained by an electric-blue sky and pulsing with an unstoppable glare. The rains do come here, albeit infrequently, and when they do the land fairly bursts into waves of birdlife and animals awakening to the wet.

Travel here admittedly favours the package tourist over the independent wanderer, but that shouldn't put off the adventurous. There's a good range of accommodation, from five-star safari chic to midrange lodges to budget camps, in the tourist hub of Kasane. That town sits at the edge of Chobe National Park, itself the size of a small country and pocked with small, independent campsites. There's a lot of room here for exploration, and if you want to rough it, that's perfectly possible. But kicking back with fusion food and fine red wine is also an option for those wanting to light some serious fires in their wallet.

HIGHLIGHTS

- Driving (or boating) along the **Chobe Riverfront** (p114), one of Africa's premier wildlife-viewing destinations

- Watching herds of buffalo thunder over **Chobe National Park** (p109)

- Getting charged by an elephant in the **Makgadikgadi Pans Game Reserve** (p106) or the adjacent **Nxai Pan National Park** (p109)

- Realising how lonely the planet can be on the remote **Kubu Island** (p105)

- Swamp-stomping amongst the incredible game in the **Linyanti Marshes** (p117)

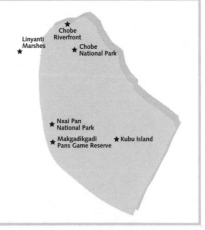

Chobe Riverfront
Linyanti Marshes
Chobe National Park
Nxai Pan National Park
Makgadikgadi Pans Game Reserve
Kubu Island

MAKGADIKGADI PANS

The Sowa (Sua), Nxai and Ntwetwe Pans together make up the 12,000-sq-km Makgadikgadi Pans. While Salar de Unyuni in Bolivia is the biggest single pan in the world, the Makgadikgadi network of parched, white dry lakes is larger. During the sizzling heat of the late winter (August), the stark pans take on a disorienting and ethereal austerity. Heat mirages destroy the senses as imaginary lakes shimmer and disappear, ostriches take flight, and stones turn to mountains and float in mid-air. But, as the annual rains begin to fall in the late spring, depressions in the pans form temporary lakes and fringing grasses turn green with life. Herd animals arrive to partake of the bounty, while water birds flock to feed on algae and tiny crustaceans.

Ancient lakeshore terraces reveal that the pans were once part of a 'superlake' of over 60,000 sq km that reached the Okavango and Chobe Rivers to the far north. However, less than 10,000 years ago, climatic changes caused the huge lake to evaporate, leaving only salt behind.

NATA

The dust-bowl town of Nata serves as the gateway to the Makgadikgadi Pans, as well as an obligatory fuel stop if you're heading to either Kasane or Maun. Be aware that elephants graze alongside the highway in this region, so take care during the day and avoid driving at night. Also, be warned: the road from Nata to Kasane is one of the worst tarred roads in the country. A 2WD can make it, but be prepared for a *lot* of potholes.

The best lodging in this area was the **Nata Lodge** (☎ 621 1260; www.natalodge.com; camping per person P55, d luxury tents P478, chalets from P572; ⍰), which burnt down in 2008. Owners say a new and better hotel is literally rising from the ashes, and the renovated Nata Lodge should be open by the time you read this. Like its predecessor, it will consist of a good mix of luxury chalets and cheap campsites, all set amidst a verdant oasis of monkey thorn, marula and *mokolane* palms. The attempts at incorporating San and desert artwork into the general vibe of the place are admirable and seem very effective.

Hourly combis (minibuses) travelling between Kasane (P50, five hours) and Francistown (P20, two hours), and Maun (P40, five hours) and Francistown (P15, two hours), pass by the North Gate Restaurant.

SOWA PAN

Sowa (also spelt Sua) Pan is mostly a single sheet of salt-encrusted mud stretching across the lowest basin in northeastern Botswana. Sowa means 'salt' in the language of the San, who once mined the pan to sell salt to the Bakalanga. Today, it is mined by the Sua Pan Soda Ash Company, which sells sodium carbonate for industrial manufacturing.

Nata Delta

During the rainy season (November to May), huge flocks of water birds congregate at the Nata Delta, which is formed when the Nata River flows into the northern end of the Sowa Pan. When the rains are at their heaviest (December to February), the pan is covered with a thin film of water that reflects the sky and obliterates the horizon. Access is via a 4WD track from the village of Nata.

Nata Bird Sanctuary

This 230-sq-km community-run **wildlife sanctuary** (☎ 71-544342; admission P25; ⍰ 7am-7pm) was proposed in 1988 by the Nata Conservation Committee and established four years later with the help of several local and international non-governmental organisations. Local people voluntarily relocated 3500 cattle and established a network of tracks throughout the northeastern end of Sowa Pan.

Although the sanctuary protects antelopes, zebras, jackals, foxes, monkeys and squirrels, the principal draw is the large population of water birds. Over 165 species of bird have been recorded here, including pied kingfishers, carmine and blue-cheeked bee-eaters, martial and black-breasted eagles, and secretary and kori bustards. When the Nata River flows in the rainy season, the sanctuary also becomes a haven for Cape and Hottentot teals, white and pink-backed pelicans, and greater and lesser flamingos. Visitors should pick up a copy of the *Comprehensive Bird List & Introductory Guide* (P4) from reception at the entrance.

In the dry season (May to October), it's possible to drive around the sanctuary in a 2WD with high clearance, though it's best to enquire about the condition of the tracks

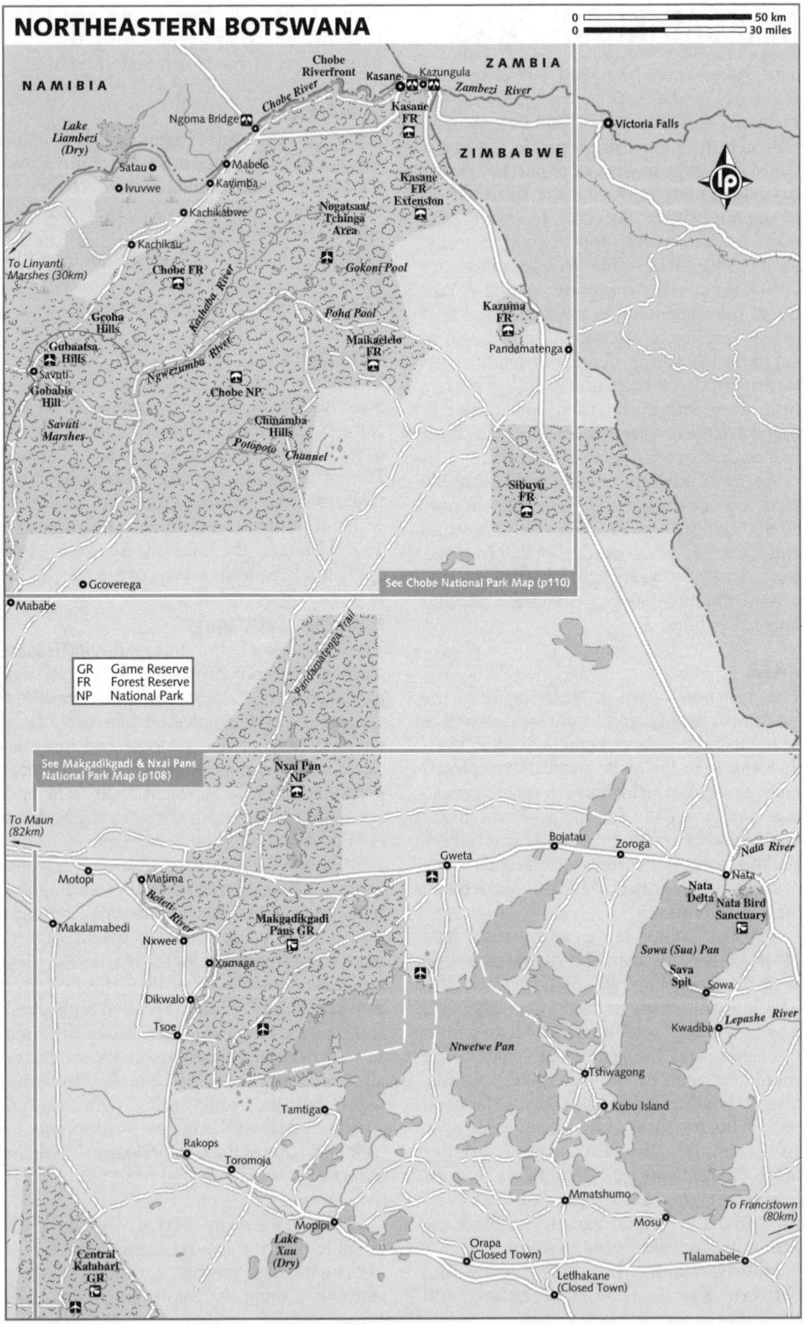
NORTHEASTERN BOTSWANA
0 50 km
0 30 miles
NAMIBIA
ZAMBIA
ZIMBABWE
Chobe Riverfront
Kasane
Kazungula
Zambezi River
Chobe River
Victoria Falls
Ngoma Bridge
Kasane FR
Lake Liambezi (Dry)
Satau
Mabele
Ivuvwe
Kavimba
Kasane FR Extension
Kachikabwe
Nogatsaa/Tchinga Area
Kachikau
To Linyanti Marshes (30km)
Chobe FR
Gokoni Pool
Kashaba River
Poha Pool
Kazuma FR
Gcoha Hills
Maikaelelo FR
Pandamatenga
Gubaatsa Hills
Savuti
Ngwezumba River
Chobe NP
Gobabis Hill
Savuti Marshes
Chinamba Hills
Potopoto Channel
Sibuyu FR
Gcoverega
See Chobe National Park Map (p110)
Mababe
Pandamatenga Trail
GR Game Reserve
FR Forest Reserve
NP National Park
See Makgadikgadi & Nxai Pans National Park Map (p108)
Nxai Pan NP
To Maun (82km)
Bojatau
Zoroga
Gweta
Nata River
Nata
Motopi
Matima
Nata Delta
Nata Bird Sanctuary
Boteti River
Makalamabedi
Makgadikgadi Pans GR
Nxwee
Sowa (Sua) Pan
Xumaga
Sava Spit
Sowa
Dikwalo
Lepashe River
Tsoe
Kwadiba
Ntwetwe Pan
Tshwagong
Kubu Island
Tamtiga
Rakops
Toromoja
Mmatshumo
To Francistown (80km)
Mosu
Mopipi
Lake Xau (Dry)
Orapa (Closed Town)
Tlalamabele
Central Kalahari GR
Letlhakane (Closed Town)

in the sanctuary before entering. During the rainy season, however, a 4WD is essential.

Nata Bird Sanctuary offers several serene and isolated campsites with clean pit toilets, braai (barbecue) pits and cold showers. Camping here costs P30 per person, and all sites are accessible by 2WD if it hasn't been raining heavily. From the campsites, it's possible to access the pan on foot (7km), though you should bring a compass with you, even if you're only walking a few hundred metres into the pan.

The entrance to the sanctuary is 15km southeast of Nata.

Sowa Spit

This long, slender protrusion extends into the heart of the pan and is the nexus of Botswana's lucrative soda-ash industry. Although security measures prevent public access to the plant, private vehicles can proceed as far as Sowa village on the pan's edge. Views of the pan from the village are limited, though they're ideal if you're travelling through the area in a 4WD.

Kubu Island

An island without an ocean: here, along the southwestern edge of Sowa Pan, is a ghostly, baobab-laden rock, entirely surrounded by a sea of salt. In Tswana, *kubu* means 'hippopotamus' (because there used to be lots here) and, as unlikely as it may seem given the current environment and climate, this desolate area may have been inhabited by people as recently as 500 years ago. On one shore lies an ancient crescent-shaped stone wall of unknown origin, which has yielded numerous artefacts, testament to those who lived here before the waters dried up (some think it served as a space in male initiation ceremonies). The **island** (www.kubuisland.com; per person/vehicle P30/40) is now protected as a national monument, administered by the local Gaing-O-Community Trust. There is a small **campsite** (☎ 297 9612; per person P40) with pit toilets, though you will have to carry in your own water.

Access to Kubu Island (GPS coordinates: S 20°53.740', E 25°49.426') involves negotiating a maze of grassy islets and salty bays. Increased traffic has now made the route considerably clearer, but drivers still need a 4WD and a compass or GPS equipment. Note that Kubu island can actually become a real island if the waters come in strong from the delta or via the rains.

From the Nata–Maun highway, the track starts near Zoroga (GPS: S 20°10.029', E 25°56.898'), about 24km west of Nata. After about 72km, the village of Thabatshukudu (GPS: S 20°42.613', E 25°47.482') will appear on a low ridge. This track then skirts the western edge of a salt pan for 10.3km before passing through a veterinary checkpoint. Just under 2km further south, a track (17km) heads southeast to the northern end of Kubu.

From the Francistown–Rakops Rd, turn north at the junction for Letlhakane and proceed 25km until you reach Mmatshumo village. About 21km further north is a veterinary checkpoint. After another 7.5km, an 18km track heads northeast to the southern end of Kubu. This turn-off (GPS: S 20°56.012', E 25°40.032') is marked by a small cairn.

GWETA

Gweta is an obligatory fuel stop if you're heading to either Kasane or Maun, a dusty crossroads on the edge of the pans framed by bushveld and big skies. The name of the village is derived from the croaking sound made by large bullfrogs, which, incredibly, bury themselves in the sand until the rains provide sufficient water for them to emerge and mate.

There are two good hotels here. In the centre of town, **Gweta Lodge** (☎ 621 2220; www.gwetalodge.com; camping per person P40, luxury tents P350, rondavels P350, r s/d from P650/800; 🖳 🖳) is a supremely friendly place that manages to combine Southern African colonial outpost (note the lithographs in the kitchen) with funky, end-of-the-world party place (note the Prince playing at the bar come evening) and make it work. Management is friendly and there's a good variety of rooms: cheap campsites if you need them, and posher digs scattered around the main grounds. In addition to the standard tours of the pans, the lodge offers activities like quadbiking, land yachting, power-kiting (all around P850) and paintballing (P350).

About 4km east of Gweta, you'll see a huge concrete aardvark (no, you're not hallucinating) that marks the turn-off for **Planet Baobab** (☎ 72-83 8334; www.unchartedafrica.com; camping per person US$13, 2-/4-person huts from US$139/227; 🖳). This is one of the most inventive lodges in the country, and can we just say: thank God there's an African resort out there that's not full of masks and wildlife pix. Instead, you get a great open-air bar filled with vintage travel posters, metal seats covered in cow hide, beer-bottle chandeliers and the like.

Outside, rondavels and chalets are scattered over the gravel, and staff contribute to a vibe as funky as it is friendly. Campers can pitch a tent beneath the shade of a baobab tree while others can choose between Bakalanga-style 'mud huts' or San-style 'grass huts' (both much plusher than they sound). The lodge is 1km off the highway (follow signs from the aardvark). Planet Baobab also arranges overnight stays to the Kalahari Surf Camp, an isolated bush camp in the interior of Ntwetwe Pan.

Hourly combis travelling between Kasane (P35, four hours) and Francistown (P30, three hours), and Maun (P25, four hours) and Francistown (US$3, three hours) pass by the Maano Restaurant.

NTWETWE PAN

Although the Ntwetwe Pan was once fed by the Boteti River, it was left permanently dry following the construction of the Mopipi Dam, which provides water for the diamond mines in Orapa (p109). Ironically, Ntwetwe is now famous for its extraordinary lunar landscape, particularly the rocky outcrops, dunes, islets, channels and spits found along the western shore.

On the Gweta–Orapa track, 27km south of Gweta, is **Green's Baobab** (GPS: S 20°25.543', E 25°13.859'), which was inscribed by the 19th-century hunters and traders Joseph Green and Hendrik Matthys van Zyl (see the boxed text, p151) as well as other ruthless characters.

About 11km further south is the turn-off to the far more impressive **Chapman's Baobab** (GPS: S 20°29.392', E 25°14.979'), which has a circumference of 25m and was historically used as a navigation beacon. It may also have been used as an early post office by passing explorers, traders and travellers, many of whom left inscriptions on its trunk.

The enormous crescent-shaped dune known as **Gabatsadi Island** has an expansive view from the crest that has managed to attract the likes of Prince Charles. (He went there to capture the indescribably lonely scene in watercolour, but the paints ran because it was so hot!) The island lies just west of the Gweta–Orapa track, about 48km south of Gweta.

If you've got some serious cash to burn, the highly recommended **Jack's Camp** (r from US$1250) and nearby **San Camp** (r from US$980) are among the most luxurious lodges in the whole of Africa. The relatively cheaper **Camp**

Kalahari (r from US$550) is honestly almost just as swish, and more aimed at families. All properties are run by **Uncharted Africa** (☎ in South Africa 27-11 447 1605; www.unchartedafrica.com), the same company that manages Planet Baobab (p105). Accommodation at the camps is in classic 1940s East African–style canvas tents furnished with regal linens and romantically lit by paraffin lanterns. Buckets of hot water are delivered on request, though flush toilets are a welcome modern concession. The central 'mess tent' operates as a field museum where local guides and world-renowned experts deliver lectures and lead discussions on the area's flora and fauna. There's also a dining tent, a drinks tent and a separate tea tent where you can indulge in high tea while relaxing on Oriental rugs and cushions. Safari expeditions put you in touch with local meerkats, rare brown hyenas and San culture. Rates include full board, wildlife drives, bush walks and a range of activities. Air fares cost P2149 per person one way from Maun.

MAKGADIKGADI & NXAI PANS NATIONAL PARK

West of Gweta, the main road between Nata and Maun slices through Makgadikgadi Pans Game Reserve and Nxai Pan National Park, which protect large tracts of salt pans, palm forests, grasslands and savannah. Since both parks complement one another in enabling wildlife migrations, Makgadikgadi Pans Game Reserve and Nxai Pan National Park were established concurrently in the early 1970s and combined into a single park in the mid-1990s.

Makgadikgadi & Nxai Pans National Park is administered by the Department of Wildlife & National Parks (DWNP), so camping is only allowed at designated campsites, which must be booked in advance at the DWNP office in Gaborone (p81) or Maun (p121). You will not be permitted into either park without a campsite reservation, unless you're on an organised tour.

Refer to the National Parks chapter, p26, for information about the opening times of the national parks as well as admission and camping costs.

Makgadikgadi Pans Game Reserve

This 3900-sq-km park extends from the Boteti River in the west to the Ntwetwe

Pan in the east. Although the Boteti River only flows after good rains, wildlife congregates along the river during the dry season when the flow is reduced to a series of shallow pools, as these are the only source of permanent water in the reserve. During years of average to low rainfall, the Boteti experiences one of Southern Africa's most spectacular wildebeest and zebra migrations between May and October.

The DWNP runs two campsites in the reserve. The Khumaga campsite (GPS: S 20°27.350', E 24°46.136') is well developed, with sit-down flush toilets, (cold) showers and running (non-drinkable) water. The Njuca Hills campsite (GPS: S 20°25.807', E 24°52.395') is less developed, with pit toilets and no running water, but the surrounding hills boast staggering views of migrating wildlife.

Leroo-La-Tau (☎ 686 0300; www.africansecrets. net/llt_home.html; s/d US$200/275; ☒) is a recommended safari lodge made up of several East African–style canvas tents with private verandahs that overlook the Boteti riverbed. Wildlife viewing in the surrounding reserve is awesome, and readers consistently rave about the spotless rooms, wonderful facilities and professional service. Rates include full board, wildlife drives, bush walks and a range of activities. Transfers from Maun cost US$100 per vehicle (with six passengers).

Basic supplies are available at the Khumaga (Xhumaga) village shop.

The main entrance to the game reserve is 141km west of Nata and 164km east of Maun. Another gate is in Khumaga to the west. A 4WD is needed to drive around the park, though the campsites and lodge are accessible by 2WD.

EXPLORING THE MAKGADIKGADI PANS

The Makgadikgadi Pans are accessed by three tracks that connect the Nata–Maun highway with the Francistown–Rakops road: along the east of Sowa Pan from Nata, along the west of Ntwetwe Pan from Gweta and down the strip between both pans (ie the access route for Kubu Island) from near Zoroga. You will also need a proper map (eg the *Shell Tourist Map of Botswana*), a compass (or preferably a GPS unit), lots of common sense and genuine confidence and experience in driving a 4WD. You must also be totally self-sufficient in food, fuel, water and spare parts, and ideally be part of a convoy of vehicles.

Prospective drivers should keep in mind that salt pans can have a mesmerising effect, and even create a sense of unfettered freedom. Once you drive out onto the salt, remember that direction, connection, reason and common sense appear to dissolve. Although you may be tempted to speed off with wild abandon into the white and empty distance, exercise caution and restrain yourself. You should be aware of where you are at all times by using a map and compass (GPS units are not foolproof).

As a general rule, always follow the tracks of other drivers – these tracks are a good indication that the route is dry. In addition, never venture out onto the pans unless you're absolutely sure the salty surface and the clay beneath are dry. Foul-smelling salt means a wet and potentially dangerous pan, which is very similar in appearance and texture to wet concrete. When underlying clay becomes saturated, vehicles can break through the crust and become irretrievably bogged. If you do get bogged and have a winch, anchor the spare wheel or the jack – anything to which the winch may be attached – by digging a hole and planting if firmly in the clay. Hopefully, you'll be able to anchor it better than the pan has anchored the vehicle.

It is important to stress that to explore the pans properly and independently requires more of a 4WD expedition than a casual drive. Lost travellers are frequently rescued from the pans, and there have been a number of fatalities over the years. And remember: *never* underestimate the effect that the pans can have on your sense of direction.

It's often safer, and sometimes cheaper in the long run, to explore the pans on an organised tour with a knowledgeable guide. The pans can be visited on day or overnight trips offered by the lodges listed in this region, or on an overnight trip from lodges in Maun (p120). Prices vary according to the length of the trip, the distance covered and the amount of activities you do. Shop around, compare prices and choose a trip that suits your needs. Whether you explore the pans by 4WD or quad bike or on foot, one thing is certain – you're in for an adventure.

NORTHEASTERN BOTSWANA

MAKGADIKGADI & NXAI PANS NATIONAL PARK

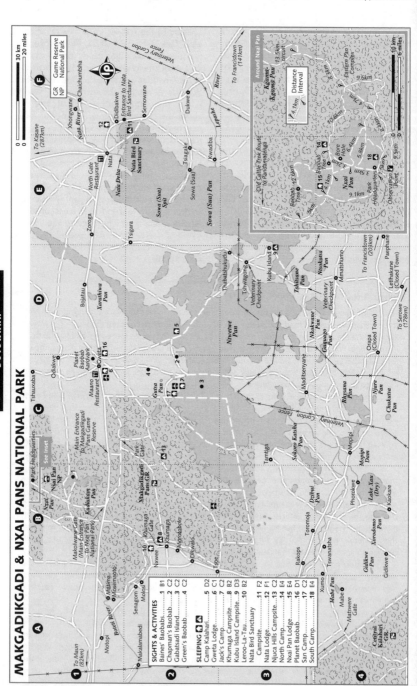

SIGHTS & ACTIVITIES

Baines' Baobabs	1 B1
Chapman's Baobab	2 C2
Gabatsadi Island	3 C2
Green's Baobab	4 C2

SLEEPING

Camp Kalahari	5 D2
Gweta Lodge	6 C1
Jack's Camp	7 C2
Khumaga Campsite	8 B2
Kubu Island Campsite	9 D3
Leroo-La-Tau	10 B2
Nata Bird Sanctuary Campsite	11 F2
Nata Lodge	12 F1
Njuca Hills Campsite	13 C2
North Camp	14 E4
Nxai Pan Lodge	15 E4
Planet Baobab	16 D1
San Camp	17 C2
South Camp	18 E4

Scale: 0 — 30 km / 0 — 20 miles

GR — Game Reserve
NP — National Park

Around Nxai Pan (inset)

Scale: 0 — 10 km / 0 — 6 miles

Distance Interval 9.1km

Nxai Pan National Park

This 2578-sq-km park lies on the old **Pandamatenga Trail**, which once connected a series of bore holes and was used until the 1960s for overland cattle drives. The grassy expanse of the park is interesting during the rains, when large animal herds migrate from the south and predators arrive to take advantage of the bounty, but it's also impressive when the land is dry and dust clouds migrate over the scrub. The region is specked with umbrella acacias, and resembles the Serengeti in Tanzania (without all the safari vehicles).

In the south of the park are the famous **Baines' Baobabs** (GPS: S 20°06.726', E 24°46.136'), which were immortalised in paintings by the artist and adventurer Thomas Baines in 1862. Baines, a self-taught naturalist, artist and cartographer, had originally been a member of David Livingstone's expedition up the Zambezi (see the boxed text, p190) but was mistakenly accused of theft by Livingstone's brother and forced to leave the party. Livingstone's brother later realised his mistake (but never publicly admitted it), yet Baines remained the subject of ridicule in Britain. Today, a comparison with Baines' paintings reveals that in almost 150 years, only one branch has broken off.

The DWNP runs two campsites in the reserve. South Camp (GPS: S 19°56.159', E 24°46.598') is about 1.5km east of the park headquarters, while North Camp (GPS: S:19°52.797', E 24°47.358') is about 7km north of the park headquarters. Both have sit-down flush toilets, running (non-drinkable) water and braai pits (though firewood is scarce).

Or, if you've got cash to splash, opt for the excellent **Nxai Pan Lodge** (☎ 686 1449; www.kwando.co.bw; r per person US$360; ❄ ➘). Eight rooms done up in a chic African-modern style curve in a crescent around an open plain; inside, smooth linens and indoor and outdoor showers do a good job of pushing the whole rustic-luxury vibe. From a large, polished deck observers can watch elephants, zebras and cheetahs cross the grassland – all from the comfort of a pool, if you want to be really indulgent.

The entrance to the park is at Makolwane Gate, which is about 140km east of Maun and 60km west of Gweta. The park headquarters is another 35.5km north along a terrible sandy track. A 4WD is required to get around the national park.

ORAPA & LETLHAKANE

To visit these self-contained diamond-mining communities, apply for a permit from **Debswana** (☎ 297 0201, 361 4200), the partly government-owned mining company based in Gaborone. Although there's nothing of interest other than diamonds, a guided tour is an excellent way to get some perspective on the lucrative diamond-mining industry. Don't even think of stopping by without permission – security here is serious business and you need to apply for a pass at least two weeks in advance.

CHOBE NATIONAL PARK

Chobe National Park, which encompasses nearly 11,000 sq km, is understandably one of the country's greatest tourist attractions. After visiting the Chobe River in the 1930s, Sir Charles Rey, the Resident Commissioner of Bechuanaland, proposed that the entire region be set aside as a wildlife preserve. Although it wasn't officially protected until 1968, Chobe has the distinction of being Botswana's first national park.

Chobe is divided into four distinct areas, each characterised by a unique ecosystem. Along the northern boundary of the park is the Chobe Riverfront, which flows annually and supports the largest wildlife concentration in the park. It is also the most accessible of the regions and thus receives the greatest volume of tourists. The other three areas – Nogatsaa/Tchinga, Savuti and Linyanti – can only be reached via 4WD expedition or fly-in, though they offer more unspoilt views.

The best time to visit Chobe is during the dry season (April to October), when wildlife congregates around permanent water sources. Try to avoid visiting here from January to March, as getting around can be difficult during the rains (although this is peak season for flying into Savuti).

KASANE & AROUND

Kasane lies in a riverine woodland at the meeting point of four countries – Botswana, Zambia, Namibia and Zimbabwe – and the confluence of two major rivers – the Chobe and the Zambezi. It's also the northern gateway to Chobe National Park, and the jumping-off point for excursions to Victoria Falls. Although it's nowhere near as large or

CHOBE NATIONAL PARK

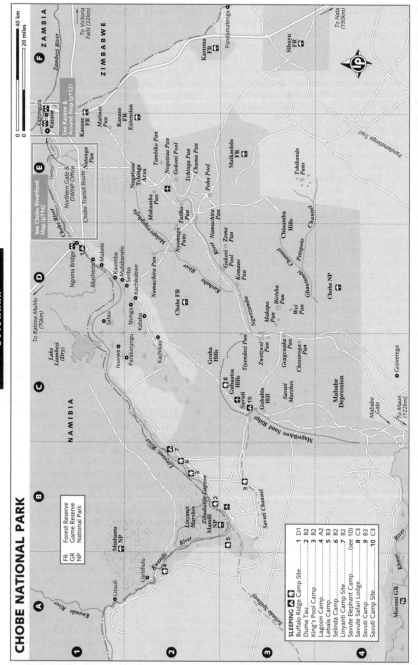

FR Forest Reserve
GR Game Reserve
NP National Park

SLEEPING 🛏
Buffalo Ridge Camp Site........1 D1
Duma Tau...............................2 B2
King's Pool Camp....................3 B2
Lagoon Camp.........................4 A2
Lebala Camp..........................5 B3
Linyanti Camp.......................6 B2
Linyanti Camp Site.................7 B2
Savute Elephant Camp....(see 10)
Savute Safari Lodge...............8 C3
Savuti Camp...........................9 B3
Savuti Camp Site.................10 C3

EXPLORING CHOBE NATIONAL PARK

Although exploring Chobe properly and independently requires more of a 4WD expedition than a casual drive, the proximity of Kasane to the national park means that it's fairly easy to visit the Chobe Riverfront by day and spend the night at any of the well-developed lodges or campsites in town. The riverfront is extremely easy to navigate, and allows independent travellers with their own 4WD vehicle to enjoy a short 'on-road' wildlife drive from Kasane. The best time to safari along the riverfront is in the late afternoon, when hippos amble onto dry land and elephants head to the banks for a cool drink and a romp in the water.

If you don't have your own wheels, any of the hotels and lodges in Kasane can help you organise a wildlife drive or boat cruise along the riverfront. Although the majority of travellers' experiences in Chobe are limited to riverfront wildlife drives and boat cruises, most people are more than satisfied with these tours. Two- to three-hour cruises and wildlife drives typically cost around P200, though you will also have to pay separate park fees. As always, shop around, compare prices and choose a trip that suits your needs.

If you're planning on independently venturing deeper into the national park, the first thing you must do is book your campsites through the DWNP in Gaborone (p81) or Maun (p121) prior to arrival in Chobe. If you're not able to contact these offices beforehand, reservations may be possible at the DWNP office at the Northern Gate to Chobe, though it's possible that all campsites may be booked by the time you get there. Unlike other parks run by the DWNP, Chobe may be entered without a DWNP campsite reservation, since most visitors visit the park on a day trip from Kasane. See the National Parks chapter, p26 for information about the opening times of the national parks as well as admission and camping costs.

In order to explore the interior of the park, you will have to be completely self-sufficient, as petrol and supplies are only available in Kasane and Maun. Water is available inside the park, though it must be boiled or treated prior to drinking. As a bare minimum, you will need a proper map (eg the *Shell Map of the Chobe National Park*), a compass (or preferably a GPS unit), lots of common sense, and genuine confidence and experience in driving a 4WD. All tracks in the national park are made of clay, sand, mud or rocks (or all four), and are frequently washed out following heavy rains. If possible, it's best to travel as part of a convoy of vehicles.

If you'd like to explore the far-flung corners of Chobe, but the prospect of driving yourself through the wilds of Botswana is a little too much to handle, the hotels and lodges in Kasane can also help you organise a multi-day overland safari through Chobe. Depending on the degree of luxury you're after, trips can cost anywhere from US$100 to US$300 per day, though prices can vary greatly according to the season. As a general rule, it's easier to get a lower price if you're booking as part of a group, so talk to a few different tour operators, always bargain hard and don't agree to a trip unless you're sure it's what you want.

developed as Maun, there's certainly no shortage of lodges competing with one another for the tourist buck.

About 12km east of Kasane is the tiny settlement of **Kazungula**, which serves as the border crossing between Botswana and Zimbabwe, and the landing for the Kazungula ferry, which connects Botswana and Zambia.

Information
EMERGENCY
Chobe Private Clinic (☎ 625 1555; President Ave) Offers 24-hour emergency services.
Kasane Hospital (☎ 625 0333; President Ave) Public hospital on the main road.

Police station (☎ 625 2444; President Ave; 24hr) Also along the main road.

INTERNET ACCESS
Kasane Computers (☎ 625 2312; per hr P30; 8am-5pm Mon-Fri, to 1pm Sat)
Kasane Internet (☎ 625 0736; Audi Centre, President Ave; per hr P30; 8am-5pm Mon-Fri, to 1pm Sat) Internet in Kasane is dead slow and unreliable.

MONEY
Barclays Bank (President Ave) Offers better exchange rates than the bureaux de change. Be sure to stock up on US dollars (post-1996) if you're heading to Zimbabwe.

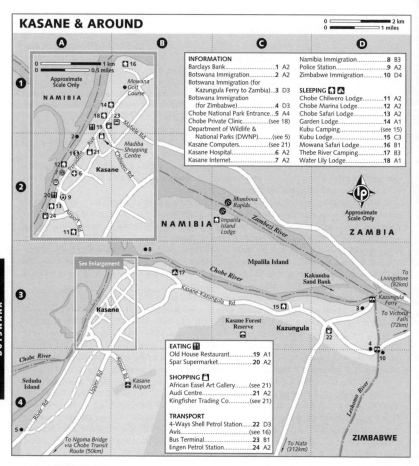

KASANE & AROUND

INFORMATION
Barclays Bank.............................1 A2
Botswana Immigration.............2 A2
Botswana Immigration (for
    Kazungula Ferry to Zambia)...3 D3
Botswana Immigration
    (for Zimbabwe)......................4 D3
Chobe National Park Entrance...5 A4
Chobe Private Clinic.............(see 18)
Department of Wildlife &
    National Parks (DWNP).......(see 5)
Kasane Computers..............(see 21)
Kasane Hospital.........................6 A2
Kasane Internet.........................7 A2

Namibia Immigration.................8 B3
Police Station..............................9 A2
Zimbabwe Immigration.........10 D4

SLEEPING
Chobe Chilwero Lodge............11 A2
Chobe Marina Lodge...............12 A2
Chobe Safari Lodge.................13 A2
Garden Lodge...........................14 A1
Kubu Camping.....................(see 15)
Kubu Lodge..............................15 C3
Mowana Safari Lodge.............16 B1
Thebe River Camping.............17 B3
Water Lily Lodge.....................18 A1

EATING
Old House Restaurant.............19 A1
Spar Supermarket....................20 A2

SHOPPING
African Easel Art Gallery........(see 21)
Audi Centre.............................21 A2
Kingfisher Trading Co............(see 21)

TRANSPORT
4-Ways Shell Petrol Station......22 D3
Avis..(see 16)
Bus Terminal...........................23 B1
Engen Petrol Station...............24 A2

TOURIST INFORMATION

Department of Wildlife & National Parks (DWNP; ☎ 625 0235; Northern Gate) This is the booking office for campsites within Chobe National Park.

Letsholo Traditional Group (☎ 74093782, 74407310) People interested in seeing traditional dance should check out this group, who occasionally practice their authentic dances along the main road.

Sleeping & Eating

Kasane primarily caters for well-to-do travellers, though there are several affordable accommodation options in town. However, if you're looking to splurge on a nice room, this is one town where indulging in a bit of luxury can make for a truly memorable occasion.

For more options along the Chobe Riverfront, see p115.

All of the hotels listed below have good attached restaurants, and there's a Spar supermarket just by Chobe Safari Lodge if you're self-catering. While closed at research time, the Old House, Kasane's only real restaurant, should be open by the time you read this.

BUDGET & MIDRANGE

Thebe River Camping (☎ 625 0314; thebe@info.bw; Kasane-Kazungula Rd; camping per person P60; ⊜) Perched alongside the Chobe River, this leafy backpackers lodge is the most budget-friendly option in Kasane. Well-groomed campsites are located near braai pits and a modern ablution block with steamy showers and flush toilets. There's also a thatched bar-restaurant that serves cheap food and cold beers – come night, if there is anything going on in Kasane, it's going on here. If you're looking to organise a budget trip to Chobe, the lodge is home to Thebe River Safaris, which specialises in multi-day overland trips through the national park.

Kubu Camping (☎ 625 0312; www.kubulodge.net; Kasane-Kazungula Rd; camping per person P60; 🖳) Adjacent to Kubu Lodge, this popular alternative to Thebe River Camping is a good option if you're looking for a more relaxed and independent scene. Although the campsite is not as attractive as Thebe, campers can take advantage of the lodge facilities, including the egg-shaped pool and open-air bar-restaurant.

Water Lily Lodge (☎ 625 1775; liyaglo@botsnet.bw; Kasane-Kazungula Rd; r P550) Although rooms at this family-run guesthouse are fairly basic, the atmosphere is warm and inviting, and the lodge is one of the more economical options in town.

Garden Lodge (☎ 625 0051; www.thegardenlodge .com; President Ave; r incl breakfast & dinner from $US180; 🖳) The simple but charming lodge is built around a tropical garden and features a number of well-furnished rooms that exude a homey atmosphere. It's a little more quirky than the average lodge in these parts, with hints of eccentricity that put it above the pack.

TOP END

All rooms have cable TV and air-con. Rates include breakfast. For more top-end options, see the Mpalila Island, Namibia, section (p282).

Chobe Safari Lodge (☎ 625 0336; www.chobesafari lodge.com; President Ave; camping US$14, r from US$134; 🖳 🖳) One of the more affordable upmarket lodges in Kasane, Chobe Safari is excellent value, especially if you're travelling with little ones. Understated but comfortable rooms are priced according to size and location, though all feature attractive mosquito-netted beds and modern furnishings.

Kubu Lodge (☎ 625 0312; www.kubulodge.net; Kasane-Kazungula Rd; s/d/tr US$290/345/300; 🖳 🖳) Located 9km east of Kasane, this riverside option lacks the stuffiness and formality found in most other top-end lodges. Rustic wooden chalets are lovingly adorned with thick rugs and wicker furniture, and scattered around an impeccably manicured lawn dotted with fig trees.

Mowana Safari Lodge (☎ 625 0300; www.cresta -hospitality.com; Kasane-Kazungula Rd; per person incl full board & activities US$500; 🖳 🖳) This flagship in the Cresta group of luxury hotels was opened by the president in 1993 and caters primarily to high-end business travellers. Botswana-inspired thatched rooms come with traditional spreads and woven wicker furniture, and have a few modern conveniences such as air-con and cable TV. There is a busy conference centre here as well as a number of bars, restaurants, pools and a spa.

Chobe Marina Lodge (☎ 625 2221; www.chobemarina lodge.com; President Ave; s/d incl all meals, activities, park fees & airport transfers US$408/544; 🖳 🖳) Occupying an attractive spot along the river, Chobe Marina Lodge is conveniently located in the centre of Kasane. The rooms, like those of the Safari Lodge, are much of a muchness in terms of their blend of African aesthetics and mod cons, but they're still pretty lovely.

Chobe Chilwero Lodge (☎ 625 1362; www.sanctuary lodges.com; Airport Rd; per person low/high season incl all meals, activities, park fees & airport transfers US$590/900; 🖳 🖳) Chilwero means 'place of high view' in Tswana, and indeed this exclusive lodge boasts panoramic views across the Chobe River. Accommodation is in one of 15 elegant bungalows featuring romantic indoor and outdoor showers, private terraced gardens and colonial fixtures adorned with plush linens. The lodge is on expansive grounds that contain a pool, a spa, an outdoor bar and a well-reviewed gourmet restaurant.

Shopping

African Easel Art Gallery (☎ 625 0828; Audi Centre, President Ave) This upmarket gallery exhibits purchasable work by artists from Botswana, Namibia, Zambia and Zimbabwe.

Kingfisher Trading Co (Audi Centre, President Ave) This simple shop sells African curios at fixed (though reasonable) prices.

Getting There & Away
AIR

Air Botswana connects Kasane to Maun (P682) and Gaborone (P1057). **Air Botswana** (☎ 625 0161) has an office at Kasane airport, which is near the centre of town.

BUS & COMBI

Combis heading to Francistown (P65, seven hours), Maun (P60, six hours), Nata (P55, five hours) and Gweta (P45, four hours) run when full from the Shell petrol station and bus terminal on Mabele Rd. Thebe River Camping, Mowana Safari Lodge and Chobe Safari Lodge also run private shuttle buses to Livingstone/ Victoria Falls (US$45, two hours). All these operations usually pick up booked passengers at their hotels around 10am.

CAR & MOTORCYCLE

The direct route between Kasane and Maun is only accessible by 4WD in the dry season, and sometimes impossible by anything but huge, state-of-the-art 4WDs during heavy rains. Also remember that there is nowhere along the Kasane–Maun road to buy fuel, food or drinks, or to get vehicle repairs. For more information, see the boxed text, p111.

All other traffic between Kasane and Maun travels via Nata, but this road is also, unfortunately, a nightmare. While a 2WD can make it, be prepared for a stunningly awful series of potholes and the like on your way up.

HITCHING

Hitching through Chobe National Park is difficult and potentially dangerous, since drivers worrying about their fuel reserves are particularly concerned about taking on additional weight (not to mention having an extra mouth to feed). In any case, all passengers have to pay entrance fees to Chobe, so it's cheaper – and eventually quicker – to go the long way round via Nata.

To go to Nata and Francistown, wait at the intersection of the Kasane-Kazungula and Kazungula–Nata roads and ask around the 4-Ways Shell petrol station nearby. To Ngoma Bridge (for Namibia), ask around the Engen petrol station near the Chobe Safari Lodge.

MOBILE SAFARIS

Other than careering through Chobe National Park in a private or rented 4WD, the only way to travel overland directly between Maun and Kasane is on a 4WD 'mobile safari'. This is a glorious way to travel through Botswana's two major attractions, but safaris are expensive and can be tough going in the middle of the wet season (January to March). For more information, contact one of the tour operators in Maun (see p123).

Getting Around

Combis travel regularly between Kasane and Kazungula, and continue to the immigration posts for Zambia and Zimbabwe if requested. The standard fare for anywhere around Kasane and Kazungula is about P20.

If you're looking to rent a car for the day, **Avis** (☎ 625 0144) has an office in the Mowana Safari Lodge.

CHOBE RIVERFRONT

The Chobe Riverfront rarely disappoints. Whether you cruise along the river in a motorboat, or drive along the banks in a 4WD, you're almost guaranteed an up-close encounter with some of the largest elephant herds on the continent. The elephant population

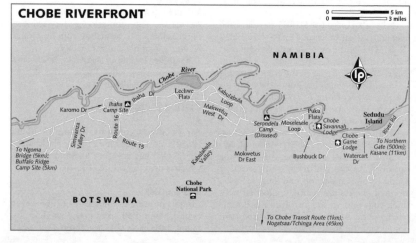

CHOBE RIVERFRONT

DIANE MOSWEU

How did you become a game guide? I started in 2005, after moving here from my home place in Shakewe. We grew up in areas with a high concentration of wildlife. I used to herd cattle in the bush before I went to school. When I left that place I didn't intend to work as a guide – I worked at the airport for three years. The people who employed me encouraged me to do this as a career.

So for you the learning part was driving. I found it very difficult. But I knew spotting wildlife from my childhood.

How do you like the work? I am enjoying the work. I like meeting people from different places and telling them more about our life in Africa, especially people who are from outside Africa.

Is it funny to see us foreigners shocked at animals? It's not a surprise because I know that where you come from is more urban. I don't like staying in urban areas. I came to Kasane because it is quieter than Maun.

Is enough of Botswana protected? Should land be opened for development? I think it is very important throughout the world to conserve these resources for future generations. They have been threatened all along, until we realised they were nearly wiped out. Some of the people I guide are very educated, and they can sensitise other people in their home places. Local people support the parks. I knew these were here from school; we learn in school it's very important to protect these lands. And even now we are teaching our parents about the financial benefits of these natural resources.

How would you improve the park system? A lot of government guys are rotated out quickly. It would be better if they were here for a long time, so they know where the wildlife is and where the poachers are.

Diane Mosweu is game guide in Kasane.

at Chobe numbers in the thousands and, although they're fairly used to being gawked at by camera-wielding tourists, being surrounded by a large herd is an awesome (and somewhat terrifying) experience.

With the exception of rhinos, the riverfront is home to virtually every mammal found in Southern Africa. The river brims with hippopotamuses, and cheetahs and lions are frequently sighted along the banks. During the dry season (April to October), herds of antelopes, giraffes, zebras, buffaloes and wildebeests congregate along the river, providing plenty of nourishment for the local crocodiles. The marshy river flood plain is also inhabited by Chobe's two trademark antelopes, namely the water-loving red lechwe and the increasingly rare puku. The latter has a face like a waterbuck but can be distinguished by its notched, inward-curving horns and its small, stocky build.

The birdlife along the riverfront is extraordinarily varied. Over 440 species of bird have been recorded here, including flashy lilac-breasted rollers, white-fronted bee-eaters, kori bustards, korhaans, secretary birds and maribou storks. Along the river, listen for the

screaming fish eagles overhead as they make precision dives for fish.

Although animals are present along the riverfront year-round, the density of wildlife can be overwhelming during the dry season. Between the months of September and October, wildlife viewing at the Chobe Riverfront is some of the best in Africa.

Sleeping

Ihaha campsite is the closest DWNP campsite (see p106) to Kasane, located along the riverfront about 27km from the Northern Gate. This well-developed campsite has sit-down flush toilets, (cold) showers and a braai area. Unfortunately, it has become a target for thieves from across the river, so campers must remain vigilant.

Buffalo Ridge Camp Site (Map p110; ☎ 625 0430; camping per person US$5.50) This basic camping area is immediately uphill from the Ngoma Bridge border crossing near the western end of the Chobe transit route. Unlike Ihaha, Buffalo Ridge is privately owned, so you do not need a reservation with the DWNP to camp here.

Chobe Game Lodge (☎ 625 0340/1761; www.chobe gamelodge.com; River Rd; per person low/high season

US$500/720; 🐾) This highly praised safari lodge is one of Botswana's pinnacles of luxury. The lodge itself is constructed in the Moorish style and flaunts high arches, barrel-vaulted ceilings and tiled floors. The individually decorated rooms are elegant yet soothing, and some have views of the Chobe River and Namibian flood plains. Service is attentive and professional, and there's a good chance you'll spot herds of elephants along the riverfront as you walk around the hotel grounds. The lodge is located about 9km west of the Northern Gate.

Getting There & Away

From central Kasane, the Northern Gate is about 6km to the southwest. Unlike all other national parks operated by the DWNP, you do not need a campsite reservation to enter, though you will be expected to leave the park prior to closing if you do not have one. All tracks along the riverfront require a 4WD vehicle, and you will not be admitted into the park without one.

You can either exit the park via the Northern Gate by backtracking along the river or via the Ngoma Bridge Gate near the Namibian border. If you exit via Ngoma, you can return to Kasane via the Chobe transit route. (If you're simply bypassing Chobe en route to/from Namibia, you do not have to pay park fees to travel on this road.) Be advised that elephants frequently cross this road, so keep your speed down and do not drive at night.

NOGATSAA/TCHINGA AREA

The Nogatsaa/Tchinga area may lack the overwhelming numbers of animals found along the riverfront or in Savuti, but it still supports herds of buffaloes and elephants as well reedbucks, gemsboks, roans and the rare oribi antelopes. Although Nogatsaa/Tchinga lacks a permanent source of water, the pans (sometimes called 'dams') present in the area store water for months after the rains have stopped.

Although there used to be two public campsites in the area, they are currently closed to private visitors.

The clay around this region is popularly known as 'black cotton', and it often defeats even the most rugged of 4WD vehicles. If you're planning on exploring the area in detail, it's best to first seek local advice, especially during the rainy season.

SAVUTI

Savuti's flat, wildlife-packed expanses are awash with distinctly African colours and vistas. The area contains the remnants of the 'superlake' that once stretched across northern Botswana, although the modern landscape has a distinctive harsh and empty feel to it. Because of the roughness of the terrain and the difficulty in reaching the area, Savuti is an obligatory stop for all 4WD enthusiasts en route between Kasane and Maun. It is also the domain of the rich and powerful – Savuti has the dubious distinction of being one of the most elite tourist destinations in Botswana.

Savuti has no perennial water sources, so animals lured into the area during wetter years face subsequent drought conditions. Those capable of escaping to the Chobe, Linyanti and Okavango River systems do so, but others, weakened, crowd into dwindling water holes, where they are picked off by opportunistic predators.

The density of wildlife, especially during the rainy season (November to May), is mind-boggling. Savuti is overrun with lions and elephants, and there are numerous documented instances of the former killing the latter. The area is also home to vast herds of buffaloes, zebras, impalas, wildebeests and antelopes, which are frequently preyed upon by cheetahs, wild dogs and hyenas.

The most famous sight in the area is **Gobabis Hill**, which features several sets of 4000-year-old rock paintings of San origin. Some lie near the base at the northern end of the hill, though the best are halfway to the summit and face east. Visitors can park their 4WDs nearby and walk to the paintings.

Sleeping
CAMPING

Savuti Camp Site (see p27 for prices) has sit-down flush toilets, braai pits, (hot!) showers and plenty of shade. Baboons are a real nuisance, though, and unwary campers have been cleaned out the second their backs have been turned. Also remember that the old Savuti Camp Site nearby was destroyed by thirsty elephants!

LODGES

The two lodges listed here must be booked in advance; all rates include meals, drinks, excursions and park fees.

THE SAVUTI CHANNEL

Northern Botswana contains a bounty of odd hydrographic phenomena. For instance, the Selinda Spillway passes water back and forth between the Okavango Delta and Linyanti Marshes. Just as odd, when the Zambezi River is particularly high, the Chobe River goes ahead and reverses the direction of its flow, causing it to spill into the area around Lake Liambezi. Historically, there was also a channel between the Khwai River system in the Okavango Delta and the Savuti Marshes.

But the strangest phenomenon of all is probably the Savuti Channel, which links the Savuti Marshes with the Linyanti Marshes and – via the Selinda Spillway – the Okavango Delta. Most confounding is the seeming complete lack of rhyme or reason to the flow of the channel. At times, it will stop flowing for years at a stretch (eg, from 1888 to 1957, 1966 to 1967, and 1979 through to the mid-1990s). When flowing, the channel creates an oasis that provides water for thirsty wildlife herds and acts as a magnet for a profusion of water birds. Between flows, the end of the channel recedes from the marshes back towards the Chobe River, while at other times the Savuti Marshes flood and expand. What's more, the flow of the channel appears to be unrelated to the water level of the Linyanti-Chobe River system itself. In 1925, when the river experienced record flooding levels, the Savuti Channel remained dry.

According to the only feasible explanation thus far put forward, the phenomenon may be attributed to tectonics. The ongoing northward shift of the Zambezi River and the frequent low-intensity earthquakes in the region reveal that the underlying geology is tectonically unstable. The flow of the Savuti Channel must be governed by an imperceptible flexing of the surface crust. The minimum change required to open or close the channel would be at least 9m, and there's evidence that this has happened at least five times in the past 100 years.

Savute Safari Lodge (per person low/high season US$476/686) Next to the former site of the legendary Lloyd's Camp, this relatively new upmarket retreat consists of 12 contemporary thatched chalets that are simple yet functional in design. The main safari lodge is home to a sitting lounge, an elegant dining room, a small library and a cocktail bar. There is also a breathtaking viewing deck where you can watch the sunset over the bush. For booking information, contact Desert & Delta Safaris (☎ 686 1243; www.desertdelta.com; Maun).

Savute Elephant Camp (per person low/high season US$615/1205; ❄) The premier camp in Savuti is made up of 12 lavishly appointed East African–style linen tents complete with antique-replica furniture. The main tent houses a dining room, lounge and bar, and is next to a swimming pool that overlooks a pumped water hole. For booking information, contact Orient-Express Safaris (☎ 686 0302; www.orient-express.com; Maun).

Getting There & Away

Chartered flights use the airstrip several kilometres north of the lodges in Savuti. Return air fares from Maun cost between P1023 and P1364 per person (slightly less from Kasane).

Under optimum conditions, it's a four-hour slog from Sedudu Gate to Savuti, though be

advised that this route is often unnavigable from January to March. Access is also possible from Maun or the Moremi Game Reserve (p132) via Mababe Gate, though the track is primarily clay and very tough going when wet. All of these routes require a state-of-the-art 4WD vehicle and some serious off-road experience. For more information on driving in Chobe, see the boxed text, p111.

LINYANTI MARSHES

In the northwest corner of Chobe National Park, the Linyanti River spreads into a 900-sq-km flooded plain that attracts stunning concentrations of wildlife during the dry season. On the Namibian side of the river, this well-watered wildlife paradise is protected by the Mudumu (p282) and Mamili National Parks (p283), but apart from 7km of frontage along the northwestern edge of Chobe National Park, the Linyanti Marshes are protected only by their remoteness.

The marshes are home to stable populations of elephants, lions, wild dogs, cheetahs and leopards – this is some of the best predator viewing in Southern Africa. But one of Linyanti's main attractions is its isolation. Since the marshes are technically not part of Chobe National Park, the lodges are not governed by the DWNP regulations, which means that night drives and wildlife walks (with armed guards) are permitted.

Sleeping
CAMPING

Linyanti Camp Site is a DWNP-operated campsite (see p27 for prices) with braai pits, hot showers, sit-down flush toilets and, in the dry season, lots of elephants – be careful.

LODGES

The first four camps listed below are run by **Wilderness Safaris** (☎ in South Africa 27-11 807 1800; www.wilderness-safaris.com) and, with the exception of King's Pool, feature luxury tents with en suite bathrooms and hot-water showers.

Lagoon Camp and Lebala are operated by **Kwando Safaris** (☎ 686 1449 www.kwando.co.bw).

All the camps must be booked in advance, and all rates include meals, drinks, excursions and airport transfers.

Selinda Camp (low/high season US$430/600) This East African vintage-style nine-person camp is the simplest and most affordable of the four camps, though it is still luxurious without any stretch of the imagination.

Savuti Camp (low/high season US$550/700) Slightly more exclusive than Selinda, this six-person camp is located next to a perennial waterhole in the Savuti Channel that attracts large concentrations of elephants and lions during the dry season.

Duma Tau (low/high season US$620/850) Slightly larger than Savuti, this 10-person camp overlooks the hippo-filled Zibadianja Lagoon from a mangosteen grove. The lagoon can be explored by boat when the water levels are high, or you can kick back in a luxury tent under thatch.

Lebala (low/high season US$670/965) The name means 'open plains', which is what you get in terms of a view, along with dense game concentrations, a serious commitment to multiple game drives and excellent bush walks. The grasslands eventually give way to the marshlands of Linyanti, which conceal heavy birdlife.

Lagoon Camp (Map p110; low/high season US$620/875) Overlooking a (guess) lagoon is this series of luxury tents, which looks out over flood plains and river tracks thick with wild dogs, lions and buffalos. Fishing trips and evening boat cruises are available.

King's Pool Camp (low/high season US$750/1075) Occupying a magical setting on a Linyanti River oxbow overlooking a lagoon, this 10-person camp is the most luxurious of the four properties. Accommodation at King's Pool is in private thatched chalets featuring indoor and outdoor showers. This place almost prides itself on being noisy – you will almost certainly be woken up by the nearby hippos, elephants, baboons and lions.

Getting There & Away

The only proper track to Linyanti Marshes starts in Savuti, but it's extremely sandy and difficult to negotiate year-round. Most guests choose to fly into their camp on a chartered flight from Maun or Kasane. Return airfares from Maun cost between P1023 and P1364 per person; fares are slightly less from Kasane.

NORTHEASTERN
BOTSWANA

Okavango Delta

The chorus of the African bush has some distinctive, as it were, earmarks: saw-throated leopard barks and the crazy whoop of a running hyena. It's a soundtrack sourced from ruggedness and, as such, we don't often think of how beautiful the gentle music is, like a *mokoro* (dugout canoe) slipping over papyrus, silk on soft.

By the same token, we often expect the Botswanan wilderness to be dry, harsh, all hills and bush and soul-spanning sky. So we can forget the subtle, less dramatic if equally arresting beauty of wind tousling reed beds and the casual incongruity of tufts of palm growing out of a flat carpet of marsh and slow streams.

The Okavango Delta, the 16,000-sq-km expansion and expiration of the Okavango River, Africa's third longest, is this continent's realisation of a different kind of scenery: the bright tinkle of water versus the thorny forest and the slow drift of flood tides versus the Kalahari sun. Indeed, the contrast the Okavango presents compared to the rest of Botswana is one of her most jarring, memorable aspects: here, in the heart of the thirst lands, is the world's largest inland river delta, an unceasing web of water, rushing, standing, flooding, dying.

And the waters do die. The never make it to the sea, soaking instead into the salt pans of central Botswana. But before they do, they sustain vast quantities of wildlife and a similarly large tourism industry. A chaotic mix of campers, bush pilots, wildlife guides and luxury-safari types are drawn to this mother of waters. Join the pack, if not the package tour, and prepare for a wholly new Africa.

OKAVANGO DELTA

HIGHLIGHTS

- Gliding through the watery mazes of the delta in a traditional **mokoro** (see the boxed text, p124)
- Going on safari in one of Africa's most pristine and exclusive wildernesses in the **Moremi Game Reserve** (p132)
- Splurging on a **luxury lodge** (see the boxed text, p131) in the delta, even if you've been shoestringing for months on end
- Chartering a plane or helicopter and taking a **scenic flight** (p125) from Maun over the full expanse of the delta
- Travelling overland from **Maun** (p120) on a mobile safari through Chobe National Park to Kasane

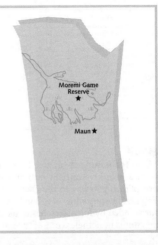

Moremi Game Reserve ★

Maun ★

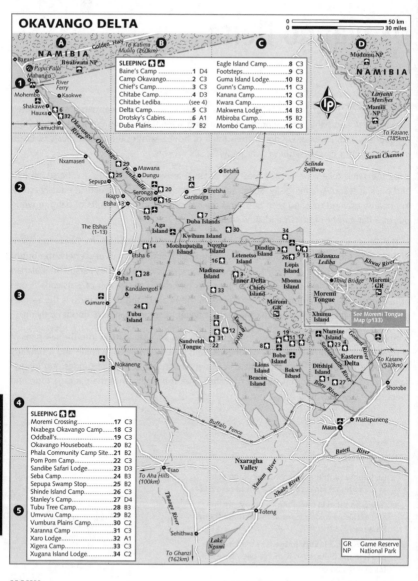

OKAVANGO DELTA

SLEEPING
Baine's Camp...................1 D4
Camp Okavango.............2 C3
Chief's Camp..................3 C3
Chitabe Camp................4 D3
Chitabe Lediba..........(see 4)
Delta Camp...................5 C3
Drotsky's Cabins...........6 A1
Duba Plains..................7 B2
Eagle Island Camp.........8 C3
Footsteps.....................9 C3
Guma Island Lodge......10 B2
Gunn's Camp...............11 C3
Kanana Camp...............12 C3
Kwara Camp................13 C3
Makwena Lodge...........14 B3
Mbiroba Camp.............15 B2
Mombo Camp..............16 C3

SLEEPING
Moremi Crossing..................17 C3
Nxabega Okavango Camp......18 C3
Oddball's............................19 C3
Okavango Houseboats.........20 B2
Phala Community Camp Site..21 B2
Pom Pom Camp..................22 C3
Sandibe Safari Lodge...........23 D3
Seba Camp.........................24 B3
Sepupa Swamp Stop............25 B2
Shinde Island Camp.............26 C3
Stanley's Camp....................27 D4
Tubu Tree Camp..................28 B3
Umvuvu Camp....................29 B2
Vumbura Plains Camp...........30 C3
Xaranna Camp.....................31 C3
Xaro Lodge........................32 A1
Xigera Camp.......................33 C3
Xugana Island Lodge............34 C2

GR Game Reserve
NP National Park

MAUN

Maun (pronounced 'mau-UUnn') is Botswana's primary tourism hub and the self-proclaimed gateway to the Okavango Delta. Essentially consisting of a few intersections surrounded by long stretches of block housing, this is nonetheless one of the more interesting towns in Botswana, attracting a reliably mad crew of bush pilots, tourists, campers, volunteers and luxury safari–philes. It's a decent enough base for a day or two, which is the amount of time most people spend here, and serves as a natural centre point between Kasane, the Makgadikgadi and the Kalahari.

Orientation

Central Maun contains most of the restaurants, shops and travel agencies, while the village of **Matlapaneng**, 8km northeast of the centre, has most of the budget lodges and campsites. In between is the village of Sedie, which has a number of hotels and tourist-oriented businesses.

Information

If you're planning on spending a few days in Maun, pick up a copy of the *Ngami Times*, which is published every Friday. If you're here in late April, make sure you check out the **Maun Festival** (www.maunfestival.com), an annual celebration of the region's music, art and dance.

BOOKSHOPS

Botswana Book Centre (☎ 686 0853; the Mall) This bookshop offers one of the best ranges of books about Botswana in the country. It also sells English-language novels and local, South African and international magazines and newspapers.

EMERGENCY

Delta Medical Centre (☎ 686 1411; Tsheke Tsheko Rd) Near the tourist office along the main road; this is the best medical facility in Maun. It offers a 24-hour emergency service.
Maun General Hospital (☎ 686 0661; Shorobe Rd) About 1km southwest of the town centre.
MedRescue (☎ 680 0598, 686 0991, 686 1831) For evacuations in the bush.
Police station (☎ 686 0223; Sir Seretse Khama Rd)

INTERNET ACCESS

Many hotels now offer internet access.
Afro-Trek I-Café (☎ 686 2574; Shorobe Rd; per hr P50) In the Sedia Hotel.
PostNet (☎ 686 5612; Maun Shopping Centre; per hr P50; ☷ 9am-6pm Mon-Fri, 9.30am-3pm Sat)

MONEY

The Mall has branches of Barclays Bank and Standard Chartered Bank, which both have foreign-exchange facilities and offer better rates than the bureaux de change. Barclays charges 2.5% commission for cash/travellers cheques, but no commission for cash advances with Visa and MasterCard. Standard Chartered charges 3% commission for cash and travellers cheques; however, it is not as well set up as Barclays.

Although you will get less favourable rates at a bureau de change, they are a convenient option if the lines at the banks are particularly long.
Sunny Bureau de Change (☎ 686 2786; Ngami Centre, Sir Seretse Khama Rd; ☷ 7am-6pm)

POST

Post office (☷ 8.15am-1pm & 2.15-4pm Mon-Fri, 8.30-11.30am Sat) Near the Mall.

TOURIST INFORMATION

Department of Wildlife & National Parks (DWNP; ☎ 686 1265; Kudu St; ☷ 7.30am-12.30pm & 1.45-4.30pm Mon-Sat, 7.30am-noon Sun) To book national parks campsites, go to the reservations office, which is housed in a caravan behind the main building.
Tourist office (☎ 686 0492; Tsheke Tsheko Rd; ☷ 7.30am-12.30pm & 1.45-4.30pm Mon-Fri) Provides information on the town's many tour companies and lodges.

Sights

NHABE MUSEUM

This **museum** (☎ 686 1346; Sir Seretse Khama Rd; admission free; ☷ 9am-4.30pm Mon-Sat) is housed in a historic building built by the British military in 1939 and used during WWII as a surveillance post keeping tabs on the German presence in Namibia. The museum offers a few displays about the history of the Ngamiland district (the sub-district of Northwestern Botswana where the delta is located) and some temporary exhibitions of photography, basket-weaving and art. Donations are welcome. The museum also houses the Bailey Arts Centre, which allows local artists to produce and sell baskets, screen prints, paintings and pottery, among other things.

CROCODILE FARM

This community-run **crocodile farm** (☎ 686 4539; admission P15; ☷ 9am-4.30pm Mon-Sat) is basically all the encouragement you need to keep your hands and feet inside the *mokoro* while cruising through the delta. The farm is about 15km south of the Maun 'Mall'. To get there, just follow the road that runs by the Barclays outside of town and you shouldn't miss it.

MAUN ENVIRONMENTAL EDUCATION CENTRE

This **centre** (☎ 686 1390; admission free; ☷ 7.30am-12.30pm & 1.45-4.40pm), located in the Maun Wildlife Reserve, is on the eastern bank of

OKAVANGO DELTA

MAUN & MATLAPANENG

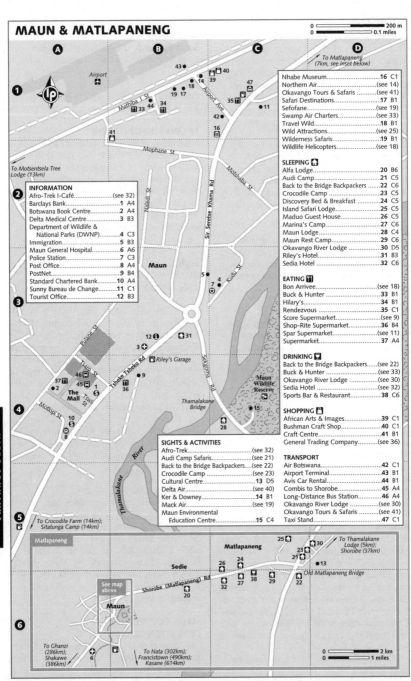

INFORMATION

Afro-Trek I-Café	(see 32)
Barclays Bank	**1** A4
Botswana Book Centre	**2** A4
Delta Medical Centre	**3** B3
Department of Wildlife & National Parks (DWNP)	**4** C3
Immigration	**5** B3
Maun General Hospital	**6** A6
Police Station	**7** C3
Post Office	**8** A4
PostNet	**9** B4
Standard Chartered Bank	**10** A4
Sunny Bureau de Change	**11** C1
Tourist Office	**12** B3

SIGHTS & ACTIVITIES

Afro-Trek	(see 32)
Audi Camp Safaris	(see 21)
Back to the Bridge Backpackers	(see 22)
Crocodile Camp	(see 23)
Cultural Centre	**13** D5
Delta Air	(see 40)
Ker & Downey	**14** B1
Mack Air	(see 19)
Maun Environmental Education Centre	**15** C4

Nhabe Museum	**16** C1
Northern Air	(see 14)
Okavango Tours & Safaris	(see 41)
Safari Destinations	**17** B1
Sefofane	(see 19)
Swamp Air Charters	(see 33)
Travel Wild	**18** B1
Wild Attractions	(see 25)
Wilderness Safaris	**19** B1
Wildlife Helicopters	(see 18)

SLEEPING

Alfa Lodge	**20** B6
Audi Camp	**21** C5
Back to the Bridge Backpackers	**22** C6
Crocodile Camp	**23** C5
Discovery Bed & Breakfast	**24** C5
Island Safari Lodge	**25** C5
Maduo Guest House	**26** C5
Marina's Camp	**27** C6
Maun Lodge	**28** C4
Maun Rest Camp	**29** C6
Okavango River Lodge	**30** D5
Riley's Hotel	**31** B3
Sedia Hotel	**32** C6

EATING

Bon Arrivee	(see 18)
Buck & Hunter	**33** B1
Hilary's	**34** B1
Rendezvous	**35** C1
Score Supermarket	(see 9)
Shop-Rite Supermarket	**36** B4
Spar Supermarket	(see 11)
Supermarket	**37** A4

DRINKING

Back to the Bridge Backpackers	(see 22)
Buck & Hunter	(see 33)
Okavango River Lodge	(see 30)
Sedia Hotel	(see 32)
Sports Bar & Restaurant	**38** C6

SHOPPING

African Arts & Images	**39** C1
Bushman Craft Shop	**40** C1
Craft Centre	**41** B1
General Trading Company	(see 36)

TRANSPORT

Air Botswana	**42** C1
Airport Terminal	**43** B1
Avis Car Rental	**44** B1
Combis to Shorobe	**45** A4
Long-Distance Bus Station	**46** A4
Okavango River Lodge	(see 30)
Okavango Tours & Safaris	(see 41)
Taxi Stand	**47** C1

OKAVANGO DELTA

the Thamalakane River, and aims to provide children with an appreciation of nature. If you're in town with kids, it may be worth bringing them here for an hour or two.

CULTURAL CENTRE

Still under construction at the time of writing, this two-storey, Moroccan-style **complex** is set to open in early 2010 across from Audi Camp (p126). Owners say they want to have a marketplace and cafe for visitors on the bottom floor, topped by studios for arts, dance and music training. The complex is generating a fair bit of buzz in town and should be worth checking out once it opens.

Tours

Maun is chock-a-block with travel agencies and safari companies, which can be absolutely headache-inducing for the uninitiated traveller. Before you fork over all your hard-earned cash to a questionable operator, pause for a moment, take a deep breath and read on – there is in fact a method to the madness.

First of all, it helps to know that most delta lodges are affiliated with specific agencies, so it pays to shop around and talk to a few different tour operators. Second, if you're planning an extended trip into the delta or intend to stay at a luxury lodge, contact one or more of the agencies or operators listed here *before* you

arrive if possible. While the cheaper lodges can usually accommodate guests at the drop of a hat, don't come to Maun and expect to jump on a plane to a safari lodge or embark on an overland safari the next day. (For more information on *mokoro* trips, see the boxed text, p124. For more information on delta lodges, see the boxed text, p131.)

From Maun, it's easy to book tours to other parts of Botswana, most notably to Chobe National Park, Tsodilo Hills and the Central Kalahari Game Reserve. These excursions are often added to the end of delta tours. Maun is also the base for overland safaris to Kasane via Chobe National Park (p128).

A good place to start is at **Travel Wild** (☎ 686 0822; www.travelwildbotswana.com; Mathiba I St), opposite the airport, which serves as a central booking and information office for lodges, safaris and other adventures. **Safari Destinations** (☎ 686 0822/3; travelwild@dynabyte.bw; Mathiba I St) serves as a good clearing house for information on booking agencies. It can't provide you with direct bookings, but it's got great contacts with all local safari providers.

The following tour operators are recommended.

African Animal Adventures (☎ 7230 1054; www.africananimaladventures.com) A very highly recommended outfit that does horse safaris into the delta and the salt pans of the northeast. Can be contacted by phone, email or

---

BONJOUR KEIPIDILE

Do you have a favourite style of music? Things like classical music I like, but jazz is my favourite to play.

Why? It's hard to explain. Guys like Bo West (Botswanan jazz guitarist), their sound is just unbelievable.

How old were you when you started playing? What got you into the guitar? I was 10 years old when I started. My family was a religious clan – we were singing every night. When I was 16, I started playing in clubs in Gabs. At the time it was mostly a band situation, and even now I prefer a nice band.

Why do you like to play? It soothes me when I'm not feeling comfortable.

People talk of an African connection to music. Do you believe in that? *[Bonjour's friend interjects]* In Africa, people used to communicate with drums. It's an inborn talent. For instance, if we were to dance, I'll go with the rhythm, and you won't. Music is something we've always done. But it's something we were born with. It's just like dogs chasing cats.

What do you like about Batswana music today? Today our music is OK. Our understanding of what people need to do in order for the music to improve needs work. Today most people think that, if you only know three chords, that's OK. And the technology around today is making playing music too simple.

Bonjour Keipidile is a Maun-based guitarist.

MOKORO TRIPS

One of the best (and also cheapest) ways to experience the Okavango Delta is to glide across the waters in a *mokoro* (plural *mekoro*), a shallow-draft dugout canoe traditionally hewn from an ebony or a sausage-tree log. With encouragement from several international conservation groups, however, the Batswana have now begun to construct more *mekoro* from fibreglass. The rationale behind this is that ebony and sausage trees take over 100 years to grow while a *mokoro* only lasts for about five years.

A *mokoro* may appear precarious at first, but it is amazingly stable and ideally suited to the shallow delta waters. It can accommodate two passengers and some limited luggage, and is propelled by a poler who stands at the back of the canoe with a *ngashi,* a long pole made from the mogonono tree.

The quality of a *mokoro* trip often depends on the passengers' enthusiasm, the meshing of personalities and the skill of the poler. Most polers (but not all) speak at least some English and can identify plants, birds and animals, and explain the cultures and myths of the delta inhabitants. Unfortunately, polers are often shy and lack confidence, so you may have to ask a lot of questions to get the information.

It's important to stress that you should not expect to see too much wildlife. From the *mokoro,* you'll certainly spot plenty of hippos and crocs (which may or may not excite you), and antelopes and elephants are frequently sighted during hikes. However, the main attraction of a *mokoro* trip is the peace and serenity you'll feel as you glide along the shallow waters of the delta. If however your main interest is viewing wildlife, consider spending a night or two in the Moremi Game Reserve (p132).

A day trip from Maun into the Eastern Delta includes a two- to three-hour return drive in a 4WD to the departure point, two to three hours in a *mokoro* (perhaps longer each day on a two- or three-day trip), and two to three hours' hiking. At the start of a *mokoro* trip, ask the poler what he has in mind, and agree to the length of time spent per day in the *mokoro,* out hiking, and relaxing at the campsite – bear in mind that travelling by *mokoro* is tiring for the poler.

In terms of pricing, catering is an important distinction. 'Self-catering' means you must bring your own food as well as cooking, sleeping and camping equipment. This option is a good way to shave a bit off the price, though most travellers prefer catered trips. It's also easier to get a lower price if you're booking as part of a group or are planning a multi-day tour. You can also save quite a bit of cash if you visit the delta during the rainy season, but be prepared to battle the elements (and the mosquitoes). Shop around, bargain hard and don't agree to a trip unless you're sure it's what you want.

Sadly, some polers do not receive a fair percentage of the rates charged by tourist agencies in Maun, and the polers just cannot compete without an office in town with a telephone and internet connection. However, several villages along the Okavango Panhandle have established community-based tourist ventures with campsites and *mokoro* trips. Their rates are lower and, importantly, profits directly benefit the communities. For more information, see the boxed text, p138.

Finally, a few other things to remember:

- ask the booking agency if you're expected to provide food for the poler (usually you're not, but polers appreciate any leftover cooked or uncooked food)
- bring good walking shoes and long trousers for hiking, a hat, and plenty of sunscreen and water
- water from the delta (despite its unpleasant colour) can be drunk if boiled or purified
- most campsites are natural, so take out all litter and burn toilet paper
- bring warm clothes for the evening between about May and September
- wildlife can be dangerous, so make sure to never swim anywhere without checking with the poler first.

through Back to the Bridge Backpackers (right) and Gweta Lodge (p105).

African Excursions (africanexcursions@botsnet.bw) Independent tour operator that does good cultural tours of Maun that include dancing, a handicrafts market and a traditional meal, all for P300.

Afro-Trek (☎ 686 2574; www.afrotrek.com; Shorobe Rd) This company specialises in midmarket safaris and is in the Sedia Hotel (p126).

Audi Camp Safaris (☎ 686 0599; www.okavangocamp.com; Shorobe Rd) Run out of the popular Audi Camp (p126).

Back to the Bridge Backpackers (☎ 686 2406; www.maun-backpackers.com; Shorobe Rd) This budget operation is run from Back to the Bridge Backpackers (right).

Crocodile Camp Safaris (☎ 686 0222; www.crocodilecamp.com; Shorobe Rd) This budget operator is at the Crocodile Camp (right).

Ker & Downey (☎ 686 0570; www.kerdowney.com; Mathiba I St) This is one of Botswana's most exclusive tour operators.

Okavango River Lodge (☎ 686 0298/3707; www.okavango-river-lodge.com; Shorobe Rd) Run out of the Okavango River Lodge (right).

Okavango Tours & Safaris (☎ 686 0220; www.okavango.bw; Mophane St) In the Power Station complex, this well-established operator specialises in upmarket lodge-based tours.

Wild Attractions (☎ 686 0300; www.africansecrets.net/wa_home.html; Mathiba I St) This excellent operation is run out of the Island Safari Lodge (p126).

Wild Lands Safaris (☎ 686 1008; www.wildlandsafaris.com) A reliable operator with a good customer-service record.

Wilderness Safaris (☎ in South Africa 27-11 807 1800; www.wilderness-safaris.com; Mathiba I St) Near the airport, this operator specialises in upmarket safaris.

SCENIC FLIGHTS

To join a scenic flight you can either contact one of the following charter companies or simply ask at the front desk about your accommodation. But plan ahead, as it's unlikely that you'll be able to contact a charter company and join a scenic flight on the same day.

The offices for all air-charter companies in Maun are either in or next to the airport. Prices vary according to the size of the plane and the number of passengers, though you can expect to pay about US$100 to US$200 per hour.

Delta Air (☎ 686 0044; synergy@info.bw; Mathiba I St) Near the Bushman Craft Shop.

Mack Air (☎ 686 0675; www.mackair.co.bw; Mathiba I St) Around the corner from Wilderness Safaris.

Moremi Air Services (☎ 686 3632; www.moremiair.com) In the airport terminal.

Northern Air (☎ 686 0385; http://kerdowney.bw/northern_air.html; Mathiba I St) Part of the Ker & Downey office.

Sefofane (☎ 686 0778; www.sefofane.com) Part of Wilderness Safaris.

Swamp Air Charters (☎ 686 0569; gunnscamp@info.bw; Mathiba I St) Near the Buck & Hunter Pub.

Wildlife Helicopters (☎ 686 0664; wildheli@info.bw; Mathiba I St) The only helicopter-ride operator in Maun.

Sleeping

All campsites, hotels and lodges listed here – except Riley's – are in either Sedie or Matlapaneng. The attraction of the latter is that the camps and lodges are quiet, secluded and pleasantly located along Thamalakane River. The downside is that they are all up to 10km from central Maun. Most are accessible by public transport, however, and each place offers transfers to/from Maun daily, usually for a small fee. Every campsite, hotel and lodge listed here also has a decent restaurant and bar.

BUDGET

Camping is also available at the Sedia Hotel.

Okavango River Lodge (☎ 686 3707/0298; www.okavango-river-lodge.com; Matlapaneng; camping per person US$3, s/d chalets US$35/40) This down-to-earth spot off Shorobe Rd has a lovely setting on the riverbank. The owners are friendly and unpretentious and pride themselves on giving travellers useful (and independent) information on trips through the delta. Between this spot and the Bridge Backpackers you'll find most of Maun's tourist and expat-oriented nightlife. On that note, we've got to give the owners credit on the excellent name of their boat: Sir Rosis of the River.

Back to the Bridge Backpackers (☎ 686 2037; hellish@info.bw; Hippo Pools, Old Matlapaneng Bridge; camping per person P30, s/d tents per person P120/90, s P80; ☐ ☑) 'The Bridge', as it's known, has a great bar-at-the-end-of-the-world kind of vibe. Bush pilots and backpackers chat each other up, dogs play with kids and a regular cast of drunks keeps the bar propped up (or is that the other way 'round?). A good range of *mokoro* trips and the like is on offer, and in general this is a place that gets the backpacker vibe down, and well. From Shorobe Rd, follow signs for the lodge as soon as you approach the Old Matlapaneng Bridge.

Crocodile Camp (☎ 686 0265; www.crocodilecamp.com; Matlapaneng; camping per person P40, tents from P140, chalets from P300; ☑) 'Croc Camp' occupies a superb spot right on the river and is a quieter place for those not needing shots of pre-safari sambuca (not that it doesn't serve sambuca). Off Shorobe Rd, the campsite has such Maun rarities as grass, though the pre-erected linen tents are a good option if you're looking for a little safari chic. There are also a number of thatched riverside chalets with en suite bathrooms.

Audi Camp (☎ 686 0599; www.okavangocamp.com; Matlapaneng; camping per person from P45, s/d tents from P240/300; ⊞ ☒) Off Shorobe Rd, Audi Camp is a fantastic campsite that's become increasingly popular with families, although independent overlanders will feel utterly welcome as well. Management is friendly and very helpful, and there's a wide range of safari activities. The restaurant does a mean steak as well. If you don't have your own tent, the pre-erected tents complete with fan are a rustically luxurious option.

Maun Rest Camp (☎ 686 2623; simonjoyce@info.bw; Shorobe Rd, Matlapaneng; camping per person from P45, tents from P300) This no-frills rest camp off Shorobe Rd is spotless and boasts what justifiably may be 'the cleanest ablution blocks in Maun'. The owners also pride themselves on turning away the overland truck and party crowd, so you can be assured of a quiet and undisturbed night's rest here.

Discovery Bed & Breakfast (☎ 680 0627; www.discoverybedandbreakfast.com; Matlapaneng; s/d from P200/300; ☒) Discovery does a cool job of creating a traditional (for tourists) African-village vibe in the midst of Maun. The thatched, rondavel-style (traditional circular houses with thatched roofs) housing looks pretty bush from the outside and feels as posh as a nice hotel on the inside. A pretty garden connects the dusty grounds, and there's a good communal fire pit for safari stories with fellow travellers.

Island Safari Lodge (☎ 686 0300; www.africansecrets.net; Matlapaneng; camping per person P40, s/d chalets P350/500) One of the original lodges in Maun, Island Safari Lodge is also still one of its best. It runs a professional, well-established series of safaris, the African-style rondavel housing is charming and comfy, and the verandah is a great spot for watching the river flow by on lazy Okavango afternoons. The campsites aren't too bad, either.

Marina's Camp (☎ 680 1231; www.marinascamp.com; Matlapaneng; s/d from P399/572; ☒) There's a bit of a bohemian vibe to this collection of African-style huts and houses, linked by stone pathways and surrounding a popular little bar. All of the rooms are clean and comfortable, and the management is friendly and very helpful for booking excursions.

MIDRANGE & TOP END
All hotels listed here – except the Alfa and the Maduo – offer rooms with cable TV, bathroom and air-con.

Sedia Hotel (☎ 686 0177; www.sedia-hotel.com; Shorobe Rd, Sedie; camping per person P20, s/d P600/675, chalets from P850; ☒ ☒) If you're in need of modern comforts, the Sedia Hotel is a good option. This resort-like hotel features an outdoor bar, a continental-inspired restaurant and a huge swimming pool. You can choose from a number of rooms and self-contained chalets, or simply pitch a tent and take advantage of all the hotel facilities.

Alfa Lodge (☎ 686 4689; Shorobe Rd, Sedie; s/d P200/337; ☒) Rumour has it that Scottish scientists have cloned the Alfa from Maduo Guest House (see below) DNA, as they are pretty much exactly alike but for their prices.

Maduo Guest House (☎ 686 0846; Shorobe Rd, Sedie; r from P398; ☒) Maduo isn't much more than a series of concrete blocks with motel-style rooms; it's clean, comfy and pretty boring. Primarily aimed at domestic tourists, it may lack character by Western standards, but this is good value for Maun, especially if you want to sit in a room with a TV and you have an aversion to camping (although, if so, really: why are you in Botswana?).

Riley's Hotel (☎ 686 0204; Tsheke Tsheko Rd; s/d P675/760, chalets from P570; ☒ ☒) Riley's is the only hotel or lodge in central Maun. It offers comfortable rooms in a convenient and quiet setting, and a remodelling of the grounds is giving the place a little more character and value for money. It's popular with Batswana business folk and government workers, but don't come here for a lodge/wilderness experience.

Maun Lodge (☎ 686 3939; www.maunlodge.com; Sekgoma Rd; r from US$99, chalets from US$86; ☒ ☒) This upmarket option is just south of the town centre and boasts all the luxuries you'd expect at this price. It's certainly a comfortable option, though it's lacking in personality and atmosphere, especially if you're coming from (or going to) any of the luxury lodges in the delta.

Thamalakane Lodge (☎ 686 4313, 7250 6184; thamalakanelodge@ngami.net; Shorobe Rd; P950; ☒ ⊞ ☒) With a beautiful setting on a sun-drenched curve of the Thamalakane River, over-looking wading hippos and waving reeds, Thamalakane wins in the location, location, location stakes. But it's also got beautiful little chalets, stuffed with modern amenities and dressed up in safari-chic tones, and a kitchen cranking out arguably the best food in Maun.

Motsentsela Tree Lodge (☎ 680 0757; treelodge@ netspread.co.bw; r from US$220; ✿ ☐ ☑) This private farm-reserve, about 13km west of the airport, is a lovely luxury option that maintains a good crew of regular visitors. These returnees are probably impressed by the resident wandering giraffe, kudu and ostrich, the large, beautifully decked out private cabins and the utter sense of calm and quiet here far away from Maun's bustle (as it were). Contact the lodge to book ahead and arrange transfers or get directions.

Eating

Besides the restaurants listed below, Maun has versions of every peri-peri obsessed fast food chain in Southern Africa and well-stocked supermarkets, including the Score Supermarket in the Maun Shopping Centre; a supermarket in both the Mokoro Shopping and Ngami Centres; and the Shop-Rite on Tsheke Tsheko Rd.

Hilary's (☎ 686 1610; meals from P40; ☉ 8am-4pm Mon-Fri, 8.30am-noon Sat) Just off Mathiba I St, this homey place offers a choice of wonderfully earthy meals, including homemade bread, baked potatoes, soups and sandwiches. It's ideal for vegetarians and anyone sick of greasy sausages and soggy chips.

Bon Arrivee (☎ 680 0330; Mathiba I St; meals P35-80) They lay on the pilot puns and flight-deck jokes very thick at this airport-themed place, which sits, of course, right across from the airport. The food is good – lots of pasta, steak and seafood – but don't come here an hour before your flight expecting a quick turnaround.

Buck & Hunter (☎ 680 1001; Mathiba I St; meals P40-80) This used to be a pretty wild pub, the northern outpost of Gaborone's own Bull & Bush. Today, thanks to stricter alcohol-consumption control, the Buck is a bit more sedate, although it's still reasonably popular with expats and locals. In any case, the beer is cold and the steak is thick, so get over here already.

Rendezvous (☎ 7287 6183; Engen Complex; dishes cafe P35-65, restaurant P50-100) Rendezvous is split into two very excellent halves. The cafe does

pretty good pizzas, sandwiches and the like, and – thank the tech gods – actually has reliable wi-fi. The attached restaurant does more upmarket, candle-lit fare, all of which is very fine for those needing a bit of white-linen civilisation.

Drinking

Every one of the lodges listed above has its own bar, but at research time the only places that really kicked off if you were in need of a party were Back to the Bridge Backpackers and Okavango River Lodge. The Sedia Hotel has a poolside English-style pub that's regularly packed with Germans, natch. Of course, there's a fair few shebeen (illegal drinking establishments) serving home-brewed sorghum beer to a local crowd; the staff at your hotel or lodge can point you in the right direction for this sort of off-licence fun. Buck & Hunter and the **Sports Bar & Restaurant** (Shorobe Rd, Sedie), near Crocodile Camp, are also good for a beer or 10.

Shopping

Craft Centre (☎ 686 3391; Mophane St) In the Power Station complex, this friendly place makes and sells pottery, paintings and handmade-paper products (from elephant dung among other things), and regularly features exhibitions of other arts and crafts.

General Trading Company (☎ 686 0025; Tsheke Tsheko Rd) This large mauve building next to the Shop-Rite supermarket sells a huge range of high-priced safari gear, books, videos, and locally produced jewellery, pottery, drums and baskets.

Bushman Craft Shop (☎ 686 0220; Mathiba I St) Although it caters more to travellers who need a last-minute souvenir before catching a flight out of town, this small shop near the airport has a decent range of books, videos and woodcarvings.

African Arts & Images (☎ 686 3584; Mathiba I St) Next to the Bushman Craft Shop on the road near the airport terminal, this upmarket shop has an impressive range of books about Botswana, photographic prints of the delta and locally made pottery.

Getting There & Away
AIR

You can fly to Gaborone (P1057) or Kasane (P682) daily with **Air Botswana** (☎ 686 0391; Airport Ave). For information about chartering a plane

---

EXPLORING THE OKAVANGO DELTA

Stretching like an open palm across north-western Botswana, the Okavango Delta is a complex and unique ecosystem as well as Botswana's premier tourist attraction. Although the size and scope of the region is often a deterrent for independent travellers, it's easier to plan a trip through the region than you might imagine, especially if you think of the delta as having four distinct areas.

- Eastern Delta – this part of the delta is far more accessible, and therefore cheaper to reach, from Maun than the Inner Delta and Moremi. You can easily base yourself in Maun, and arrange a day trip by *mokoro* or an overnight bush-camping trip for far less than the cost of staying in (and getting to) a lodge in the Inner Delta or Moremi.

- Inner Delta – the area west, north and south of Moremi is classic delta scenery where you can truly be seduced by the calming spell of the region. Accommodation is in top-end luxury lodges, almost all of which are only accessible by expensive chartered flights.

- Moremi Game Reserve – this region includes Chiefs Island and the Moremi Tongue, and is one of the most popular destinations within the delta. The Moremi Game Reserve is the only protected area within the delta, so wildlife is plentiful, but you will have to pay daily park entry fees. Moremi has a few campsites run by the DWNP as well as several truly decadent lodges with jaw-dropping prices. Refer to the National Parks chapter, p26, for information about the opening times of the national parks as well as the costs of admission and camping. The Moremi Game Reserve is accessible by 4WD from Maun or Chobe as well as by charter flight.

---

in Maun, see p178. Also see p170 for details about international flights between Maun and Johannesburg (South Africa), Victoria Falls (Zimbabwe) and Livingstone (Zambia).

BUS & COMBI
The station for long-distance buses and combis (minibuses) is along Tsaro St. One bus leaves at least every hour between 6.30am and 4.30pm for Francistown (P55 to P60, five hours), via Gweta (P35, four hours) and Nata (P45, five hours). Combis also leave for Kasane (P60, six hours) when full. For Gaborone, you will have to change in either Ghanzi or Francistown.

To Ghanzi (P35 to P40, five hours), via D'kar (P28 to P32, 3½ hours), buses leave at about 7.30am and 10.30am, but it is best to check at the station or tourist office for current schedules. To Shakawe (P70, seven hours), five or six buses leave between 7.30am and 3.30pm, and stop at Gumare and Etsha 6. Combis to Shorobe (P3, one hour) leave when full from a spot just up from the bus station.

For more information about public buses and shuttle minibuses between Maun and Namibia, Zambia and Zimbabwe, see p174.

CAR & MOTORCYCLE
The direct route between Kasane and Maun is only accessible by 4WD in the dry season, and sometimes impossible by anything but huge, state-of-the-art 4WDs during heavy rains. Also remember that there is nowhere along this direct route to buy fuel, food or drinks, or get vehicle repairs. For more information, see the boxed text, p111. All other traffic between Maun and Kasane travels via Nata.

HITCHING
For eastbound travellers, the best hitching spot is Ema Reje Restaurant on the road towards Nata; for Ghanzi, try outside Sitatunga Camp. Hitching between Maun and Kasane, via Chobe National Park, can be difficult since drivers will be watching their fuel (and food) reserves. All passengers have to pay entrance fees to Chobe, so it's cheaper – and quicker in the long run – to go round via Nata.

MOBILE SAFARIS
Other than careering through Chobe National Park in a private or rented 4WD, the only way to travel overland directly between Maun and Kasane is on a 4WD 'mobile safari'. This is a glorious way to travel though Botswana's two major attractions as you'll see a plethora of wildlife while exploring some of the country's most rugged corners, though safaris are expensive, and can be tough going in the middle of the wet season (January to March). For

OKAVANGO DELTA

■ Okavango Panhandle – this swampy extension of the Inner Delta stretches northwest towards the Namibian border and is the main population centre in the region. Although this area does not offer the classic delta experience, it is growing in popularity due to its ease of accessibility via public transport or 2WD. Since the area is not controlled by a lodge or the DWNP, a number of villages in the panhandle have established accessible campsites and also offer some great affordable *mokoro* trips and fishing expeditions.

If you're planning a 4WD expedition through the park, you will have to be completely self-sufficient as petrol and supplies are only available in Kasane and Maun. As a bare minimum, you'll need a proper map (eg the *Shell Map of the Okavango Delta*), a compass (or preferably a GPS unit), lots of common sense, and genuine confidence and experience in driving a 4WD. Tracks can get extremely muddy, and trails are often washed out during and after the rains. From January to March, the Moremi Game Reserve can be inaccessible, even with a state-of-the-art 4WD. If possible, it's best to travel as part of a convoy of vehicles. If the prospect of driving yourself through the wilds of Botswana seems too daunting, the hotels and lodges in Maun can also help you organise a trip through the delta.

Generally, the best time to visit the delta is from July to September, when the water levels are high and the weather is dry. Bear in mind that several lodges close down for part or all of the rainy season. Those that remain open will provide a unique delta experience, as most tourists avoid the region altogether during these months.

Not surprisingly, mosquitoes are prevalent, especially in the wet season (November to March). Malaria is also rife in this part of the country, so take all necessary precautions – see the Health chapter, p390, for info.

more information, contact one of the tour operators listed on p123.

Getting Around
TO/FROM THE AIRPORT
Maun airport is close to the town centre, so taxis rarely bother hanging around the terminal when planes arrive. If you have prebooked accommodation at an upmarket hotel or lodge in Maun or the Okavango Delta, make sure it provides a (free) courtesy minibus. Others will have to ask the courtesy minibus driver for a lift (P10), or walk about 300m down Airport Rd to Sir Seretse Khama Rd and catch a combi.

CAR & BICYCLE RENTAL
Avis Car Rental (☎ 686 0039; Mathiba I St) has a good selection of both 2WD and 4WD vehicles, though it's recommended that you book ahead, especially during the dry season.

A mountain bike is a great way to travel around town, especially if you're staying in Matlapaneng. Don't worry – the road from Maun to Matlapaneng is flat. **Okavango Tours & Safaris** (☎ 686 0220; Mophane St) rents mountain bikes for US$4 per day.

COMBIS & TAXIS
Combis marked 'Maun Route 1' or 'Sedie Route 1' travel every few minutes during day-light hours between the station in town and a stop near Crocodile Camp in Matlapaneng. The standard fare for all local trips is P2.70.

Taxis also ply the main road and are the only form of public transport in the evening. They also hang around a stand along Pulane St in the town centre. A typical fare from central Maun to Matlapaneng costs about P10/30 in a shared/private taxi. To pre-order a taxi, try **Atol Taxi Cabs** (☎ 686 4770/1).

SHOROBE
If you're in the market for traditional baskets, visit the Shorobe Baskets Cooperative. Under the patronage of Conservation International, this cooperative of about 70 local women produces Ngamiland-style baskets with beautiful and elaborate patterns. Combis heading to Shorobe (P5, one hour), situated about 40km north of Maun, depart from Maun when full.

EASTERN DELTA
The Eastern Delta includes the wetlands between the southern boundary of Moremi Game Reserve and the buffalo fence that crosses the Boro and Santandadibe Rivers, north of Matlapaneng. If you're short of time and/or money, this part of the Okavango Delta remains an affordable and accessible

OKAVANGO DELTA

option. From Maun, it is easy to arrange a day trip on a *mokoro* or a two- or three-night *mokoro* trip combined with bush camping (see p123 for tour operators).

Sleeping

Although most excursions through the Eastern Delta are budget trips that involve bush camping, there are a handful of up-market lodges in the region if you're looking for a little luxury. See the boxed text, opposite, for an explanation of lodge rates and services.

Chitabe Camp (☎ in South Africa 27-11 807 1800; www.wilderness-safaris.com; per person low/high season US$365/700; ☒) Near the Santandadibe River, at the southern edge of Moremi Game Reserve, Chitabe is an island oasis (only accessible by boat or plane) renowned for the presence of Cape hunting dogs and other less common wildlife. Accommodation is in East African–style en suite luxury tents, which are built on wooden decks and sheltered beneath the shade of a lush canopy.

Chitabe Lediba (☎ in South Africa 27-11 807 1800; www.wilderness-safaris.com; per person low/high season US$365/700; ☒) On the other side of the island from Chitabe Camp is the baby brother in the family. With only five tents and a more natural aesthetic, Chitabe Lediba has a warm and intimate atmosphere.

Sandibe Safari Lodge (☎ in South Africa 27-11 809 4300; www.andbeyondafrica.com; per person low/shoulder/high season US$400/600/945; ☒) Understated elegance is the theme at this riverine forest retreat, which consists of eight ochre-washed chalets surrounded by thick bush and towering trees. Dinner is served by candlelight and lantern in the main adobe-walled compound, while the night's festivities revolve around a campfire in a scenic clearing next to the water.

Getting There & Away

If you're either on a *mokoro* day trip or a multi-day bush-camping expedition from Maun, you will be transported to/from the Eastern Delta by 4WD. However, if you're planning to stay at any of the lodges listed in the Sleeping section (above) you will have to take a charter flight. Flights to the Eastern Delta typically cost between US$150 and US$200 return. A *mokoro* or 4WD vehicle will meet your plane and take you to the lodge.

INNER DELTA

Roughly defined, the Inner Delta occupies the areas west of Chiefs Island and between Chiefs Island and the base of the Okavango Panhandle. *Mokoro* trips through the Inner Delta are almost invariably arranged with licensed polers affiliated with specific lodges, and operate roughly between June and December, depending on the water level. To see the most wildlife, you will have to pay park fees to land on Chiefs Island or other parts of Moremi Game Reserve. Also, be sure to advise the poler if you'd like to break the trip with bushwalks around the palm islands.

Sleeping

See the boxed text, opposite, for an explanation of lodge rates and services.

Oddball's (☎ 686 1154; www.oddballs-camp.com; tents low/shoulder/high season from US$200/275/325) Although it occupies a less-than-exciting woodland beside an airstrip, Oddball's is within walking distance of some classic delta scenery. For years, this lodge catered primarily to backpackers and was by far the most affordable option in the delta. Although it's still one of the cheapest lodges in the region, Oddball's has gone up market in recent years; its new price tag is a little high considering you're still staying in budget dome tents.

Gunn's Camp (☎ 686 0023; www.gunnscamp.com; s/d US$375/470) Gunn's is a beautiful option for those wanting the amenities of a high-end safari – expertly cooked meals, attentive service and wonderful views over its island location in the delta – with a more rugged sense of place. The elegant tented rooms are as comfy and soft as you please, but there is more of a feeling of being engaged with the wilderness, what with the hippos, warthogs and even elephants that occasionally wander through the grounds.

Kanana Camp (☎ 686 0375; www.kerdowney botswana.com; low/high season US$425/500) This classy retreat occupies a watery site in a maze of grass and palm-covered islands. It's an excellent base for wildlife-viewing by *mokoro* around Chiefs Island or fishing in the surrounding waterways. Accommodation is in eight well-furnished linen tents that are shaded by towering riverine forest.

Moremi Crossing (☎ 686 0023; www.gunns-camp. com/moremi_crossing.php; s/d US$425/650) A collection of lovely chalets flanks a simply gorgeous (and enormous) thatched dining and

DELTA LODGES

If you've got a little bulge in your budget, the delta is one place where it's worth dusting off the tailcoat and living it up to your heart's content.

The rates for all lodges in the Eastern Delta, Inner Delta and Moremi Game Reserve include accommodation or camping equipment, all meals and several activities or excursions, such as *mokoro* trips, nature walks and wildlife drives. The more expensive places also include drinks (beer and wine only), and entry fees to Moremi Game Reserve. All rooms, chalets and tents have private bathrooms (unless stated otherwise).

Transfers (if required) by road or, more usually by air, from Maun are never included in normal daily rates, though they may be included in package deals. Air fares listed are per person return from Maun. Most lodges and booking agencies deal exclusively with a particular Maun-based air-charter company, so your chances of finding other charter companies offering discounted fares to a certain lodge are negligible.

Most lodges have different rates for 'high season' (about July to October) and 'low season' (about November to June), but if only one rate is listed, this is the rate charged all year. Some places offer unadvertised discounted rates for 'shoulder seasons' (early March to mid-June and mid-October to late November), but you'll have to ask. The rates listed are always per person sharing a twin or double room. Single supplements are usually charged but will normally be waived if a single traveller is willing to share twin accommodation with another single traveller. Rates listed include all government taxes and service charges. Tips are always extra.

The rates shown in this chapter are for 'foreigners'; most lodges offer substantial (but rarely published) discounts to citizens and residents of Botswana and to citizens of 'regional countries', ie mainly South Africa and Namibia. Although tariffs are quoted in US dollars by the lodges, payment is possible in pula – but at a rate that suits the lodge. Payment by credit card may incur an additional surcharge, so check first with the lodge.

All lodges in the Eastern Delta, Inner Delta and Moremi Game Reserve must be prebooked, preferably before you arrive in Maun. Although each camp has a unique atmosphere and location, accommodation is usually in one of a handful of safari-chic linen tents or chalets, which surround a central mess tent where you can dine, socialise or unwind.

---

bar area that overlooks a long flood plain where you can often see wandering giraffes and elephants. The management is friendly as hell, and the camp is to be commended for pioneering a plumbing system that minimises environmental impact (it's also quite a feat of engineering – ask to see how it all works). Moremi is located a short boat trip from Gunn's Camp and owned by the same company.

Delta Camp (☎ 686 1154; per person low/high season from US$486/694) This long-standing camp is beautifully situated beside a flowing channel near the southern end of Chiefs Island. Unlike most other camps, which house guests in en suite luxury tents, Delta Camp consists of 10 thatched huts with en suite bathrooms and private verandahs.

Pom Pom Camp (☎ 686 0023; www.pompomcamp.com; per person low/shoulder/high season US$405/450/680) This intimate camp was one of the original luxury retreats in the delta, though frequent renovations have kept it up to speed with

recent properties. Six linen tents are skilfully placed around a scenic lagoon, which contributes to the tranquil and soothing atmosphere.

Nxabega Okavango Camp (☎ in South Africa 27-11 809 4300; www.andbeyondafrica.com; per person low/high season from US$400/950) In a grove of ebony trees on the flats near the Boro River, this exquisitely designed tented camp has sweeping views of the delta flood plains. Ten tents with private verandahs surround an impressively built thatched lodge that oozes style and sophistication.

Vumbura Plains Camp (☎ 686 0086; www.wilderness-safaris.com; per person low/high season US$600/800) This regally luxurious twin camp is on the Duba Plains at the transition zone between the savannahs and swamps north of the delta, and is famous for attracting large buffalo herds. Accommodation is in either the six-tent Vumbura camp or the slightly smaller five-tent Little Vumbura, which occupies a nearby island.

OKAVANGO DELTA

Tubu Tree Camp (☎ 686 0086; www.wilderness
-safaris.com; per person low/high season US$600/900) Get
your khaki and pith-helmet fix from the
gorgeous tilted accommodation that hovers
over this pretty little corner of the Okavango.
Porches look out from your accommodation
over one of the largest consistent dry areas
of the delta, which often teems with a good
variety of wildlife.

Xigera Camp (☎ 686 0086; www.wilderness-saf
aris.com; per person low/high season from US$600/900)
Pronounced kee-*jera*, this isolated spot is deep
in the heart of the Inner Delta and renowned
for its rich birdlife. The area surrounding
the camp is permanent wetland, which gives
Xigera a lush and tropical atmosphere that is
intoxicating from the moment you first step
on the grounds. Accommodation is in eight
hybrid tent-chalets that are well furnished
and a unique departure from the traditional
linen tent.

Duba Plains (☎ 686 0086; www.wilderness-safaris.
com; per person low/high season US$770/1030) North of
the Moremi Game Reserve, Duba Plains is
one of the most remote camps in the delta.
The intimate layout of the grounds (there are
only six tents) and the virtual isolation of this
part of the delta both contribute to a unique
wilderness experience.

Seba Camp (☎ 686 0086; www.wilderness-safaris.
com; per person low/high season US$845/900) Seba, the
lovely Tswana word meaning whisper, is set
in an equally lovely riverine forest. While it
offers many of the same aristocratic offer-
ings as other top-end safari lodges, what sets
it apart is the emphasis on family service;
unlike other properties, this one welcomes
children. Youngsters (and oldsters) can pass
their days watching researchers study nearby
elephants that have been re-released into the
wild from captivity.

Eagle Island Camp (☎ 686 0302; www.orient_
express_safaris.com; per person low/shoulder/high season
US$805/1000/1245) Widely considered to be one
of the most beautiful camps in the delta, Eagle
Island occupies a fairly stunning concession
deep in the waters. You'll be shacked up in
silk-soft luxury tents and helicopter safaris
are part of your stay, plus the usual range of
wildlife drives, walks, lavish meals and the
rest, you lucky thing.

Footsteps (☎ 686 0375; www.kerdowneybotswana.
com) This relatively new program, run by Ker
& Downey safaris, places an emphasis on
walking and *mokoro* safaris across the delta

flood plains. As such it's the sort of thing that
rewards fit travellers, but with that said, the
rest camps are still impressively posh – the
theme is old Africa exploration, but we doubt
Livingstone ever laid his bushy beard on the
soft sheets K&D provides.

Getting There & Away
The only way into and out of the Inner Delta
for most visitors is by air. This is an expensive
extra, but the pain is alleviated if you look
at it as two scenic flights. Chartered flights
to the lodges listed in Sleeping (p130) typically cost about US$150 to US$200 return
to/from Mekoro, or 4WD vehicles will meet
your plane and take you to the lodge.

MOREMI GAME RESERVE
Moremi Game Reserve (sometimes called
Moremi Wildlife Reserve) is the only part of
the Okavango Delta that is officially cordoned
off for the preservation of wildlife. It was set
aside as a reserve in 1963 when it became
apparent that poaching was decimating wildlife populations. Named after the Batawana
chief Moremi III, the reserve has been extended over the years and now encompasses
almost 5000 sq km – over one-third of the
entire delta.

Moremi has a distinctly dual personality,
with large areas of dry land rising between vast
wetlands. The most prominent 'islands' are
Chiefs Island, accessible by *mokoro* from the
Inner Delta lodges, and Moremi Tongue at the
eastern end of the reserve, which is mostly accessible by 4WD. Habitats in the reserve range
from mopane woodland and thorn scrub to
dry savannah, riparian woodland, grassland,
flood plain, marsh, and permanent waterways,
lagoons and islands.

The reserve is a massive oasis where the
density of many wildlife species reaches its
peak for the entire country. With the recent
reintroduction of the rhino, Moremi is now
home to the Big Five (lion, leopard, buffalo,
elephant and rhino), and notably the largest population of red lechwe in the whole
of Africa. The reserve also protects one of
the largest remaining populations of African
wild dogs as well as the full complement of
feline predators (see the boxed text, p134).
Birding in Moremi is also incredibly varied
and rich, and it's arguably the best place in
Africa to view the rare and secretive Pel's
fishing owl.

Although wildlife viewing in the delta is at times an exercise in patience, Moremi is an animal lover's paradise, particularly during the dry season, when wildlife concentrations are truly mind-boggling. However, Moremi is regarded as one of the most exclusive destinations in Botswana, so unless you're planning a 4WD bush-camping expedition, you're going to have to dig deep for the privilege of staying in one of the reserve's luxury lodges.

Information

The Moremi Game Reserve is administered by the DWNP, and entry and camping fees must be paid for *in advance* at the DWNP office in Maun (p121). You *cannot* pay the entrance fee at the gate. DWNP campsites are often booked well in advance, especially during South African school holidays (mid-April, July, September, and December to January), so try to book as early as possible.

Refer to the National Parks chapter, p26, for information about the opening times of the national parks as well as for admission and camping costs.

The best time to see wildlife in Moremi is the late dry season (July to October), when animals are forced to congregate around permanent water sources, which are accessible to wildlife (and humans). September and October are optimum times for spotting wildlife and birdlife, but these are also the hottest two months. January and February are normally very wet and driving around Moremi at this time can be difficult.

To explore the reserve by private 4WD vehicle, you will have to be completely self-sufficient, as petrol and supplies are only available in Kasane and Maun. Water is available inside the reserve, though it must be boiled or treated prior to drinking. As a bare minimum, you will need a proper map (eg the *Shell Map of the Moremi Game Reserve*), a compass (or preferably a GPS unit), lots of common sense, and genuine confidence and experience in driving a 4WD. Tracks in the reserve are mostly clay and are frequently impassable during the rainy season. If possible, it's best to travel as part of a convoy of vehicles.

Visitors must pay entry fees and camp at either of the two main gates. From Maun,

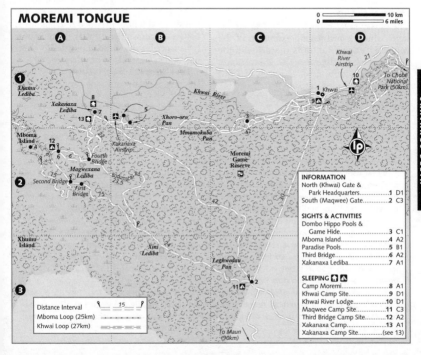

the entrance is located at South (Maqwee) Gate, about 99km north of Maun along a sandy 4WD track, via Shorobe. From the east, a track links Chobe National Park with Moremi across a shaky wooden bridge over the Khwai River. The other gate – and the park headquarters – is located at North (Khwai) Gate.

The village of Khwai has a couple of shops that sell basic supplies, and locally made baskets are often for sale along the village road.

Sights

THIRD BRIDGE

Literally the third log bridge after entering the reserve at South Gate, this rustic and beautiful bridge spans a sandy, tannin-coloured pool on the Sekiri River – an idyllic spot to camp and enjoy a picnic. Contrary to official advice, and despite DWNP regulations, many ignorant visitors swim here, but it's a *very* bad idea. The foolhardy should only do so in broad daylight and keep close watch among the reeds for hippos and crocs.

MBOMA ISLAND

The grassy savannah of this 100-sq-km island, which is just a long extension of the Moremi Tongue, contrasts sharply with the surrounding landscapes. The 25km sandy Mboma Loop starts about 2km west of Third Bridge and is a pleasant side trip.

XAKANAXA LEDIBA

With one of Africa's largest heronries, Xakanaxa Lediba (Xakanaxa Lagoon) is renowned as a bird-watchers' paradise. Potential sightings here include herons, marabous, saddle-bill storks, egrets and ibises (wood, sacred and glossy). The area also supports an array of wildlife and large numbers of fish.

The lagoon is home to several upmarket lodges that operate boat and *mokoro* trips for guests. The public may be able to join an organised boat or *mokoro* trip for a high – but negotiable – fee.

The drive between North Gate and Xakanaxa Lediba follows one of Botswana's most scenic tracks. Worthwhile stops include **Dombo Hippo Pool** (about 14km southwest of North Gate), where hippos crowd along the shore. Their shenanigans can be enjoyed in relative safety from an elevated observation post. The two waterholes at **Paradise Pools** are as lovely as the name suggests.

Sleeping

CAMPING

The DWNP operates each of the four campsites in the Moremi Game Reserve. Each site has an ablutions block with cold showers (or hot showers if you have firewood to crank up the boilers), sit-down flush toilets, running water (which needs to be boiled or purified for drinking) and picnic tables. For prices, see p27.

Khwai Camp Site (Map p133; North Gate) The campsite here is shady and well developed. There

---

THE CARNIVORE CHAIN OF COMMAND

With such an abundance of large carnivores, Moremi is one of the finest reserves for witnessing interactions between the super-predators. As competitors for the same resources, they share no affinity, and encounters between them are typically hostile.

By far the largest African carnivore, the lion sits pretty much unchallenged at the top of the pecking order and is usually able to kill anything it can get hold of, including other predators. Adult lions usually only worry about other lions, though large hyena clans occasionally kill injured or adolescent lions, and they're certainly able to drive small prides from their kills.

Hyenas also trail after other predators in the hopes of getting a free meal. At Moremi, it's fairly common to see spotted hyena clans trailing African wild dogs on the hunt. Again, strength in numbers is a key factor: a few hyenas can lord over an entire pack of wild dogs, though a single hyena is easily harassed into retreating. Coincidentally, both hyena clans and wild-dog packs dominate leopards, but individuals do so at their peril as leopards will occasionally bring down a lone hyena or wild dog.

At the very bottom of the hierarchy is the world's fastest land predator, the cheetah. By sacrificing brute force for incredible speed, cheetahs are simply unable to overpower other predators. Nor can they afford the risk of injury and invariably give way to other super-predators, regardless of numbers.

are a couple of small shops in Khwai village on the other side of the river selling food and other supplies.

Maqwee Camp Site (Map p133; South Gate) This campsite is reasonably developed, though the ablution blocks are a bit rundown. Be careful not to leave any food lying about, as the baboons here are aggressive and ill-tempered.

Third Bridge Camp Site (Map p133; Third Bridge) On the edge of a lagoon (so watch out for hippos and crocs), the most popular campsite in Moremi is starting to show its age, though it's still a beautiful place to pitch for the night. However, the Third Bridge area is overrun with baboons, so again, be careful not to leave any food lying about. Also, avoid camping on the bridge or sleeping in the open because wildlife – especially lions – use the bridge as a thoroughfare.

Xakanaxa Camp Site (Map p133; Xakanaxa Lediba) Occupying a narrow strip of land, this campsite is surrounded by marshes and lagoons. But watch out for wildlife – campers are frequently woken during the night by elephants, and a young boy was tragically killed by hyenas here in 2000.

LODGES

See the boxed text, p131, for an explanation of lodge rates and services. You'll note that the lodges run by Desert & Delta all have essentially the same rates.

Camp Moremi (Map p133; ☎ 686 1244; www. desertdelta.com; per person low/shoulder/high season US$396/476/686) This long-standing wilderness retreat sits amid giant ebony trees next to Xakanaxa Lediba and is surrounded by wildlife-rich grasslands. The most famous attraction in Moremi is Pavarotti, a retired hippo who has adopted the camp as his home. Accommodation is in East African–style linen tents that are attractively furnished with wooden fixtures.

Camp Okavango (Map p120; ☎ 686 1243; www. desertdelta.com; per person low/shoulder/high season US$396/476/686, ste US$616/726/915) Set amid sausage and jackalberry trees just outside Moremi, this charming lodge is very elegant, and the staff are famous for their meticulous attention to detail. If you want Okavango served up with silver tea service, candelabras and fine china, this is the place for you.

Khwai River Lodge (Map p133; ☎ 686 1244; www.desertdelta.com; per person low/shoulder/high season US$396/476/686) Perched on the northern shores of the Khwai River, this opulent lodge overlooks the Moremi Game Reserve, and is frequently visited by large numbers of hippos and elephants. Accommodation is in 15 luxury en suite tents that are larger and more extravagant than most upmarket hotel rooms.

Xugana Island Lodge (Map p120; ☎ 686 1244; www.desertdelta.com; per person low/shoulder/high season US$396/476/686) Set on a pristine lagoon just north of Moremi, this lodge offers superb bird-watching and fishing. This area was historically frequented by ancient San hunters, and Xugana means 'kneel down to drink' – a reference to the welcome sight of perennial water after a long hunt. Accommodation is in thatched chalets with modern furnishings.

Stanley's Camp (Map p120; ☎ in South Africa 27-11 438 4650; www.sanctuarylodges.com; per person low/high season US$520/790) Although it is significantly less ostentatious than other lodges in Moremi, Stanley's, located near the Boro River, lacks the formality and pretence commonly found in this corner of the country. En suite tents are simple but spacious, though the real attraction is the lively (and at times rambunctious) atmosphere in the communal dining tent. You can book through any of the operators in Maun (see p123).

Xakanaxa Camp (Map p133; ☎ in South Africa 27 -11 463 3999; www.xakanaxa-camp.com; per person low/ shoulder/high season from US$520/620/875) This camp, much loved by locals, offers a pleasant mix of delta and savannah habitat, and teems with huge herds of elephants and other wildlife. However, it's most famous for its legendary bird-watching, especially along the shores of the nearby Xakanaxa Lediba. They're very good at providing the luxury safari experience here.

Kwara Camp (Map p120; ☎ 686 1449; www.kwando. com; per person low/high season US$550/800) This island camp lies in an area of subterranean springs. These form pools that support enough fish to attract flocks of pelicans (hence its name, which means 'where the pelicans feed'). These pools also attract heavy concentrations of wildlife, which is the drawcard for the lodge. Although the place is luxurious, the atmosphere is informal and relaxed.

Xaranna Camp (Map p120; ☎ in South Africa 27-11 809 4300; www.andbeyondafrica.com; per person low/shoulder/ high season US$550/770/1375) With its own island

FLORA & FAUNA OF THE OKAVANGO DELTA

Although the profuse flora of the Okavango Delta is magnificent, the wildlife will probably seem quite elusive unless you're staying in or travelling around the Moremi Game Reserve (p132). It's easy enough to deduce that such an abundance of water wouldn't be overlooked by the thirsty creatures of the Kalahari, but with a swampy surfeit of hiding places the wildlife is simply not easy to spot.

While sitting in a *mokoro*, you may think that the delta is just a papyrus-choked swamp dotted with palm islands. While that impression is not without some validity, the delta's hydrography is more complex, as there are also deeper and faster-flowing river channels and serene lagoons, known as *madiba* (singular *lediba*), which are more or less permanent and remain largely free of vegetation. The reeds and papyrus, however, are rife. They wave and cluster along channels, blocking the *mokoro*-level view, but the slower-moving channels and even the *madiba* are festooned with the purple-bottomed leaves and pink-and-white blooms of water lilies. When they are roasted, the roots of these lilies are delicious, and even the flowers can be eaten.

Vegetation on the palm islands is diverse. In addition to the profuse *mokolane* palms, there are savannah grasses, leadwood willows, marulas, strangler figs, acacia thorn, ebony and whimsical sausage trees with long and unmistakable fruits (these yield an agent that has proven effective against some forms of skin cancer). If you're visiting in January, you'll be able to sample the fruits of the African mangosteen and marula.

The delta's reptilian realm is dominated by the Nile crocodile, which lounges lazily along the island shorelines or lies quietly in the water with only its eyes and snout breaking the surface. For this reason, you should always talk to the poler before entering the water; also be careful not to dangle any limbs you want to keep in the water. Other reptiles include the immense carnivorous *leguaan* (water monitor), which either swims through the shallows or basks on the sand.

The amphibian world is represented by the tiny frogs that inhabit the reeds – and sometimes plop into your lap as you're poled in a *mokoro* through reed thickets. Their resonant peeping is one of the delta's unforgettable sounds, while the tinkle-like cries of bell frogs and the croaking of the larger and more sonorous bullfrogs provide a lovely evening chorus.

Birds will probably provide the bulk of your wildlife viewing and include African jacanas (which strut across lily pads), bee-eaters, snakebirds, storks, egrets, shrikes, kingfishers, hornbills and herons. More unusual are the psychedelic pygmy geese (actually a well-disguised duck), and the brilliantly plumed, lilac-breasted rollers, with bright-blue wings and a green and lilac underside. Watch also for birds of prey, like Pel's fishing owls, goshawks, bateleur eagles and African fish eagles.

The northeast corner of the delta is home to rare sitatungas – splay-hoofed swamp antelopes, which are particularly adept at manoeuvring over soft, saturated mud and soggy, mashed vegetation. When frightened, they submerge like hippos, leaving only their tiny nostrils above the surface. Red *lechwes*, of which there are an estimated 30,000, are easily distinguished by their large rumps. In the shallow and still pools of the palm islands, reedbucks wade and graze on water plants, and the islands are also inhabited by large herds of impala.

The most commonly sighted mammals in the delta are hippos, which are submerged throughout most of the day, only to emerge in the late afternoon and evening to graze on the riverbanks. Hippos are easily startled and prone to attack, especially when accompanied by their young, so don't be surprised if your poler exhibits an extra degree of attention and care when they're present.

The delta also supports a stable population of predators, including lions, cheetahs, leopards and hyenas, who strut around the tall grasses of the Moremi Game Reserve. At the canine end of the spectrum, Moremi is also home to 30% of the world's remaining African wild dogs.

The Okavango Delta is incredibly diverse in terms of flora and fauna, though it will take some time to fully appreciate this unique ecosystem. Be patient – you never know what's around the next river bend.

and 25,000-hectare concession, Xaranna has a lot of room for wildlife, which you can often see from the nine gorgeous en suite tents that overlook a syrup-slow channel of the delta.

Shinde Island Camp (Map p120; ☎ 686 0375; www.kerdowneybotswana.com; per person low/high season US$581/797) This lagoon-side camp sits just north of Moremi, between the savannah and the delta, and is one of the oldest camps in the delta. Eight linen tents surround a central lodge known for its class and formality.

Baine's Camp (Map p120; ☎ in South Africa 27-11 438 4650; www.sanctuarylodges.com; per person low/high season US$620/1030) Five elevated suits overlook a tree line that conceals (but not too much) great wildlife viewing in a shady, woodsy area of the delta. There's a very private, world-in-its-infancy sense of fresh beauty in the place; you'd be forgiven for thinking a naked couple arguing over an apple was about to emerge from the landscape.

Chief's Camp (Map p120; ☎ in South Africa 27-11 438 4650; www.sanctuarylodges.com; per person low/high season US$900/1450) Considered by many to be one of the premier camps in the delta, Chief's blends into its marshy surroundings like a hunter in a duck blind. Except you're not trying to pot-shot wildlife here – just photograph or watch it from 12 pretty incredible luxury 'bush pavilions'.

Mombo Camp (Map p120; ☎ 686 0302; www.orient_ex press_safaris.com; per person low/high season US$1630/1770) Mombo Camp (and its sister camp, Little Mombo) are on the northwest corner of Chief's Island and offer what is arguably the best wildlife viewing in all of Botswana. It's possible to see the Big Five literally out your window, though you will have to pay dearly for the privilege. The ambience is as super luxurious as you'd expect, and each of the 12 linen tents (nine at Mombo, three at Little Mombo) could compete with most five-star hotel rooms. Just as well, at these prices.

Getting There & Away

There are public airstrips at Khwai River and Xakanaxa Lediba, and most lodges have access to private landing strips. The more remote lodges are only accessible by air, and flights to these lodges are normally arranged by the lodges or booking agencies in Maun. Chartered flights to the lodges listed in Sleeping (p134) typically cost between US$150 and US$200 return.

Lodges and campsites in the Moremi Tongue area are normally accessible by 4WD. If you're driving from Maun, take the paved road to Shorobe, where the road turns into good gravel. Soon enough, it deteriorates into terrible sand that is only accessible by 4WD. From South Gate to Third Bridge, it's about 52km (two hours) along a poor sandy track, but the route runs through beautiful, wildlife-rich country. It's about 25km (one hour) from Third Bridge to Xakanaxa Lediba, and another 45km (1½ hours) from there to North Gate.

The other tracks around Moremi are mostly either clay, which is almost impossible to drive along in the wet season, particularly near any mopane forests, or sand, which is terrible in the dry, particularly around Third Bridge. The tracks sometimes become so bad that the reserve is temporarily closed. Check the road conditions with the DWNP offices in Gaborone or Maun, and/or with other drivers, before attempting to drive into Moremi during the wet season.

OKAVANGO PANHANDLE

The Okavango Panhandle is a narrow strip of swampland that extends for about 100km from Etsha 13 to the Namibian border, and is the result of a 15km-wide geological fault that constricts the meandering river until it's released into the main delta. In the panhandle the waters spread across the valley on either side to form vast reed beds and papyrus-choked lagoons. Here a cosmopolitan mix of people (Mbukushu, Yei, Tswana, Herero, European and San, as well as Angolan refugees) occupy clusters of fishing villages and extract their livelihoods from the rich waters.

As the rest of the delta grows more expensive for tourists, the Okavango Panhandle is booming as a result of local cooperatives (see the boxed text, p138) that offer affordable accommodation and *mokoro* trips. Although it is arguably not the 'real delta', the panhandle is the main population centre in the region, which gives it a unique character and atmosphere that is virtually absent from other parts of the delta. The panhandle also has permanent water year-round, which means it's always possible to organise a *mokoro* trip. And finally, although the size and scope of the panhandle are modest, it boasts the same flora and fauna (see the boxed text, opposite) found in other parts of the delta. Of course, you'll still have to part with a bit of cash to

OKAVANGO DELTA

THE OKAVANGO POLERS TRUST

Established in 1998 by the people of Seronga, the **Okavango Polers Trust** (☎ 687 6861; www
.okavangodelta.co.bw) provides cheaper and more accessible *mokoro* trips and accommodation for
visitors. Since the collective is run entirely by the village, all profits are shared by the workers,
invested into the trust and used to provide the community with better facilities. The trust directly employs nearly 100 people, including polers, dancers, cooks, managers and drivers. Since
no travel agency or safari operator is involved, the cooperative can afford to charge reasonable
prices for *mokoro* trips. Although it's not uncommon to pay upwards of US$200 per day for a
mokoro trip out of Maun, the trust charges around P500 per day for *two* people. Keep in mind,
however, that you must self-cater (ie, bring your own food, water and, if necessary, camping
and cooking equipment).

There's no longer a daily bus from Mohembo to Seronga, but it's almost always possible to
hitch from the free Okavango River ferry in Mohembo. Plan on paying about P5 for a lift. When
they're operating, water taxis run along the Okavango between Sepupa Swamp Stop (below) and
Seronga (P30, two hours); transfers from the Seronga dock to Mbiroba Camp (below), 3km away,
cost P70. Otherwise, Sepupa Swamp Stop charters 18-passenger boats for P700.

---

explore the delta properly, but at least you'll
have enough in the bank when it's all done to
print your photos.

Villages along the road between Maun
and Shakawe that are not directly linked to
the Okavango Panhandle, namely Gumare,
Etsha 6 and Shakawe, are covered in the
Northwestern Botswana chapter (p140).

Activities

The most popular leisure activity in the
panhandle is **fishing**. Anglers from southern
Botswana and South Africa flock here to hook
tigerfish, pike, barbel (catfish) and bream.
Tigerfish season is from September to June,
while barbel are present from mid-September
to December.

Most lodges and campsites along the panhandle can arrange fishing trips, and hire out
gear for about US$5 per person per day.

Sleeping

Panhandle camps are mostly in the middle
range, and have until recently catered mainly
for the sport-fishing crowd. However, this is
changing along with the recent increase in
travellers looking for affordable delta trips.

CAMPING

Camping is also available at most of the
lodges.

Phala Community Camp Site (Ganitsuga; camping
per person US$4) This rustic campsite is friendly,
welcoming and far from the tourist crowd.
Phala is near Ganitsuga village, about 23km
east of Seronga and accessible by a sturdy

2WD or hitching from Seronga. A basic shop
sells provisions and drinks.

LODGES

Umvuvu Camp (☎ 7153 4340; www.okavangopanhandle.
com; camping per person P40, s/d tents P150/200) Umvuvu
is friendly as hell and a good spot to enjoy
the slow pace of river life minus the amenities of the safari package tourist. The location
is beautiful and the lodge well managed, so
you're never far from an excursion or the wet
wilderness itself.

Sepupa Swamp Stop (☎ 687 7073; www.swampstop.
co.bw; Sepupa; camping per person P40, tents from P120) This
laid-back riverside campsite is secluded, handy
to Sepupa village, very affordable and accessible (3km) from the Maun–Shakawe road.
The lodge can arrange *mokoro* trips through
the Okavango Polers Trust (see the boxed text,
above) and transfers to Sepupa, as well as boat
trips for US$14/91 per hour/day.

Mbiroba Camp (☎ 687 6861; www.okavangodelta.
co.bw; camping per person P55, rondavels P110, chalets
from P250) This impressive camp is run by the
Okavango Polers Trust (see the boxed text,
above) and is the usual launching point for
mokoro trips into the delta. The camp features a well-groomed and shady campsite,
an outdoor bar, a traditional restaurant and
rustic two-storey chalets. Mbiroba is 3km
from Seronga village.

Makwena Lodge (☎ 687 4299; backpackers from P220,
camping per person P340) Located on Qhaaxhwa
(Birthplace of the Hippo) Lagoon, at the base
of the panhandle, this stretch of water closely
resembles the Inner Delta. Guests often see

red *lechwes* and sitatungas, as well as water birds and raptors. Inexpensive *mokoro* trips can be arranged, and there's an attached bar-restaurant that serves up tasty and cheap grub. Makwena is operated by Drotsky's Cabins (see below). Those without a 4WD can prearrange transfers from Etsha 6 (P70 per person).

Drotsky's Cabins (☎ 687 5035; drotskys@info.bw; camping P120, A-frames from P400, 5-person chalets P950) This lovely, welcoming lodge lies beside a channel of the Okavango River about 5km southeast of Shakawe and about 4km east of the main road. Set amid a thick riverine forest, it's very secluded, with fabulous bird-watching and fine views across the reeds and papyrus. Rowing boats can be rented for P200 per hour. There is a small outdoor bar-restaurant offering cheap eats.

Xaro Lodge (s/d chalets P350/550) Run by the son of the owners of Drotsky's Cabins (see above), this lodge is remote – about 10km downstream from Drotksy's – but serene and extremely picturesque. Accommodation is in several clean and tidy chalets that surround a modest bar-restaurant. The main activity at the lodge is fishing, though it also makes for a great retreat. Transfers by boat from Drotksy's Cabins cost P100 per person. Book through Drotksy's.

Guma Island Lodge (☎ 687 4022; www.ngumalodge.com; camping per person P50, family chalets P1000) Fishing is the focus at this secluded camp, which lies east of Etsha 13, on the Thaoge River. However, Guma Island also advertises itself as a 'family resort', so if you're travelling with little ones, they will be well catered for. Chalet rates include half-board, boat trips, fishing-tackle hire and *mokoro* trips. The final 16km from Etsha 13 requires a 4WD, but the lodge provides safe parking facilities and transfers from Etsha 13 (around P300 per trip).

Okavango Houseboats (☎ 686 0802; www.okavangohouseboats.com; houseboats from P4500) Floating down the river in one of these houseboats, which vaguely resemble Mississippi steamboats that got lost somewhere in Angola, gives a new, aquatic twist to the 'mobile safari' experience. The craft depart from Seronga, and should be booked well in advance. Expect some amazing birding and riverside wildlife viewing. The boats accommodate six to 20 people.

Getting There & Away
The road between Maun and Shakawe, via Sehithwa, is paved and continues into Namibia. The roads into the major villages, such as Gumare, Etsha 6 and Sepupa, are also paved, while tracks to the lodges and campsites are normally accessible by 2WD (unless stated otherwise).

To reach Sepupa, catch a bus towards Shakawe from Maun, disembark at the turnoff to the village (P50, six hours) and hitch a lift or walk (about 3km) into Sepupa. To get to Seronga, there are several options: ask Sepupa Swamp Stop about a boat transfer (P150 per person, minimum of six people) or wait for the public boat (P30 per person, two hours), which leaves Sepupa more frequently in the afternoon. Alternatively, catch the bus all the way from Maun to Shakawe (P70, seven hours); jump on a combi (P5, 30 minutes) up to Mohembo; take the free car ferry (45 minutes, 6.30am to 6.30pm) across the river; and then hitch (which is usually easy enough) along the good sandy road (accessible by 2WD) to Seronga. Otherwise, drive via Shakawe and Mohembo, or fly to Seronga from Maun – try **Mack Air** (☎ 686 0675; www.mackair.co.bw).

From Seronga to the Phala Community Camp Site, hitch a lift or organise a transfer with Mbiroba Camp.

Northwestern Botswana

First off: you are to be congratulated for even reaching this remote, little-visited corner of the country. The far northwest of Botswana, outside of the Okavango Delta, is a wild border space of small towns and cattle posts separated by long, windy stretches of yellow grass and bleached thornbush. Elsewhere are marshy outflows wrapped in reeds, the latter used in the construction of some of the country's prettiest crafts. Scattered throughout are rocky outcroppings, the sides of their walls daubed with pigments and paintings from the San and their relatives.

This land may not necessarily be ignored by the government, but it's safe to say it doesn't usually take top priority in the national agenda. As a result, driving your own vehicle through this region has the distinct feeling of peeling off the path, leaving the safety of accessible hubs like Maun, Kasane, Ghanzi and the rest in the east, and truly giving yourself over to Botswanan chance.

Agriculture and fishing are the main industries here, and tourism infrastructure remains essentially undeveloped. That means you can see the 'desert louvre' of the Tsodilo Hills, for example, almost completely on your own. This sort of thing adds to the adventure for a certain type of traveller, and if that's you, pack that 4WD, load up your jerry cans with petrol, get some water in reserve and (to paraphrase Mark Twain) light out for Botswana's territory ahead of the rest.

HIGHLIGHTS

- Marvelling at the ancient San rock art scattered among the mystical **Tsodilo Hills** (p144)
- Spelunking where few have spelunked before at **Gcwihaba (Drotsky's) Cave** (p142)
- Relishing the disarming solitude of the largely unexplored **Aha Hills** (p143)
- Going birding (for the time being) on the ephemeral shores of **Lake Ngami** (p142)
- Shopping for curios in the tiny village of **Gumare** (p143)

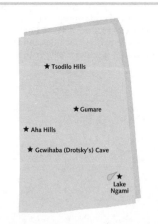

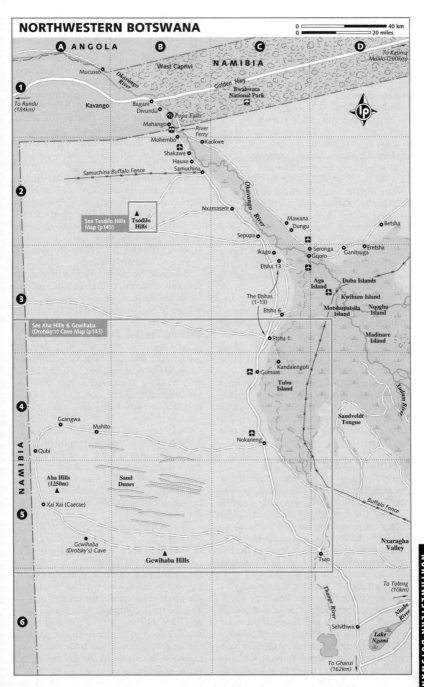

NORTHWESTERN BOTSWANA

0 ———— 40 km
0 ———— 20 miles

A ANGOLA   **B**   **C**   **D**

To Katima
Mulilo (200km)

Mucusso

West Caprivi   N A M I B I A

Golden Hwy

Bwabwata
National Park

To Rundu
(184km)

Kavango   Bagani
Divundu   Popa Falls

Mahango   River
Ferry

Mohembo

Shakawe   Kaokwe

Hauxa

Samuchina Buffalo Fence   Samuchina

See Tsodilo Hills
Map (p145)   Tsodilo
Hills   Nxamasere

Mawana
Dungu   Betsha

Sepupa

Seronga   Eretsha
Ikago   Gqoro   Ganitsuga

Etsha 13

Aga   Duba Islands
Island   Kwihum Island

The Etshas
(1-13)   Motshupatsila   Nqogha
Etsha 6   Island   Island

See Aha Hills & Gcwihaba
(Drotsky's) Cave Map (p143)   Etsha 1   Madinare
Island

Kandalengoti

Gumare   Tubu
Island

Gcangwa   Mahito   Sandveldt
Tongue

Qubi

Nokaneng

Aha Hills
(1250m)   Sand
Dunes

Xai Xai (Caecae)   Buffalo Fence

Gcwihaba
(Drotsky's) Cave   Nxaragha
Valley

Gcwihaba Hills   Tsao

To Toteng
(10km)

Thaoge River   Nhabe
River

Sehithwa   Lake
Ngami

To Ghanzi   To Ghanzi
(162km)

N A M I B I A

Okavango River

Okavango River

LAKE NGAMI

Arriving at the shores of Lake Ngami in 1849, Dr David Livingstone (p190) witnessed a magnificent expanse of water teeming with animals and birdlife. He estimated the area of the lake to be around 810 sq km, though the ancient shoreline revealed that Ngami may have been as large as 1800 sq km. However, for reasons not completely known, the lake disappeared entirely a few years later, reappearing briefly towards the end of the 19th century, a pattern that has continued.

Lake Ngami lacks an outflow and can only be filled by an overflow from the Okavango Delta down the Nhabe River. Following heavy rains in 1962, the lake reappeared once more, covering an area of 250 sq km. Although the lake was present for nearly 20 years, it mysteriously disappeared again in 1982, only to reappear once more in 2000. Since then, heavy rains have kept the lake partially filled at various times, though it's anyone's guess when it will dry up again.

Following heavy rains, the lake attracts flocks of flamingos, ibises, pelicans, eagles, storks, terns, gulls and kingfishers. Although there is no accommodation around the lake, unofficial camping is possible along the lakeshore, though you will need to be entirely self-sufficient.

All (unsigned) tracks heading south from the paved road between Toteng and Sehitwa lead to the lake. These tracks are accessible by 2WD in the dry season, but not when it has been raining (which is, of course, the best time to go).

GCWIHABA (DROTSKY'S) CAVE

In 1932 a group of San showed Gcwihaba (meaning 'hyena's hole') to a farmer named Martinus Drotsky, who promptly decided to name the cave after himself. Although Drotsky is most likely the first European to have explored the cave, legend has it that the fabulously wealthy Hendrik Matthys van Zyl (see the boxed text, p151) stashed a portion of his fortune here in the late 1800s.

The interior of the cave is defined by its 10m-long stalagmites and stalactites, which were formed by dripping water that seeped through the ground and dissolved the dolomite rock. The cave is home to large colonies of Commerson's leaf-nosed bats (which have a wingspan of up to 60cm) and common slit-faced bats (distinguished by their long ears),

which, although harmless, can make your expedition a hair-raising experience.

Information

Gcwihaba (Drotsky's) Cave is not developed for tourism: the interior of the cave is completely dark, and there are no lights or route markings. You should carry in several gas lamps or strong torches (flashlights), as well as emergency light sources such as matches and cigarette lighters. It's also a good idea to travel in pairs, and to let someone else know where you're going to be.

It is possible to walk (about 1km) through the cave from one entrance to the other, but venturing far inside the cave is *only* for those with proper lighting and some experience and confidence. The main entrance is signposted from the end of the track, and is near a noticeboard. The cave is permanently open and there is no admission charge.

Unofficial camping is possible beneath the thorn trees around both entrances, and bore water and basic supplies are available at the villages of Xai Xai (Caecae) and Gcangwa.

Getting There & Away

A fully equipped 4WD with high clearance is essential for visiting Gcwihaba (Drotsky's) Cave (GPS coordinates: S 20°01.302', E 21°21.275'). There are two turn-offs from the Sehitwa–Shakawe road, so it is possible to combine a visit to the cave with a visit to the Aha Hills.

One turn-off (GPS: S 20°09.033', E 22°26.028') is poorly signposted 1.5km north of Tsao and heads west towards Xai Xai village. After 93km look for the signposted turn-off to Xhaba Bore Hole and follow the track (53.8km) to the cave. This track is more scenic, more direct and better in the dry season.

The second turn-off (GPS: S 19°39.587', E 22°11.013') is at Nokaneng, 70km north of Tsao and 37km south of Gumare. This track heads west (121.5km) to Gcangwa and then south (45km) along sharp, tyre-bursting rock to Xai Xai, via the Aha Hills (which rise up on either side of the track). From Xai Xai, the track continues 9.1km to the turn-off (GPS: S 19°54.326', E 21°09.433') for the track (27km) to the cave. This is certainly the long way round. The track is also very sandy, so it's worse in the dry season but better in the wet.

AHA HILLS

Straddling the Botswana–Namibia border, the 700-million-year-old limestone and dolomite Aha Hills (1250m) rise 300m from the flat, thorny Kalahari scrub. Due to the almost total absence of water, there is an eerie dearth of animal life – there are no birds and only the occasional insect. However, the main attraction of the Aha Hills is their beguiling solitude and isolation. When night falls, the characteristic sounds of Southern Africa are conspicuously absent, though the resulting stillness is near perfect.

Much of this area remains unexplored, so there are precious few reliable maps. However, the Aha Hills present the perfect opportunity to put the guidebook down and explore a region that few tourists visit.

There are no facilities here, but unofficial camping is allowed within 100m of the main track. Basic supplies and drinkable bore water are available in the villages of Xai Xai and Gcangwa.

The GPS coordinates for the Aha Hills are S 19°47.244', E 21°03.981'. From the Sehitwa–Shakawe road, there are two turn-offs: one near Tsao and another at Nokaneng. The hills are located about 33km south of Gcangwa and about 12km north of Xai Xai. See opposite for information on travelling onward to Gcwihaba (Drotsky's) Cave.

GUMARE

The tiny village of Gumare is home to the **Ngwao Boswa Curio Shop** (☎ 687 4074), which makes and sells Ngamiland baskets under the label Ngwao Boswa Basket Enterprises (*ngwao boswa* means 'inherited tradition' in Tswana). The cooperative is run by village women and prices are reasonable and fixed.

Daily combis (minibuses) between Maun and Shakawe stop in Gumare, though the demand for seats far exceeds supply – line up and prepare to defend your spot.

ETSHA 6

Etsha 6 is the largest of the 13 Etsha villages strung along the Sehitwa–Shakawe road. During the early days of Angola's civil war, the Mbukushu fled southwards and were granted refugee status in Botswana. In 1969 they organised themselves into 13 groups based on

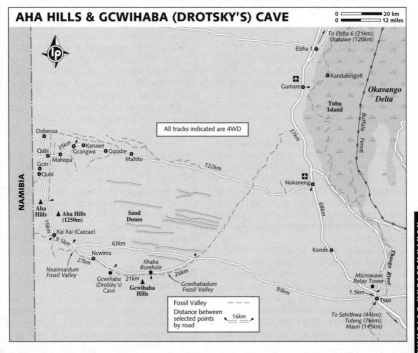

AHA HILLS & GCWIHABA (DROTSKY'S) CAVE

0 — 20 km
0 — 12 miles

All tracks indicated are 4WD

To Etsha 6 (21km);
Shakawe (125km)

Etsha 1

Etsha 6

Kandalengoti

Gumare

Okavango Delta

Tubu Island

Buffalo Fence

Dobecoa

35km
Karuwe
Qabi Gcangwa Gqoshe
Mahopa Mahito

Gcin
Qubi

37km

122km

Nokaneng

NAMIBIA

Aha Hills

Aha Hills (1250m)

Sand Dunes

15km

Xai Xai (Caecae)

9.1km

63km

Konde

68km

Ncwima

27km

Xhaba Borehole

Nxainxaidum Fossil Valley

Gcwihaba (Drotsky's) Cave

21km

Gewihaba Hills

26km

Gcwihabadum Fossil Valley

93km

Microwave Relay Tower

1.5km

Thaoge River

Tsao

Fossil Valley — — —
Distance between selected points by road   16km

To Sehithwa (44km);
Toteng (76km);
Maun (145km)

the clan and social structure they carried over from Angola. Each group proceeded to settle in a village 1km from the next, and were subsequently named Etsha 1, Etsha 2 and so on by the Botswanan government.

If you want to stretch your legs, visit the **House of the River People** (admission P10), a museum and cultural centre featuring the traditions and artistry of the Bayei, Mbukushu and San people of the Okavango region. The adjacent Okavango Basket Shop is an excellent place to buy Ngamiland baskets, pottery and carvings.

If you want to break up the driving, you can crash for the night at the **Etsha Guesthouse & Camping** (camping per person P30, s/d with shared bathroom P10/20), which has four thatched chalets, braai (barbecue) pits and an ablutions block.

Cheap and filling takeaway food is available at Ellen's Cafe, beside the Shell petrol station (a rarity in these parts). Even if you think you have enough petrol to make it to either Maun or Shakawe, play it safe and fill up the tank here.

Six daily combis between Maun and Shakawe stop in Etsha 6, though the demand for seats far exceeds supply – again, line up aggressively. Etsha 6 is 3km east of the main road.

TSODILO HILLS

The Tsodilo Hills are lonely chunks of quartzite schist that rise abruptly from a rippled, ocean-like expanse of desert. They are imbued with myth, legend and spiritual significance for the original San inhabitants as well as the Mbukushu newcomers.

Excavations of flaked stone tools indicate that Bantu people arrived as early as AD 500, but layers of superimposed rock paintings and other archaeological remnants suggest that ancestors of the San have been here for up to 30,000 years. The San believe the Tsodilo Hills are the site of the first Creation, and the Mbukushu claim that the gods lowered the people and their cattle onto Female Hill.

The Tsodilo Hills were the 'Slippery Hills' described by Sir Laurens van der Post. It was here that his cameras inexplicably jammed, his tape recorders ceased functioning and his group was attacked by swarms of bees on three consecutive mornings. When he learned that two members of his party had ignored a long-established protocol by killing a warthog

and steenbok while approaching the sacred hills, van der Post buried a note of apology beneath the panel of paintings that now bears his name.

The Tsodilo Hills are famous for their extensive outline-style rock art. To date, about 2750 paintings at over 200 sites have been found and catalogued.

Orientation

Four chunks of rock make up the Tsodilo Hills: Male Hill, Female Hill, Child Hill and a distant hillock known as North Hill, which remained nameless until recently. (According to one San legend, North Hill was an argumentative wife of the Male Hill who was sent away.) Distinguished by their streaks of vivid natural hues – mauve, orange, yellow, turquoise and lavender – the Male and Female Hills are the most accessible.

Information

The Tsodilo Hills are now a national monument and under the auspices of the National Museum in Gaborone. All visitors must report to the headquarters at the Main (Rhino) Camp, about 2.5km north of the airstrip. Admission to the hills is free.

There's a small museum near Main (Rhino) Camp extolling the undeniably spiritual nature of the hills. However, if you're looking for more detailed information on the hills, look for *Contested Images*, published by the University of Witwatersrand, Johannesburg, which contains a chapter on the Tsodilo Hills by Alec Campbell. Alternatively, try Tom Dowson's erudite *Conference Proceedings on Southern African Rock Paintings*.

The best way to get around the hills is to walk, though some trails require guides (a guide will also greatly improve your understanding of the paintings). Official guides from the headquarters charge about P100 per group (with about five people) per day.

The best time to visit is during winter (April to October) as daytime temperatures in the summertime can be excruciatingly hot. From December to February, watch out for bees.

Sights & Activities
ROCK PAINTINGS
Most of the paintings are executed in ochres or whites using natural pigments. The older paintings, which are thought to date from the Later Stone Age to the Iron Age, are

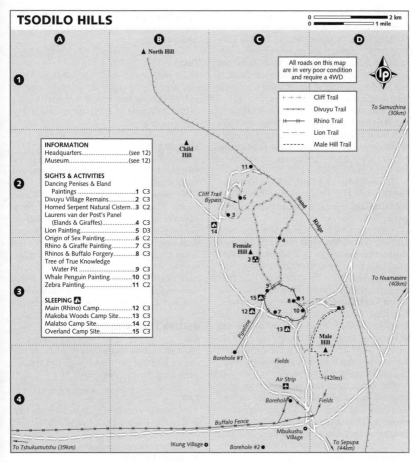

TSODILO HILLS

INFORMATION
Headquarters.........................(see 12)
Museum..............................(see 12)

SIGHTS & ACTIVITIES
Dancing Penises & Eland
  Paintings 1 C3
Divuyu Village Remains..............2 C3
Horned Serpent Natural Cistern..3 C2
Laurens van der Post's Panel
  (Elands & Giraffes)..................4 C3
Lion Painting.............................5 D3
Origin of Sex Painting................6 C2
Rhino & Giraffe Painting............7 C3
Rhinos & Buffalo Forgery............8 C3
Tree of True Knowledge
  Water Pit 9 C3
Whale Penguin Painting...........10 C3
Zebra Painting.........................11 C2

SLEEPING
Main (Rhino) Camp.................12 C3
Makoba Woods Camp Site.......13 C3
Malatso Camp Site...................14 C2
Overland Camp Site.................15 C3

All roads on this map are in very poor condition and require a 4WD

Cliff Trail / Divuyu Trail / Rhino Trail / Lion Trail / Male Hill Trail

generally attributed to the San. However, it's fairly certain that the most recent works were painted by 'copycat' Bantu artists. Interestingly, neither the San nor the Mbukushu accept responsibility for any of the works, maintaining that the paintings have been there longer than even legend can recall.

One of the most fascinating paintings is the **zebra painting** on a small outcrop north of Female Hill. This stylised equine figure is now used as the logo of Botswana National Museums & Monuments. The amazing **whale and penguin paintings** on the southeast corner of Female Hill suggest a link between the early San and the Namibian coast. However, sceptics have suggested that the paintings

are naive representations of a local bird and fish from the shallow lake that once existed northwest of Female Hill.

Around the corner and to the west, the **rhino and giraffe painting** portrays a rhino family and an authentic-looking giraffe. Inside the deepest hollow of Female Hill is another rhino painting, which also includes a 'forgery' of a buffalo that was created more recently. Directly across the hollow, one of the few Tsodilo paintings containing human figures depicts a dancing crowd of sexually excited male figures – Alec Campbell, the foremost expert on the hills and their paintings, has amusedly dubbed it the **'Dancing Penises'**. On the northern face of Male Hill is a painting of a solitary **male lion**.

NORTHWESTERN BOTSWANA

WALKS

The hills can be explored along any of the five walking trails, as shown on the Tsodilo Hills map (p145). Some trails require a guide, while others, such as the popular Rhino Trail, can be explored individually with a map. Contact the headquarters at Main (Rhino) Camp for advice, maps and guides.

The summit of Male Hill is accessible along the **Male Hill Trail** by climbing from the hill's base near the male lion painting. The route is rough, rocky and plagued by false crests, but the view from the summit may well be the finest in the Kalahari.

Between Male and Female Hills, and linking the Male Hill Trail with the Rhino Trail, is the **Lion Trail**, though it doesn't pass anything particularly interesting.

From the Overland Camp Site, the steep and signposted **Rhino Trail** climbs past several distinctive paintings to a water pit where dragonflies and butterflies flit around a slimy green puddle. Near this site is an odd tree, once described to Laurens van der Post as the **Tree of True Knowledge** by the San guide who led him there. According to the guide, the greatest spirit knelt beside this fetid pool on the day of Creation. In the rocks beyond this pool are several 'hoof prints', which the Mbukushu believe were made by the cattle lowered onto the hill by the god Ngambe.

The Rhino Trail continues over the crest of a hill into a bizarre grassy valley flanked by peaks that seem a bit like an alternative universe. The route passes several rocky outcrops and rock paintings and then descends into the prominent hollow in the southeastern side of Female Hill.

On Female Hill, a short but hazardously rocky climb along the **Divuyu Trail** leads to Laurens van der Post's Panel, which contains elands and giraffes. This trail also leads to the Divuyu Village Remains.

Another route, the partially marked **Cliff Trail**, goes past the unassuming site known as the 'Origin of Sex' painting and around the northern end of Female Hill and into a deep and mysterious hidden valley. This trail also passes an amazing natural cistern (in a rock grotto near the northwestern corner of Female Hill), which has held water year-round for as long as anyone can remember. The San believe that this natural tank is inhabited by a great serpent with twisted horns, so visitors should warn the occupant of their approach by tossing a small stone into the water. This impressive feature is also flanked by several rock paintings.

Tours

Most lodges and tour operators in Maun can organise one-day air charters starting at US$5000 for five people, but they'll allow only a little time to climb or explore in this remarkable area.

Sleeping

Unofficial camping is possible anywhere, but be wary of wild animals, and please be respectful of local people.

Visitors can also camp at Main (Rhino) Camp, Malatso Camp, Overland Camp or Makoba Woods Camp for around P40 per person per night. Each campsite offers some shade and has pit toilets, though running water is not available. There is, however, drinkable bore water at Main (Rhino) Camp and at the borehole about 300m south of the airstrip. Basic supplies are available at Mbukushu village, but it's best to carry in your own food.

Getting There & Away

AIR

Most air-charter companies in Maun (p125) charge US$500 per plane (with five passengers) for a day trip to the hills.

CAR

Three routes from the Sehitwa–Shakawe road lead to the Tsodilo Hills (for which the GPS coordinates are S 18°45.677', E 21°44.833'). Each track is very sandy and rocky and only accessible by 4WD.

One southernmost turn-off (GPS: S 18°45.160', E 22°10.639') is signposted and starts 600m south of Sepupa, from where it's about 50km (2½ hours) to the headquarters. This is probably the best track (which is still not much of a recommendation) because it's the easiest to find and the one where you're most likely to come across other vehicles for a lift (or to be hauled out of the sand if stuck).

The northernmost turn-off (GPS: S 18°29.261', E 21°55.135') starts at the Samuchina Buffalo Fence (39.2km northwest of Sepopa and 17.2km southeast of Shakawe), but it's poorly signed. Follow the fence west for 7.6km, turn left (southwest) at the blue sign reading I-3 and follow the trail (a total of 36.2km from the main road). This is a contender for the Planet's Worst Drive, though – it's akin to spending three to four hours on a bucking bronco.

The third turn-off (GPS: S 18°35.836', E 21°59.956') starts 2.3km southeast of the turn-off to Nxamasere (ie 26km northwest of Sepupa and 32.7km southeast of Shakawe) but is not signposted, and the track is almost never used. Much of this track (37.6km in length) winds and twists through deep sand, passes abandoned villages and squeezes through disconcertingly narrow gaps among the dead trees.

SHAKAWE

For travellers, the sleepy outpost of Shakawe serves as a Botswanan entry or exit stamp, a staging point for trips into the Tsodilo Hills, or fishing or *mokoro* trips in the Okavango Panhandle, which stretches northwest from the delta to the Namibian border.

The heart of Shakawe is Wright's Trading Store, which has a self-service supermarket and bottle shop, and can often exchange pula for Namibian dollars or South African rand. There is now also a Barclay's ATM and a Shoprite supermarket where you can change money.

Six daily combis connect Shakawe with Maun (P80, seven hours), with stops in Gumare and Etsha 6. There's also a petrol station (no sign) east of the main road immediately before the turning into the centre, though it's not reliable, sometimes having no petrol. There's a small airport (well, runway) used for charter flights.

Kalahari

Botswana's landscapes are primeval, recalling in stone, thorns and brush the earliest memories of the human experience. But even in this country there is a space older than space, a land that speaks to some deep-seated essence within the DNA, a hearkening back to a sort of racial infancy. This impression of whence time began is utterly realised in the hot winds and snap of thorn bush under a tracker's feet in the Kalahari.

The Tswana call it the Kgalagadi: Land of Thirst. And this is dry, parched country. If not a land of sand dunes, then it's certainly a land painted by a sand palette: blood and mud reds and bleached bone yellow; dust that bites you back as you taste it in the morning. But come the nights this hard end of the colour wheel shifts into its cooler, sometimes white-cold shades: indigo nights that fade to deepest black, and blue stars ice-speckling the impossibly long horizon. Indeed, the local San insist that here you can hear 'the stars in song' behind the dark.

The Kalahari's 1.2-million-sq-km basin stretches across parts of the Democratic Republic of the Congo, Angola, Zambia, Namibia, Botswana, Zimbabwe and South Africa. The land is harsh, but it is also covered with trees and criss-crossed by ephemeral rivers and fossilised watercourses that burst with life when kissed by the rains.

Was this once the Garden of Eden? In some ancestral memory, perhaps. The land feels ancient, as do the San, its indigenous peoples, although the latter are also admirably adapting to the realities of the 21st century while trying to maintain the old ways. Visit them, and look into yourself in an elder place that makes you feel very, very young.

HIGHLIGHTS

- Feeling the wind strip you to primal happiness in the **Central Kalahari Game Reserve** (p155)
- Watching the moon rise as the sun sets and vice versa in **Kgalagadi Transfrontier Park** (p152)
- Getting a taste for the Kalahari at the small but accessible **Khutse Game Reserve** (p154)
- Learning at the feet of one of mankind's oldest cultures in **D'kar** (p150)
- Exploring the **Kgalagadi Villages** (p151), one of the most remote population centres in Botswana

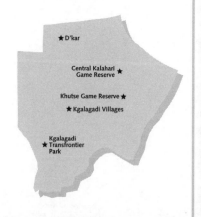

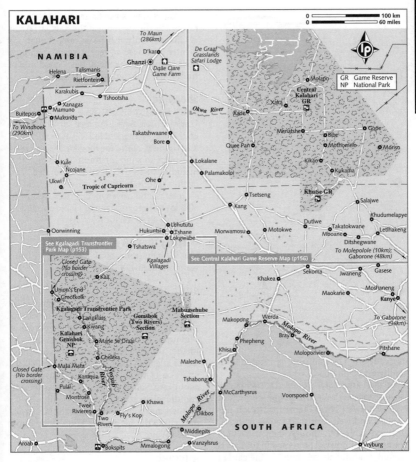

KALAHARI

See Kgalagadi Transfrontier Park Map (p153)

See Central Kalahari Game Reserve Map (p156)

GR Game Reserve
NP National Park

GHANZI

The 'capital of the Kalahari' isn't much more than a break in the dust. It may be difficult to understand how a town could prosper in such inhospitable terrain, but it helps that Ghanzi sits atop a 500km-long limestone ridge containing vast amounts of artesian water.

Although the town is not without a certain outback charm, travellers stop in Ghanzi either to fill up on petrol and stock up on supplies, or to break up the monotonous drive between Windhoek (Namibia) and Maun.

Interestingly enough, the name 'Ghanzi' comes from the San word for a one-stringed musical instrument with a gourd soundbox and *not* the Tswana word *gantsi* (flies), though this would arguably be more appropriate.

Sleeping

All of the below options can hook you up with wildlife drives, San cultural activities and the like.

Interesting alternatives to staying in Ghanzi are the Dqãe Qare Game Farm (p151) in nearby D'kar and De Graaf Grassland Safari Lodge (p151), 60km east.

Thakadu Bush Camp (☎ 659 6959, 7212 0695; www.thakadubushcamp.com; camping per person P30, s/d chalets P200/330; ☒) This popular campsite is a fun place to stop for a night or three, enjoying the boozy, friendly ambience and letting the stars soar overhead. There's a refreshing swimming pool on site and a pub-style restaurant and bar. The rough access road is just passable to low-slung 2WD vehicles –

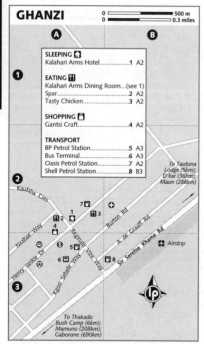

GHANZI

```
0          500 m
0          0.3 miles
```

SLEEPING 🏠
Kalahari Arms Hotel................1 A2

EATING 🍴
Kalahari Arms Dining Room...(see 1)
Spar..2 A2
Tasty Chicken........................3 A2

SHOPPING 🛍
Gantsi Craft.............................4 A2

TRANSPORT
BP Petrol Station.....................5 A3
Bus Terminal..........................6 A3
Oasis Petrol Station................7 A2
Shell Petrol Station.................8 B3

To Tautona
Lodge (5km);
D'kar (38km);
Maun (286km)

Kautsha Cres

Burton Rd

A de Graaff Rd

Sir Seretse Khama Rd

Airstrip

Nxabae Way

Henry Jankie Dr

Reginald Vize Way

Kgosi Sebele Way

To Thakadu
Bush Camp (6km);
Mamuno (208km);
Gaborone (690km)

use caution. The campsite is located 6km
southwest of Ghanzi.

Kalahari Arms Hotel (☎ 659 6298; www.kalahari
armshotel.com; Henry Jankie Dr; camping per person P30, s/d
P400/460; ❄ ⛲) This Ghanzi institution has
modern and well-furnished rooms with air-
con and cable TV, though the campsite is
cramped and noisy. The rooms in rondavels
(round, traditional-style huts) in the garden
by the pool are nicest and cost the same as
other accommodation.

Tautona Lodge (☎ 659 7499; www.tautonalodge.com;
camping per person P30, s/d 377/500; ❄ ⛲) This luxury lodge is 5km northeast of Ghanzi, and has
expansive grounds featuring t wo swimming
pools and a watering hole that is frequented by
antelopes. Spacious rooms in Batswana-style
thatched buildings have air-con and cable TV
and are decorated with traditional spreads.

Eating
If you're self-catering, there's a **Spar** (Reginald Vize
Way) supermarket in the centre of town.

Tasty Chicken (Henry Jankie Dr; meals US$2-4) The
local greasy spoon serves little more than fried
chicken and chips.

Kalahari Arms Dining Room (☎ 659 6298; meals
P35-70) The dining room at the Kalahari Arms
is Ghanzi's only real restaurant, though it's
greatly improved in recent years. Although
it's a bit pricey, the menu has a good mix of
traditional and continental dishes.

Shopping
Gantsi Craft (☎ 659 6241; Henry Jankie Dr; ⏰ 8am-
12.30pm & 2-5pm Mon-Fri, 8am-noon Sat) This cooperative was established in 1953 as a craft outlet
and training centre for the San. It's an excellent place to shop for traditional San crafts,
including hand-dyed textiles, decorated bags,
leather aprons, bows and arrows, musical instruments, and woven mats. Prices are 30% to
50% lower than in Maun or Gaborone and all
proceeds go to the local artists.

Getting There & Away
For information about travelling to/from
Namibia, see p174.

BUS & COMBI
To Maun (P40, five hours), one bus leaves
at 9am and another at 3.30pm, travelling
via D'kar (P8, 45 minutes). To the border at
Mamuno (P20, three hours) – but not any
further into Namibia – a combi (minibus)
leaves at about 10am. To Gaborone (P80, 11
hours), a TJ Motlogewa's Express bus leaves at
about 7am, 9am and 10am most days (best to
enquire with your accommodation).

Buses and combis leave from the bus terminal behind the BP petrol station along Kgosi
Sebele Way.

HITCHING
Most traffic heading northeast is bound for
Maun, so it's easy to hitch a ride there from
anywhere past the airport along Sir Seretse
Khama Rd. To get to Gaborone, look for a lift
at the Oasis petrol station on Henry Jankie Dr
or the Shell station on A de Graaff Rd.

D'KAR
This small village just north of Ghanzi is
home to a large community of Ncoakhoe San
who operate an art gallery, cultural centre
and wildlife ranch under the auspices of the
Kuru Family of Organisations (KFO; www.kuru.co.bw),
an affiliated group of non-governmental
organisations (NGOs) working towards the
empowerment of the indigenous peoples of
Southern Africa.

HENDRIK MATTHYS VAN ZYL

Since the 19th century, Ghanzi has served as a rest stop for traders and travellers crossing the Kalahari. Although the town has seen its fair share of odd characters, perhaps the most infamous (and ruthless) individual to pass through was a man by the name of Hendrik Matthys van Zyl.

During the 1860s and '70s, this former politician from the Transvaal in South Africa crossed the Kalahari on several occasions, trading munitions, shooting elephants and killing San along the way. From 1877 to 1878 Van Zyl based himself in the town of Ghanzi and proceeded to shoot more than 400 elephants, which yielded no less than 4 tonnes of ivory. With the proceeds from the ivory sales, Van Zyl built a two-storey mansion with stained-glass windows, filled it with imported furniture, and lived like a king in the poverty-stricken wilderness.

However, Van Zyl was suddenly and mysteriously killed in 1880, which gave rise to a series of legends surrounding the cause of his death. According to one tale, Van Zyl was murdered by a revenge-seeking San, possibly one of his own servants. Another tale claims that he was murdered by the Khoikhoi people in retaliation for past injustices. Shortly after his death, Van Zyl's wife, daughter and three sons disappeared to the Transvaal and were never heard of again.

Prior to his death, a rumour circulated that Van Zyl hid a large portion of his fortune in Gcwihaba (Drotsky's) Cave (p142), although nothing has been recovered to date.

The **Contemporary San Art Gallery & Craft Shop** (☎ 659 7242; admission free; ☷ 8am-12.30pm & 2-5pm Mon-Fri) provides opportunities for local artists to create and sell arts, crafts and paintings. There is also a small gift shop with a wonderful assortment of souvenirs, including ostrich-eggshell jewellery, CDs of San music, leather products, the requisite bow and arrow set, and a few carvings. The gallery acts as a de facto tourist office, and an adjacent shop sells basic supplies and drinks. It's situated along D'kar's only road, near the turn-off to the Ghanzi–Maun highway.

The **Cultural Centre, Museum & Art Workshop** (☎ 659 7704; admission free; ☷ 8am-12.30pm & 2-5pm Mon-Fri) contains several exhibits on San culture, while the attached workshop works in conjunction with the art gallery to encourage local participation in KFO-run projects. The complex is behind the Reformed Church, and is well signposted from along the village road.

Dqãe Qare Game Farm (☎ 7252 7321; www.kuru. co.bw; admission P15, camping per person P30, San huts per person with/without half-board P320/250) is a 7500-hectare private reserve where visitors can participate in traditional activities organised by the local San community. There are guided bushwalks (P50 per hour) and plenty of opportunities to gain insights into traditional hunting and gathering techniques. Money spent at the farm is invested in the community. Although it's possible to drop by for an hour or two, spending a night either camping or in one of the San huts is a great opportu-

nity to meet locals in a relaxed setting. The ranch is 15km southeast of D'kar and only accessible by 4WD. If you don't have a 4WD, arrange transport at the ranch office at the back of the art gallery and craft shop in D'kar. These transfers cost US$25 per four-passenger vehicle to the farm.

Unaffiliated with KFO but highly recommended by readers is **Grassland Safari Lodge** (☎ 7210 4270; www.grasslandlodge.com; r low/shoulder/high season US$375/400/475), located well off the beaten track about 60km from main Ghanzi–Maun road. This admirable lodge runs a predator-protection program that temporarily houses lions, cheetahs, leopards and wild dogs that are often shot by farmers protecting their livestock. It also conducts wildlife drives and horse safaris and hosts excellent cultural activities with local San – Grassland's owner, Nelltjie Bowers, can speak the clicking Naro language. Road transfers are available from Maun (US$140) and Ghanzi (US$30), and there are charter flights from Maun (US$300) as well – all of the above require a minimum of two guests. Contact the lodge in advance for directions to the property.

KGALAGADI VILLAGES

Hukuntsi, Tshane, Lokgwabe and Lehututu are collectively known as the Kgalagadi Villages, and were one of the most remote areas in Botswana prior to the paving of the road leading to Kang. For travellers, the villages serve as the jumping-off point for Kgalagadi Transfrontier Park.

The main commercial centre for the four villages, **Hukuntsi**, is a good place to fill up on petrol and stock up on supplies. Along the route from Hukuntsi to Tshatswa (about 60km to the southwest) are sparkling-white salt pans that fill with water during the rainy season and support large populations of gemsbok, ostriches and hartebeest.

Tshane is 12km east of Hukuntsi and has a colonial police station dating from the early 1900s.

Lokgwabe, which lies 11km south of Hukuntsi, was settled by the Nama leader Simon Kooper, who sought British protection in Bechuanaland after leading the 1904 Nama rebellion in Namibia. He was subsequently pursued across the Kalahari by German troops and 800 camels. German detritus, including empty tins of corned beef, still litters the route.

Named after the sound made by ground hornbills, **Lehututu**, located 10km northwest of Tshane, was once a major trading post but is now little more than a spot in the desert.

There are no hotels in the area – visitors must either know someone to stay with or carry a tent. If you're camping, ask for permission and advice about a suitable campsite from the *kgosi* (chief) in any of the villages.

Hukuntsi is 114km southwest along a paved road from Kang and 271km north of Tshabong along a sandy 4WD track.

KGALAGADI TRANSFRONTIER PARK

In 2000 the former Mabuasehube-Gemsbok National Park was combined with South Africa's former Kalahari Gemsbok National Park to create the new Kgalagadi Transfrontier Park. The result is a 28,400-sq-km bi-national park that is one of the largest and most pristine wilderness areas on the continent. The park is also the only place in Botswana where you'll see the shifting sand dunes that many mistakenly believe to be typical of the Kalahari. This is true desert; in the summer it can reach 45°C, and at night it can drop to -10°C.

Kgalagadi is home to large herds of springbok, gemsbok, eland and wildebeest as well as a full complement of predators, including lions, cheetahs, leopards, wild dogs, jackals and hyenas. Over 250 bird species are present, including several endemic species of larks and bustards.

Information

The park is geographically and administratively divided into three sections: Gemsbok (Two Rivers) Section and Mabuasehube Section in Botswana and the Kalahari Gemsbok National Park in South Africa.

The two sections of the park in Botswana are administered by the Department of Wildlife & National Parks (DWNP), so camping is only allowed at designated campsites and must be booked at the DWNP office in Gaborone (p81) or Maun (p121). You will not be permitted into the Botswana side of the park without a campsite reservation.

Refer to the National Parks chapter, p26, for information about the opening times and admission and camping costs for the national parks.

The two main gates (where entry permits are bought) are at Twee Rivieren (South Africa) and Two Rivers (Botswana). To reach the Mabuasehube Section, there are gates along the tracks from the south, north and east, but entry permits must be bought at the park headquarters (Game Scout Camp at Mpaathutlwa Pan). There is also a 4WD track from Tshatswa to the new northern gate of the Gemsbok (Two Rivers) Section at Kaa.

Campers staying at the Polentswa and Rooiputs campsites can pick up firewood at Two Rivers campsite (Botswana), while petrol and basic food supplies are available at Twee Rivieren (South Africa). There are also reliable petrol supplies at Hukuntsi, Jwaneng, Kang and Tshabong. Maps of the combined park are available at the gates at Two Rivers and Twee Rivieren.

The best time to visit is from December to May.

Sights
MABUASEHUBE SECTION

The Mabuasehube section of the park covers 1800 sq km, and focuses on the low red dunes around three major and several minor salt-pan complexes. The largest, Mabuasehube Pan, is used as a salt lick by migrating herds in late winter and early spring.

TWO RIVERS SECTION

Although you can now reach the Two Rivers section from either Kaa or Mabuasehube, access is still easiest from South Africa. The pools of rainwater that collect in the dry riverbeds of the Auob and Nossob Rivers provide

the best opportunities for wildlife viewing in
the park.

KALAHARI GEMSBOK NATIONAL PARK (SOUTH AFRICA)
This section is characterised by a semi-desert
landscape of Kalahari dunes, camelthorn-
dotted grasslands and the dry beds of the
Auob and Nossob Rivers. One advantage of
visiting this side of the park is that many roads
are accessible by 2WD.

Activities
WILDERNESS TRAILS
There are several challenging wilderness tracks
through this remote corner of Botswana. The
Nossob Eco Trail is a four-day jaunt, entirely self-
catered, that stops at basic campsites along
the way. Hand-held radios are provided for
the journey, which requires a minimum of
two and a maximum of five vehicles. The
cost per vehicle (maximum five occupants) is
R1730. You must prebook through the DWNP
in Gaborone (☎ 318 0774). The **Swartbas
Wilderness Trail** is a two-day hiking track with
basic camping facilities accessible by sturdy
4WD. It is closed from April to November;
book on ☎ 054-561 2000.

Sleeping
All campsites in the Botswana sections of the
park must be booked in advance; see opposite.

Bookings for huts and chalets on the South
African side are recommended from June to

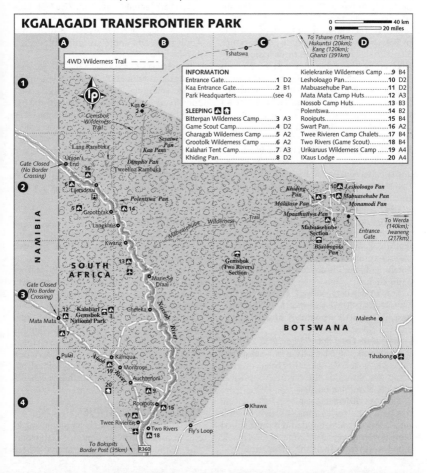

September and during all weekends and public and school holidays. Contact the **National Parks Board** (☎ Pretoria 012-428 9111; PO Box 787, Pretoria, 0001) or the park directly on ☎ 054-561 2000.

MABUASEHUBE SECTION
There are rudimentary campsites at Lesholoago Pan, Game Scout Camp, Khiding Pan and Mabuasehube Pan. Facilities are limited to pit latrines, but all (except Khiding Pan) have waterholes for viewing wildlife. Water (not suitable for drinking) is reliably available at Game Scout Camp.

TWO RIVERS SECTION
Two Rivers (Game Scout; not to be confused with Game Scout Camp in the Mabuasehube Section), opposite Twee Rivieren (South Africa), has cold showers and sit-down flush toilets. It is accessible from north of Bokspits in Botswana without having to go into South Africa first. There are also three basic campsites along the Botswana side of Nossob River: Rooiputs, with shade and rustic ablution blocks about 30km up from Two Rivers; Polentswa, with shade and latrines but no running water; and Swart Pan, which can only be accessed from the South African side.

KALAHARI GEMSBOK NATIONAL PARK
Huts and chalets are all equipped with bedding and cooking equipment. Each place has a shop that sells basic supplies, such as food, drinks (including alcohol) and usually petrol.

Twee Rivieren Camp Chalets (camping R120-130, chalets R520-740; 🞱 🞲) The most accessible and popular rest camp on either side of the river features a swimming pool and an outdoor bar-restaurant. Rustic chalets have modern amenities including air-con, hot showers and a full kitchen.

Nossob Camp Huts (camping R130, chalets from R460, 4-bed guest houses R910, 6-bed cottages R730) This fairly basic rest camp is attractively situated alongside the Nossob River.

Mata Mata Camp Huts (camping R130, 2 bed with shared bathroom R450, 6-bed cottages for 1-4 people with kitchen & bathroom R760) Also fairly basic, this rest camp lies alongside the scenic Auob River near the Namibian border.

Bitterpan Wilderness Camp (tents R690) Getting out here requires coming through Nossob on a one-way route, but damn if these stilted tents hovering over a shimmering waterhole aren't worth it for their sheer romance.

Gharagab Wilderness Camp (cabins R720) Blending into the wiry bush of the northern portion of the park, Gharagab is a dusty, surreally beautiful spot for watching sunsets over the local waterhole.

Grootolk Wilderness Camp (cabins R760) Only 20km from the Botswana–Namibia–South African border and several eons from the modern world, these desert cabins are a desert escapist's dream.

Kielekranke Wilderness Camp (cabins R760) Another gorgeous set of tented cabins set deep within the Kalahari.

Urikaruus Wilderness Camp (cabins R760) A stilted camp hidden amidst camelthorn trees that has good wildlife viewing near its dry riverbed and waterhole.

Kalahari Tented Camp (tents R790-885) This series of 15 tents (including a honeymoon pitch - nice) perches over the dried-out Auob river and some stunning blood-red thirst lands.

!Xaus Lodge (☎ in South Africa 27 21-701 7860; www.xauslodge.co.za; chalets R2200; 🞱 🞲) If you really feel like splurging, book a night in Kgalagadi's only luxury accommodation. Owned and operated by the local San community, the lodge is a dry, dreamy fantasy in ochre, decorated with wall hangings made by a local women's sewing collective (see more of their work at www.vezokuhle.heksie.co.za) The on-site pool feels a little much, but the San staff, cultural activities and excellent wildlife drives are all suitably mind-blowing.

Getting There & Away
Airstrips (for chartered flights only) are located at Ghanzi, Tshabong, Twee Rivieren and Nossob Camp.

The Two Rivers Section is accessible from the south via Two Rivers and from the north via Kaa. Access to the Kalahari Gemsbok National Park is via Twee Rivieren – both are about 53km north of the Bokspits border crossing. The border crossings to Namibia at Union's End and Mata Mata are closed because traffic disturbs the wildlife. Access to the Mabuasehube Section is possible from the south (via Tshabong), north (via Tshane) and east (via Werda).

KHUTSE GAME RESERVE
This 2500-sq-km reserve is a popular weekend excursion for residents of Gaborone. The name Khutse, which means 'where

---

THE KALAHARI CONSERVATION SOCIETY

The Kalahari Conservation Society (KCS) is a non-governmental organisation (NGO) that was established in 1982 by former president of Botswana Sir Ketumile Masire. KCS was formed in recognition of the pressures on Botswana's wildlife and has spent the last two decades actively collaborating with other NGOs and government departments to help conserve the country's environment and natural resources. To date, the organisation has been involved in more than 50 conservation projects in the Kalahari, Chobe National Park, Moremi Game Reserve and the Okavango Delta.

The KCS aims to promote knowledge of Botswana's rich wildlife resources and its environment through education and publicity; to encourage, and sometimes finance, research into issues affecting these resources and their conservation; and to promote and support policies of conservation towards wildlife and its habitat. To achieve these objectives, the KCS relies on private donations, and encourages a membership (US$50 per year) for interested parties.

For more information, visit the website at www.kcs.org.bw.

---

one kneels to drink' in Sekwena (the local dialect of Tswana), indicates that the area once had water, though today the reserve experiences continual droughts. Although wildlife concentrations in the reserve are minimal, its popularity is due to its ease of accessibility and the solitude of the pans and savannah scrub.

Information

Khutse is administered by the DWNP, so camping is only allowed at designated campsites (see p152). You will not be permitted into the park without a campsite reservation.

Refer to the National Parks chapter, p26, for information about the opening times of the national parks as well as for admission and camping costs.

The last reliable petrol supply is at Molepolole, while food and drinks are available at Molepolole, Letlhakeng and Salajwe.

The best time to visit Khutse is during spring and autumn. Try to avoid weekends and holidays, as Khutse will be full of visitors.

Sleeping

Khutse boasts several superbly located campsites, though visitors should bring their own drinking water and food.

Wildlife Camp (Map p156; Game Scout Camp) is the only camp with running (non-drinkable) water, sit-down flush toilets and (cold) showers. It's near the entry gate to the reserve.

Between Khutse I Pan & Khutse II Pan, Khutse Camp Site (Map p156) lacks facilities, though it is popular and accessible.

Both the following basic campsites are near vital water sources, which are popular with wildlife, including cheetahs.

Molose Waterhole (Map p156; S 23°23.023', E 24°11.182')

Moreswe Pan (Map p156; S 23°33.510', E 24°06.826')

Getting There & Away

The entrance gate and park office are 55km from Gaborone. The road is paved until Letlhakeng, though it's a long (103km) and sandy (4WD only) road to Khutse.

CENTRAL KALAHARI GAME RESERVE

The dry heart of the dry south of a dry continent, the Central Kalahari Game Reserve (CKGR) is, at all times, awe inspiring. Trekkers, overlanders and wanderers return from here with fuller beards, sunken eyes and dazed smiles. There is…something in the dry air, and the seemingly empty landscape conceals a very deep sense of meaningful connection to those who enter it.

Covering 52,000 sq km (about the size of Denmark), this is Africa's largest protected area. Although it was originally established in 1961 as a private reservation for the San, today it functions primarily as a wildlife reserve. The southern and western parts of the CKGR are still home to small populations of San, although a recent wave of forced relocations has greatly reduced this population. (For more information on the San's history and their contemporary situation, see p63).

CKGR is perhaps best known for Deception (Letiahau) Valley, the site of Mark and Delia Owens' 1974 to 1981 brown hyena study, which is described in their book *Cry of the Kalahari*.

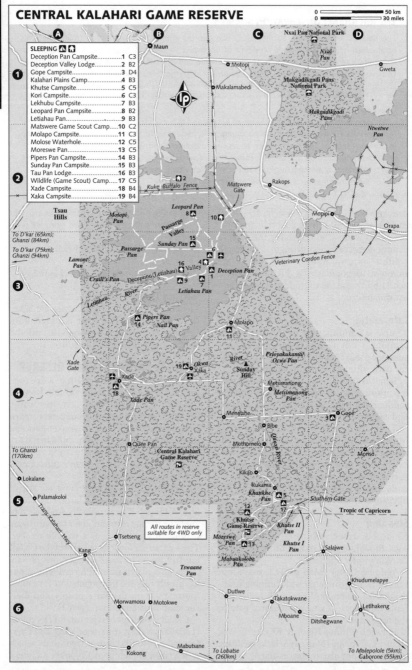

CENTRAL KALAHARI GAME RESERVE

| | | |
|0| |50 km|
|0| |30 miles|

SLEEPING
Deception Pan Campsite	1	C3
Deception Valley Lodge	2	B2
Gope Campsite	3	D4
Kalahari Plains Camp	4	B3
Khutse Campsite	5	C5
Kori Campsite	6	C3
Lekhubu Campsite	7	B3
Leopard Campsite	8	B2
Letiahau Pan	9	B3
Matswere Game Scout Camp	10	C2
Molapo Campsite	11	C3
Molose Waterhole	12	C5
Moreswe Pan	13	C5
Pipers Pan Campsite	14	B3
Sunday Pan Campsite	15	B3
Tau Pan Lodge	16	B3
Wildlife (Game Scout) Camp	17	C5
Xade Campsite	18	B4
Xaka Campsite	19	B4

All routes in reserve suitable for 4WD only

Three similar fossil valleys – the Okwa, the Quoxo (Meratswe) and the Passarge – also bring topographical relief to the virtually featureless expanses, although the rivers ceased flowing more than 16,000 years ago.

Most visitors base themselves in and around Deception (Letiahau) Valley, which attracts large amounts of wildlife, especially after the rains. The reserve is renowned for brown hyenas, which emerge just after dark, and you may also see lions, giraffes, wildebeest, springbok and, just perhaps, cheetahs and leopards. The pans in the northern part of the reserve – Letiahau, Pipers, Sunday and Passarge – are artificially pumped to provide water for animals.

Information

The CKGR is administered by the DWNP, so camping is only allowed at designated campsites, which must be booked in advance (see p152). You will not be permitted into the park without a campsite reservation.

Refer to the National Parks chapter, p26, for information about the opening times of the national parks as well as the costs of admission and camping.

The nearest reliable petrol supplies are located in Molepolole, Ghanzi, Maun and Rakops. The best time to visit is April/May and September/October. Collecting firewood is banned in the CKGR (and is virtually impossible anyway), so bring your own.

Tours

Most lodges and tour operators in Maun (p123) can organise trips around the CKGR when there's enough demand. Trips can cost anywhere from US$150 to US$250 per day, though prices can vary greatly according to the season. It's generally easier to get a lower price if you're booking as part of a group, so talk to a few different tour operators, bargain hard and don't agree to a trip unless you're sure it's what you want.

Sleeping

There are basic campsites at Deception Pan, Leopard Pan, Kori, Lekhubu, Letiahau Pan, Sunday Pan and Pipers Pan, but all lack facilities. The well-known Deception Pan enjoys a few rare, shady acacia trees, while Pipers Pan is known for its bizarre ghost trees. Other remote campsites include those at Xaka, Molapo, Gope and Xade in the southern part of the reserve. Marginally drinkable water is available only at the Matswere Game Scout Camp, near the northeastern gates of the reserve.

Within the CKGR, Tau Pan Lodge and Kalahari Plains Camp are each usually accessed via charter flight; see below.

Deception Valley Lodge (☎ in UK 1212 868393; www .deceptionvalley.co.za; per person low/high season US$550/750; 🏠) On the edge of the reserve, this exclusive bush retreat was designed to blend into the surrounding nature without detracting from its ambience. Soothing rooms blend Victorian and African design elements, and feature a private lounge and outdoor shower. The lodge is about 120km south of Maun, and the route is accessible to 2WD vehicles during the dry season.

Tau Pan Lodge (☎ 686 1449 www.kwando.co.bw; per person US$360) The first camp to be opened within the CKGR, this solar-powered luxury lodge overlooks magnificent Tau Pan from a rugged sand ridge. Wildlife drives and San-led bushwalks are the order of the day, and neither disappoint, especially when the rains hit and this becomes one of Southern Africa's best wildlife-viewing locations. The lodge maintains a strong eco sensibility throughout, and comes highly recommended by former guests.

Kalahari Plains Camp (☎ in South Africa 27-11 807 1800; www.wilderness-safaris.com) Run by the reliably luxurious Wilderness Safaris, these six posh, solar-powered tents are maintained in impeccable style in a gorgeous location near Deception Pass. Rare black-maned Kalahari lions prowl nearby, and the exclusive service plus total isolation makes for serious out-of-body travel joy.

Getting There & Away

Airstrips (for chartered flights only) are located near Xade, Xaka and Deception Pan.

A 4WD is essential to get around the reserve, and a compass (or GPS equipment) and petrol reserves are also recommended. Several 4WD tracks lead into the CKGR, but only three are official entrances. The main one is Matswere Gate (GPS: S 21°09.047', E 24°00.445') – from Rakops, take the 4WD track north for 2.5km, turn west and follow the signs; and from Maun, take the Maun–Nata highway for 54km, turn south to Makalamabedi and follow the signs.

The Southern Gate (GPS: S 23°21.388', E 24°36.470') is along a track from Khutse Game Reserve. The turn-off to Xade Gate (not far from Xade Wildlife Camp) starts near D'kar.

Botswana Directory

CONTENTS

ACCOMMODATION

Botswana has a number of comfortable campsites and an array of upper-midrange hotels and top-end lodges – but there is little in between. Budget travellers who do not want to camp may have to, so it is recommended to take a tent anyway.

Where appropriate, accommodation options are split into budget, midrange and top-end categories for ease of reference. Upmarket places tend to price in US dollars as opposed to pula, and we have listed prices using both currencies. In general, a budget double room is anything under P350. Midrange accommodation is priced anywhere from P350 to P800. Note that there's a real dearth of midrange places

in the Okavango Delta, which is largely given over to luxury camps and top-end lodges that can set you back around US$500, although this can rise stratospherically to around US$1000 in the delta. Discounted rates for children are rare, although a number of lodges do offer special family rooms.

While most budget and lower-midrange options tend to have a standard room price, many top-end places change their prices according to season. High season is from June to November, low season corresponds to the rains (December to March or April) and the shoulder is a short April and May window. A 10% government tax is levied on hotels and lodges (but not all campsites) and is included in prices listed in this book.

Camping

Just about everywhere of interest, including all major national parks, has a campsite. Public camping areas in the national parks and reserves are run by the Department of Wildlife and National Parks (DWNP) and are invariably basic, often with pit latrines and cold showers, but they are always in superb locations. These campsites *must* be booked in advance and they fill up fast in busy periods like school holidays. For more information on how to make bookings, see p28.

A number of privately run campsites offer better facilities than the DWNP, and some hotels and lodges also provide camping areas. Most private and hotel/lodge campsites have sit-down toilets, showers (often hot), braai (barbecue) pits and washing areas. One definite attraction is that campers can use the hotel bars and restaurants and splash around the hotel swimming pool for free. These

---

BOOK ACCOMMODATION ONLINE

For more accommodation reviews and recommendations by Lonely Planet authors, check out the online booking service at www.lonelyplanet.com. You'll find the true, insider lowdown on the best places to stay. Reviews are thorough and independent. Best of all, you can book online.

PRACTICALITIES

- Botswana uses the metric system for weights and measures (see inside front cover).

- Buy or watch videos on the PAL system.

- Two types of plugs are used; the South African type, with three round pins, and the UK type, with three square pins; the current is 220/240V, 50Hz.

- The government-owned *Daily News* covers government issues as well as some limited international news. Of more interest to visitors is the *Botswana Advertiser*, available in Gaborone and eastern Botswana. Gaborone newspapers include the *Mirror*, the *Botswana Gazette*, the *Botswana Guardian*, the *Midweek Sun* and *Mmegi/Reporter*, which has an Arts & Culture Review. Elsewhere, regional weeklies like Maun's *Ngami Times* are a better source of local information.

- Several radio stations broadcast news in English and Tswana and play local and foreign music. Yarona (106.6FM) and GABZFM (96.2FM) broadcast around Gaborone, while RB2 (103FM) is the commercial network of Radio Botswana. With a short-wave radio, you can easily pick up the BBC World Service and international services from Europe.

- The Botswana TV (BTV) broadcasts news (in Tswana) and sports (in English and Tswana) and an array of US sitcoms. Gaborone Broadcasting Corporation (GBCTV) can be picked up around the capital. Government-run South African stations are also available. Most midrange hotels offer M-Net, a pay-TV station, and most top-end hotels also offer satellite TV.

---

campsites cost about P30 to P60 (rarely up to P100) per person per night. Advance bookings are not normally required and some campsites do not accept bookings anyway.

Camping in the wild is permitted outside national parks, reserves, private land and away from government freehold areas. If you want to camp near a village, obtain permission from the village leader or police station and enquire about a suitable site.

Hotels

Every major town has at least one hotel, and the larger towns and tourist areas, like Gaborone and Maun, offer several in different price ranges. However, you won't find anything as cheap as the budget accommodation in Namibia, and the really cheap places in Botswana are likely to double as brothels. There's a relatively high demand for hotel rooms in Gaborone from business travellers, so it pays to book ahead. Elsewhere in Botswana, advance booking is not normally necessary.

The range of hotel accommodation listed in this book includes rondavels, which are detached rooms or cottages with a private bathroom; B&B-type places, often with a shared bathroom – mostly in Gaborone; motel-style units with a private bathroom and, sometimes, cooking facilities – usually along the

highways of eastern Botswana; and luxury hotels in major towns.

Lodges

Most of Botswana's lodges (sometimes called 'camps') are found in Chobe National Park, the Tuli Block, Moremi Game Reserve and all over the Okavango Delta. It's impossible to generalise about them: some lie along the highways and others occupy remote wilderness areas, and they range from tiny sites with established luxury tents to large areas with brick or reed-built chalets.

Prices at lodges are always high, though: US$500/700 per person per night in the low/high season is not uncommon. And most places are only accessible by 4WD transfer or air, an extra US$100 to US$200.

ACTIVITIES

Most holidays to Botswana are an action-packed blur of 4WD off-road trails, bush trekking and poling gently along the Okavango Delta's waterways in a traditional *mokoro* (dugout canoe). In all fairness, the eye-watering prices of nearly all top-end lodges include any number of exciting activities, and over the last few years a heartening number of local cooperatives have begun to spring up and are offering exciting adventures at a more affordable price.

Hiking

Major hiking trails are not a feature of Botswana's activity landscape in the same way they are in Namibia. This is largely because the main areas of attraction in Botswana are densely vegetated national parks that are full of wild animals red in tooth and claw.

However, most lodges in the Okavango Delta, along with those in the Central Kalahari Game Reserve and the Makgadikgadi Pans offer nature trails. The treks run out of Jack's Camp in the Makgadikgadi Pans (p106), for example, are a fascinating opportunity to explore the salt pans with San guides, who can point out the hidden details of the landscape and its specially adapted flora and fauna. Another top hiking spot is the Tsodilo Hills (p146) in north-western Botswana, where trails lead up to thousands of rock-art sites. Other popular walking spots are Gaborone Dam (p92), Kgale Hill (p92), Kanye (p93), the Mokolodi Nature Reserve (p92) and Mochudi (p89) – all near Gaborone.

Organised hikes with a guide can be arranged for guests through most lodges, and can usually form part of a *mokoro* trip in the Okavango Delta. Many tour operators are now also offering multi-day hikes between camps.

Horse Riding

Cantering among herds of zebras and wildebeest is an unforgettable experience and the horse-riding safaris in Botswana are second to none. You'll need to be an experienced rider as most horseback safaris in Botswana don't take beginners – after all, you need to be able to get yourself out of trouble should you encounter it. The privately owned Mashatu Game Reserve (p101) in the arid Tuli Block is one of the few places where novice riders can also have a go, as is African Animal Adventures (p123) in Maun.

Mokoro Trips

Travelling around the channels of the Okavango Delta on a *mokoro* is a wonderful experience that is not to be missed. The *mokoro* is poled along the waterways by a skilled poler, much like an African gondola. Although you won't be spotting much wildlife from such a low viewpoint, it's a great way to appreciate the delta's birdlife. For more info on *mokoro* trips in the delta, see the boxed texts, p138 and p124.

Motorboat & Fishing Trips

The only two places where motorboats can operate for wildlife cruises and fishing trips are along the Okavango River and Chobe River. The most popular form of freshwater fishing is fly fishing for tigerfish, for which you'll need to head for the deeper and faster-flowing waters of the Okavango Panhandle to places like Drotsky's Cabins (p139) and Xaro Lodge (p139). The fly-fishing season is from August to November; remember that it is considered good sport to catch and release the fish.

Quadbikes

Some lodges in the Makgadikgadi Pans area in northeastern Botswana offer trips across the expansive salt pans on four-wheeled quadbikes, also called ATVs (all-terrain vehicles). These are safe to drive, require no experience, do not need a car or motorbike licence and are great fun.

Scenic Flights

Another thrilling activity on offer in the Okavango Delta is a scenic flight of fancy in a light aircraft or helicopter (see p125). These can be arranged either in Maun directly with the operator or through your accommodation. Prices range between US$100 and US$200 per person.

BUSINESS HOURS

Opening hours across Botswana are fairly standard and it seems the whole country closes down on Sunday.

Private businesses and shops are open from 8am or 9am to 5pm or 6pm Monday to Friday (but often close for lunch between noon and 2pm), and 9am to 1pm Saturday. Banks are open from 8am to 3pm Monday to Friday, and 8am to 12.30pm Saturday. Post offices normally operate from 7.30am to 12.30pm and 2pm to 4.30pm Monday to Friday, and 7.30am to 12.30pm Saturday. All government offices are open from 7.30am to 12.30pm and 2pm to 4.30pm Monday to Friday. Restaurant opening hours are fairly standard, with most places opening all day between around 10.30am to 11pm Monday to Saturday. Throughout this guide we have only listed non-standard opening hours.

CHILDREN

You will find it very difficult to enjoy the best of Botswana while travelling with very young children. In fact only a few camps even welcome kids, and those that do usually have an age minimum of about 12 or 16 years, so check first. A notable exception is Seba Camp (p132).

All this is really just common sense, as small children and wild animals don't tend to mix well. It's also very uncommon to find high chairs in restaurants, cots for kids in hotels, nappy (diaper) changing facilities or babysitting agencies.

Practicalities

As a parent you will need to be extra vigilant in the bush. Almost no private or public campsite in the country has enough fencing to keep animals out and children in, and there are the additional hazards of camp fires, mosquitos, snakes and biting/stinging insects. Remember that most mosquito repellents with high levels of DEET may be unsuitable for young children.

The heat and dust, and the long and boring trips by bus or car, may take their toll; so come well prepared with lots of activity books, CDs and games. Road safety is also a big issue and if you're travelling with kids you'd be wise to invest in car hire. You should also check in advance whether you can hire car seats from your rental firm; to be on the safe side it's a good idea to bring your own.

Health-wise, Botswana is a comparatively safe country, and medical facilities are good.

The Botswanan government makes some concessions to travellers with children: eg entry fees to national parks and reserves are free for children under eight and half-price for those aged from eight to 17 years old.

For invaluable general advice on taking the family abroad, see Lonely Planet's *Travel with Children* by Brigitte Barta et al.

Sights & Activities

Travelling by camper van and camping or 'faking it' in luxury tented lodges are thrilling experiences for young and old alike, while attractions such as viewing the abundant wildlife in Chobe National Park (p109) or quadbiking across the Makgadikgadi Pans provide ample entertainment.

Other activities like horse riding, cycling safaris, scenic flights over the Okavango Delta

and *mokoro* trips are the stuff of dreams for most kids, and you can always nip over the border to Zambia for some extreme activities like rafting, lion walks, river boarding and cruising (see p183). Camps in Botswana that do allow children often offer specialist children's guides and imaginative activity programs, which might include things like making paper from elephant dung!

Full-scale safaris are generally suited to older children. Remember that hours of driving and animal viewing can be an eternity for children, so you'll need to break trips up with plenty of pit stops and time spent poolside where possible.

CLIMATE CHARTS

Botswana has a subtropical desert climate, characterised by extremes of temperature between day and night, low rainfall and sometimes stifling humidity. December to February is the wettest time of the year, characterised by torrential downpours and high humidity (typically 50% to 80%). Daytime temperatures can often reach 40°C, although they tend to average around the high 20s. Flooding is frequent and in years of high rainfall, like 2005, it can bring parts of the country to a standstill.

From March to May the rains ease off and the temperature subsides to an ambient 25°C, making this one of the best times of the year to visit. From late May to August, rain is rare anywhere in the country. Days are normally

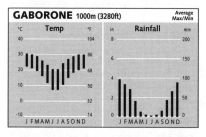

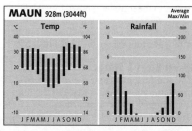

clear and warm, but nights can be cold. In the Kalahari, below-freezing temperatures are possible in June and July and, where there's enough humidity, frost.

The driest part of the year is September to October, when temperatures start to rise again. Typical daytime temperatures are around 30°C and humidity is between 20% and 40%. Also see p15 for the best times of the year to travel in Botswana.

CUSTOMS REGULATIONS

Most items from elsewhere in the Southern African Customs Union (SACU) – Namibia, South Africa, Lesotho and Swaziland – may be imported duty free. Major goods brought into Botswana from any other country are subject to normal duties.

Visitors may bring into Botswana the following amounts of duty-free items: up to 400 cigarettes, 50 cigars or 250g of tobacco; 2L of wine or 1L of beer or spirits; and 50mL of perfume or 250mL of eau de cologne. Animal products like meat, milk and eggs cannot be brought into the country.

Firearms require a temporary import permit and must be declared at the time of arrival, and cars may not be sold in Botswana without payment of duty.

There is no restriction on currency; however, you will need to declare any pula or foreign currency you have on you when entering the country. Foreigners can export up to P10,000, or the equivalent in foreign currency, without declaring it.

DANGERS & ANNOYANCES

Botswana is not your average African country. It is modern and developed and most things work. You can safely drink the tap water in the towns and cities and you do not need protection against cholera or yellow fever.

HIV/AIDS is a serious issue but, unless you fail to take common-sense precautions, there should be no undue risk. In fact, the greatest danger to the traveller is posed by wildlife and the inherent risks of driving in the bush. For tips on how to avoid any close encounters with wild animals, see the boxed text, p50.

Insect Bites & Stings

The south, south-central and southwest of the country are malaria free and the disease is a minimal threat in the remainder of the country in winter (May to July). For the rest of the time you should use prophylactic treatment. The right clothing, mosquito nets and appropriate repellents are 80% of the battle.

Another waterborne disease is bilharzia, which is usually present in stagnant or slow-moving water.

Snake bites and scorpion stings are another potential hazard. Both snakes and scorpions love dark hidey-holes. If you're camping or trekking always pack away your sleeping bag when it's not in use and tap out your boots. Don't walk around barefoot or stick your hand in holes in the ground or in rocks. Another sensible precaution is to shake out your clothes before you put them on. Remember, snakes don't bite unless threatened or stepped on.

For more information on these and other health risks, see the Health chapter, p387.

Police & Military

Although police and veterinary roadblocks, bureaucracy and bored officials may be tiresome, they're mostly harmless. Careful scrutiny is rare, but drivers may have to unpack their luggage for closer inspection at a border or veterinary checkpoint.

The Botswana Defence Force (BDF), on the other hand, takes its duties seriously and is best not crossed. The most sensitive base, which is operated jointly with the US government, lies in a remote area off the Lobatse road, southwest of Gaborone. Don't stumble upon it accidentally! Also avoid State House, the official residence of the president in Gaborone, especially after dark. It's located near the government enclave, where there's not much else going on in the evening, so anyone caught 'hanging around' is viewed suspiciously.

Road Safety

The most significant concern for independent travellers is road safety. Botswana has one of the highest accident rates in the world, and drunk and reckless driving are common, especially at month's end (wage day). Cattle, goats, sheep, donkeys and even elephants are deadly hazards on the road, especially at dusk and after dark when visibility is poor. To drive in Botswana you need to be prepared for the unexpected and observe the speed limits on unsurfaced roads.

DISCOUNT CARDS

There is no uniformly accepted discount-card scheme in Botswana, but a residence permit entitles you to claim favourable residents' rates at hotels. Hostel cards are also of little use, but student cards score a 15% discount on Intercape Mainliner buses and occasionally attract discounts on museum admissions. Seniors over 60, with proof of age, also receive a 15% discount on Intercape Mainliner buses and good discounts on domestic Air Namibia fares.

The only other discounts available are the concessions on entry fees to the national wildlife parks, where children between the ages of eight and 17 pay half price.

EMBASSIES & HIGH COMMISSIONS
Botswanan Embassies & High Commissions
Botswana does not have much representation overseas, but visas can be issued to most visitors on arrival.

Australia (☎ 612-6290 7500; fax 6286 2566; 52 Culgoa Circuit, O'Malley, ACT 2606, Canberra)

Namibia (☎ 264-61-221 941/2/7; fax 236 034; 101 Nelson Mandela Ave, PO Box 20359, Windhoek)

South Africa Cape Town (☎ 021-421 1045; fax 421 1046; 4th fl, Southern Life Centre, 5 Riebeeck St, PO Box 3288, Cape Town); Johannesburg (☎ 011-403 3748; fax 403 1384; 33 Hoofd St, Braampark, Forum Ii, 4th fl, PO Box 32051, Braamfontien, Johannesburg)

UK (☎ 0207-499 0031; http://botswana.embassy homepage.com; 6 Stratford Place, London W1C 1AY)

USA (☎ 202-244 4990/1; www.botswanaembassy.org; 1531 New Hampshire Ave NW, Washington DC 2008)

Zambia (☎ 01-250 019/555; fax 253 895; 5201 Pandit Nehru Rd, Diplomatic Triangle, PO Box 31910, Lusaka)

Zimbabwe (☎ 04-794 645/7/8; fax 793 030; 22 Phillips Ave, Belgravia, PO Box 563, Harare)

Embassies & Consulates in Botswana
All the diplomatic missions listed below are located in Gaborone (Map pp82–3). Many more countries have embassies or consulates in South Africa.

Angola (☎ 390 0204; fax 397 5089; Plot 13232 Khama Cres, Nelson Mandela Dr, PO Box 111)

France (☎ 397 3863; www.ambafrance-bw.org; 761 Robinson Rd, PO Box 1424; 🕑 8am-4pm Mon-Fri)

Germany (☎ 395 3143; www.gaborone.diplo.de; 3rd fl, Professional House, Broadhurst Mall, Segoditshane Way)

Namibia (☎ 390 2181; fax 390 2248; 2nd fl, Debswana House, PO Box 987; 🕑 7.30am-1pm & 2-4.30pm Mon-Fri)

South Africa (☎ 390 4800/1/2/3; sahcgabs@botsnet. bw; Plot 29, 29 Queens Rd, PO Box 00402; 🕑 8am-12.45pm & 1.30-4.30pm Mon-Fri)

UK (☎ 395 2841; www.britishhighcommission.gov. uk/botswana; Plot 1079-1084 Main Mall, Queens Rd, PO Box 0023; 🕑 8am-12.30pm & 1.30-4.30pm Mon-Thu, 8am-1pm Fri)

USA (☎ 395 3982; http://gaborone.usembassy.gov; Embassy Dr, PO Box 90; 🕑 9am-4pm Mon-Fri)

Zambia (☎ 395 1951; fax 395 3952; Plot No 1118 Queens Rd, the Mall, PO Box 362; 🕑 8.30am-12.30pm & 2-4.30pm Mon-Fri)

Zimbabwe (☎ 391 4495; fax 390 5863; Government Enclave, Plot 8850, PO Box 1232; 🕑 8am-1pm & 2-4.30pm Mon-Fri)

FESTIVALS & EVENTS
The Maitisong Festival, which is held in Gaborone over one week in March and/or April, is the highlight of the calendar for lovers of local and regional music, dance and drama (see the boxed text, p85). The capital also hosts the annual **Traditional Dance Competition**, held in late March. Another worthwhile cultural festival is the **Kuru Traditional Dance and Music Festival**, held in D'kar in August, when all aspects of traditional bushman culture are on display. In 2009, Maun hosted the first annual **Maun Festival**, with plenty of music, craftwork, dance and food; it will be repeated yearly in late April/early May.

FOOD
In this book we've used the term budget to describe places where you can get a meal for less than P40. These meals are very simple and tend towards grilled meats, chicken and rice or chips, burgers or pizza, as well as some cafe snacks. At midrange restaurants you should be able to get a decent meal between P50 and P80, while the very most you'll pay at a top-end place is around P120. At most remote lodges and camps all your meals and possibly soft drinks will be included in the price of your room. Throughout this guide we've also listed local shops and supermarkets where you can buy fresh fruit and veg and other camping/self-catering supplies.

Drinks
Bottles of beer cost around P15 in a bar but less in a supermarket or bottle shop. Bottled beer is always a lot cheaper than canned beer (which is what is usually sold in restaurants).

Supermarkets and bottle shops are well stocked with imported beer, wine and spirits at prices comparable to those in Europe or North America. You may want to sample some of the superb red and white wines produced in the Cape region of South Africa.

Bottled water is also available at supermarkets and restaurants. A 1L bottle will set you back around P7. If you're planning on camping for an extended period of time it's probably worth carrying purification tablets.

GAY & LESBIAN TRAVELLERS

Homosexuality, both gay and lesbian, is illegal in Botswana and carries a minimum sentence of seven years if you're caught. Intolerance has increased further over the last five years due to the homophobic statements of national leaders in neighbouring Namibia and Zimbabwe.

To tackle this widespread homophobia, a group of lesbians, gays and bisexuals established the group **LeGaBiBo** (Lesbians, Gays and Bisexuals of Botswana; ☎ 393 2516; www.legabibo.org.bw; 5062 Medical Mews, Fairgrounds, Gaborone) in 1998. The first thing they did was to publish a human-rights charter under the auspices of Ditshwanelo, the Botswana Centre for Human Rights. In conjunction with LeGaBiBo, Ditshwanelo held a safe-sex workshop in 2001 to highlight the risks of HIV/AIDS, which was attended by government policy makers and representatives from the UN Development Programme.

However, since then the Botswana High Court has ruled on a case involving two gay men. In its judgment, passed in July 2003, it found that 'the time has not yet arrived to decriminalise homosexual practices even between consenting adult males in private'. In light of this, Ditshwanelo continues to advocate and lobby for the decriminalisation of homosexuality.

Given the sensitivity of the subject and the strongly held views of many Batswana, it is advisable to refrain from any overt displays of affection in public. As there are no public organisations in Botswana besides LeGaBiBo, which can only provide limited information, the most useful resource is the South African website **Behind the Mask** (www.mask.org.za).

HOLIDAYS

During official public holidays, all banks, government offices and major businesses are closed. However, hotels, restaurants, bars, smaller shops, petrol stations, museums and national parks and reserves stay open, while border posts and public transport continue operating as normal. Government offices, banks and some businesses also take the day off after New Year's Day, President's Day, Botswana/Independence Day and Boxing Day.

New Year's Day 1 January
Easter March/April – Good Friday, Easter Saturday and Easter Monday
Labour Day 1 May
Ascension Day May/June, 40 days after Easter Sunday
Sir Seretse Khama Day 1 July
President's Day Third Friday in July
Botswana/Independence Day 30 September
Christmas Day 25 December
Boxing Day 26 December

INSURANCE

A travel-insurance policy to cover theft, loss and medical problems is a good idea. Some policies offer lower and higher medical-expense options; the higher ones are chiefly for countries that have extremely high medical costs, such as the USA. Some policies specifically exclude 'dangerous activities', which can be defined to mean scuba diving, motorcycling and even trekking. If 'risky' activities are on your agenda, as they may well be, you'll need the most comprehensive policy.

You may prefer to have an insurance policy that pays doctors or hospitals directly rather than your having to pay on the spot and claim later. If you have to claim later, make sure you keep all documentation. Some policies ask you to call back (reverse charges) to a centre in your home country, where an immediate assessment of your problem is made. Check that the policy covers ambulances or an emergency flight home.

For details on health insurance, see p387; for more details on car insurance, see p179.

INTERNET ACCESS

Despite the fact that Botswana has one of the most well-developed telecommunications networks on the continent, internet access is surprisingly poor and connection is unreliable and slow. VoIP (Voice over Internet Protocol) is also officially banned at the moment, although Botswana has a significant number of registered Skype users.

Main towns like Gaborone, Francistown, Kasane and Maun all have internet cafes. Plan on spending between P20 and P50 per hour online. Some hotels and lodges offer internet access, except for those at the top of the range in main urban centres.

Bearing all this in mind it's probably not worth bringing a laptop unless you have important work to do. Only a few hotels have in-room internet access and most of these are in Gaborone. Also, you should be aware that your modem may not work once you leave your home country – for more information, see www.teleadapt.com.

LEGAL MATTERS

Botswana has a strong criminal code and constitution and, as much as humanly possible, arrests, tries and convicts without prejudice. Police rarely abuse their powers and foreigners are not usually targeted by the police or military for bribes or anything else. In fact, bribery of officials is taken very seriously indeed and should not be attempted under any circumstances.

All drugs are illegal in Botswana and penalties are at least as stiff as those imposed in Western countries. So don't think about bringing anything over the borders or buying it while you're there. The police are allowed to use entrapment techniques, such as posing as drug pushers, to catch criminals, so don't be tempted.

The legal age of sexual consent is 16 for girls and 14 for boys, although rather confusingly parents can consent to marrying off their daughters at 14. Rape laws in Botswana currently only protect women, although marital rape is not recognised (see p65).

If you do get into trouble with the police or military, you are in theory allowed a phone call to your embassy or high commission.

MAPS

The most accurate country map, which is very useful if you're driving, is the *Shell Tourist Map of Botswana* (1:1,750,000), and is available at major bookshops in Botswana and South Africa. It includes detailed coverage of all major parks and reserves, as well as the Tuli Block, the Tsodilo Hills, Gcwihaba (Drotsky's) Cave and the Makgadikgadi Pans. It also lists dozens of vital Global Positioning System (GPS) coordinates.

Shell also produces maps to Chobe National Park, Moremi Game Reserve, the Okavango Delta and Linyanti Marshes, and the Kgalagadi Transfrontier Park. These maps give fantastically detailed coverage of the wildlife-viewing tracks in the parks along with GPS coordinates. All of these maps cost around US$2.50.

GeoCentre produces a more general country road map of Botswana at a scale of 1:1,650,000, as does Macmillan (1:1,750,000).

The best place to purchase maps in Botswana is at petrol stations, although you can get your hands on more general maps at local bookshops.

In the USA, **Maplink** (www.maplink.com) is an excellent and exhaustive source for maps of Botswana. A similar selection of maps is available in the UK from **Stanfords** (www.stanfords.co.uk) and in Australia from **MapLand** (www.mapland.com.au).

MONEY

Throughout this book prices have been quoted in US dollars and Botswanan pula (P). At top-end hotels, lodges and camps, things are priced and you can pay in US dollars. Otherwise, you'll be making most transactions in Botswana pula.

Pula means 'blessings' or 'rain', the latter of which is as precious as money in this largely desert country. Notes come in denominations of P10, P20, P50 and P100, and coins (thebe, or 'shield') are in denominations of 5t, 10t, 25t, 50t, P1, P2 and P5.

Most banks and foreign exchange offices won't touch Zambian kwacha and Namibian dollars, so make sure to buy/sell these currencies at or near the respective borders.

There are five commercial banks in the country with branches in all the main towns and major villages. Outside these you won't find any facilities. There are, however, exchange bureaux at border posts.

There is no black market in Botswana. Anyone offering to exchange money on the street is doing so illegally and is probably setting you up for a scam, the exception being the guys who change pula for South African rand in front of South Africa–bound minibuses – locals use their services, so they can be trusted.

See the inside front cover for a table of exchange rates or log on to www.oanda.com; also see p16 for further information on costs.

ATMs

Credit cards can be used in ATMs displaying the appropriate sign, or to obtain cash advances over the counter in many banks – Visa and MasterCard are among the most widely recognised.

You'll find ATMs at all the main bank branches throughout Botswana, including in Gaborone, Maun and Kasane, and this is undoubtedly the simplest (and safest) way to handle your money while travelling.

Cash

Most common foreign currencies can be exchanged, but not every branch of every bank will do so. Therefore, it's best to stick to US dollars, euros (or UK pounds) and South African rand, which are all easy to change.

Foreign currency, typically US dollars, is also accepted by a number of midrange and top-end hotels, lodges and tour operators. South African rand can also be used on Botswanan combis (minibuses) and buses going to/from South Africa, and to pay for Botswanan vehicle taxes at South African/Botswanan borders.

Cash transfers from foreign banks are possible at the head offices of Barclays and Standard Chartered, and through Western Union, in Gaborone.

Credit/Debit Cards

All major credit cards, including Visa, MasterCard, American Express and Diners Club, are widely accepted in most shops, restaurants and hotels (but not petrol stations).

Major branches of Barclays Bank and Standard Chartered Bank also deal with cash advances over the counter. Almost every town has at least one branch of Barclays and/or Standard Chartered that offers foreign-exchange facilities, but not all have the authority or technology for cash advances.

Tipping

While tipping isn't obligatory, the government's official policy of promoting upmarket tourism has raised expectations in many hotels and restaurants. A service charge may be added as a matter of course, in which case there's no need to leave a tip. If there is no service charge and the service has been good, leave about 10%.

It is also a good idea to tip the men who watch your car in public car parks and the attendants at service stations who wash your windscreens. A tip of around P2 to P5 is appropriate.

Travellers Cheques

Travellers cheques can be cashed at most banks and exchange offices. American Express (Amex), Thomas Cook and Visa are the most widely accepted brands.

It is preferable to buy travellers cheques in US dollars, euros or UK pounds rather than any other currency. Get most of the cheques in largish denominations to save on per-cheque exchange rates.

You must take your passport with you when cashing cheques.

PHOTOGRAPHY & VIDEO

While many Batswana enjoy being photographed, others do not; the main point is that you should always respect the wishes of the person in question and don't snap a picture if permission is denied. You should also avoid taking pictures of bridges, dams, airports, military equipment, government buildings and anything that could be considered strategic.

Print and slide film, batteries and most accessories, as well as video cartridges, are available in Gaborone, Francistown and Maun. However, nothing is cheap and you may not find your preferred brand, so it's best to bring your own. A roll of Fuji 24/36 print film costs about P30 and about P40 for slide film (without processing).

Film can be developed in all major towns; it costs about P70 for a roll of 24/36 colour prints.

Digital memory cards, CDs and the like can be purchased in Gaborone in large malls like Game City. They're a bit harder to find in Maun and Kasane, but it's possible. In Maun, there are convenience stores across from the airport that may be able to help you; in Kasane, try Kasane Internet (p111)

POST

Botswana Post (www.botspost.co.bw) is generally reliable, although it can be slow, so allow at least two weeks for delivery to or from any overseas address. Postcards and standard letters (weighing up to 10g) cost P3.30 to other African countries, P4.10 to Europe and P4.90 to the rest of the world.

There is a poste restante service in all major towns, but the most reliable is at the Central Post Office along the Mall in Gaborone. To send or receive parcels, go to the parcel office at the Central Post Office, fill out the customs forms and pay the duties (if required). Parcels may be plastered with all the sticky tape you like, but they must also be tied up with string and sealing wax, so bring matches to seal knots with the red wax provided. To pick up parcels, you must present photo ID.

SHOPPING

The standard of Botswana handicrafts is generally high, particularly the beautifully decorative 'Botswana baskets', which are originally produced in Ngamiland (northwestern Botswana). Baskets can be bought cheaply at workshops in Etsha 6 (p143) and Gumare (p143) villages, both just off the Sehitwha–Shakawe road in northwestern Botswana. Equally high-quality baskets are produced in Shorobe (near Maun; p129) and Francistown (p99).

San jewellery and leatherwork is another highlight. Souvenirs include leather aprons and bags, ostrich-eggshell beads (which may not be imported into some countries) and strands of seeds and nuts (which likewise may be not be imported into some countries). These can be bought in remote northwestern villages, such as Xai Xai (Caecae; p142) and Ghanzi (p150). But one of the best outlets is the cooperative at D'kar (p151). Leather products are also made at Pilane, near Gaborone, and Francistown.

Beautiful weavings, textiles and fabrics are also available, although the most inspired pieces are justifiably expensive given the quality of the workmanship. The best and least expensive work is normally found right at its source, eg the cooperatives at Oodi (near Gaborone; see the boxed text, p91) and Francistown (p99).

Other cooperatives at Maun (p127), and Gabane (p91) and Thamaga (p91), both a short distance from Gaborone, make and sell excellent pottery, including cups, pots and vases – all at reasonable prices. Tours of the workshop at Thamaga can be arranged. Modern and traditional art can be found in Gaborone (p88).

For more information about Botswana's handicrafts, see p67.

SOLO TRAVELLERS

Botswana can be a difficult destination for the solo traveller. The backpacking scene is limited, prices are high (unless you're camping) and, outside of Maun, there is no network of hostels where you can meet up with fellow travellers. In addition, the single supplements levied at most lodges and camps are extremely high, sometimes as much as US$200 extra on top of prices that may already be hovering around US$500.

It's also well nigh impossible to reach many areas of interest on public transport, so if you can't hook up with other travellers you'll be paying through the nose for car hire. Even in Maun, the tourist hub of the country, single travellers are few and far between, and compared with Namibia the scene is disappointing. Having said that, the best places for solo travellers to head are the Audi Camp (see p126), Okavango River Lodge (see p125) and Back to the Bridge Backpackers (see p125), all in Maun. This is where you'll have the best chance of hitching up with other groups for activities in the Okavango Delta.

Of course, some people love the solitary spaces of solo travel, and Botswana, with its scenic capacity for always making you feel small and enlarged all at once, is perfect for this sort of traveller.

TELEPHONE

Botswana Telecom (www.btc.bw) is the operator of Botswana's fixed-line telephone service, which now also offers ASDL links that service many Botswanan businesses.

Local calls at peak times cost P20 per minute. Domestic calls (eg Gaborone to Lobatse) cost P33 per minute, depending on the distance. International calls vary depending on the country; see www.btc.bw/doc/btc_rates.pdf for a full list of rates, but at peak times it's P1.90/2.40 per minute to a UK landline/mobile, P1.60/2.10 to a German landline/mobile and a flat P1.60 to the USA.

Off-peak discounts of 33% for local and domestic calls and 20% for international calls are available from 8pm to 7am Monday to Friday, 1pm to midnight Saturday and all day Sunday – but not if you use the operator.

The Botswana Telecom website also allows access to an online telephone directory, the white pages for residential numbers and the yellow pages for business numbers. **AC Braby** (www.brabys.com/bw) also has a good online phone directory.

Mobile Phones

Botswana has two global mobile (cell) phone networks, **Mascom Wireless** (www.mascom.bw) and **Orange Botswana** (www.orange.co.bw), of which Mascom is by far the largest provider. Still even Mascom's coverage is patchy, confined to the eastern corridor from Gaborone in the southeast to Francistown in the east of the country. Outside these areas reception is minimal. Maun, Ghanzi and Mamuno have good coverage, but reception will be patchy in other areas. That said, the main highway system is generally

BOTSWANA DIRECTORY

covered and thanks to an expanding market, coverage is increasing on a steady basis.

If you're travelling for an extended period of time a cheaper alternative might be a pre-paid mobile phone, which you can pick up for around P500. You can pick up subsequent pay-as-you-go cards at Mascom dealers in main towns.

Most Botswana mobile numbers begin with 071 or 072.

Phone Codes

Botswana's country code is ☎ 267. There are no internal area codes, so when phoning Botswana from outside the country, dial ☎ 267 and then the actual telephone number. When dialling an international number from Botswana, the international access code is ☎ 00; this is then followed by the desired country code, area code (if applicable) and telephone number.

Phonecards

Telephone booths can be used for local, domestic and international calls and can be found in and outside all Botswana Telecom (BTC) offices, outside all post offices and around all shopping centres and malls. Blue booths (with the English and Tswana words 'coin' and *madi*) take coins, and the green booths (with the words 'card' and *karata*) use phonecards.

Phonecards can be bought at BTC offices, post offices and some small grocery shops. Local and long-distance telephone calls can also be made from private telephone agencies, often called 'phone shops'.

TIME

Botswana is two hours ahead of GMT/UTC, so when it's noon in Botswana, it's 10am in London, 5am in New York, 2am in Los Angeles and 8pm in Sydney (not taking into account daylight-saving time in these countries). There is no daylight-saving time in Botswana.

TOURIST INFORMATION
Local Tourist Offices

For many years the tourism industry in Botswana was controlled by a few exclusive operators who brought guests from abroad and ferried them hither and thither until their departure date. There was little need for a local network of tourist offices as people simply didn't require them.

More recently, independent travel to Botswana has been on the rise and the government is finally acknowledging the need for some sort of network of information offices both inside and outside the country, but within Botswana there's still very limited support.

The main tourist office in the capital is the **Department of Tourism** (☎ 391 3111; www.botswana tourism.co.bw; 2nd fl, Standard Chartered Bank Bldg, The Mall). The department also has information offices in Maun, Kasane and Selebi-Phikwe.

Also in Gaborone are the offices of the **Department of Wildlife and National Parks** (DWNP; ☎ 397 1405; dwnp@gov.bw; PO Box 131, Government Enclave, Khama Cres), where you can make reservations at the national campsites. For more information on the DWNP see p26.

Tourist Offices Abroad

Botswana has no dedicated tourist offices overseas, but several foreign companies serve as agencies for the Department of Tourism:

Germany (☎ 030-4208 464; www.botswanatourism.de; Karl-Marx-Allee 91A, 10243 Berlin)
UK (☎ 01344 298 982; www.botswanatourism.org.uk; Old Boundary House, London Rd, Sunningdale, Berkshire SL5 0DJ)
USA (☎ 888-675-7600; www.botswanatourism.us; 128 Lubrano Dr, Annapolis, MD 21401)

Another useful contact is the **Regional Tourism Organisation of Southern Africa** (☎ in South Africa 011-315 2420; www.retosa.co.za; PO Box 7381, Halfway House, Johannesburg 1685, South Africa), which promotes tourism throughout Southern Africa, including Botswana.

TRAVELLERS WITH DISABILITIES

People with limited mobility will have a difficult time in travelling around Botswana – although there are many disabled people living in the country, facilities here are very few. Along streets and footpaths, kerbs and uneven surfaces will often present problems for wheelchair users and only a very few up-market hotels/lodges and restaurants have installed ramps and railings. Also getting to and around any of the major lodges or camps in the national wildlife parks will be extremely difficult given their remote and wild locations.

If you are contemplating travelling to Botswana, make sure to choose the areas you visit carefully. The swampy environs of the Okavango Delta will be particularly challenging for people who have special needs, although the lodges in both the Kalahari (p148) and the Makgadikgadi Pans (p103) are relatively accessible, providing you are travelling with an able-bodied companion. It is also worth bearing in mind that almost any destination in Botswana will require a long trip in a 4WD and/or a small plane.

VISAS

Most visitors can obtain tourist visas at the international airports and borders (and the nearest police stations in lieu of an immigration official at remote border crossings). Visas that are valid for 30 days – and possibly up to 90 days if requested at the time of entry – are available for free to passport holders from most Commonwealth countries (but not Ghana, India, Nigeria, Pakistan and Sri Lanka); all EU countries (except Spain and Portugal); the USA; and countries in the Southern African Customs Union (SACU), ie South Africa, Namibia, Lesotho and Swaziland. If you hold a passport from any other country, apply for a 30-day tourist visa at an overseas Botswanan embassy or consulate. Where there is no Botswanan representation, try going to a British embassy or consulate.

Tourists are allowed to stay in Botswana for a maximum of 90 days every 12 months, so a 30-day visa can be extended twice. Visas can be extended for free at immigration offices in Gaborone (Map pp82–3), Francistown, Maun (Map p122) and Kasane (Map p112). Whether you're required to show an onward ticket and/or sufficient funds at this time depends on the official(s).

Anyone travelling to Botswana from an area infected with yellow fever needs proof of vaccination before they can enter the country.

VOLUNTEERING

There are very few volunteering opportunities in Botswana. The community and conservation projects that exist are usually small, focused grassroots projects that simply aren't set up for drop-in volunteers. Another factor is that Botswana is a pretty well-organised, wealthy country and the need for volunteer projects simply doesn't exist, with the exception of non-governmental organisations (NGOs) working with HIV/AIDS sufferers.

Having said that, if you are still keen on working in Botswana it pays to contact the organisation you're interested in working for well in advance of when you plan to travel. This way you'll be able to let it know what skills you might bring to the project and give it time to make the necessary arrangements. Throughout this guide we've highlighted a number of conservation and community-based projects.

Outside that, you could get in touch with the following international organisations.

Australian Volunteers International (☎ 03-9279 1788; www.australianvolunteers.com; 71 Argyle St, PO Box 350, Fitzroy, VIC 3065, Australia) This organisation places experienced and qualified volunteers for two years.

Project Trust (☎ 01879-230444; www.projecttrust.org .uk; The Hebridean Centre, Isle of Coll, Argyll, Scotland, PA78 6TE, UK) The UK's oldest gap-year organisation, Project Trust arranges one-year placements for school leavers. It currently has volunteers working at a school near Maun in Botswana.

UN Volunteers (UNV; ☎ 228-815 2000; www.unv.org; Postfach 260 111, Bonn, Germany) This is an umbrella organisation that places experienced and qualified volunteers. It has an office in Gaborone (www.unbotswana.org.bw/unv. html; UN Place, Khama Cres, Plot 22, PO Box 54, Gaborone).

Another useful organisation is **Volunteer Work Information Service** (VWIS; ☎ +44 1935 864 458; www .workingabroad.com; The Old School House, Pendomer, Yeovil, Somerset, BA22 9PH, UK), which can research volunteer-work opportunities in over 150 countries.

WOMEN TRAVELLERS

In general, travelling around Botswana poses no particular difficulties for women travellers. For the most part, men are polite and respectful, especially if you are clearly not interested in their advances, and women can meet and communicate with local men without their intentions necessarily being misconstrued. However, unaccompanied women should be cautious in nightclubs or bars, as generally most instances of hassle tend to be the advances of men who have had one too many drinks.

The threat of sexual assault isn't any greater in Botswana than in Europe, but women should still avoid walking alone in parks and backstreets, especially at night. Don't hitch alone or at night and, if you can, find a companion for trips through sparsely populated areas. Use common sense and things should go well.

Dress modestly. Short sleeves are fine, and baggy shorts and loose T-shirts are acceptable where foreigners are common, but in villages and rural areas try to cover up as much as possible.

Botswana Transport

BOTSWANA TRANSPORT

GETTING THERE & AWAY

Botswana is not the easiest or cheapest place in the world to get to. Surprisingly few international airlines fly to and from Botswana; the long-distance airlines prefer to fly into Johannesburg (Jo'burg) or Cape Town in South Africa, where connecting airline flights depart to Maun or Gaborone. Many people prefer to enter the country overland from South Africa or, more recently, Namibia as part of a longer safari. Flights, tours and rail tickets can be booked online at www.lonelyplanet.com/travel_services.

THINGS CHANGE...

The information in this chapter is particularly vulnerable to change. Check directly with the airline or a travel agent to make sure you understand how a fare (and ticket you may buy) works and be aware of the security requirements for international travel. Shop carefully. The details given in this chapter should be regarded as pointers and are not a substitute for your own careful, up-to-date research.

ENTERING THE COUNTRY

Entering Botswana is straightforward and tourists are warmly welcomed. Visas (see p169) are typically available on arrival for most nationalities. If you're crossing into the country overland you may well be questioned about the duration of your stay and how you intend to fund your trip, but you'll never be hassled by officialdom. You will, however, need to have all the necessary documentation for your vehicle (see p175).

Passport

All visitors entering Botswana must hold a passport that is valid for at least six months. Also, allow a few empty pages for stamp-happy immigration officials, especially if you're crossing over to Zimbabwe and/or Zambia to see Victoria Falls.

Residents of the EU (except those from Spain and Portugal), Argentina, Brazil, Mexico, USA, South Africa, Scandinavia, Balkan countries and all members of the Commonwealth (with the exception of Ghana, India, Mauritius, Nigeria, Pakistan and Sri Lanka) will be granted a one-month entry permit on arrival. For further information on entry requirements see p169.

AIR
Airports & Airlines

Botswana's main airport is **Sir Seretse Khama International Airport** (GBE; Map pp82-3; ☎ 391 4401), located 11km north of the capital, Gaborone. Although this is well served with flights from Jo'burg and Harare it is seldom used by tourists as an entry point into the country. Far more popular are **Maun Airport** (MUB; Map p122; ☎ 686 1559) and **Kasane Airport** (BBK; Map p112; ☎ 625 0133). There is also an airstrip near Pont Drift (in the Tuli Block) for chartered flights from South Africa.

The national carrier is Air Botswana, which flies routes within Southern Africa. Air Botswana has offices in Gaborone (Map pp82-3), Francistown (Map p98), Maun (Map p122), Kasane and Victoria Falls (Zimbabwe). It's worth noting that at present you cannot reserve tickets via its website.

CLIMATE CHANGE & TRAVEL

Climate change is a serious threat to the ecosystems that humans rely upon, and air travel is the fastest-growing contributor to the problem. Lonely Planet regards travel, overall, as a global benefit, but believes we all have a responsibility to limit our personal impact on global warming.

Flying & Climate Change

Pretty much every form of motorised travel generates CO_2 (the main cause of human-induced climate change) but planes are far and away the worst offenders, not just because of the sheer distances they allow us to travel, but because they release greenhouse gases high into the atmosphere. The statistics are frightening: two people taking a return flight between Europe and the USA will contribute as much to climate change as an average household's gas and electricity consumption over a whole year.

Carbon-Offset Schemes

Climatecare.org and other websites use 'carbon calculators' that allow travellers to offset the level of greenhouse gases they are responsible for with financial contributions to sustainable-travel schemes that reduce global warming – including projects in India, Honduras, Kazakhstan and Uganda.

Lonely Planet, together with Rough Guides and other concerned partners in the travel industry, supports the carbon-offset scheme run by climatecare.org. Lonely Planet offsets all of its staff and author travel.

For more information check out our website: www.lonelyplanet.com.

AIRLINES FLYING TO/FROM BOTSWANA

No European or North American airline flies directly into Botswana. The country is only served by two airlines and a number of special charter flights. Most travellers fly into either Jo'burg or Cape Town in South Africa (both of which are served by an array of international and domestic carriers) and hop on a connecting flight.

Air Botswana (BP; ☎ 390 5500; www.airbotswana .co.bw)

South African Airways (☎ Gaborone airport 390 5740, international 27-11 978 5313; www.flysaa.com)

Tickets

All visitors to Botswana will need to carry a return ticket. The major gateway to Botswana is through Jo'burg, which is reflected in the following information. Return flights from Jo'burg to Gaborone or Maun are US$200 to US$300, although if you book your internal flight at the same time as your main flight you'll nearly always get a better deal (as well as ensuring the most speedy transit).

You'll nearly always find the best deals through tour operators or discount flight centres. Paying by credit card generally offers some protection against cancellation. Similar protection can be obtained by buying a ticket from a bonded agent, such as one covered by the **Air Travel Organiser's Licence** (ATOL; www.atol.org.uk) scheme in the UK.

The airport departure tax for international flights is included in the cost of your plane ticket.

Africa

The only scheduled flights to Botswana come from Jo'burg and Cape Town (South Africa), Victoria Falls and Harare (Zimbabwe), Lusaka (Zambia) and Windhoek (Namibia). To get to/from any other country in Africa, get a connection in either Jo'burg (best for Southern Africa) or Harare (for Eastern Africa).

FROM NAMIBIA

Air Namibia (www.airnamibia.com) now runs a flight from Windhoek to Maun three times a week. It also operates a further three flights to Victoria Falls (Zimbabwe), which transit through Maun. This is a popular route and is often filled months in advance, so you'll need some forward planning.

FROM SOUTH AFRICA

Jo'burg is the best place in South Africa to buy tickets. Air Botswana flies between Gaborone and Jo'burg about 40 times a week, with additional services run by South African Airways. Air Botswana also offers flights daily between

Maun and Jo'burg and a direct service between Jo'burg and Kasane three times a week.

Rennies Travel (www.renniestravel.com) and **STA Travel** (www.statravel.co.za) have offices throughout Southern Africa. Check their websites for branch locations. Other competitive agents are **Flight Centre** (www.flightcentre.co.za) and **Africa Travel Company** (www.africatravelco.com) in Cape Town.

FROM ZIMBABWE & ZAMBIA

Air Botswana flies between Gaborone and Harare (Zimbabwe) on Monday, Wednesday, Friday and Saturday. All flights (except the one on Saturday) are timed to enable immediate connections on Air Zimbabwe to Lusaka (Zambia). Air Botswana also flies from Victoria Falls (Zimbabwe) to Maun on Tuesday, Wednesday, Friday and Sunday.

Given all the disruption in neighbouring Zimbabwe, Livingstone (Zambia) is currently experiencing something of a boom and a new runway was being built at the time of research. The plan is that all the big regional carriers like Kenya Airways, South African Airways and Namibian Airways will service the new airport.

Asia

South African Airways services a plethora of routes to Asia, including Bangkok and Hong Kong. You might also consider flying **Kenya Airways** (www.kenya-airways.com), which offers similar routes, or **Qantas** (www.qantas.com.au), which operates flights to Jo'burg from Beijing, Shanghai and Singapore via Australia.

STA Travel (Bangkok www.statravel.co.th; Hong Kong www.statravel.hk; Japan www.statravel.co.jp; Singapore www.statravel.co.sg) has branches throughout Asia. In Hong Kong you can also try **Four Seas Tours** (www.fourseastravel.com).

Australia

Qantas (www.qantas.com.au) flies from Perth and Sydney to Jo'burg several times a week; and British Airways also flies between Perth and Jo'burg three or four times a week. From Perth, expect to pay about A$1500 return to Jo'burg; from Sydney and Melbourne, about A$2000 return.

Round-the-world (RTW) tickets are often good value; it can sometimes work out cheaper to keep going right around the world on a RTW ticket than to do a U-turn on a return ticket.

STA Travel (☎ 1300 733 035; www.statravel.com.au) and **Flight Centre** (☎ 133 133; www.flightcentre.com.au) are well-known agents for cheap fares, with offices throughout Australia. For online booking try www.travel.com.au. Cheap fares are also advertised in the travel sections of weekend newspapers, such as the *Age* in Melbourne and the *Sydney Morning Herald*.

Canada

From Canada to Botswana, get a flight to New York, Atlanta or Chicago, or Europe, and a connection to Jo'burg.

Canadian air fares tend to be about 10% higher than those sold in the USA. **Travel Cuts** (www.travelcuts.com) is Canada's national student-travel agency and has offices in all major cities. For online bookings, try www.expedia.ca and www.travelocity.ca.

Continental Europe

Most major European airlines, including **Lufthansa** (www.lufthansa.com), **Air France** (www.airfrance.com), **Alitalia** (www.alitalia.it) and **KLM** (www.klm.com), fly to Jo'burg several times a week each. Return fares range from €600 to €1000, depending on the season. Be sure to plan in advance during high season (July to October) as flights fill up fast.

STA Travel (Austria www.statravel.at; Denmark www.statravel.dk; Finland www.statravel.fi; Germany www.statravel.de; Norway www.statravel.no; Sweden www.statravel.se; Switzerland www.statravel.ch), the international student- and youth-travel giant, has branches in many European nations. There are also many **STA-affiliated travel agencies** (www.statravelgroup.com) across Europe.

Other recommended travel agencies across Europe include the following.

BELGIUM
Acotra Student Travel Agency (☎ 02 512 7079)

FRANCE
Anyway (☎ 0892 302 301; www.anyway.fr)
Lastminute (www.fr.lastminute.com)
Nouvelles Frontières (☎ 01 4920 6587; www.nouvelles-frontieres.fr)
Voyageurs du Monde (www.vdm.com)

GERMANY
Expedia (www.expedia.de)
Kilroy Travel Group (www.kilroygroups.com)
Lastminute (☎ 01805 284 366; www.lastminute.de)

ITALY
CTS Viaggi (☎ 06 4411166; www.cts.it)

NETHERLANDS
Airfair (☎ 0900-7 717 717; www.airfair.nl)
Holland International (www.hollandinternational.nl)
NBBS Reizen (☎ 0180-393 377; www.nbbs.nl)

SCANDINAVIA
Kilroy Travel Group (www.kilroygroups.com)

SPAIN
Barcelo Viajes (☎ 902 200 400; www.barceloviajes.com)
Viajes Zeppelin (☎ 91 542 51 54; www.viajeszeppelin. com)

India

Flights between South Africa and Mumbai (Bombay) are common given the fairly large Indian population in South Africa; South African Airways and Kenya Airways are the main carriers. Typical fares to Jo'burg are between US$800 and US$1200.

Although most of India's discount-travel agents are in Delhi, there are also some reliable agents in Mumbai. **STIC Travels** (www.stictravel. com) has offices in dozens of Indian cities.

New Zealand

Inevitably, Kiwis will need a connection through Australia. RTW fares for travel to or from New Zealand are worth checking out as they are often good value. The *New Zealand Herald* also has a good travel section with plenty of advertised fares.

Flight Centre (☎ 0800 243 544; www.flightcentre. co.nz) and **STA Travel** (☎ 0800 474 400; www.statravel. co.nz) have branches throughout the country.

UK & Ireland

Both **British Airways** (www.ba.com) and **SAA** (www. flysaa.com) fly non stop between London and Jo'burg (and Cape Town) at least once a day. **Virgin Atlantic** (www.virgin-atlantic.com), which also offers flights several times a week between London and Jo'burg, usually offers the cheapest fares: about UK£480 return for this route.

Advertisements for many travel agencies appear in the travel pages of the weekend broadsheet newspapers, in *Time Out,* the *Evening Standard* and in the free magazine *TNT* (www.tntmagazine.com).

For students or travellers under 26 years, popular travel agencies include **STA Travel** (☎ 0871 230 0040; www.statravel.co.uk) and **Trailfinders**

(☎ 0845 058 5858; www.trailfinders.co.uk). Both of these agencies sell tickets to all travellers, but they cater especially for young people and students.

Other recommended travel agencies:
ebookers.com (☎ 0871 223 5000; www.ebookers.com)
Flight Centre (☎ 0870 499 0040; www.flightcentre. co.uk)
North-South Travel (☎ 01245-608291; www.north southtravel.co.uk) Donates part of its profit to projects in the developing world.
Quest Travel (☎ 0845 263 6963; www.questtravel.com)
Travel Bag (☎ 0871 703 4698; www.travelbag.co.uk)

USA

From the east coast, the cheapest and most direct way to Botswana is by **Delta Air Lines** (www. delta.com) or South African Airways directly to Jo'burg, and then a connection to Gaborone. Expect to pay at least US$1500 return from New York or Washington to Jo'burg.

It may actually be cheaper to buy a US–London return fare and then buy a new ticket in the UK for the London–Botswana section of your journey. Otherwise check out the fares from other European capitals.

Delta and **United Airlines** (www.united.com) offer weekly flights from Chicago and/or Atlanta to Jo'burg. Air fares from the west coast, via Chicago, Atlanta, New York or Europe, to Jo'burg cost between US$1800 and US$2200 return.

San Francisco is the ticket-consolidator capital of America, although some good deals can be found in Los Angeles, New York and some other big cities. **STA Travel** (☎ 800-781 4040; www.statravel.com) has offices in Boston, Chicago, Miami, New York, Philadelphia, San Francisco and other major cities.

The following websites are recommended for online bookings.

- www.cheaptickets.com
- www.expedia.com
- www.kayak.com
- www.orbitz.com
- www.sta.com
- www.travelocity.com

LAND

Overland entry into Botswana is quite straightforward. Border posts are usually open from either 6am to 4pm or 8am to 6pm. For a useful map showing all the border crossings and up-to-date information on opening hours, check out the government website at www.botswana-tourism.gov.bw/entry_req/border_posts.html.

If you're driving a hire car into Botswana you will need to present a letter of permission from the rental company saying the car is allowed to cross the border. For more information on taking a vehicle into Botswana see opposite.

Border Crossings

Botswana has a well-developed road network with easy access from neighbouring countries. Gaborone is only 280km as the crow flies from Jo'burg along a good road link. The main border crossings into Botswana are as follows.

- From South Africa – Martin's Drift (from Northern Transvaal), Tlokweng (from Jo'burg), Ramatlabama (from Mafikeng)
- From Namibia – Mamuno, Mohembo and Ngoma Bridge
- From Zimbabwe – Kazungula, Ramokgweban/Plumtree and Pandamatenga
- From Zambia – Kazungula Ferry

All borders are open daily. It is advisable to try to reach the crossings as early in the day as possible to allow time for any potential delays. Immigration posts at some smaller border crossings close for lunch between 12.30pm and 1.45pm. At remote borders on the Botswanan side you may need to get your visa at the nearest police station in lieu of an immigration post.

Bus

Trying to enter and travel around Botswana on public transport is a big headache. Public transport is aimed at moving people between population centres and will rarely deliver you to the more exciting tourist spots.

There is, however, one mainline route run by Intercape Mainliner (see right) between Jo'burg and Gaborone. These double-decker buses are extremely comfortable with on-board TV and air-conditioning.

NAMIBIA

The public transport options between the two countries are few. One option is to catch the daily combi (minibus) from Ghanzi to Mamuno (three hours) and then to cross the borders on foot, bearing in mind that this crossing is about a kilometre long. You will then have to hitch a ride from the Namibian

side at least to Gobabis, where you can catch a train or other transport to Windhoek. It's time-consuming and unreliable at best.

SOUTH AFRICA

Intercape Mainliner (☎ in South Africa 0861 287 287, in Botswana 397 4294; www.intercape.co.za) runs a service from Jo'burg to Gaborone (from SAR180, 6½ hours, one daily); while you need to get off the bus to sort out any necessary visa formalities, you'll rarely be held up for too long at the border. That said, arranging your visa in advance will save time.

You can also travel between South Africa and Botswana by combi. From the far (back) end of the bus station in Gaborone, combis leave when full to a number of South African destinations including Jo'burg (P140/SAR160, five to seven hours). Be warned that you'll be dropped in Jo'burg's Park Station, which is *not* a safe place to linger in. Combis also travel from Selebi-Phikwe to the border at Martin's Drift (P20, two hours).

Public transport between the two countries bears South African number plates and/or signs on the door marked 'ZA Cross Border Transport'.

ZIMBABWE

Incredibly, there is *no* public transport between Kasane, the gateway to one of Botswana's major attractions (ie Chobe National Park), and Victoria Falls. Other than hitching, the only method of transport is the tourist 'shuttle minibus' (about one hour). There is little or no coordination between combi companies in either town, so combis often return from Victoria Falls to Kasane empty. Most combis won't leave unless they have at least two passengers.

From Kasane, Thebe River Camping (p112) and Chobe Safari Lodge (p113) offer private transfers to Livingstone/Victoria Falls (US$50, two hours). Both these operations usually pick up booked passengers at their hotels around 10am.

Book at Audi Camp, Chobe Safari Lodge (p113) in Kasane or Backpackers Bazaar (p186) in Victoria Falls. Backpackers Bazaar can also provide you with information on local shuttle buses running between Victoria Falls and Kasane.

From Victoria Falls, several travel agencies and hotels offer transfers to Kasane, but in reality they only go as far as the Zimbabwe border, where you will be met by someone on the Zimbabwe side. Some hotels and hostels in Zimbabwe (p195) will still arrange for your transport from the border, but you need to contact them beforehand.

Between Francistown and Bulawayo, several combis (P30, two hours) leave in both directions daily. For anywhere else in western Zimbabwe, get a connection in Bulawayo.

Car & Motorcycle

Crossing land borders with your own vehicle or a hire car is generally straightforward as long as you have the necessary paperwork – the vehicle registration documents if you own the car, or a letter from the hire company stating that you have permission to take the car over the border, and proof of insurance.

A vehicle registered outside Botswana can be driven around the country for six months, and an insurance policy purchased in a member country of the South African Customs Union (SACU; South Africa, Botswana, Namibia, Lesotho and Swaziland) is valid in Botswana for six months. If you don't have third-party insurance from another SACU country, you must buy it at a Botswanan border. Everyone driving into Botswana must pay road tax (officially called the National Road Safety Fund Levy), which costs around P100 per vehicle and is valid until the end of the current year.

See p178 for information about driving around Botswana.

NAMIBIA

The most common – and safest – crossing is at Mamuno, between Ghanzi and Windhoek, but the border post at Mohembo is also popular. The only other real option is the crossing at Ngoma Bridge across the Chobe River. The Kasane/Mpalila Island border is only available to guests who have prebooked accommodation at upmarket lodges on the island (see p282).

Drivers crossing the border at Mohembo must secure an entry permit for Mahango Game Reserve at Popa Falls. This is free if you're transiting, or N$80 per person per day plus N$40 per vehicle per day if you want to drive around the reserve (which is possible in a 2WD). From Divundu turn northwest towards Rundu and Windhoek, or east towards Katima Mulilo (Namibia), Kasane (Botswana)

and Victoria Falls (Zimbabwe), or take the ferry to Zambia.

SOUTH AFRICA

Most people travelling overland between Botswana and South Africa use the borders at Ramatlabama (between Lobatse and Mafikeng), Tlokweng Gate (between Gaborone and Zeerust) or Pioneer Gate (between Lobatse and Zeerust). The other border crossings serve back roads across the Limpopo River in the Tuli Block region and the Molopo River in southern Botswana.

It is vital to note that some crossings over the Limpopo and Molopo Rivers are drifts (river fords) that cannot be crossed by 2WD in wet weather. In times of very high water, these crossings may be closed to all traffic.

Hiring a Car in South Africa

Renting a car in South Africa will probably work out cheaper than renting one in Botswana. All major international car-rental companies (see p179) have offices all over South Africa. We'd also recommend the competitive local agencies **Around About Cars** (☎ 0860 422 4022; www .aroundaboutcars.com), **Britz** (☎ 011 396 1860; www.britz .co.za) and **Buffalo Campers** (☎ 27-11 021 0385; www .buffalo.co.za), which offers a 4WD for about R776 per day, including insurance, free kilometres and also cooking/camping equipment.

The cheapest 2WD will end up costing about SAR310 per day (with a minimum of five days) and a 4WD will cost in the region of SAR660 per day.

Purchasing a Car in South Africa

If you are planning an extended trip (three months or more) in Botswana it may be worth considering purchasing a second-hand car in South Africa and then selling it at the end of the trip.

Jo'burg is the best place to buy a car and start a trip to Botswana because of its proximity to Gaborone. It's also worth noting that cars bought in Cape Town will be viewed less favourably at sale given that Cape Town cars are considered to be at risk of rust given the city's seaside location. Newspapers in Jo'burg are obviously one place to start looking; also ask around the hostels. Used-car dealers won't advertise the fact, but they may buy back a car bought from them after about three months for about 60% of the purchase price – if the car is returned in good condition.

WILD DRIVING IN BOTSWANA & NAMIBIA

Below are road-tested tips to help you plan a safe and successful 4WD expedition. For more info on specific driving trips, see the boxed texts, p107, p111 and p128.

- Invest in a good Global Positioning System (GPS). You should always be able to identify your location on a map, though, even if you're navigating with a GPS.

- Stock up on emergency provisions, even on main highways. Fill up whenever you pass a station. For long expeditions, carry the requisite amount of fuel in metal jerry cans (off-road driving burns nearly twice as much fuel as highway driving). Carry 5L of water per person per day, as well as a plenty of high-calorie, non-perishable emergency food items.

- You should have a tow rope, a shovel, an extra fan belt, vehicle fluids, spark plugs, bailing wire, jump leads, fuses, hoses, a good jack and a wooden plank (to use as a base in sand and salt), several spare tyres and a pump. A good Swiss Army knife or Leatherman and a roll of gaffer tape can save your vehicle's life in a pinch.

- Essential camping equipment includes a waterproof tent, a three-season sleeping bag (or a warmer bag in the winter), a ground mat, fire-starting supplies, firewood, a basic first-aid kit and a torch (flashlight) with extra batteries.

- Sand tracks are least likely to bog vehicles in the cool mornings and evenings, when air spaces between sand grains are smaller. Move as quickly as possible and keep the revs up, but avoid sudden acceleration. Shift down gears before deep sandy patches or the vehicle may stall and bog. When negotiating a straight course through rutted sand, allow the vehicle to wander along the path of least resistance. Anticipate corners and turn the wheel slightly earlier than you would on a solid surface – this allows the vehicle to skid round smoothly – then accelerate gently out of the turn.

- Driving in the Kalahari is often through high grass, and the seeds it disperses can quickly foul radiators and cause overheating. If the temperature gauge begins to climb, remove as much plant material as you can from the grille.

- Keep your tyre pressure slightly lower than on sealed roads.

Naturally, check the vehicle documents from the previous owner. A roadworthy certificate (usually included when a car is bought from a used-car dealer) is required, as is a certificate from the police (also provided by most car dealers) to prove that the car isn't stolen. Once it's bought, re-register the vehicle at a Motor Vehicle Registration Division in a major city. Also recommended is a roadworthiness test by the Automobile Association (R115 to R350, membership not required) before you buy anything.

For a *very* rough idea of prices, don't expect to buy a vehicle for less than SAR31,000 to SAR46,500. A 4WD Land Rover will cost around R62,000.

ZIMBABWE

The two most commonly used borders are at Ramokgwebana/Plumtree and Kazungula.

There's also a lesser-used back-road crossing at Pandamatenga.

RIVER CROSSING

Botswana and Zambia share what is probably the world's shortest international border: about 750m across the Zambezi River. The only way across the river is by ferry from Kazungula, which normally operates from 6am to 6pm daily. Expect the ferry to cost about US$0.75 per person, US$10 for a motorbike, US$15 for a car and US$25 for a 4WD.

There is no regular public transport from the Zambian side of the river, although there is one combi that goes to Dambwa (P30, one hour), 3km west of Livingstone. If you don't have a vehicle, ask for a lift to Livingstone, Lusaka or points beyond at the ferry terminal or on the ferry itself.

- Avoid travelling at night, when dust and distance may create confusing mirages.
- Keep your speed to a maximum of 100km/h.
- Follow ruts made by other vehicles.
- If the road is corrugated, gradually increase your speed until you find the correct speed – it'll be obvious when the rattling stops.
- Be especially careful on bends – slow right down before attempting the turn.
- If you have a tyre blowout, do *not* hit the brakes or you'll lose control and the car will roll. Instead, steer straight ahead as best you can, and let the car slow itself down before you bring it to a complete stop.
- To avoid dust clouds when a vehicle approaches from the opposite direction, reduce your speed and keep as far left as possible.
- In rainy weather, gravel roads can turn to quagmires and desert washes may fill with water. If you're uncertain, get out and check the depth, and only cross when it's safe for the type of vehicle you're driving.
- Be on the lookout for animals.
- Avoid swerving sharply or braking suddenly on a gravel road or you risk losing control of the vehicle. If the rear wheels begin to skid, steer gently in the direction of the skid until you regain control. If the front wheels skid, take a firm hand on the wheel and steer in the opposite direction of the skid.
- Wrap food, clothing and camera equipment in dustproof plastic or keep them in sealed containers.
- In dusty conditions, switch on your headlights so you can be seen more easily.
- Overtaking can be extremely dangerous because your view may be obscured by dust kicked up by the car ahead. Flash your high beams at the driver in front to indicate that you want to overtake (this isn't considered obnoxious in Southern Africa). If someone behind you flashes their lights, move as far to the left as possible.

GETTING AROUND

Botswana's public-transport network is limited. Although domestic air services are fairly frequent and usually reliable, Air Botswana (and charter flights) is not cheap and only a handful of towns are regularly served. The railway service is inexpensive and dependable, but it is terribly slow and is restricted to one line along the thin populated strip of eastern Botswana. Public buses and combis (minibuses) are also cheap and reasonably frequent but confined to paved roads between towns. All in all, hiring a vehicle is the best and most practical option.

AIR

The national carrier, Air Botswana, operates a limited number of domestic flights between Gaborone and Francistown (US$100), Maun (US$155) and Kasane (US$155). Keep in mind these prices are all very subject to change. It also runs occasional packages between Gaborone and Maun, including hotels and sightseeing tours – check with the airline, or look for advertisements in the local English-language newspapers.

One-way fares are more expensive than return fares, so plan your itinerary accordingly; children aged under two sitting on the lap of an adult cost 10% of the fare and children aged between two and 12 cost 50% of the fare. Passengers are allowed 20kg of luggage (unofficially, a little more is often permitted if the flight is not full).

For details about the costs and frequency of domestic flights, and the contact details for Air Botswana offices, see Getting There & Away in the regional chapters of this book.

Charter Flights

Charter flights are often the best – and sometimes the only – way to reach remote lodges and isolated villages, but they are an expensive extra cost.

On average, a one-way fare between Maun and a remote lodge in the Okavango Delta will set you back around US$100 to US$200. These services are now highly regulated and flights must be booked as part of a safari package with a mandatory reservation at one of the lodges. This is essential as you can't simply turn up in these remote locations and expect to find a bed for the night, as many lodges are very small. Likewise, you are not permitted to book accommodation at a remote lodge in the delta without also booking a return air fare at the same time. Packages can be booked through agencies in Maun.

It is very important to note that passengers on charter flights are only allowed 10kg to 12kg of luggage each (check the exact amount when booking). However, if you have an extra 2kg to 3kg the pilot will usually only mind if the plane is full of passengers.

If you can't stretch the budget to staying in a remote lodge you can still book a flight over the delta with one of the scenic flight companies in Maun – see p125 for details.

BICYCLE

Botswana is largely flat – and that's about the only concession it makes to cyclists. Unless you're an experienced cyclist and equipped for the extreme conditions, abandon any ideas you may have about a Botswanan bicycle adventure. Distances are great and horizons are vast; the climate and landscapes are hot and dry; and, even along major routes, water is scarce and villages are widely spaced. What's more, the sun is intense and prolonged exposure to the burning ultraviolet rays is hazardous. Also bear in mind that bicycles are not permitted in Botswana's national parks and reserves and cyclists may encounter potentially dangerous wildlife while travelling along any highway or road.

BUS & COMBI

Buses and combis regularly travel to all major towns and villages throughout Botswana but are less frequent in sparsely populated areas such as western Botswana and the Kalahari. Public transport to smaller villages is often nonexistent, unless the village is along a major route.

The extent and frequency of buses and combis also depends on the quantity and quality of roads – for example, there is no public transport along the direct route between Maun and Kasane (ie through Chobe National Park) – and services are suspended if roads are flooded. Also, bear in mind that there are very few long-distance services, so anyone travelling between Gaborone and Kasane or Maun, for example, will need a connection in Francistown. For more detail about these regional routes refer to the relevant regional chapter.

Buses are usually comfortable, and normally leave at a set time regardless of whether they're full or not. Finding out the departure times for buses is a matter of asking around the bus station, because schedules are not posted anywhere. Combis leave when full, usually from the same station as the buses. Tickets for all public buses and combis cannot be bought in advance; they can only be purchased on board.

CAR & MOTORCYCLE

The best way to travel around Botswana is to hire a vehicle. With your own car you can avoid public transport and organised tours. The downside is that distances are long and the cost of hiring a vehicle is high in Botswana – but probably cheaper in South Africa (see p175).

You cannot hire a motorbike in Botswana and, unlike Namibia, the terrain is not well suited to biking. It's also important to note that motorbikes are *not* permitted in national parks and reserves for safety reasons.

Driving Licence

Your home driving licence is valid for six months in Botswana, but if it isn't written in English you must provide a certified translation. In any case, it is advisable to obtain an International Driving Permit (IDP). Your national automobile association can issue this and it is valid for 12 months.

Fuel & Spare Parts

The cost of fuel (petrol) is relatively expensive in Botswana, around P75 per litre, but prices vary according to the remoteness of the petrol station. Petrol stations are open 24 hours in Gaborone, Francistown, Maun, Mahalapye and Palapye; elsewhere, they open from about 7am to 7pm daily.

Hire

To rent a car you must be aged at least 21 (some companies require drivers to be over 25) and have been a licensed driver in your home country for at least two years (sometimes five).

Most major international car-rental companies will allow you to take a vehicle to South Africa, Lesotho, Swaziland, Namibia and Zimbabwe, but only if you have cleared it with the company beforehand so it can sort out the paperwork. It is also possible to hire a car, for example, in Gaborone and return it to Jo'burg (South Africa) or Windhoek (Namibia), but this will cost extra. Rental companies are less happy about drivers going to Zambia, and will not allow you to go anywhere else in Africa (apart from those listed above).

Naturally, always check the paperwork carefully and thoroughly examine the vehicle before accepting it; make sure the 4WD engages properly and that you understand how it works. Also, check the vehicle fluids, brakes, battery and so on – the Kalahari is a harsh place to find out that the company (or you) has overlooked something important.

It is probably best to deal with one of the major car-rental companies listed below. For information about hiring a car in South Africa and then driving it to Botswana, see p175.

Avis (www.avis.com) Offices in Gaborone, Francistown, Maun, Kasane and all over Southern Africa.

Budget (www.budget.co.za) Offices in Gaborone, as well as in South Africa, Zimbabwe and Namibia.

Europcar (www.europcar.co.za) Offices in Gaborone and in the major cities of South Africa, Namibia and Zambia.

Tempest (www.tempestcarhire.co.za) This large South Africa–based company has offices in Gaborone, throughout South Africa and in Namibia.

Additional charges will be levied for the following: dropping off or picking up the car at your hotel (rather than the car-rental office); a 'tourism levy' of 1% is sometimes charged (but this seems fairly arbitrary); each additional driver; a 'cleaning fee' (which can amount to P400!) may be incurred – at the discretion of the rental company; and a 'service fee' may be added. Also check to make sure the government sales tax (10%) is included.

It is nearly always advisable to pay with a 'gold level' credit card, which will offer you some protection should anything go wrong

and will possibly cover you for collision as well.

Insurance

Insurance is *strongly* recommended. No matter who you hire your car from, make sure you understand what is included in the price (such as unlimited kilometres, tax and so on) and what your liabilities are. Most local insurance policies do not include cover for damage to windshields and tyres.

Third-party motor insurance is a minimum requirement in Botswana. However, it is also advisable to take Damage (Collision) Waiver, which costs around P150 extra per day for a 2WD and about P300 per day for a 4WD. Loss (Theft) Waiver is also an extra worth having. For both types of insurance, the excess liability is about P4450 for a 2WD and P8900 for a 4WD. If you're only going for a short period of time it may be worth taking out the Super Collision Waiver, which covers absolutely everything, albeit at a price.

Purchase

Unless you're going to be staying in Botswana for several years, it's not worth purchasing a vehicle in the country. The best place to buy a vehicle is across the border in South Africa (see p175).

If you do buy a car with hard currency and resell it in Botswana, you can remit the same amount of hard currency to your home country without hassles – just keep the papers and inform the bank in advance.

Road Conditions

Good paved roads link all major population centres. Tracks with sand, mud, gravel and rocks (and sometimes all four) – but normally accessible by 2WD except during exceptional rains – connect most villages and cross a few national parks. The important Nata–Kasane road was in a miserable state at research time.

Most other 'roads' are poorly defined – and badly mapped – tracks that should only be attempted by 4WD. In the worst of the wet season (December to February), 4WDs should carry a winch on some tracks (eg through Chobe National Park). A compass or, better, Global Positioning System (GPS) equipment, is essential for driving by 4WD around the salt pans of the Kalahari or northeastern Botswana at any time.

BOTSWANA TRANSPORT

Road Rules

To drive a car in Botswana, you must be at least 18 years old. Like most other Southern African countries, traffic keeps to the left side of the road. The national speed limit is 120km/h on paved roads, 80km/h on gravel roads and 40km/h in all national parks and reserves. When passing through towns and villages, assume a speed limit of 60km/h, even in the absence of any signs.

Highway police use radar and love to fine motorists for speeding (about P100, plus additional charges according to the rate at which you were exceeding the limit). Sitting on the roof of a moving vehicle is illegal, and wearing seat belts (where installed) is compulsory in the front (but not back) seats. Drink-driving is also against the law, and your insurance policy will be invalid if you have an accident while drunk. Driving without a licence is also a serious offence.

If you have an accident causing injury, it must be reported to the authorities within 48 hours. If vehicles have sustained only minor damage and there are no injuries – and all parties agree – you can exchange names and addresses and sort it out later through your insurance companies.

In theory, owners are responsible for keeping their livestock off the road, but in practice animals wander wherever they want. If you hit a domestic animal, your distress (and possible vehicle damage) will be compounded by trying to find the owner and the red tape involved when filing a claim. Wild animals, including elephants and the estimated three million wild donkeys in Botswana, are a hazard, even along the highways. The Maun–Nata and Nata–Kasane roads are frequently traversed by elephants. The chances of hitting a wild or domestic animal is far, far greater after dark, so driving at night is definitely not recommended.

One common, but minor, annoyance are the so-called 'buffalo fences' (officially called Veterinary Cordon Fences; see p75). These are set up to stop the spread of disease from wild animals to livestock. Unless you're driving, or travelling in, a cattle truck, simply slow down while the gate is opened and make an effort to offer a friendly wave to the bored gate attendant.

HITCHING

Hitching in Botswana is an accepted way to get around, given that public transport is sometimes erratic, or nonexistent, in remote areas. There are even established rates for main routes. Travellers who decide to hitch, however, should understand that they are taking a small but potentially serious risk. People who do choose to hitch will be safer if they travel in pairs and let someone know where they are planning to go.

The equivalent of a bus fare will frequently be requested in exchange for a lift, but to prevent uncomfortable situations at the end of the ride determine a price before climbing in. Information on hitching along the main routes is given throughout this guide.

It is totally inadvisable to hitch along the back roads, for example through the Tuli Block or from Maun to Kasane through Chobe National Park. This is because traffic along these roads is virtually nonexistent; in fact, vehicles may only come past a few times a day, leaving the hopeful hitchhiker at risk of exposure or, even worse, running out of water. One way to circumvent this problem is to arrange a lift in advance at a nearby lodge.

LOCAL TRANSPORT

Public transport in Botswana is geared towards the needs of the local populace and is confined to main roads between major population centres. Although cheap and reliable, it is of little use to the traveller as most of Botswana's tourist attractions lie off the beaten track.

Combi

Combis, recognisable by their blue number plates, circulate according to set routes around major towns, ie Gaborone, Kasane, Ghanzi, Molepolole, Mahalapye, Palapye, Francistown, Selebi-Phikwe, Lobatse and Kanye. They are very frequent, inexpensive and generally reliable. However, they aren't terribly safe (drive too fast), especially on long journeys, and they only serve the major towns, which aren't of much interest to tourists. They can also be crowded.

Taxi

Licensed taxis are also recognisable by their blue number plates. They rarely bother hanging around the airports at Gaborone, Francistown, Kasane and Maun, so the only reliable transport from the airport is usually a courtesy bus operated by a top-end hotel or lodge. These are free for guests, but anyone else can normally negotiate a fare with the bus driver. Taxis are always available *to* the airports, however.

It is not normal for taxis to cruise the streets for fares – even in Gaborone. If you need one, telephone a taxi company to arrange a pick-up or go to a taxi stand (usually near the bus or train stations). Some taxi companies include **Speedy Cabs** (☎ 395 0070) and **Final Bravo Cab** (☎ 312 1785). Fares for taxis are negotiable, but fares for occasional shared taxis are fixed. Taxis can be chartered – about P300 to P400 per day, although this is negotiable depending on how far you want to go.

TRAIN

The Botswana Railways system is limited to one line running along eastern Botswana. It stretches from Ramokgwebana on the Zimbabwean border to Ramatlabama on the South African border, and was once part of the glorious Johannesburg–Bulawayo service,

which is now sadly defunct. Although cheap and reliable, it is painfully slow and serves places of little or no interest to the tourist.

There are two different types of train – the quicker and more expensive 'day train', and the slower and cheaper 'night train'. Both travel the route between Lobatse and Francistown, via Gaborone, Pilane, Mahalapye, Palapye, Serule and other villages. The most useful route is the Gaborone–Francistown service (club/economy class P30/60, 6½ hours, daily at 10am). A sleeper train also services this route but is considerably dearer (1st-class sleeper/2nd-class sleeper/economy P175/140/35, 8¼ hours, daily at 9pm).

Schedules and tickets are available at all train stations, but reservations are only pos-sible at Gaborone, Francistown and Lobatse (for trips beyond Gaborone). For 1st and 2nd class, advance bookings are essential; economy-class passengers can buy a ticket in advance or on the train.

BOTSWANA TRANSPORT

Victoria Falls

Victoria Falls is the largest, most beautiful and most majestic waterfall on the planet, and is the Seventh Natural Wonder of the World as well as being a Unesco World Heritage Site. A trip to Southern Africa would not be complete without visiting this unforgettable place. But it isn't just the one million litres of water that fall – per second – down a 108m drop along a 1.7km wide strip in the Zambezi Gorge that makes Victoria Falls so awesome; it's the whole natural context in which the falls are located that makes Victoria Falls so special.

Jump into the gorge, get drenched by the spray of the falls, raft along the rapids or cruise gently along the great Zambezi River. Whether it's wildlife that attracts you or the chance to fill your life with wildness, this place is rare and extraordinary and yet easy and unspoilt. Victoria Falls is to be seen, heard, tasted and touched: it is a treat that few other places in the world can offer, a Must See Before You Die spot.

Victoria Falls has a wet and dry season: when the river is higher and the falls fuller it's the Wet and when the river is lower and the falls aren't smothered in spray it's the Dry. The falls are spectacular at any time of year, except if all you want to do is ride those famous rapids, in which case you want the river low, the rocks exposed and the rapids pumping. The weather is never too hot or too cold, and all else on offer – from fine dining to zipping across a border on a high wire – are also there year round. The high seasons are June to August and Christmas, but April, with all the spray, is special too. Although Zimbabwe and Zambia share it, Victoria Falls is a place all of its own, which is why we give it its own chapter.

HIGHLIGHTS

- Gazing in amazement at Victoria Falls from the **Zambian** (p193) or **Zimbabwean** (p198) side (or preferably both)

- Visiting the falls during the full moon and seeing the enigmatic **lunar rainbow** (p193)

- Drinking a cocktail at the **Royal Livingstone Hotel** (p191) on a deck on the river near the lip of the falls

- Enjoying a spot of high tea at the **Terrace** (p197) at the elegant Victoria Falls Hotel

- Getting your **adrenaline kicks** (opposite) with bungee jumping, microlighting, white-water rafting, jet-boating or a Gorge Swing

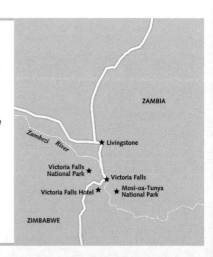

ACTIVITIES: A-Z

Face fear and enjoy the rush: Victoria Falls has got it all! Activities listed in this section can be booked through your accommodation and started from either Livingstone (Zambia) or Victoria Falls (Zimbabwe) for about the same cost. Confirm any extra costs such as park or visa fees, at the time of booking. All operators give package prices too and for around US$125 you can sample all the adrenalin leaps. The operators usually offer photos and videos of your escapades as well (US$35 for videos, US$15 for single shots, US$45 for both). Note that rates given in this section are approximate and subject to change.

Abseiling

Spend the day rappelling down cliffs and swinging across the canyons and gorges the rushing Zambezi cuts through in the scenic Batoka Gorge. Half-/full-day excursions cost US$80/100.

Bird Walk

Check out the amazing birds that inhabit the area around the falls for around US$70.

Botswana/Chobe Day Trip

Located a mere one-hour's drive from Victoria Falls, this day trip includes a breakfast boat cruise, a game drive in Chobe National Park, lunch and transfer back to Victoria Falls by 5pm. Wildlife viewing is excellent: lions, elephants, wild dogs, cheetahs, buffaloes and plenty of antelopes. The price is US$150 per person.

Bungee Jumping

Tackling the third-highest jump in the world (111m) costs single/tandem US$105/$130. There are two main spots, and both jumps are from the same height.

Canoeing & Kayaking

Half-/full-day trips along the Zambezi River cost US$60/75; overnight jaunts cost US$150, and three-night trips start at US$300.

Clay Pigeon Shooting

Morning, lunch and afternoon sessions are available, the latter with dinner, which you eat in a boma with panoramic views over the rolling African bush. Situated only 3km from Victoria Falls, these sessions are of an international standard with instructors and are good for both beginners and the experienced. Costs start at US$55.

Elephant-Back Safaris

Take a journey on the back of an elephant through stunning national parkland or nature reserves. See the boxed text, p185, for information on some issues with wild animal encounters.

Fishing

Tackle the mighty tiger fish of the Zambezi with a half-day trip including tackle, rods, lures and bait, all for around US$90.

Fixed-Wing Flights

Whether you fly in a modern Cessna or a vintage Tiger Moth, you'll have amazing views of the falls, the spray and the river from above. Flights range from US$80 to US$160 depending on the type of craft and the route.

Flying Fox

Zip across the Batoka Gorge for just US$25.

Game Drives & Walks

Take a morning or evening guided safari in a national park, either in a 4WD or by foot. Enjoy the African landscape at its best in the gentle morning or early evening light. Costs are from US$50 per person or game walks US$70. Note that this is for group bookings only.

Golf

Enjoy scenic game drives between rounds on immaculate fairways on both sides of the border, in Zimbabwe at The Elephant Hills Hotel or in Zambia at Livingstone Royal Golf & Country Club. A game of nine holes costs US$10 (equipment hire US$10) and 18 holes costs $US20 (equipment hire US$20). Caddy fees are US$5 extra.

Gorge Slide

This is a lot like the Flying Fox but you whiz down into the Batoka Gorge and back up the other side (single/tandem $35/45) – an adrenalin rush for starters.

Gorge Swing

For those who want to be brave enough to bungee jump but never will be, this is perfect. It's located at the Batoka Gorge.

Jump

Jump feet first, free fall for four seconds but you'll end up the right-way-up, swinging but not upside down. There are tandem options of this too. There are two main spots, one right off the Victoria Falls Bridge, and the other a bit further along the gorge. Costs are US$75.

Helicopters

The 'Flight of the Angels' is a 15-minute joy ride (US$115 excluding park fees) over the falls or 30 minutes (US$260) across the falls and Zambezi National Park.

Hiking

Embark on a hike with guides around the Zambezi National Park (Zimbabwe) or Mosi-oa-Tunya National Park (Zambia). Day hikes cost US$50, while overnight camping is an additional US$10.

Horse-Riding

Tracks go alongside the Zambezi, and you can indulge in a bit of wildlife spotting from horseback. Two-/three-hour rides cost about US$45/60, while half-/full-day rides are about US$85/160.

Hwange Day Trips

Don't miss the park with one of the largest number of elephants in the world. A day trip will cost around US$250.

Interactive Drumming

Spend an evening by a campfire drumming under the southern African sky. A one-hour session followed by a traditional meal costs US$25.

Jet Boats

Go straight into whirlpools! This hair-raising trip costs US$90, and is combined with a cable-car ride down into the Batoka Gorge.

Microlights & Ultralights

These motorised hang-gliders offer fabulous aerial views, and the pilot will take pictures for you with a camera fixed to the wing. Prices are US$104 for 15 minutes over the falls and US$185 for 30 minutes for the falls and Zambezi National Park.

> **ZAMBEZI RIVER: HIGHS & LOWS**
>
> During the rainy season (March to May), the Zambezi's flow can be 10 times higher, while in the dry season (September to December), the volume of water can be as low as 4% of the peak flow.

Night Game Drives

Only available on the Zimbabwean side, these take place in the Zambezi National Park, and cost US$90 for a full night drive.

Quadbiking

Discover the spectacular landscape surrounding Livingstone, Zambia, and the Batoka Gorge, spotting wildlife as you go on all-terrain quad bikes. These ultimate adventure vehicles allow all riders to go at their own pace, under supervision of qualified guides. Trips vary from eco trail riding at Batoka Land to longer range cultural trips in the African Bush. A one-hour spin costs US$60.

Rafting

There are high-water runs through rapids 11 to 18 (or 23), which are relatively mild and can be done between 1 July and 15 August, though in high rainfall years they may begin as early as mid-May. Wilder low-water runs operate from roughly 15 August to late December, taking in the winding 22km from rapids 4 to 18 (or 23) if you put in on the Zimbabwean side, and from Rapids 1 to 18 (or 23) if you put in on the Zambian side. Half-/full-day trips cost about US$110/125, and overnight trips about US$165. Longer jaunts can also be arranged.

Retail Therapy

You'll find markets located in Victoria Falls town and on the Zambian side of the bridge after immigration, near the entrance to the National Park and the falls.

Rhino Walks

These and other nature walks are done on the Zambian side, through the Masi-oa-Tunya National Park. It must be noted that, as with all safaris, although guides do their best, viewing of particular animals cannot be guaranteed. Walks costs $US85 per person, for groups of up to eight. Organised by Bwaato Adventures, you can book online through www.zambiatour

---

NATIONAL PARK FEES

You can pay your park fees at the national park entrances and national park offices inside the parks.

- US$10 Victoria Falls Entrance – from the Zambian side
- US$20 for overseas residents in Zimbabwe
- US$15 for regional residents in Zimbabwe
- US$20 Victoria Falls Entrance – from the Zimbabwean side

---

ism.com, but this can also be booked through your hotel or hostel.

River-Boarding

How about lying on a boogie board and careering down the rapids? 'Waterfall surfing', as it's sometimes called, costs from US$135/150 for a half/full day. The best time of year for river-boarding is February to June.

Sitting

Not to be underestimated is the fine art of sitting while at Victoria Falls and soaking up the atmosphere, gazing about you while watching the world go by. You can sit either at a restaurant (Zambezi Waterfront for example; see p189) or bar (Royal Livingstone for preference; see p191) with the river rushing underneath you, or have the falls and bungee jumpers plummeting in front of you (Drop Zone Viewing Platform) on the Zambian side of the Bridge. In Zimbabwe you can make like a local and sit on The Rock, which is near The Big Tree – stunning! And absolutely free.

Steam Train Trips

A variety of steam train tours ranging from the Royal Tea Run to the Victoria Falls Bridge, to an *Out of Africa* Bush Breakfast or sunset steamer (only for prebooked groups, a minimum of 25) cost about US$95.

Traditional Dancing

Great as a spectator sport or you can join in for US$40.

Victoria Falls Tour

The best way to see the falls is on the Zimbabwean side. You enter through the

National Park gates (open from 6am to 6pm), show your passport and pay a US$20 fee per person. Hire a raincoat and umbrella just inside those gates if you go in April, or you may as well walk in your swimming suit – you *will* get drenched! The walk is along the top of the gorge on a path, which is signposted with the best vantage points and can sometimes be shared with monkeys and warthogs. The former are cheeky and the latter are shy. Note that you can get to the bridge, but not onto it, from this path.

Wildlife Drives

Head out on a guided safari in Mosi-oa-Tunya Game Park, Zambia, which is a great place to see white rhinos. Wildlife drives here cost around US$50. Or choose a river safari on the Zambezi. River cruises along the Zambezi range from civilised jaunts on the *African Queen* to full-on, all-you-can-drink sunset booze cruises. Prices range from US$30 to US$60. Great for spotting wildlife, though some tourists get just as much enjoyment out of the free drinks!

TRAVEL & ADVENTURE COMPANIES

What's so easy is that 99% of all bookings for activities in the falls are done through the lodge, hotel or backpacking hostel you are staying in. Prices for activities are all basically the same, and arranging it from where you stay means transfers are included.

You can also go directly to tour operators who have activities operators on their books too. Try **Wild Horizons** (☎ 44571; www.wildhorizons .co.zw) with an office in Victoria Falls town,

---

ANIMAL ENCOUNTERS: SHOULD YOU AVOID THEM?

There are some dodgy operators out there, so do think about what they are offering in terms of the welfare of the animals. For example, what happens to the young lion cubs or elephants when they get older? If elephants are to be used for commercial purposes, there are a few good operations in Africa that are 'using' elephants in the right way, ie by doing walks with elephants rather than riding them. This serves to educate the public about elephants and satisfies the desire for tourists to have close contact with elephants, which is after all an extraordinary privilege.

VISAS

You will need a visa to cross sides from Zim to Zam or vice versa. These are applicable to most nationalities and they are available at the border posts.

- Day visit: US$20 for 24 hours
- Single entry: US$50
- Double/multi-entry: US$80
- Multi-entry: on application

African Horizons (☎ 323432; www.adventure-africa.com) in Livingstone, or **Safari Par Excellence** (☎ in Zambia 326629, 421190, 011205306; www.safpar.net) which all cover activities on either side.

If you want independent advice, visit **Backpackers Bazaar** (Map p196; ☎ 013-45828; bazaar@ mweb.co.zw; off Parkway; ⏰ 8am-5pm Mon-Fri, 8am-4pm Sat & Sun) in the town of Victoria Falls.

ZAMBIA

While Zimbabwe is working hard to rekindle its economy, Zambia is stable; the 73 tribes coexist peacefully and the currency (the kwacha) is strengthening. The recent tourist swing to the Zambian side of Victoria Falls due to Zimbabwe's troubles has initiated a construction boom. Local business owners are riding the tourism wave and are building and renovating for even more expected growth. The Zambezi River waterfront is rapidly being tastefully developed as one of the most exclusive destinations in Southern Africa.

LIVINGSTONE
☎ 0213

The historic town of Livingstone, named after the first European to set eyes on Victoria Falls, sprung to life following the construction of the Victoria Falls Bridge in 1904. During the remainder of the 20th century, Livingstone existed as a quiet provincial capital. However, during the political and economic troubles in Zimbabwe, Livingstone quickly lifted its game and was able to cater for a new wave of tourists. Historic buildings got much-needed facelifts, new construction projects began and plans were hatched for increased transport links.

Today, Livingstone is the preferred base for backpackers visiting Victoria Falls. The town is not much to look at but it is a fun place for backpackers: It's set 11km away from the falls and unless you've gone for the option of staying on the Zambezi riverfront, you are not staying in a natural setting, but an African border town. That said, it has excellent (read: fun, cheap and well-organised) hostels, all with internet access and the full gamut of activities on offer within, plus restaurants and bars in town catering to every type of traveller – from those on a shoestring to those on a once in a lifetime event such as a honeymoon.

History
Although several explorers and artists visited the area following its 'discovery', Victoria Falls were largely ignored by Europeans until the construction of Cecil Rhodes' railway in 1905. During the British colonial era and the early years of Zambian and Zimbabwean independence, the falls emerged as one of the most popular tourist destinations in southern Africa. However, tourist numbers plummeted in the late 1960s in response to the guerrilla warfare in Zimbabwe, and the climate of suspicion aimed at foreigners under the rule of Zambian President Kenneth Kaunda.

During the 1980s, tourism surged once more as travellers started flocking to the region in search of adrenaline highs. The town of Victoria Falls (p194) in Zimbabwe billed itself as a centre for extreme sports, while sleepy Livingstone absorbed some of the tourist overflow. By the end of the 20th century, Victoria Falls was receiving over a quarter of a million visitors each year, and the future (on both sides of the falls) was looking bright.

In a few short years however, the civil unrest resulting from Zimbabwean President Robert Mugabe's controversial land reform program brought tourism in the town of Victoria Falls to a halt. Although foreigners safely remained on the sidelines of the political conflict, hyperinflation of the currency, lack of goods and services and the absence of commodities such as petrol all served as significant deterrents to tourism.

On the Zambian side of the falls however, business is booming. After years of playing second fiddle to the town of Victoria Falls, Livingstone has been reaping the benefits of Zimbabwe's decline. New hotels, restaurants

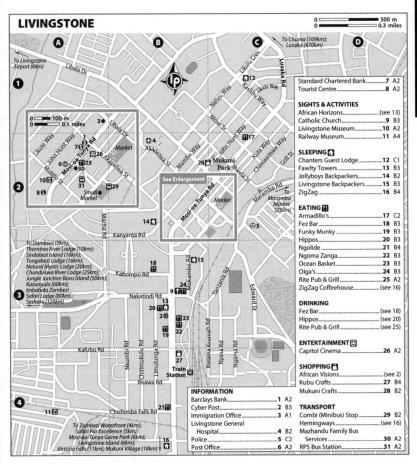

LIVINGSTONE

Standard Chartered Bank..............**7** A2	
Tourist Centre..............**8** A2	

SIGHTS & ACTIVITIES
African Horizons..............(see 13)	
Catholic Church..............**9** B3	
Livingstone Museum..............**10** A2	
Railway Museum..............**11** A4	

SLEEPING 🛏
Chanters Guest Lodge..............**12** C1	
Fawlty Towers..............**13** B3	
Jollyboys Backpackers..............**14** B2	
Livingstone Backpackers..............**15** B3	
ZigZag..............**16** B4	

EATING 🍴
Armadillo's..............**17** C2	
Fez Bar..............**18** B3	
Funky Munky..............**19** B3	
Hippos..............**20** B3	
Ngolide..............**21** B4	
Ngoma Zanga..............**22** B3	
Ocean Basket..............**23** B3	
Olga's..............**24** B3	
Rite Pub & Grill..............**25** A2	
ZigZag Coffeehouse..............(see 16)	

DRINKING
Fez Bar..............(see 18)	
Hippos..............(see 20)	
Rite Pub & Grill..............(see 25)	

ENTERTAINMENT 🎬
Capitol Cinema..............**26** A2	

SHOPPING 🛍
African Visions..............(see 2)	
Kubu Crafts..............**27** B4	
Mukuni Crafts..............**28** B2	

TRANSPORT
Combi (Minibus) Stop..............**29** B2	
Hemingways..............(see 16)	
Mazhandu Family Bus	
Services..............**30** A2	
RPS Bus Station..............**31** A2	

INFORMATION
Barclays Bank..............**1** A2	
Cyber Post..............**2** B3	
Immigration Office..............**3** A1	
Livingstone General	
Hospital..............**4** B2	
Police..............**5** C2	
Post Office..............**6** A2	

and shopping malls are popping up all over town and along the Zambezi riverfront, while increased flights and bus routes are making it easier for travellers to arrive en masse. While Zimbabwe still has political tensions, the dollarisation and other moves to revitalise the economy will no doubt have their effect here on Livingstone.

Orientation

Livingstone is a small African town that has taken on the role of a backpacking mecca. The town centres itself around one main road, Mosi-oa-Tunya Rd, meaning 'The Smoke That Thunders', which is exactly what the falls look like from Livingstone. The town centre itself is 11km from the entrance to the

falls. Several establishments are set right on the Zambezi River, but most of the action is set a bit back from the waterfront.

Information

Barclays Bank (cnr Mosi-oa-Tunya Rd & Akapelwa St) Accepts major brands of travellers cheques, offers cash advances on Visa and MasterCard and changes money.

Cyber Post (216 Mosi-oa-Tunya Rd; per hr US$4) Also offers international phone calls and faxes. All the hostels now have wi-fi or at least internet access.

Livingstone General Hospital (☎ 321475; Akapelwa St)

Police (☎ 320116; Maramba Rd)

Post office (Mosi-oa-Tunya Rd) Has a poste restante and fax service.

Standard Chartered Bank (Mosi-oa-Tunya Rd) Accepts major brands of travellers cheques, offers cash advances on Visa and MasterCard and changes money.

Tourist Centre (☎ 321404; Mosi-oa-Tunya Rd; ☺ 8am-1pm & 2-5pm Mon-Fri, 8am-12pm Sat) This is mildly useful and has a few brochures and maps, but really, the hostels are heaving with all the information you need.

Dangers & Annoyances

Don't walk from town to the falls as there have been a number of muggings along this stretch of road – even tourists on bicycles have been attacked. It's a long and not a terribly interesting walk anyway. Take a blue taxi for US$10.

Sights & Activities

One of the most popular sights is **Livingstone Island** (Map pp192–3), in the middle of the Zambezi River at the top of the falls, so you can literally hang your feet off the edge. A trip to the island costs about US$45 and can be arranged at your hotel or hostel.

African Culture, Language and Meals Experiences (☎ 323432; www.adventure-africa.com; 559 Makambo Rd), which can be organised through Fawlty Towers, is an African experience at Ngoma Zanga with a meal, singing, drumming and dancing. It's good value.

Mukuni Village (admission US$3; ☺ dawn-dusk) is a 'traditional' Leva village that welcomes tourists on guided tours. Although the village can be inundated with tourists at times, the admission fee does fund community projects.

The **Capitol Cinema** (Mosi-oa-Tunya Rd), located quite close to the Jollyboys, caters for travellers and at the time of writing it was showing a James Bond Film Festival. They also screen football matches.

The stately **Livingstone Museum** (Mosi-oa-Tunya Rd; adult US$2; ☺ 9am-4.30pm) is divided into five sections covering archaeology, history, ethnography, natural history and art, and is highlighted by Tonga ritual artefacts, a life-sized model African village, a collection of David Livingstone memorabilia and historic maps dating back to 1690.

The **Railway Museum** (Chishimba Falls Rd; admission US$5; ☺ 8.30am-4.30pm) features a charming but motley collection of locomotives, rolling stock and rail-related antiques. Unless you're a ravenous railway buff however, it probably isn't worth visiting.

Sleeping

Accommodation on the Zambian side of Victoria Falls is located either in Livingstone or along the Zambezi waterfront. In town you are within walking distance of all the bars and restaurants; along the riverfront you can relax in seclusion along some gorgeous stretches of the Zambezi. It is certainly stunning to be able to be simultaneously on the edge of the river and on the lip of the falls where the river rushes at great speed and you can see the spray. Or if you're staying further away, it's just as amazing to be down the river where it opens up more and you can see extraordinary amounts of elephants and other wildlife including hundreds of species of birds, right from the hotel.

TOWN CENTRE
Budget

Livingstone Backpackers (☎ 323432; www.adventure-africa.com; 559 Makambo Rd; camping US$3; dm from US$5, private room US$20; ☒) This is a brand new offering; it's Fawlty Towers Mark II set in a nearby location, only this is bigger, better and cheaper than ever. It has an outdoor bar, nice pool,

---

VISITING ZAM FROM ZIM (OR VICE VERSA)

From Victoria Falls you can walk, take a taxi, or a complimentary bus service from your hotel to the Zimbabwean immigration post, and then continue 1.3km on foot over the Victoria Falls Bridge. Enjoy the thrilling atmosphere of the bungee jumpers, and their audiences, halfway across the bridge. Just past the bridge is the Zambian border crossing, and 100m beyond it, the entrance to Mosi-oa-Tunya National Park.

Take a blue taxi (US$10) to Livingstone, about 11km away. Mugging is common along this route and it's too far to walk.

Most travel agencies and hotels in Victoria Falls and Livingstone charge about US$25 for minibus transfers between the two towns. If you're crossing into Zambia for the day, advise the Zimbabwean officials before leaving the country so you won't need to buy a new visa when you return later in the day.

Jacuzzi, snazzy open-air living room, climbing wall, pool table, DSTV (a digital satellite TV company) with all the sport channels and self-catering kitchen. In total it offers 78 beds, and is a great deal for both groups or individuals.

Jollyboys Backpackers (☎ 324229; www.backpackzambia.com; 34 Kanyanta Rd; camping per person US$6, dm from US$6, d from US$25; ☒) Located behind the museum, this place won the prize for the best hostel in Zambia in 2008. From the sunken pillow lounge to the pool, cheap restaurant, bar, barbeque, DSTV and lofty observation tower, everything has been carefully designed by the fun-loving owners. At night, management will not let you bring in people who are not staying at the hostel.

Midrange

Fawlty Towers (☎ 323432; www.adventure-africa.com; 216 Mosi-oa-Tunya Rd; s/d half board US$25/45; ☐ ☒) This backpacking institution has been renovated into a guest house, full of upmarket touches: free internet and wi-fi, hip bar, shady lawn, a great pool plus a well-organised, on-the-pulse vibe, which comes directly from its owner, Richard Sheppard, a campaigner for bringing back budget travel. There is also a towering thatched bar-restaurant on the premises called Hippos (p191) which is one of the hottest nightspots in town.

ZigZag (☎ 322814; www.zigzagzambia.com; Mosi-oa-Tunya Rd; s/d US$45/70, f US$90; ℗ ☐ ☒) This place consists of 12 motel-style rooms, a lovely swimming pool and a small craft shop. Comfortably and peacefully set in a 1.5 acre garden, this very friendly family-run business has all the mod cons such as air-con and wi-fi. Lovely baking really takes the cake here, though. It also has ZigZag Coffee House (p191).

Chanters Guest Lodge (☎ 323412; www.chanters-livingstone.com; Likulu Cres; s/d incl breakfast US$55/65, f incl breakfast US$85; ℗ ☒) This lodge has 10 motel-style rooms in suburban Livingstone, a pool and restaurant and is set in quiet surroundings. This is a good option for families.

ZAMBEZI RIVERFRONT

Prebooking for hotels along the riverfront is necessary.

Budget

Jungle Junction Bovu Island (☎ 323708; www.junglejunction.info; camping per person US$10-15, huts per person $20-30; ℗ ☒) Hippos, hammocks and harmony. Located on a lush island in the middle of the Zambezi River, Jungle Junction attracts

travellers who want to do nothing more than lounge beneath the palm trees, or engage in some fishing. Meals are available (from US$7 to US$12).

Midrange

All prices include meals and transfers from Livingstone.

Zambezi Waterfront (☎ 320606; www.safpar.net; camping per person US$10, s/d pre-set tents US$30/20, s/d incl breakfast per person from US$125/110, f US$200; ℗ ☒ ☒) Accommodation is varied, and includes luxury tents, standard and riverside chalets as well as executive rooms and family suites. It includes a great open-air beer garden right on the Zambezi River.

Natural Mystic Lodge (☎ 324436; www.naturalmysticlodge.com; s/d from US$85/95; ℗ ☒) The atmosphere at Natural Mystic is significantly less lavish than at some of the more upmarket lodges, though it makes for a peaceful retreat. It's 20km from Livingstone and 30km from the falls. Transfers are usually provided.

Top End

Chundukwa River Lodge (☎ 324452; info@maplanga.co.za; camping per person US$10, huts per person US$125; ℗ ☒) This simple but rustic lodge consists of thatched huts perched directly on the water. Sightings of elephants and hippos from the rooms are commonplace, there is a cooling plunge pool right on the riverbank and yummy home-cooking Zambian style.

Imbabala Zambezi Safari Lodge (☎ in South Africa 27 11 921 0225; per person from US$157) Set on a riverine fringe of the Zambezi River where Zimbabwe, Botswana and Zambia converge, 80km west of Victoria Falls, this lodge offers amazing game viewing and bird watching. It is set in a national parks concession bordering the Chobe Forest Reserve – a park renowned for its massive elephant population.

Thorntree River Lodge (☎ 324480; www.safpar.com/thorntree.htm; chalets per person US$250; ℗ ☒ ☒) The Thorntree River Lodge is located within the borders of Mosi-oa-Tunya National Park, and features rustic chalets with panoramic views of elephants frolicking along the Zambezi River. Prices include full board.

Zambezi Sun (Map pp192-3; ☎ 321122; www.sunint.co.za; s/d from US$275/300; ℗ ☒ ☒) The closest Zambian hotel to the falls, this huge complex, with restaurants, bars and a casino, is Moroccan-inspired, and designed to simulate

THE MAN, THE MYTH, THE LEGEND

David Livingstone is one of a few European explorers who is still revered by modern-day Africans. His legendary exploits on the continent border the realm of fiction, though his life's mission to end the slave trade was very real (and ultimately very successful).

Born into rural poverty in the south of Scotland on March 19, 1813, Livingstone began working in a local cotton mill at the age of 10, though his first passion was for the classics. After studying Greek, medicine and theology at the University of Glasgow, he worked in London for several years before being ordained as a missionary in 1840. The following year, Livingstone arrived in Bechuanaland (now Botswana) and began travelling inland, looking for converts and seeking to end the slave trade.

As early as 1842, Livingstone had already become the first European to penetrate the northern reaches of the Kalahari. For the next several years, Livingstone explored the African interior with the purpose of opening up trade routes and establishing missions. In 1854, Livingstone discovered a route to the Atlantic coast, and arrived in present-day Luanda. However, his most famous discovery occurred in 1855 when he first set eyes on Victoria Falls during his epic boat journey down the Zambezi River.

Livingstone returned to Britain a national hero, and recounted his travels in the 1857 publication *Missionary Travels and Researches in South Africa*. Livingstone's oft-cited motto was "Christianity, Commerce and Civilization", and he believed that navigating and ultimately controlling the Zambezi was crucial to this agenda.

In 1858, Livingstone returned to Africa as the head of the 'Zambezi Expedition', a government-funded venture that aimed to identify natural resource reserves in the region. Unfortunately for Livingstone, the expedition ended when a previously unexplored section of the Zambezi turned out to be unnavigable. The British press labelled the expedition as a failure, and Livingstone was forced to return home in 1864 after the government recalled the mission.

In 1866, Livingstone returned to Africa, and arrived in Zanzibar with the goal of seeking out the source of the Nile River. Although the British explorer John Hanning Speke arrived on the shores of Lake Victoria in 1858, the scientific community was divided over the legitimacy of his discovery (in actuality, the Nile descends from the mountains of Burundi halfway between Lake Tanganyika and Lake Victoria).

In 1869, Livingstone reached Lake Tanganyika despite failing health, though several of his followers abandoned the expedition en-route. These desertions were headline news in Britain, sparking rumours regarding Livingstone's health and sanity. In response to the growing mystery surrounding Livingstone's whereabouts, the *New York Herald* newspaper arranged a publicity stunt by sending journalist Henry Morton Stanley to find Livingstone.

According to Stanley's published account, the journalist had once asked the paper's manager how much he was allowed to spend on the expedition. The famous reply was simple: "Draw £1000 now, and when you have gone through that, draw another £1000, and when that is spent, draw another £1000, and when you have finished that, draw another £1000, and so on – but find Livingstone!"

After arriving in Zanzibar and setting out with nearly 200 porters, Stanley finally found Livingstone on November 10, 1871 in Ujiji near Lake Tanganyika. Although Livingstone may well have been the only European in the entire region, Stanley famously greeted him with the line 'Dr Livingstone, I presume?'.

Although Stanley urged him to leave the continent, Livingstone was determined to find the source of the Nile. Livingstone penetrated deeper into the continent than any European prior. On May 1, 1873, Livingstone died from malaria and dysentery near Lake Bangweula in present-day Zambia. His body was carried for thousands of kilometres by his attendants, and now lies in the ground at Westminster Abbey in London.

a north African kasbah. It contains a great playground for kids.

Royal Livingstone (Map pp192-3; ☎ 321122; www .sunint.co.za; s/d from US$415/450; ℗ ⛾ ☎) Very stylish colonial accommodation with a manicured lawn leading to the river, the hotel has an atmosphere of indulgence and yesteryear glamour, and is absolutely fab for a honeymoon.

Tongabezi Lodge (☎ 323235; www.tongabezi.com; cottages/houses per person US$430/530; ℗ ⛾ ☎) Here you'll find sumptuous spacious cottages and open-faced 'houses', with trees as part of the structure and private dining decks. Guests are invited to spend an evening on nearby Sindabezi Island (per person per night US$350), selected by the *Sunday Times* as the best remote place to stay in the world.

Eating & Drinking

Livingstone is home to a number of high-quality tourist-oriented restaurants, including a batch of excellent newcomers.

Royal Livingstone (Map pp192-3; ☎ 321122; www .sunint.co.za; cocktails US$4) Try a refreshing beverage on the extraordinary drinks deck upon the water not far from the lip of the falls.

Funky Munky (216 Mosi-oa-Tunya Rd; snacks & mains US$5) This laid-back bistro is a popular backpackers' hang out and prepares baguettes, salads and pizzas in a comfortable setting.

ZigZag Coffee House (Mosi-oa-Tunya Rd; mains US$5) This place offers an eclectic range of dishes, from tacos to tandoori, and is ideal for a coffee or milk shake.

Olga's (cnr Mosi-oa-Tunya & Nakatindi Rds; mains US$5-10) This new place is a good bet for pizza. It's opposite Fawlty Towers and behind the Catholic church.

Armadillo's (Mosi-oa-Tunya Rd; mains US$5-10) Located in the centre of town, this is a new and homey but nice place, with 'international' dishes cooked by an internationally trained chef: fish as well as local food. It can cater for large groups.

Ngolide (Mosi-oa-Tunya Rd; mains US$5-10) This place is a very popular Indian tandoori restaurant which also sells spicy chicken, so is popular with the locals as well as tourists. The chef is from India and it is good value for money. Groups are welcome and takeaways are available.

Ocean Basket (82 Mosi-oa-Tunya Rd; mains US$5-10) This popular South African restaurant specialises in (not surprisingly) fish. Sure, you're dining in a landlocked country but the quality and selection here is good.

Fez Bar (Kabompo Rd; mains US$6) This Moroccan-inspired bar and lounge serves tasty and eclectic meals throughout the day, though things really get kicking here once the sun goes down.

Hippos (Limulunga Rd; mains US$6) This raucous but newly renovated bar-cum-restaurant at the back of Fawlty Towers is housed underneath a soaring two-storey thatched roof.

Rite Pub & Grill (Mosi-oa-Tunya Rd; mains US$7) This centrally located pub draws in a good mix of travellers and locals, and serves tasty pub grub amid a kitschy Wild West setting.

Ngoma Zanga (Mosi-oa-Tunya Rd; meal US$25) This restaurant allows you to release your inner tourist! It has comparatively expensive but excellent African cuisine, in a typical 'traditional' scenario, from the welcoming routine to the performances while you eat the local fare.

Shopping

African Visions (216 Mosi-oa-Tunya Rd) Near the Livingstone Adventure Centre, this is a charming place selling quality fabrics and crafts from all over Africa.

Kubu Crafts (Mosi-oa-Tunya Rd) This shop offers a vast selection of classy souvenirs. You can admire your purchases while sipping a tea or coffee in the shady tea garden.

Mukuni Crafts (Mosi-oa-Tunya Rd) The craft stalls in the southern corner of this park are a pleasant, and relatively hassle-free place to browse for souvenirs.

Getting There & Away

AIR

Proflight Zambia (☎ 0211-271032; www.proflight-zambia .com) connects Livingstone to destinations throughout Zambia, Botswana and Namibia. **South African Airways** (www.flysaa.com) and **British Airways** (www.britishairways.com) both have daily flights to and from Johannesburg, and the cheapest economy fare starts at around US$450 return.

BICYCLE

Bikes can be ridden to/from Zimbabwe; do be cautious as cyclists have been mugged while riding to/from the Zambian border and Victoria Falls.

BUS & COMBI (MINIBUS)
Domestic

RPS (Mutelo St) has two bus services a day travelling to Lusaka (K65,380 to K84,060),

VICTORIA FALLS & MOSI-OA-TUNYA NATIONAL PARKS

seven hours). **CR Carriers** (cnr Mosi-oa-Tunya Rd & Akapelwa St) runs four services a day to Lusaka (K65,380 to K84,060, seven hours). Buses to Shesheke (K32,690, five hours) leave at around 10am from Mingongo bus station next to the Catholic church at Dambwa village, 3km west of the town centre. Direct buses to Mongu (K51,370, nine hours) leave at midnight from Maramba market, though you might feel more comfortable on a morning bus to Sesheke, and then transfer to a Mongu bus (K23,350, four hours).

Combis (minibuses) to the Botswana border at Kazungula (K18,680, one hour) depart from Dambwa, 3km west of the town centre, on Nakatindi Rd.

International

For information about travelling to Botswana, and crossing the Zambia–Botswana border at Kazungula, see p174. For information about travelling to Namibia, and crossing the Zambia–Namibia border at Katima Mulilo, see p381. For information about crossing into Zimbabwe along the Victoria Falls Bridge, see p188.

CAR & MOTORCYCLE

If you're driving a rented car or motorcycle, be advised that the vast majority of companies do not insure their vehicles in Zambia.

HITCHING

With patience, it's fairly easy to hitch from Kazungula, Botswana, and Katima Mulilo,

Namibia, to Livingstone. The best place in all three towns to arrange a lift is at any petrol station. See warnings about hitching on p180 and p386.

TRAIN

The *Zambezi Express* leaves Livingstone for Lusaka (US$4/5/7/8 economy/standard/1st class/sleeper, 15 hours), via Choma, on Tuesday, Thursday and Sunday at 7pm. Reservations are available at the **train station** (☎ 320001), which is signed off Mosi-oa-Tunya Rd.

Getting Around
TO/FROM THE AIRPORT

Livingstone Airport is located 6km northwest of town, and is easily accessible by taxi (US$10 each way).

CAR & MOTORCYCLE

If you're planning on renting a car in Zambia, consider using **Hemingways** (☎ 320996, 323097; www.hemingwayszambia.com), based in Livingstone. They have new Toyota Hi-Lux campers, fully kitted.

COMBIS & TAXIS

Combis run regularly along Mosi-oa-Tunya Rd to Victoria Falls and the Zambian border, and cost US$0.50 for 15 minutes. Taxis, which are blue, cost US$10.

MOSI-OA-TUNYA NATIONAL PARK

Zambia's smallest national park is located 11km from Livingstone, and is divided into

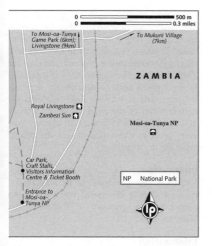

two sections – the Victoria Falls World Heritage National Monument Site and Mosi-oa-Tunya Game Park.

Victoria Falls World Heritage National Monument Site

The entrance to the **park** (admission US$10, ☉ 6am-6pm) is located just before the Zambian border post. From the entrance, a path leads to the visitor information centre, which has modest displays on local fauna, geology and culture as well as a healthy number of craft stalls.

From the centre, a network of paths leads through thick vegetation to various viewpoints. You can walk upstream along a path mercifully free of fences – and warning notices (so take care!) – to watch the Zambezi waters glide smoothly through rocks and little islands towards the lip of the falls.

For close-up views of the **Eastern Cataract**, nothing beats the hair-raising (and hair-wetting) walk across the **footbridge**, through swirling clouds of mist, to a sheer buttress called the **Knife Edge**. If the water is low, or the wind is favourable, you'll be treated to a magnificent view of the falls as well as the yawning abyss below. Otherwise, your vision (and your clothes) will be drenched by spray. Then you can walk down a steep track to the banks of the great Zambezi to see the huge whirlpool called the **Boiling Pot**.

Like its counterpart on the Zimbabwean side, the park is open again in the evenings during (and just before and after) a full

moon in order to see the amazing **lunar rainbow**. The tickets cost an extra US$10 – hours of operation vary, though you can inquire through your accommodation.

Mosi-oa-Tunya Game Park

Upriver from the falls, and only 3km southwest of Livingstone, is this tiny **wildlife sanctuary** (per person US$10; ☉ 6am-6pm), which has a surprising range of animals including rhinos, zebras, giraffes, buffaloes, elephants and antelopes.

Getting There & Away

The Zambian side of the falls is 11km south of Livingstone and along the main road to the border with Zimbabwe. Plenty of minibuses and shared taxis ply the route from the minibus terminal along Senanga Rd in Livingstone. As muggings have been reported, it is best to take a taxi.

ZIMBABWE

Although Zimbabwe was long the preferred base for visiting Victoria Falls, in recent years travellers have been reluctant to cross the border. In all fairness, there were plenty of reasons to be alarmed, especially since the international media held a glaring spotlight on stories of petrol rationing, hyperinflation, rampant land reform and food shortages. At the time of research, the US-based *Foreign Policy* magazine ranked Zimbabwe second (after Somalia) in their top 10 list of failed states.

As a testament to their resilience, however, Zimbabweans always believe this will get better and fortunately tourists and tourist locations are not targets for political violence. So foreign tourists continue to remain safely on the sidelines of the majority of Zimbabwe's ongoing problems.

Despite the threat of nation-state collapse, Zimbabwe has always been on the map for certain groups of intrepid travellers. For the luxury-seeking international jet setters, the generator-fuelled power in the five-star lodges has never flickered, and the imported fine wine has never stopped flowing. For shoestringers looking to bolster their travel resumes with a bit of street cred, travelling around Zim has always had undeniable appeal. But Victoria Falls is good for Granny, adrenaline junkies, nature freaks and everyone in between.

While it is recommended that you monitor the situation closely before visiting Zimbabwe, at the time of research the recent introduction of the US dollar means shortages are not an issue in Vic Falls, and that the town is safe to visit. The farcical Zim dollar is now just being sold as a souvenir, and while dollarisation hasn't helped everyone in the country, food is back in the stores and petrol is back in the pumps. And, although it remains to be seen whether or not newly elected Prime Minister Morgan Tsvangirai can continue to share power with the country's big man, President Robert Mugabe, a coalition government was a fascinating development in Zimbabwean politics.

Walking through the streets of Vic Falls can make you wonder how it looked when it was heaving. Locals eke out a meagre living by tending to the few remaining tourists. As when making plans to visit any African country, remember that situations can change. Zimbabwe is the path less travelled right now, yet it is extraordinary and unforgettable.

VICTORIA FALLS
☎ 013

Unlike Livingstone, the town of Victoria Falls (or simply Vic Falls) was built for tourism. It is right upon the falls with neat, walkable streets lined with hotels, bars, shops and craft markets. These days, however, Vic Falls feels like a resort in off-season. The off-season for this side has been long and tragic, but it's no longer deserved. The Zimbabwean side is a safe, calm and fully functional tourist resort.

Remote in terms of the rest of Zimbabwe, Vic Falls remained largely untouched by the violent troubles elsewhere in the country. And with road access to and from Zambia, Namibia and Botswana, the lodges and smart hotels remained relatively well-stocked even in the hard times. Dollarisation happened in Vic Falls years ahead of the rest of the country, but now the place sells Zim dollars as souvenirs! And yes, there was a Z100 trillion dollar note.

The people of the town are passionate about their home and boy have they got some generous hospitality to offer too. However, it isn't all-paradise here and visitors can expect to be approached by touts.

All this, together with an active organisation of community-minded and resourceful tourism operators leading a campaign called gotovictoriafalls.com, means tourism should be/could be *the* economic anchor for Zimbabwe. Social responsibility is ingrained in their plans and, being entirely dependent on tourism, Victoria Falls residents are very mindful of the need for safety, quality and stability and to ensure all visitors take away positive memories of this stunningly beautiful destination.

Orientation
Vic Falls was designed to be walkable – it's just over a kilometre from the town centre to the entrance to Victoria Falls National Park.

Information
EMERGENCY
Medical Air Rescue Service (MARS; ☎ 44764)
Police (☎ 44206; Livingstone Way)
Victoria Falls Surgery (☎ 43356; West Dr)

INTERNET ACCESS
Telco (☎ 43441; Phumula Centre; per hr US$1; ☺ 8am-6pm) Surprisingly reliable internet access.

MONEY
Barclays Bank (off Livingstone Way)
Standard Chartered Bank (off Livingstone Way)

POST
Post office (off Livingstone Way)

TELEPHONE
Telephone calls can be made at telephone offices and travel agencies upstairs in Soper's Arcade. To dial Livingstone you don't need the country or city code – simply dial ☎ 8, then the local number.

TOURIST INFORMATION
Zimbabwe Tourism Authority (☎ 44376; zta@vicfalls .ztazim.co.zw; 258 Adam Stander Dr; ☺ 8am-4.30pm Mon-Fri) gives away a few brochures and can book accommodation throughout the country.

Dangers & Annoyances
Mugging is not such a problem in Victoria Falls any more, but at dawn and dusk wild animals such as lions, elephants and warthogs do roam the streets away from the town centre, so take taxis at these times. Although it's

perfectly safe to walk to and from the falls, it's advisable to stick to the more touristed areas.

Sights & Activities

The **Big Tree**, which is a huge baobab tree with a 20m circumference and historical importance, is on Zambezi Dr heading north from near the entrance to the falls. This was the main trading spot for Zimbabweans and Zambians – the latter canoed across the river before the bridge was built.

Further on from there, take the first broad and clear path leading to the river. It leads to a spot called **The Rock**, a wonderful place to watch the wildly rushing water right at the lip of the falls. Local guides can take you. Ask them also about **The Lookout**, 8km out of town, another local secret, where you really hear the sound of the Smoke That Thunders.

The **Falls Craft Village** (☎ 44309; Adam Stander Dr; ☯ 8am-5pm) is a touristy mock-up of a traditional Zimbabwean village. Souvenirs start at US$20. It offers the chance to watch craftspeople at work, consult with a *nganga* (fortune teller) and see some remarkable 'pole dancing' (but not the sort you might find in a Western strip joint).

The **Crocodile Ranch and Wildlife Nature Sanctuary** (☎ 40509-11; Parkway; admission incl guided tour US$10; ☯ 8am-5pm) offers lots of crocs, lions and leopards.

The impressive **Victoria Falls Aquarium** (Livingstone Way; admission US$5; ☯ 9.30am-5.30pm) is apparently the largest freshwater aquarium in Africa. It's worth a visit for the bright and imaginative displays about the aquatic life in the Zambezi River.

The **Elephant's Walk Museum** (Elephant's Walk Shopping Village, off Adam Stander Dr; admission free; ☯ 8am-5pm) houses a small but worthwhile private collection detailing the cultural heritage of local ethnic groups.

The **Zambezi Nature Sanctuary** (☎ 44604; Parkway; admission incl guided tour US$5; ☯ 8am-5pm) offers lots of crocs, as well as lions and leopards. It shows informative videos, and houses a museum, aviary and insect collection. Try to get there for the lion and croc feeding, which takes place around 4pm daily.

Sleeping

There are budget and midrange places in Zimbabwe but on the whole, accommodation in Zimbabwe is expensive.

BUDGET & MIDRANGE

Victoria Falls Backpackers (☎ 42209; www.victoriafallsbackpackers.com; 357 Gibson Rd; camping per person US$4, dm US$8, s/d with shared bathroom US$10/20; P ⬛ ☮) Although it's a bit further out than other places, Victoria Falls Backpackers is superbly set up for independent and budget travellers.

Shoestrings Backpackers (☎ 40167; 12 West Dr; camping per person US$6, dm US$9, d US$35; P ☮) Shoestrings is a popular stop for the overland truck crowd, though the laid-back ambience also draws in a good number of independent travellers.

ZIM OR ZAM?

Victoria Falls straddle the border between Zimbabwe and Zambia, and is easily accessible from both countries. However, the big question for most travellers is: do I visit the falls from the town of Victoria Falls, Zimbabwe or from Livingstone, Zambia? The answer is simple: Visit the falls from both sides and, if possible, stay in both towns.

From the Zimbabwean side, you're further from the falls, though the overall views are better. From the Zambian side, you can almost stand on top of the falls, though your perspective is narrowed. Admission is cheaper on the Zambian side, though the Zimbabwean side is less-touristed and much quieter.

The town of Victoria Falls was built for tourists, so it's easily walkable and located right next to the entrance to the Falls. It has a natural African bush beauty.

Livingstone is an attractive town with a relaxed ambience and a proud, historic air. Since the town of Victoria Falls was the main tourist centre for so many years, Livingstone feels more authentic, perhaps because locals earn their livelihood through means other than tourism. Livingstone is bustling with travellers year round, though the town is fairly spread out, and located 11km from the falls.

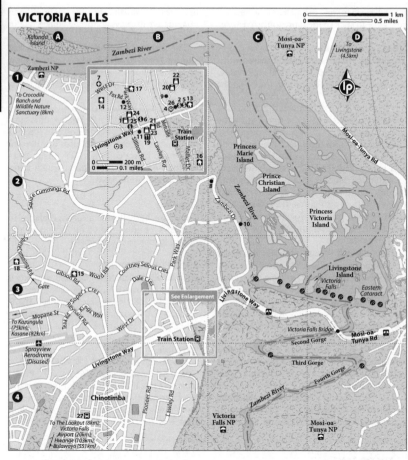

Victoria Falls Restcamp & Lodges (☎ 40509-11; www.vicfallsrestcamp.com; cnr Parkway & West Drs; camping US$10, dm US$11, s/d chalets with shared bathroom US$25/34, fitted dome tents US$60, s/d cottages with bathroom US$67; [P] [🏊]) Now run by the same people who do the sumptuous Ilala Lodge Hotel. This institution still has a great pool and the restaurant, In-Da-Belly (see opposite), but is doing well under new management. The rooms are very clean and you can now book all your falls activities here. Everything under one roof.

TOP END
Victoria Falls Safari Lodge (☎ 43201; www.vfsl.com; Squire Cummings Rd; s/d incl breakfast from US$315/395; [P] [🍴] [🏊]) If you were only coming to Victoria Falls on your Africa trip, staying here would

give you it all: set in a national park you get the bush experience of a tented camp complete with waterhole where wildlife drink at sunset (as you drink your sundowner or dine on gourmet bush cuisine), on top of your trips to the falls and the river.

Victoria Falls Hotel (☎ 44751; www.victoriafalls hotel.com; Mallet Dr; s/d incl breakfast from US$216/232; [P] [🍴] [🏊]) This historic hotel (the oldest in Zimbabwe) oozes elegance and sophistication, and occupies an impossibly scenic location. Looking across manicured lawns to the gorge and bridge, you can't see the falls as such but, they are just there, and you do see the spray. High tea here is an institution.

Ilala Lodge (☎ 44737; www.ilalalodge.com; 411 Livingstone Way; s/d incl breakfast from US$256/320;

P X S) This hotel is situated just 300m from the main entrance to the mighty Victoria Falls and is a truly magnificent hotel. A colonial relic, it is adorned with mounted rifles, hunting trophies and oil paintings; classically decorated rooms face out towards the manicured lawns and elaborate gardens.

Matetsi Water Lodge (☎ 04 731295; www.andbeyond .com; per person sharing US$435; ☒) Situated 30km from the falls, along the banks of the Zambezi, this shows Zimbabwean finesse in hospitality at its best. Each uber-luxurious bungalow has its own pool yet is set in the wild. There are very good specials throughout the year so contact them for cheaper rates.

Eating

In-Da-Belly Restaurant (☎ 332077; Victoria Falls Restcamp & Lodges; meals US$5-8) The name is a play on Ndebele, one of the two major population tribes in Zimbabwe, and it serves good bistro-style cuisine.

Mama Africa (☎ 41725; meals US$5-8) This perennial tourist haunt behind the Landela Centre specialises in local dishes, steaks and game meats when available.

River Cafe (☎ 42994; Landela Centre) This cafe serves a variety of cafe-style meals. It's a nice spot to hang out and have a meal or drinks. You can shop for curios in the complex too.

Terrace (Victoria Falls Hotel, Mallet Dr; meals US$20) The Terrace at the stately Victoria Falls Hotel overlooks the hotel gardens and the Victoria Falls Bridge, and brims with English colonial ambience. High tea here is a must – just do it.

Boma (☎ 43201; Victoria Falls Safari Lodge, Squire Cummings Rd; meals US$40 buffet) Boma is the place to release your inner tourist without being tacky and enjoy a taste of Africa: do interactive drumming or get your fortune told by a witch doctor.

Drinking

There's unfortunately not much life in Vic Falls after sunset, though the bar at **Shoestrings Backpackers** (☎ 40167; 12 West Dr; drinks from US$3) is the place to go. Here you can meet the local guides off duty, and they can give you local knowledge on places to visit.

Shopping

The **craft market** (Adam Stander Dr) has loads of curios, while the nearby Elephant's Walk Shopping Village complex stocks mainly upmarket crafts. The craftsmen eke out a mea-

---

FURTHER READING

Want to know a bit more about Victoria Falls? We suggest having a read or a look at:

- *Exploring Victoria Falls* by Prof Lee Berger and Brett Hilton-Barber
- *Mosi-oa-Tunya: Handbook to the Victoria Falls Region* by DW Phillipson
- www.wildzambezi.com
- www.gotovictoriafalls.com
- www.africaalbidatourism.com
- www.africanencounter.com
- www.zctf.mweb.co.zw – Zimbabwe Conservation Task Force
- www.zimbabwe-art.com – Zimbabwe Conservation Art Programme

THE MIGHTY ZAMBEZI RIVER

The Zambezi River emerges from the northwestern tip of Zambia, one of the greatest rivers of Africa. It descends from 1500m above sea level and traverses six countries before its epic 2574km journey ends. The Indian Ocean receives its largest fresh water discharge through this incredible catchment. The Zambezi has a basin of more than 1,570,000 square kms and is the lifeblood of the people that reside on the river. The life it supports – from people to vast populations of animals – is as wild as it is captivating.

---

gre living by selling to tourists, so it would be good for lots of reasons to go shopping! African items are often made from recycled items and they do look good at home.

The Phumula Centre is a small mall of shops for locals and tourists, supermarkets and small restaurants.

Getting There & Away
AIR
Check out www.flightsite.co.za, where you can search all the airlines including low cost carriers (and car hire companies) for the cheapest flights and book yourself. **South African Airways** (☎ 011-808678; www.flysaa.com) and **British Airways** (www.britishairways.com) fly every day to Johannesburg from around US$320 return. **Air Namibia** (www.airnamibia.com) flies to Windhoek for around US$530 return.

BICYCLE
Bikes can be ridden to/from Zambia, however, bear in mind that cyclists have been mugged while riding to/from the Zambian border and the falls.

BUS & MINIBUS
Minibuses or combis are no longer recommended to travellers as they become so neglected and overused that they break down and are frequently involved in fatal accidents.

For information on travelling to Botswana, and crossing the Zimbabwe–Botswana border at Kazungula, see p174. For information about travelling to Namibia, see p381. For information about crossing into Zambia along the Victoria Falls Bridge, see p188.

CAR & MOTORCYCLE
If you're driving a rented car or motorcycle from Zambia, you'll need a letter from your rental company stating that you are permitted to enter Zimbabwe.

HITCHING
It's fairly easy to hitch between Victoria Falls and Kazungula, Botswana. If you head to the petrol station in both towns you'll have the best chance of a lift; see also p180.

TRAIN
The *Mosi-oa-Tunya* train leaves Victoria Falls daily at 6.30pm for Bulawayo, Zimbabwe (economy/2nd/1st class, US$1/3/4, 12 hours). Make reservations at the **ticket office** (☎ 44391; ☺ 7am-12pm & 2-4pm Mon-Fri, 7am-10am Sat & Sun) inside the train station.

Getting Around
TO/FROM THE AIRPORT
Victoria Falls Airport is located 20km southeast of town, and is easily accessible by taxi (US$20 each way).

CAR & MOTORCYCLE
When planning your trip, find out what the situation is with petrol availability, as this is an issue that has cycles all of its own. At the time of writing, petrol was readily available in petrol stations but this may change.

TAXIS
A taxi around town costs about US$10 and slightly more after dark. Taxis don't use meters, so you'll have to bargain. The taxi cabs themselves are all pretty shabby, but they get you from A to B.

VICTORIA FALLS NATIONAL PARK
The entrance to the **national park** (Map pp192-3; admission US$20, ☺ 6am-6pm) is located just before the Zimbabwean border post. The admission price must be paid in US dollars. One of the most dramatic spots is the westernmost point known as **Cataract View**. Another track leads to the aptly named **Danger Point**, where a sheer, unfenced 100m drop-off will rattle your nerves. From there, you can follow a side track for a view of the **Victoria Falls Bridge**.

Like its counterpart on the Zimbabwean side, the park is open again in the evenings during (and just before and after) a full moon in order to see the amazing **lunar rainbow**. The tickets cost an extra US$10 – hours of operation vary, though you can inquire through your accommodation.

ZAMBEZI NATIONAL PARK

This **national park** (Map p196; admission US$10; 6am-6.30pm) consists of 40km of Zambezi River frontage and a spread of wildlife-rich mopane forest and savannah. The park is best known for its herds of sable antelopes, but it is also home to lions, giraffes and elephants. The entrance to the park is situated only 5km northwest of the Victoria Falls town centre, and is easily accessible by private vehicle. If you don't have your own wheels (or your petrol is running low), tour operators on both sides of the border offer wildlife drives, guided hikes and fishing expeditions in the park.

Namibia

Namibia History

IN THE BEGINNING

Namibia's history extends back into the mists of time, a piece in the jigsaw that saw the evolution of the earliest human beings. The camps and stone tools of *homo erectus* (literally 'man who stands upright') have been found scattered throughout the region. One archaeological site in the Namib Desert provides evidence that these early people were hunting the ancestors of present-day elephants, and butchering their remains with stone hand-axes as early as 750,000 years ago.

By the middle Stone Age, which lasted until 20,000 years ago, the Boskop, the presumed ancestors of the San (see p63), had developed into an organised hunting and gathering society. Use of fire was universal, tools (made from wood and animal products as well as stone) had become more sophisticated and natural pigments were being used for personal adornment. From around 8000 BC (the late Stone Age) they began producing pottery, and started to occupy rock shelters and caves such as those at Twyfelfontein (p294), Brandberg (p293) and the Tsodilo Hills (p144) in Botswana.

To catch up on all the hot topics facing Namibia today, log on to the *Namibian* newspaper's excellent website, www.namibian.com.na.

THE SETTLEMENT OF NAMIBIA

The archaeological connection between the late–Stone Age people and the first Khoisan arrivals isn't clear, but it is generally accepted that the earliest documented inhabitants of Southern Africa were the San, a nomadic people organised into extended family groups who were able to adapt to the severe terrain.

During the early Iron Age, between 2300 and 2400 years ago, rudimentary farming techniques appeared on the plateaus of south-central Africa. However, whether or not the earliest farmers were Khoisan, who had adapted to a settled existence or migrants from East and Central Africa, remains in question. Regardless, as the centuries came and went, Bantu-speaking groups began to arrive in sporadic southward waves.

The first agriculturists and iron-workers of definite Bantu origin belonged to the Gokomere culture. They settled the temperate savannah and cooler uplands of southeastern Zimbabwe, and were the first occupants of the Great Zimbabwe site. Cattle ranching became the mainstay of the community, and earlier hunting and gathering San groups retreated to the west, or were enslaved and/or absorbed.

An interesting source of information on just some of the development projects afoot in Namibia is the USAID website, http://namibia.usaid.gov.

At the same time, the San communities were also coming under pressure from the Khoikhoi (the ancestors of the Nama), who probably entered the region from the south. The Khoikhoi were organised loosely into tribal groups, and were distinguished by their reliance on raising livestock. They

TIMELINE

pre 30,000 BC	30,000–10,000 BC	8000 BC
Early Homo sapiens unintentionally deposit well-preserved fragments of prehistoric stone tools in middens, indicating some of the region's first modern human habitation and material culture.	The Boskop people, the presumed ancestors of the San, develop as a sophisticated hunting and gathering society, ushering in a new era of the Stone Age.	Technological advancements in the late Stone Age, namely a mastery over natural dyes and pigments, enable humans to start adorning rock shelters and caves with complex rock art.

gradually displaced the San, becoming the dominant group in the region until around 1500 AD.

During the 16th century, the Herero arrived in Namibia from the Zambezi Valley, and proceeded to occupy the north and west of the country. As ambitious pastoralists, they inevitably came into conflict with the Khoikhoi over the best grazing lands and water sources. Eventually, given their superior strength and numbers, the Herero forced nearly all of the indigenous Namibian groups to submit to their domination. By the late 19th century a new Bantu group, the Owambo, settled in the north along the Okavango and Kunene Rivers.

Republished in 2001, Charles John Anderson's *Notes of Travel in South-Western Africa* is a fascinating account of the country through the eyes of one of the first traders of the mid-19th century.

EUROPEAN EXPLORATION & INCURSION

In 1486, the Portuguese captain Diego Cão sailed as far south as Cape Cross, where he erected a stone cross in tribute to his royal patron, João II. The following year, another cross was erected by Bartolomeu Dias at Lüderitz, but it wasn't really until the early 17th century that Dutch sailors from the Cape colonies began to explore the desert coastline, although they refrained from setting up any permanent stations.

Soon after, however, growing European commercial and territorial interests were to send ambitious men deeper into Namibia's interior, and in 1750, the Dutch elephant hunter Jacobus Coetsee became the first European to cross the Orange River. In his wake came a series of traders, hunters and missionaries, and by the early 19th century, there were mission stations at Bethanie, Windhoek, Rehoboth, Keetmanshoop and various other sites. In 1844 the German Rhenish Missionary Society, under Dr Hugo Hahn, began working among the Herero. More successful were the Finnish Lutherans who arrived in the north in 1870, and established missions among the Owambo.

By 1843 the rich coastal guano deposits of the southern Namib Desert were attracting commercial attention. In 1867, the guano islands were annexed by the British, who then proceeded to take over Walvis Bay in 1878. The Brits also mediated the largely inconclusive Khoisan–Herero wars during this period.

Adolf Lüderitz bought the port and surrounding area of Angra Pequena for 100 rifles and £200.

THE SCRAMBLE FOR AFRICA

The Germans, under Chancellor Otto von Bismarck, were late entering the European scramble for Africa. Bismarck had always been against colonies; he considered them an expensive illusion, famously stating, 'My map of Africa is here in Europe'. But he was to be pushed into an ill-starred colonial venture by the actions of a Bremen merchant called Adolf Lüderitz.

Having already set up a trading station in Lagos, Nigeria in 1881, Lüderitz convinced the Nama chief, Joseph Fredericks, to sell Angra Pequena, where he established his second station trading in guano (made from excrement, this manure was an effective fertiliser and gunpowder ingredient). He then

AD 500–1500	1487	1500–1600
Khoikhoi migrate north from South Africa, gradually displacing the San as the dominant ethnic group in the region, until the arrival of other peoples in 1500.	Portuguese explorer Bartolomeu Dias erects a stone cross at Lüderitz before rounding the Cape of Good Hope in a bid to secure a maritime route to South Asia.	Groups of ethnic Herero arrive in Namibia, occupying the northern and western reaches of the country, and effortlessly crushing local resistance with mere strength of numbers.

petitioned the German chancellor for protection. Bismarck, still trying to stay out of Africa, politely requested the British at Walvis Bay to say whether they had any interest in the matter, but they never bothered to reply. Subsequently, in 1884, Lüderitz was officially declared part of the German Empire.

Initially, German interests were minimal, and between 1885 and 1890, the colonial administration amounted to three public administrators. Their interests were served largely through a colonial company (along the lines of the British East India Company in India prior to the Raj), but the organisation couldn't maintain law and order.

So in the 1880s, due to renewed fighting between the Nama and Herero, the German government dispatched Curt von François and 23 soldiers to restrict the supply of arms from British-administered Walvis Bay. This seemingly innocuous peacekeeping regiment slowly evolved into the more powerful Schutztruppe (German Imperial Army), which constructed forts around the country to combat growing opposition.

At this stage, Namibia became a fully fledged protectorate known as German South West Africa. The first German farmers arrived in 1892 to take up expropriated land on the central plateau, and were soon followed by merchants and other settlers. In the late 1890s the Germans, the Portuguese in Angola and the British in Bechuanaland (present-day Botswana) agreed on Namibia's boundaries.

> For a chilling account of Germany's colonial conduct in South West Africa, get hold of Mark Cocker's excellent book, *Rivers of Blood, Rivers of Gold: Europe's Conflict with Tribal Peoples*.

REAPING THE WHIRLWIND

Meanwhile, in the south, diamonds had been discovered at Grasplatz, east of Lüderitz, by a South African labourer Zacharias Lewala. Despite the assessment of diamond-mining giant De Beers that the find probably wouldn't amount to much, prospectors flooded in to stake their claims. By 1910, the German authorities had branded the entire area between Lüderitz and the Orange River a *Sperrgebiet* (closed area), chucked out the prospectors and granted exclusive rights to Deutsche Diamanten Gesellschaft (German Diamond Company).

But for all the devastation visited upon the local populace, Germany was never to benefit from the diamond riches they found. The outbreak of WWI in 1914 was to mark the end of German colonial rule in South West Africa. By this time, however, the Germans had all but succeeded in devastating the Herero tribal structures, and taken over all Khoikhoi and Herero lands. The more fortunate Owambo, in the north, managed to avoid German conquest, and they were only subsequently overrun during WWI by Portuguese forces fighting on the side of the Allies.

In 1914, at the beginning of WWI, Britain pressured South Africa into invading Namibia. The South Africans, under the command of Prime Minister Louis Botha and General Jan Smuts, pushed northwards, forcing the outnumbered Schutztruppe to retreat. In May 1915, the Germans faced

1750	1828	19th century
Dutch elephant hunter Jacobus Coetsee became the first European to cross the Orange River, followed by a series of traders, hunters and missionaires.	The amalgamation of the Rhenish Missionary Society results in Germany's first missionaries setting up stations in South Africa, from where they gradually proceed north into Namibia.	Coastal guano deposits attract commercial attention. Bremen merchant Adolf Lüderitz establishes his second guano trading station, and petitions the German government for protection.

their final defeat at Khorab near Tsumeb, and a week later, a South African administration was set up in Windhoek.

By 1920, many German farms had been sold to Afrikaans-speaking settlers, and the German diamond-mining interests in the south were handed over to the South Africa–based Consolidated Diamond Mines (CDM), which later gave way to the Namdeb Diamond Corporation Limited (Namdeb).

SOUTH AFRICAN OCCUPATION

Under the Treaty of Versailles in 1919, Germany was required to renounce all of its colonial claims, and in 1920, the League of Nations granted South Africa a formal mandate to administer Namibia as part of the Union.

While the mandate was renewed by the UN following WWII, South Africa was more interested in annexing South West Africa as a full province in the Union, and decided to scrap the terms of the mandate and rewrite the constitution. In response, the International Court of Justice determined that South Africa had overstepped its boundaries, and the UN established the Committee on South West Africa to enforce the original terms of the mandate. In 1956 the UN further decided that South African control should be terminated.

Undeterred, the South African government tightened its grip on the territory, and in 1949, granted the white population parliamentary representation in Pretoria. The bulk of Namibia's viable farmland was parcelled into some 6000 farms for white settlers, while other ethnic groups were relegated to newly demarcated 'tribal homelands'. The official intent was ostensibly to 'channel economic development into predominantly poor rural areas', but it was all too obvious that it was simply a convenient way of retaining the majority of the country for white settlement and ranching.

As a result, a prominent line of demarcation appeared between the predominantly white ranching lands in the central and southern parts of the country, and the poorer but better-watered tribal areas to the north. This arrangement was retained until Namibian independence in 1990, and to some extent continues to the present day.

SWAPO

Throughout the 1950s, despite mounting pressure from the UN, South Africa refused to release its grip on Namibia. This intransigence was based on its fears of having yet another antagonistic government on its doorstep, and of losing the income that it derived from the mining operations there.

Forced labour had been the lot of most Namibians since the German annexation, and was one of the main factors that led to mass demonstrations and the increasingly nationalist sentiments in the late 1950s. Among the parties was the Owamboland People's Congress, founded in Cape Town under the leadership of Samuel Daniel Shafiishuna Nujoma and Herman Andimba Toivo ya Toivo.

Henno Martin's *The Sheltering Desert* is a Namibian classic, recounting the adventures of two German geologists who spent WWII hiding out in the Namib Desert.

1884	1884–1915	1892–1905
Otto von Bismarck invites other dominant European powers to participate in the Berlin Conference, which officially began the 'Scramble for Africa', and marked Germany's emergence as an imperial power.	Bismarck establishes the colony of German South West Africa, despite the fact that the territorial holding is more than one and a half times the size of Germany.	The Schutztruppe (German Imperial Army) violently suppresses Herero and Nama uprisings against colonial rule: 65,000 Herero and 10,000 Nama are killed, leaving more than 15,000 refugees.

In 1959, the party's name was changed to the Owamboland People's Organisation, and Nujoma took the issue of South African occupation to the UN in New York. By 1960 his party had gathered increased support, and they eventually coalesced into the South-West African People's Organisation (Swapo), with its headquarters in Dar es Salaam, Tanzania.

DARK TIMES

Once the Germans had completed their inventory of Namibia's natural resources, it is difficult to see how they could have avoided the stark picture that presented itself. Their new colony was a drought-afflicted land enveloped by desert, with a nonexistent transport network, highly restricted agricultural opportunities, unknown mineral resources and a sparse, well-armed indigenous population. In fact, the only option that presented itself was to follow the example of the Herero, and pursue a system of seminomadic pastoralism. But the problem with this was that all the best land fell within the territories of either the Herero or the Nama.

In 1904, the paramount chief of the Herero invited his Nama, Baster and Owambo counterparts to join forces with him to resist the growing German presence. This was an unlikely alliance between traditional enemies. Driven almost all the way back to Windhoek, the German Schutztruppe brought in reinforcements, and under the ruthless hand of General von Trotha went out to meet the Herero forces at their Waterberg camp.

On 11 August 1904, the Battle of Waterberg commenced. Although casualties on the day were fairly light, the Herero fled from the scene of battle east into the forbidding Omaheke Desert. Seizing the opportunity, von Trotha ordered his troops to pursue them to their death. In the four weeks that followed, some 65,000 Herero were killed or died of heat, thirst and exhaustion. In fact, the horror only concluded when German troops themselves began to succumb to exhaustion and typhoid, but by then, some 80% of the entire Herero population had been wiped out.

Since the early 1990s, traditional Herero leaders have been lobbying for an official apology as well as monetary compensation from the German government. Finally in 2004, on the 100th anniversary of the Battle of Waterberg, Heidemarie Wieczorek-Zeul, Germany's development aid minister, apologised for the genocide, and in 2005 Germany pledged US$28 million to Namibia over a 10-year period as a reconciliation initiative.

Still many problems remain. The Namibian government, almost exclusively made up of Owambo members, believes that any compensation should be channelled through it rather than go directly to the Herero, citing its policy of nontribalism as a key concern. But as the chairman of the Namibian National Society for Human Rights points out, 'Not all the country suffered from the genocide, so it is ridiculous to say that the Hereros should not be specifically compensated'.

What may have been a minor episode in German colonial history was a cataclysm for the Herero nation. Demographic analysts suggest there would be 1.8 million Herero in Namibia today if it were not for the killings, making it the dominant ethnic group rather than the Owambo. In reality there are only about 120,000 Herero. For many this is a bitter pill to swallow, as the comments of Chief Kuaima Riruako illustrate. 'We ought to be in control of this country,' he said, 'and yet we are not.' Old rivalries still run deep.

1910	1915–19	1920
The diamond-rich area between Lüderitz and the Orange River is sealed and dubbed the Sperrgebiet (Forbidden), though prospecting operations come to a grinding halt following the outbreak of WWI.	After being defeated at Tsumeb by South African forces in May 1915, Germany loses control of its colony, and in 1919, formally renounces all colonial holdings under the jurisdiction of the Treaty of Versailles.	The League of Nations grants the Union of South Africa a mandate to administer South West Africa, though it is denied its requests to fully incorporate the colony as a province.

In 1966, Swapo took the issue of South African occupation to the International Court of Justice. The court upheld South Africa's right to govern South West Africa, but the UN General Assembly voted to terminate South Africa's mandate and replace it with a Council for South West Africa (renamed the Commission for Namibia in 1973) to administer the territory.

In response, on 26 August 1966 (now called Heroes' Day), Swapo launched its campaign of guerrilla warfare at Ongulumbashe in northern Namibia. The next year, one of Swapo's founders, Toivo ya Toivo, was convicted of terrorism and imprisoned in South Africa, where he would remain until 1984. Nujoma, however, stayed in Tanzania, and avoided criminal prosecution. In 1972, the UN finally declared the South African occupation of South West Africa officially illegal and called for a withdrawal, proclaiming Swapo the legitimate representative of the Namibian people.

In 1975, Angola gained independence under the Cuban-backed Popular Movement for the Liberation of Angola (MPLA). Sympathetic to Swapo's struggle for independence in neighbouring Namibia, the fledgling government allowed it a safe base in the south of the country from where it could step up its guerrilla campaign against South Africa.

South Africa responded by invading Angola in support of the opposition party National Union for the Total Independence of Angola (Unita), an act that prompted the Cuban government to send hundreds of troops to the country to bolster up the MPLA. Although the South African invasion failed, and troops had to be withdrawn in March 1976, furious and bloody incursions into Angola continued well into the 1980s.

In the end, it was neither solely the activities of Swapo nor international sanctions that forced the South Africans to the negotiating table. On the contrary, all players were growing tired of the war, and the South African economy was suffering badly. By 1985, the war was costing some R480 million (around US$250 million) per year, and conscription was widespread. Mineral exports, which once provided around 88% of the country's gross domestic product (GDP), had plummeted to just 27% by 1984.

INDEPENDENCE

In December 1988, a deal was finally struck between Cuba, Angola, South Africa and Swapo that provided for the withdrawal of Cuban troops from Angola and South African troops from Namibia. It also stipulated that the transition to Namibian independence would formally begin on 1 April 1989, and would be followed by UN-monitored elections held in November 1989 on the basis of universal suffrage. Although minor score settling and unrest among some Swapo troops threatened to derail the whole process, the plan went ahead, and in September, Sam Nujoma returned from his 30-year exile. In the elections, Swapo garnered two-thirds

A valuable addition to the library of Namibian resistance is John Masson's biography of the famed resistance fighter Jakob Marengo.

Told in his own words, *To Free Namibia: The Life of the First President of Namibia* is Sam Nujoma's account of Namibia's liberation and his personal role as 'Father of the Nation'.

1949	1959	1966
The Union of South Africa grants parliamentary representation to whites living in South West Africa, prompting the International Court of Justice to launch a full investigation into the legality of the matter.	After the UN calls for the Union of South Africa to abandon South West Africa, the Owamboland People's Congress is established, which subsequently becomes the South-West Africa People's Organisation (Swapo).	Swapo begins its long campaign of guerrilla resistance against its colonial occupiers, marking the public emergence of one of Namibia's most famous freedom fighters and future president, Sam Nujoma.

of the votes, but the numbers were insufficient to give the party the sole mandate to write the new constitution, an outcome that went some way to allaying fears that Namibia's minority groups would be excluded from the democratic process.

In the country's first elections in November 1989, 710,000 Namibians voted in the members of the National Assembly – a staggering 97% turnout.

Following negotiations between the Constituent Assembly (soon to become the National Assembly) and international advisers, including the USA, France, Germany and the former USSR, a constitution was drafted. The new constitution established a multiparty system alongside an impressive bill of rights. It also limited the presidential executive to two five-year terms. The new constitution was adopted in February 1990, and independence was granted a month later, with Sam Nujoma being sworn in as Namibia's first president.

POST-INDEPENDENCE

In those first optimistic years of his presidency, Sam Nujoma and his Swapo party based their policies on a national reconciliation program aimed at healing the wounds left by 25 years of armed struggle. They also embarked on a reconstruction program based on the retention of a mixed economy and partnership with the private sector.

These moderate policies and the stability they afforded were well received, and in 1994, President Nujoma and his party were re-elected with a 68% landslide victory over the main opposition party, the Democratic Turnhalle Alliance (DTA). Similarly in 1999, Swapo won 76.8% of the vote, although concerns arose when President Nujoma amended the constitution to allow himself a rather unconstitutional third term.

Other political problems included growing unrest in the Caprivi Strip. On 2 August 1999, rebels – mainly members of Namibia's Lozi minority led by Mishake Muyongo, a former vice president of Swapo and a long-time proponent of Caprivian independence – attempted to seize Katima Mulilo. However, the poorly trained perpetrators failed to capture any of their intended targets, and after only a few hours, they were summarily put down by the Namibian Defence Force (NDF).

Later that year, Nujoma also committed troops from the NDF to support the Angolan government in its civil war against Unita rebels – an act that triggered years of strife for the inhabitants of the Caprivi Strip, where fighting and lawlessness spilled over the border. When a family of French tourists was robbed and murdered while driving between Kongola and Divundu, the issue exploded in the international press, causing tourist numbers to plummet. Continuing reports of fighting, attacks on civilians and land-mine detonations caused a huge exodus of people from the region, and kept tourists firmly away until the cessation of the conflict in 2002.

In 2004, the world watched warily to see if Nujoma would cling to the office of power for a fourth term, and an almost audible sigh of relief could

1972   **1975**   **1989**

The UN General Assembly rules that South Africa's occupation of South West Africa is illegal, declares that Namibia is rightfully controlled by Swapo and calls for the release of the organisation's imprisoned leaders in South Africa.

Angola gains independence under the Cuban-backed Popular Movement for the Liberation of Angola (MPLA) and provides a safe base for Swapo's guerrilla campagn.

One of Africa's youngest countries, second only to Eritrea, Namibia officially becomes independent on 1 April 1989 after a multiparty peace deal is brokered between Cuba, Angola, South Africa and Swapo.

THE POVERTY AGENDA

In 2006, 18 expropriation orders were served on Namibia's commercial farmers. In total, the government eventually hopes to resettle some 250,000 landless Namibians through the compulsory purchase of some 9 million hectares of commercial farmland.

The move to compulsory purchase is not unexpected. For more than 15 years the government has been pursuing a policy of 'willing seller, willing buyer', whereby they have compensated those who have voluntarily chosen to sell their farms. According to the Namibia Agricultural Union (NAU), some 600 white-owned farms have been acquired this way since independence, and now nearly 50% of Namibia's arable land either belongs to, or is being utilised by, the black majority. But according to President Pohamba, this still isn't enough. And in 2006 he was quoted as saying that there was no more time to waste, 'otherwise the peace and stability that we enjoy in this country can easily be disturbed, and a revolution by the landless…might happen.' Ominous words from a man who, along with Namibia's previous president Sam Nujoma, has a long affiliation with Zimbabwe's president, Robert Mugabe.

That same year, Namibia's land minister, Isak Katali, made waves on a state visit to Zimbabwe, where he declared how impressed he was by Zimbabwe's 'successful land-reform program'. His later statement, 'it's good to keep your dignity rather than a full stomach', prompted a concerned article in the *Namibian* newspaper beseeching the government to put aside political rhetoric, and assess the real benefits of land reform in bringing positive development to the economy.

Sceptics would say there are few economic benefits to be had. Although in principle many people support land reform, Namibia's arid environment is badly suited to a system of small holdings farmed by poor Namibians who have neither the economic nor technical resources to develop the land. The real social issue, some say, is not so much land reform, but the government's failure to provide work opportunities for ordinary Namibians.

Whatever the problems, it is clear that most Namibians don't relish the economic and social chaos in neighbouring Zimbabwe, where hyperinflation reached lofty percentages usually reserved for astronomical calculations. As the *Namibian* article so succinctly concludes, 'We emulate them at our peril.'

be heard in Namibia when he announced that he would finally be stepping down in favour of his chosen successor, Hifikepunye Pohamba.

Like Sam Nujoma, Pohamba is a Swapo veteran, and swept to power with nearly 77% of the vote. He leaves behind the land ministry where he presided over one of Namibia's most controversial schemes – the expropriation of land from white farmers (see the boxed text above). This 'poverty agenda', along with Namibia's HIV/AIDS crisis and a nascent secessionist movement in the Caprivi Strip, will be remembered as the defining issues of his presidency.

BASKING IN THE LIMELIGHT

Namibia has been riding high on the headlines in recent times. In 2006, Brad Pitt and Angelina Jolie chose the country to host the birth of their daughter,

1990	1994	1999
UN-administered general elections are held on the basis of universal suffrage, and Sam Nujoma returns to Namibia after a 30-year exile to be sworn in as the country's first president.	A comprehensive reconstruction program, which ushered in four years of relative stability, is widely deemed a success, catapulting President Nujoma and Swapo to re-election by a landslide victory.	Nujoma is re-elected to a controversial third term as president, though his victory is short-lived as a state of emergency is declared in the Caprivi Strip following a series of attacks by separatists.

Shiloh Nouvel. The media feeding-frenzy has delighted the Namibian government, although critics have sourly dismissed it as celebrity colonialism. Whatever the case may be, the exposure has undoubtedly given a huge boost to the country's tourism industry.

In 2006 filming of a movie about Sam Nujoma was called to a halt as actors and crew complained they had not been paid. The film stars Danny Glover and Carl Lumbly (as the young Nujoma); both actors worked on the film for free.

Namibia was also the location for part of internationally renowned photographer Sebastião Salgado's Genesis project, which aims to document undeveloped landscapes across the planet. Salgado travelled deep into the Namib to capture amazing images of this timeless desert, and nowhere in his journey thus far has he captured the essence of the project's title so succinctly.

Namibia has also profited considerably in the new millennium from the extraction and processing of minerals for export. Rich alluvial diamond deposits alongside uranium and other metal reserves put the country's budget into surplus in 2007 for the first time since independence. Compared to other sub-Saharan countries, Namibia has one of the highest per capita GDP, though this statistic is masked by one of the world's most unequal income distributions.

Although Swapo continues to largely dominate the political climate, Namibia is presently one of the better performing democracies in Africa, and scores comparatively well in world development indicators assessed by the World Bank. In November 2009, Swapo will once again defend its presidential and parliamentary positions as Namibia enters its general election season.

The political battlefield is set to heat up as President Pohamba seeks re-election and a populist reaffirmation of his ruling party. Fortunately, however, most domestic and international political observers are fairly confident that the country will be spared the violence and controversy that has marred so many elections on the continent.

2004	2006	2009
Germany offers an official state-level apology for killing tens of thousands of Herero and Nama during the colonial era, but rules out financial compensation to living descendants.	In a highly publicised act mirroring neighbouring Zimbabwe, the Namibian government commences the expropriation of white-owned farms as part of a hotly contested land-reform program.	At 77 years of age, Sam Nujoma graduates from the University of Namibia with a Masters Degree in Geology, promising the public that the country's vast mineral wealth has not yet been fully exploited.

Namibia Culture

THE NATIONAL PSYCHE

On a national level, Namibia is still struggling to attain a cohesive identity, and history weighs heavy on the generations who grew up during the struggle for independence. As a direct and unfortunate result, some formidable tensions still endure between various social and racial groups.

Although the vast majority of travellers will be greeted with great warmth and curiosity, some people may experience unpleasant racism or unwarranted hostility – this is not confined to black/white relations, and can affect travellers of all ethnicities as Namibia's ethnic groups are extremely varied. Acquainting yourself with Namibia's complex and often turbulent past will hopefully alert you to potentially difficult or awkward situations. Taking care of basic etiquette like dressing appropriately, greeting people warmly or learning a few words of the local languages will also stand you in good stead.

Socially, Namibians enjoy a rock-solid sense of community thanks to the clan-based system. Members of your clan are people you can turn to in times of need. Conversely, if someone from your clan is in trouble, you are obligated to help, whether that means providing food for someone who is hungry, care for someone who is sick, or even the adoption of an orphaned child in some cases. This inclusiveness also extends to others, and it is not uncommon for travellers to be asked to participate in a spontaneous game of football or a family meal.

Such an all-embracing social structure also means that the traditional family nucleus is greatly extended. Many Namibian families will include innumerable aunts and uncles, some of whom might even be referred to as mother or father. Likewise, cousins and siblings are interchangeable, and in some rural areas, men may have dozens of children, some of whom they might not even recognise. In fact, it is this fluid system that has enabled families to deal in some way with the devastation wreaked by the HIV/AIDS crisis – for more information, see the boxed text, p219.

LIFESTYLE

On the whole, Namibians are a conservative and God-fearing people – an estimated 80% to 90% of the country is Christian – so modesty in dress is important. Keeping up appearances extends to behaving modestly and respectfully to one's elders and social superiors, performing religious and social duties, and fulfilling all essential family obligations.

Education, too, is very important and the motivation to get a good education is high. But getting an education is by no means easy for everyone, and for families living in remote rural areas, it often means that very young children must be sent to schools far away where they board in hostels. The literacy rate for Namibia is 85%.

Indeed, most Namibians still live in homesteads in rural areas, and lead typical village lives. Villages tend to be family- and clan-based, and are presided over by an elected *elenga* (headman). The *elenga* is responsible for local affairs, everything from settling disputes to determining how communal lands are managed.

The sad reality is that life is a struggle for the vast majority of Namibians (see the boxed text, p213). Unemployment is high, and the economy remains dependent on the mining industry, and to a lesser ex-

To receive a gift politely, accept it with both hands and perhaps bow slightly. If you're receiving something minor, receive it with your right hand while touching your left hand to your right elbow.

GREETINGS

The Namibia greeting is practically an art form and goes something like this: *Did you get up well? Yes. Are you fine? Yes. Did you get up well? Yes. Are you fine? Yes.*

This is an example of just the most minimal greeting; in some cases greetings can continue at great length with repeated inquiries about your health, your crops and your family, which will demand great patience if you are in a hurry.

However, it is absolutely essential that you greet everyone you meet, from the most casual encounter in the corner store, to an important first meeting with a business associate. Failure to greet people is considered extremely rude, and it is without a doubt the most common mistake made by outsiders.

Learn the local words for 'hello' and 'goodbye,' and use them unsparingly. If you have the time and inclination, consider broadening your lexicon to include longer and more complex phrases. For an overview of the many Namibian local tongues, see the Language chapter on p394.

Even if you find yourself tongue-tied, handshakes are also a crucial icebreaker. The African handshake consists of three parts: the normal Western handshake, followed by the linking of bent fingers while touching the ends of upward-pointing thumbs, and then a repeat of the conventional handshake.

tent fishing and canning. In recent years, tourism has grown considerably throughout the country, though white Namibians still largely control the industry.

ECONOMY

The Namibian economy is dominated by the extraction and processing of minerals for export. Although mining only accounts for 8% of the GDP, it provides more than half of foreign exchange earnings. Most famously, Namibia's large alluvial diamond deposits have earned it the enviable reputation as one of the world's primary sources for gem-quality stones. However, the country is also regarded as a prominent producer of uranium, lead, zinc, tin, silver and tungsten.

Although the per-capita GDP of US$5500 is high by African standards, the statistic masks the inequalities between population groups. In reality, around 5% of the population controls three-fourths of the economy, and the UN Development Program's 2005 Human Development Report showed that 55% of the population lives on US$2 per day. The net result is a continuing exodus of people from rural communities to urban centres, a trend that is taking its toll on traditional lifestyles and culture.

Furthermore, the mining sector employs only about 3% of the population, while about half of the population depends on subsistence agriculture for its livelihood. In fact, Namibia normally imports about 50% of its cereal requirements, and in drought years, food shortages are a major problem in rural areas. Although the fishing industry is also a large economic force, catches are typically canned and marked for export.

The Namibian economy is closely linked to the regional powerhouse of South Africa, and the Namibian dollar pegged one-to-one to the South African rand. In 2007, payments from the Southern African Customs Union (SACU) put Namibia's budget into surplus for the first time since independence.

At the time of press, however, it was evident that the global recession had also greatly impacted Namibia's economic sector. Rising costs for mineral extraction and fish canning were denting the profit margins on lucrative exports, not to mention the global decline in the demand for precious metals.

The website www.arasa .info is an alliance of 14 nongovernmental organisations working in all Southern African Development Community (SADC) countries promoting a human rights-based response to HIV/AIDS.

POPULATION

According to the CIA World Factbook, Namibia's population in 2009 was estimated at 2,108,000 people, with an annual population growth rate of 0.95%. This figure takes into account the effects of excess mortality due to AIDS, which became the leading cause of death in Namibia in 1996. At approximately two people per square kilometre Namibia has one of Africa's lowest population densities.

The population of Namibia comprises 12 major ethnic groups. The majority of people come from the Owambo tribe (50%), with other ethnic groups making up a relatively small percentage of the population: Kavango (9%), Herero/Himba (7%), Damara (7%), Caprivian (4%), Nama (5%), Afrikaner and German (6%), Baster (6.5%), San (1%) and Tswana (0.5%).

Like nearly all other Sub-Saharan nations, Namibia is struggling to contain its HIV/AIDS epidemic, which is impacting heavily on average life expectancy and population growth rates. According to the CIA World Factbook, life expectancy in Namibia has dropped to 51 years, although some other estimates place it as low as 43. In 2007, 15.3% of the population were HIV-positive, and by 2021, it is estimated that up to a third of Namibia's children under the age of 15 could be orphaned.

Although Namibia is one of the world's least densely populated countries, its rich mix of ethnic groupings provides a wealth of social and cultural diversity. The indigenous people of Namibia, the Khoisan (comprised of San hunter-gatherers and Nama pastoralists), have inhabited the region from time immemorial. They were followed by Bantu-speaking herders, with the first Europeans trickling in during the 17th century.

Although English was chosen by the government as the official language, Afrikaans is spoken by the majority of the population due to the legacy of South African occupation.

San

For information on the San people, see p63.

AN ARGUMENT FOR MINIMUM WAGE *Ian Ketcheson*

A teller at the import/export shops in Oshikango can expect to earn around US$75 per month. These are the same shops that sell, in US dollars, everything from fridges to kitchen cupboards and motorcycles. The US$75 per month wage is not unusual, and would compare to salaries paid to most service-sector workers. Manual labourers and farm workers generally receive less.

To begin her day, the teller would need to walk several kilometres to her job in Oshikango. Transport into town costs one dollar each way, so it would eat up half of her salary. She would have to bring her own food and drink, as a Coke costs about US$0.75 and even the simplest lunch would cost at least US$2.

One night at the motel in Oshikango would cost her the equivalent of three weeks' salary; a tank of petrol would eat up a month-and-a-half of wages; and she would have to save all her salary for 15 years to buy a used truck. All this while she sells US$5000 motorcycles and US$500 fridges to wealthy Angolans, and converts their US hundred-dollar bills into Namibian dollars.

Like South Africa, Namibia's economy has been built on the apartheid system's legacy of cheap labour, and as a result, has produced an incredible gap between rich and poor in the country. While many things have changed in the years since independence, this gap remains.

At the time of research, Namibia still lacked a statutory minimum wage law. As a result, the mining, construction and agricultural sectors continue to set basic levels of pay through collective bargaining practices, which some economists have criticised for being extremely cumbersome and even exploitative.

Owambo

As a sort of loose confederation, the Owambo have always been strong enough to deter outsiders, including the slavers of yore and the German invaders of the last century. They were historically an aggressive culture, which made them the obvious candidates to fight the war of independence. They also make up Namibia's largest ethnic group (about 50% of the population) and, not surprisingly, most of the ruling South West Africa People's Organisation (Swapo) party.

The Owambo traditionally inhabited the north of the country, and are subdivided into 12 distinct groups. Four of these occupy the Kunene region of southern Angola, while the other eight comprise the Owambo groups in Namibia. The most numerous group is the Kwanyama, which makes up 35% of Namibia's Owambo population and dominates the government.

For in-depth articles covering the economy, health and politics of Namibia and its neighbours log on to www.osisa.org.

Recently large numbers of Owambo have migrated southwards to Windhoek, or to the larger towns in the north, to work as professionals, craftspeople and labourers. They have enjoyed considerable favour from the government over the years, and with the exception of white Namibians of European descent, are among the most successful tribal group.

Kavango

The Kavango originated from the Wambo tribe of East Africa, who first settled on the Kwando River in Angola before moving south in the late 18th century to the northern edges of the Okavango. Since the outbreak of civil war in Angola in the 1970s, however, many Kavango have emigrated further south, swelling the local Namibian population, and making them Namibia's second largest ethnic group. They are divided into five distinct subgroups: the Mbukushu, the Sambiyu, the Kwangari, the Mbunza and the Geiriku.

The Kavango are famous for their highly skilled woodcarvers. However, as with other groups in northern Namibia, large numbers of Kavango are now migrating southwards in search of employment on farms, in mines and around urban areas.

Herero/Himba

Namibia's 100,000 Herero occupy several regions of the country, and are divided into several subgroups. The largest groups include the Tjimba and Ndamuranda groups in Kaokoveld, the Maherero around Okahandja, and the Zeraua, who are centred on Omaruru. The Himba of the Kaokoveld are also a Herero subgroup (see the boxed text, opposite), as are the Mbandero, who occupy the colonially demarcated territory formerly known as Hereroland, around Gobabis in eastern Namibia.

The Herero were originally part of the early Bantu migrations south from central Africa. They arrived in present-day Namibia in the mid-16th century, and after a 200-year sojourn in the Kaokoveld, they moved southwards to occupy the Swakop Valley and the Central Plateau. Until the colonial period, they remained as seminomadic pastoralists in this relatively rich grassland, herding and grazing cattle and sheep.

However, bloody clashes with the northwards migrating Nama, as well as with German colonial troops and settlers, led to a violent uprising in the late 19th century, which culminated in the devastating Battle of Waterberg in August 1904 (see p206). In the aftermath, 80% of the country's Herero population was wiped out, and the remainder were dispersed around the country, terrified and demoralised. Large numbers fled into neighbouring Botswana, where they settled down to a life of subsistence agriculture (although they have since prospered to become the country's richest herders).

The characteristic Herero women's dress is derived from Victorian-era German missionaries. It consists of an enormous crinoline worn over a series of petticoats, with a horn-shaped hat or headdress. If you happen to be in Okahandja on the nearest weekend to 23 August, you can witness the gathering of thousands of Hereros immaculately turned out in their traditional dress who come to honour their fallen chiefs on Maherero Day (see p370).

Damara

The Damara resemblance to some Bantu of West Africa has led some anthropologists to believe they were among the first people to migrate into Namibia from the north, and that perhaps early trade with the Nama and San caused them to adopt Khoisan as a lingua franca.

What is known is that prior to the 1870s, the Damara occupied much of central Namibia from around the site of Rehoboth, westwards to the Swakop and Kuiseb Rivers, and north to present-day Outjo and Khorixas. When the Herero and Nama began expanding their domains into traditional Damara lands, large numbers of Damara were displaced, killed or captured and enslaved. The enmity between them resulted in Damara support for the Germans against the Herero during the colonial period. As a reward,

---

BEYOND THE CLICHÉS: A TRAVELLER'S PERSPECTIVE *Ian Ketcheson*

It's hard to write about the Himba in a way that doesn't sound like a cliché or a National Geographic article. They are the widely photographed subject of many travel brochures and glossy coffee-table books. They are often portrayed as an 'early people' who have lived untouched by outside influence for thousands of years. Their practice of smearing red ochre over their bodies, and their not-so-modest attire of leather miniskirts and loincloths, has also made them quite popular on the tourist circuit for those wishing to travel to a remote corner of the continent for a glimpse of 'traditional' Africa.

While these stereotypes might seem accurate at first glance, the reality is much more complex. In fact, the Himba have only lived in this part of Namibia for about 200 years. After being on the losing end of many ethnic battles during the 18th and 19th centuries, this group of people managed some success on the battlefield in the late 19th century, stole a bunch of cattle and goats, and headed off to the remote northwestern corner of the country where they could finally get some peace and quiet – at least until the tourists started turning up in the 1990s.

As for their attire, it's just a sign of the lack of success that Christian missionaries have had in colonising the Himba. One of the top priorities of missionaries across Namibia (and beyond) was to convince people that the first thing a 'civilised' person could do was to put on hot, uncomfortable and expensive clothes. After they had proper clothes, all they had to do was get a 'real' (read Christian) name, renounce polygamy and sit through long church services. Next stop, heaven.

Although the Himba are also widely portrayed as victims of the steady march of modernisation, their leaders have shown themselves to be quite adept at dealing with the outside world. In the late 1990s, the Namibian government was moving ahead with plans to dam Epupa Falls in order to reduce the country's dependence on imported electricity. The plan would have flooded large areas of Himba land, and posed a major threat to their way of life.

Chief Kapika, the Himba leader for the area bordering the falls, with the assistance of some of the top lawyers in the country, mounted a campaign of opposition to the scheme that included a high-profile trip to Europe, where he spoke to foreign investors, NGOs and activists. Chief Kapika quite successfully managed to shine a bit of the international spotlight on his cause, attracting attention and generating support to help in the fight against the government. In recent years, the dam proposal has fallen through, and it's unlikely that the government will raise the issue again in the near future.

the Damara were granted an enlarged homeland, now the southern half of Kunene province.

When Europeans first arrived in the region, the Damara were described as seminomadic pastoralists, who also maintained small-scale mining, smelting and trading operations. However, during the colonial period, they settled down to relatively sedentary subsistence herding and agriculture. In the 1960s, the South African administration purchased for the Damara over 4.5 million hectares of marginal European-owned ranch land in the desolate expanses of present-day Damaraland.

Not that it has done them much good – the soil in this region is generally poor, most of the land is communally owned, and it lacks the good grazing that prevails in central and southern Namibia. Nowadays, most of Namibia's 80,000 Damara work in urban areas and on European farms, and only about a quarter of them actually occupy Damaraland.

Namibians of European Descent

There were no European settlers in Namibia until 1884 when the Germans set up a trading depot at Lüderitz Bay. By the late 1890s, Namibia was a German colony, and settlers began to arrive in ever-greater numbers. At the same time, Boers (white South Africans of Dutch origins) were migrating north from the Cape. Their numbers continued to increase after Namibia came under South African control following WWI.

Nowadays, there are around 85,000 white Namibians, most of whom are of Afrikaans descent. They are concentrated in the urban, central and southern parts of the country, and are involved mainly in ranching, commerce, manufacturing and administration. Furthermore, white Namibians also almost exclusively manage and control the tourism industry.

Caprivians

The female protagonist of Wilbur Smith's pageturner *The Burning Shore* (1987) is shipwrecked on the Skeleton Coast and survives by adapting to indigenous life with a San couple.

In the extreme northeast, along the fertile Zambezi and Kwando riverbanks, live the 80,000 Caprivians, comprising five main tribal groups: the Lozi, Mafwe, Subia, Yei and Mbukushu. Most Caprivians derive their livelihood from fishing, subsistence farming and herding cattle.

Until the late 19th century, the Caprivi Strip was under the control of the Lozi kings. Today, the lingua franca of the various Caprivian tribes is known as Rotse, which is a derivative of the Lozi language still spoken in parts of Zambia and Angola.

Nama

Sharing a similar language to the San of Botswana and South Africa, the Nama are another Khoisan group, and are one of Namibia's oldest indigenous peoples.

The Nama's origins are in the southern Cape. However, during the early days of European settlement, they were either exterminated or pushed northwards by colonial farmers. They eventually came to rest in Namaqualand, around the Orange River, where they lived as seminomadic pastoralists until the mid-19th century, when their leader, Jan Jonker Afrikaner, led them to the area of present-day Windhoek.

On Namibia's Central Plateau, they came into conflict with the Herero, who had already occupied that area, and the two groups fought a series of bloody wars. Eventually, the German government enforced the peace by confining both groups to separate reserves.

Today, there are around 60,000 Nama in Namibia, and they occupy the region colonially designated as Namaqualand, which stretches from Mariental southwards to Keetmanshoop. They're known especially for their traditional

music, folk tales, proverbs and praise poetry, which have been handed down
through the generations to form a basis for their culture today.

Topnaar

The Topnaar (or Aonin), who are technically a branch of the Nama, mainly occupy the western central Namib Desert, in and around Walvis Bay. However,
unlike the Nama, who historically had a tradition of communal land ownership, the Topnaar passed their lands down through family lines.

Today the Topnaar are arguably the most marginalised group in Namibia.
Historically, they were dependent upon the !nara melon, which was supplemented by hunting. Now their hunting grounds are tied up in Namib-
Naukluft Park. Those that remain in the desert eke out a living growing !nara
melons and raising stock (mainly goats).

Most Topnaar have migrated to Walvis Bay and settled in the township of
Narraville, from where they commute to fish-canning factories. Others live
around the perimeter in shanty towns. In the Topnaar community, southeast
of Walvis Bay, a primary school and hostel have been provided, although
only a minority of students come from the Topnaar community.

Coloureds

After the transfer of German South West Africa (as Namibia used to be
known) to South African control after WWI, the South African administration began to introduce the racial laws of apartheid. Thus, at the beginning
of the 1950s, cohabitation of mixed-race couples became illegal, although
marriage was still allowed. On Afrikaans and German farms all over the
territory, farmers married Damara and Herero women; but a few years later
marriage, too, was forbidden.

This left the children of these unions in an unenviable position, shunned by
black and white communities alike. There are now around 52,000 coloureds
in Namibia living mainly in Windhoek, Keetmanshoop and Lüderitz.

Basters

Although distinct from coloureds, Basters are also the result of mixed unions,
specifically between the Nama and Dutch farmers in the Cape Colony. In the
late 1860s, after coming under pressure from the Boer settlers in the Cape,
they moved north of the Orange River and established the settlement of
Rehoboth in 1871. There they established their own system of government
with a headman (Kaptein) and legislative council (Volksraad). They also
benefited from supporting the Germans during the colonial period with
increased privileges and recognition of their land rights.

Most of Namibia's 35,000 Basters still live around Rehoboth, and either
follow an urban lifestyle or raise livestock.

Tswana

Namibia's 8000 Tswana make up the country's smallest ethnic group. They
are related to the Tswana of South Africa and Botswana, the Batswana (see
p62), and live mainly in the eastern areas of the country, around Aminuis
and Epukiro.

RELIGION

About 80% to 90% of Namibians profess Christianity, and German
Lutheranism is the dominant sect in most of the country. As a result of
early missionary activity and Portuguese influence from Angola, there is
also a substantial Roman Catholic population, mainly in the central and
northern areas.

Most non-Christian Namibians – mainly Himba, San and some Herero – live in the north, and continue to follow animist traditions. In general, their beliefs are characterised by ancestor veneration, and most practitioners believe that deceased ancestors continue to interact with the living, and serve as messengers between their descendants and the gods.

WOMEN IN NAMIBIA

In a culture where male power is mythologised, it's unsurprising that women's rights lag behind. Even today, it's not uncommon for men to have multiple sexual partners, and until recently, in cases where husbands abandoned their wives and their children, there was very little course for redress. Since independence, the Namibian government has been committed to improving women's rights with bills like the Married Persons Equality Act (1996), which equalised property rights and gave women rights of custody over their children.

Even the government acknowledges that achieving gender equality is more about changing grass-roots attitudes than passing laws, as a survey into domestic violence in 2000 revealed. Of the women interviewed in Lüderitz, Karasburg and Keetmanshoop, 25% said they had been abused or raped by their husbands. Endemic social problems, such as poverty, alcoholism and the feeling of powerlessness engendered by long-term unemployment, only increase feelings of disaffection and fuel the flames of abuse. Although the government in recent years passed one of the most comprehensive legislative acts against rape in the world, it remains to be seen how effectively it is enforced.

Namibian women do feature prominently in local and civic life, and many a Namibian woman took a heroic stance in the struggle for independence, as the impressive stories in *Histories of Namibia* (p17) reveal. They are also undoubtedly the linchpin of the Namibian home. They also shoulder a double responsibility in raising children and caring for family members as well as contributing to the family income. This load has only increased with the horrendous effects of HIV/AIDS on the family structure.

For a no-holds-barred opinion of the ups and downs of politics, as well as some excellent book reviews, look no further than www.africa-confidential.com.

ARTS

With its harsh environment and historically disparate and poor population, Namibia does not have a formal legacy of art and architecture. What it does have in abundance is a wealth of material arts: carvings, basketry, tapestry, beadwork and textile weaving. The best places to browse and purchase such items are the Namibia Crafts Centre (p245) in Windhoek, and the Penduka craft village (p245), a cooperative located at the Goreangab Dam, about 10km outside Windhoek.

Literature

Dogged by centuries of oppression, isolation, lack of education and poverty, it is hardly surprising that prior to independence there was a complete absence of written literature in Namibia, though there was a rich tradition of oral literature. What there was boils down to a few German colonial novels – most importantly Gustav Frenssen's *Peter Moor's Journey to Southwest Africa* (original 1905, English translation 1908) – and some Afrikaans writing. The best-known work from the colonial period is undoubtedly Henno Martin's *The Sheltering Desert* (1956, English edition 1957), which records two years spent by the geologist author and his friend Hermann Korn avoiding internment as prisoners of war during WWII.

Only with the independence struggle did an indigenous literature begin to take root. One of contemporary Namibia's most significant writers is Joseph

Diescho (born 1955), whose first novel, *Born of the Sun,* was published in 1988, when he was living in the USA. To date, this refreshingly unpretentious work remains the most renowned Namibian effort. As with most African literature, it's largely autobiographical, describing the protagonist's early life in a tribal village, his coming of age and his first contact with Christianity. It then follows his path through the South African mines and his ultimate political awakening. Diescho's second novel, *Troubled Waters* (1993), focuses on a white South African protagonist, who is sent to Namibia on military duty and develops a political conscience.

A new and increasingly apparent branch of Namibian work comes from women writers. Literature written by Namibian women after independence deals primarily with their experiences as women during the liberation struggle and in exile, as well as with the social conditions in the country after independence. Thus, the writing of Ellen Namhila (*The Price of Freedom;* 1998), Kaleni Hiyalwa (*Meekulu's Children;* 2000) and Neshani Andreas (*The Purple Violet of Oshaantu;* 2001) gives us a great insight into the sociopolitical world of post-colonial Namibia.

A New Initiation Song (1994) is a collection of poetry and short fiction published by the Sister Namibia collective. This volume's seven sections cover memories of girlhood, body images, and heterosexual and lesbian relationships. Among the best works are those of Liz Frank and Elizabeth !Khaxas.

> The website www .africaresource.com is an educational portal with some fantastic cultural content, including peer-reviewed journals, poetry, art, essays and exhibitions as well as some interesting academic research.

LEARNING TO SURVIVE *Ian Ketcheson*

Before my wife, daughter and I moved to the small northern Namibia community of Odibo, we thought we were well aware of the impact of HIV/AIDS on Namibia.

What we weren't prepared for, though, were the funerals. We lived next door to a large Anglican church, a massive white building that on any given Sunday will hold more than 1000 people for the marathon four-hour church services. During the rest of the week, the steady flow of funeral processions past our front door was a daily reminder of the deeply personal impact of the HIV/AIDS pandemic on the community. According to a former nurse and local historian, the number of funerals held at the church has risen almost five-fold in the last decade, from 37 in 1992 to 177 in 2003.

At the same time, the tremendous stigma that surrounds the disease has made it very difficult for Namibians to be open about their status. As is the case across much of Africa, HIV/AIDS is shrouded in denial and silence, and reinforced by fear, shame and a lack of understanding of the disease. Despite the prevalence of HIV/AIDS in Namibia, a study carried out by the Namibian government in 2000 found that two-thirds of women in the Ohangwena region said they would not buy food from a person they knew to be HIV positive.

In the midst of these seemingly insurmountable challenges, there are thousands of community workers and volunteers struggling to overcome the stigma and help those affected. In the small community in which we lived, projects include the Anglican Home-Based Care Project, which provides training and distributes home-based care kits to volunteers who visit patients too ill to leave their homesteads, and Omwene Tu Talulula (OTTA; the name means 'Learn to Survive'), a group of HIV-positive activists that travels to schools, churches and other community gatherings encouraging people to come out about their status, and calling for an end to discrimination.

While some progress has been made to improve conditions for people living with HIV/AIDS with improved access to antiretrovirals over the last few years, the challenges remain daunting. For many residents of Ohangwena region in Northern Namibia, it is difficult or impossible to make the long trip to a hospital or clinic, and people often don't have enough food to help them digest their medicine. I was amazed to discover on a visit to homesteads served by the Anglican Home-Based Care Project that volunteers dropped off a loaf of bread in most of the homesteads they visited. For many it would be their only substantial food of the day, and would mean that they would be able to tolerate that day's medication.

The most outstanding short stories include 'Uerieta' by Jane Katjavivi, which describes a white woman's coming to terms with African life, and 'When the Rains Came' by Marialena van Tonder, in which a farm couple narrowly survives a drought. One contributor, Nepeti Nicanor, along with Marjorie Orford, also edited another volume, *Coming on Strong* (1996).

Those who read German will appreciate the works of Giselher Hoffmann (born 1958), which address historical and current Namibian issues. His first novel, *Im Bunde der Dritte* (Three's Company; 1984), is about poaching. *Die Erstgeboren* (The Firstborn; 1991) is told from the perspective of a San group that finds itself pitted against German settlers. Similarly, the Nama-Herero conflict of the late 19th century is described from the Nama perspective in *Die Schweigenden Feuer* (The Silent Fires; 1994). It's also concerned with the impact of modernisation on indigenous cultures.

> For an interesting study of Namibian literature get hold of a copy of Dorian Haarhoff's *The Wild South-West* (1991), which explores the dynamics of colonial literature and provides a survey of indigenous literary response.

Cinema

Since 2002, the Namibian Film Commission has been encouraging local film production and promoting the country as a film location. In the same year, a little known film called *Beyond Borders,* about the Ethiopian famine in 1984, was shot in the country. Little could anyone have guessed how significant it would be when the film's star Angelina Jolie returned in 2006 to give birth to her daughter. On a more serious note, the annual **Wild Cinema Festival** (www .wildcinema.org) is gaining impressive ground, attracting thousands of theatre goers every autumn.

In 2006 another important film project got off the ground. *Where Others Wavered* is the story of Namibia's first president, Sam Nujoma, and his struggle to lead the country to independence. Directed by Charles Burnett, and with Hollywood heavyweights Danny Glover and Carl Lumbly (Sam Nujoma) on the cast list, this film would have provided for some interesting viewing, had production not ground to halt in 2006 after the crew walked away without pay, although critics of Nujoma have already condemned it as just another vanity project in the 'cult of Sam'.

> Capturing the beauty of the landscape and the infamy of conflict diamonds (those mined in conflict areas, which are then sold illicitly), Eric Valli's film *The Trail* (2006) tells the story of a geologist taken hostage by diamond poachers.

Music

Namibia's earliest musicians were the San, whose music probably emulated the sounds of animals, and was sung to accompany dances and storytelling. The early Nama, who had a more developed musical technique, used drums, flutes and basic stringed instruments also to accompany dances. Some of these were adopted and adapted by the later-arriving Bantu, who added marimbas, gourd rattles and animal-horn trumpets to the range. Nowadays, drums, marimbas and rattles are still popular, and it isn't unusual to see dancers wearing belts of soft-drink (soda) cans filled with pebbles to provide rhythmic accompaniment to their steps.

A prominent European contribution to Namibian music is the choir. Early in the colonial period, missionaries established religious choral groups among local people, and both school and church choirs still perform regularly. Namibia's most renowned ensembles are the Cantare Audire Choir and the **Mascato Coastal Youth Choir** (www.mascatoyouthchoir.com), the country's national youth choir. Naturally, the German colonists also introduced their traditional 'oompah' bands, which feature mainly at Oktoberfest (see p240) and at other German-oriented festivals.

Architecture

While most visitors to Namibia have already set their sights on the country's natural wonders, there are a surprising number of architectural wonders to discover as well. More than a century later, striking German colonial

---

ARTS FESTIVALS

In 2001 the government of Namibia drew up its first cultural policy. Its slogan is 'unity in diversity', and its aim is to foster a mutual understanding and respect between Namibia's historically divided people. Much of this effort is focused on the younger generation, with art and culture now forming an integral part of the school curriculum.

In pursuit of this cultural utopia the government sponsors the /AE//Gams Arts Festival, which is held in venues around Windhoek in October. This is a great opportunity to see local musicians, dancers, choirs and poets in action as they compete for various prizes. Another highlight of the festival is the traditional food on sale at venues around town.

Another patron of the festival is Bank Windhoek, a bank that shows a surprising cultural bent. In 2003, when the bank decided to rebrand, it chose to sponsor its own arts festival. The Bank Windhoek Arts Festival has since become the largest arts festival in the country, with a program running from March until September. To find out more about events, venues and how you can purchase tickets, log on to www.bankwindhoekarts.com.na.

---

structures continue to stand as testament to the former European occupation of Namibia.

While most of Windhoek has modernised with the chock-a-block concrete structures that typify most African cities, there are a few 'diamonds-in-the-rough', so to speak. Towering over the city is the German Lutheran Christuskirche, which masterfully uses local sandstone in its European-leaning neo-Gothic construction.

Another notable structure is the Alte Fest or 'Old Fort,' which was constructed in 1890 by Curt of Francois and his men to serve as the barracks for the German army. It remains the oldest surviving building in the city, though it serves a much more peaceful function as the National Museum.

Of course, if you truly want to experience the shining jewels in Namibia's architectural crown, you're going to need to head out to the coast. Here, improbably squeezed between the frozen waters of the South Atlantic and the overbearing heat of the Namib Desert, are the surreal colonial relics of Swakopmund and Lüderitz.

Walking the streets of either city, you'd be easily forgiven for thinking that you were in a Bavarian *dorfchen* (small village), albeit one on the African continent. Somewhat forgotten by time and history, both cities are characterised by a handsome blend of German imperial and art nouveau styles, which become all the more bizarre when viewed against the backdrop of soaring dunes and raging seas.

Dance

Each group in Namibia has its own dances, but common threads run through most of them. First, all dances are intended to express social values, to some extent, and many dances reflect the environment in which they're performed.

Dances of the Ju/hoansi !Kung men (a San group in northeastern Namibia) tend to mimic the animals they hunt, or involve other elements that are important to them. For example, the 'melon dance' involves tossing and catching a *tsama* melon according to a fixed rhythm. The Himba dance *ondjongo* must be performed by a cattle owner, and involves representing care and ownership.

Specific dances are also used for various rituals, including rites of passage, political events, social gatherings and spiritual ceremonies. The Ju/hoansi male initiation dance, the *tcòcmà,* for example, may not even be viewed by women. In the Kavango and Caprivi region, dances performed by traditional healers require the dancer to constantly shake rattles held in both hands. Most festive dances, such as the animated Kavango *epera* and *dipera,* have roles for both men and women, but are performed in lines with the genders separated.

Visual Arts

The majority of Namibia's established modern painters and photographers are of European origin, and concentrate largely on the country's colourful landscapes, bewitching light, native wildlife and, more recently, its diverse peoples. Well-known names include François de Necker, Axel Eriksson, Fritz Krampe and Adolph Jentsch. The well-known colonial landscape artists Carl Ossman and Ernst Vollbehr are exhibited in Germany. The work of many of these artists is exhibited in the permanent collection of the National Art Gallery (p238) in Windhoek, which also hosts changing exhibitions of local and international artists.

Non-European Namibians who have concentrated on three-dimensional and material arts have been developing their own traditions. Township art – largely sculpture made out of reclaimed materials like drink cans and galvanised wire – develops sober themes in an expressive and colourful manner. It first appeared in the townships of South Africa during the apartheid years. Over the past decade, it has taken hold in Namibia, and is developing into a popular art form. Names to keep an eye on include Tembo Masala and Joseph Madisia.

In an effort to raise the standard and awareness of the visual arts in Namibia, a working group of artists – including Joseph Madesia and François Necker – established the **Tulipamwe International Artists' Workshop** (www.artshost .org/tulipamwe) in 1994. Since then they have held a long list of workshops in farms and in wildlife lodges around Namibia where Namibian, African and international artists can come together and share ideas and develop their skills base.

FOOD & DRINK
Staples & Specialities

Traditional Namibian food consists of a few staples, the most common of which is *oshifima,* a dough-like paste made from millet, and usually served with a stew of vegetables or meat. Other common dishes include *oshiwambo,* a rather tasty combination of spinach and beef, and *mealie pap,* an extremely basic porridge.

As a foreigner you'll rarely find such dishes on the menu. Most Namibian restaurants serve a variation on European-style foods, like Italian or French, alongside an abundance of seafood dishes. Such gourmet pretensions are confined to big towns like Windhoek, Swakopmund and Lüderitz; outside of these you'll rapidly become familiar with fried-food joints and pizza parlours.

Whatever the sign above the door, you'll find that most menus are meat-orientated, although you might be lucky to find a few vegetarian side dishes. The reason for this is pretty obvious – Namibia is a vast desert, and the country imports much of its fresh fruit and vegetables from South Africa. What is available locally is the delicious gem squash and varieties of pumpkin such as butternut squash. In season, Namibian oranges are delicious; in the Kavango region, papayas are served with a squeeze of lemon or lime.

More than anything else, German influences can be found in Namibia's *konditoreien* (cake shops), where you can pig out on *Apfelstrudel* (apple strudel), *Sachertorte* (a rich chocolate cake layered with apricot jam), *Schwartzwälder Kirschtorte* (Black Forest cake), and other delicious pas-

The African staple, maize or sorghum meal, is the centre of nearly every meal. It is normally taken with the right hand from a communal pot, rolled into balls and dipped into some sort of relish.

tries and cakes. Several places in Windhoek and Swakopmund are national institutions. You may also want to try Afrikaners' sticky-sweet *koeksesters* (small doughnuts dripping with honey) and *melktart* (milk tart).

Cooked breakfasts include bacon and *boerewors* (farmer's sausage), and don't be surprised to find something bizarre – curried kidneys, for example – alongside your eggs. Beef in varying forms also makes an occasional appearance at breakfast time.

Evening meals feature meat – normally beef or game. A huge beef fillet steak or a kudu cutlet will set you back no more than N$75. Fish and seafood are best represented by kingklip, kabeljou and several types of shellfish. These are available all over Namibia, but are best at finer restaurants in Windhoek, Swakopmund and Lüderitz, where they'll normally be fresh from the sea.

Drinks

In the rural Owambo areas, people socialise in tiny makeshift bars, enjoying local brews like *oshikundu* (beer made from mahango, or millet), *mataku* (watermelon wine), *tambo* (fermented millet and sugar) or *mushokolo* (a beer made from a small local seed) and *walende,* which is distilled from the *makalani* palm and tastes similar to vodka. All of these concoctions, except *walende,* are brewed in the morning and drunk the same day, and they're all dirt cheap, costing less than US$0.25 per glass.

For more conventional palates, Namibia is awash with locally brewed lagers. The most popular drop is the light and refreshing Windhoek Lager, but the brewery also produces Tafel Lager, the stronger and bitterer Windhoek Export, and the slightly rough Windhoek Special. Windhoek Light and DAS Pilsener are both drunk as soft drinks (DAS is often called 'breakfast beer'!), and in winter, Namibia Breweries also brews a 7% stout known as Urbock. South African beers like Lion, Castle and Black Label are also widely available.

Although beer is the drink of choice for most Namibians, Namibia also has its own winery, the Kristall Kellerei, 3km east of Omaruru. Here it produces Cabernet (the best), colombard (also good), prickly-pear-cactus schnapps (a good blast) and grappa (a rough, powerful blast). South African wines are also widely available. Among the best are the Cabernet and pinot varieties grown in the Stellenbosch region of Western Cape Province. A good bottle of wine will set you back between N$75 and N$150.

Windhoek Lager is brewed according to the 1516 German purity law of *Reinheitsgebot,* which states that beer can only contain barley, hops and water.

Namibia Environment

THE LAND

It's the oldest desert in the world, a garden of burned and blackened-red basalt that spilled out of the earth 130 million years ago in southwest Africa, hardening to form the arid landscape of Namibia, the driest country south of the Sahara. Precious little can grow or thrive in this merciless environment, with the exception of a few uniquely adapted animals and plants, which illustrate the sheer ingenuity of life on earth.

Arid Namibia enjoys a wide variety of geographical and geological features. Broadly speaking, its topography can be divided into five main sections: the Namib Desert and the coastal plains of the south and central interior; the eastward-sloping central plateau, with its flat-topped inselbergs (isolated mountains); the Kalahari sands along the Botswana and South Africa borders; and the densely wooded bushveld of the Kavango and Caprivi regions. Most famous of all are the scorched dunes of the impossibly eerie but always captivating Skeleton Coast.

The Namib Desert extends along the country's entire Atlantic coast, and is scored by a number of rivers, which rise in the central plateau, but often run dry. Some, like the ephemeral Tsauchab, once reached the sea, but now end in calcrete pans. Others flow only during the summer rainy season, but at some former stage, carried huge volumes of water, and carved out dramatic canyons like the Fish River and Kuiseb, where Henno Martin and Hermann Korn struggled to survive WWII (see p218).

In wild contrast to the bleached-blue skies and vast, open expanses of the majority of the country, the Kavango and Caprivi regions are a well-watered paradise. Bordering Angola to the north, they are bounded by four great rivers – the Kunene, Okavango, Kwando/Mashi/Linyanti/Chobe and Zambezi – that flow year-round.

WILDLIFE

For big game watchers, there are really only three significant areas in Namibia: Kaokoland, where elusive desert elephants and black rhinos follow the river courses running to the Skeleton Coast; the isolated and rarely visited Khaudom, where Namibia's last African wild dogs find refuge; and Etosha National Park, one of the world's finest game reserves.

Further south is the largest game reserve in Africa, the Namib-Naukluft Park, which covers an astonishing 6% of Namibia's area. Much of it is true desert, and large mammals occur in extremely low densities, though local specials include Hartmann's mountain zebras as well as more widespread Southern African endemics like springboks and gemsboks. For aficionados of smaller life, the Namib is an endemism hotspot: on the dunes, Gray's larks, dune larks, slip-face lizards and fog-basking beetles are found, while the scattered rocky plateaus host long-billed larks, rockrunners and Herero chats.

The severe Namibian coast is no place to expect abundant big game, though it's the only spot in the world where massive fur-seal colonies are patrolled by hunting brown hyenas and black-backed jackals. The coast also hosts massive flocks of summer waders, including sanderlings, turnstones and grey plovers, while Heaviside's and dusky dolphins can often be seen in the shallow offshore waters.

In 2009, the Namibian government opened Sperrgebiet National Park, a vast 16,000 sq km expanse of land home to the threatened desert rain frog, dramatic rock formations and disused diamond mines. The area's haunting

At 161km long and almost 550m deep, the Fish River Canyon is second only in size to Arizona's Grand Canyon and is one of Africa's least-visited geological wonders.

Surface temperatures in the Namib Desert can reach as high as 70°C (158°F), so many reptiles and plants derive their moisture by condensing fog on their bodies or leaves.

For tips on how to build a fire, avoid uncomfortable situations with dangerous animals and find something edible amid the scrub, dip into *An Explorer's Handbook* by Christina Dodwell.

beauty, which is highlighted by shimmering salt pans and saffron-coloured sand dunes, provide one of the world's most dramatic backdrops for adventurous wildlife watchers.

For a rundown of all of Namibia's national parks and their highlights refer to the National Parks and Reserves chapter on p28.

Mammals

Nowhere else on earth does such diverse mammal life exist in such harsh conditions. On the gravel plains live ostriches, zebras, gemsboks, springboks, mongooses, ground squirrels and small numbers of other animals, such as black-backed jackals, bat-eared foxes, caracals, aardwolfs and brown hyenas. Along the coast, penguins and seals thrive in the chilly Atlantic currents, and in the barren Erongo mountains and Waterberg plateau the last wild black rhinoceros populations are slowly recovering.

Namibia's largest and best-known wildlife park is Etosha (see p264). Its name means 'Place of Mirages', for the dusty saltpan that sits at its centre. During the dry season, huge herds of elephants, zebras, antelope and giraffes, as well as rare black rhinos, congregate here against an eerie bleached-white backdrop.

To see the elusive wild dog, Khaudom Game Reserve (p277) is your best bet. Namibia's other major parks for good wildlife viewing are Bwabwata National Park (p278), Mudumu National Park (p282) and Mamili National Park (p283).

Not all of Namibia's wildlife is confined to national parks. Unprotected Damaraland (p292), in Namibia's northwest, is home to numerous antelope species and other ungulates, and is also a haven for desert rhinos, elephants and other specially adapted subspecies. Hikers in the Naukluft and other desert ranges may catch sight of the elusive Hartmann's mountain zebra, and along the desert coasts you can see jackass penguins, flamingos, Cape fur seals and perhaps even the legendary brown hyena, or *strandwolf*.

For more in-depth information about the array of mammalian wildlife found in Namibia, refer to p33 or pick up *Watching Wildlife Southern Africa* published by Lonely Planet.

Reptiles

The dry lands of Namibia boast more than 70 species of snake, including three species of spitting cobra. It is actually the African puff adder that causes the most problems for humans, since it inhabits dry, sandy riverbeds. Horned adders and sand snakes inhabit the gravel plains of the Namib, and the sidewinder adder lives in the Namib dune sea. Other venomous snakes include the slender green vine snake; both the green and black mamba; the dangerous zebra snake; and the boomslang (Afrikaans for 'tree snake'), a slender 2m aquamarine affair with black-tipped scales.

Lizards, too, are ubiquitous. The largest of these is the leguaan or water monitor, a docile creature that reaches over 2m in length, swims and spends a lot of time laying around water holes, probably dreaming of becoming a crocodile. A smaller version, the savannah leguaan, inhabits *kopjes* (small hills) and drier areas. Also present in large numbers are geckos, chameleons, legless lizards, rock-plated lizards and a host of others.

The Namib Desert supports a wide range of lizards, including a large vegetarian species, *Angolosaurus skoogi,* and the sand-diving lizard, *Aprosaura achietae,* known for its 'thermal dance'. The unusual bug-eyed palmato gecko inhabits the high dunes and there's a species of chameleon.

In the watery marshes and rivers of the north of the country, you'll find Namibia's reptile extraordinaire, the Nile crocodile. It is one of the largest

If you must take home one of those luscious photographic tomes – and Namibia is so photogenic – then pick up Amy Shoeman's *The Skeleton Coast*. Beautiful photography combined with excellent text.

Namib Desert brown hyenas are ecologically unique, as they scavenge almost exclusively on Cape fur seal pups. To find out more about the efforts being made to conserve their numbers log on to www.strand wolf.org.za.

species of crocodile on the planet, and can reach 5m to 6m in length. It has a reputation as a 'man-eater,' but this is probably because it lives in close proximity to human populations. In the past, there have been concerns over excessive hunting of the crocodile, but these days numbers are well up, and it's more at risk from pollution and accidental entanglement in fishing nets.

Insects & Spiders

Although Namibia doesn't enjoy the profusion of bug life found in countries further north, a few interesting specimens buzz, creep and crawl around the place. Over 500 species of colourful butterflies – including the African monarch, the commodore and the citrus swallowtail – are resident, as well as many fly-by-night moths.

Interesting buggy types include the large and rarely noticed stick insects, the similarly large (and frighteningly hairy) baboon spider, and the ubiquitous and leggy *shongololo* (millipede), which can be up to 30cm long.

The Namib Desert has several wonderful species of spider. The tarantula-like 'white lady of the dunes' is a white hairy affair that is attracted to light. There's also a rare false spider known as a solifluge, or sun spider. You can see its circulatory system through its light-coloured translucent outer skeleton. The dunes are also known for their extraordinary variety of *tenebrionid* (known as *toktokkie*) beetles.

Common insects such as ants, stink bugs, grasshoppers, mopane worms and locusts, sometimes find their way into frying pans for snacks. For travellers, it takes something of a culinary daredevil to dive into a newspaper wrapped ball of fried bugs, though for locals, the practice provides essential protein supplements.

Birds

Namibia's desert landscape is too harsh and inhospitable to support a great variety of birdlife. The exception to this is the lush green Caprivi Strip, which borders the Okavango Delta. Here, in the Mahango Game Reserve (p278), you'll find the same exotic range of species as in Botswana, including the gorgeous lilac-breasted rollers, pygmy geese (actually a duck) and white-fronted, carmine and little bee-eaters. Other wetland species include the African jacanas, snakebirds, ibis, storks, egrets, shrikes, kingfishers, great white herons, and purple and green-backed herons. Birds of prey include Pel's fishing owl, goshawks, several species of vultures, and both bateleurs and African fish eagles.

Likewise, the coastal wildfowl reserves support an especially wide range of birdlife: white pelicans, flamingos, cormorants and hundreds of other wetland birds. Further south, around Walvis Bay and Lüderitz, flamingos and jackass penguins share the same desert shoreline.

Situated on a key migration route, Namibia also hosts a range of migratory birds, especially raptors, who arrive around September and October, and remain until April. The canyons and riverbeds slicing across the central Namib Desert are home to nine species of raptor, as well as the hoopoe, the unusual red-eyed bulbul and a small bird known as the familiar chat. Throughout the desert regions, you'll also see the intriguing social weaver, which builds an enormous nest that's the avian equivalent of a 10-storey block of flats. Central Namibia also boasts bird species found nowhere else, such as the Namaqua sand-grouse and Grey's lark.

Fish

The Namibian coastal waters are considered some of the world's richest, mainly thanks to the cold Benguela Current, which flows northwards from

Around 90% of all South African flamingos winter in the lagoon at Walvis Bay, which supports up to 160,000 birds.

The most comprehensive field guide to birds in Southern Africa is Kenneth Newman's *Birds of Southern Africa;* all species are identified in colour or black-and-white illustrations.

the Antarctic. It's exceptionally rich in plankton, which accounts for the abundance of anchovies, pilchards, mackerels and other whitefish. But the limited offshore fishing rights have caused problems, and there is resentment that such countries as Spain and Russia have legal access to offshore fish stocks. Namibia has now declared a 200-nautical-mile exclusive economic zone to make Namibian fisheries competitive.

PLANTS

Because Namibia is mostly arid, much of the flora is typical African dryland vegetation: scrub brush and succulents, such as euphorbia. Along the coastal plain around Swakopmund are the world's most extensive and diverse fields of lichen; they remain dormant during dry periods, but with the addition of water, they burst into colourful bloom (see p295).

Most of the country is covered by tree-dotted, scrub savannah grasses of the genera *Stipagrostis, Eragrostis* and *Aristida*. In the south, the grass is interrupted by ephemeral watercourses lined with tamarisks, buffalo thorn and camelthorn. Unique floral oddities here include the *kokerboom* (quiver tree), a species of aloe that grows only in southern Namibia.

In the sandy plains of southeastern Namibia, raisin bushes *(Grewia)* and candlethorn grow among the scrubby trees, while hillsides are blanketed with green-flowered *Aloe viridiflora* and camphor bush.

The eastern fringes of Namib-Naukluft Park are dominated by semidesert scrub savannah vegetation, including some rare aloe species *(Aloe karasbergensis* and *Aloe sladeniana)*. On the gravel plains east of the Skeleton Coast grows the bizarre *Welwitschia mirabilis*, a slow-growing, ground-hugging conifer that lives for more than 1000 years (see p318).

In areas with higher rainfall, the characteristic grass savannah gives way to acacia woodlands, and Etosha National Park enjoys two distinct environments: the wooded savannah in the east and thorn-scrub savannah in the west. The higher rainfall of Caprivi and Kavango sustains extensive mopane woodland, and the riverine areas support scattered wetland vegetation, grasslands and stands of acacias. The area around Katima Mulilo is dominated by mixed subtropical woodland containing copalwood, Zambezi teak and leadwood, among other hardwood species.

The Namib, by Dr Mary Seely, is a fantastically useful handbook about the desert, its flora and fauna, written by none other than the director of the Desert Research Unit.

ENDANGERED SPECIES

Overfishing and the 1993–94 outbreak of 'red tide' along the Skeleton Coast have decimated the sea lion population, both through starvation and commercially inspired culling. Also, the poaching of desert rhinos, elephants and other Damaraland species has caused their numbers to decrease, and the desert lion, which once roamed the Skeleton Coast, is now considered extinct.

For the rest of Namibia's lions, survival is also precarious. From a high of 700 animals in 1980, the number has now decreased to no more than 400. Of these, nearly 85% are confined to Etosha National Park and Khaudom Game Reserve. One problem is that reserve fences are penetrable, and once the lions have left protected areas, it's only a matter of time before they're shot by ranchers to protect cattle.

The stability of other bird and plant species, such as the lichen fields, the welwitschia plant, the Damara tern (p321), the Cape vulture and numerous lesser-known species, has been undoubtedly compromised by human activities (including tourism and recreation) in formerly remote areas. However, awareness of the perils faced by these species is increasing among operators and tourists alike, which adds a glimmer of hope to the prospects of their future survival.

ENVIRONMENTAL ISSUES

With a small human population spread over a large land area, Namibia is in better environmental shape than most African countries, but challenges remain. Key environmental issues include water schemes and water quality, uneven population distribution, bush and wildlife management, trophy-hunting policies, attitudes of farmers and villagers towards wildlife, conservation methods and ecotourism issues.

The Looming Energy Crisis

In recent years, Namibia's energy crisis has deepened to worrying levels. Since 2006, NamPower has been at the forefront of an energy conservation awareness campaign, and the Windhoek City Council has jumped on board by asking residents to switch off gas-fired water heaters in an attempt to manage the power shortages. But this barely begins to tackle the problem, especially since Namibia continues to import more than 45% of its energy from South Africa. Even though the country's energy problems are not readily obvious, at least to the casual traveller, it's important to keep these issues in mind at all times, and try to limit your energy usage by turning off lights, taking shorter showers and being reasonable with the air-con.

It is this looming crisis that lies behind Namibia's many dam proposals, like the Epupa and Popa Falls dams, the hydroelectric plant proposal on the Kunene River, and, worst of all, the proposal for a pipeline diverting water from the Okavango River direct to Windhoek. At the time of research, all of these projects were either on hold or undergoing further environmental study. And, as a member of the Okavango River Basin Commission (OKACOM), Namibia is working with Angola and Botswana to create a sustainable management plan for the waters of the Okavango Basin (see p76).

But this doesn't solve the immediate crisis, and in 2006 the government ruffled more feathers when it mooted the idea of a nuclear power plant at its Roessing uranium mine. Mines and Energy Secretary Joseph Iita was quick to add that it was just one idea being considered in light of Namibia's huge uranium resources. The Ministry of Mines and Energy is also supporting a new project investigating the viability of renewable energy (Namibia Renewable Energy Programme). The project is investigating the potential of solar energy as part of Namibia's Vision 2030.

Hunting

Like Botswana, hunting is legal in Namibia, although it is strictly regulated and licensed. The Ministry of the Environment and Tourism along with the Namibia Professional Hunting Association (NAPHA) regulate hunting, which accounts for 5% of the country's revenue from wildlife.

The Namibian government views its hunting laws as a practical form of wildlife management and conservation. Many foreign hunters are willing to pay handsomely for big wildlife trophies (a leopard, for example, will fetch at least US$2500, while an elephant provides many times that amount) and farmers and ranchers frequently complain about the ravages of wildlife on their stock. The idea is to provide farmers with financial incentives to protect free-ranging wildlife. Management strategies include encouraging hunting of older animals, evaluating the condition of trophies and setting bag limits in accordance with population fluctuations.

In addition, quite a few private farms are set aside for hunting. The owners stock these farms with wildlife bred by suppliers – mainly in South Africa – and turn it loose into the farm environment. Although community-based hunting concessions have appeared in the Bushmanland area, these still aren't widespread.

No more than 5% of the Sperrgebiet is actively mined, yet current mining and prospecting licences cover more than one-third of the land area.

Want to know what the Ministry of Environment and Tourism is up to? To find out more about its projects and proposals, log on to www.met.gov.na.

Culling

Increasingly across the region, park authorities are facing elephant overpopulation. Proposed solutions include relocation (where herds are permanently transplanted to other areas) and contraception. The only other alternative is to cull herds, sometimes in large numbers; this seems a bizarre paradox, but illustrates the seriousness of the problem. In the West people generally hold a preservationist viewpoint: that elephant herds should be conserved for their own sake or for aesthetic reasons. However, the local sentiment maintains that the elephant must justify its existence on long-term economic grounds for the benefit of local people, or for the country as a whole.

This is an issue sure to generate much debate, with proponents citing the health of the parks, including other wildlife and the elephants themselves, and organisations such as the International Fund for Animal Welfare (IFAW) appalled at such a solution, which they claim is cruel, unethical and scientifically unsound. IFAW believes aerial surveys of elephant numbers are inaccurate, population growth has not been accurately surveyed and that other solutions have not been looked at carefully enough, including more transfrontier parks crossing national borders.

Furthermore, there is much dispute about whether controlled ivory sales should be reintroduced, with countries with excessive elephant populations and large ivory stockpiles pushing hard for a relaxation on the ban. Some argue that countries with large tracts of protected land are paying for the inability of other African countries to properly manage and protect their wildlife. Indeed, it remains to be seen whether a lift on the ban will occur, but meanwhile debate about the ivory trade, and the culling solution to overpopulation, rages on.

If you're interested in community-based tourism, log on to www .nnf.org.na, the website of Namibia's Nature Foundation, whose aim is to promote sustainable development alongside the ethical use of natural resources.

Travelling Sustainably

As one of Africa's most iconic destinations, Namibia spoils visitors with a never-ending assortment of natural landscapes. At the same time, the greatest challenge to responsible travellers in the region is preserving the purity of the environment for future generations. Quite simply, each of us bears the responsibility to minimise the impact of our stay and to travel in the most sustainable way possible. Fortunately, ecotourism initiatives

---

CONSERVATION ORGANISATIONS

Anyone with a genuine interest in a specific ecological issue is invited to contact one or more of the following organisations. These organisations do not, however, provide tourist information or offer organised tours (unless stated otherwise).

AfriCat Foundation (www.africat.org) A nonprofit organisation focusing on research and the reintroduction of large cats into the wild. There's also an onsite education centre and a specialist veterinary clinic; see p255.

BirdLife International (www.birdlife.org) BirdLife International is actively involved in conservation projects, such as building observation posts, and organising bird-watching trips. Despite Namibia's variety of birdlife the organisation has no in-country affiliations.

Cheetah Conservation Fund (CCF; www.cheetah.org) A centre of research and education on cheetah populations and how they are conserved. It's possible to volunteer with this organisation.

Integrated Rural Development and Nature Conservation (IRDNC; www.irdnc.org.na) IRDNC aims to improve the lives of rural people by diversifying their economic opportunities to include wildlife management and other valuable natural resources. Its two main projects are in the Kunene region and the Caprivi Strip.

Save the Rhino Trust (SRT; www.savetherhino.org) SRT has worked tirelessly to implement community-based conservation since the early 1980s. By 2030, it hopes that its efforts will have succeeded in re-establishing the black rhino in Namibia in healthy, breeding populations. For details, see p297.

are spreading throughout Namibia, and you can find a full listing of environmentally sensitive listings on p423.

The continuous growth of the travel industry has brought incredible economic success to parts of Namibia. However, this growth has also placed enormous stress on both biological and cultural habitats, and threatens to destroy the very destinations that tourists are seeking out. In recent years, the term 'sustainable tourism' has emerged as a buzzword in the industry, and refers to striking the ideal balance between the traveller and their surrounding environment.

One of the most important tenets of sustainable tourism is the notion of respecting local communities. Cultural ruin of a destination is irreversible, but community preservation is one area where travellers can make the biggest individual difference. While in Namibia, talk to locals, and ask them about their customs and traditions. An eagerness to learn on the part of the traveller may reassure a local that others value their customs, even if everything is changing around them.

An immediate benefit of tourism is a strong financial boost to the local economy. Regardless of whether you're shoestringing or living it up in five-star hotels, please respect the fact that international travel in any capacity is a luxury that the majority of the world's people will never be able to enjoy. If the opportunity arises to spend money at a locally run business or vendor arises, don't hesitate to give a little back.

Finally, one of the simplest things you can do before embarking on a trip to Namibia is to learn about pressing conservation and environmental issues. Keeping these issues in mind, do your best to do business with and support hotels, lodges, tour operators and environmental groups that promote conservation initiatives and have public long-term management plans.

Windhoek

Compared to African heavyweights like Johannesburg, Nairobi, Cairo and Lagos, Windhoek is more akin to an oversized village than a capital city. With a relatively small population, and a compact and surprisingly pedestrian-friendly city centre, Windhoek is relaxed, relatively hassle-free and utterly cosmopolitan. On the streets you'll see Owambo, Kavango, Herero, Damara and Caprivian people, together with Nama, San, coloureds, Afrikaaners and Europeans, all contributing to the city's optimistic outlook that sets an example for all of Africa.

Largely influenced by its German colonial heritage, Windhoek's architecture is colourful and inspiring, and there are a few streets in the capital where colonial styling still radiates. Neo-Baroque cathedral spires, as well as a few seemingly misplaced German castles, punctuate the skyline, and complement the steel and glass high-rises that emerged from Namibia's rapid growth and development. Indeed, Windhoek is an extremely well-heeled city that stands in marked contrast to the desolate hinterlands that serve as Namibia's main tourist drawcards.

With so much open space lying beyond the borders of the capital, most foreign visitors treat Windhoek as little more than a springboard for their onward travels. But a few days in the city can be treated as an opportunity to gain perspective on the complexities of one of the world's youngest nations. From the posh bars and exclusive eateries dotting the eastern suburbs, to the bustling markets and heaving streets of the black townships, Windhoek is where rich and poor alike give shape and form to the face of modern Namibia.

HIGHLIGHTS

- Exploring Windhoek's humble collection of **colonial buildings** (p234) and informative **museums** (p237)

- Wandering down **Post St Mall** (p234), where you can check out the Gibeon meteorites while shopping for curios

- Enjoying a meal in any of the city's fine **restaurants** (p243) before heading to (or after coming back from) the bush

- Indulging in cold beers and hot beats in any of the city's pumping **bars and clubs** (p244)

- Driving (or hiking) through **Daan Viljoen Game Park** (p238), a proper safari park lying on the outskirts of the city

Daan Viljoen
Game Park
★

★ Windhoek

- TELEPHONE CODE: 06   ■ POPULATION: less than 250,000   ■ ELEVATION: 1660M

WINDHOEK

HISTORY

The city of Windhoek has existed for just over a century, but its history is as diverse as its population. During the German colonial occupation, it became the headquarters for the German Schutztruppe (Imperial Army), which was ostensibly charged with brokering peace between the warring Herero and Nama in exchange for whatever lands their efforts would gain for German occupation. For over 10 years at the turn of the 20th century, Windhoek served as the administrative capital of German South West Africa.

In 1902, a narrow-gauge railway was built to connect Windhoek to the coast at Swakopmund, and the city experienced a sudden spurt of growth. During this period, Windhoek began to evolve into the business, commercial and administrative centre of the country, although the modern city wasn't officially founded until 1965. Under South African administration, racial separation created the unfortunate pattern of poor black and rich white suburbs seen at present.

Today, Windhoek is now home to all of Namibia's government ministries and functions, as well as most of the country's commercial concerns. Furthermore, a recent spate of growth has seen the construction of middle-income housing in the west and southeast of the city that is seeking to bring all races together, and subsequently erase decades of apartheid-inspired residential policies.

ORIENTATION

Set among low hills, Windhoek enjoys dry, clean air, and a healthy highland climate. For the early German colonists, the city's high elevation and cool temperatures were conducive to comfortable residential living without fear of malaria.

Central Windhoek is bisected by Independence Ave, where most shopping and administrative functions are concentrated. The shopping district is focused on the Post St pedestrian mall and the nearby Gustav Voigts Centre, Wernhill Park Centre and Levinson Arcade. Zoo Park, beside the main post office, provides a green lawn and shady lunch spots.

North along Independence Ave are the industrial expanses of Windhoek's Northern Industrial Area. To the west and northwest are the high-density townships of Khomasdal and Katutura, which are slowly developing into amenable neighbourhoods, but still have several pockets of serious poverty. In other directions, middle- and upper-class suburbs such as Klein Windhoek and Eros Park sprawl across the hills that encircle the city, affording impressive views.

Immediately beyond the city limits, the wild country begins. Approximately 45km to the east lies Hosea Kutako International Airport, completely surrounded by the encroaching bush. Just to the west is Daan Viljoen Game Park, where wild animals roam in the shadow of the capital.

Maps

Free city plans are available from the tourist offices. You can purchase topographic sheets of much of Namibia for a small fee from the map section of the **Office of the Surveyor General** (Map p236; ☎ 245055; cnr Robert Mugabe Ave & Korn St).

INFORMATION
Emergency
Ambulance & Fire Brigade (☎ 211111)
Crime report (☎ 290 2239) A 24-hour phone service.
National police (☎ 10111)
Police (☎ 228328)

WHAT'S IN A NAME?

Windhoek's original settlement, in what is now Klein Windhoek, was called /AE//Gams (Fire Waters) by the Nama, and Otjomuise (Smoky Place) by the Herero. These two names refer to the hot springs that attracted early tribal attention and settlement. On a visit in 1836, British prospector Sir James Alexander took the liberty of renaming it Queen Adelaide's Bath, although it's fairly certain the monarch never did soak there. In 1842, for reasons known only to them, a pair of German missionaries named the settlement Elbersfeld, but in 1844, the rival Wesleyan mission decided a better name would be Concordiaville. Meanwhile, in 1840, Nama leader Jan Jonker Afrikaner and his followers arrived and began referring to it as Winterhoek, after the Cape Province farm where he was born. The modern name, which means Windy Corner, was probably corrupted from Winterhoek by the Germans sometime around the turn of the 20th century.

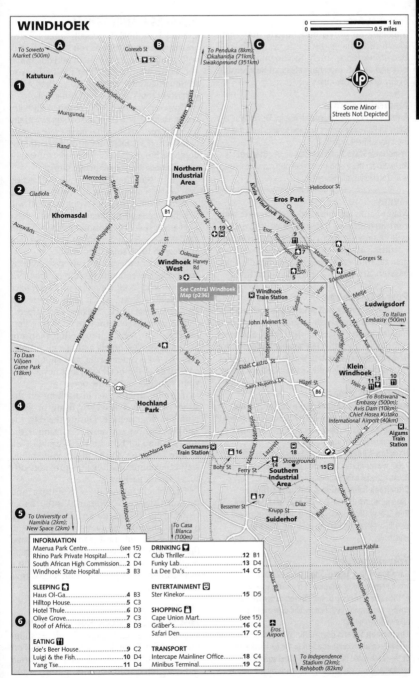

WINDHOEK

INFORMATION
Maerua Park Centre.....................(see 15)
Rhino Park Private Hospital............**1** C2
South African High Commission....**2** D4
Windhoek State Hospital...............**3** B3

SLEEPING
Haus Ol-Ga.....................................**4** B3
Hilltop House...................................**5** C3
Hotel Thule.....................................**6** D3
Olive Grove.....................................**7** C3
Roof of Africa................................**8** D3

EATING
Joe's Beer House..............................**9** C2
Luigi & the Fish............................**10** D4
Yang Tse.......................................**11** D4

DRINKING
Club Thriller..................................**12** B1
Funky Lab.....................................**13** D4
La Dee Da's...................................**14** C5

ENTERTAINMENT
Ster Kinekor.................................**15** D5

SHOPPING
Cape Union Mart.......................(see 15)
Gräber's.......................................**16** C4
Safari Den....................................**17** C5

TRANSPORT
Intercape Mainliner Office...........**18** C4
Minibus Terminal..........................**19** C2

Internet Access

Virtually all hotels and hostels now offer cheap and reliable internet access, with wi-fi becoming increasingly the norm. If you're out and about, internet cafes can be found in every mall in the city.

Medical Services

Rhino Park Private Hospital (Map p233; ☎ 225434; Sauer St) Provides excellent care and service, but patients must pay up front.
Windhoek State Hospital (Map p233; ☎ 303 9111) An option for those who are short of cash but have time to wait. Located just off Harvey Rd.

Money

Major banks and bureaux de change are concentrated around Independence Ave, and all will change foreign currency and travellers cheques and give credit-card advances. As a general rule, ATMs in Namibia handle Visa, MasterCard and home ATM transactions.

Post & Telephone

The modern **main post office** (Map p236; Independence Ave) can readily handle overseas post. It also has telephone boxes in the lobby, and next door is located the **Telecommunications Office** (Map p236; Independence Ave), where you can make international calls and send or receive faxes.

Tourist Information

Namibia Tourism Board (Map p236; ☎ 290 6000; www.namibiatourism.com.na; 1st Fl, Channel Life Towers, 39 Post St Mall) The national tourist office can provide information from all over the country.
Namibia Wildlife Resorts (NWR; Map p236; ☎ 285 7200; www.nwr.com.na; Erkrath Bldg, Independence Ave) Books national park accommodation and hikes.
Windhoek Information & Publicity Office (Map p236; ☎ 290 2058; www.cityofwindhoek.org.na; Post St Mall) This friendly office answers questions and distributes local publications, including *What's On in Windhoek*.

Travel Agencies

Cardboard Box Travel Shop (Map p236; ☎ 256580; www.namibian.org) Attached to the backpacker hostel of the same name (see p240), this recommended travel agency can arrange both budget and upmarket bookings all over the country.
Chameleon Safaris (Map p236; ☎ 247668; www .chameleonsafaris.com) Attached to the backpacker hostel of the same name (see p240), this travel agency is also recommended for all types of safaris around the country.

DANGERS & ANNOYANCES

Central Windhoek is actually quite relaxed and hassle free. As long as you stay alert, walk with confidence, keep a hand on your wallet and avoid wearing anything too flashy, you should encounter nothing worse than a few persistent touts and the odd con artist.

However, you do need to be especially wary when walking with any kind of bag, especially on backstreets, as there has been a recent spate of muggings at knifepoint. Most importantly, don't use bumbags or carry swanky camera or video totes – they're all prime targets.

In the event that you are mugged, never, ever resist – simply give up your valuables and, more often than not, your assailant will flee the scene rapidly. Remember that a petty thief and a violent aggressor are very different kinds of people, so don't give your assailant any reason to do something rash.

As an extra precaution, always travel by taxi at night, even in the wealthy suburbs. The streets in Windhoek are ominously quiet once the sun goes down, which sadly means that foreign tourists quickly become easy targets.

The most likely annoyance for travellers is petty theft, which more often than not occurs at budget hotels and hostels around the city. As a general rule, you should take advantage of the hotel safe, and never leave your valuables out in the open.

If you're driving, avoid parking on the street, and never leave anything of value visible in your vehicle. During the day, the safest and most convenient parking is the underground lot beneath the Wernhill Park Centre (Map p236). At night, you should stay at accommodation that provides off-street secure parking.

The black township of Katutura and the northwestern industrial suburbs of Goreangab, Wanaheda and Hakahana are not as dangerous as their counterparts in South Africa, and are reasonably safe during the daytime. However, if you do visit these neighbourhoods, it's best to either go with a local contact or as part of an organised tour (see the boxed text, p239).

SIGHTS

Post St Mall & Gibeon Meteorite Exhibit

The throbbing heart of the Windhoek shopping district is the bizarrely colourful **Post St Mall** (Map p236), an elevated pedestrian walkway lined with vendors selling curios, artwork, clothing and practically anything else that may be of interest to tourists. Even if you're not in the mood for shopping, you can always sit down at one of the many alfresco cafes and sip an espresso while people watching, or alternatively throw down a meat pie or two and join the thronging crowds.

Scattered around the centre of the mall is a display of **meteorites** from the Gibeon meteor shower, which deposited upwards of 21 tonnes of mostly ferrous extraterrestrial boulders around the town of Gibeon in southern Namibia. For more information, see the boxed text, p344.

Zoo Park

Although this leafy **park** (Map p236; ☾ dawn-dusk) served as a public zoo until 1962, today it functions primarily as a picnic spot and shady retreat for lunching office workers. Of course, 5000 years ago the park was the site of a Stone Age elephant hunt, as evidenced by the remains of two elephants and several quartz tools found here in the early 1960s. This prehistoric event is honoured by the park's prominent **elephant column**, designed by Namibian sculptor Dörthe Berner.

A rather anachronous mate to the elephant column is the **Kriegerdenkmal** (War Memorial), topped by a rather frightening golden imperial eagle, which was dedicated in 1987 to the memory of German Schutztruppe soldiers who died in the Nama wars of 1893–94.

Christuskirche

Windhoek's best-recognised landmark, and something of the unofficial symbol of the city, this German Lutheran **church** (Map p236; Fidel Castro St) stands on a traffic island and lords over the city centre. This unusual building, which was constructed from local sandstone in 1907, was designed by architect Gottlieb Redecker in conflicting neo-Gothic and Art-Nouveau styles. The resulting design looks strangely edible, and is somewhat reminiscent of a whimsical gingerbread house. The altarpiece, the *Resurrection of Lazarus*, is a copy of the renowned work by Rubens. To view the interior, pick up the key during business hours from the nearby church office on Peter Müller St.

Tintenpalast

The former administrative headquarters of German South West Africa have been given a new mandate as the Namibian **parliament building** (Map p236; ☎ 288 2583; www.parliament.gov .na; admission free; ☾ tours 9-11am & 3-4pm Mon-Fri). As a fitting homage to the bureaucracy of government, the name of the building means 'Ink Palace', in honour of all the ink spent on typically excessive official paperwork.

The building is remarkable mainly for its construction from indigenous materials. The surrounding gardens, which were laid out in the 1930s, include an olive grove and a proper bowling green. In the front, have a look at Namibia's first post-independence monument, a bronze-cast statue of the Herero chief Hosea Kutako, who was best known for his vehement opposition to South African rule.

Hofmeyer Walk

This **walking track** (Map p233) through Klein Windhoek Valley starts from Sinclair St and heads south through the bushland to finish at the point where Orban St becomes Anderson St. The walk takes about an hour at a leisurely pace, and affords panoramic views over the city as well as a close-up look at the aloes that characterise the hillside vegetation. These cactus-like plants are at their best in winter, when their bright red flowers attract tiny sunbirds, mousebirds and bulbuls.

Hikers have been robbed along this route, so don't go alone and avoid carrying valuables.

State House

The residence of the German colonial governor once graced the present site of **State House** (Map p236; Robert Mugabe Ave), though the mansion was razed in 1958. Soon after, it was replaced by the present building, which was occupied by yet another colonist the South African Administrator. After independence, control of State House finally returned to Namibia, as it became the official residence of the Namibian president. All that remains of the original building is part of the old garden wall.

Gathemann's Complex

Along Independence Ave are three colonial-era buildings, all designed by the famous architect Willi Sander. The one furthest south was built in 1902 as the Kronprinz Hotel, which later joined Gathemann House (now home to a gourmet restaurant) to function as a private business. The most notable of the three is the Erkrath Building, which was constructed in 1910 as a private home and

CENTRAL WINDHOEK

business, but now serves as the headquarters of Namibian Wildlife Resorts (p234).

Turnhalle

The **Turnhalle** (Map p236; Bahnoff St) was built in 1909 as a practise hall for the Windhoek Gymnastic Club, though in 1975 it was modernised and turned into a conference hall. On 1 September of that year, it served as the venue for the first Constitutional Conference on Independence for South West Africa, which subsequently – and more conveniently – came to be called the Turnhalle Conference. During the 1980s, the building hosted several political summits and debates that paved the way to Namibian independence. Unfortunately, a fire ravaged

the Turnhalle in 2007, which calls into question its future role in state affairs.

Old Magistrates' Court

This old **courthouse** (Map p236; cnr Lüderitz & Park Sts; ☽ 8am-1pm & 2-5pm Mon-Fri, 8am-1pm Sat) was built in 189–98 for Carl Ludwig, the state architect, but it was never used and was eventually drafted into service as the magistrates' court. Take a look at the verandah on the south side, which provided a shady sitting area for people waiting for their cases to be called. The building has been given new life as the Namibia Conservatorium.

Kaiserliche Realschule

Windhoek's first German **primary school** (Map p236; Robert Mugabe Ave) was built in 1908, and opened the following year with a class size of 74 students. Notice the curious turret with wooden slats, which was designed to provide ventilation for European children unaccustomed to the African heat. The building later housed Windhoek's first German high school, an English middle school and today the administrative headquarters of the National Museum of Namibia.

Castles

Believe it or not, Windhoek is home to no fewer than three castles, which serve as austere reminders of German colonisation. Uphill from Robert Mugabe Ave are **Schwerinsburg Castle** (1913; Map p236), which now serves as a private home, **Sanderburg Castle** (1917; Map p236), which is the Italian ambassador's stately residence, and **Heinitzburg Castle** (1914; Map p236), which now houses a fine hotel and restaurant.

Oode Voorpost

This classically elegant **building** (1902; Map p236; John Meinert St) originally held the colonial surveyors' offices. Today, it's more famous for the nearby bronze **kudu statue** (cnr Independence Ave &

John Meinert St), which honours the many kudu (a kind of antelope) who died from the 1896 rinderpest epidemic – only in Namibia!

Museums
NATIONAL MUSEUM OF NAMIBIA

The whitewashed ramparts of Alte Feste, Windhoek's oldest surviving building, date from the early 1890s, and originally served as the headquarters of the German Schutztruppe. Today the building houses the historical section of the **National Museum of Namibia** (Map p236; ☎ 293 4437; Robert Mugabe Ave; admission free; ⏰ 9am-6pm Mon-Fri, 3-6pm Sat & Sun), which contains memorabilia and photos from the colonial period as well as indigenous artefacts. There is also an excellent display on Namibia's independence, which provides some enlightening context to the struggles of this young country.

Outside the museum, don't miss the somewhat incongruous collection of railway engines and coaches, which together formed one of the country's first narrow-gauge trains. This open-air exhibit is lorded over by a bronze statue known as the **Reiterdenkmal** (Rider's Memorial), which commemorates

Schutztruppe soldiers killed during the Herero-Nama wars of 1904–08. For history buffs, note that the statue was unveiled on 27 January 1912, which coincided with Kaiser Wilhelm II's birthday.

OWELA MUSEUM & NATIONAL THEATRE OF NAMIBIA

The other half of the National Museum of Namibia, about 600m from the main building, is known as the **Owela Museum** (Map p236; State Museum; ☎ 293 4358; 4 Robert Mugabe Ave; admission free; 🕑 9am-6pm Mon-Fri, 3-6pm Sat & Sun). Exhibits focus on Namibia's natural and cultural history.

Practically next door is the **National Theatre of Namibia** (Map p236; ☎ 237966; 12 Robert Mugabe St), built in 1960 by the Arts Association of Namibia and continuing to serve as one of Windhoek's major cultural centres.

TRANS-NAMIB TRANSPORT MUSEUM

Windhoek's beautiful old Cape Dutch–style train station on Bahnhof St was constructed by the Germans in 1912, and was expanded in 1929 by the South African administration. Across the driveway from the entrance is the German steam locomotive 'Poor Old Joe', which was shipped to Swakopmund in 1899 and reassembled for the treacherous journey across the desert to Windhoek. Upstairs in the train station is the small but worthwhile **Trans-Namib Transport Museum** (Map p236; ☎ 298 2186; admission N$5; 🕑 9am-noon & 2-4pm Mon-Fri) outlining Namibian transport history, particularly that of the railway.

At the entry to the station parking area, you'll see the **Owambo Campaign Memorial**, which was erected in 1919 to commemorate the 1917 British and South African campaign against Chief Mandume of the Kwanyama Owambo. Heavily outmatched by the colonial armies, the chief depleted all of his firepower and committed suicide rather than surrendering.

NATIONAL ART GALLERY

This **art gallery** (Map p236; ☎ 240930; cnr Robert Mugabe Ave & John Meinert St; admission free; 🕑 8am-5pm Mon-Fri, to 1pm Sat) contains a permanent collection of works reflecting Namibia's historical and natural heritage.

Around Windhoek

DAAN VILJOEN GAME PARK

This beautiful **wildlife park** (Map p238; per person/vehicle N$40/10; 🕑 visitors sunrise-6pm) sits in the Khomas Hochland about 18km west of Windhoek, though unfortunately it was being juggled between owners at the time of research. Once operated under the jurisdiction of Namibian Wildlife Resorts (NWR), the property is now privately owned and no longer open to overnight guests. However, there are rumours circulating that a much-needed face lift is under way, and that the campsite and resort will re-open in the years to come.

Because there are no seriously dangerous animals (eg big cats), you can walk to your heart's content through lovely wildlife-rich desert hills, and spot gemsbok, kudu, mountain zebras, springbok, hartebeests, warthogs and elands. Daan Viljoen is also known for its birdlife, and over 200 species have been recorded, including the rare green-backed heron and pin-tailed whydah.

Daan Viljoen's hills are covered with open thorn-scrub vegetation that allows excellent wildlife viewing, and three walking tracks have been laid out. The 3km **Wag-'n-Bietjie Trail** follows a dry riverbed from near the park office to Stengel Dam. A 9km circuit, the **Rooibos Trail** crosses hills and ridges and affords great

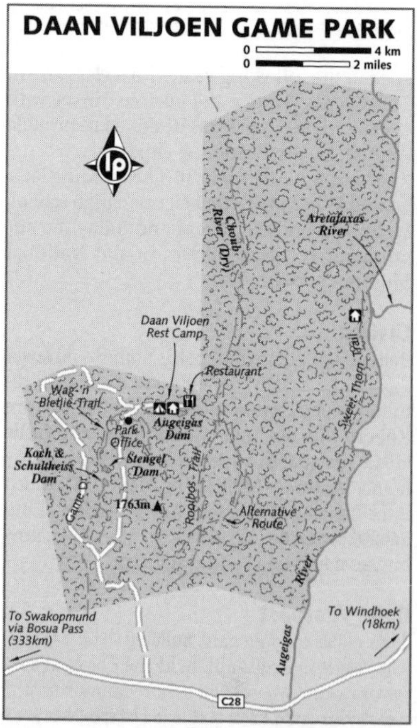

KATUTURA – A PERMANENT PLACE?

In 1912, during the days of the South African mandate – and apartheid – the Windhoek town council set aside two 'locations', which were open to settlement by black Africans working in the city: the Main Location, which was west of the city centre, and Klein Windhoek, to the east. The following year, people were forcibly relocated to these areas, which effectively became haphazard settlements. In the early 1930s, streets were laid out in the Main Location and the area was divided into regions. Each subdivision within these regions was assigned to an ethnic group and referred to by that name (eg Herero, Nama, Owambo, Damara), followed by a soulless numerical reference.

In the 1950s, the Windhoek municipal council, with encouragement from the South African government (which regarded Namibia as a province of South Africa), decided to 'take back' Klein Windhoek and consolidate all 'location' residents into a single settlement northwest of the main city. There was strong opposition to the move, and in early December 1959 a group of Herero women launched a protest march and boycott against the city government. On 10 December, unrest escalated into a confrontation with the police, resulting in 11 deaths and 44 serious injuries. Frightened, the roughly 4000 residents of the Main Location submitted and moved to the new settlement, which was ultimately named 'Katutura'. In Herero the name means 'We Have No Permanent Place', though it can also be translated as 'The Place We Do Not Want To Settle'.

Today in independent Namibia, Katutura is a vibrant Windhoek suburb – Namibia's Soweto – where poverty and affluence brush elbows. The town council has extended municipal water, power and telephone services to most areas of Katutura, and has also established the colourful and perpetually busy Soweto Market (off Map p233), where traders sell just about anything imaginable. Unlike its South African counterparts, Katutura is relatively safe by day, assuming of course you find a trustworthy local who can act as a guide. The **Namibia Community Based Tourism Association** (Nacobta; ☎ 250558; www.nacobta.com.na) sponsors township tours with **Face-to-Face Tours** (☎ 265446; www.face2face.co.za), which can be arranged by phoning ahead or sending an email. Alternatively, you can simply book through your accommodation; the backpacker hostels in particular run extremely worthwhile tours.

views back to Windhoek in the distance. The 34km **Sweet-Thorn Trail** circuits the empty eastern reaches of the reserve.

To get to Daan Viljoen, take the C28 west from Windhoek; Daan Viljoen is clearly signposted off the Bosua Pass Hwy, about 18km from the city.

AVIS DAM

Just east of Windhoek on the road to the airport, Avis Dam offers bird-watching, quiet waterside hikes and some of the best sunset viewpoints in the capital. You'll need a private vehicle – and the company of a few good friends – to make the trip worthwhile, but it's a popular locals' destination that few tourists get the chance to visit.

ACTIVITIES

Major sporting events, including rugby, football, netball and track and field, are held at Independence Stadium (Map p233) off the B1, about 2km south of town. See local papers and fliers for event announcements.

FESTIVALS & EVENTS

Bank Windhoek Arts Festival Largest arts festival in the country, with events running from March to September (see the boxed text, p221).

Mbapira/Enjando Street Festival Windhoek's first big annual bash. It's held in March around the city centre. It features colourful gatherings of dancers, musicians and people in ethnic dress.

Independence Day On 21 March; also usually celebrated in grand style, with a parade and sports events.

Windhoek Karnival (WIKA) The German-style carnival takes place in late April and features a week of events and balls.

Wild Cinema Festival (www.wildcinema.org) An annual international film festival that takes place in late spring and early summer.

Windhoek Agricultural, Commercial & Industrial Show In late September or early October, the city holds this on the showgrounds near the corner of Jan Jonker and Centaurus Sts.

/AE//Gams Arts Festival Held in venues around Windhoek in October (see the boxed text, p221).

WINDHOEK

Oktoberfest True to its partially Teutonic background, Windhoek stages this festival towards the end of October – beer lovers should not miss it.

SLEEPING

Whether you bed down in a bunkhouse or slumber the night away in a historic castle, Windhoek has no shortage of appealing accommodation options. Compared to the rest of the country, prices in the capital are on average relatively high, though you can be assured of a corresponding level of quality. Note that in a city this small, space is limited, so consider booking your bed well in advance, especially if you're travelling during the high season, holidays or even on busy weekends.

Budget

Cardboard Box Backpackers (Map p236; ☎ 228994; www.cardboardbox.com.na; 15 Johann Albrecht St; camping per site N$40, dm N$80, r from N$220; ☐ ☎) 'The Box' has been doing it for years, namely rocking the spot as Windhoek's wildest backpackers. Centred on a dreamy swimming pool that fronts a fully stocked bar, travellers have a tough time leaving this oasis of affordable luxury, though no one seems to be bothered in the slightest! If you do decide to motivate yourself the city centre is just a short walk away, and the excellent on-site Travel Shop gives unbiased information and can help sort out all your future travel plans.

Chameleon Backpackers Lodge & Guesthouse (Map p236; ☎ 244347; www.chameleonbackpackers.com; 5-7 Voight St; camping per site N$50, dm from N$90, r from N$325; ☐ ☎) This well-matched rival to the Cardboard Box caters to a slightly more subdued crowd, offering luxurious African-chic en suite rooms and spick-and-span dorms at shoestring prices. Of course, Chameleon is a backpackers at its core, so you can be sure that the bar sees plenty of action, and the on-site safari centre offers some of the most affordable trips in Namibia. Here's the best part: you can check your ecoguilt at the door thanks to the solar-heated showers, comprehensive recycling program and compost heap!

Haus Ol-Ga (Map p233; ☎ 235853; 91 Bach St; s/d N$300/400) The name of this German-oriented place is derived from the owners' names: Gesa Oldach and Erno Gauerke, who go out of their way to provide a good measure of Deutsch hospitality here in Namibia. Haus Ol-Ga enjoys a nice, quiet garden atmosphere in Windhoek West, and is a good choice if you're looking for accommodation that is more reminiscent of a homestay.

Midrange

Puccini House (Map p236; ☎ 236355; www.puccini-namibia.com; 4 & 6 Puccini St; s/d/tr N$385/450/630, s/d without bathroom N$215/360; ☐ ☎) The closest backpacker option to the city centre is conveniently located near the Wernhill Park Centre, yet retains its intimate atmosphere with only 14 rooms and a very welcoming management. The best part of staying here is the wonderful menu featuring home-cooked meals, braai (barbecue) pits and even wood-fired pizza.

Rivendell Guest House (Map p236; ☎ 250006; www.rivendell.com; 40 Beethoven St; s/d N$345/460, s/d with shared bathroom from N$265/340; ☐ ☎) A very relaxed guest house located in a shady suburb within easy walking distance of the city centre, Rivendell is a quieter alternative to some of the more bustling backpackers. Bright and airy rooms open to a tranquil garden and a sparkling pool, ensuring quiet vibes and easy times.

Guesthouse Tamboti (Map p236; ☎ 235515; www.guesthouse-tamboti.com; 9 Kerby St; s/d from N$350/495; ☒ ☐ ☎) An adorable German-run guest house situated on a small hill just above the city centre, Tamboti is a very friendly and relaxed place, where guests can help themselves to the honour bar and then lounge on the poolside deck with a cold lager. It's one of the more affordable midrange options in town, spacious rooms with fine furnishings yet only have to part with half the money required at competitive spots.

Hotel-Pension Handke (Map p236; ☎ 234904; www.natron.net/handke/main.html; 3 Rossini St; s/d/tr N$435/595/735) Run by a caring mother-and-son duo, this homey option in Windhoek West is more reminiscent of a stay with family friends than a guest house. Guests can catch up on their reading in the manicured garden, or chat the day away with the friendly owners.

Hotel-Pension Steiner (Map p236; ☎ 222898; www.natron.net/tour; 11 Wecke St; s/d from N$450/685; ☎) Although it has an excellent city-centre location just a few minutes' walk from Independence Ave, this small hotel-pension is sheltered from the hustle and bustle of the street scene. Simple but comfortable rooms open to a thatched bar and swimming pool, where you can quickly unwind after walking up and down the streets.

Casa Blanca (off Map p233; ☎ 249623; www.casablancahotelnamibia.com; 52 Fritsche St; s/d from N$540/740; ☎)

This Spanish-Moorish influenced 'white house' is more akin to a castle, complete with wrought-iron balustrades, terracotta tiling and impeccable gardens brimming with verdant plants and vibrant flowers. A boutique hotel through and through, Casa Blanca offers discerning travellers a slice of European sophistication in the peaceful Pioneer's Park suburb of the city.

Olive Grove (Map p233; ☎ 234971; www.olivegrove -namibia.com; 20 Promenaden Rd; s/d standard N$595/695, luxury N$795/925, ste from N$1350; 🞐) Refined elegance is the order of the day at this boutique hotel in Klein Windhoek, which features 10 individually decorated rooms and two suites awash in fine linens, hand-crafted furniture and all-around good taste. Guests in need of some pampering can indulge in a massage, or warm their toes on a cold Windhoek night in front of the crackling fire.

Roof of Africa (Map p233; ☎ 254708; www.roofofafrica .com; 124-126 Nelson Mandela Ave; s/d standard N$595/795, deluxe N$695/895, luxury N$895/1095; 🞐 🖳 🞐) Despite its humble origins as a backpackers lodge, the Roof of Africa is all grown up, and proud of its rebranded image as a sophisticated hotel and conference centre. A pleasant haven located about 30 minutes by foot from the city centre, Roof of Africa has a rustic barnyard feel, offering well-designed rooms of varying price and luxury that attract laid-back travellers looking for a quiet retreat from the city.

Hilltop House (Map p233; ☎ 249116; www.thehilltop house.com; 12 Lessing St; r per person from N$625; 🞐) A historic Bavarian mansion built into the side of a hill decades ago, this tiny guest house oozes personality at every turn. Atmospheric rooms reflect the house's history as an artists' studio, and are located off a shady verandah that has panoramic views over the Klein Windhoek valley.

Top End
Villa Verdi (Map p236; ☎ 221994; www.leadinglodges .com/villaverdi.htm; 4 Verdi St; s/d standard N$670/1080, luxury N$815/1340; 🞐 🖳 🞐) This utterly unique Mediterranean-African hybrid features whimsically decorated rooms complete with original paintings and arty touches. Straddling the divide between midrange and top-end properties, Villa Verdi competes in opulence and class with the bigger hitters on the block, yet offers more affordably priced rooms by targeting the boutique market rather than the tour-group crowd.

Hotel Thule (Map p233; ☎ 371950; www.thule-na mibia.com; 1 Gorges St; s/d from N$935/1380; 🞐 🖳 🞐) Perched on a towering hilltop in Eros Park, which is something along the lines of the Beverly Hills of Windhoek, Hotel Thule commands some of the most impressive views of any hotel in the capital. Cavernous rooms with a touch of European elegance are complemented by an award-winning restaurant and wraparound sundowner bar where you can sip a cocktail while watching the twinkling lights of the city switch on for the night.

Kalahari Sands Hotel & Casino (Map p236; ☎ 222300; www.suninternational.com; Gustav Voigts Centre, 129 Independence Ave; r from N$1850; 🞐 🖳 🞐) This high-rise hotel in the heart of the city primarily appeals to business travellers with its international four-star standards. All of the 187 rooms are fully equipped with plush furnishings and first-class amenities, and guests can also take advantage of the attached casino as well as the on-site gym, sauna, rooftop pool, and wide assortment of bars and restaurants. Be sure to book in advance over the internet as discount rates are frequently available.

Hotel Heinitzburg (Map p236; ☎ 249597; www .heinitzburg.com; 22 Heinitzburg St; s/d from €150/230; 🞐) This is Windhoek's most royal B&B option – quite literally – as it's located inside Heinitzburg Castle, which was commissioned in 1914 by Count von Schwerin for his fiancée, Margarethe von Heinitz. A member of the prestigious Relais & Chateaux hotel group, the Heinitzburg is far and beyond the most personable upmarket accommodation in Windhoek. Rooms have been updated for the 21st century with satellite TV and air-con, though the highlight of the hotel is the palatial dining room, which offers excellent gourmet cuisine and an extensive wine dungeon.

EATING
Namibia's multicultural capital provides a stunning range of restaurants, and the best of the best here can easily compete with any you'd find in culinary capitals around the world. Indeed, most first-timers to Windhoek are pleasantly surprised by the overwhelming quality and diversity of the restaurant scene. It's certainly worth stretching your budget and indulging the gourmand lifestyle while you're in town. Be advised that reservations are a very good idea on Friday and Saturday nights, when long lines at Windhoek's all-star eateries are not uncommon.

WINDHOEK

HANNAH NAOMI KIM

This Korean-American artist has been living and working in Windhoek. Over a cold bottle of Windhoek lager, she shared her thoughts on generational change in Namibia.

What was the original aim of your Fulbright research? I have always been fascinated by the unique history of Namibia, particularly the fact that it was doubly colonised, first by Germany and later by South Africa, and only very recently gained its independence. As an artist, I was interested in studying the visual culture that emerged from this post-colonial identity, and in observing how Namibians view themselves within the scope of their history. And, of course, I was looking for artistic inspiration from Namibia's dramatic desert landscapes.

Why did you choose to base yourself in Windhoek? Quite simply, Windhoek is a microcosm of the world. While vast stretches of the country are defined by towering dunes and jagged coastlines, Windhoek is a surprisingly modern and cosmopolitan city. Far beyond being the most populous city in one of the least populated countries in the world, Windhoek is home to increasingly global citizens who are savvy about world news and politics. At the same time, however, the outskirts of the capital are home to impoverished shantytowns where survival unfortunately remains a daily struggle. But it is precisely this striking contrast that so closely mirrors the global wealth disparity.

What were the findings of your research? Through a series of paintings that combined archival and personal photography, I attempted to locate contemporary Namibian identity by juxtaposing different ways of Namibian living. But my findings, so to speak, were that being a young person in a relatively young country is fraught with complexity. For instance, the young generation is politically removed from earlier freedom fighters who struggled against the Germans and later the Afrikaners. The adoption of English as the official language has created a sort of cultural veneer; although it's an equalising force, as a result, many young people are mostly interested in following global trends in popular culture. So you see, there exists an enormous generation gap that underlies this complexity, and I realised that the present realities of Namibia superseded my original project aims. In this current climate, the country is building momentum as young Namibians rise to the challenge of forming their own identities on the world stage, and moving away from their colonial roots.

How does Namibia inspire your artistic work? Namibia is a painter's paradise. The landscapes here are saturated with colour and, perhaps more importantly, there is so much space to absorb this colour. Whenever I think about the Namibian landscape, I imagine an endless horizon punctuated by moments of luminosity. But Namibia isn't just a stark and barren country of wilderness. There is an inherent beauty in the complexity that stems from the collision of modern conceptions of identity upon a backdrop of ancient landscapes.

What has been the most defining aspect of your time in Namibia? Reconciling my identity as a Korean-American has been far and away the most defining aspect of my time here, mainly because Namibians are so profoundly aware of race. The fact that colonialism has only recently been dismantled means that a residue of racial tension still remains in this country. But I do believe that racial reconciliation will ultimately happen, through generational change. In the younger generations, you find more of an understanding of race, and an individual is more likely to view someone different with the proverbial clean slate. For the older generations, however, it is more difficult for people to forgive and forget the injustices of apartheid.

So you believe that there is hope for the future? Absolutely. When I engage younger Namibians in conversation, they don't just see me as having an Asian face, and they aren't at all surprised that I can speak fluent English. As I alluded to before, this is a population segment that grew up watching Beyonce, 50 Cent and other celebrities on satellite TV, and they are aware that people can have multiple ethnicities and multiple identities. So there is hope that generational change will ultimately result in racial reconciliation, with the optimism that this youth movement spreads throughout the country, and bring new vision to the nation.

This Korean-American artist has been living and working in Windhoek as a Fulbright Scholar.

Budget

Windhoek is a grocery paradise for self-caterers. The big names are **Pick & Pay** (Map p236; Wernhill Park Centre) and **Checkers** (Map p236; Gustav Voigts Centre).

Namibians have something of a sordid love affair with fast food, and you'll find chicken and burger joints everywhere you look, including KFC, Nando's Chicken, Spur and Wimpy's. Although you'll pay more for a value meal here than you would back home, fast food is still quick, easy and comparatively cheap.

King Pies (Map p236; ☎ 248978; Levinson Arcade; pies N$10-15) If you're looking for a quick and filling bite, this popular Namibian chain sells a variety of filled meat and vegetable pies.

Sardinia's Pizzeria (Map p236; ☎ 225600; 39 Independence Ave; dishes N$20-50) An energetic restaurant that sells decent pizza by the slice and other Italian classic dishes, as well as strong coffee and sugary gelato.

Café Zoo (Map p236; ☎ 223479; Zoo Park, Independence Av; coffee N$10-15; light meals $25-50) A storied Windhoeker cafe that's part of a long line of cafes stretching back nearly a century, this sheltered spot beneath a giant rubber tree on the edge of Zoo Park is just lovely for a cappuccino accompanied by a light meal.

Yang Tse (Map p233; ☎ 234779; /AE//Gams Shopping Centre, 351 Sam Nujoma Dr; mains N$30-60) This cheap Chinese joint, which has a long list of traditional mainland dishes and more Westernised treats, is a nice change if you're growing tired of standard Namibian fare.

Midrange

Gourmet (Map p236; ☎ 232360; Kaiserkrone Centre, Post St Mall; mains N$40-80) Tucked away in a nondescript courtyard just off Post St Mall, this alfresco bistro has one of the most comprehensive menus you've ever seen. The unifying trend is its adherence to using gourmet ingredients to create a blend of Namibian, German, French and Italian dishes that are as innovative as they are delicious.

Taal (Map p236; ☎ 221958; 416 Independence Ave; mains N$45-85) Indian food may not have as strong a following in Namibia as it does in neighbouring South Africa, but this fresh new eatery is set to change that. Offering the full set of Indian dishes from the subcontinent, Taal introduces some much-needed spice and heat into Windhoek's restaurant scene.

Restaurant Africa (☎ 247178; Alte Fest, Robert Mugabe Ave; mains from N$45-90) This pan-African restaurant is part of the historic Alte Fest, Windhoek's oldest building, which presently houses the National Museum of Namibia. After perusing the galleries and working up an appetite, choose from a wide list of dishes from across the continent, including everyone's local favourite – stir-fried mopane worms!

Abyssinia (Map p236; ☎ 254891; Lossen St; mains N$50-90) Drawing its name from the ancient kingdom that eventually became modern Ethiopia, Abyssinia offers spongy *injera* (sourdough flatbread) alongside family-style meat and veggie stews. While getting comfy on the cushion-covered floor, you can also try some of the potent coffee that has made Ethiopia a brand name in cafes across the world.

Luigi & the Fish (Map p233; ☎ 256399; 320 Sam Nujoma Dr; mains N$50-100) Often described as the ocean equivalent to Joe's Beer House, this equally famous Windhoek institution specialises in (you guessed it!) fish, serving up Namibian regulars such as hake, butterfish, mussel hotpots and crayfish cocktails alongside meats, pizza, game dishes and vegetarian fare. A huge complex punctuated by open-air beer gardens and lively dining halls ensures a warm familial atmosphere and a memorable night out.

La Marmite (Map p236; ☎ 248022; Independence Ave; mains N$60-120) Commanding a veritable legion of devoted followers, this stylish yet humble West African eatery deserves its long-garnered popularity. Here you can sample wonderful North and West African cuisine, including Algerian, Senegalese, Ivorian, Cameroonian and Nigerian dishes, all of which are prepared with the finesse of the finest French haute cuisine.

nice (Map p236; ☎ 300710; cnr Mozart St & Hosea Kutako Dr; mains N$65-110) The Namibian Institute of Culinary Education – or 'nice' for short – operates this wonderfully conceived 'living classroom' where apprentice chefs can field test their cooking skills. Spanning several indoor and outdoor rooms, the restaurant itself is more akin to a stylish gallery, while the rotating menu of edible delights sits well with the more permanent sushi and wine bar.

Top End

Restaurant Gathemann (Map p236; ☎ 223853; 179 Independence Ave; mains N$95-220) Located in a prominent colonial building (see p235) overlooking Independence Ave, this splash-out spot serves gourmet Namibian cuisine that fully utilises

WINDHOEK

EAT AT JOE'S

A legendary Windhoek institution that is something of an obligatory stop for foreign visitors, **Joe's Beer House** (Map p233; ☎ 232457; Green Market Sq, 160 Nelson Mandela Ave; beers N\$10-30, mains N\$50-100; 🕒 5pm-late) is where you can indulge (albeit with a little guilt…) in flame-broiled fillets of all those amazing animals you've seen on safari! Seriously. We're talking huge cuts of zebra tenderloin, ostrich skewers, peppered springbok steak, oryx medallions, crocodile on a hotplate, and the house speciality: sliced and marinated kudu. True to its moniker, Joe's also stocks a wide assortment of Namibian and German beers, and you can count on prolonged drinking here until early in the morning. Sure, it's touristy, but there's a lot of fun to be had here, especially on a warm evening when you can throw back a few cold ones underneath a faux-African hut. Reservations are recommended.

this country's unique list of ingredients. From Kalahari truffles (see p323) and Owamboland legumes to tender cuts of game meat and Walvis Bay oysters, Restaurant Gathemann is a wholly unique establishment that earns the respect of even the finickiest of foodies.

Leo's (Map p236; ☎ 249597; www.heinitzburg .com; 22 Heinitzburg St; mains N\$175-300) Arguably Windhoek's finest restaurant, Leo's takes its regal setting in Heinitzburg Castle to heart by welcoming diners into its banquet hall that has previously served the likes of royalty. The formal settings of bone china and polished crystal glassware are almost as extravagant as the food itself, which spans cuisines and continents and land and sea.

DRINKING

Although what's hip is constantly changing, there are a few perennially popular spots where you can enjoy a few drinks and maybe even a bit of dancing. In addition to the places listed below, most restaurants double as late-night watering holes, particularly tourist-friendly establishments such as Joe's Beer House (see the boxed text, above) and Luigi & the Fish (see p243). While the nightlife scene in Windhoek is relaxed and generally trouble-free, you should always travel by taxi when heading to and from establishments.

Club Thriller (Map p233; Goreseb St, Katutura; admission varies; ☎ 11pm-late) Lies in a rough area, but beyond the weapons search at the door, the music is Western and African and the atmosphere upbeat and relatively secure. However, avoid carrying valuables or wearing jewellery; foreigners may also have to fend off strangers hitting on them for beers and cash. Women travelling alone may not feel comfortable here.

El Cubano (Map p236; ☎ 291 7192; cnr Sam Nujoma Dr & Tal St; ☎ 5.30pm-late) Offering up a little bit of Havana, El Cubano is a popular lounge as well as the preferred nightspot for lovers of fine cigars and expertly crafted mojitos.

Funky Lab (Map p233; ☎ 271946; /AE//Gams Shopping Centre; 🕒 4pm-late Sun-Thu, 2pm-late Fri & Sat) This very popular club is one of Windhoek's hottest night-time dancing spots, especially if you're craving a little disco in your life.

La Dee Da's (Map p233; ☎ 081 2434 432; Ferry St, Southern Industrial Area; admission varies; 🕒 10.30pm-4am Thu-Sat) Another stalwart on the Windhoek clubbing scene; here you can dance to Angolan *kizomba* (fast-paced Portuguese-African music), hip-hop, rave, traditional African, rock and commercial pop accompanied by special effects.

Wine Bar (Map p236; ☎ 226514; 3 Garten St; 🕒 5.30-11pm) A relative newcomer on the drinking scene but rapidly becoming one of the city's most happening nightspots, Wine Bar occupies a historic mansion on a quiet side street. Playing off this ambience, your hosts will satiate your palette with one of the city's best wine selections, paired with Mediterranean-style tapas and small snacks.

ENTERTAINMENT

Whether you're in the mood for a night out at the theatre or a Hollywood screening, Windhoek can provide.

National Theatre of Namibia (Map p236; ☎ 237 966; www.namibiatheatre.org; Robert Mugabe St) Located south of the National Art Gallery, the national theatre stages infrequent theatrical performances; for information see the Friday edition of the *Namibian*.

New Space (off Map p233; ☎ 206 3111; University of Namibia complex) New Space sometimes stages theatre productions.

Ster Kinekor (Map p233; ☎ 249267; Maerua Park Centre) Off Robert Mugabe Ave, this place shows recent films and has half-price admission on Tuesday.

Warehouse Theatre (Map p236; ☎ 225059; Old South-West Brewery Bldg, 48 Tal St; admission varies) A delightfully integrated club staging live African and European music and theatre productions.

Windhoek Conservatorium (Map p236; ☎ 293 3111; Fidel Castro St) The conservatorium occasionally holds classical concerts.

The outdoor performing group Theatre in the Park stages two live shows each month, and also promotes children's theatre and screens African films. For the latest schedules, see the Windhoek Information & Publicity Office (p234).

SHOPPING

The handicrafts sold in Post St Mall are largely imported from neighbouring countries, though there is still an excellent selection of woodcarvings, baskets and other African curios on offer. You're going to have to bargain hard if you want to secure a good price, though maintain your cool and always flash a smile – you'll win out with politeness in the end! For higher quality items, check out the listings below.

Mall culture is alive and well in Windhoek, and you'll find them scattered throughout the city centre and out in the 'burbs. Most of the stores are South African standards, which generally offer high-quality goods at a fraction of the price back home. Katutura's Soweto Market (see p239) is more reminiscent of a traditional African market, though it's best to visit either with a local or as part of an organised tour.

Namibia Crafts Centre (Map p236; ☎ 222236; 40 Tal St; ✆ 9am-5.30pm Mon-Fri, to 1pm Sat) This place is an outlet for heaps of wonderful Namibian inspiration – leatherwork, basketry, pottery, jewellery, needlework, hand-painted textiles and other material arts – and the artist and origin of each piece is documented. The attached snack bar is well known for its coffee and healthy snacks.

House of Gems (Map p236; ☎ 225202; scrap@iafrica .com.na; 131 Stübel St) This is the most reputable shop in Windhoek for buying both raw and polished minerals and gemstones. For more information, see the boxed text, below.

Penduka (off Map p233; ☎ 257210; www.penduka.com) Penduka, which means 'wake up', operates a nonprofit women's needlework project at Goreangab Dam, 8km northwest of the city centre. You can purchase needlework, baskets, carvings and fabric creations for fair prices and be assured that all proceeds go to the producers. To get there, take the Western Bypass north and turn left on Monte Cristo Rd, left on Otjomuise Rd, right on Eveline St and right again on Green Mountain Dam Rd. Then follow the signs to Goreangab Dam/Penduka.

Camping Gear

Cymot Greensport (Map p236; ☎ 234131; 60 Mandume Ndemufayo St) is good for quality camping, hiking, cycling and vehicle outfitting equipment, as is **Cape Union Mart** (Map p233; Maerua Park Centre). Gear for 4WD expeditions is sold at **Safari Den** (Map p233; ☎ 231931; 20 Bessemer St); alternatively, try **Gräber's** (Map p233; ☎ 222732; Bohr St) in the Southern Industrial Area.

GETTING THERE & AWAY
Air

Chief Hosea Kutako International Airport, which is located about 40km east of the city centre, serves most international flights into and out of Windhoek. **Air Namibia** (☎ 299 6333; www.airnamibia.com) operates flights daily between Windhoek and Cape Town and

---

GEM CONSCIOUSNESS

The former owner of House of Gems, Sid Pieters, who passed away in 2003, was once Namibia's foremost gem expert. In 1974, along the Namib coast, Pieters uncovered 45 crystals of jeremejevite, a sea-blue tourmaline containing boron – the rarest gem on earth. His discovery was only the second ever; the first was in Siberia in the mid-19th century. Another of his finds was the marvellously streaky 'crocidolite pietersite' (named for Pieters himself), from near Outjo in North-Central Namibia. Pietersite, a beautiful form of jasper shot through with asbestos fibres, is certainly one of the world's most beautiful and unusual minerals, and some believe that it has special energy- and consciousness-promoting qualities. Other New Age practitioners maintain that it holds the 'keys to the kingdom of heaven'; stare at it long enough and perhaps you'll agree.

CYCLING THE ELEPHANT HIGHWAY *Mara Vorhees*

When I was contemplating the possibility of a bike ride across Botswana and Namibia, I turned to my trusty Lonely Planet: 'Unless you're an experienced cyclist and equipped for the extreme conditions, abandon any ideas you may have about a…bicycle adventure'. The book went on to emphasise the scorching sun, the paucity of water and the vast distances. 'If you try to ride your bike here,' I inferred, 'you will die.' What had I gotten myself into?

I was reassured by the fact that I would be riding as a part of an organised tour. The **Tour d'Afrique** (TDA; www.tourdafrique.com) is an 11,800km expedition from Cairo to Cape Town that is divided into eight legs. As a member of a Lonely Planet relay team, I would ride the penultimate leg – the Elephant Hwy – from Victoria Falls to Windhoek.

So, thankfully, I did not have to worry about pesky details like drinking water. Namibia and especially Botswana are sparsely populated countries. Even on the country's major highways, we rode for hours at a time without passing any sign of civilisation. In fact, we spent every second night at a bush camp, sleeping in the wilderness with no facilities except those provided by the TDA truck. Remember that this is the desert. Without a support vehicle, cyclists should be prepared to carry or pull at least two days' worth of food and water.

The other aspect of the climate – the heat – was also not a major concern, since my trip took place in April. As it turns out, autumn in Southern Africa offers conditions that are close to per-fect for cycling. We would set out at sunrise to take advantage of the cool morning air. I always needed a jacket to start, but that never lasted long; by midday it would be hot. Of course, by midday the speedier riders had already reached our destination. As one of the slower riders, I endured some hot afternoons, but the temperature rarely went above 30°C.

The sun is brutal, no doubt, and the application of sunscreen was a ritual that took place every morning and every few hours on the road. Some cyclists wore a long-sleeved, lightweight base layer under their jerseys to protect their arms from the sun. In any case, there was no escaping the 'biker's tan' showing off the line from the chamois shorts.

So I could handle the heat and the limited water supply, but what about the distances? At 1576km, the Elephant Hwy is one of the longest sections of the tour and it was certainly further than I had ever ridden my bike. The good news is that the landscape is mostly flat and the roads are paved. The bad news is that it can be monotonous when you are riding for six to eight hours a day. So how to prepare? Take care of your body: make sure you have trained properly by log-ging many, many kilometres. Take care of your mind: bring an iPod.

Desolate landscapes aside, there's plenty to see along the Elephant Hwy. Yes, *elephants*. They are frequently sighted along the main road north and west of Nata. I was thrilled when I cycled past a group of ellies congregating around a watering hole and, later when a big one created a roadblock ahead of me. I was not so thrilled when I saw – or rather smelt – a carcass at the side of the road.

In case you're wondering, an elephant's top speed is 40km/h when he is alarmed or upset. Fortunately, he can't sustain this speed for more than a few seconds. So, as long as you get a head start on your bike, you can probably outride him.

There is other wildlife in the vicinity, although it can be difficult to spot from the road: keep your eyes peeled for giraffes, warthogs, various antelopes, iguanas and plenty of birds.

That said, if wildlife watching is your game, you'll want to schedule some time out of the saddle. Park your bike in Maun (p120) and take an excursion into the Okavango Delta (p119). Spend a few nights at a lodge between Nata and Maun so you can explore the Makgadikgadi Pans (p103). Trade your bike for a boat in Kasane (p109) and cruise along the Zambezi River. Cyclists are not permitted in the national parks, for good reason: nobody wants to be meals on wheels.

Author Mara Vorhees was one of 16 Lonely Planet riders to participate in the 2009 Tour d'Afrique. She rode 1546km of the Elephant Hwy.

Johannesburg, as well as twice-weekly flights to/from Frankfurt. (Flights to London were suspended at the time of writing.) Several airlines also offer international services to/from Maun, Botswana, and Victoria Falls, Zimbabwe. For more information, see p377.

Eros Airport, immediately south of the city centre, serves most domestic flights into and out of Windhoek. Air Namibia offers occasional flights to/from Katima Mulilo, Lüderitz, Ondangwa, Rundu, Swakopmund/Walvis Bay and Tsumeb.

Coming from Windhoek, make sure the taxi driver knows which airport you are going to.

Other airlines with flights into and out of Windhoek:

British Airways (☎ 248528; www.ba.com)
Lufthansa Airlines (☎ 226662; www.lufthansa.com)
South African Airways (☎ 237670; www.flysaa.com)
TAAG Angola (www.taag.com.br)

All of these airlines have offices at Chief Hosea Kutako International Airport, though you can easily make travel arrangements in advance by going online.

Bus

From the main long-distance bus terminal (Map p236; cnr Fidel Castro & Rev Michael Scott Sts), the **Intercape Mainliner** (www.intercape.co.za) runs to/from Cape Town, Johannesburg, Victoria Falls and Swakopmund, serving a variety of local destinations along the way. Tickets can be purchased either though your accommodation, from the Intercape Mainliner Office (Map p233) or over the internet – given the popularity of these routes, advance reservations are recommended. For specific fare information, see the various destination chapters.

Local *combis* (minibuses) leave when full from the Rhino Park petrol station and can get you to most urban centres in Namibia. However, these routes do not serve the vast majority of Namibia's tourist destinations, which are located well beyond major population centres. Still, they're a fine way to travel if you want to visit some of the country's smaller towns and cities, and it's great fun to roll up your sleeves and jump into the bus with the locals. Again, for specific fare information, see the various destination chapters.

Car & Motorcycle

Windhoek is literally the crossroads of Namibia – the point where the main north–south route (the B1) and east–west routes (B2 and B6) cross – and all approaches to the city are extremely scenic, passing through beautiful desert hills. Roads are clearly signposted; those travelling between northern and southern Namibia can avoid the city centre by taking the Western Bypass.

Hitching

Due to its location and traffic, hitching to or from Windhoek is easier than anywhere else in Namibia. For more information on hitching in the country, see p386.

Train

Windhoek train station has a **booking office** (☎ 2982 175; ☺ 7.30am-4pm Mon-Fri) where you are able to reserve seats on any of the country's public rail lines. Routes are varied, and include overnight trains to Keetmanshoop, Tsumeb and Swakopmund, though irregular schedules, lengthy travel times and far better bus connections make train travel of little interest for the majority of overseas travellers.

GETTING AROUND

City buses have been phased out in favour of inexpensive shared taxis and minibuses. Collective taxis from the main ranks at Wernhill Park Centre follow set routes to Khomasdal and Katutura, and if your destination is along the way, you'll pay around N$5 to N$10. With taxis from the main bus terminals or by radio dispatch, fares are either metered or are calculated on a per-kilometre basis, but you may be able to negotiate a set fare per journey. Plan on N$25 to N$50 to anywhere around the city.

If you're arriving at Hosea Kutako International Airport, taxis typically wait outside the arrivals area. It's a long drive into the city, so you can expect to pay anywhere from N$250 to N$300 depending on your destination. For Eros Airport, fares are much more modest at around N$30 to N$50, though in all instances you're going to need to negotiate hard.

North-Central Namibia

With little more than a car window separating you from the surrounding white plains, a thermos of early-morning coffee and cameras ready, there are few places that can match the wildlife prospects of dawn in Etosha National Park. Home to a network of artificial water-holes and naturally up-welling springs, the southern boundary of the Etosha Pan harbours enormous congregations of African animals. Just one day of wildlife watching at a single waterhole can produce literally thousands of sightings, which has justifiably earned Etosha the reputation as one of the best reserves in the world.

Unlike the vast majority of safari parks in Africa, all roads inside Etosha are 2WD accessible and open to private vehicles. This, of course, means that if you've been fortunate enough to rent your own vehicle, you're in for one of the most memorable safaris of your life. Anyone can tell their friends and family back home how quickly their guide spotted a pride of lions, but how many people can say that they drove on the edges of a salt pan while tracking herds of zebra in the distance?

The crown jewel in Namibia's rich treasure trove of national parks, Etosha dominates the tourism circuit in North-Central Namibia. However, there are plenty of worthwhile opportunities here for hiking and exploring, and there's a good chance that the tourist crowds will be elsewhere. If you have the time to spare, don't overlook the region's other highlights, which run the gamut from lofty plateaus and art-laden caves to hulking meteorites and dino footprints.

HIGHLIGHTS

- Going on a self-drive safari in **Etosha National Park** (p264), one of the world's premier wildlife venues
- Hiking to the top of the **Waterberg Plateau** (p256) for a view that takes your breath away
- Spelunking for rock art at **Phillips Cave** (p253) in the Erongo Mountains (Erongoberg)
- Checking out the world's largest **meteorite** (p260), located just outside the town of Grootfontein
- Looking for dinosaurs, or at least their **tracks** (p254), on the Otjihaenamparero Farm near Kalkfeld

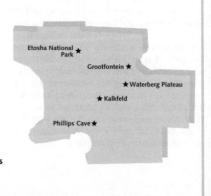

Etosha National Park ★

Grootfontein ★

★ Waterberg Plateau

★ Kalkfeld

Phillips Cave ★

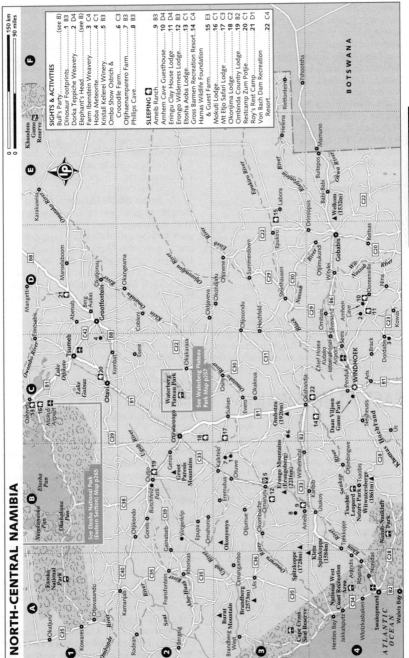

NORTH-CENTRAL NAMIBIA

SIGHTS & ACTIVITIES	
Bull's Party	(see 8)
Dinosaur Footprints	1 B3
Dorka Teppiche Weavery	2 D4
Elephant's Head	(see 8)
Farm Ibenstein Weavery	3 C4
Hoba Meteorite	4 C1
Kristall Kellerei Winery	5 B3
Ombo Show Ostrich &	
Crocodile Farm	6 C3
Otjihaenamparero Farm	7 B3
Phillips Cave	8 B3

SLEEPING 🏠	
Ameib Ranch	9 B3
Arnhem Cave Guesthouse	10 D4
Eningu Clay House Lodge	11 D4
Erongo Wilderness Lodge	12 B3
Etosha Aoba Lodge	13 C1
Gross Barmen Recreation Resort	14 C4
Harnas Wildlife Foundation	
& Guest Farm	15 E3
Mokuti Lodge	16 C1
Mt Etjo Safari Lodge	17 C3
Okonjima Lodge	18 C2
Ombinda Country Lodge	19 B2
Restcamp Zum Potjie	20 C1
Roy's Rest Camp	21 D1
Von Bach Dam Recreation	
Resort	22 C4

Geography

Although Etosha Pan is the most prominent feature in the region, the area is primarily known as a mining and cattle-ranching centre. Large-scale mining, particularly in the Tsumeb area, dates back to the early 1900s, while pastoralism, especially among the Herero, pre-dates the German colonial era. North-Central Namibia is also known for its unique natural landscapes, particularly the Waterberg Plateau Park, a lovely island in the sky, and the Erongo Mountains (Erongoberg), which form a dramatic backdrop along the route from Windhoek to Swakopmund.

Getting Around

Since the majority of sites in North-Central Namibia are outside population centres, you will need a private vehicle to access most of the region. Etosha itself is easy enough to visit as part of an organised tour, but most visitors prefer the thrill and excitement of a self-drive safari. Even in the rainy season, the paved approach to the park, in addition to all internal roads, is easily accessible to 2WD vehicles.

Outside of Etosha, North-Central Namibia benefits from an excellent network of tarred roads. This is one region where a 4WD vehicle is largely unnecessary, aside from a few minor access roads in the Erongo Mountains.

EAST TO BOTSWANA

The seemingly never-ending B6 runs east from Windhoek to the Botswana border, passing through the heart of one of Namibia's most important ranching centres. Together, the 970 farms of the Omaheke region cover nearly 5 million hectares, and provide over one-third of Namibia's beef. While passionate carnivores can certainly rejoice at these numbers, the road east to Botswana is a long and monotonous slog to the border, though fortunately the road is paved, flat and in excellent condition.

GOBABIS
☎ 062

Gobabis is situated on the Wit-Nossob River, 120km from the Botswana border at Buitepos. The name is Khoikhoi for 'Place of Strife', but a slight misspelling (Goabbis) renders it 'Place of Elephants', which locals

seem to prefer despite its obvious shortage of elephants.

Although Gobabis is the main service centre of the Namibian Kalahari, there isn't a lot to look at. The town's only historic building is the old military hospital, the **Lazarett**, which once served as a town museum. It's not officially open, but you can pick up a key at the library in the centre of town.

If you get stuck in town for the night, the centrally located **Big 5 Central Hotel** (☎ 562094; Voortrekker St; camping per person N$50, s/d from N$250/380) offers wary drivers a wide range of clean and comfortable rooms, as well as a decent restaurant specialising in huge flame-grilled cuts of the local beefsteak.

The **Harnas Wildlife Foundation & Guest Farm** (Map p249; ☎ 568788; www.harnas.de; camping per person N$185, igloo/cottage per person N$485/605, igloo/cottage per person incl full board N$1330/1630) is a rural development project that likens itself to Noah's Ark. Here you can see wildlife close up, and get the chance to cuddle baby cheetahs, leopards and lions, if they haven't already grown too big for that sort of thing. Many of the animals here are caged, but since they were either orphaned or injured, they would be unable to survive were it not for the foundation. A wide range of accommodation is available, including options for full board, and there are plenty of activities here to keep you amused for a couple of days. To get here, turn north on the C22 past Gobabis and continue for 50km, then turn east on the D1668. After 42km, turn left at the Harnas gate and continue 8km to the farm.

Public transport is unreliable along this route, and it's recommended that you head east from Windhoek in a private vehicle. If you're planning on crossing into Botswana in a rental car, be sure in advance that all of your paperwork is in order (see p170).

BUITEPOS

Buitepos, a wide spot in the desert at the Namibia–Botswana border crossing, is little more than a petrol station and customs and immigration post. The border itself is open from 8am to 6pm, though you should cross with plenty of daylight since it's a long drive to Ghanzi, the next settlement of major size along the Trans-Kalahari Hwy.

If you arrive in Buitepos too late to cross, the **East Gate Service Station & Rest Camp** (☎ 560405; Trans-Kalahari Hwy; camping per person N$90, cabins without bathroom per person N$145, 2-person bunga-lows N$520; [icon]) rises from the desert like a mirage, and is a decent enough place to crash if you're not particularly fussy.

On the other side of the border, the paved road continues to Ghanzi (see p149).

NORTH TO ETOSHA

The immaculate B1 heads north from Windhoek, and provides access to Outjo as well the Golden Triangle of Otavi, Tsumeb and Grootfontein. Prominent towns in their own right, together they serve as the launching point for excursions into nearby Etosha National Park. While it's very tempting to strike north with safari fever, it's definitely worth slowing down and taking a bit of time to explore the quirky sights of this comparatively untouristed section of North-Central Namibia.

OKAHANDJA & AROUND

☎ 062

Okahandja is the administrative centre for the Herero people, who settled in this former Nama homeland in the early 19th century, sparking a series of tribal wars. From the mid-19th century to the early 20th century the town served as a German-run mission and a colonial administrative centre, remnants of which still dot the town centre. Beyond its historical significance, Okahandja is the main service centre and highway junction between Windhoek, Swakopmund and the north, as well as the jumping-off point for a couple of recreation resorts.

Sights

CEMETERIES

In the churchyard and across the road from the 1876 **Friedenskirche** (Church of Peace; Kerk St; [icon] dawn-dusk) are the graves of several historical figures, including Herero leader Willem Maherero, Nama leader Jan Jonker Afrikaner and Hosea Kutako, the 'father of Namibian independence', who was the first politician to petition the UN against the South African occupation of Namibia.

East of Kerk St is the **Herero Heroes Cemetery**, which has the graves of several Herero war heroes. The cemetery is the starting point of the annual procession by the Red Flag Herero to pay respect to their leaders and,

OKAHANDJA

SIGHTS & ACTIVITIES	
Friedenskirche & Graves............	1 B3
Herero Heroes Cemetery.........	2 B3
Moordkoppie............................	3 A3

SLEEPING	
Okahandja Rest Camp..............	4 A1
Sylvanette Guest House...........	5 A2

EATING	
Bäckerei Dekker & Café...........	6 B3
Lewcor Biltong Factory............	7 B3

in the spirit of unity, to former enemy Jan Jonker Afrikaner.

MOORDKOPPIE

The historical animosity between the Nama and the Herero had its most emphatic expression at the **Battle of Moordkoppie** (Afrikaans for 'Murder Hill') on 23 August 1850. During the battle, 700 Herero under the command of chief Katjihene were massacred by Nama forces. Half of the victims were women and children, whose bodies were dismembered for the copper bangles on their arms and legs. The scene of this tragedy was a small rocky hill near the centre of town between the B2 and the railway line, 500m north of the Gross Barmen turn-off.

OMBO SHOW OSTRICH & CROCODILE FARM

On the D2110, 2km north of the town centre, is the **Ombo Show Ostrich & Crocodile Farm** (Map p249; ☎ 501176; tours per person N$15). Here you can feed ostriches, sit on one, watch them hatching and dancing, and – of course – eat them. You can also take photographs of crocodiles lazing in the sun as well as watch artisans make Herero dolls and Kavango woodcarvings.

Festivals & Events

On the weekend nearest 26 August is **Maherero Day**, which is when the Red Flag Herero people meet in traditional dress in memory of their fallen chiefs, killed in battles with the Nama and the Germans. A similar event is held by the Mbanderu, or Green Flag Herero, on the weekend nearest 11 June.

Sleeping & Eating

IN TOWN

Okahandja Rest Camp (☎ 504086; Voortrekker St; camping per person N$50, rondavels per person from N$150) This sheltered camp offers modern ablution blocks, communal kitchens, braai (barbecue) facilities and a few basic rondavels with shared facilities. The camp is located north of town opposite the Shell petrol station.

Sylvanette Guest House (☎ 501213; www.sylvanette .com; Anderson St; s/d from N$390/600; ⚄ 🖳 ⚄) This cosy little guest house is located in a quiet and garden-like suburban setting and centred on a refreshing swimming pool surrounded by all manners of potted plants. Well-priced rooms pay tribute to the wilds of Namibia with ample animal prints, and there's even a strong wi-fi signal here.

Bäckerei Dekker & Café (☎ 501962; Main St; meals & snacks N$20-45) This German cafe and bakery serves full breakfasts, toasted sandwiches, healthy snacks, pies, light lunches and desserts.

Lewcor Biltong Factory (Main St) *Biltong* (dried meat) fans will love this place – try the delicious chilli bites seasoned with peri-peri, a hot pepper sauce of Portuguese/Angolan origin.

AROUND TOWN

Gross Barmen Recreation Resort (Map p249; ☎ 501091; www.nwr.com.na; per vehicle N$10, camping per site N$50, per person N$80, 2-/4-bed chalets N$450/600) Located 26km southwest of Okahandja, the former mission station of Gross Barmen is Namibia's most popular hot-spring resort. Known as Otikango or 'weak spring in the rocks' in Herero, the site is home to naturally occurring mineral springs, through there have been plenty of more recent additions, including tennis courts, heated pools, and an open-air bar and restaurant – the whole package feels something like a cross between an oasis and a health farm. You can try showing up without

a reservation, but it's best to book in advance through Namibia Wildlife Resorts (NWR) in Windhoek (see p234).

Von Bach Dam Recreation Resort (Map p249; ☎ 501475; www.nwr.com.na; per vehicle N$10, camping per site N$50, per person N$80) Located just south of Okahandja on the B1, this comparatively less trafficked resort has good fishing prospects thanks to several years of heavy rains. Although this may not last for long, even non-anglers can enjoy picnics, bird-watching or bushwalking. Once again, all visits should be prebooked through NWR in Windhoek (see p234). Fishing licences may be purchased at the gate.

Getting There & Away

BUS

Several weekly buses make the one-hour journey between Windhoek and Okahandja on the **Intercape Mainliner** (www.intercape.co.za); fares cost from N$150. Book your tickets in advance online as this service continues on to Victoria Falls and fills up quickly.

Combis (minibuses) also run up and down the B1 with fairly regular frequency, and a ride between Windhoek and Okahandja shouldn't cost more than N$75. Okahandja is also a minor public-transport hub, serving various regional destinations by combi with fares averaging between N$30 and N$50.

CAR

Okahandja is 70km north of Windhoek on the B1, the country's main north-south highway.

TRAIN

Trans-Namib (☎ 061-298 2175) operates trains on Monday and Wednesday between Windhoek and Okahandja (fares from N$75), though very limited early-morning and late-night departures are inconvenient for most.

ERONGO MOUNTAINS (ERONGOBERG)
☎ 064

The volcanic Erongo Mountains, often referred to as the Erongoberg, rise as a 2216m massif north of Karibib and Usakos. After the original period of volcanism some 150 million years ago, the volcano collapsed on its magma chamber, allowing the basin to fill with slow-cooling igneous material. The result is this hard granite-like core, which withstood the erosion that washed away the surrounding rock. Much later in prehistory, the site was occupied by the San (see p63), who left behind a rich legacy of cave paintings and rock art that has weathered remarkably well throughout the ages.

Sights

The Erongo range is best known for its caves and rock paintings, particularly the 50m-deep **Phillips Cave** (Map p249; day permit N\$30). This cave, 3km off the road, contains the famous humpbacked white elephant painting. Superimposed on the elephant is a large humpbacked antelope (perhaps an eland), and around it frolic ostriches and giraffes. The Ameib paintings were brought to attention in the book *Phillips Cave* by prehistorian Abbè Breuil, but his speculations about their Mediterranean origins have now been discounted. The site is open to day hikers via Ameib Ranch (see below).

The Ameib picnic site is backed up by outcrops of stacked boulders, one of which, the notable Bull's Party, resembles a circle of gossiping bovines. Other formations that are often photographed include one resembling an elephant's head and another that recalls a Herero woman in traditional dress, standing with two children.

Sleeping

Ameib Ranch (Map p249; ☎ 530803; www.natron .net/tour/ameib; camping per person N\$70, half-/full board per person from N\$500; ▣) Located at the base of the Erongo foothills, the 'Green Hill' Ranch was established in 1864 as a Rhenish mission station, though it operates today as a guest farm and campsite. Accommodation is in the historic farmhouse, which is adjacent to a landscaped pool, a lapa (a circular area with a fire pit, used for socialising) and the well-maintained campsite. Ameib Ranch owns the concessions on Phillips Cave, and issues permits for the sight in addition to guided hikes and day tours.

Erongo Wilderness Lodge (Map p249; ☎ 570537; www.erongowilderness.com; per person tented bungalows incl full board from N\$1350; ▣ ▣ ▣) This highly acclaimed wilderness retreat combines spectacular mountain scenery, wildlife viewing, bird-watching and environmentally sensitive architecture to create one of Namibia's most memorable lodges. Accommodation is in one of 10 tented bungalows, which are built on wooden stilts and situated among towering

granite pillars. When you're not lounging in front of the fireplace in the main lodge, you can choose from a variety of activities (cost included in the full-board price), including hiking, birding or going on a wildlife drive. To get to the lodge, go to Omaruru, turn west on the D2315 (off the Karibib road 1km south of town) and continue for 10km.

Getting There & Away

North of Ameib, the D1935 skirts the Erongo Mountains before heading north into Damaraland. Alternatively, you can head east towards Omaruru on the D1937. This route virtually encircles the Erongo massif and provides access to minor 4WD roads into the heart of the mountains. These roads will take you to some excellent wild bushwalking if you're looking to really get away from it all.

OMARURU
☎ 064

Omaruru's dry and dusty setting beside the shady Omaruru riverbed lends it a real outback feel. Its name means 'Bitter, Thick Milk' in Herero, and refers to the milk produced by cattle that have grazed on bitterbush – in dry periods, this hardy plant remains green and tasty long after other vegetation has become insipid.

The town was founded in 1870 as a trading post and mission station, and it was here that the New Testament and the liturgies were first translated into Herero. Evidence of this history abounds, and it's worth taking a look around town before pressing on to either Swakopmund or Otjiwarongo.

Sights
FRANKE TOWER

In January 1904 Omaruru was attacked by Herero forces under chief Manassa. German captain Victor Franke, who had been engaged in suppressing an uprising in southern Namibia, petitioned Governor Leutwein for permission to march north and relieve the besieged town. After a 20-day, 900km march, Franke arrived in Omaruru and led the cavalry charge, which defeated the Herero attack.

For his efforts Franke received the highest German military honours, and in 1908 the grateful German residents of Omaruru erected the Franke Tower in his honour. The tower, which was declared a national monument in 1963, holds a historical plaque and affords a view over the town. It's normally locked, though if you want to climb it, you can pick up a key at the Central Hotel.

KRISTALL KELLEREI WINERY

Namibia's only **winery** (Map p249; ☎ 570083; ⌚ 10am-10pm Mon-Fri, 9am-2pm Sat) grows red and white grapes to produce ruby cabernet, co-lombard, blanc de noir, sparkling wine and grappa, as well as prickly-pear cactus to pro-duce its famous cactus schnapps (definitely an acquired taste). In the afternoon you can enjoy light meals – cheese and cold-meat plat-ters, salads and schnitzels – while tasting the wines and other products; dinners are also available by prebooking. The winery is 4km east of town on the D2328.

RHENISH MISSION STATION & MUSEUM

Constructed in 1872 by missionary Gottlieb Viehe, the **Rhenish Mission Station & Museum** (Wilhelm Zeraua St; admission free) now houses the town museum. Displays include 19th-century household and farming implements, an old drinks dispenser and lots of historical pho-tographs. Opposite is the cemetery where Herero chief Wilhelm Zeraua and several early German residents are buried. Pick up the museum keys from the Central Hotel.

Festivals & Events

Each year on the weekend nearest to 10 October the White Flag Herero people hold a **procession** from the Ozonde suburb to the graveyard, opposite the mission station, where their chief Wilhelm Zeraua was buried after his defeat in the German-Herero wars.

Sleeping & Eating

Omaruru Rest Camp (☎ 570516; camping per person N$50, rondavels per person from N$150; ▣) This mu-nicipal rest camp at the edge of town has basic campsites and rondavels, though there is plenty of hot water and reliable internet access. The sports bar and restaurant is quite popular and attracts a good mix of people from around the area.

Central Hotel Omaruru (☎ 570030; Wilhelm Zeraua St; s/d from N$190/440; ▣ ▣) Owing to a recent overhaul, this is now the best place to stay for the night in Omaruru, offering affordable but thoroughly modern rooms in a historic colo-nial building. The main dining room caters to both guests and locals, and serves Namibian standards and Continental favourites.

Omaruru Souvenirs & Kaffestube (☎ 570230; Wilhelm Zeraua St; meals N$20-55) The building hous-ing this intimate cafe dates from 1907. This place is a good choice for a strong cup of cof-fee and traditional German baked goods, as well as for a cold pint of Hansa and some pub grub in the outdoor beer garden.

Getting There & Away

With your own vehicle, the paved C33 passes through Omaruru, and provides the quickest route between Swakopmund and Etosha.

KALKFELD
☎ 067

Around 200 million years ago, Namibia was covered in a shallow sea, which gradu-ally filled with wind-blown sand and eroded silt. Near the tiny town of Kalkfeld, these sandstone layers bear the evidence of a 25m-long dinosaur stroll, which took place an estimated 170 million years ago. The tracks were made in what was then soft clay by a three-toed dinosaur that walked on its hind legs – probably a forerunner of modern birds.

The **dinosaur footprints** (Map p249) are 29km from Kalkfeld on Otjihaenamparero Farm (Map p249), just off route D2414. The site was declared a national monument in 1951, but individual visits are still subject to the farmer's permission. Alternatively, Mt Etjo Safari Lodge (below) provides access to a smaller set of nearby tracks.

There's no accommodation in Kalkfeld, but nearby **Mt Etjo Safari Lodge** (Map p249; ☎ 304464; www.mount-etjo.com; camping per 4-person private site N$550, d/ste incl half-board N$1300/3200; ▣ ▣ ▣), in the heart of a private nature reserve, is a good option. 'Mt Etjo' means place of refuge, and refers to the nearby table mountain. Its place in history was sealed in April 1989 when the Mt Etjo Peace Agreement was signed, ending South-West African People's Organisation's (Swapo) liberation struggle and setting the stage for Namibian independence the following March (see p205). Impressive history aside, this is your best base if you want to ensure a guaranteed viewing of the dino tracks, which are located on the edge of the appropriately named Dinosaur Campsite. Accommodation is either in the main safari lodge, a mod-est, upmarket affair that benefits from the beauty of the surrounding nature, or in the expensive but entirely private campsite, located a few kilometres down the road. The lodge is situated 35km from Kalkfeld via the D2414 and the D2483 – just follow the brightly painted signs.

Kalkfeld is located just off the C33 approximately halfway between Omaruru and Otjiwarongo.

OTJIWARONGO
☎ 067

After the 1891 treaty between German missionaries and the Herero chief Kambazembi, a Rhenish mission station was established here, and a German military garrison arrived later in 1904. The town was officially founded in 1906 with the arrival of the narrow-gauge railway from Swakopmund to the mines at Otavi and Tsumeb. An old locomotive still rests in town, proudly marking this historical legacy.

Sights
LOCOMOTIVE NO 41
At the train station stands Locomotive No 41, which was manufactured in 1912 by the Henschel company of Kassel, Germany, and then brought all the way to Namibia to haul ore between the Tsumeb mines and the port at Swakopmund. It was retired from service in 1960 when the 0.6m narrow gauge was replaced with the wider 1.067m gauge.

CROCODILE RANCH
Otjiwarongo is home to Namibia's first **crocodile ranch** (☎ 302121; cnr Zingel & Hospital Sts; admission N$20; ☼ 9am-4pm Mon-Fri, 11am-2pm Sat & Sun). This ranch produces skins for export, though you can score some cheap prices on high-quality belts, wallets, shoes and even jackets. There is also a small cafe serving snacks, light meals and crocodile cutlets.

Sleeping
The roads between Windhoek, Swakopmund, Outjo and the Golden Triangle converge at the agricultural and ranching centre of Otjiwarongo. Known as the Pleasant Place in Herero, Otjiwarongo is particularly pleasant in September and October when the town explodes with the vivid colours of blooming jacaranda and bougainvillea.

Out of Africa Town Lodge (☎ 303397; www.out-of-afrika.com; Long St; s/d N$270/350; ☒ ☒) This attractive whitewashed, colonial-style lodge is

a nice place to break up the drive to Etosha if you accidentally get a late start. Lofty rooms retain their historical accents, though frequent renovations have kept them in sync with the times.

C'est Si Bon Hotel (☎ 301240; Swembad St; s/d N$670/885; ☒ ☒) Named after a common French expression that translates to 'it is good', this charmer of a hotel takes its moniker to heart, blending Namibian design with European flourishes. After a few laps in the pool, a cappuccino on the sundeck and a glass of wine in the bar, you'll certainly agree that everything is indeed *c'est si bon*.

Okonjima Lodge (Map p249; ☎ 304563; www.okonjima.com; per person incl full board low/high season from N$990/2000) The Place of Baboons is home to the AfriCat Foundation, which sponsors a cheetah and leopard rehabilitation centre as well as a sanctuary for orphaned or problem lions, cheetahs and other cats. Guests are able to participate in cheetah- and leopard-tracking expeditions, in addition to more relaxing activities, including hiking, bird-watching and wildlife drives. Accommodation is in a variety of chalets, luxury tents and en suite rooms that are scattered throughout the reserve. To reach Okonjima, turn west onto the D2515, 49km south of Otjiwarongo; follow this road for 15km and then turn left onto the farm road for the last 10km.

Getting There & Away
The Intercape Mainliner service between Windhoek and Victoria Falls passes through Otjiwarongo, and minibuses between Windhoek and the north stop at the Engen petrol station. All train services between Tsumeb and Windhoek or Walvis Bay (via Swakopmund) also pass through.

OUTJO
☎ 067

Outjo was established in 1880 by the trader Tom Lambert and thus never functioned as a mission station, though in the mid-1890s it did a short, uneventful stint as a German garrison town. At present, Outjo's environs boast citrus groves and pastureland, with most of the economy revolving squarely around cattle ranching. For visitors, Outjo is the last major rest stop before reaching Okaukuejo, the administrative headquarters of and western gateway to Etosha National Park.

Sights

NAULILA MONUMENT
This monument commemorates the 19 October 1914 massacre of German soldiers and officials by the Portuguese near Fort Naulila on the Kunene River in Angola. It also commemorates soldiers killed on 18 December 1914, under Major Franke, who was sent to avenge earlier losses.

FRANKE HOUSE MUSEUM
Originally called the Kliphuis or stone house, the **Franke House** (admission free; 10am-12.30pm & 3-5pm Mon-Fri) is one of Outjo's earliest buildings. It was constructed in 1899 by order of Major von Estorff as a residence for himself and subsequent German commanders. It was later occupied by Major Franke, who posthumously gave it his name, though the current focus of the museum is political and natural history.

WINDMILL TOWER
Outjo's old 9.5m stone windmill tower was constructed in 1900 to provide fresh water for German soldiers, their horses and the colonial hospital. It rises above the C39, immediately east of Outjo.

Sleeping & Eating
Etosha Garden Hotel (313130; www.etosha-garden-hotel.com; s/d N$390/660;) Just a short walk from the town centre, this Austrian-run oasis features curio-filled rooms surrounding plush greenery and a sparkling-clear swimming pool. The dining room features a varied menu of imaginative dishes, including zebra steak with blueberry and red-wine sauce, and roast kudu with red apple, cabbage, croquettes and pears.

Ombinda Country Lodge (Map p249; 313181; ombinda@ovt.namib.com; camping per person US$90, s/d from N$455/785;) This jacaranda-studded lodge is located 1km south of town and consists of traditional reed-and-thatch chalets that have been brought up to date with amenities such as satellite TV and air-con. The adjacent campsite is well looked after, and campers are granted full use of the lodge including access to the pool.

Outjo Cafe-Bäckerei (313055; light meals N$35-55) An Outjo institution, and something of an obligatory stop for German tour buses en route to Etosha, this Deutschland-inspired cafe and bakery is famous for its bread and sweet treats, and is also a good choice for light meals, including chicken, schnitzels and burgers.

Getting There & Away
Combis run between the OK supermarket in Outjo to towns and cities around North-Central Namibia, though there is no public transport leading up to Okakuejo and the Andersson Gate of Etosha National Park. If you're driving, however, the paved route continues north as far as the park gate. (Keep your speed under control, though, as wildlife is frequently seen along the sides of the highway. Smashing into a warthog – or, worse, an impala – can seriously ruin your onward safari plans.)

WATERBERG PLATEAU PARK
Waterberg Plateau Park takes in a 50km-long, 16km-wide Etjo sandstone plateau, looming 150m above the desert plains. Rainwater is absorbed by the sandstone layers and percolates through the strata until it reaches the southwest tilting mudstone, forming an aquifer that emerges in springs at the cliff base.

Around this sheer-sided 'lost world' is an abundance of watering holes that support a mosaic of lush trees and rare wildlife. In addition to the standard complement of African herbivores, the park protects rare and threatened species, including sable and roan antelopes, white and black rhinos, and even wild dogs.

History
While Waterberg is known among tourists as a unique safari park, the plateau has played a prominent role in Namibian history.

In 1873 a Rhenish mission station was established at Waterberg, but it was destroyed in 1880 during the Herero-Nama wars. In 1904 it was the site of the decisive Battle of the Waterberg between German colonial forces and the Herero resistance. Due to superior weaponry and communications, the Germans prevailed and the remaining Herero were forced to flee east into the Kalahari. The final death blow was dealt by German soldiers, who were sent ahead to refuse the retreating Herero access to the region's few waterholes.

Information
Waterberg Plateau Park (per person per day N$80, plus per vehicle N$10, wildlife drives per person N$450) is accessible by private vehicle, though visitors

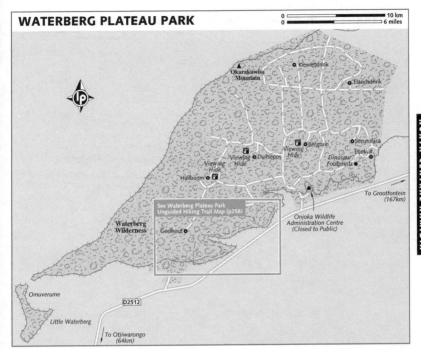

WATERBERG PLATEAU PARK

0   10 km
0   6 miles

Okarakuwisa Mountain

Kiewietdrink

Elandsdrink

Bergtuin

Securidaca

Viewing Hide

Duitsepos

Viewing Hide

Etjokui

Dinosaur Footprints

Viewing Hide

Huilboom

To Grootfontein (167km)

See Waterberg Plateau Park Unguided Hiking Trail Map (p258)

Onjoka Wildlife Administration Centre (Closed to Public)

Waterberg Wilderness

Geelhout

Omuverume

D2512

Little Waterberg

To Otjiwarongo (64km)

must explore the plateau either on foot or as part of an official wildlife drive conducted by NWR.

Open-top safari vehicles driven by park rangers depart from the Waterberg Resort at 7am and 3pm, and advance reservations must be made through the NWR office in Windhoek (see p234).

With the exception of walking trails around the Waterberg Resort, both unguided and guided hiking routes in Waterberg must be booked well in advance. For more information, see the Activities section, below.

Activities
HIKING
Waterberg Unguided Hiking Trail

A four-day, 42km unguided hike around a figure-eight track begins at 9am every Wednesday from April to November. It costs N$50 per person, and groups are limited to between three and 10 people. Book through NWR in Windhoek (see p234).

Hikers stay in basic shelters along the course and don't need to carry a tent but must otherwise be self-sufficient, ie carry

food, sleeping bag, torch (flashlight) etc. Shelters have drinking water, but you'll need to carry enough to last you between times – plan on drinking 3L to 4L per day, especially in the hot summer months.

The first day begins at the visitors centre (which is the Waterberg Resort), and follows the escarpment for 13km to Otjozongombe shelter. The second day's walk to Otjomapenda shelter is just a three-hour, 7km walk. The third day consists of an 8km route that loops back to Otjomapenda for the third night. The fourth and final day is a six-hour, 14km return to the visitors centre.

Waterberg Wilderness Trail

From April to November the four-day, guided Waterberg Wilderness Trail operates every second, third and fourth Thursday of the month. The walks, which are led by armed guides, accommodate groups of six to eight people. They begin at 2pm on Thursday from the visitors centre and end early on Sunday afternoon. They cost N$100 per person and also must be prebooked

NORTH-CENTRAL NAMIBIA

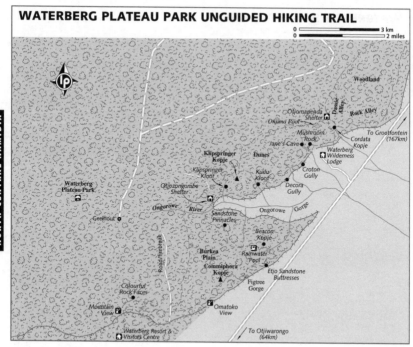

WATERBERG PLATEAU PARK UNGUIDED HIKING TRAIL

through NWR in Windhoek (see p234). There's no set route, and the itinerary is left to the whims of the guide. Accommodation is in simple huts, but participants must carry their own food and sleeping bags.

Resort Walking Trails

Around the pink-sandstone-enclosed rest camp are nine short walking tracks, including one up to the plateau rim at Mountain View. They're great for a pleasant day of easy walking, but watch for snakes, which sun themselves on rocks and even on the tracks themselves. No reservations are required for these trails.

Sleeping

The Waterberg Resort must be booked in advance through NWR in Windhoek (see p234). The Waterberg Wilderness Lodge is privately owned and accepts walk-ins, though advance reservations are recommended given its popularity.

Waterberg Resort (camping per site N$100, s/d N$650/1000, s/d bush chalets from N$800/1300) Together with its sibling properties in Etosha, the

Waterberg Resort is part of NWR's Classic Collection, which has benefited from significant investment and total refurbishment over the past several years. At Waterberg, campers can pitch a tent in any number of immaculate sites (complete with power points) scattered around hot-water ablution blocks, braai pits and picnic tables. If you're looking for a bit of bush luxury, newly constructed luxury chalets benefit from good design sense. Campers can pick up firewood, alcohol, basic groceries and other supplies from the shop, while others can sink their teeth into a fine oryx steak at the restaurant and wash it down with a glass of South African Pinotage from the bar. One word of warning, though: Waterberg is overrun with crafty baboons, so keep your tents zipped and your doors closed, and watch where you leave your food.

Waterberg Wilderness Lodge (☎ 687018; www .waterberg-wilderness.com; camping N$120, s/d incl half-board from N$1070/2100; 🕅 🖳 🖳) While it's considerably more expensive than the NWR resort, Waterberg Wilderness occupies a vast private concession within the park and is a wonderful upmarket alternative if you've got a bit of extra cash to burn. The Rust family has painstakingly transformed the property (formerly a cattle farm) by repopulating game animals and allowing nature to return to its pregrazed state. The main lodge rests in a sun-drenched meadow at the end of a valley, where you'll find red-sandstone chalets adorned with rich hardwood furniture. Alternatively, you can choose from a handful of more secluded chalets perched high on a rock terrace deeper in the concession, or save a bit of money and pitch your own tent in the high-lying plateau campsite. To reach Waterberg Wilderness, take the D2512 gravel road 8km northeast of the park entrance.

Getting There & Away
Waterberg Plateau Park is only accessible by private car – motorcycles are not permitted anywhere within the park boundaries. From Otjiwarongo it's about 90km to the park gate via the B1, C22 and the gravel D512. While this route is passable to 2WD vehicles, go slow in the final stretches as the road is torn apart in several spots. If you have a high-clearance 4WD (and a bit of extra time on your hands), you might want to leave or arrive on the particularly scenic D2512, which runs between Waterberg and Grootfontein.

OTAVI
☎ 067
Between Otjiwarongo and Tsumeb, the B1 passes Otavi, the Place of Water, near the mountains of the same name. The town was originally a German garrison, and a natural spring was used to irrigate the surrounding land to cultivate wheat. Otavi grew after 1906, when it became a copper-mining centre and was linked to Swakopmund by a narrow-gauge railway. In 1991, French and US palaeontologists uncovered the jawbone of a prehistoric ape-like creature, which has since become known as the Otavi Ape and has shed some light on our prehistoric missing link.

Sights
The **Khorab Memorial**, 2km north of Otavi, was erected in 1920 to commemorate the German troops who surrendered to the South African army under General Louis Botha on 9 July 1915. From the hotel, it's over the railway line and right along the signposted track.

Sleeping & Eating
Palmenecke Guest House (☎ 234199; www.palmenecke .co.za; 96 Hertzog Ave; s/d N$195/350; ✖ 🖳 🕿) This centrally located guest house is situated in Otavi proper, and greets guests with its cool blue hues and soaring palm trees. Palmenecke is surprisingly well priced given its poolside lapa and air-conditioned rooms with appealing enough decor; the restaurant-bar serves dinner to guests and lunch to anyone passing through town.

Restcamp Zum Potjie (Map p249; ☎ 234300; www .zumpotjie.com; camping per person N$95, s/d bungalows N$460/790; ✖ 🖳 🕿) Set amid rolling countryside just about 8km from Otavi on the Tsumeb road, this long-standing rest camp offers basic en suite accommodation and camping. The bizarre name (pronounced 'tsoom-poykee') blends German and Afrikaans, and means roughly 'in the pot'. True to its moniker, *potjie* meals (the stew cooked in the iron three-legged pot of the same name) are most definitely available and easily the highlight of staying here.

Getting There & Away
All minibuses between Windhoek and Tsumeb or Oshakati pass through Otavi.

GROOTFONTEIN
☎ 067
With a pronounced colonial feel, Grootfontein (Afrikaans for Big Spring) has an air of uprightness and respectability, with local limestone constructions and avenues of jacaranda trees that bloom in the autumn. The springboard for excursions out to Khaudom Game Reserve (p277) and the San villages in Otjozondjupa (p284), Grootfontein is the last town of any real significance before heading out into the deep, deep bush. Prior to embarking on your journey, fill the tank and pick up last-minute supplies, though save some time to check out the nearby Hoba Meteorite (p260), which is quite simply a hulking mass of extraterrestrial space rock.

History
It was the town's eponymous spring that managed to attract Grootfontein's earliest travellers, and in 1885 the Dorsland (Afrikaans for Thirst Land) trekkers set up the short-lived Republic of Upingtonia. By 1887 the settlement was gone, but six years later Grootfontein became the headquarters for the

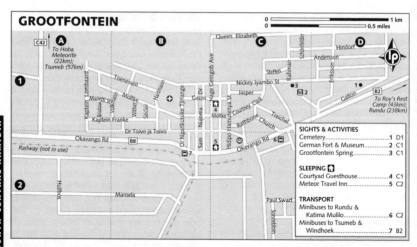

NORTH-CENTRAL NAMIBIA

German South-West Africa Company, thanks to the area's abundant mineral wealth. In 1896 the German Schutztruppe constructed a fort using local labour, and Grootfontein became a heavily fortified garrison town. The fort and nearby colonial cemetery are still local landmarks, as is the spring that put the town on the map in the first place.

Sights

GROOTFONTEIN SPRING

The Herero knew this area as 'Otjiwanda tjongue', or 'Leopard's Crest', but the current name, Afrikaans for Big Spring, parallels the Nama name Gei-aus, which means the same thing. This reliable source of water has attracted both people and wildlife for thousands of years, and also became a halt for European hunters as early as the 1860s.

The water also attracted the area's first European settlers. In 1885, 40 families of Dorsland trekkers arrived from Angola to settle this land, which had been purchased by their leader, Will Jordan, from the Owambo chief Kambonde.

The spring and adjacent tree park can be seen near the swimming pool at the eastern end of town.

GERMAN FORT & MUSEUM

The 1896 fort was enlarged several times in the early 20th century and in 1922 a large limestone extension was added. Later the building served as a boarding school, but in 1968 it fell into disuse.

Only a last-minute public appeal saved the structure from demolition, and in 1974 it was restored to become the **Alte Forte Museum** (admission free; 9am-12.30pm & 2pm-4.30pm Mon-Fri). Displays outline the area's mineral wealth, early industries and colonial history, and there are collections of minerals, domestic items, old cameras and typewriters, and a restored carpentry and blacksmith's shop.

CEMETERY

In the town **cemetery**, off Okavango Rd, you can wander the graves of several Schutztruppe soldiers who died in combat with local forces around the turn of the century.

AROUND GROOTFONTEIN
Hoba Meteorite

Near the Hoba Farm, the world's largest **meteorite** (Map p249; admission N$10; dawn-dusk) was discovered in 1920 by hunter Jacobus Brits. This cuboid bit of space debris is composed of 82% iron, 16% nickel and 0.8% cobalt, along with traces of other metals. No one knows when it fell to earth (it's thought to have been around 80,000 years ago), but since it weighs around 54,000kg, it must have made a hell of a thump.

In 1955, after souvenir hunters began hacking off bits to take home, the site was declared a national monument, and a conservation project was launched with funds from the Rössing Foundation. There's now a visitors information board, a short nature trail and a shady picnic area.

From Grootfontein, follow the C42 towards Tsumeb. After 4km, turn west on the D2859 and continue 18km to the Hoba Farm; then follow the clearly marked signs until you reach the complex.

Sleeping & Eating

Roy's Rest Camp (Map p249; ☎ 240302; camping per person N$100, s/d N$550/920; ⌘) Sleeping accommodation in this recommended place looks like a fairy-tale illustration – the handmade wooden furnishings are all fabulously rustic, while the thatched bungalows sit tranquilly beneath towering trees. Hiking and mountain-biking possibilities include 3km and 5km trails, and there are also opportunities for multiday camping trips led by San guides. Roy's is located 43km outside Grootfontein on the road towards Rundu, and it's a convenient stop if you're heading to Tsumkwe (p286).

Meteor Travel Inn (☎ 242078; s/d from N$250/400; ⌘) Conveniently located in the centre of town, the rooms at this long-standing Grootfontein establishment have seen better years, but they'll suffice if you're not too fussy. The restaurant, however, is as good as ever, and its popular game dishes and homemade pizzas pack in hungry locals on most nights.

Courtyard Guesthouse (☎ 240027; www.natron .net/tour/courtyard; 2 Gauss St; s/d N$425/605; ⌘ ⌘ ⌘) The top spot in Grootfontein is modest by any standard, but its truly enormous rooms leave you plenty of space to unpack your bag and take stock of your gear. If you're about to embark on a bush outing, spend the afternoon poolside and bask in comfort while you can.

Getting There & Away

Minibuses run frequently between Grootfontein and Tsumeb, Rundu, Katima Mulilo and Windhoek, departing when full from informal bus stops along Okavango Rd at the appropriate ends of town. The Intercape Mainliner bus between Windhoek and Victoria Falls also passes through.

If you're heading out to Tsumkwe, you will need a private vehicle. The gravel road into town is accessible by 2WD if you take it slow, but you will need a high-clearance vehicle to reach the various villages in Otjozondjupa and a 4WD might be necessary in the rainy season. If you're heading to Khaudom, a sturdy 4WD is a requirement, as is travelling as part of a well-equipped convoy.

TSUMEB
☎ 067

The name of this town, situated at the apex of the Golden Triangle, was derived from the melding of the San word *tsoumsoub* (to dig in loose ground) and the Herero word *otjisume* (place of frogs). To fathom the latter derivation requires some imagination: Tsumeb isn't really known for its frog population, but the red, brown, green and grey streaks created by minerals looked like dried scum that had been scooped out of a pond and splattered on the rocks. As a result, both the frogs and the digging equipment appear on the town crest.

The prosperity of this mining town is based on the presence of 184 known minerals, including 10 that are unique to this area. Its deposits of copper ore and a phenomenal range of other metals and minerals (lead, silver, germanium, cadmium and many others), brought to the surface in a volcanic pipe, as well as Africa's

NORTH-CENTRAL NAMIBIA

THE RED LINE

Between Grootfontein and Rundu, and Tsumeb and Ondangwa, the B8 and B1 cross the 'Red Line', the Animal Disease Control Checkpoint veterinary control fence separating the commercial cattle ranches of the south from the communal subsistence lands to the north. This fence bars the north–south movement of animals as a precaution against foot-and-mouth disease and rinderpest, and animals bred north of this line may not be sold to the south or exported to overseas markets.

As a result, the Red Line also marks the effective boundary between the developed and developing world. The landscape south of the line is characterised by a dry, scrubby bushveld (open grassland) of vast ranches, which are home only to cattle and a few scattered ranchers. North of the Animal Disease Control Checkpoint, travellers enter a landscape of dense bush, baobab trees, mopane scrub and small kraals (farms), where the majority of individuals struggle to maintain subsistence lifestyles.

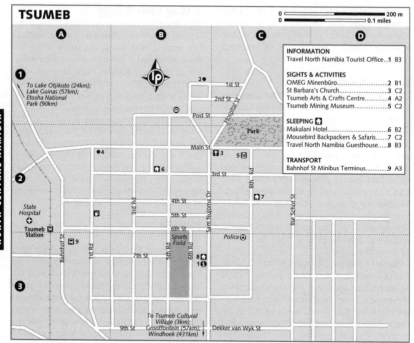

TSUMEB

most productive lead mine (the world's fifth largest), give it the distinction of being a metallurgical and mineralogical wonder of the world. Tsumeb specimens have found their way into museum collections around the globe, but you'll also see a respectable assembly of the region's mineralogical largesse and historical data in the town museum.

Information
Travel North Namibia Tourist Office (☎ 220728; travelnn@tsu.namib.com; 1551 Sam Nujoma) The friendly office provides nationwide information, arranges accommodation, transport, car hire and Etosha bookings, and has internet access.

Sights & Activities
TSUMEB MINING MUSEUM
Tsumeb's history is told in this **museum** (cnr Main St & 8th Rd; admission N$15; ☺ 9am-noon & 3-6pm Mon-Fri, 3-6pm Sat), which is housed in a 1915 colonial building that once served as both a school and a hospital for German troops. In addition to outstanding mineral displays (you've never seen anything like psitticinite!), the museum also houses mining machinery, stuffed birds, Himba and Herero

artefacts, and weapons recovered from Lake Otjikoto (see the boxed text, opposite). There is also a large collection of militaria, which was dumped here by German troops prior to their surrender to the South Africans in 1915.

TSUMEB ARTS & CRAFTS CENTRE
This **craft centre** (☎ 220257; 18 Main St; ☺ 8.30am-1pm & 2.30-5.30pm Mon-Fri, 8.30am-1pm Sat) markets Caprivian woodwork, San arts, Owambo basketry, European-Namibian leatherwork, karakul weavings, and other traditional northern Namibian arts and crafts.

ST BARBARA'S CHURCH
Tsumeb's distinctive Roman Catholic **church** (cnr Main St & Sam Nujoma) was consecrated in 1914 and dedicated to St Barbara, the patron saint of mineworkers. It contains some fine colonial murals and an odd tower, which makes it look less like a church than a municipal building in some small German town.

OMEG MINENBÜRO
Due to its soaring spire, the **OMEG Minenbüro building** (Otavi Minen und Eisenbahn Gesellschaft Bldg; 1st

St) is frequently mistaken for a church – in fact, it looks more like a church than St Barbara's. It's probably Tsumeb's most imposing building – and few would guess that it dates back to 1907.

TSUMEB CULTURAL VILLAGE

This **complex** (☎ 220787; admission N$10; ⊙ 8.30am-1pm Mon-Fri, 2.30-5.30pm Sat), located 3km outside the town on the road to Grootfontein, showcases examples of housing styles, cultural demonstrations and artefacts from all major Namibian traditions.

LAKE GUINAS

Southwest of Lake Otjikoto lies the geologically similar Lake Guinas, which is used to irrigate surrounding farmland. It's smaller than its counterpart but is also less touristy and twice as deep. It's also less accessible. Drive 27km northwest of Tsumeb on the B1 and turn southwest on the D3043. After 20km, turn southeast onto the D3031. The lake is 5km further along.

Sleeping & Eating

Mousebird Backpackers & Safaris (☎ 221777; www .mousebird.com; 533 4th St; camping per person N$125, dm N$185, s/d from N$390/420; ⌨) Tsumeb's long-standing backpacker spot continues to stay true to its roots, offering economical accommodation without sacrificing personality or character. Rooms are simple, but colourfully adorned to help brighten your day, and it's easy to arrange onward camping safaris to Etosha and points beyond if you don't have your own car.

Travel North Namibia Guesthouse (☎ 220728; http://natron.net/tnn/index.htm; Sam Nujoma Dr; s/d N$350/480; ⌨ ✹) Situated adjacent to the tourist office, which is also run by the wife-and-husband duo of Regina and Johann, this budget guest house is a wonderful spot if you're counting your Nam dollars. Airy private rooms are on offer here, as are customisable safaris throughout the whole of northern Namibia.

Makalani Hotel (☎ 221051; www.makalanihotel .com; 3rd St; s/d from N$420/610 ✹ ⌨ ✹) Situated in the town centre, the upmarket Makalani Hotel exudes a positively Caribbean vibe, complete with shady palms, tranquil (pool) waters, and vibrant shades of yellow, blue and red. The sun-drenched beer garden is a popular spot for an icy Windhoek lager, while the comprehensive restaurant underneath the lapa is arguably the best eating place in town.

NORTH-CENTRAL NAMIBIA

LAKE OTJIKOTO

In May 1851, explorers Charles Andersson and Francis Galton stumbled across the unusual **Lake Otjikoto** (admission N$15; ⊙ 8am-6.30pm summer, to 5.30pm winter). The name of the lake is Herero for Deep Hole, and its waters fill a limestone sinkhole measuring 100m by 150m, reaching depths of 55m. Interestingly, Lake Otjikoto and nearby Lake Guinas are the only natural lakes in Namibia, and they're also the only known habitats of the unusual mouth-brooding cichlid fish. These fish are psychedelic in appearance – ranging from dark green to bright red, yellow and blue – and are believed by biologists to eschew camouflage due to the absence of predators in this isolated environment. It's thought that these fish evolved from tilapia (bream) washed into the lake by ancient floods.

In 1915 the retreating German army dumped weaponry and ammunition into the lake to prevent it from falling into South African hands. It's rumoured that they jettisoned five cannon, 10 cannon bases, three Gatling guns and between 300 and 400 wagonloads of ammunition. Some of this stuff was salvaged in 1916 at great cost and effort by the South African Army, the Tsumeb Corporation and the National Museum of Namibia. In 1970, divers discovered a Krupp ammunition wagon 41m below the surface; it's on display at the Owela Museum (p238) in Windhoek. In 1977 and 1983, two more ammunition carriers were salvaged as well as a large cannon, and are now on display at the Tsumeb Mining Museum.

Lake Otjikoto is located 25km north of Tsumeb along the B1, and there are signs marking the turn-off. Although the site is undeveloped, there are a ticket booth, an adjacent car park and several small kiosks selling cold drinks and small snacks. While treasure seekers have been known to don scuba gear and search the lake under cover of night, diving (and swimming for that matter) is presently forbidden.

Getting There & Away

BUS

Several weekly **Intercape Mainliner** (www.intercape .co.za) buses make the six-hour trip between Windhoek and the Travel North office. Book your tickets (fares from N$350) in advance online as this service continues on to Victoria Falls and fills up quickly.

Combis also run up and down the B1 with fairly regular frequency, and a ride between Windhoek and Tsumeb shouldn't cost more than N$200. Combis depart from the minibus terminus in town. If you're continuing on to Etosha National Park, be advised that there is no public transport serving this route.

CAR

Tsumeb is an easy day's drive from Windhoek along paved roads and serves as the jumping-off point for Namutoni and the Von Lindequist Gate of Etosha National Park. The paved route continues north as far as the park gate, though keep your speed under control as wildlife is frequently seen along the sides of the highway.

TRAIN

Trans-Namib (☎ 061-298 2175) operates trains on Monday and Wednesday between Windhoek and Tsumeb (fares from N$175), though the very limited early-morning and late-night departures are inconvenient for most.

ETOSHA NATIONAL PARK

☎ 067

Covering an area of more than 20,000 sq km, Etosha National Park ranks as one of the world's greatest wildlife-viewing venues. Its name, which means Great White Place of Dry Water, is taken from the vast greenish-white Etosha Pan, an immense, flat, saline desert covering over 5000 sq km that for a few days each year is converted by the rains into a shallow lagoon teeming with flamingos and pelicans. However, it's the surrounding bush and grasslands that provide habitat for Etosha's diverse wildlife. Although it may look barren, the landscape fringing the pan is home to 114 mammal species as well as 340 bird species, 16 reptile and amphibian species, one fish species and countless insects.

Unlike many other parks in Africa, where you can spend days looking for animals across the plains, one of Etosha's charms is its ability to bring the animals to you. The usual routine here (if you're fortunate enough to have your own car) is to park next to one of the many waterholes, wait with bated breath and watch while a host of animals comes by – lions, elephants, springboks, the whole lot – not two by two but in the hundreds. An impressive network of campsites and bush chalets also means that you can bed down inside the park, and continue your wildlife watching even under cover of night.

HISTORY

The first Europeans in Etosha were traders and explorers John Andersson and Francis Galton, who arrived by wagon at Namutoni in 1851. They were later followed in 1876 by an American trader G McKeirnan, who observed: 'All the menageries in the world turned loose would not compare to the sight I saw that day'.

However, Etosha didn't attract the interest of tourists or conservationists until after the turn of the 20th century, when the governor of German South West Africa, Dr von Lindequist, became concerned about diminishing animal numbers and founded a 99,526-sq-km reserve, which included Etosha Pan.

At the time, the land was still unfenced and animals could follow their normal migration routes. In subsequent years, however, the park boundaries were altered a few times, and by 1970 Etosha had been reduced to its present size.

ORIENTATION & INFORMATION

Only the eastern two-thirds of Etosha are open to the general public; the western third is reserved exclusively for tour operators. Etosha's three main entry gates are Von Lindequist (Namutoni), west of Tsumeb; King Nehale, southeast of Ondangwa; and Andersson (Okaukuejo), north of Outjo.

Visitors are encouraged to check in at either Von Lindequist Gate or Andersson Gate (King Nehale Gate is frequently closed), where you then must purchase a permit costing N$80 per person plus N$10 per vehicle per day. The permits are to be presented at your reserved rest camp, where you pay any outstanding camping or accommodation fees.

Although fees are normally prepaid through NWR in Windhoek (see p234), it is sometimes possible to reserve accommodation at either

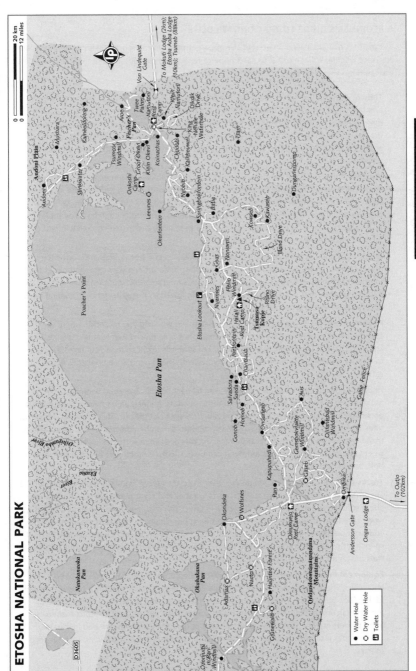

A BEGINNER'S GUIDE TO TRACKING WILDLIFE

Visitors to Africa are always amazed at the apparent ease with which professional guides locate and spot wildlife. While most of us can't hope to replicate their skills in a brief visit, a few pointers can hone your approach.

- **Time of day** This is possibly the most important factor for determining animal movements and behaviours. Dawn and dusk tend to be the most productive periods for mammals and many birds. They're the coolest parts of the day, and also produce the richest light for photographs. Although the middle of the day is usually too hot for much action, this is when some antelopes feel less vulnerable at a watering hole, and when raptors and reptiles are most obvious.

- **Weather** Prevailing conditions can greatly affect your wildlife-viewing experience. For example, high winds may drive herbivores and birds into cover, so concentrate your search in sheltered areas. Summer thunderstorms are often followed by a flurry of activity as insect colonies and frogs emerge, followed by their predators. Overcast or cool days may prolong activity such as hunting by normally crepuscular predators, and extremely cold winter nights force nocturnal species to stay active at dawn.

- **Water** Most animals drink daily when water is available, so water sources are worthwhile places to invest time, particularly in the dry season. Predators and very large herbivores tend to drink early in the day or at dusk, while antelopes tend to drink from the early morning to midday. On the coast, receding tides are usually followed by the appearance of wading birds and detritus feeders such as crabs.

- **Food sources** Knowing what the different species eat will help you to decide where to spend most of your time. A flowering aloe might not hold much interest at first glance, but knowing that it is irresistible to many species of sunbirds might change your mind. Fruiting trees attract monkeys, while herds of herbivores with their young are a predator's dessert cart.

- **Habitat** Knowing which habitats are preferred by each species is a good beginning, but just as important is knowing where to look in those habitats. Animals aren't merely randomly dispersed within their favoured habitats. Instead, they seek out specific sites to shelter – hollows, trees, caves and high points on plains. Many predators use open grasslands but also gravitate towards available cover, such as large trees, thickets or even grass tussocks. 'Ecotones' – where one habitat merges into another – can be particularly productive because species from both habitats overlap.

- **Tracks and signs** Even when you don't see animals, they leave many signs of their presence. Spoor (tracks), scat (droppings), pellets, nests, scrapes and scent marks provide information about wildlife, and may even help to locate it. Check dirt and sand roads when driving – it won't take long for you to recognise interesting spoor. Elephant footprints are unmistakable, and large predator tracks are fairly obvious. Also, many wild cats and dogs use roads to hunt, so look for where the tracks leave the road – often they mark the point where they began a stalk or sought out a nearby bush for shade.

- **Equipment** Probably the most important piece of equipment you can have is a good pair of binoculars. These help you not only spot wildlife but also correctly identify it (this is essential for birding). Binoculars are also useful for viewing species and behaviours where close approaches are impossible. Field guides, which are pocket-sized books that depict mammals, birds, flowers etc of a specific area with photos or colour illustrations, are also invaluable. These guides also provide important identification pointers and a distribution map for each species.

NORTH-CENTRAL NAMIBIA

gate. However, be advised that the park can get very busy on weekends, especially during the dry season – if you can manage it, pre-booking is recommended.

Etosha is open to day visitors, but it's impossible to see much of the park in less than two or three days. Most visitors spend a couple of nights at one of the three rest camps, Namutoni, Halali and Okaukuejo, which are spaced at 70km intervals. Each has its own character, so it's worth visiting more than one if you have the time.

The main camps are open year-round, and have restaurants, bars, shops, swimming pools, picnic sites, petrol stations, kiosks and floodlit watering holes that attract game throughout the night. The recently constructed ultra-luxury camp at Onkoshi is a largely private affair, but certainly worth staying at if you have a serious bit of cash to burn.

Those booked into the rest camps must show up before sunset, and can only leave after sunrise; specific times are posted on the gates. Anyone returning later is locked out; if this happens, a blast on your car horn will send someone running to open the gate, but violators can expect a lecture on the evils of staying out late, a black mark on their park permit and perhaps even a fine.

The park speed limit is set at 60km/h both to protect wildlife and keep down the dust. If any of your belongings won't tolerate a heavy dusting, pack them away in plastic. Car-cleaning services are available at any of the rest camps for a small fee.

All roads in the eastern section of Etosha are passable to 2WD vehicles, but wildlife viewing is best from the vantage point offered by a high-clearance vehicle. The park road between Namutoni and Okaukuejo skirts Etosha Pan, providing great views of its vast spaces. Driving isn't permitted on the pan, but a network of gravel roads threads through the surrounding savannahs and mopane woodland and even extends out to a viewing site, the Etosha Lookout, in the middle of the salt desert.

The best time for wildlife drives is at first light and late in the evening, though visitors aren't permitted outside the camps after dark. While self-drivers should definitely wake up at twilight, when animals are most active, guided night drives (N$600 per person) can be booked through any of the main camps and are your best chance to see lions hunting as well as various nocturnal species. Each of the camps also has a visitor register, which describes any recent sightings in the vicinity.

Pedestrians, bicycles, motorcycles and hitching are prohibited in Etosha, and open trucks must be screened off. Outside the rest camps, visitors must stay in their vehicles (except at toilet stops).

ACTIVITIES
Wildlife Watching
Etosha's most widespread vegetation type is mopane woodland, which fringes the pan and constitutes about 80% of the vegetation. The park also has umbrella-thorn acacias and other trees that are favoured by browsing animals, and from December to March this sparse bush country has a pleasant green hue.

Depending on the season, you may observe elephants, giraffes, Burchell's zebras, springboks, red hartebeests, blue wildebeests, gemsboks, elands, kudus, roans, ostriches, jackals, hyenas, lions, and even cheetahs and leopards. Among the endangered animal species are the black-faced impala and the black rhinoceros.

The park's wildlife density varies with the local ecology. As its Afrikaans name would suggest, Oliphantsbad (near Okaukuejo) is attractive to elephants, but for rhinos you couldn't do better than the floodlit waterhole at Okaukuejo. In general, the further east you go in the park, the more wildebeests, kudus and impalas join the springboks and gemsboks. The area around Namutoni, which averages 443mm of rain annually (compared with 412mm at Okaukuejo), is the best place to see the black-faced impala and the Damara dik-dik, Africa's smallest antelope. Etosha is also home to numerous smaller species, including both yellow and slender mongooses, honey badgers and leguaans.

In the dry winter season, wildlife clusters around waterholes, while in the hot, wet summer months, animals disperse and spend the days sheltering in the bush. In the afternoon, even in the dry season, look carefully for animals resting beneath the trees, especially prides of lions lazing about. Summer temperatures can reach 44°C, which isn't fun when you're confined to a vehicle, but this is the calving season, and you may catch a glimpse of tiny zebra foals and fragile newborn springboks.

Birdlife is also profuse. Yellow-billed hornbills are common, and on the ground you

NORTH-CENTRAL NAMIBIA

THE NAME OF THE GAME

The word 'game' actually hails from hunting: originally the game was the thrill of the sport, but gradually the quarry itself came to be called game. Derivation notwithstanding, the term pops up regularly in Southern Africa when people refer to wildlife, and it doesn't necessarily mean that some poor beast is about to receive a lethal dose of lead poisoning. 'Game viewing' is the most common local term for wildlife watching and is usually done on a 'game drive', a guided tour by vehicle. 'Big Game' is, of course, the Big Five (lion, leopard, buffalo, black rhino, elephant) whereas 'general game' collectively refers to the diverse herbivore community, ranging from duikers to giraffes. Of course, while 'game' in its various forms is used widely, hunters also still employ the term, most often as 'Big Game' as well as 'Plains Game', their term for herbivores.

---

should look for the huge kori bustard, which weighs 15kg and seldom flies. You may also observe ostriches, korhaans, marabous, white-backed vultures and many smaller species.

SLEEPING & EATING
In the Park

Prebooking for the NWR-run camps listed below is mandatory. Although it is sometimes possible to reserve a space at either of the park gates, it's best to contact the NWR office in Windhoek (see p234) well in advance of your visit.

Okaukuejo Rest Camp (camping per site N$200, plus per person N$100, s/d from N$800/1300, chalets from N$900/1500, luxury chalets per person N$1600; 🛒 🍴) Pronounced 'o-ka-kui-yo', this the site of the Etosha Research Station, and it functions as the official park headquarters and main visitors centre. The Okaukuejo waterhole is probably Etosha's best rhino-viewing venue, particularly between 8pm and 10pm, though you're almost guaranteed to spot zebras, wildebeest, jackals and even elephants virtually any time of the day. Also popular is the sunset photo frenzy from Okaukuejo's landmark stone tower, which affords a view across the spaces to the distant Ondundozonananandana (Lost Shepherd Boy) Mountains; try saying that after a bottle of beer (or even before!). Okaukuejo's Campsite can get very crowded, but the shared facilities are excellent, and include washing stations, braai pits, and bathroom and toilet facilities with hot water. The self-catering accommodation is the nicest in the park (excluding Onkoshi; opposite), and includes older but recently refurbished rooms alongside stand-alone chalets. If you want to splurge, the luxury chalet is a stunning two-storey affair complete with a furnished centre-stage balcony boasting unmatched views of animals lining up to drink.

Halali Rest Camp (camping per site N$200, plus per person N$100, s/d from N$800/1300, chalets from N$900/1500; 🛒 🍴) Etosha's middle camp, Halali, nestles between several incongruous dolomite outcrops. The name is derived from a German term for the ritual horn-blowing to signal the end of a hunt, and a horn now serves as Halali's motif. The short Tsumasa hiking track leads up Tsumasa Kopje, the hill nearest the rest camp, from where you can snap wonderful panoramic shots of the park. The best feature of Halali is its floodlit waterhole, which is a 10-minute walk from the rest camp and is sheltered by a glen of trees with huge boulders strewn about. While it's not as dramatic in scope as Okaukuejo, it's a wonderfully intimate setting where you can savour a glass of wine in peace, all the while scanning the bush for rhinos and lions, which frequently stop to drink in the late evening hours. Like Okaukuejo, there is a very well-serviced campsite here, in addition to a fine collection of luxury chalets that make for a wonderfully relaxed night of sleep despite being deep in the middle of the African bush.

Namutoni Rest Camp (camping per site N$200, plus per person N$100, s/d from N$1400/1800, chalets from N$2000/3000; 🍴 🛒) Etosha's easternmost camp is defined by its landmark whitewashed German fort, a colonial relic that casts a surreal shadow over the rest of the camp. The structure originally served as an outpost for German troops, but it was fortified n 1899 by the German cavalry in order to quell Owambo uprisings. In the battle of Namutoni, on 28 January 1904, seven German soldiers unsuccessfully tried to defend the fort against 500 Owambo warriors. Two years later, the damaged structure was renovated and pressed into service as a police station. In 1956 it was restored to its original specifications, and two years later it was opened as tourist accommodation. In recent years the entire interior has been painstakingly updated, and the building now serves as Etosha's boutique accommodation.

Even if you're not staying here, the tower and ramparts provide a great view, and every evening a crowd gathers to watch the sunset; arrive early to stake out a good vantage point. Each night the flag is lowered, and a ceremonial bugle call signals sundown. In the morning, a similar ritual drags you out of your bed. Beside the fort is a lovely freshwater limestone spring and the floodlit King Nehale waterhole, which is filled with reed beds and some extremely vociferous frogs. The viewing benches are nice for lunch or watching the pleasant riverbank scene, but unfortunately the spot attracts surprisingly few thirsty animals. Again, like Okakuejo and Halali, Namutoni also offers an immaculate campsite in addition to a few luxury chalets on the edge of the bush.

Onkoshi Camp (s/d incl activities, entrance fees & transfers from Namutoni from N$5500/9000; 🔀 🖳) Although it's an enormous splash-out that requires some serious purchasing power, the brand-new Onkoshi Camp at Etosha National Park is the shining crown jewel of NWR's Premier Collection. Upon arrival in Namutoni, you will be chauffeured to a secluded peninsula on the rim of the pan, and then given the keys to one of only 15 thatch-and-canvas chalets that rest on elevated wooden decks and occupy exclusive locations well beyond the standard tourist route. The interiors, which blend rich hardwoods, delicate bamboo, elaborate metal flourishing, finely crafted furniture, hand-painted artwork and fine porcelain fixtures, create an overwhelmingly opulent atmosphere. While the temptation certainly exists to spend your days lounging about such regal settings, guests are treated to personalised wildlife drives conducted by Etosha's finest guides, and dinners are multicourse affairs that are illuminated by candlelight.

Outside the Park

There are literally dozens and dozens of top-end lodges located on the periphery of Etosha, though only a few are listed below. At all of these properties, prebooking is essential, and access is via private vehicle or charter flight.

All published rates are for the high season and include full board and wildlife drives; transfers from Windhoek are also possible with advance notice.

Etosha Aoba Lodge (Map p249; ☎ 229100; www.etosha-aoba-lodge.com; s/d from N$895/1390; 🔀 🖳 🐾) Situated on a 70-sq-km private concession about 10km east of von Lindequist Gate, this tranquil lodge is located in tamboti forest next to a dry river bed. The property comprises 10 cottages that blend effortlessly into their riverine environment. The atmosphere is peaceful and relaxing, though the main lodge is conducive to unwinding with other guests after a long day on safari. The restaurant offers gourmet dishes, including kudu terrine with Kalahari truffles and zebra steaks with locally harvested wild mushrooms.

Mokuti Lodge (Map p249; ☎ 229084; www.namibsunhotels.com.na; s/d from N$965/1375; 🔀 🖳 🐾) This sprawling lodge, located just 2km from von Lindequist Gate, has over 100 rooms as well as several swimming pools and tennis courts, though the low-profile buildings create an illusion of intimacy. The lodge seeks to create an informal, relaxed atmosphere, which makes this a good choice if you're travelling with the little ones. Don't miss the attached reptile park and its resident snake collection, which features locals captured around the lodge property – now that's a comforting thought!

Ongava Lodge (Map p265; ☎ 061-274500; www.wilderness-safaris.com; per person from N$2530; 🔀 🖳 🐾) The most exclusive luxury lodge in the Etosha area is located on a private game reserve near Andersson Gate that protects several prides of lions, a few black and white rhinos, and your standard assortment of herd animals. Ongava is actually divided into two properties; the main Ongava Lodge is a collection of safari-chic chalets surrounding a small waterhole, while the Ongava Tented Camp consists of six East African–style canvas tents situated a bit deeper in the bush.

GETTING THERE & AWAY

There's no public transport into and around the park, which means that you must visit either in a private vehicle or as part of an organised tour.

Northern Namibia

Windhoek may be Namibia's capital, but Northern Namibia is the country's most densely populated region, and undeniably its cultural heartland. Home to Owambo people, including Namibia's first president, Sam Nujoma, the north served as the base for the South-West African People's Organisation (Swapo) during the Namibian War of Independence. From 1966 to 1988, a bloody guerrilla war was fought on this soil, though peace and calm have returned to the area. Today, most Owambo follow subsistence agricultural lifestyles, growing staple crops and raising cattle and goats.

Northern Namibia also takes form and identity from the Caprivi Strip, where broad flood plains enable the Mafwe, Subia, Bayei and Mbukushu peoples to cultivate plantations and catch vast quantities of river fish. Alongside these traditional villages are a collection of national parks, which are finally being repopulated with wildlife after so many decades of war and conflict. At the time of independence, these parks had been virtually depleted by poachers, though years of progressive wildlife management have firmly placed the region back on the safari circuit.

Although largely confined to eastern Otjozondjupa, the San (pejoratively referred to as Bushmen) once roamed the entire region, and indeed much of Southern Africa. Unfortunately, Kalahari cultures have been forced to contend with serious lifestyle changes over the generations, and sadly are no longer able to continue their ancestral hunting and gathering patterns. Still, a visit to these communities opens a window into a way of life once followed by all of humankind.

HIGHLIGHTS

- Learning about the ways of the past from modern San in **Otjozondjupa** (p284)
- Exploring the wildlife reserves on the **Caprivi Strip** (p278) while they're still undiscovered
- Testing your 4WD mettle on an expedition through the remote **Khaudom Game Reserve** (p277)
- Living it up in luxury at one of the lodges on the wildlife-rich **Mpalila Island** (p282)
- Saying you've been to Angola (sort of) by crossing the border (halfway) at **Ruacana Falls** (p275)

Geography

Known as the Land of Rivers, Northern Namibia is bounded by the Kunene and Okavango Rivers along the Angolan border, and in the east by the Zambezi and the Kwando/Mashe/Linyanti/Chobe river systems. In the northeast, the gently rolling Kavango region is dominated by the Okavango River. East of Kavango is the spindly Caprivi Strip, a flat, unexceptional landscape that is characterised by expanses of acacia forest. Along the border with Botswana is the Otjozondjupa region, a wild and thinly populated strip of scrub forest that is home to several scattered San villages.

Getting Around

As a major population centre, Owamboland is comparatively well served by combis (minibuses), and hitching here is fairly easy due to the higher density of people. The C46 and B1 here are both sealed and in good condition, but off these routes, road maintenance is poor, and a 4WD is required in places, especially after the rain. Petrol is available at Oshakati, Ondangwa, Oshikango and Uutapi (Ombalantu).

If you're transiting the Caprivi Strip en route to Victoria Falls, Intercape Mainliner connects Livingstone, Zambia, to Windhoek. If you have a private vehicle, this route is tarred in its entirety and suitable for all 2WD vehicles. However, a high-clearance vehicle, preferably with 4WD, is necessary for visiting any of the national parks.

Finally, the town of Tsumkwe in Otjozondjupa can be reached by 2WD, though you will need a sturdier vehicle if you plan to visit outlying San villages. If you're continuing on to Khaudom Game Reserve, a fully equipped 4WD vehicle is a necessity, and ideally you'll be travelling as part of a convoy.

THE NORTH

The regions of Omusati, Oshana, Ohangwena and Otjikoto comprise the homeland of the Owambo people, Namibia's largest population group. Although there's little in terms of tourist attractions in this region, Owambo country is home to a healthy and prosperous rural society that buzzes with activity. It's also a good place to stock up on the region's high-quality basketry and sugar-cane work, which is often sold at roadside stalls. Designs are simple and graceful, usually incorporating a brown geometric pattern woven into the pale-yellow reed.

ONDANGWA
☎ 065

The second-largest Owambo town is known for its large number of warehouses, which provide stock to the 6000 tiny cuca shops (small bush shops named after the brand of Angolan beer they once sold) that serve the area's rural residents. Aside from being a population and distribution centre, Ondangwa is also a minor transport hub, with combis fanning out from here to other cities and towns in the north.

Sights

The main attraction in the area is **Lake Oponono**, a large wetland fed by the Culevai *oshanas* (underground river channels). After a heavy rainy season, the lakeshores attract a variety of birdlife, including saddlebill storks, crowned cranes, flamingos and pelicans. The edge of lake is located 27km south of Ondangwa.

Also worthwhile is the **Nakambale House** (admission N$5; ⏰ 8am-1pm & 2-5pm Mon-Fri, 8am-1pm Sat, noon-5pm Sun), which was built in the late 1870s by Finnish missionary Martti Rauttanen, and is believed to be the oldest building in northern Namibia. It now houses a small museum on Owambo history and culture. Nakambale is part of Olukonda village, which is located 6km southeast of Ondangwa on the D3606.

Sleeping & Eating

Nakambale Campsite (Map pp272-3; ☎ 245668; www .nacobta.com.na; camping N$50, huts per person N$100) Here's your opportunity to sleep in a basic hut that would have been used historically by an Owambo chief or one of his wives. A member of Nacobta, a collective of various organisations that aims to foster increased community-based tourism, Nakambale is located on the outskirts of Olukonda village, 6km southeast of Ondangwa on the D3606.

Protea Hotel Ondangwa (Map pp272-3; ☎ 241900; www.proteahotels.com; s/d from N$730/915; 🖧 🕿) This plush business hotel features bright rooms decorated with tasteful artwork as well as modern furnishings. The attached Chatters restaurant does decent Continental-inspired cuisine, and there's also a small espresso shop and takeaway in the lobby.

NORTHERN NAMIBIA

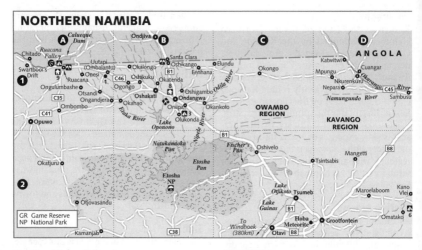

NORTHERN NAMIBIA

Getting There & Away

AIR

Air Namibia flies to and from Windhoek's Eros Airport daily. Note that the airstrip in Oshakati is for private charters only, which means that Ondangwa serves as the main access point in the north for airborne travellers.

BUS

Combis run up and down the B1 with fairly regular frequency, and a ride between Windhoek to Ondangwa shouldn't cost more than N$150. From Ondangwa, a complex network of combi routes serves population centres throughout the north, with fares typically costing less than N$30 a ride.

CAR

The B1 is paved all the way from Windhoek to Ondangwa and out to Oshakati.

The Oshikango border crossing to Santa Clara in Angola, 60km north of Ondangwa, is open and carries frequent cross-border truck traffic. During the day, you may be able to hop across for a quick look around, but to stay overnight or travel further north, you'll need an Angolan visa that allows overland travel.

TRAIN

Trans-Namib (☎ 061-298 2175) operates a new passenger line between Windhoek and Ondangwa (fares from N$110). Overnight trains leave Windhoek at 5.30pm on Friday, and return from Ondangwa at 1pm on Sunday.

OSHAKATI
☎ 065

The Owambo capital is an uninspiring commercial centre that is little more than a strip of characterless development along the highway. But it's worth spending an hour or so

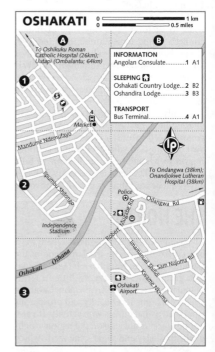

OSHAKATI

| 0 | 1 km |
| 0 | 0.5 miles |

INFORMATION
Angolan Consulate............1 A1

SLEEPING 🏠
Oshakati Country Lodge....2 B2
Oshandira Lodge.............3 B3

TRANSPORT
Bus Terminal....................4 A1

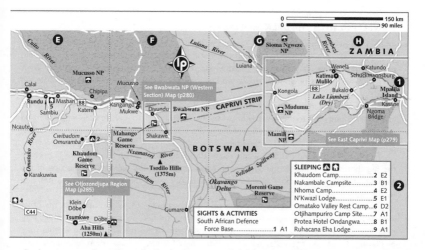

SIGHTS & ACTIVITIES
South African Defence
Force Base.......................1 A1

SLEEPING
Khaudom Camp..................2 E2
Nakambale Campsite...........3 B1
Nhoma Camp.....................4 E2
N'Kwazi Lodge...................5 E1
Omatako Valley Rest Camp...6 D2
Otjihampuriro Camp Site.......7 A1
Protea Hotel Ondangwa.......8 B1
Ruhacana Eha Lodge 9 A1

See Bwabwata NP (Western Section) Map (p280)

See East Caprivi Map (p279)

See Otjozondjupa Region Map (p285)

at the large covered market, which proffers everything from clothing and baskets to mopane worms and glasses of freshly brewed *tambo* (beer).

If for some reason you get stuck here for the night, **Oshandira Lodge** (☎ 220443; oshandira@ iway.na; s/d N$425/695; ☒), next to the airstrip, offers simple but spacious rooms that surround a landscaped pool and thatched open-air restaurant.

A slightly more upmarket option is the **Oshakati Country Lodge** (☎ 222380; countrylodge@ mweb.com; Robert Mugabe Rd; s/d N$695/1010; ☒ ☐ ☒), a favourite of visiting government dignitaries and businessmen, though it's your best bet if you're a slave to modern comforts.

From the bus terminal at the market, combis leave frequently for destinations in the north.

UUTAPI (OMBALANTU) & AROUND
☎ 065

The area around Uutapi (also known as Ombalantu), which lies on the C46 between Oshakati and Ruacana, is home to a number of widely revered national heritage sites, and warrants a quick visit if you've got your own wheels and are passing through the area.

The most famous attraction in Uutapi is the former **South African Defence Force (SADF) base** (Map pp272–3), which is dominated by an enormous baobab tree. This tree, known locally as *omukwa*, was once used to shelter cattle from invaders, and later was used as a turret from which to ambush invading tribes.

It didn't work with the South African forces, however, who invaded and used the tree for everything from a chapel to a coffee shop.

To reach the fort, turn left at the police station 350m south of the Total petrol station and look for an obscure grassy track winding between desultory buildings towards the conspicuous baobab.

Another famous destination is the town of **Ongulumbashe**, which is regarded as the birthplace of modern Namibia. On 26 August 1966 the first shots of the war for Namibian independence were fired from this patch of scrubland. The site is also where the People's Liberation Army of Namibia enjoyed its first victory over the South African troops, who had been charged with rooting out and quelling potential guerrilla activities. At the site, you can still see some reconstructed bunkers and the 'needle' monument marking the battle. An etching on the reverse side honours the Pistolet-Pulemyot Shpagina (PPSh), the Russian-made automatic rifle that played a major role in the conflict.

From Uutapi, turn south on the D3612 to the village of Otsandi (Tsandi). At the eastern edge of the village, turn west down an unnumbered track and continue 20km to Ongulumbashe. Be advised that this area is considered to be politically sensitive – you will need permission to visit the site from the Swapo office in Uutapi.

If you're feeling especially patriotic you can also visit the town of **Ongandjera**, which is the birthplace of former president Sam Nujoma.

TRAVELLING WITH CHILDREN *Ian Ketcheson*

In 2003 we packed up our home in Toronto and set off on a 15-month Namibian adventure. We knew that travelling halfway around the world with our daughter, Renée, would be a big undertaking, but we saw ourselves as experienced travellers ready to handle anything. What we didn't realise was how much the world changes when you are travelling with a little kid in tow.

Our biggest challenge in our first weeks in Namibia was adjusting not to the differences of life in another country but to the new rhythm of family life, and finding ways to keep Renée amused in a country with endless open road, where the other kids spoke little or no English, and when we often spent all day, every day, together.

We also quickly found out that when you're travelling with a child, the little things become the big things. While Renée quickly became blasé about spotting baboons by the side of the road, she fussed over the differences in the taste of soy sauce and ketchup and was petrified by the most innocuous insects.

It also took her several weeks to muster up enough courage to go and play with the other kids. Several months in, however, it was not uncommon for her to spend most of the day running from our house to our neighbour's, making pretend sand meals, shucking marula fruit, or playing dodge ball and other games with her new friends. This was soon followed by the acquisition of more vocabulary than both my wife and I combined, and produced the great moment when she was able to tell our neighbour, in fluent Oshikwanyama, that she wanted to go to Oshikango to buy a chicken.

Namibia is a country of wide-open spaces, and there are places where you can drive hundreds of kilometres with only a bend or two in the road. Music and books on tape were our salvation on these trips, with Renée settling in with her handful of children's tapes on a steady loop in the back seat.

With all that time on the road, safety became one of our big concerns. All parents travelling with children to Namibia should make sure they bring their own car seat with them, and be prepared for vehicles and drivers that have never seen one installed before. You should also never drive after dark, never take a white-knuckle taxi ride on the long journeys between cities and you should avoid minibuses.

Wildlife parks gained another level of interest for us, as we got to experience safaris through a kid's eyes. We had great discussions about why we can't rub noses with lions and sang wonderful songs about how we could lure elephants out of the bushes with peanut butter. Most days in Etosha (p264), Renée would wear herself out by early afternoon and would often fall asleep while watching zebras and elephants, only to rouse herself for ice cream and a late-afternoon swim back at the camp.

Be warned, however, that Namibia does not have a lot of kid-friendly activities on offer, so it is important to try and plan some surprises for them, and it's a good idea to bring your own entertainment with you. Renée would put up with a lot of long driving on the promise of a quick game of soccer at a dusty roadside stop, or perhaps a picnic in a dried-up riverbed. We always made sure that her menagerie of indestructible Fisher-Price figurines, sand toys and colouring books were close at hand. Although toys tend to be rather expensive in Namibia, we made sure that when we made a trip to Oshakati or Windhoek we swung by the Game or Pick & Pay department stores to pick up a new colouring book, or yet another set of sand toys.

Looking back on our time in Namibia, we are thankful that so many of our memories are preserved in the writings from my blog. Even if you aren't able to bring your own computer, it is worth spending an hour or two in an internet cafe every once in a while jotting down your thoughts and memories. Your child's grandparents will thank you immediately, and you'll thank yourself long after you have returned home.

Canadian Ian Ketcheson lived for two years in the village of Odibo
with his wife and young daughter.

The rose-coloured kraal that was his boyhood home is now a national shrine, and is distinguished from its neighbours by a prominent Swapo flag hung in a tree. It's fine to look from a distance, but the kraal remains a private home and isn't open to the public.

Ongandjera lies on the D3612, 52km southeast of Uutapi near Okahao. It's also accessible via the C41 from Oshakati.

RUACANA
☎ 065

The tiny Kunene River town of Ruacana (from the Herero words *orua hakahana* – the rapids) was built as a company town to serve the 320-megawatt underground Ruacana hydroelectric project, which now supplies over half of Namibia's power requirements. Here, the Kunene River splits into several channels before plunging 85m over a dramatic escarpment and through a 2km-long gorge of its own making.

Sights

At one time, **Ruacana Falls** was a natural wonder, though all that changed thanks to Angola's Calueque Dam, 20km upstream, and NamPower's Ruacana power plant. What little water makes it past the first barrage is collected by an intake weir, 1km above the falls, which ushers it into the hydroelectric plant to turn the turbines. On the rare occasions when there's a surfeit of water, Ruacana returns to its former glory. In wetter years, it's no exaggeration to say it rivals Victoria Falls – if you hear that it's flowing, you certainly won't regret a side trip to see it (and it may be the closest you ever get to Angola).

To reach the falls, turn north 15km west of Ruacana and follow the signs towards the border crossing. To visit the gorge, visitors must temporarily exit Namibia by signing the immigration register. From the Namibian border crossing, bear left (to the right lies the decrepit Angolan border crossing) to the end of the road. There you can look around the ruins of the old power station, which was destroyed by Namibian liberation forces. The buildings are pockmarked with scars from mortar rounds and gunfire, providing a stark contrast to the otherwise peaceful scene.

Sleeping

Otjihampuriro Camp Site (Map pp272-3; ☎ 270120; www .nacombta.com.an; camping per person N$50) This community-run campsite sits alongside the river and has a good measure of shade and privacy. There are also braai (barbecue) pits, hot showers and environmentally friendly pit toilets. Local community members can organise trips to Ruacana Falls or to nearby Himba villages for a small fee.

Ruhacana Eha Lodge (Map pp272-3; ☎ 271500; www .ruacanaehalodge.com.na; Springbom Ave; camping per person N$55; huts per person N$180; s/d N$630/860; ⬚ ⬚ ⬚) This upmarket lodge appeals to travellers of all budgets by offering manicured campsites and rustic A-frame huts alongside its polished rooms. An attractive oasis in the middle of Ruacana, the Eha Lodge is highlighted by its lush gardens and refreshing plunge pool.

Getting There & Away

Ruacana is near the junction of roads between Opuwo, Owambo country and the rough 4WD route along the Kunene River to Swartbooi's Drift (p301). Note that mileage signs along the C46 confuse Ruacana town and the power plant, which are 15km apart. Both are signposted 'Ruacana' – don't let them throw you too badly.

For westbound travellers, the 24-hour BP petrol station is the last before the Atlantic; it's also the terminal for afternoon minibuses to and from Oshakati and Ondangwa, costing around N$30.

The Angolan border crossing is open to Namibians, though others need an Angolan visa that allows overland entry.

KAVANGO REGION

The heavily wooded and gently rolling Kavango region is dominated by the Okavango River and its broad flood plains. The rich soil and fishing grounds support large communities of Mbukushu, Sambiyu and Caprivi peoples, who are renowned for their high-quality woodcarvings – animal figures, masks, wooden beer mugs, walking sticks and boxes are carved in the light *dolfhout* (wild teak) hardwood and make excellent souvenirs. Although there's little wildlife nowadays outside Khaudom, the game reserve itself arguably rivals Etosha as Namibia's top safari experience.

Rundu is also a convenient overnight spot to break up the long drive to/from the Caprivi Strip, and the musical sound of Portuguese in

NORTHERN NAMIBIA

the air is a nice contrast to more anglophone parts of the country.

At Sambiu, east of Rundu and 30km along the Okavango River road, is a **Roman Catholic mission museum** (☎ 251111; admission free; ☺ by appointment), which exhibits crafts and woodcarvings from Angola and Kavango. Phone to arrange a visit, or take your chances and simply stop by during daylight hours.

RUNDU
☎ 066

Rundu, a sultry tropical outpost on the bluffs above the Okavango River, is a major centre of activity for Namibia's growing Angolan community. Although the town has little of specific interest for tourists, the area is home to a number of wonderful lodges where you can laze along the riverside, and spot crocs and hippos doing pretty much the same.

Take a stroll around the large covered **market**, which is one of Africa's most sophisticated informal sales outlets. From July to September, don't miss the fresh papayas, sold straight from the trees. Alternatively, head for the **Khemo Open Market** (☎ daily),

where you can shop for both African staples and Kavango handicrafts.

Sleeping & Eating
Lodges in Rundu and the surrounding region offer a variety of excursions, including sunset cruises, canoeing, fishing, horse riding and day trips to Angola (though you will need to arrange for a visa in advance).

Self-caterers will find supplies at the well-stocked Spar Supermarket in the town centre.

Sarasungu River Lodge (☎ 255161; www.sarasunguriverlodge.com; camping per person N$70, s/d/tr N$445/620/830; ☒) The newest lodge in the Rundu area is situated in a secluded riverine clearing 4km from the town centre, and has attractive thatched chalets that surround a landscaped pool.

Hakusembe Lodge (☎ 257010; www.natron.net /hakusembe; camping per person N$80, chalets per person incl half board from N$880; ☒ ☒) This secluded hideaway sits amid lush riverside gardens, and comprises eight luxury chalets (one of which is floating) decked out in safari prints and locally crafted furniture. It lies 17km down the Nkurenkuru Rd, then 2km north to the riverbank.

Ozzy's Beer House (☎ 256723; meals N$35-60) A popular stop with passing motorists, Ozzy's has plenty of kilojoule-loaded meals to fuel hungry drivers, as well as ice-cold draft beer if you're retiring in Rundu for the night.

Getting There & Away
BUS
Several weekly **Intercape Mainliner** (www.intercape .co.za) buses make the seven-hour trip between Windhoek and Rundu (fares from N$365). Book your tickets in advance online as this service continues on to Victoria Falls and fills up quickly.

Combis connect Windhoek and Rundu with fairly regular frequency, and a ride shouldn't cost more than N$200. From Rundu, routes fan out to various towns and cities in the north, with fares costing less than N$30 a ride. Both buses and combis depart and drop-off at the Shell petrol station.

CAR & MOTORCYCLE
Drivers travelling to and from Grootfontein should take special care due to the many pedestrians, animals and potholes that create road hazards. Note that military convoys

along the Caprivi Strip are no longer necessary, and the route has been considered safe for self-drivers since the end of the Angolan Civil War in 2002.

FERRY

The rowboat ferry between Rundu and Calai in Angola operates on demand from the riverbanks.

KHAUDOM GAME RESERVE
☎ 066

Exploring the largely undeveloped 384,000-hectare Khaudom Game Reserve is an intense wilderness challenge that is guaranteed not to disappoint. Meandering sand tracks lure you through pristine bush and across *omiramba* (fossil river valleys), which run parallel to the east–west-oriented Kalahari dunes. As there is virtually no signage, and navigation is largely based on GPS coordinates and topographic maps, few tourists make the effort to extend their safari experience beyond the secure confines of Etosha.

But that is precisely why Khaudom is worth exploring – as one of Namibia's most important game reserves, Khaudom is home to one of only two protected populations of lions, and it's the only place in the country where African wild dogs can be spotted. The reserve also protects large populations of elephants, zebras, giraffes, wildebeests, kudus, oryxes and tsessebes, and there's a good chance you'll be able to spot large herds of roan antelopes here. If you're an avid birder, Khaudom sup-

ports 320 different species, including summer migratory birds such as storks, crakes, bitterns, orioles, eagles and falcons.

As an added bonus, you are actually allowed to get out of your car in Khaudom at any point, an action that is largely prohibited at the majority of wildlife reserves in Namibia. If you use this privilege judiciously, you can check the muddy edges of waterholes: fresh predator tracks indicate areas in which to invest some time. However, always exercise extreme caution when searching around waterholes and never walk around alone. In Khaudom, perhaps more than anywhere else in the country, do not forget that you truly are in the wild.

Orientation & Information

In order to explore the reserve by private 4WD vehicle, you will have to be completely self-sufficient, as petrol and supplies are only available in towns along the Caprivi Strip. Water is available inside the reserve, though it must be boiled or treated prior to drinking. At a bare minimum, you will need a GPS unit, a proper topographic map and a compass, and lots of common sense and genuine confidence and experience in driving a 4WD.

Tracks in the reserve are mostly sand, though they deteriorate into mud slicks after the rains. As a result, Namibia Wildlife Resorts (NWR) requires that parties travel in a convoy of at least two self-sufficient 4WDs, and are equipped with enough food, water and petrol to survive for at least three days. Caravans, trailers and motorcycles are prohibited.

Wildlife viewing is best from June to October, when herds congregate around the waterholes and along the *omiramba*. November to April is the richest time to visit for bird-watchers, though you will have to be prepared for a difficult slog through muddy tracks.

Sleeping

In the past, NWR used to administer two official campsites in the park, though after one too many episodes of elephants gone wild, it's decided to close up shop. The remains of the camps are still present, and you're encouraged to camp there (the alternative is pitching a tent in the bush), though once again we need to stress that you must be completely self-sufficient before visiting Khaudom.

Sikereti Camp (Map p285) 'Cigarette' camp is located in a shady grove of terminalia trees, though full appreciation of this place requires sensitivity to its subtle charms, namely isolation and silence.

Khaudom Camp (Map pp272–3) This dune-top camp overlooks an ephemeral waterhole, and is somewhat akin to the Kalahari in miniature.

Getting There & Away

From the north, take the sandy track from Katere on the B8 (signposted 'Khaudom'), 120km east of Rundu. After 45km you'll reach the Cwibadom Omuramba, where you should turn east into the park.

From the south, you can reach Sikereti Camp via Tsumkwe. From Tsumkwe, it's 20km to Groote Döbe and another 15km from there to the Dorslandboom turning (see the Map p285). It's then 25km north to Sikereti Camp.

THE CAPRIVI STRIP

Namibia's spindly northeastern appendage, the Caprivi Strip is typified by expanses of mopane and terminalia broadleaf forest, and punctuated by *shonas* or fossilised parallel dunes that are the remnants of a drier climate. For most travellers, the Caprivi serves as the easiest access route connecting the main body of Namibia with Victoria Falls and Botswana's Chobe National Park. However, visitors with time and patience can get off the beaten path here, exploring such hidden gems as Mudumu, Mamili and Bwabwata National Parks.

BWABWATA NATIONAL PARK
☎ 066

First gazetted in 1999 but only very recently recognised as a national park, Bwabwata was established to rehabilitate local wildlife populations. Prior to the 2002 Angolan ceasefire, this area saw almost no visitors, and wildlife populations had been virtually wiped out by rampant poaching instigated by ongoing conflict. Now that peace has returned, the animals are miraculously back again, and tourism is starting to pick up once more.

If you come here expecting Etosha, you'll be severely disappointed, though if you're looking to get off the beaten path, this is a great area to explore while it's still relatively undiscovered.

Orientation

Bwabwata includes five main zones: the Divundu area, the West Caprivi Triangle, the Mahango Game Reserve, Popa Falls and the now-defunct West Caprivi Game Reserve. The Mahango Game Reserve presently has the largest concentrations of wildlife, and is resultantly the focus of most safaris in the area.

Divundu, with two (nominally) 24-hour petrol stations and a relatively well-stocked supermarket, is merely a product of the road junction. The real population centres are the neighbouring villages of Mukwe, Andara and Bagani. Divundu is marked as Bagani on some maps and road signs, though technically they're separate places about 2km apart.

The West Caprivi Triangle, the wedge bounded by Angola to the north, Botswana to the south and the Kwando River to the east, was formerly the richest wildlife area in the Caprivi. Poaching, bush clearing, burning and human settlement have greatly reduced wildlife, though you can still access the area via the road along the western bank of the Kwando River near Kongola.

Finally, the Golden Hwy between Rundu and Katima Mulilo traverses the former West Caprivi Game Reserve. Although this was once a haven for large herds of elephants, it served as a pantry for local hunters and poachers for decades and is now largely devoid of wildlife.

Sights
MAHANGO GAME RESERVE

This small but diverse 25,000-hectare **park** (per person/vehicle N$40/10; ☉ sunrise-sunset) occupies a broad flood plain north of the Botswana border and west of the Okavango River. It attracts large concentrations of thirsty elephants and herd animals, particularly in the dry season. As in Khaudom Game Reserve, you are permitted to leave your vehicle, but exercise caution at all times.

With a 2WD vehicle, you can either zip through on the Mahango transit route or follow the Scenic Loop Drive past Kwetche picnic site, east of the main road. With a 4WD you can also explore the 20km Circular Drive Loop, which follows the *omiramba* and offers the best wildlife viewing. It's particularly nice to stop beside the river in the afternoon and watch the elephants swimming and drinking among hippos and crocodiles.

POPA FALLS

Near Bagani, the Okavango River plunges down a broad series of cascades known as **Popa Falls** (per person/vehicle N$40/10; ☼ sunrise-sunset). The falls are nothing to get steamed up about, especially if Victoria Falls lies in your sights. In fact, the falls are actually little more than large rapids, though periods

of low water do expose a drop of 4m. Aside from the 'falls', there are good opportunities here for hiking and bird-watching, though swimming is definitely not safe as there are hungry crocs about.

Sleeping

While private concessions here handle their own bookings, the campsite at Popa Falls is run by NWR and must be prebooked through its main office in Windhoek (see p234).

WESTERN SECTION

Ngepi Camp (Map p280; ☎ 259903; www.ngepicamp .com; camping per person N$50; bush/tree huts per person N$300/430) Travellers rave about this place, and we agree: it's probably one of the best backpacker lodges in Namibia. You can swim in the Okavango River 'cage' (it keeps you and the crocs at a safe distance from one another) and spend evenings in the inviting bush bar. Crash for the night in a bush or tree hut, or pitch a tent by the river and let the sounds of hippos splashing ease you into a restful sleep. Ngepi is not a luxury camp – showers are

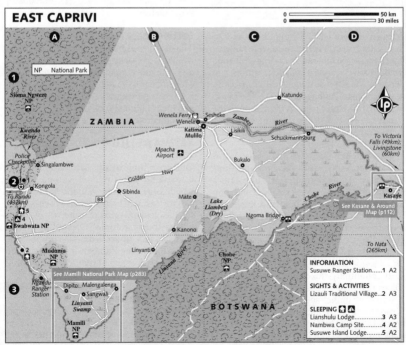

EAST CAPRIVI

INFORMATION
Susuwe Ranger Station......1 A2

SIGHTS & ACTIVITIES
Lizauli Traditional Village..2 A3

SLEEPING
Lianshulu Lodge..............3 A3
Nambwa Camp Site..........4 A2
Susuwe Island Lodge........5 A2

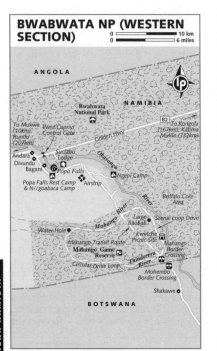

BWABWATA NP (WESTERN SECTION)

EASTERN SECTION
At the eastern end of the park are several accommodation options. See also p282.

Nambwa Camp Site (Map p279; camping per person N$50) Nambwa, 14km south of Kongola, lacks facilities, but it's the only official camp in the park, and it provides easy access to the wildlife-rich oxbow lagoon, about 5km south. Book and pick up a permit at the Susuwe ranger station, about 4km north of Kongola (4WD access only) on the west bank of the river. To reach the camp, follow the 4WD track south along the western bank of the Kwando River.

Susuwe Island Lodge (Map p279; ☎ in South Africa 27-11 706 7207; www.islandsinafrica.com; per person low/high season from N$2480/3220; ☒ ☐ ☒) This posh safari lodge is located on a remote island in the Kwando River and surrounded by a diverse habitat of savannah, woodland and wetland. Accommodation is in six stylish brick and thatch chalets adorned in soft earth tones. Amenities include an open-fire lounge, a gourmet bar-restaurant, private plunge pools and an outdoor viewing deck for taking in the beauty of the area. Susuwe is accessible only by charter flight or 4WD. Prebooking is mandatory.

Getting There & Away
The paved road between Rundu and Katima Mulilo is perfectly suited to 2WD vehicles, as is the gravel road between Divundu and Mohembo (on the Botswana border). Drivers may transit the park without charge, but you will incur national park entry fees if you use the loop drive through the park.

KATIMA MULILO
☎ 066
Out on a limb at the eastern end of the Caprivi Strip lies remote Katima Mulilo, which is as far from Windhoek (1200km) as you can get in Namibia. Once known for the elephants that marched through the village streets, Katima is devoid of wildlife these days – apart from the hippos and crocodiles in the Zambezi – though it continues to thrive as a border town and minor commercial centre.

Sleeping & Eating
Mukusi Cabins (☎ 253255; Engen petrol station; camping N$50, s/d from N$300/350; ☒) Although it lacks the riverside location of other properties in the

rough and there's no TV – but this all adds to the rustic charm. There's also a wide range of inexpensive excursions, including Mahango wildlife drives, canoe trips, booze cruises, and *mokoro* (traditional dugout canoe) trips in the Okavango Panhandle (p137). The camp is located 4km off the main road, though the sandy access can prove difficult without a high-clearance vehicle. Phone the lodge if you need a lift from Divundu.

Popa Falls Rest Camp (Map p280; camping per person N$50, s/d cabins N$350/500) Recent renovations have turned this humble rest camp into a sparkling riverside spot. A small on-site shop sells the essentials, while a field kitchen is available for self-catering. Facilities include hot showers, sit-down flush toilets and braai pits.

N//goabaca Camp (Map p280; www.nacobta.com.na; camping per person N$50, s/d cabins N$350/500) This leafy community-run campsite sits beside the Okavango River opposite the Popa Falls Rest Camp. Any money spent here supports local Kxao (Bushmen) communities, and there are trackers on the staff here who can arrange walking ventures out into the bush.

area, this oasis behind the petrol station has a good range of accommodation, from simple rooms with fans to small but comfortable air-con cabins. The lovely bar-restaurant dishes up a range of unexpected options – including calamari, snails and kingklip – as well steak and chicken standbys.

Caprivi River Lodge (☎ 253300; www.capririverlodge.info; camping per person N$50, s N$305-800, d N$445-1075; ❷ ⚄) This diverse lodge offers options to suit travellers of all budgets, from a grassy campsite and rustic chalets with shared bathrooms to slightly more luxurious wooden cabins with en suite bathrooms. It offers a decent variety of activities, including kayaking, boating, fishing and wildlife drives in the various Caprivi parks. The lodge is located 5km from town along Ngoma Rd.

Protea Hotel Zambezi Lodge (☎ 253149; http://namibweb.com/zambezilodge.htm; camping per person N$50, s/d from N$650/955; ❷ ▢ ⚄) This stunning riverside lodge is perched on the banks of the Zambezi and features a floating bar where you can watch the crocs and hippos below. The campsite is amid a flowery garden, while accommodation is in well-equipped modern

rooms that open up to small verandahs and ample views.

Shopping

Caprivi Arts Centre (⊙ 8am-5.30pm) Run by the Caprivi Art & Cultural Association, the centre is a good place to look for local curios and crafts, including elephant and hippo wood-carvings, baskets, bowls, kitchen implements, and traditional knives and spears.

Getting There & Away

With a private vehicle, the **Ngoma Bridge border crossing** (⊙ 7am-6pm) enables you to access Chobe National Park (Botswana), Kasane (Botswana) and Victoria Falls (Zimbabwe) in just a couple of hours. If you stick to the Chobe National Park Transit Route, you're excused from paying Botswana park fees.

The new 1km-long **Wenela bridge** (⊙ 7am-6pm) spans the Zambezi between Katima Mulilo and Wenela, providing easy access to Livingstone and other destinations in Zambia. If you're heading to the falls, the road is now tarred all the way to Livingstone, and is accessible by 2WD vehicle, even in the rainy season.

AIR

Air Namibia has several weekly departures between Windhoek's Eros Airport and Katima's Mpacha Airport, located 18km southwest of town.

BUS & MINIBUS

Several weekly **Intercape Mainliner** (www.intercape.co.za) buses make the 17-hour run between Windhoek and Katima Mulilo. Book your tickets (fares from N$350) in advance online as this service continues on to Victoria Falls and fills up quickly.

Combis connect Windhoek and Katima with fairly regular frequency, and a ride shouldn't cost more than N$225. From Katima, routes fan out to various towns and cities in the north, with fares costing less than N$30 a ride.

CAR

The paved Golden Hwy runs between Katima Mulilo and Rundu and is accessible to all 2WD vehicles.

HITCHING

The best places to wait for lifts between Katima Mulilo and Rundu are at the petrol

KATIMA MULILO

0	300 m
0	0.2 miles

ZAMBIA

Zambezi River

Ngoma Rd

To Wenela Bridge to Zambia (4km)

To Protea Hotel Zambezi Lodge (700m); Caprivi River Lodge (5km); Ngoma Bridge (67km)

Police

Market

Bank of Windhoek

To Mpacha Airport (18km); Kongola (119km); Rundu (553km); Windhoek (1253km)

SLEEPING 🛏
Mukusi Cabins....................**1** A2

SHOPPING 🛍
Caprivi Arts Centre............**2** B2

TRANSPORT
Combi Stop.....................(see 3)
Mainliner Bus Stop............**3** A2

stations in Divundu and Kongola. Chances are that any eastbound/westbound vehicle from Rundu/Katima Mulilo will be doing the entire route.

MPALILA ISLAND
☎ 066

Mpalila (Impalilia) Island, a wedge driven between the Chobe and Zambezi Rivers, represents Namibia's outer limits at the 'four-corners meeting' of Zimbabwe, Botswana, Namibia and Zambia. The island itself, which is within easy reach by boat from Chobe National Park, is home to a handful of exclusive lodges catering to upmarket tourists in search of luxurious isolation.

Prebooking is essential for all accommodation on the island. All lodges offer a variety of activities for guests, including cruises on the Chobe River, guided wildlife drives, fishing expeditions, island walks and *mokoro* trips. Rates include full board and transfers.

Overlooking the impressive Mombova rapids, **Impalila Island Lodge** (Map p112; ☎ in South Africa 27-11 706 7207; www.islandsinafrica.com; per person low/high season US$350/550; ☒ ☒) is a stylish retreat of eight luxury chalets built on elevated decks at the water's edge. The centrepiece of the lodge is a pair of ancient baobab trees, which tower majestically over the grounds.

The most famous spot on the island is **Chobe Savannah Lodge** (Map p114; ☎ 686 1243; www.desertdelta.com; per person low/high season US$375/650; ☒ ☒), which is renowned for its panoramic views of the wildlife-rich Puku Flats. Each stylishly decorated room has a private verandah where you can spot animals without ever having to change out of your pyjamas.

Access to Mpalila Island is either by charter flight or by boat from Kasane (Botswana) though lodges will organise all transport for their booked guests.

MUDUMU NATIONAL PARK
☎ 066

Mudumu National Park has a tragic history of environmental abuse and neglect, though it's back on the map once again thanks largely to the efforts of Grant Burton and Marie Holstensen of Lianshulu Lodge (see right). As the owners of a vast private concession within the park boundaries, Grant and Marie have worked closely with both local communities and the Ministry of Environment and Tourism (MET) to link conservation, sustain-

able land use and economic development in the Caprivi.

Although Mudumu was once one of Namibia's most stunning wildlife habitats, by the late 1980s the park had become an unofficial hunting concession gone mad. In under a decade, the wildlife was decimated by trophy hunters, which prompted MET to gazette Mudumu National Park in a last-ditch effort to rescue the area from total devastation. Mudumu's wildlife has begun to return, but it will take years of wise policy making and community awareness before the area approaches its former glory. In the meantime, a visit here lends further support to an ambitious project that aims to improve the local economy while restoring some of Mudumu's lost splendour.

Sights

A joint partnership between the owners of Lianshulu Lodge, MET, private benefactors and the Lizauli community, the **Lizauli Traditional Village** (Map p279; per person N$20; ☒ 9am-5pm Mon-Sat) was established to educate visitors about traditional Caprivian lifestyles, and to provide insight into the local diet, fishing and farming methods, village politics, music, games, traditional medicine, basketry and tool making. After the guided tour, visitors can shop for good-value local handicrafts without the sales pressure.

The aforementioned partnership also recruits Mudumu game scouts from Lizauli and other villages, and has been given responsibility for community conservation and antipoaching education. Most importantly, the project provides a forum in which locals can interact with tourists, and benefit both economically and culturally from the adoption of a strict policy of environmental protection.

Sleeping

Lianshulu Lodge (Map p279; ☎ in South Africa 27-11 257 5111; r per person from N$3299; ☒) Dominated by an impressive bar and dining area that overlooks the surrounding wetlands, Lianshulu Lodge has some of the most beautifully situated accommodation in all of Namibia. Around lunchtime, leguaans (water monitors) can be seen about the place, while at dinnertime, hippos emerge from the river to graze on the lawns. In the late evening you will be serenaded by an enchanting wetland chorus of insects and the haunting 'tink-tink' of bell frogs, before you fall asleep in one of only 10 exclusive stand-alone chalets. The lodge offers a range of excursions, including the popular pontoon river cruise, where you are likely to see herds of elephants as well as nesting colonies of carmine bee-eaters.

Getting There & Away
To reach Lianshulu Lodge, follow the D3511 about 40km south of Kongola, and then turn west on the signposted track.

MAMILI NATIONAL PARK
In years of good rains, this wild and seldom-visited **national park** (per person/vehicle N$40/10) becomes Namibia's equivalent of Botswana's Okavango Delta. Forested islands fringed by

reed and papyrus marshes foster some of the country's richest bird-watching, with more than 430 recorded species to count. Poaching has taken a toll, though Mamili's wildlife, mainly semiaquatic species such as hippos, crocodiles, pukus, red lechwes, sitatungas and otters, will still impress.

Birding is best from December to March, though the vast majority of the park is inaccessible during this time. Wildlife viewing is best from June to August, and is especially good on Nkasa and Lupala islands.

There is a sparse network of unmaintained wilderness campsites in the park, though you must bring in everything, including your own water, and be prepared for extremely rough road conditions. Although there is a generally

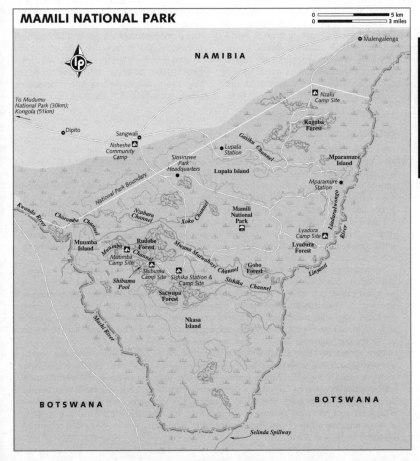

MAMILI NATIONAL PARK

a ranger to collect park fees at the entrance gate, you're all alone once inside, and it's highly recommended that you travel as part of a convoy. Needless to say, a 4WD vehicle with high clearance is mandatory, and you can expect lots and lots of deep mud.

Access to the park is by 4WD track from Malengalenga, northeast of the park, or from Sangwali village, which is due north.

OTJOZONDJUPA

Otjozondjupa is commonly referred to as Bushmanland, a pejorative term that unfortunately seems to resist dying away. A largely flat landscape of scrub desert lying at the edge of the Kalahari, Otjozondjupa is part of the traditional homeland of the Ju/hoansi San, who were among the original habitants of Southern Africa. Following a spurt in worldwide interest in Kalahari cultures, tourist traffic has increased throughout the region, though any expectations you might have of witnessing an entirely self-sufficient hunter-gatherer society will, sadly, not be met here.

For some people, witnessing the stark reality of the modern Ju/hoansi San lifestyle is a sobering experience fraught with disappointments. Hunting is forbidden throughout the region, and most communities have largely abandoned foraging in favour of cheap, high-calorie foods such as *pap* (corn meal) and rice, which are purchased in bulk from shops. Try to look beyond the dire realities of the San's economic situation, and attempt to use the experience as a rare chance to interact with the modern-day descendants of perhaps all of our ancestors.

HISTORY

The word San is a collective term referring to the traditional groups of hunter-gatherers that occupy sub-Saharan Africa, and whose languages belong to the Khoisan family of languages. According to archaeological evidence, San communities were present in Namibia as early as 20,000 years ago, and left behind written records in the form of rock paintings. By AD 1000, however, the southward Bantu migration pushed the San into inhospitable areas, including the Kalahari. Regardless,

---

THE SHAPE OF THINGS PAST

The Caprivi Strip's notably odd shape is a story in itself. When Germany laid claim to British-administered Zanzibar in 1890, Britain naturally objected, and soon after the Berlin Conference was called to settle the dispute. In the end, Britain kept Zanzibar, but Germany was offered a vast strip of land from the British-administered Bechuanaland protectorate (now Botswana). Named the Caprivi Strip after German chancellor General Count Georg Leo von Caprivi di Caprara di Montecuccoli, this vital tract of land provided Germany with access to the Zambezi River.

For the Germans, the motivation for this swap was to ultimately create a colonial empire that spanned from the South Atlantic coast to Tanganyika (now Tanzania) and the Indian Ocean. Unfortunately for them, the British colonisation of Rhodesia stopped the Germans well upstream of Victoria Falls, which proved a considerable barrier to navigation on the Zambezi.

Interestingly enough, the absorption of the Caprivi Strip into German South West Africa didn't make world news, and it was nearly 20 years before some of its population discovered that they were under German control. In 1908 the German government finally dispatched one Hauptmann Streitwolf to oversee local administration, a move that prompted the Lozi tribe to round up all the cattle – including those belonging to rival tribes – and drive them out of the area. The cattle were eventually returned to their rightful owners, but most of the Lozi people chose to remain in Zambia and Angola rather than submit to German rule.

On 4 August 1914 Britain declared war on Germany and, just over a month later, the German administrative seat at Schuckmannsburg was attacked by the British from their base at Sesheke and then seized by the police. An apocryphal tale recounts that German governor Von Frankenberg was entertaining the English resident administrator of Northern Rhodesia (now Zambia) when a servant presented a message from British authorities in Livingstone. After reading it, the British official declared his host a prisoner of war, and thus, Schuckmannsburg fell into British hands. Whether the story is true or not, the seizure of Schuckmannsburg was the first Allied occupation of enemy territory in WWI.

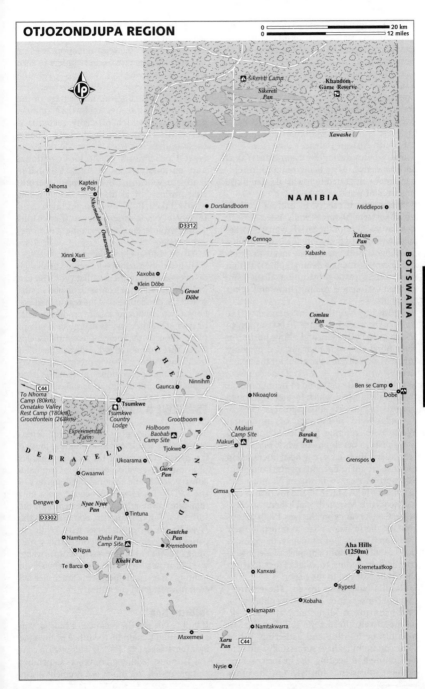

OTJOZONDJUPA REGION

0 ____ 20 km
0 ____ 12 miles

Sikereti Camp

Sikereti Pan

Khaudom Game Reserve

Xawashe

NAMIBIA

Nhoma

Kaptein se Pos

Nhomadom Omuramba

Dorslandboom

Middlepos

D3312

Cennqo

Xeixoa Pan

Xabashe

Xinni Xuri

Xaxoba

Klein Döbe

Groot Döbe

Comlau Pan

B O T S W A N A

THE

Gaunca

Ninnihm

Nkoaqǃosi

Ben se Camp

Dobe

C44

To Nhoma Camp (80km); Omatako Valley Rest Camp (180km); Grootfontein (268km)

Tsumkwe

Tsumkwe Country Lodge

Grootboom

Makuri Camp Site

Baraka Pan

Holboom Baobab Camp Site

Makuri

Experimental Farm

Tjokwe

Grenspos

D E B R A N E L D

Ukoarama

Gura Pan

P A N V E L D

Gwaanwi

Gimsa

Dengwe

Nyae Nyae Pan

Tintuna

D3302

Gautcha Pan

Aha Hills (1250m)

Namtsoa

Khebi Pan Camp Site

Kremeboom

Kremetaatkop

Ngua

Kanxasi

Te Barcu

Khebi Pan

Ryperd

Xobaha

Namapan

Namtakwarra

Maxemesi

Xaru Pan

C44

Nysie

NORTHERN NAMIBIA

anthropologists have dubbed the San our 'genetic Adam', stating that all living humans can ultimately trace back their lineage to this population group.

Of the six sub-Saharan countries where the San reside, Namibia is home to the second-largest population, numbering nearly 33,000 individuals. Although they once controlled expansive n!oresi (lands where one's heart is), these homelands were commandeered by the South African Defence Force (SADF) as military bases during the Namibian War of Independence. After being reduced to refugees, many migrated to towns like Tsumkwe in search of work.

Some San succeeded in finding work as unskilled farm labourers, while others worked as army trackers for the SADF, who were waging a war against Swapo in northern Namibia and Angola. Still, the majority met with grinding unemployment, a demographic shift that resulted in disease, prostitution, alcoholism, domestic violence, malnutrition and other social ills.

Following Namibian independence, the San territory shrank from 70,000 sq km to less than 10,000 sq km, and a large portion of their boreholes were expropriated by other interests, possibly in retaliation for their partnership with SADF. As a result, the San were left without sufficient land to maintain their traditional lifestyle, which further aggravated pre-existing poverty and dispossession.

Fortunately, a number of influential Westerners, ranging from academics and journalists to development workers and cultural survivalists, have long been interested in the advocacy of indigenous rights throughout Southern Africa. In northern Namibia, US filmmaker John Marshall and his British colleague Claire Marshall established the Nyae Nyae Conservancy in the late 1980s to encourage the Ju/hoansi San to return to their traditional lands. Unfortunately, the foundation has suffered from a number of ideological conflicts, including to what extent tourism should be fostered in the region.

Results have been mixed. The enforcement of conservation laws, most notably the establishment of Khaudom National Park, has negatively affected the ability of the San to continue hunting and gathering. While some communities have successfully shifted to agriculture and herding, the majority scrape by on a subsistence lifestyle. On the other hand, the Ju/hoansi San are permitted to hunt with traditional bows and arrows within their concession, and the reintroduction of game has enabled some successful hunters to earn a respectable living.

The Nyae Nyae Conservancy was also successful in facilitating the passage of the Traditional Authorities Act by the Namibian government, which officially recognised the political power of local chiefs. Today, these individuals work alongside the Nyae Nyae Conservancy at the local, regional and national levels to find sustainable land-use solutions. Furthermore, despite past philosophical disputes, tourism has firmly taken hold in Otjozondjupa, and the Nyae Nyae Conservancy now envisions Tsumkwe emerging as a prominent ecotourism hot spot.

While visiting Otjozondjupa, please be extremely sensitive to the plight of the San, though do take comfort in the fact that your visit can indeed help. Revenue from tourism plays a vital role in the development of the region, particularly if you are buying locally produced crafts or paying for the services of a guide. Perhaps more importantly, indigenous tourism helps to reassure communities like the San that their traditional culture is worth preserving, ensuring that future generations can continue learn about our common human heritage.

TSUMKWE & AROUND
☎ 064

Tsumkwe is the only real permanent settlement in the whole of Otjozondjupa, though it's merely a wide spot in the sand that consists of a few rust-covered buildings. Originally constructed as the regional headquarters of the SADF, Tsumkwe has been given a new mandate as the administrative centre of the Ju/hoansi San community, and home to the Nyae Nyae Conservancy (see left). While organised tourism in the region is still something of a work in progress, Tsumkwe is where you can arrange everything from bushwalks to hunting safaris, and inject some much-needed cash into the local community.

Information

If you're visiting the region as a tourist, you are required to stop by the office of the **Nyae Nyae Conservancy** (☎ 244011; ☾ irregular hrs) in central Tsumkwe. Although travellers sometimes complain that the office is extremely disorganised, it's still recommended that you book activities through the official channels rather than striking off on your own. This practice ensures that the money you spend ends up in the community fund rather than in the pockets of one or two individuals.

There are no officially posted prices for activities, though you can expect to be charged a reasonably modest amount for every person that accompanies you. English-speaking guides command the largest fee, generally in the realm of N$200 to N$250 per day plus food, while hunters and foragers expect around N$75 to N$100 per outing. You need to be very clear from the outset how many people you plan to pay as the conservancy will sometimes assign as many as five hunters and gatherers to accompany you on an outing. It is also possible to arrange overnight stays in villages, and traditional music and performances are also on offer.

While you are out travelling in the bush, you will inevitably come across San communities, and the temptation to snap photos without permission inevitably exists. However photogenic a situation might be, it is important to always ask permission before taking a photo, especially since your subject will generally ask for either money or a small gift. Before leaving Tsumkwe, it's a good idea to stock up on small bills, or better yet, do some grocery shopping in town and be prepared to trade healthy food items for snapshots. The San have a long history of gift giving, and an appreciation of this tradition will quickly win you respect.

When visiting San villages, visitors are expected to either purchase or trade for beadwork, walking sticks, ostrich-shell necklaces, bow and arrow sets, and so on. Trading is a wonderful practice worth encouraging, and prized items include T-shirts, shoes, trousers, baseball caps and other useful items. People will also ask for sugar and tobacco – you'll have to decide whether to trade these products, given their attendant health risks. In any case, please trade fairly, avoid excessive payment and help keep local dignity intact by resisting the urge to hand out gifts for nothing.

Sights
VILLAGE VISITS
While stereotypes of the San abound from misleading Hollywood cinematic representations to misconstrued notions of a primitive people living in the bush, San society is extremely complex. Before visiting a San village, take some time to read up on their wonderfully rich cultural heritage – doing so will not only provide some context to your visit but also help you better engage your hosts. For a quick overview of the San, see p63.

Decades of anthropological research have provided some incredible insight into the nature of hunter-gatherer societies. In the case of the San, one of the most striking findings was that traditional communities were nonhierarchical and egalitarian, and grouped together based on kinship and tribal membership. Since groups were never able to build up a surplus of food, full-time leaders and bureaucrats never emerged.

Although village elders did wield a measure of influence over the mobile group, the sharpest division in status was between the sexes. Men provided for their families by hunting game, while women supplemented this diet by foraging for wild fruits, vegetables and nuts. While Thomas Hobbes famously noted in the 17th century that this lifestyle was 'solitary, poor, nasty, brutish and short', recent ethnographic data has shown that hunter-gatherers worked fewer hours and enjoyed more leisure time than members of industrial societies.

Hunting and foraging trips are the highlight of any visit to Otjozondjupa. Much as they have for generations, the San still use traditional gear, namely a bow with poisoned arrows for men, and a digging stick and sling for women. In the past, men would be gone for several days at a time in pursuit of herds, so you shouldn't expect to take down any big game on an afternoon excursion. But it's fascinating to see trackers in pursuit of their quarry, and you're likely to come across spoor and maybe even an antelope or two.

Foraging is very likely to turn up edible roots and tubers, wild fruits and nuts, and even medicinal plants. At the end of your excursion, the women will be more than happy to slice up a bush potato for you, which tastes particularly wonderful when roasted over a bed of hot coals. Baobab fruit is also surprisingly sweet and tangy, while protein-rich nuts are an exotic yet nutritious desert treat.

AROUND TSUMKWE
In addition to village visits, the area around Tsumkwe is home to a number of natural attractions that are accessible by private 4WD vehicle.

The Panveld

Forming an arc east of Tsumkwe is a remote landscape of phosphate-rich pans. After the rains, the largest of these, **Nyae Nyae**, **Khebi** and **Gautcha** (all at the southern end of the arc), are transformed into superb wetlands. These ephemeral water sources attract itinerant water birds – including throngs of flamingos – but they are also breeding sites for water-fowl: ducks, spurwing geese, cranes, crakes, egrets and herons. Other commonly observed birds include teals, sandpipers and reeves, as well as the rare black-tailed godwit and the great snipe.

The Baobabs

The dry, crusty landscape around Tsumkwe supports several large baobab trees, some of which have grown quite huge. The imaginatively named **Grootboom** (Big Tree) is one of the largest, with a circumference of over 30m. One tree with historical significance is the **Dorslandboom**, which was visited by the Dorsland (Thirst Land) trekkers who camped here on their trek to Angola in 1891 and carved their names into the tree. Another notable tree, the immense **Holboom** (Hollow Tree), dominates the bush near the village of Tjokwe.

Aha Hills

Up against the Botswana border, the flat landscape is broken only by the **Aha Hills**. Given the nearly featureless landscape that surrounds them, you may imagine that these low limestone outcrops were named when the first traveller uttered 'Aha, some hills'. In fact, it's a rendition of the sound made by the endemic barking gecko.

The region is pockmarked with unexplored caves and sinkholes, but don't attempt to enter them unless you have extensive caving experience. The hills are also accessible from the Botswana side (see p143). A border crossing is open between Tsumkwe (though this is 30km to the west of the border) and Dobe.

Sleeping & Eating

There's a restaurant at the Tsumkwe Country Lodge, and the Tsumkwe Winkel in town sells limited groceries, but self-caterers would be wise to stock up on supplies before driving out here.

Nyae Nyae Conservancy Camp Sites (camping per person from N$50) The Nyae Nyae Conservancy has several campsites, the most popular being the Holboom Baobab at Tjokwe, southeast of Tsumkwe; Makuri, a few kilometres east of that; and Khebi Pan, well out in the bush south of Tsumkwe. Water is sometimes available in adjacent villages, but generally it's best to carry in all of your supplies and be entirely self-sufficient. Avoid building fires near the baobabs – it damages the trees' roots.

Omatako Valley Rest Camp (Map pp272-3; ☎ 255977; www.nacobta.com.na; camping per person N$50) Outside the conservancy at the junction of the C44 and D3306, this community-run camp has solar power, a water pump, hot showers and a staff of local San. It offers both hunting and gathering trips as well as traditional music presentations.

Tsumkwe Country Lodge (☎ 061-37475; www.namibialodges.com/tsumkwe.html; camping per person N$115, s/d from N$720/1040; ✖ ❑ ☎) The only tourist lodge in Tsumkwe proper changed hands in 2008 and is now run under the umbrella of the upmarket Country Lodge association. At the time of research there were promises of a wider network of affiliated luxury campsites deep in the bush. In the meantime, guests can easily base themselves here, and visit surrounding villages as part of an organised tour.

Nhoma Camp (☎ 273 4606; www.tsumkwel.iway.na/NhomaCamp.htm; half-/full board per person N$1199/2399; ☎) The former owners of the Tsumkwe Country Lodge, Arno and Estelle, have lived in the area for much of their lives and are well respected by the local San communities. Their new project is a luxury tented camp perched between a fossilised river valley and a verdant teak grove, though the main attraction continues to be their wonderful excursions into local San villages. The camp is located 280km east of Grootfontein and 80km west of Tsumkwe along the C44.

Getting There & Away

There are no sealed roads in the region, and only the C44 is passable to 2WD vehicles. Petrol is sometimes available at the Tsumkwe Country Lodge, though it's best to carry a few jerry cans with you. If you're planning to explore the bush around Tsumkwe, it is recommended that you hire a local guide and travel as part of a convoy

The Dobe border crossing to Botswana requires 4WD and extra fuel to reach the petrol stations at Maun or Etsha 6, which are accessed by a difficult sand track through northwestern Botswana.

Northwestern Namibia

For off-road enthusiasts and rugged survivalists alike, Northwestern Namibia is a desolate environment where some of the most incredible landscapes imaginable lie astride 4WD tracks. Along the Skeleton Coast, one of the most publicised stretches of the country, seemingly end-less expanses of foggy beach are punctuated by rusting shipwrecks and flanked by wandering dunes. Here, travellers are left entirely alone to bask in this splendid isolation, bothered only by the concern of whether their vehicles can survive the journey unscathed.

Not to be outdone by the barren coastline, the Kaokoveld is a photographer's dream-scape of wide-open vistas, lonely desert roads and hardly another person around to ruin your shot. A vast repository of desert mountains, this is one of the least developed regions of the country, and arguably Namibia at its most primeval. The Kaokoveld is also the an-cestral home of the Himba people, a culturally rich tribal group that has retained their striking appearance and dress. Much as they have for generations, Himba women smear a mixture of ochre butter and herbs on their bodies, which shines a radiant burnt orange beneath the desert sun.

And then there's Damaraland, home to the Brandberg Massif, Namibia's highest peak, and Twyfelfontein, which together contain some of Southern Africa's finest prehistoric rock paintings and engravings. A veritable window in the past, these two sites help to illuminate the hidden inner workings of our collective forebears, who roamed the African savannah so many eons ago.

NORTHWESTERN NAMIBIA

HIGHLIGHTS

- Having a face-to-face encounter in **Opuwo** (p298) with the Himba, one of Namibia's most iconic tribes
- Admiring the ancient petroglyphs at **Brandberg** (p293) and **Twyfelfontein** (p294)
- Getting off the beaten track (and the tarred road) on the **Skeleton Coast** (p304) and in the **Kaokoveld** (p298)
- Being mesmerised by the sight (and the smell!) of the enormous seal colony at **Cape Cross** (p306)
- Climbing Namibia's landmark mountain, the mighty **Spitzkoppe** (p292)

NORTHWESTERN NAMIBIA

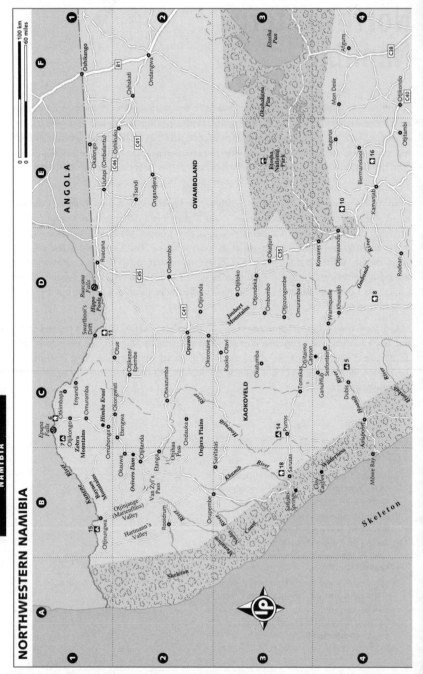

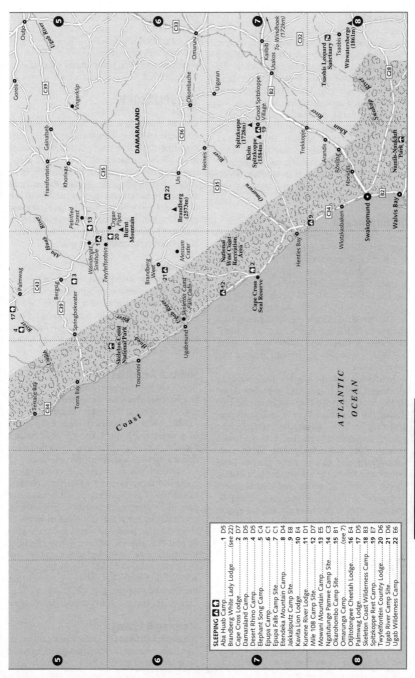

SLEEPING

Aba Huab Camp	1 D5
Brandberg White Lady Lodge	(see 22)
Cape Cross Lodge	2 D7
Damaraland Camp	3 D5
Desert Rhino Camp	4 D5
Elephant Song Camp	5 C4
Epupa Camp	6 C1
Epupa Falls Camp Site	7 C1
Etendeka Mountain Camp	8 D4
Jakkalsputz Camp Site	9 E8
Kavita Lion Lodge	10 E4
Kunene River Lodge	11 D1
Mile 108 Camp Site	12 D7
Mowani Mountain Camp	13 E5
Ngatutunge Pamwe Camp Site	14 C3
Okarohombo Camp Site	15 B1
Omarunga Camp	(see 7)
Otjitotongwe Cheetah Camp	16 E4
Palmwag Lodge	17 D5
Skeleton Coast Wilderness Camp	18 B3
Spitzkoppe Rest Camp	19 E7
Twyfelfontein Country Lodge	20 D6
Ugab River Camp Site	21 D6
Ugab Wilderness Camp	22 E6

NORTHWESTERN NAMIBIA

Geography

Northwestern Namibia is synonymous with the Skeleton Coast, a formidable desert coastline engulfed by icy breakers. As one moves inland, the sinister fogs give way to the wondrous desert wilderness of Damaraland and the Kaokoveld. The former is known for its unique geological features, including volcanic mounds, petrified forests, red-rock mesas and petroglyph-engraved sandstone slabs. The latter is known as one of the last great wildernesses in Southern Africa. Despite their unimaginably harsh conditions, both regions are also rich in wildlife, which have adapted to the arid environment and subsequently thrived.

Getting Around

Since there is virtually no public transport anywhere in the region and hitching is practically impossible, the best way to explore Northwestern Namibia is with a private vehicle. A 2WD vehicle is suitable for the paved highway to Opuwo, as well as the graded dirt C-roads and most D-roads in Damaraland. However, be advised that the roads in the Kaokoveld require a high-clearance vehicle, and some may require a 4WD, especially if driving during the rainy season.

Routes through the western Kaokoveld are all rugged 4WD tracks that were laid down by the South African Defence Force (SADF) during the Namibian War of Independence, and they've been maintained only by the wheels of passing vehicles. Off the main tourist route from Sesfontein to Opuwo, Okongwati and Epupa Falls, there's little traffic, and the scattered villages lack hotels, shops, showers, hospitals, and vehicle spares or repairs. If that makes you uncomfortable, you may want to consider visiting the region with an established tour operator or as part of a larger convoy.

DAMARALAND

Moving inland from the dunes and plains of the bleak Skeleton Coast, the terrain gradually rises through wild desert mountains towards the scrubby plateaus of central Namibia. Damaraland, which occupies much of this transition zone, is laced with springs and ephemeral rivers that provide streaks of greenery and moisture for wildlife, people and livestock. Its broad spaces are one of Africa's last 'unofficial' wildlife areas, and you can still see zebras, giraffes, antelopes, elephants and even black rhinos ranging outside national parks or protected reserves.

THE SPITZKOPPE
☎ 064

One of Namibia's most recognisable landmarks, the 1728m-high Spitzkoppe rises mirage-like above the dusty pro-Namib plains of southern Damaraland. Its dramatic shape has inspired its nickname, the Matterhorn of Africa, but similarities between this ancient volcanic remnant and the glaciated Swiss alp begin and end with its sharp peak. First summited in 1946, the Spitzkoppe continues to attract hard-core rock climbers bent on tackling Namibia's most challenging peak.

Information

The **Spitzkoppe** (Groot Spitzkoppe village; per person/car N$50/10; ☘ sunrise-sunset) is administered by the Ministry of Environment & Tourism (MET), and attended to by the local community. Local guides are also available for a negotiable price, and they provide some illuminating context to this rich cultural site.

Sights & Activities

Beside the Spitzkoppe rise the equally impressive **Pondoks**, which are composed of enormous granite domes. At the eastern end of this rocky jumble, a wire cable climbs the granite slopes to a vegetated hollow known as **Bushman's Paradise**, where an overhang shelters a vandalised panel of ancient rhino paintings.

Although you do not need technical equipment and expertise to go scrambling, **climbing** to the top of the Spitzkoppe is a serious and potentially dangerous endeavour. For starters, you must be fully self-sufficient in terms of climbing gear, food and water, and preferably be part of a large expedition. Before climbing the Spitzkoppe, seek local advice and be sure to inform others of your intentions. Also be advised that it can get extremely hot during the day and surprisingly cold at night and at higher elevations – bring proper protection.

Sleeping & Eating

Spitzkoppe Rest Camp (☎ 530879; www.nacobta.com.na; Groot Spitzkoppe village; camping per person N$35, bungalows per person N$100) This excellent community-run camp includes a number of sites that are dotted around the base of the Spitzkoppe and surrounding outcrops. Most are set in magical rock hollows and provide a sense of real isolation. Facilities at the entrance include a reception office, ecofriendly ablutions blocks and braai (barbecue) stands. There's also a small stand selling local crafts and minerals, as well as a bar and restaurant. Proceeds from the site benefit the adjoining village of Groot Spitzkoppe.

Getting There & Away

Under normal dry conditions, a 2WD is sufficient to reach the mountain. Turn northwest off the B2 onto the D1918 towards Henties Bay then, after 1km, turn north onto the D1930. After 27km (you actually pass the mountain) turn southwest onto the D3716 until you reach Groot Spitzkoppe village; here you turn west into the site.

THE BRANDBERG

The Brandberg (Fire Mountain) is named for the effect created by the setting sun on its western face, which causes this granite massif to resemble a burning slag heap. Its summit, Königstein, is Namibia's highest peak at 2573m, though the Brandberg is best known for its petroglyphs. In 1918, inside the Tsisab or Leopard ravine, German surveyor Reinhard Maack was the first European to discover what is now regarded as one of the finest remnants of prehistoric art on the African continent.

Sights

TSISAB RAVINE

The most famous figure in the ravine is the **White Lady of the Brandberg**, which is located in Maack's Shelter. The figure, which isn't necessarily a lady (it's still open to interpretation), stands about 40cm high, and is part of a larger painting that depicts a bizarre hunting procession. In one hand, the figure is carrying what appears to be a flower or possibly a feather. In the other, the figure is carrying a bow and arrows. However, the painting is distinct because 'her' hair is straight and light-coloured – distinctly un-African – and the body is painted white from the chest down.

The first assessment of the painting was in 1948, when Abbé Henri Breuil speculated that the work had Egyptian or Cretan origins, based on similar ancient art he'd seen around the Mediterranean. However, this claim was eventually dismissed, and recent scholars now believe the white lady may in fact be a San boy, who is covered in white clay as part of an initiation ceremony.

From the car park it's a well-marked 45-minute walk up a scenic track to Maack's Shelter. Along the way, watch for baboons, klipspringers and mountain zebras, and be sure to carry plenty of water. Further up the ravine are several other shelters and overhangs containing ancient paintings. As you climb higher, the terrain grows more difficult and, in places, the route becomes a harrowing scramble over house-sized boulders.

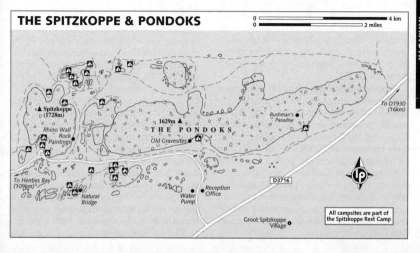

NUMAS RAVINE

Numas Ravine, slicing through the western face of the Brandberg, is another treasure house of ancient paintings. Without a guide, your hunt for ancient art may wind up as more of a pleasant stroll through a dramatic ravine. Most people try to find the rock facing the southern bank of the riverbed, which bears paintings of a snake, a giraffe and an antelope. It lies about 30 minutes' walk up the ravine. After another half-hour you'll reach an oasis-like freshwater spring and several more paintings in the immediate surroundings.

Activities
CLIMBING
As with Spitzkoppe, you do not need technical equipment and expertise to go scrambling, though an ascent to the top of Königstein is a serious and potentially dangerous endeavour. Again, you must be fully self-sufficient in terms of climbing gear, food and water, and preferably go as part of a large expedition. Seek local advice before you climb Königstein, and always inform someone of your intentions. It can get extremely hot during the day and very cold at night and at higher elevations, so be sure to bring adequate protection.

Sleeping
There are unofficial campsites near the mouths of both the Numas and Tsisab Ravines, but neither has water or facilities.

Ugab Wilderness Camp (www.nacobta.com.na; camping per person N$35, bungalows per person N$100) Ugab is another member of Nacobta, a collective of various organisations that aims to foster increased community-based tourism. Facilities are basic, though the camp is well run and a good base for organising guided Brandberg hikes or climbs. The turn-off is signposted from the D2359.

Brandberg White Lady Lodge (☎ 684004; www .brandbergwllodge.com; camping per person N$50, bungalows/ chalets from N$300/450) A brand-new lodge that is rapidly becoming one of the most popular base camps in the area, the Brandberg White Lady has something for just about every kind of traveller. Campers can pitch a tent along the riverine valley, all the while taking advantage of the lodge's upmarket facilities, while lovers of their creature comforts can choose from rustic bungalows and chalets that are highlighted by their stone interiors and wraparound patios.

Getting There & Away
To reach Tsisab Ravine from Uis, head 15km north on the D2369 and turn west on the D2359, which leads 26km to the Tsisab car park. To reach Numas Ravine from the westward turning 14km south of Uis, follow the D2342 for 55km, where you'll see a rough track turning eastward. After about 10km, you'll reach a fork; the 4WD track on the right leads to the Numas Ravine car park.

MESSUM CRATER
One of Damaraland's most remote natural attractions is the highly mysterious-looking Messum Crater, which comprises two concentric circles of hills created by a collapsed volcano in the Goboboseb Mountains. The crater measures more than 20km in diameter, creating a vast lost world that you're likely to have all to yourself.

Camping is prohibited inside the crater.

Of its three main entrances, Messum is best accessed along the Messum River from the D2342 west of the Brandberg. Note that you must stick to the tracks at all times, especially if you choose either route involving the fragile lichen plains of the National West Coast Recreation Area (see the boxed text, opposite). If you are driving in this area, you will require the relevant topographic sheets, which are available from the Office of the Surveyor General in Windhoek (see p232).

TWYFELFONTEIN & AROUND
☎ 067

Twyfelfontein (Doubtful Spring), at the head of the grassy Aba Huab Valley, is one of the most extensive rock-art galleries on the continent. The original name of this water source was /Ui-//Ais (Surrounded by Rocks), but in 1947 it was renamed by European settler D Levin, who deemed its daily output of 1 cu metre of water insufficient for survival.

In the ancient past, this perennial spring most likely attracted bounteous wildlife, and created a paradise for the hunters who eventually left their marks on the surrounding rocks. Animals, animal tracks and geometric designs are well represented here, though there are surprisingly few human figures. Many of the engravings depict animals that are no longer found in the area – elephants, rhinos, giraffes and lions – and an engraving of a sea lion

LICHEN FIELDS

Neither plants nor animals, lichens actually consist of two components – an alga and a fungus – and perhaps provide nature's most perfect example of symbiosis between two living things. The fungus portion absorbs moisture from the air, while the alga contains chlorophyll, which produces sugar and starch to provide carbohydrate energy. Both algae and fungi are cryptogams, which means that they lack the sex organs necessary to produce flowers and seeds, and are therefore unable to reproduce as plants do.

Lichens come in many varieties, including crustose, which form orange, black, brown or pale-green ring patterns on rocks, and foliose, which are actually free-standing. In fact, the gravel plains of the Namib Desert support the world's most extensive fields of foliose lichen, which provide stability for the loose soil in this land of little vegetation. These fields are composed mostly of stationary grey lichen, free-standing black lichen and the rarer orange lichen, which is surprisingly bushy and can grow up to 10cm high.

By day, the lichen fields very much resemble thickets of dead, shrivelled shrubs. However, when heavy fogs roll in during the night-time, the dull grey and black fields slowly uncurl, and burst into blue, green and orange blooms. Water droplets are absorbed by the fungus component of the lichen, which also provides the root system and physical rigidity. At the first light of dawn, however, the alga kicks in with its contribution by using the water droplets, light and carbon dioxide to photosynthesise carbohydrates for both itself and the fungus.

The best places to observe lichen fields are southwest of Messum Crater, in scattered areas along the salt road between Swakopmund (p311) and Terrace Bay, and near the start of the Welwitschia Drive (p316), east of Swakopmund.

Please keep in mind that lichens are incredibly fragile and slow growing, and the slightest disturbance can crush them. Once that happens, it may take 40 or 50 years before any regeneration is apparent. In particular, you should never thoughtlessly drive off-road, and always follow pre-existing tracks when you're bush driving.

indicates contact with the coast more than 100km away.

To date, over 2500 engravings have been discovered, and Twyfelfontein became a national monument in 1952. Unfortunately, the site did not receive formal protection until 1986, when MET designated Twyfelfontein a natural reserve. In the interim, many petroglyphs were damaged by vandals, and some were even removed altogether.

A significant amount of restoration work has taken place here in recent years, a welcome development that hasn't gone unnoticed by the international community. In 2007 Twyfelfontein was declared a Unesco World Heritage Site, the first such distinction in the whole of Namibia.

Sights
ROCK ENGRAVINGS

Most dating back at least 6000 years to the early Stone Age, Twyfelfontein's **rock engravings** (per person N$50; ☼ sunrise-sunset) were probably the work of ancient San hunters, and were made by cutting through the hard patina covering the local sandstone. In time, this skin reformed over the engravings, protecting them from erosion. From colour differentiation and weathering, researchers have identified at least six distinct phases, but some are clearly the work of copycat artists and are thought to date from the 19th century. Guides are compulsory; note that tips are their only source of income.

AROUND TWYFELFONTEIN
Burnt Mountain & Organ Pipes

Southeast of Twyfelfontein rises a barren 12km-long volcanic ridge, at the foot of which lies the hill known as **Burnt Mountain**, an expanse of volcanic clinker that appears to have been literally exposed to fire. Virtually nothing grows in this eerie panorama of desolation. Burnt Mountain lies beside the D3254, 3km south of the Twyfelfontein turn-off.

Over the road, you can follow an obvious path into a small gorge that contains a 100m stretch of unusual 4m-high dolerite (coarse-grained basalt) columns known as the **Organ Pipes**.

Petrified Forest

The **petrified forest** (per person N$50; ☉ sunrise-sunset) is an area of open veld scattered with petrified tree trunks up to 34m long and 6m in circumference, which are estimated to be around 260 million years old. The original trees belonged to an ancient group of cone-bearing plants that are known as *Gymnospermae*, which includes such modern plants as conifers, cycads and welwitschias. Because of the lack of root or branch remnants, it's thought that the trunks were transported to the site in a flood.

About 50 individual trees are visible, some half buried in sandstone and many perfectly petrified in silica – complete with bark and tree rings. In 1950, after souvenir hunters had begun to take their toll, the site was declared a national monument, and it's now strictly forbidden to carry off even a small scrap of petrified wood.

The Petrified Forest, signposted 'Versteende Woud', lies 40km west of Khorixas on the C39.

Wondergat

Wondergat is an enormous **sinkhole** with daunting views into the subterranean world. Turn west off the D3254, 4km north of the D2612 junction. It's about 500m further on to Wondergat, and 10km north of Twyfelfontein.

Sleeping & Eating

Aba Huab Camp (☎ 697981; www.nacobta.com.na; camping per person N$50, A-frames from N$300) This popular community-run campsite is attractively perched beside the Aba Huab riverbed immediately north of the Twyfelfontein turn-off. If you don't want to pitch a tent, you can opt for the open-sided A-frame shelters, though you will need to bring your own bedding. A very lively bar that attracts locals injects a lot of life into the place, and meals are available if you give prior notice.

Twyfelfontein Country Lodge (☎ 374750; www .namibialodges.com; s/d from N$1150/1730; ❄ 🖳 🏊) Over the hill from Twyfelfontein, this architectural wonder is embedded in the red rock. On your way in, be sure not to miss the ancient rock engravings, as well as the swimming pool with its incongruous desert waterfall. The lodge boasts stylish rooms, an immense and airy elevated dining room, and a good variety of excursions throughout

Damaraland. It's fairly well-signposted from Twyfelfontein and easy to find.

Mowani Mountain Camp (☎ 232009; www.mowani .com; tents per person incl full board from N$2600; 🖳 🏊) There's little to prepare you for this beautiful lodge – hidden among a jumble of boulders, its domed buildings seem to disappear into the landscape and you don't see it until you're there. The main buildings all enjoy an ingenious natural air-conditioning system, and the tented accommodation nestles out of sight amid the boulders. The mountain camp is located 5km north of the Twyfelfontein turn-off from the D2612.

Getting There & Away

There's no public transport in the area and little traffic. Turn off the C39, 73km west of Khorixas, turn south on the D3254 and continue 15km to a right turning signposted Twyfelfontein. It's 5km to the petroglyph site.

KAMANJAB

☎ 067

Flanked by lovely low rock formations, tiny Kamanjab functions as a minor service centre for northern Damaraland, and serves as an appealing stopover en route between Damaraland and Kaokoveld. Kamanjab's scenic hinterland also supports a pair of wonderful lodges that are in the business of protecting Namibia's population of feline predators.

Sleeping & Eating

Oase Guest House (☎ 330032; s/d N$420/650; 🏊) This delightful guest house is located in the heart of Kamanjab and features warm and cosy rooms. The bar-restaurant is the centre of nightlife in town, and is staffed by a friendly and welcoming cast of characters. Even if you're not staying here, it's worth stopping by for a cold beer and a fresh cut of kudu or gemsbok. The owners also arrange tours to nearby Himba villages as well as local rock-art galleries.

Otjitotongwe Cheetah Lodge (☎ 687056; s/d incl full board N$960/1760; 🏊) Otjitotongwe is run by cheetah aficionados Tollie and Roeleen Nel, who keep tame cheetahs around their home, and have set up a 40-hectare enclosure for wilder specimens, which they feed every afternoon. The project started when the Nels trapped several wild cheetahs that were poaching their livestock, in the hopes of releasing them in Etosha National Park (see

The **Save the Rhino Trust** (SRT; www.rhino-trust.org.na) is overseen by a concerned group of in-dividuals who are dedicated to stopping illegal poaching. Since the trust was formed, it has actively collaborated with both the Namibian government and local communities in order to provide security for the rhino, monitor population size, and bring benefit to the locals through conservation and tourism initiatives.

SRT operates in Damaraland, a sparsely populated region that is lacking in resources and deficient in employment opportunities. As a result, SRT has worked to include locals in con-servation efforts in the hope that they will benefit from the preservation of the species. This is especially important as Damaraland does not have a formal conservation status and thus does not receive government funding. To date, SRT has successfully protected the only free-ranging black-rhino population in the world, and allowed the group to expand in size. In fact, the International Union for Conservation of Nature (IUCN) has identified the population as the fastest growing in Africa.

Although the organisation has been incredibly successful in stabilising rhino populations, SRT still faces challenges, such as the increasing demand in Namibia for arable farmland. According to SRT, the future of the rhino is dependent on the effective resolution of this issue, and govern-ment policy must include the establishment of stable rhino populations in parks, reserves and private lands throughout the country. However, census results have revealed that SRT has helped preserve a population of 1130 rhinos, with an annual growth rate of 5%.

For visitors interested in tracking black rhinos through the bush, SRT operates the exclusive **Desert Rhino Camp** (☎ 061-225178; www.wilderness-safaris.com; per person from US$650), a joint venture with Wilderness Safaris. Accommodation is in eight East Africa–style linen tents with en suite toilets and hot-water bucket showers. Rates include all meals, wildlife drives and rhino-tracking excursions. Prebooking is essential; 4WD transfers and air charters are available.

p264). After learning that the government was opposed to the idea, they released the animals into the wild, though they kept a litter of cubs born in captivity. Since then, the Nels have taken in a number of recovered cheetahs and operate the wildlife farm in the hope of increasing awareness of the plight of these endangered predators. Otjitotongwe is located 24km south of Kamanjab on the C40.

Kavita Lion Lodge (☎ 330224; s/d incl full board N$1090/1340; ▣) This lodge, run by Uwe and Tammy Hoth, is situated on the borders of Etosha National Park, and is the home of the Afri-Leo Foundation. This nonprofit organ-isation works in cooperation with MET as well as other nongovernmental organisations (NGOs) to ensure the long-term survival of lions in Namibia. In addition to advocacy, the Hoths also take care of injured and un-ruly lions. As well as guided wildlife walks and drives through their private reserve, they can also organise trips to Etosha and into the Kaokoveld. Accommodation at Kavita is in attractive thatched chalets that surround the main lodge, which contains a formal dining room and bar. Kavita is located 34km north of Kamanjab on the C35.

Getting There & Away
The good road north to Ruacana is open to 2WD vehicles, though you need to exercise caution once you cross the Red Line (see the boxed text, p261). Just north of Etosha, this veterinary cordon fence marks the bound-ary between commercial ranching and subsistence herding.

PALMWAG
Palmwag is a rich wildlife area amid stark red hills and plains, surrounded by a bizarre landscape of uniformly sized stones – how this came about is anyone's guess. The area is home to a handful of luxury lodges, and also serves as a study centre for the Save the Rhino Trust (SRT; see the boxed text, above).

Sleeping
All of the lodges below must be prebooked. Rates include all meals and activities. Transfers by 4WD and air charters are available through the operator.

Palmwag Lodge (☎ 064-404459; www.palmwag .com.na; camping per person N$80, s/d incl full board from N$1100/1500; ▣) The oldest but most affordable accommodation in the Palmwag area is situated on a private concession adjacent to the Uniab River. The property contains several excellent hiking routes, and the human watering hole (swimming pool) has a front-row view of its palm-fringed elephantine counterpart – even black rhinos drop by occasionally.

Etendeka Mountain Camp (☎ 061-226979; www .natron.net/tour/logufa; r per person from US$330; 🏊) Environmental experts Barbara and Dennis Liebenberg run this tented camp beneath the foothills of the Grootberg Mountains. The focus of Etendeka is on conservation, not luxury, and guests usually check out with an in-depth understanding of the Damaraland environment. A portion of your accommodation fee is donated to the local community as an incentive to promote conservation in the region.

Damaraland Camp (☎ 061-225178; www.wilderness -safaris.com; r per person from US$420; 🏊) This solar-powered desert outpost with distant views of stark truncated hills is an oasis of luxury amid a truly feral and outlandish setting. When you're not living out your end-of-the-world fantasies in your en suite luxury tent, you can do a few laps in the novel pool that occupies a rocky gorge formed by past lava flows. Damaraland Camp is extremely active in promoting community development and is continually investing profits into the surrounding area.

Getting There & Away
Palmwag is situated on the D3706, 157km from Khorixas and 105km from Sesfontein. Coming from the south, you'll cross the Red Line (see the boxed text, p261), 1km south of Palmwag Lodge.

SESFONTEIN
Damaraland's most northerly outpost is almost entirely encircled by the Kaokoveld, and is somewhat reminiscent of a remote oasis in the middle of the Sahara. Fed by six springs (hence its name), the town was established as a military outpost in 1896 following a rinderpest outbreak. A barracks was added in 1901, and four years later a fort was constructed to control cattle disease, arms smuggling and poaching. This arrangement lasted until 1909, when the fort appeared to be redundant and was requisitioned by the police, who used it until the outbreak of WWI. In 1987 the fort was restored by the Damara Administration

(regional government) and converted into a comfortable lodge, which is now one of the most unusual accommodation options in the whole of Namibia.

For adventurers who dream of uncharted territory, the spectacular and little-known **Otjitaimo Canyon** lurks about 10km north of the main road, along the western flanks of the north–south mountain range east of Sesfontein. To get here would involve a major expedition on foot, but if you're up for it, pick up the topographic sheets from the Office of the Surveyor General in Windhoek (p232), pack lots of water (at least 4L per person per day) and expect unimaginable scenery and solitude.

Ever fancy spending the night in a colonial fort out in the middle of the desert? At **Fort Sesfontein** (☎ 065-275534; www.fort-sesfontein.com; r per person N$780; 🏊) you and 63 other guests can live out all your Lawrence of Arabia fantasies! Accommodation is basic but incredibly atmospheric, and it has a good restaurant here that serves German-inspired (what a surprise!) dishes.

The road between Palmwag and Sesfontein is good gravel, and you'll only have problems if the Hoanib River is flowing. Unless it has been raining, the gravel road from Sesfontein to Opuwo is accessible to all vehicles.

THE KAOKOVELD

Often described as one of the last true wildernesses in Southern Africa, the Kaokoveld is largely devoid of roads and is crossed only by sandy tracks laid down by the SADF decades ago. In this harsh wilderness of dry and arid conditions, wildlife has been forced to adapt in miraculous ways – consider the critically endangered desert elephant, which has especially spindly legs suited for long walks in search of precious water. Beyond wildlife, the Kaokoveld is also home to the Himba, a group of nomadic pastoralists who are famous for covering their skin with a traditional mixture of ochre butter and herbs to protect themselves from the sun.

OPUWO
☎ 065
In the Herero language, Opuwo means The End, which is certainly a fitting name for this dusty collection of concrete commercial buildings ringed by traditional rondavels and

EXPLORING THE KAOKOVELD

Even if you're undaunted by extreme 4WD exploration, you still must make careful preparations for any trip off the Sesfontein–Opuwo and the Ruacana–Opuwo–Epupa Falls routes. To summarise, you will need a robust 4WD vehicle, plenty of time and enough supplies to see you through the journey – this includes enough food and water for the entire trip. It's also useful to take a guide who knows the region, and to travel in a convoy of at least two vehicles. Carry several spare tyres for each vehicle, a tyre iron, a good puncture-repair kit and a range of vehicle spares, as well as twice as much petrol as the distances would suggest.

For navigation, use a compass, or preferably a global positioning system (GPS). Relevant topographic sheets are also extremely helpful. Poor conditions on some tracks may limit your progress to 5km/h, but after rains, streams and mud can stop a vehicle in its tracks. Allow a full day to travel between Opuwo and Epupa Falls, and several days each way from Opuwo to Hartmann's Valley and Otjinjange (Marienflüss) Valley. Note that Van Zyl's Pass may be crossed only from east to west. Alternative access is through the Rooidrum road junction north of Orupembe (via Otjihaa Pass).

Camping in the Kaokoveld requires awareness of the environment and people. Avoid camping in shady and inviting riverbeds, as large animals often use them as thoroughfares, and even when there's not a cloud in the sky, flash floods can roar down them with alarming force. In the interests of the delicate landscape and flora, keep to obvious vehicle tracks; in this dry climate, damage caused by off-road driving may be visible for hundreds of years to come.

Furthermore, because natural water sources are vital to local people, stock and wildlife, please don't use clear streams, springs or waterholes for washing yourself or your gear. Similarly, avoid camping near springs or waterholes lest you frighten the animals and inadvertently prevent them from drinking. You should always ask permission before entering or camping near a settlement. Remember that other travellers will pass through the region long after you've gone, so, for the sake of future tourism, please be considerate and respect the local environment and culture.

huts. While first impressions are unlikely to be very positive, a visit to Opuwo is truly one of the highlights of Namibia, particularly for anyone interested in interacting with the Himba people. As the unofficial capital of Himbaland, Opuwo serves as a convenient jumping-off point for excursions into the nearby villages, and there is a good assortment of lodges and campsites in the area to choose from.

However, Opuwo is much more than just a base for trips to see the Himba, especially since people from all across the Kaokoveld gravitate to the town's 'bright lights'. Walking up and down the main shopping drag, you'll encounter plenty of ochre-painted and barebreasted Himba women, strutting alongside Herero women decked out in traditional Victorian dress. Add to the mix the darker-skinned Zena people from Angola, as well as plenty of locals from all tribes who have adopted Western dress, and you've got yourself one of the most dynamic street scenes in all of Namibia.

Information

Kaoko Information Centre (☎ 273420; ☉ 8am-6pm) KK and Kemuu, the friendly guys at this information centre (look for the tiny, tiny yellow shack), can arrange visits to local Himba villages in addition to providing useful information for your trip through the Kaokoveld region.

Sights & Activities
HIMBA VISITS

Even if you've never heard of the Himba prior to visiting Namibia, you'll quickly become enamoured with them. A tribal group numbering not more than 50,000 people, the Himba are a seminomadic pastoral people that are closely related to the Herero, yet continue to live much as they have for generations on end.

The women in particular are famous for smearing themselves with a fragrant mixture of ochre, butter and bush herbs, which dyes their skin a burnt-orange hue, and serves as a natural sunblock and insect repellent. As if this wasn't striking enough, they also use the mixture to cover their braided hair, which

NORTHWESTERN NAMIBIA

has an effect similar to dreadlocking. Instead of wearing Western clothes, they prefer to dress traditionally, bare-breasted, with little more than a pleated animal-skin skirt in the way of clothing.

Similar to the Masai of Kenya and Tanzania, the Himba breed and care for herds of cattle in addition to goats and sheep. Unlike the East African savannah, Himba homelands are among the most extreme environments in the world, and their survival is ultimately dependent on maintaining strong community alliances. Coincidently, it was this very climactic harshness and resulting seclusion from outside influences that enabled the Himba to maintain their cultural heritage over the centuries.

During the 1980s and early 1990s, the Himba were severely threatened by war and drought, though they have experienced a tremendous resurgence in past years. At present, the population as a whole has succeeded in gaining control of their homelands, and in exerting real political power on the national stage. For more information, see the boxed text, p215.

Tourism is booming in Himbaland, as evidenced by the recent paving of the road all the way up to Opuwo (but not to the border with Angola!), and the inauguration of the Opuwo Country Hotel by the Namibian president himself. Ever-so-photogenic shots of Himba women appear on just about every Namibian tourism brochure, and busloads of tourists can be seen whizzing through Opuwo's dusty streets virtually every day.

It's not all positive, though – in the past, rural Himba people were willing models for photography. These days, however, you are likely to encounter traditionally dressed Himba people who will wave you down and ask for tips in exchange for having their photograph taken. Naturally, whether you accept is up to you, but bear in mind that encouraging this trade works to draw people away from their traditional lifestyle, and propels them towards a cash economy that undermines long-standing values and community cooperation.

Alternatively, it's recommended that you trade basic commodities for photographs. In times of plenty, Himba grow maize to supplement their largely meat- and milk-based diet, though rain is highly unpredictable in Namibia. *Pap* (corn meal) is a very desirable gift for the Himba, as is rice, bread, potatoes and other starches. Try to resist giving sugar, soft drinks and other sweets, as the majority of Himba may never meet a dentist in their lifetime.

Throughout Opuwo you will see Himba wherever you go – they will be walking the streets, shopping in the stores and even waiting in line behind you at the supermarket! However tempting it might be, please do not sneak a quick picture of them, as no one appreciates having a camera unwillingly waved in front of their face.

If you would like to have free rein with the camera, visiting a traditional village – if done in the proper fashion – can yield some truly amazing shots. Needless to say, a guide who speaks both English and the Himba language is essential to the experience. There are a few ways to go about this: you can either join an organised tour through your accommodation, stop by the Kaoko Information Centre (see p299) or find an independent guide somewhere in Opuwo.

OPUWO

INFORMATION
Kaoko Information Centre...........1 B3

SLEEPING
Kunene Village Rest Camp.........2 A2
Ohakane Lodge.....................3 B3

EATING
OK Grocer.........................4 B3

SHOPPING
Kunene Crafts Centre..............5 B3

Before arriving in the village, please do spend some time shopping for gifts – entering a village with food items will garner a warm welcome from the villagers, who will subsequently be more willing to tolerate photography. At the end of your time in the village, buying small bracelets and trinkets directly from the artisan is also a greatly appreciated gesture.

Finally, don't be afraid to ask lots of questions with the aid of your translator, and spend some time interacting with the Himba rather than just photographing them. Showing respect and admiration helps the Himba reinforce their belief that their tradition and way of life is something worth preserving.

For some more insight on the Himba people, see the boxed text, p302.

Sleeping & Eating

For self-caterers, there's an OK Grocer in town.

Kunene Village Rest Camp (☎ 273043; www.nacobta .com.na; camping per person N$40, s/d huts N$140/170) This amenable community-run rest camp has well-groomed campsites with adequate facilities as well as basic thatched huts with shared bathrooms. Follow the signposted turn-off from the government housing project at the edge of town, en route to Sesfontein.

Ohakane Lodge (☎ 273031; www.natron.net/tour /ohakane/lodgee.html; s/d N$450/800; ⊗ ⊠) This well-established and centrally located lodge sits along the main drag in Opuwo and does good business with tour groups. Fairly standard but fully modern rooms are comfortable enough, but if it's in your budget, it's worth shelling out a bit more for a bungalow at the Opuwo Country Hotel.

Opuwo Country Hotel (☎ 061-374750; www.nam ibialodges.com/opuwo.html; camping per person N$125, s/d N$1234/1748; ⊗ ⊡ ⊠) Far and away the area's swankiest accommodation option, the hilltop Opuwo Country Hotel is an enormous thatched building (reportedly the largest in Namibia) that elegantly lords it over the town below. Accommodation is in a small handful of exclusive bungalows facing across the valley towards the Angolan foothills, though most of your time here will be spent soaking your cares away in the infinity-edge pool. Even if you can't afford a bungalow here, consider pitching a tent in the secluded campsite, which grants you complete access to the hotel's amenities, including a fully stocked wine

bar and a regal dining hall. The turn-off leading up to the hotel is a bit tricky to find, but there are signs posted throughout the town.

Shopping

Kunene Crafts Centre (☎ 273209; ⊗ 8am-5pm Mon-Fri, 9am-1pm Sat) Opuwo's brightly painted self-help curio shop sells local arts and crafts on consignment. You'll find all sorts of Himba adornments smeared with ochre: conch-shell pendants, wrist bands, chest pieces and even the headdresses worn by Himba brides. There's also a range of original jewellery, appliquéd pillowslips, Himba and Herero dolls, drums and wooden carvings.

Getting There & Away

The marvellously paved C41 runs from Outjo to Opuwo, which makes Himbaland accessible even to 2WD vehicles. Although there is a temptation to speed along this long and lonely highway, keep your lead foot off the pedal north of the veterinary control fence as herds of cattle commonly stray across the road. If you're heading deeper into the Kaokoveld, be advised that Opuwo is the last opportunity to buy petrol before Kamanjab, Ruacana or Sesfontein.

SWARTBOOI'S DRIFT
☎ 065

From Ruacana, a rough track heads west along the Kunene to Swartbooi's Drift, where a monument commemorates the Dorsland trekkers who passed en route to their future homesteads in Angola. The town is a good place to break up the drive to Epupa Falls, and it's also a good base to go white-water rafting on the Kunene.

With a minimum of four participants, the Kunene River Lodge (see below) operates half-day, full-day and multiday **white-water rafting** trips, starting at N$380 per person, on the Kunene River, from the class IV Ondarusu rapids (upstream from Swartbooi's Drift) to Epupa Falls.

The very friendly **Kunene River Lodge** (☎ 274300; www.kuneneriverlodge.com; camping per person N$80, s/d chalets N$370/930, bungalows N$660/1100; ⊠), approximately 5km east of Swartbooi's Drift, makes an idyllic riverside stop. Campsites are sheltered beneath towering trees, and the thatched chalets and bungalows enjoy a pleasant garden setting. Guests can hire canoes, mountain bikes and fishing rods,

QUEEN ELIZABETH

Queen Elizabeth is a Himba woman who works in town as an independent tour guide. (If you'd like to visit a local Himba village with her, you can phone her on ☎ 081 213 8326, or look for her outside the OK Grocer at the entrance to Opuwo.) While showing us around her birthplace, she helped us understand a bit more about what it means to be Himba.

What do the Himba like to eat?
We keep all sorts of animals, so there is always milk and meat in the villages. Our water is only from rain. No rain, no crops. But this year we had so much rain, so look at all this maize we have now! You see this structure here? It's made from sand and cow dung and mopane wood, the same as our houses. We dry the corn here, and keep it for eating and for planting. We also mash the maize on stones to make mealie meal, which we boil and mix with bush herbs. Of course we prefer to eat meat, but maize keeps our bellies full when we get hungry.

What beliefs are important to the Himba?
The holy fire at the centre of each village is very important to us. Our chief watches over the holy fire and talks to our ancestors through the flame. When you get married, you pray to the holy fire for a good life. When a baby is born, you ask the holy fire to give the child a good name. Actually, today is a special day because twin calves were born, which is very lucky for us! So, tonight we will light the holy fire and have a ceremony to honour them. You see, cows are very important to our people. When you turn 11, we take out the bottom four teeth. It's painful, my dear! But we admire cows and we take after the cows so we like to have the same mouth as them. We also circumcise our boys. They don't like it, of course! They can't walk for a few days, but we rub mopane leaves on the cut to stop infection.

What is the secret to your beauty?
We Himba women have pride because of our beauty. We still cover our bodies with powdered ochre, which we get from a few secret places. Actually, the best stuff comes from Angola! We never take a shower, forever. So, we mix the powder with cow butter and special perfume we make from herbs, so we can smell nice. The colour is also important to us. Our bodies turn the same colour as the red earth, which is where all life comes from. We also like big, big hair. We style our hair with oil and ochre, but it's not always big enough. So we can buy extensions in the market place and we weave this into our hair.

What about your jewellery?
Our jewellery is made from beads and wires and cowry shells. You see these ankle bracelets – one stripe means you have no children or one baby, two stripes means you have two or more. These anklets also protect our legs from snakebites when we're out in the bush. After a woman's first menstruation, we have a big party, and the woman goes to the special menstruation hut. Then we make her a special headdress and sometimes a skirt out of lambskin. She can also start wearing metal belts instead of plastic belts. So you see, you can tell a lot about a woman just by looking at her dress!

Himba woman Queen Elizabeth was born in a small village just outside Opuwo.

as well as go on bird-watching excursions, quadbiking trips and booze cruises.

At Otjikeze/Epembe, 73km northwest of Opuwo, an eastward turning onto the D3701 leads 60km to Swartbooi's Drift. This is the easiest access route, and it's open to 2WD vehicles. The river road from Ruacana is extremely rough, but in dry conditions it can be negotiated by high-clearance 2WD vehicles. On the other hand, the 93km river road to Epupa Falls – along the lovely 'Namibian

riviera' – is extremely challenging even with a 4WD and can take several days.

EPUPA FALLS

At Epupa, which means Falling Waters in Herero, the Kunene River fans out into a vast flood plain and is ushered through a 500m-wide series of parallel channels, dropping a total of 60m over 1.5km. The greatest single drop, an estimated 37m, is commonly identified as the Epupa Falls. Here the river tumbles into a dark, narrow, rainbow-wrapped cleft, which is a spectacular sight to behold, particularly when the Kunene is in peak flow from April to May.

Although you'd think this remote corner of the Kaokoveld would be off the tourist trail, Epupa Falls is a popular stopover for overland trucks and organised safaris, and unfortunately can get swamped with tourists. But if you're passing through the area, a dip in the falls is certainly worth the detour, and the sight of so much water in the middle of the dry Kaokoveld is miraculous to say the least.

Sights & Activities

During periods of low water, the **pools** above the Epupa Falls make fabulous natural Jacuzzis. You're safe from crocodiles in the eddies and rapids, but hang onto the rocks and keep away from the lip of the falls; once you're caught by the current, there's no way to prevent being swept over. Every couple of years, some unfortunate locals and foreign tourists drown in the river, and it's difficult at best to retrieve their bodies. Swimming here is most definitely not suitable for children.

There's also excellent **hiking** along the river west of the falls, and plenty of mountains to climb, affording panoramic views along the river and far into Angola. Keen hikers can manage the route along the 'Namibian riviera' from Swartbooi's Drift to Epupa Falls (93km, five days) or from Ruacana to Epupa Falls (150km, eight days). You're never far from water, but there are lots of crocodiles and, even in winter, the heat can be oppressive and draining. It's wise to plan your trip around a full moon, when you can beat the heat by walking at night.

As with most adventure activities in Kaokoveld, you need to be self-sufficient, as there is no support network here to help you in the event of trouble. Carry extra supplies, especially since you may have to wait for lifts back. And, whenever possible, always alert someone of your intended route and itinerary before striking out into the deep bush.

Sleeping

Epupa Falls Camp Site (☎ 695 1065; www.nacobta .com.na; camping per person N$50) This community-run camp has hot showers and flush toilets and is conveniently located right at the falls.

Unfortunately, it can get very crowded and extremely noisy as it tends to get colonised by the overland crowd, but it's definitely your best bet if you want a sociable place to rest your head.

Omarunga Camp (☎ 064-403096; www.natron .net/omarunga-camp/main.html; camping per person N$80, s/d tents incl half-board N$935/1610) This German-run camp operates through a concession granted by a local chief, and has a well-groomed campsite with modern facilities as well as a handful of luxury tents. It's a very attractive spot, and a much quieter alternative to the community campsite, but it can't hold a candle to the slightly more upmarket Epupa Camp.

Epupa Camp (☎ 061-232740; www.epupa.com.na; s/d incl full board N$$1499/1999; ▨) Located 800m upstream from the falls, this former engineering camp for a now-shelved hydroelectric project has been converted into beautifully situated accommodation among a grove of towering baobab trees. There are 12 luxury tents filled to the brim with curios, and a slew of activities is on offer, including Himba visits, sundowner hikes, bird-watching walks, and trips to rock-art sites.

Getting There & Away

The road from Okongwati is accessible to high-clearance 2WD vehicles, but it's still quite rough. As the rugged 93km 4WD river route from Swartbooi's Drift may take several days, it's far quicker to make the trip via Otjiveze/Epembe.

THE NORTHWEST CORNER

West of Epupa Falls is the Kaokoveld of travellers' dreams: stark, rugged desert peaks, vast landscapes, sparse, scrubby vegetation, drought-resistant wildlife, and nomadic bands of Himba people and their tiny settlements of beehive huts. This region, which is contiguous with the Skeleton Coast Wilderness (see p304), has now been designated the Kaokoveld Conservation Area.

Sights

VAN ZYL'S PASS

The beautiful but frightfully steep and challenging Van Zyl's Pass forms a dramatic transition between the Kaokoveld plateaus and the vast, grassy expanses of Otjijange Valley (Marienflüss). This winding 13km stretch isn't suitable for trailers and may only be passed from east to west, which means you'll have to return via Otjihaa Pass or through Purros.

OTJINJANGE & HARTMANN'S VALLEYS

Allow plenty of time to explore the wild and magical Otjinjange (better known as Marienflüss) and Hartmann's Valleys – broad sandy and grassy expanses descending gently to the Kunene River. Note that camping outside campsites is prohibited at both valleys.

Sleeping

Except for in Otjinjange (Marienflüss) and Hartmann's Valleys, unofficial bush camping is possible throughout the northwest corner (for more information, see the boxed text, p299).

Okarohombo Camp Site (www.nacobta.com.na; camping per person N$50) This community-run campsite is located at the mouth of the Otjinjange Valley. Facilities are limited to long-drop toilets and a water tap, and you must be entirely self-sufficient.

Ngatutunge Pamwe Camp Site (www.nacobta.com .na; camping per person N$50; ⚑) Another community-run campsite, Ngatutunge is perched along the Hoarusib River in Purros, and, surprisingly, has hot showers, flush toilets, well-appointed bungalows, a communal kitchen and (believe it or not!) a swimming pool. The campsite is also a good spot for hiring guides to visit Himba villages or observe desert-adapted wildlife.

Elephant Song Camp (☎ 064-403829; www.na cobta.com.na; camping per person N$50) Yet another community-run campsite, Elephant Song is located in the Palmwag Concession, a very rough 25km down the Hoanib River from Sesfontein. This camp caters to outdoorsy types with great views, hiking, bird-watching and the chance to see rare desert elephants.

Getting There & Away

From Okongwati, the westward route through Etengwa leads to either Van Zyl's Pass or Otjihaa Pass. From Okauwa (with a landmark broken windmill) to the road fork at Otjitanda (which is a Himba chief's kraal), the journey is extremely rough and slow going – along the way, stop for a swim at beautiful Ovivero Dam. From Otjitanda, you must decide whether you're heading west over Van Zyl's Pass (which may only be traversed from east to west!) into Otjinjange

(Marienflüss) and Hartmann's Valleys, or south over the equally beautiful but much easier Otjihaa Pass towards Orupembe.

You can also access Otjinjange (Marienflüss) and Hartmann's Valleys without crossing Van Zyl's Pass by turning north at the three-way junction in the middle of the Onjuva Plains, 12km north of Orupembe. At the T-junction in Rooidrum (Red Drum), you can decide which valley you want. Turn right for Otjinjange (Marienflüss) and left for Hartmann's. West of this junction, 17km from Rooidrum, you can also turn south along the fairly good route to Orupembe, Purros (provided that the Hoarusib River isn't flowing) and on to Sesfontein.

Alternatively, you can head west from Opuwo on the D3703, which leads 105km to Etanga; 19km beyond Etanga, you'll reach a road junction marked by a stone sign painted with white birds. At this point, you can turn north toward Otjitanda (27km away) or south towards Otjihaa Pass and Orupembe.

THE SKELETON COAST

This treacherous coast – a foggy region with rocky and sandy coastal shallows – has long been a graveyard for unwary ships and their crews, hence its forbidding name. Early Portuguese sailors called it *As Areias do Inferno* (the Sands of Hell), as once a ship washed ashore the fate of the crew was sealed. This protected area stretches from just north of Swakopmund to the Kunene River, taking in nearly 2 million hectares of dunes and gravel plains to form one of the world's most inhospitable waterless areas.

NATIONAL WEST COAST RECREATION AREA

The National West Coast Recreation Area, a 200km-long and 25km-wide strip that extends from Swakopmund to the Ugab River, makes up the southern end of the Skeleton Coast. The area is extremely popular with South African fishermen, who flock here to tackle such saltwater species as galjoens, steenbras, kabeljous and blacktails. In fact, between Swakopmund and the Ugab River are hundreds of concrete buildings, spaced at intervals of about 200m. Although these

NORTHWESTERN NAMIBIA

SKELETONS ON THE COAST

Despite prominent images of rusting ships embedded in the hostile sands of the Skeleton Coast, the most famous shipwrecks have long since disappeared. The harsh winds and dense fog that roll off the South Atlantic are strong forces of erosion, and today there are little more than traces of the countless ships that were swept ashore during the height of the mercantile era. In addition, the few remaining vessels are often in remote and inaccessible locations.

One such example is the *Dunedin Star,* which was deliberately run aground in 1942 just south of the Angolan border after hitting some offshore rocks. The ship was en route from Britain around the Cape of Good Hope to the Middle East war zone, and was carrying more than 100 passengers, a military crew and cargo.

When a rescue ship arrived two days later, getting the castaways off the beach proved an impossible task. At first, the rescuers attempted to haul the castaways onto their vessel by using a line through the surf. However, as the surge grew stronger, the rescue vessel was swept onto the rocks and wrecked alongside the *Dunedin Star*. Meanwhile, a rescue aircraft, which managed to land on the beach alongside the castaways, became bogged in the sand. Eventually all the passengers were rescued, though they were evacuated with the help of an overland truck convoy. The journey back to civilisation was two weeks of hard slog across 1000km of desert.

Further south on the Skeleton Coast – and nearly as difficult to reach – are several more intact wrecks. The *Eduard Bohlen* ran aground south of Walvis Bay in 1909 while carrying equipment to the diamond fields in the far south. Over the past century, the shoreline has changed so much that the ship now lies beached in a dune nearly 1km from the shore.

On picturesque Spencer Bay, 200km further south and just north of the abandoned mining town of Saddle Hill, is the dramatic wreck of the *Otavi*. This cargo ship beached in 1945 following a strong storm, and is now dramatically perched on Dolphin's Head, the highest point on the coast between Cape Town's Table Mountain and the Angolan border. Spencer Bay also claimed the Korean cargo ship *Tong Taw* in 1972, which is currently one of the most intact vessels along the entirety of the Skeleton Coast.

appear to be coastal bunkers guarding against an offshore attack, they are actually toilet blocks for fishermen and campers.

Henties Bay
☎ 064

At Henties Bay, 80km north of Swakopmund, the relatively reliable Omaruru River issues into the Atlantic (don't miss the novel golf course in the riverbed!). It was named for Hentie van der Merwe, who visited its spring in 1929. Today it consists mainly of holiday homes and refuelling and provisioning businesses for anglers headed up the coast.

Lying 9km south of Henties Bay, **Jakkalsputz Camp Site** (per person N$30), a bleak strip of beach that is completely exposed to the wind, sand and drizzle. Having said that, it's one of the world's more unusual places to pitch a tent.

The **De Duine Country Hotel** (☎ 061-374750; www.namibialodges.com; s/d from N$485/700; ❂ ☖), the most established hotel in Henties Bay, sits on the coast, though not a single room has a

sea view – go figure! The German colonial–style property does feature rooms with swimming pool and garden views, though. Lunch and dinner are available at its (what else?) seafood restaurant, and the front desk can organise fishing trips, scenic flights and coastal tours.

The C34 salt road, which begins in Swakopmund and ends 70km north of Terrace Bay, provides access to the National West Coast Recreation Area and the southern half of the Skeleton Coast National Park. The park is also accessible via the C39 gravel road that links Khorixas with Torra Bay. Henties Bay lies at the junction of the coastal salt road and the C35, which turns inland towards Damaraland.

Note that motorcycles are not permitted in Skeleton Coast National Park. No permits are required to transit the area, and the salt road from Swakopmund is passable year-round with a 2WD. The only petrol in the area is available at Mile 108 Camp Site (p307) and in Swakopmund.

Cape Cross Seal Reserve

The best-known breeding colony of Cape fur seals along the Namib coast is this **reserve** (per person N$45; ☻ 10am-5pm), where the population has grown large and fat by taking advantage of the rich concentrations of fish in the cold Benguela current. The sight of more than 100,000 seals basking on the beach and frolicking in the surf is impressive to behold, though you're going to have to contend with the overwhelming odoriferousness of piles and piles of stinky seal poo. Bring a handkerchief or bandana to cover your nose – seriously, you'll thank us for the recommendation.

HISTORY

Although it's primarily known for the seals, Cape Cross has a long and illustrious history. In 1485 Portuguese explorer Diego Cão, the first European to set foot in Namibia, planted a 2m-high, 360kg *padrão* (a tribute to Portuguese king João II) at Cape Cross in honour of King John I of Portugal.

In 1893, however, a German sailor Captain Becker of the *Falke* removed the cross and hauled it off to Germany. The following year, Kaiser Wilhelm II ordered that a replica be made with the original inscriptions in Latin and Portuguese, as well as a commemorative inscription in German. This cross remains at the site, in addition to a second cross, made of dolerite, which was erected in 1980 on the site of Cão's original cross.

ORIENTATION & INFORMATION

A pattern of concrete circles near the crosses contains information on the area's history. It's laid out in the shape of the Southern Cross, the constellation that guided Diego Cão's original expedition. There's also a nearby snack bar, though good luck holding onto your appetite once you catch a whiff of seal stench.

No pets or motorcycles are permitted, and visitors may not cross the low barrier between the seal-viewing area and the rocks where the colony lounges.

CAPE FUR SEALS

There are seven seal species in Southern African waters, but except for very occasional vagrants from the Antarctic and sub-Antarctic islands, the only mainland species is the Cape fur seal. Communal to the extreme, this massive population is divided between only about 25 colonies; a few of them, like Cape Cross on Namibia's western coast, number more than 100,000.

Despite their gregariousness, Cape fur seals are not especially sociable; colony living makes sense for breeding opportunities, and to reduce the chance of predators sneaking up, but individual seals are essentially loners on land, and they constantly quarrel over their own little patch. Except for pups playing with each other in crèche-like 'playgrounds', virtually every other interaction in the colony is hostile, creating extraordinary opportunities for watching behaviour.

Cape fur seals have a thick layer of short fur beneath the coarser guard hairs, which remain dry and trap air for insulation. This enables the animals to maintain an internal body temperature of 37°C and spend long periods in cold waters.

Male Cape fur seals weigh less than 200kg on average, but during the breeding season they take on a particularly thick accumulation of blubber and balloon out to more than 360kg. Females are much smaller, averaging 75kg, and give birth to a single, blue-eyed pup during late November or early December. About 90% of the colony's pups are born within just over a month.

Pups begin to suckle less than an hour after birth but are soon left in communal nurseries while their mothers leave to forage for food. When the mothers return to the colony, they identify their own pup by a combination of scent and call.

The pups moult at the age of four to five months, turning from a dark grey to olive brown. Mortality rates in the colony are high, and up to a quarter of the pups fail to survive their first year, with the bulk of deaths occurring during the first week after birth. The main predators are the brown hyena and the black-backed jackal, which account for 25% of pup deaths. Those pups that do survive may remain with their mothers for up to a year.

Cape fur seals eat about 8% of their body weight each day, and the colonies along the western coast of Southern Africa annually consume more than 1 million tonnes of fish and other marine life (mainly shoaling fish and squid). That's about 300,000 tonnes more than is taken by the fishing industries of Namibia and South Africa put together!

SLEEPING

Cape Cross Lodge (☎ 064-694012; www.capecross.org; per person standard/luxury r incl half-board from N$750/935; ❄ 🖳) The odd but strangely appealing architecture is self-described as a cross between Cape Dutch and fishing village style, but it's actually very well designed and properly sheltered from the bleating seal colony. The nicer rooms have spacious outdoor patios that overlook the coastline, though you really can't choose a bad room at this all-around stunner of a lodge, conveniently located just before the official reserve entrance.

GETTING THERE & AWAY

Cape Cross is located 46km north of Henties Bay along the coastal salt road.

SKELETON COAST NATIONAL PARK

At Ugabmund, 110km north of Cape Cross, the salt road passes through the entry gate to the Skeleton Coast National Park. UK journalist Nigel Tisdall once wrote: 'If hell has a coat of arms, it probably looks like the entrance to Namibia's Skeleton Coast Park'. If the fog is rolling in and the sand is blowing, you're likely to agree with that assessment.

Despite the enduring fame of this coastline, surprisingly few travellers ever reach points north of Cape Cross. The reason: in order to preserve this incredibly fragile environment, Namibian Wildlife Resorts (NWR) imposes very strict regulations on individual travellers seeking to enter the park.

Although this can be a deterrent for some, permits are easily obtainable if you do some planning. And, while you may have to sacrifice a bit of spontaneity to gain admittance to the park, the enigmatic Skeleton Coast really does live up to all the hype.

Orientation & Information

The zone south of the Hoanib River is open to individual travellers, but you need a permit, which costs N$80 per person and N$10 per vehicle per day. These are available through the NWR office in Windhoek (p234). Accommodation is available only at Terrace Bay and Torra Bay (the latter is open only in December and January), either of which must be booked at NWR concurrently with your permit. To stay in either camp, you must pass the Ugabmund entrance before 3pm and/or Springbokwater before 5pm.

No day visits to the park are allowed, but you can obtain a transit permit to pass between Ugabmund and Springbokwater, which can be purchased at the gates. To transit the park, you must pass the entry gate before 1pm and exit through the other gate before 3pm the same day. Note that transit permits aren't valid for Torra Bay or Terrace Bay.

Activities

The 50km-long **Ugab River Guided Hiking Route** is open to groups of between six and eight people on the second and fourth Tuesday of each month from April to October. Hikes start at 9am from Ugabmund and finish on Thursday afternoon. Most hikers stay Monday night at the **Mile 108 Camp Site** (per person N$30), 40km south of Ugabmund, which allows you to arrive at Ugabmund in time for the hike. The hike costs N$200 per person and must be booked through NWR – hikers must provide and carry their own food and camping equipment. The route begins by crossing the coastal plain, then climbs into the hills and follows a double loop through lichen fields and past caves, natural springs and unusual geological formations.

Sleeping

All accommodation (with the exception of the Ugab River Camp Site) must be prebooked through NWR.

Ugab River Camp Site (www.rhino-trust.org.na; camping per person N$50) Outside the Skeleton Coast park, this campsite is administered by the Save the Rhino Trust (see the boxed text, p297). This remote landscape is truly enigmatic, and those who've visited have only glowing comments. It's also one of the best places in Namibia to see the elusive black rhino – multiday rhino-tracking expeditions can be arranged, though you must book in advance and supply your own food, water and camping gear. To get there, turn east onto the D2303, 67km north of Cape Cross; it's then 76km to the camp.

Torra Bay Camping Ground (per person N$50; ☽ Dec & Jan) This campsite, which is open to coincide with the Namibian school holidays, is flanked by a textbook field of barchan dunes. These dunes are actually the southernmost extension of a vast sand sea that stretches all the way to the Curoca River in Angola. Petrol, water, firewood and basic supplies are available, and campers may use the restaurant at Terrace Bay. Torra Bay is located 215km north of Cape Cross.

Terrace Bay Resort (s/d N$950/1400, 8-person beach chalets N$3200) Open year-round, this resort is a luxurious alternative to camping at Torra Bay. Around the camp you may spot black-backed jackals or brown hyenas, and the scenery of sparse coastal vegetation and lonely dunes is the Skeleton Coast at its finest. The site has a restaurant, a shop and a petrol station. Terrace Bay is located 49km north of Torra Bay.

Getting There & Away

The Skeleton Coast National Park is accessed via the salt road from Swakopmund, which ends 70km north of Terrace Bay. The park is also accessible via the C39 gravel road which runs between Khorixas and Torra Bay. Note that motorcycles are not permitted in the Skeleton Coast National Park. Hitchhikers may be discouraged by the bleak landscape, cold sea winds, fog, sandstorms and sparse traffic.

SKELETON COAST WILDERNESS AREA

The Skeleton Coast Wilderness, stretching between the Hoanib and Kunene Rivers, makes up the northern third of the Skeleton Coast. This section of coastline is among the most remote and inaccessible areas in Namibia, though it's here in the wilderness that you can truly live out your Skeleton Coast fantasies. Since the entire area is a private concession, you're going to have to part with some serious cash to visit. Access is via charter flight, and the sole accommodation is at the extraordinary Skeleton Coast Wilderness Camp.

History

In the early 1960s, Windhoek lawyer Louw Schoemann began bringing business clients to the region, and became involved in a consortium to construct a harbour at Möwe Bay, at the southern end of the present-day Skeleton Coast Wilderness. In 1969, however, the South African government dropped the project, and in 1971 it declared the region a protected reserve. Five years later, when the government decided to permit limited tourism, the concession was put up for bid, and Schoemann's was the only tender.

For the next 18 years, his company, Skeleton Coast Fly-In Safaris, led small group tours and practised ecotourism long before it became a buzz word. Sadly, Louw Schoemann passed away after losing the concession in 1993, but the family carried on with the business. Currently, the concession is held by Wilderness Safaris Namibia, which continues to conserve this wilderness while still managing to provide unforgettable experiences.

Sights & Activities

The wonders of this region defy description. For instance, the **barchan dunes** of the northern Skeleton Coast hold a unique distinction: they roar. If you don't believe it, sit down on a lee face, dig in your feet and slide slowly down. If you feel a jarring vibration and hear a roar akin to a four-engine cargo plane flying low, don't bother looking up – it's just the sand producing its marvellous acoustic effect. It's thought that the roar is created when air pockets between electrically charged particles are forced to the surface. The effect is especially pronounced in the warmth of the late afternoon, when spaces between the sand particles are at their greatest.

Sleeping

Skeleton Coast Wilderness Camp (☎ 061-274500; www.wilderness-safaris.com; 4-/5-day trips per person from US$2500/3000) If your budget stretches this far, it's most definitely worth visiting. Located near Sarusas Springs, this exclusive luxury retreat is the most remote camp in the Wilderness Safari collection. Activities include viewing desert elephants along the Hoarusib River, ocean fishing, dune climbing, hiking through the Clay Castles and basking in veritable isolation. Rates are variable but always include accommodation, air transfers from Windhoek, meals, drinks and activities. Prebooking is mandatory.

Getting There & Away

The Skeleton Coast Wilderness Area is closed to private vehicles. Access is restricted to fly-in trips operated by Wilderness Safaris. The flights in and out travel one way over the Kaokoveld highlands and the other way along the Skeleton Coast (which is magnificent – plan on filling up half your memory card with digital snaps!).

NORTHWESTERN NAMIBIA

Central Namibia

Central Namibia is defined by the Namib Desert, a barren and desolate landscape of undulating apricot-coloured dunes interspersed with dry pans. Indeed, the Nama word 'Namib', which inspired the name of the entire country, rather prosaically means 'Vast Dry Plain'. Nowhere is this truer than at Sossusvlei, Namibia's most famous strip of sand, where gargantuan dunes tower more than 300m above the underlying strata. With camera in hand, you can capture some of the very same iconic images that have catapulted Namibia into the consciousness of so many desert-bound travellers.

Although it's difficult to imagine that civilisation could flourish in such a harsh and unforgiving environment, Central Namibia is home to two large cities, Walvis Bay and Swakopmund, which were originally established as port towns during the colonial era. The former, Walvis Bay, is one of the most important maritime centres and commercial fisheries in the whole of the South Atlantic. Just beyond the city limits, however, lie several crucial wetland areas, which support the country's largest density of flamingos.

The latter, Swakopmund, welcomes visitors with its bizarre German-colonial flair, and keeps their adrenaline levels surging by offering a full complement of adventure sports. From quad biking up the crest of a soaring seaside dune to jumping out of a plane at 3000m with a parachute strapped to your back, Swakop – as it's affectionately known by locals – is where you can test your limits, push your envelope and go wild amid a stunningly beautiful natural setting unlike any other on the planet.

HIGHLIGHTS

- Watching the sun rise from the tops of fiery-coloured dunes at **Sossusvlei** (p336)
- Getting your adrenaline fix at **Swakopmund** (p311), the extreme-sports capital of Namibia
- Photographing some of the largest flocks of flamingos in Africa near **Walvis Bay** (p325)
- Testing your endurance on remote hiking trails through the remote **Naukluft Mountains** (p332)
- Admiring the tenacity of the ancient yet slow-growing Welwitschia plants along **Welwitschia Drive** (p316)

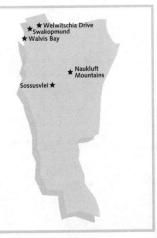

CENTRAL NAMIBIA

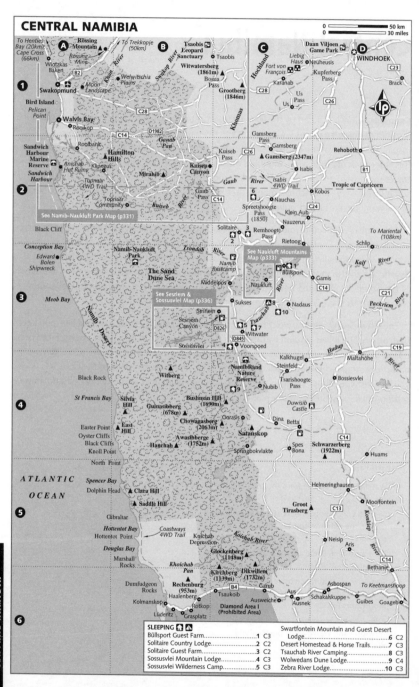

CENTRAL NAMIBIA

0 — 50 km
0 — 30 miles

CENTRAL NAMIBIA

Geography

The Namib Desert is one of the oldest and driest deserts in the world. As with the Atacama in northern Chile, it is the result of a cold current – in this case, the Benguela Current – sweeping north from Antarctica, which captures and condenses humid air that would otherwise be blown ashore. Although travellers to Namibia and Botswana are surprised (and even a bit disappointed) by the lushness of the Kalahari, the soaring sand dunes of the Namib rarely cease to amaze. Much of the surface between Walvis Bay and Lüderitz is covered by enormous linear dunes, which roll back from the sea towards the inland gravel plains that are occasionally interrupted by isolated mountain ranges.

Getting Around

If you don't have a private vehicle, Swakopmund is serviced by a variety of transport options, and Sossusvlei is visited on virtually every organised tour of Namibia. Like the rest of the country though, you really need your own wheels to fully appreciate the full expanse of the desert.

Paved roads connect Windhoek to Swakopmund and continue south to Sesriem, the base town for Sossusvlei. If you have a 2WD vehicle, you can get within a couple kilometres of Sossusvlei, though the final stretch is only accessible by 4WD (taxis are available). Otherwise, most of the region is 2WD accessible, aside from a few minor 4WD roads in and around Namib-Naukluft Park.

THE NORTHERN REACHES

From Windhoek, the Khomas Hochland mountain range stretches west to form a scenic transition zone between the high central plateau and the Namib plains. En route to Swakopmund and Walvis Bay, this scenic landform facilitates some truly pleasurable driving, though the real highlight awaits you on the coast. Just as the road begins to flatten out, falling in line with surrounding gravel plains, deep orange dunes appear on your left, while your nose first catches the salty breeze of the ocean just ahead – welcome to Swakopmund!

SWAKOPMUND

☎ 064

Often described as being more German than Germany, Swakopmund is a quirky mix of German-Namibian residents and overseas German tourists, who feel right at home with the town's pervasive *Gemütlichkeit*, a distinctively German appreciation of comfort and hospitality. With its seaside promenades, half-timbered homes and colonial-era buildings, it seems that only the wind-blown sand and the palm trees distinguish Swakop (as it is familiarly known) from holiday towns along Germany's North Sea and Baltic coasts.

Swakop is Namibia's most popular holiday destination, and it attracts surfers, anglers and beach lovers from all over Southern Africa. However, the city has recently reinvented itself as the adventure sports capital of Namibia, and now attracts adrenaline junkies jonesing for a quick fix. Whether you slide down the dunes on a greased up snowboard, or go against your survival instincts by hurling yourself out of a Cessna, Swakop has no shortage of gut-curdling activities to choose from.

History

Small bands of Nama people have occupied the Swakop River mouth from time immemorial, but the first permanent settlers were Germans who didn't arrive until early 1892. Because nearby Walvis Bay had been annexed by the British-controlled Cape Colony in 1878, Swakopmund remained German South West Africa's only harbour, and resultantly rose to greater prominence than its poor harbour conditions would have otherwise warranted. Early passengers were landed in small dories, but after the pier was constructed, they were winched over from the ships in basketlike cages.

Construction began on the first building, the Alte Kaserne (Old Barracks), in September 1892. By the following year it housed 120 Schutztruppe (German Imperial Army) soldiers, and ordinary settlers arrived soon after to put down roots. The first civilian homes were prefabricated in Germany, and then transported by ship. By 1909, Swakopmund had officially become a municipality.

The port emerged as the leading trade funnel for all of German South West Africa, and attracted government agencies and transport companies. During WWI however, South West Africa was taken over by South Africa,

CENTRAL NAMIBIA

CENTRAL NAMIBIA

SWAKOPMUND

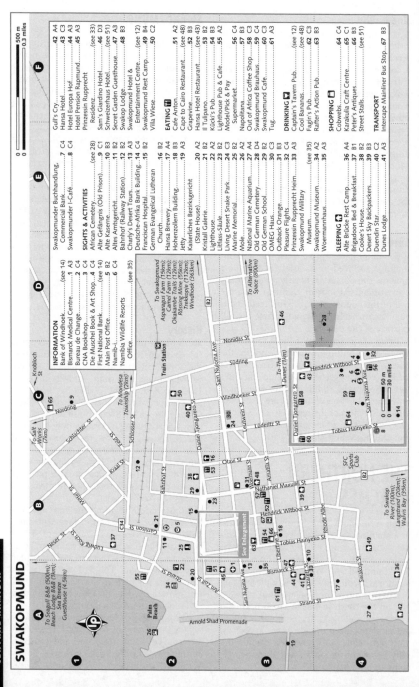

and the harbour was allowed to silt up as maritime operations moved to nearby Walvis Bay. Strangely enough, this ultimately turned Swakopmund into a holiday resort, which is why the city is generally more pleasant on the eye than the industrial-looking Walvis Bay.

Information

Thanks to the mild temperatures and negligible rainfall, Swakopmund enjoys a statistically superb climate (25°C in the summer and 15°C in the winter), but there's a bit of grit in the oyster. When an easterly wind blows, the town gets a good sandblasting, and the cold winter sea fogs often create an incessant drizzle and an unimaginably dreary atmosphere. However, take comfort in the fact that this fog rolls up to 50km inland, and provides life-sustaining moisture for desert plants and animals.

BOOKSHOPS
CNA bookshop (Hendrick Witbooi St) Sells popular paperbacks.
Die Muschel Book & Art Shop (☎ 402874; Hendrick Witbooi St) Esoteric works on art and local history are available here.
Swakopmunder Büchhandlung (☎ 402613; Sam Nujoma Ave) A wide selection of literature from various genres.

EMERGENCY
Ambulance (☎ 405731)
Fire brigade (☎ day 402411, after hours pager 405544).
Police (☎ 10111)

INTERNET ACCESS
Swakopmunder I-café (Tobias Hainyeko St & Sam Nujoma Ave; per hr N$10; ☺ 7am-10pm Mon-Sat, 10am-10pm Sun)

MEDICAL SERVICES
Bismarck Medical Centre (☎ 405000; Bismarck St) For doctors' visits, see this recommended centre.

MONEY
Bureau de Change (Sam Nujoma Ave; ☺ 7am-7pm daily) The most convenient option for changing money. Charges no commission to change travellers cheques – the catch is that you'll need the slips verifying proof of purchase.

POST
Main post office (Garnison St) Also sells telephone cards and offers fax services.

TOURIST INFORMATION
Namib-i (☎ 404827; www.natron.net/tour/swakop /infoe.htm; Sam Nujoma Ave, PO Box 829; ☺ 8am-1pm & 2-5pm Mon-Fri, 9am-noon & 3.30-5.30pm Sat, 9.30am-noon & 3.30-5pm Sun) This tourist information centre is a very helpful resource. In addition to helping you get your bearing, it can also act as a booking agent for any activities and tours that happen to take your fancy.
Namibia Wildlife Resorts office (NWR; ☎ 204172; www.nwr.com.na; Woermannhaus, Bismarck St; ☺ 8am-1pm & 2-5pm Mon-Fri) Like its big brother in Windhoek (see p234), this office sells Namib-Naukluft Park and Skeleton Coast permits, and can also make reservations for any NWR-administered property in the country.

Dangers & Annoyances

Although the palm-fringed streets and cool sea breezes in Swakopmund are unlikely to make you tense, you should always keep your guard up in town. Regardless of how relaxed the ambience might be, petty crime is unfortunately on the rise.

If you have a private vehicle, never leave your car unattended. Be sure that you leave it in clear sight, all locked up with no possessions inside visible during the day. At night, you need to make sure you're parked in a gated parking lot and not on the street. Also, when you're choosing a hotel or hostel, be sure that the security precautions (ie an electric fence and/or a guard) are up to your standards. Finally, although Swakopmund is generally safe at night, it's best to stay in a group, and when possible, take a taxi to and from your accommodation.

Sights
HISTORICAL BUILDINGS

Swakopmund brims with numerous historic examples of traditional German architecture. For further information on the town's colonial sites, pick up *Swakopmund – A Chronicle of the Town's People, Places and Progress*, which is sold at Swakopmund Museum and in local bookshops.

Woermannhaus
From the shore, the delightful German-style Woermannhaus, located on Bismarck St, stands out above surrounding buildings. Built in 1905 as the main offices of the Damara & Namaqua Trading Company, it was taken over in four years later by the Woermann & Brock Trading Company, which supplied the current name. In the 1920s, it was used as a school dormitory, and later served as a

merchant sailors' hostel. It eventually fell into disrepair, but was declared a national monument and restored in 1976.

For years, the prominent Damara tower (formerly a water tower) provided a landmark for ships at sea as well as for traders arriving by ox wagon from the interior. It now affords a splendid panorama, and houses the **Swakopmund Military Museum** (admission N$10; ⏰ 10am-noon Mon & Tue, Thu-Sat & 3-6pm Mon-Thu) and a gallery of historic paintings. You can pay the admission fee and pick up a key at the library.

The Jetty

In 1905, the need for a good cargo- and passenger-landing site led Swakopmund's founders to construct the original wooden pier. In the years that followed, it was battered by the high seas and damaged by woodworm, and in 1911, construction began on a 500m iron jetty. When the South African forces occupied Swakopmund, the port became redundant (they already controlled Walvis Bay), so the old wooden pier was removed in 1916 and the unfinished iron pier was left to the elements. In 1985 it was closed for safety purposes, but a year later, a public appeal raised 250,000 rand to restore the structure. It's now open to the general public, but again suffers from neglect.

The Mole

In 1899, architect FW Ortloff's sea wall (better known as the Mole) was intended to enhance Swakopmund's poor harbour and create a mooring place for large cargo vessels. But Mr Ortloff was unfamiliar with the Benguela Current, which sweeps northwards along the coast, carrying with it a load of sand from the southern deserts. Within less than five years, the harbour entrance was choked off by a sand bank, and two years later, the harbour itself had been invaded by sand to create what is now called Palm Beach. The Mole is currently used as a mooring for pleasure boats.

Altes Amtsgericht

This gabled building, located on the corner of Garnison and Bahnhof Sts, was constructed in 1908 as a private school. When the funds ran out, the government took over the project and requisitioned it as a magistrates' court. In the 1960s it functioned as a school dormitory, and now houses municipal offices. Just so no

one can doubt its identity, the words 'Altes Amtsgericht' (German for 'Old Magistrates' Court') are painted across the front.

Kaiserliches Bezirksgericht (State House)

This rather stately building on Daniel Tjongarero St was constructed in 1902 to serve as the district magistrates' court. It was extended in 1905, and again in 1945 when a tower was added. After WWI it was converted into the official holiday home of the territorial administrator. In keeping with that tradition, it's now the official Swakopmund residence of the president.

Bahnhof (Railway Station)

This ornate railway station, built in 1901 as the terminal for the *Kaiserliche Eisenbahn Verwaltung* (Imperial Railway Authority), connected Swakopmund to Windhoek. In 1910, when the railway closed down, the building assumed the role as main station for the narrow-gauge mine railway between Swakopmund and Otavi. It was declared a national monument in 1972, and now houses the Swakopmund Hotel & Entertainment Centre (see p323).

Marine Memorial

Often known by its German name, Marine Denkmal, this memorial was commissioned in 1907 by the Marine Infantry in Kiel, Germany, and designed by sculptor AM Wolff. Located on Daniel Tjongarero St, it commemorates the German First Marine Expedition Corps, which helped beat back the Herero uprisings of 1904. As a national historical monument, it will continue to stand, but one has to wonder how long it will be before the Herero erect a memorial of their own.

Historical Cemeteries

It's worth having a quick wander past the historical cemeteries beside the Swakop River. The neatly manicured Old German Cemetery dates from the colonial era, and the tombstones, which are still maintained by resident families, tell countless stories. The adjoining African cemetery makes an equally intriguing cultural statement, and has plenty of stories of its own.

Prinzessin Rupprecht Heim

The single-storey Prinzessin Rupprecht Heim, located on Lazarett St, was constructed in 1902 as a military hospital. In 1914 it was transferred to the Bavarian Women's Red Cross, which named it after its patron, Princess Rupprecht, wife of the Bavarian crown prince. The idea was to expose convalescents to the healthy effects of the sea breeze. The building currently operates as a hotel (see p322).

Alte Gefängnis (Old Prison)
This impressive 1909 structure, located on Nordring St, was built as a prison, but if you didn't know this, you'd swear it was either an early train station or a health-spa hotel. The main building was used only for staff housing, while the prisoners were relegated to much less opulent quarters on one side.

Hohenzollern Building
This imposing baroque-style building, situated on Libertine St, was constructed in 1906 to serve as a hotel. Its rather outlandish décor is crowned by a fibreglass cast of Atlas supporting the world, which replaced the precarious cement version that graced the roof prior to renovations in 1988.

Litfass-Saule
In 1855, the Berlin printer Litfass came up with the notion of erecting advertising pillars on German street corners. For the citizens of early Swakopmund, they became a common source of information and advertising. This remaining example is on the corner of Daniel Tjongarero and Nathaniel Maxulili Sts.

OMEG Haus
Thanks to the narrow-gauge railway to the coast, the colonial company Otavi Minen und Eisenbahn Gesellschaft (OMEG), which oversaw the rich Otavi and Tsumeb mines, also maintained an office in Swakopmund, situated on Sam Nujoma Ave.

Deutsche-Afrika Bank Building
This handsome neo-classical building near the corner of Woermann and Tobias Hainyeko Sts was opened in 1909 as a branch office of the Deutsche-Afrika Bank. It's now a functioning Bank of Windhoek branch.

Lighthouse
This operational lighthouse, an endearing Swakopmund landmark just off Strand St, was constructed in 1902. It was originally built 11m high, but an additional 10m was added in 1910.

Franciscan Hospital
Built in 1907, Franciscan Hospital was originally called the St Antonius Gebaude Hospital, and functioned continuously until 1987. It is located on Daniel Tjongarero St.

German Evangelical Lutheran Church
This neo-baroque church on Daniel Tjongarero Av was built in 1906 to accommodate the growing Lutheran congregation of Dr Heinrich Vedde – it still holds regular services.

Old German School
This 1912 baroque-style building on Post St was the result of competition won by budding German architect Emil Krause.

MUSEUMS & GALLERIES
Swakopmund Museum
When ill winds blow, head for this **museum** (☎ 402046; Strand St; adults/students N$18/12; ☼ 10am-12.30pm & 3-5.30pm), at the foot of the lighthouse, where you can hole up and learn about the town history. The museum occupies the site of the old harbour warehouse, which was destroyed in 1914 by a 'lucky' shot from a British warship.

Displays include exhibits on Namibia's history and ethnology, including information on local flora and fauna. Especially good is the display on the !nara melon (see boxed text, p335), a fruit which was vital to the early Khoikhoi people of the Namib region.

It also harbours a reconstructed colonial home interior, Emil Kiewitand's apothecary shop and an informative display on the Rössing Mine. Military buffs will appreciate the stifling uniforms of the Camel Corps and the Shell furniture, so called because it was homemade from 1930s depression-era petrol and paraffin tins.

National Marine Aquarium
This waterfront **aquarium** (Strand St; admission N$30; ☼ 10am-6pm Tue-Sat, 11am-5pm Sun, closed Mon except public holidays) provides an excellent introduction to the cold offshore world in the South Atlantic Ocean. Most impressive is the tunnel through the largest aquarium, which allows close-up views of graceful rays, toothy sharks (you can literally count all the teeth!)

THE MARTIN LUTHER

In the desert 4km east of Swakopmund, a lonely and forlorn steam locomotive languished for several years. The 14,000kg machine was imported to Walvis Bay from Halberstadt, Germany, in 1896 to replace the ox wagons used to transport freight between Swakopmund and the interior. However, its inauguration into service was delayed by the outbreak of the Nama-Herero wars, and in the interim, its locomotive engineer returned to Germany without having revealed the secret of its operation.

A US prospector eventually got it running, but it consumed enormous quantities of locally precious water. It took three months to complete its initial trip from Walvis Bay to Swakopmund, and subsequently survived just a couple of short trips before grinding to a halt just east of town. Clearly this particular technology wasn't making life easier for anyone, and it was abandoned and dubbed the *Martin Luther,* in reference to the great reformer's famous words to the Diet of Reichstag in 1521: 'Here I stand. May God help me, I cannot do otherwise.'

Although the Martin Luther was partially restored in 1975, and concurrently declared a national monument, it continued to suffer from the ravages of nature. Fortunately, in 2005 students from the Namibian Institute of Mining and Technology restored the locomotive to its former grandeur. They also built a protective encasement that should keep the Martin Luther around at least for another century.

and other little marine beasties found on Namibia's seafood platters.

Kristall Galerie

This architecturally astute **gallery** (☎ 406080; Bahnhof St; admission N$20; ⊙ 9am-5pm Mon-Sat) features some of the planet's most incredible crystal formations, including the largest quartz crystal that has ever been found. The adjacent shop sells lovely mineral samples, crystal jewellery, and intriguing plates, cups and wine glasses that are carved from the local stone.

Living Desert Snake Park

This **park** (☎ 405100; Sam Nujoma Ave; admission N$15; ⊙ 8.30am-5pm Mon-Fri, 8.30am-3pm) houses an array of serpentine sorts. The owner knows everything you'd ever want to know – or not know – about snakes, scorpions, spiders and other widely misunderstood creatures.

BEACHES & DUNES

Swakopmund is Namibia's main beach resort, but even in summer, the water is never warmer than around 15°C (remember, the Benguela Current sweeps upwards from Antarctica). Swimming in the sea is best in the lee of the Mole sea wall.

At the lagoon at the Swakop River mouth you can watch ducks, flamingos, pelicans, cormorants, gulls, waders and other birds. North of town you can stroll along kilometres and kilometres of deserted beaches stretching towards the Skeleton Coast. The best surfing is at Nordstrand (Thick Lip) near Vineta Point.

A fascinating short hike will take you across the Swakop River to the large dune fields south of town. The dune formations and unique vegetation are great for solo exploring.

HANSA BREWERY

Aficionados of the amber nectar will want to visit the **Hansa Brewery** (☎ 405021; 9 Rhode Allee; admission free), which is the source of Swakopmund's favourite drop. Free tours – with ample opportunity to sample the product – run on Tuesday and Thursday, but advanced reservations are necessary.

AROUND SWAKOPMUND
Welwitschia Drive

This worthwhile excursion by vehicle or organised tour is recommended if you want to see one of Namibia's most unusual desert plants, the Welwitschia (see the boxed text, p318). Welwitschias reach their greatest concentrations on the Welwitschia Plains east of Swakopmund, near the confluence of the Khan and Swakop Rivers, where they're the dominant plant species.

In addition to this wilted wonder itself, Welwitschia Drive also takes in grey and black **lichen fields** (see p295), which were featured in the BBC production *The Private Life of Plants.* It was here that David Attenborough pointed out these delightful examples of plant-animal symbiosis, which burst into 'bloom' with the

CENTRAL NAMIBIA

addition of fog droplets. If you're not visiting during a fog, sprinkle a few drops of water on them and watch the magic.

Another interesting stop is the **Baaiweg (Bay Rd)**, the ox-wagon track that was historically used to move supplies between the coast and central Namibia. The tracks remain visible because the lichen that were destroyed when it was built have grown back at a rate of only 1mm per year, and the ruts aren't yet obscured.

Further east is the **Moon Landscape** (Map p331), a vista across eroded hills and valleys carved by the Swakop River. Here you may want to take a quick 12km return side-trip north to the farm and oasis of **Goanikontes** (Map p331), which dates from 1848. It lies beside the Swakop River amid fabulous desert mountains, and serves as an excellent picnic site.

To the east along the main loop is further evidence of human impact in the form of a **campsite** used by South African troops for a few days in 1915. They were clearly not minimum-impact campers!

A few kilometres beyond the South African troop camp, the route turns north. Shortly thereafter, you'll approach a prominent black **dolerite dyke** splitting a ridgetop. This was created when molten igneous material forced its way up through a crack in the overlying granite and cooled.

Camping is available at the **Welwitschia campsite** (Map p331; campsite N$50 plus per person N$10), near the Swakop River crossing on the Welwitschia Plains detour, is available for parties of up to eight people. Book through NWR offices in either Windhoek (p234) or Swakopmund (p313).

The Welwitschia Drive, which turns off the Bosua Pass route east of Swakopmund, lies inside the Namib-Naukluft Park. Most often visited as a day trip from Swakopmund, the drive can be completed in two hours, but allow more time to experience this other-worldly landscape.

Swakopmund Salt Works

When the Klein family began extracting salt from here in 1933, it was thought that the area was nothing more than a low, salty depression along the desert coast. But when the **salt works** (Map p331; ☎ 402611; ⏰ Mon to Fri, reservations necessary) lasted for 20 years, they decided to excavate a series of shallow evaporation pans

to concentrate and extract the minerals. Now water is pumped into the pans directly from the sea and the onshore breeze provides an ideal catalyst for evaporation.

Water is moved through the several pans over a period of 12 to 18 months. The waterborne minerals are concentrated by evaporation and eventually crystals of sodium chloride and other salts develop. Thanks to the variety of algae in the mineral soup that's created at the various stages, each pond takes on a different brilliant colour: purple, red, orange, yellow and even greenish hues. From aloft, they take on the appearance of a colourful stained-glass window.

Thanks to the sheltered environment, the ponds provide a habitat for small fish as well as birds, including flamingos, avocets, sandpipers, teals, grebes, gulls, cormorants and terns. The Kleins have now registered the site as a private bird reserve, and they've also erected a large wooden platform – an artificial island – which is used by cormorants as a breeding site. After the breeding season, scrapers are sent onto the platform to collect the guano deposits.

Rössing Mine

This **mine** (off Map p331; ☎ 402046), 55km east of Swakopmund, is the world's largest open-cast uranium mine. Uranium was first discovered here in the 1920s by Peter Louw, though his attempts at developing the mine quickly failed. In 1965, the concession was transferred to Rio Tinto-Zinc, and comprehensive surveys determined that the formation measured 3km long and 1km wide. Ore extraction came on line in 1970, but didn't reach capacity for another eight years. The current scale of operations is staggering: at full capacity the mine produces one million tonnes of ore per week.

Rössing, with 2500 employees, is currently a major player in Swakopmund's economy. The affiliated Rössing Foundation provides an educational and training centre in Arandis, northeast of the mine, as well as medical facilities and housing for its Swakopmund-based workers. It has promised that the eventual decommissioning of the site will entail a massive clean-up, but you may want to temper your enthusiasm about its environmental commitments until something is actually forthcoming.

Three-hour **mine tours** (per person N$50) leave from Cafe Anton at 10am on the first and

WELWITSCHIAS

Among Namibia's many botanical curiosities, the extraordinary *Welwitschia mirabilis,* which exists only on the gravel plains of the northern Namib Desert from the Kuiseb River to southern Angola, is probably the strangest of all. It was first noted in 1859, when Austrian botanist and medical doctor Friedrich Welwitsch stumbled upon a large specimen east of Swakopmund. He first suggested that it be named *tumboa,* which was the local name for the plant. However, his discovery was considered to be so important that Welwitsch humbly decided to name it after himself instead. More recently, the Afrikaners have dubbed it *tweeblaarkanniedood* or 'two-leaf can't die', which is, more than anything else, a reference to its longevity.

Although these plants are the ugly ducklings of the vegetable world, they're remarkably adapted to their harsh habitat. It was once thought that the plant had a tap root down through clay pipes to access the water table 100m or more beneath the surface. In fact, the root is never more than 3m long and it's now generally accepted that, although the plant gets some water from underground sources, most of its moisture is derived from condensed fog. In fact, pores in the leaves trap moisture, and longer leaves actually water the plant's own roots by channelling droplets onto the surrounding sand.

Despite their dishevelled appearance, welwitschias actually have only two long and leathery leaves, which grow from opposite sides of the corklike stem. Over the years, these leaves are darkened in the sun and torn by the wind into tattered strips, causing the plant to resemble a giant wilted lettuce.

Strangely, welwitschias are considered to be trees and are related to conifers, specifically pines, but they also share some characteristics of flowering plants and club mosses. Females bear the larger greenish-yellow to brown cones, which contain the plant's seeds, while the males have more cones, but they're smaller and salmon coloured. They're a dioeceous species, meaning that male and female plants are distinct, but their exact method of pollination remains in question. It's thought that the large sticky pollen grains are carried by insects, specifically wasps.

Welwitschias have a slow growth rate, and it's believed that the largest ones, whose tangled masses of leaf strips can measure up to 2m across, may have been growing for up to 2000 years! However, most midsized plants are less than 1000 years old. The plants don't even flower until they've been growing for at least 20 years. This longevity is probably only possible because they contain some compounds that are unpalatable to grazing animals, although black rhinos have been known to enjoy the odd plant.

The plants' most prominent inhabitant is the yellow and black pyrrhocorid bug, which lives by sucking sap from the plant. It's commonly called the push-me-pull-you bug, due to its almost continuous back-to-back mating.

third Friday of each month; book in advance at the Swakopmund Museum. You can also arrange a visit through any of the tour companies listed on p320 in this section.

Trekkopje

The **military cemetery** at Trekkopje is located 112km northeast of Swakopmund along the B2. In January 1915, after Swakopmund was occupied by South African forces, the Germans retreated and cut off supplies to the city by damaging the Otavi and State railway lines. However, the South Africans had already begun to replace the narrow-gauge track with a standard-gauge one, and at Trekkopje, their crew met German forces. When the Germans attacked their camp on

26 April 1915, the South Africans defended themselves with guns mounted on armoured vehicles and won easily. All fatalities of this battle are buried in the Trekkopje cemetery, which is immediately north of the railway line, near the old train station.

Swakopmund Asparagus Farm

You surely never thought that an **asparagus farm** (off Map p312; ☎ 405134; admission free; ☼ 9am-4pm Mon-Fri) could be a tourist attraction, but Swakopmund's delicious green gold grows in the wildest desert, and makes for an interesting quick visit and taste test. To reach the farm, take the Windhoek road 11km east of town and turn off at El Jada; it's 4km from there.

CENTRAL NAMIBIA

Activities

After aspiring for years to become a dry version of Victoria Falls, Swakopmund is one of the top destinations in Southern Africa for extreme sports enthusiasts. Although filling your days with adrenaline-soaked activities is certainly not cheap, there are few places in the world where you can climb up, race down and soar over towering sand dunes.

Most activity operators don't have offices in town, which means that you need to arrange all of your activities through either your accommodation or the Namib-i (see p313) tourist information centre.

Alternatively, you can stop by Outback Orange (see below). Although it specialises in quadbiking, the friendly staff members here are more than happy to phone a few operators for you.

SANDBOARDING

Sandboarding with **Alter Action** (☎ 402737; lie-down/stand-up N$340/550) is certain to increase your heart rate while going easy on your wallet (it's by far the cheapest trip in town). If you have any experience snowboarding or surfing, it's highly recommended that you have a go at the stand-up option. You will be given a snowboard, gloves, goggles and enough polish to ensure a smooth ride. While you can't expect the same speeds as you would on the mountain, you can't beat the experience of carving a dune face, and falling on sands hurts a lot less than ice!

The lie-down option (which makes use of a greased-up sheet of masonite) requires much less finesse but is equally fun. The highlight is an 80km/h 'schuss' down a 120m mountain of sand, which finishes with a big jump at the end. Slogging up the dunes can be rather taxing work, so you need to be physically fit and healthy. Trips depart in the morning and last for approximately four hours. The price includes the equipment rental, transport to and from the dunes, instruction, lunch and either a beer or soda upon completion.

QUADBIKING

Outback Orange (Map p312; ☎ 400 968; www.outback -orange.com; 42 Nathaniel Maxulili St; 1/2hr trip N$250/395) offers stomach dropping tours on quad-bikes (motorcycle-style 4WD) through the enormous dune field adjacent to Swakop. If you've ever wanted to recreate the *Star Wars* experience of riding a speeder through the deserts of Tatooine, this is your chance! In two hours, you'll travel over 60km and race up and down countless dunes, all the while enjoying panoramic views of sand and sea. These tours are definitely not for the weak-hearted as you can pick up some serious speed on these bikes, and there are plenty of hair-pin turns and sheer drops to contend with throughout the trip.

Outback Orange is recommended for its safety-conscious and environmentally sensitive staff. While quadbiking will never be an eco-activity, tours follow predemarcated routes, which means that you will not be stirring up new tracts of sand and avoiding the gravel plains all together. This ensures the continued survival of the highly endangered Damara Tern (p321). The guides also tailor trips to ability: experienced riders are allowed to drive manual bikes, while novice riders are given automatics. If you do get your bearings quickly and you want to let loose a bit, go ahead and ask your guide to let you fly down one of the really big dunes.

SKYDIVING

Ground Rush Adventures (☎ 402841; www.skydiveswa kop.com.na; tandem jump N$1900, handycam/professional video N$450/850) provides the ultimate rush, and skydiving in Swakopmund is sweetened by the outstanding dune and ocean backdrop. The crew at Ground Rush has an impeccable safety record to date, and they make even the most nervous participant feel comfortable about jumping out of a plane at 3000m and freefalling for 30 seconds at 220km/h. If you're having any second thoughts taking the plunge, know that your tandem master has been pulling the chord several times a day for years and years on end!

The price also includes a 25-minute scenic flight in a tiny Cessna aircraft, which provides striking views of the coastline between Swakop and Walvis Bay to the south. It is worth pointing out that the ascent can often be the scariest part, especially if you're afraid of flying (though it certainly makes the jump that much easier!). If you want physical evidence of your momentary lapse of reason, there are two photo/video options available: one is a handycam strapped to your tandem master, while the other is a professional photographer jumping out of the plane alongside you and filming the entire descent. Have a light breakfast – you'll thank us later!

CENTRAL NAMIBIA

SCENIC FLIGHTS

Pleasure Flights (Map p312; ☎ 404500; www.pleasure flights.com.na; Sam Nujoma Ave; prices variable) One of the most reputable light-plane operators in Namibia, Pleasure Flights has been offering scenic aerial cruises for more than 15 years. Considering that so much of the South Atlantic coastline is inaccessible on the ground, taking to the skies is a wonderful way to appreciate the wild nature that typifies most of the region. Several uniquely designed routes are available for your choosing, which take in a range of destinations, including the Salt Works, Sandwich Harbour, Welwitschia Drive, the Brandberg Mountains, Sossusvlei, the Skeleton Coast and beyond.

Prices start at around N$750 to N$800 per person for a one-hour circuit, though prices are dependent on the length of the flight and the number of passengers on board as well as the fluctuating price of aviation fuel. Generally speaking, if you can put together a large group, and you spring for the longer flight, you will get much better value for your dollars. Regardless, chartering a private plane is a privileged experience that is well worth the splurge, and there are few places in the world that can rival the beauty and grandeur of Central Namibia.

HORSEBACK RIDING

Okakambe Trails (☎ 402799; www.okakambe.iway .na; 12km east of Swakopmund on the D1901; prices variable) Meaning 'horse' in the local Herero and Oshivambo languages, Okakambe specialises in horseback riding and trekking through the desert. The German owner cares immensely for her horses, so you can be assured that they're well fed and looked after. Prices for a one-hour solo ride along the Swakop River to the Moon Landscape start at N$450, but discounts are available for larger groups and longer outings. More experienced riders can organize multiday treks with full board, as well as moonlight outings and jaunts along the beach and through the dunes.

CAMELBACK RIDING

If you want to live out all your *Lawrence of Arabia*–inspired Saharan fantasies, visit the **Camel Farm** (Map p331; ☎ 400363; ☒ 2-5pm), which is adjacent to Okakambe Trails. After donning the necessary amount of Bedouin kitsch, you can mount your dromedary and make haste for the horizon. While camels run the gamut from uncouth to downright mean-tempered, don't underestimate their speed and grace! A camel galloping in full stride can cover an enormous distance, and their unique physiology justifiably earns them the nickname 'ships of the deserts'.

KAYAKING & MARINE SAFARIS

If you're interested in taking to the high seas, see p329 for more activities in nearby Walvis Bay.

Tours

If you've arrived in Swakopmund by public transport, and don't have access to a private vehicle, then consider booking a tour through one of the operators listed below. Central Swakop is compact and easily walkable, but you need to escape the city confines if you really want to explore the area.

Prices are variable depending on the size of your party and the length of tour. As with activities in Swakop, money stretches further if you get together with a few friends and combine a few destinations to make a longer outing.

Possible tours include: sundowner on the dunes the Cape Cross seal colony (p306); Rössing Mine gem tours; Welwitschia Drive; Walvis Bay Lagoon (see p328); and various destinations in the Namib Desert and Naukluft Mountains (see p330).

The most popular operators are **Charly's Desert Tours** (Map p312; ☎ 404341; www.charlysdesert tours.com; Sam Nujoma Ave), **Namib Tours and Safaris** (☎ 404072; www.namibia-tours-safaris.com) and **Turnstone Tours** (☎ 403123; www.turnstone-tours. com). With the exception of Charly's, the operators listed in this section do not have central offices, so it's best to make arrangements through your accommodation.

If you're interested in arranging a visit to the Mondesa township, **Hata-Angu Cultural Tours** (☎ 461118; www.culturalactivities.in.na) runs a variety of different excursions that provide insight into how the other half of Skakopmunders live.

Sleeping

Swakopmund has a number of budget hotels and hostels that are all of high standard, as well as several family-run guesthouses and B&Bs. There are also a handful of attractive midrange and top-end hotels that are definitely worth the splurge.

A TERN FOR THE WORSE

Around 90% of the world population of the tiny Damara tern, of which less than 2000 breeding pairs remain, are endemic to the open shores and sandy bays of the Namib coast from South Africa to Angola. Adult Damara terns, which have a grey back and wings, a black head and white breast, measure just 22cm long, and are more similar in appearance to swallows than to other terns.

Damara terns nest on the Namib gravel flats well away from jackals, hyenas and other predators, though their small size renders them incapable of carrying food for long distances. As a result, they must always remain near a food source, which usually consists of prawns and larval fishes.

When alarmed, Damara terns try to divert the threat by flying off screaming. Since the nest is usually sufficiently well camouflaged to escape detection, this is an effective behaviour. However, if the breeding place is in any way disturbed, the parent tern abandons the nest and sacrifices the egg or chick to the elements. The following year, it seeks out a new nesting site, but more often than not, it discovers that potential alternatives are already overpopulated by other species, which it instinctively spurns.

Over the past few seasons, this has been a serious problem along the Namib coast, mainly due to the proliferation of unregulated off-road driving along the shoreline between Swakopmund and Terrace Bay. This problem is further compounded by the fact that Damara terns usually hatch only a single chick each year. In recent years, the terns have failed to breed successfully, and if the current situation continues, they may well be extinct within just a few years.

Although the biggest risk to the Damara tern continues to be off-road drivers, the increase in tourist activities on the dunes is also taking its toll. One way of reducing the environmental impact of activities is for a company to operate in a confined area. When you're booking through a company, inquire about its conservation policies. The companies listed in this guide are among the most reputable tour operators in town.

Given Swakopmund's chilly climate, air-conditioning is absent at most hotels, though you won't miss it once the sea air starts blowing through your room. On the contrary, a heater is something of a requirement in the winter months when the mercury drops along the coast.

During the school holidays in December and January, accommodation books up well in advance – make reservations as early as possible.

BUDGET
Camping
Gull's Cry (☎ 461591; campsites per person N$150) This campsite sits right on the sand at the beach front, sheltered from the wind by lovely tamarisk trees. It's convenient to the city centre, but facilities are basic, and it can get very crowded and noisy at times.

Alte Brücke Rest Camp (☎ 404918; www.altebrucke.com; Strand St; 6-person campsite N$200, s/d chalet from N$535/680) This upmarket version of the Gull's Cry features spacious campsites with private braai (barbecue) pits and power points, as well as fully equipped chalets featuring modern kitchens, full bathrooms, TV lounges and private patios. The Alte Brücke has an attrac-

tive location on the flats at the mouth of the Swakop River.

Hostels, Hotels & Lodges
Desert Sky Backpackers (☎ 402339; dsbackpackers@swakop.com; 35 Lazarett St; camping per person N$50, dm N$60, r per person N$160; 🖳) This centrally located backpackers haunt is an excellent place to drop anchor in Swakopmund. The indoor lounge is simple and homey, while the outdoor picnic tables are a nice spot for a cold beer and warm conversation. The friendly staff offers everything you've come to expect from a well-appointed backpacker lodge: kitchen facilities, storage lockers, internet access and laundry services. Free coffee is available all day, and you're within stumbling distance of the pubs if you want something stronger.

Cooke's House (☎ 462837; 32 Daniel Tjongarero St; s/d N$160/240) Housed in a 1910 historic home, this three-bedroom inn is an excellent choice if you're looking for personalised attention at the hands of the delightful owners. Darryl and Hannelore pride themselves on offering affordable accommodation with plenty of character.

Swakopmund Rest Camp (☎ 410 4333; www.swakopmund-restcamp.com; Swakop St; 2-/4-bed cabins from

N$175/200, flat from N$320) This municipal rest camp is comprised of basic shacks plopped orderly in the desert, in addition to a handful of self-contained flats with basic cooking facilities. A far less sociable option than the backpacker spots, the rest camp caters primarily to fishermen and their families, though the price is right if you're travelling with a few friends.

Seagull B&B (☎ 405278; www.seagullbandb.com.na; 60 Strand St North; s/d from N$240/300) This budget B&B is run by an accommodating Brit, and features a variety of rooms to suit travellers with wallets of varying sizes. Just a short walk north of town along Neser St, it's one of the most affordable B&Bs in Swakopmund, and is a much more personal place than some of the larger backpacker joints.

Dunes Lodge (☎ 463139; www.dunes.com.na; 12 Lazarett St; camping per person N$50, dm N$110, r from N$300; 🖳 🟊) The Dunes Lodge is an upmarket backpackers featuring a number of attractive perks, including an indoor pool and billiards table, as well as traditional backpacker amenities, including a communal kitchen, internet, TV lounge and laundry service. Both the dorm rooms and private rooms sparkle with bright paint, and you're only a few blocks from the beach.

Prinzessin Rupprecht Residenz (☎ 412540; www.prinzrupp.com.na; 15 Lazarett St; s/d from N$290/570) Housed in the former colonial military hospital, this pension appeals to history buffs looking to catch a glimpse of the Swakopmund of old. The interior has been largely retained, and you can still stroll along the hospital corridors and try to picture the building's former life.

Alternative Space (☎ 402713; nam0352@mweb.com .na; 46 Dr Alfons Weber St; s/d from N$300/400; 🖳) Located on the desert fringe, 800m east of town, this delightfully alternative budget choice is run by Frenus and Sybille Rorich. The main attractions are the castle-like architecture, saturation artwork and an industrial scrap-recycling theme. The catch is that only 'friends of Frenus and Sybille' are welcome, though they're great people and are very welcoming. Dune carts (free to guests) are guaranteed to provide a thrilling experience, especially with the dunes lying just off in the distance. Be advised that this is most definitely not a party place.

Villa Wiese (☎ 407105; www.villawiese.com; cnr Bahnhof & Windhoeker Sts; dm US$110, s/d N$330/385; 🖳) Villa Wiese is a friendly and funky guest lodge

occupying historic colonial mansion complete with vaulted ceilings, rock gardens and period furniture. It draws a very eclectic mix of overlanders, backpackers and independent travellers, and serves as a slightly more sophisticated alternative to other budget options in town. The nearby Duendin Star is its overflow property, and has similar costs and atmosphere.

Swakop Lodge (☎ 402030; 14 Nathaniel Maxuilili St; dm N$135, s/d N$415/600; 🖳) This backpacker-orientated hotel is the epicentre of the action in Swakopmund, especially since this is where many of the adrenaline activities depart from and return to, and where many of the videos are screened each night. The hotel is extremely popular with overland trucks, so it's a safe bet that the attached bar (see Drinking, p325) is probably bumping and grinding most nights of the week.

Midrange

Sea Breeze Guesthouse (☎ 463348; www.seabreeze.com.na; Turmalin St; per person N$260; 🖳) This very affordable guest house is right on the beach about 4.5km north of town, and is an excellent option if you're looking for a secluded retreat. The Italian owners have an incredible design sense, which is evident the moment you enter. Ask to see a few of the rooms as several of them have spectacular sea views, and there's no extra cost.

Hotel Pension Rapmund (☎ 402035; www.hotel pensionrapmund.com; 6-8 Bismarck St; s/d N$420/615) Overlooking the park promenade, this long-standing hotel pension is under new ownership, and has benefited from some extensive renovations. Light and airy rooms are adorned with rich woods and plenty of African and German-inspired flourishing to create an attractive accommodation spot that typifies Swakopmund.

Schweizerhaus Hotel (☎ 400331; www.schweizer haus.net; 1 Bismarck St; s/d from N$510/850; 🖳) Although it's best known for the landmark institution that is Cafe Anton (see p324), the Schweizerhaus Hotel itself is also a class act. Standard but comfortable rooms benefit from spectacular views of the beach and the adjacent lighthouse, which lights up the sky when the heavy fog rolls in from sea.

Secret Garden Guesthouse (☎ 404037; www.natron .net/tour/secretgarden; 36 Bismarck St; r per person N$450; 🖳) The 'secret garden' is the lush, palm-fringed courtyard in the centre of the guesthouse, which is the perfect oasis if you're in search of a little solitude and an intimate and tranquil retreat, especially since the beach is only a few hundred metres away.

Brigadoon Bed & Breakfast (☎ 406064; www.briga doonswakopmund.com; 16 Ludwig Koch St; s/d N$555/745; ☒) This Scottish-run B&B occupies a pleasant garden setting opposite Palm Beach, and consists of Victorian-style cottages with period furniture. For something slightly more modern, you can visit the main building and use the heated indoor pool, which is a nice consolation if the ocean is too cold for swimming.

Hotel Europa Hof (☎ 405061; www.europahof. com; 39 Bismarck St; s/d N$610/915; ☒) The Europa Hof resembles a proper Bavarian chalet, and overflows with Continental atmosphere, complete with colourful flower boxes, a German-style beer garden and European flags flying from the windows. Room interiors are fairly standard and a bit dull in comparison to the rest of the property, but they're reasonably priced, making this hotel all-around good value.

Beach Lodge (☎ 400933; www.beachlodge.com.na; Stint St; s/d from N$640/870; ☒) This boat-shaped place, which sits right on the sand about 1km north of town, allows you to watch the sea through your very own personal porthole. Rooms vary in size and amenities, and some come complete with window-side bathtubs and working fireplaces to keep you warm when the cool fog rolls in.

Top End

Sam's Giardino Hotel (☎ 403210; www.giardino.com .na; 89 Lazarett St; s/d from N$900/1150; ☒) A slice of central Europe in the desert, Sam's Giardino Hotel mixes Swiss and Italian hospitality and architecture while emphasising superb wines, fine cigars and relaxing in the rose garden with a Saint Bernard named Ornelia. The resulting combination is an incredibly sophisticated yet wholly relaxed environment where guests can live it up in the lap of luxury while not being afraid to put their feet up.

Hansa Hotel (☎ 400311; www.hansahotel.com .na; 3 Hendrick Witbooi St; s/d from N$1230/1730; ☒) Swakopmund's most established upmarket hotel bills itself as 'luxury in the desert', and makes much of the fact that it has hosted the likes of Aristotle Onassis, Sir Laurens van der Post, Eartha Kitt, Oliver Reed and Ernest Borgnine. Individually decorated rooms with lofty ceilings and picture windows are tasteful and elegant, though the highlight of the property is its classic dining hall with white glove service, bone china, sterling silver and fine crystal stemware.

Swakopmund Hotel & Entertainment Centre (☎ 400800; www.legacyhotels.co.za; off Bahnhof St; s/d from N$1599/2399; ☒ ☒) This Las Vegas–style hotel and entertainment complex is located in the shell of the historic railway station, and boasts a casino, a cinema, several restaurants, a large swimming pool, a conference centre, a gymnasium and a spa. The grounds are opulently decorated with palm trees and fountains, and the rooms are – in true Vegas fashion – lavish to the point of excessiveness.

Eating

True to its Teutonic roots, Swakopmund's restaurants have a heavy German influence, though there's certainly no shortage of local seafood and traditional Namibian favourites, as well as a surprising offering of truly cosmopolitan fare. While Windhoekers might disagree, Swakopmund can easily contend for the title of Namibia's culinary capital, and you should certainly spend your time here eating out as much as your budget will allow.

BUDGET

Self-caterers can head for the well-stocked Model/Pick & Pay supermarket on Sam

---

KALAHARI TRUFFLES

There is certainly no shortage of gourmet foods on the menu in Swakop, though one of the more heavenly items for foodies is the much-celebrated Kalahari truffle. A somewhat distant cousin of the more widely known European truffle, the Kalahari truffle is a *terfeziaceae* (desert truffle), which is endemic to arid and semi-arid areas of Africa and the Middle East. In the Kalahari, they can grow to several centimetres across, and reach weights of up to 300g. Although their flavour is not nearly as rich as the white and black truffles from Italy and France, Kalahari truffles are much more common, and thus much, much more affordable. When thinly sliced, braised in olive oil and served over a fine cut of ostrich steak, Kalahari truffles are simply divine.

Nujoma Ave near the corner with Hendrick Witbooi St. All of the backpacker spots listed in the Sleeping section have kitchens on the premises.

Out of Africa Coffee Shop (☎ 404752; 13 Daniel Tjongarero St; snacks & coffee N$15-35) This place has the motto 'Life is too short to drink bad coffee', and it does something about it! It welcomes you in the morning with some of Namibia's best coffee – espresso, cappuccino, latte and other caffeinated specialities – served up in French-style cups, along with freshly-baked muffins and light meals.

Swakopmund Cafe (☎ 402333; 5 Tobias Hainyeko St; light meals N$35-55) Swakopmunders loves their cafes, and hopping from one to the next is standard fare. At this excellent bistro, you can tuck into imaginative breakfasts, lunches and dinners, including a variety of salads, crepes, gyros, steaks and seafood specials.

Cafe Anton (☎ 402419; 1 Bismarck St; light meals N$35-65) This much-loved local institution, located in Hotel Schweizerhaus, serves superb coffee, *Apfelstrudel*, *Kugelhopf* (cake with nuts and raisins), *Mohnkuchen* (poppy seed cake), *Linzertorte* (cake flavoured with almond meal, lemon and spices, and spread with jam) and other European delights. The outdoor seating is inviting for afternoon snacks in the sun.

MIDRANGE

Napolitana (☎ 402773; 33 Nathaniel Maxuilili St; mains N$50-85) This quaint and intimate Italian-bistro specialises in gourmet pizzas and pasta, as well as heartier meat and seafood dishes. Portions are large and ingredients are fresh, and there's nothing quite like a hot steaming pie to get your stamina back after a day of adrenaline sports.

Swakopmund Brauhaus (☎ 402214; 22 Sam Nujoma Ave; mains N$60-90) This excellent restaurant and boutique brewery offers one of Swakopmund's most sought-after commodities, namely authentic German-style beer. And, not to break with tradition, feel free to accompany your frothy brew with a plate of mixed sausages, piled sauerkraut and a healthy dollop of spicy mustard.

Cape to Cairo Restaurant (☎ 463160; 7 Nathaniel Maxuilili St; mains N$60-95) This popular tourist restaurant serves a wide variety of dishes from across the African continent. The speciality here is game meat, served up in fillets, stews and burgers, though vegetarians will have no problem feasting on chapattis, ratatouilles and other veggie treats.

Kücki's Pub (☎ 402407; Tobias Hainyeko St; meals N$60-100) Another Swakopmund institution, Kücki's has been in the bar and restaurant biz for a couple of decades running. Although the menu is full of pub grub and comfort food, everything is masterfully prepared, and the warm and congenial atmosphere is a welcome complement.

Lighthouse Pub & Cafe (☎ 400894; Palm Beach; mains US$60-110) With a postcard-perfect view of the beach and crashing surf, the Lighthouse Pub & Cafe is an atmospheric choice for lovers of fine seafood. Depending on what the fishermen are catching in their nets, lines and pots, you'll find everything from kingklip and lobster to kabeljou and calamari.

Tug (☎ 402356; mains US$75-125) Housed in the beached tugboat *Danie Hugo* near the jetty, the Tug is something of an obligatory destination for any dinner-goer in Swakopmund. Regarded by many as the best restaurant in town, the Tug is an atmospheric, upmarket choice for meat and seafood, though a sundowner cocktail will do just fine. Due its extreme popularity and small size, advance bookings are recommended.

TOP END

Grapevine (☎ 404770; Libertine St; mains N$80-155) True to its moniker, the emphasis at this upmarket bistro is on the fruit of the vine, and you'll be allotted plenty of time to select your vintage from the veritable novel of a wine list. Once you've selected your vino, ask your server to help you match your food and drink, and the rest of the evening is guaranteed to be a heavenly affair.

Il Tulipano (☎ 400122; 37 Daniel Tjongarero St; mains N$95-165) Italian food is loved the world over, but it's an all-together different cuisine when an Italian is preparing it. At Il Tulipano, you can expect the real deal, namely handmade semolina pastas, light and fluffy risottos and fragrant lamb and veal dishes, topped off with fresh-baked breads, carefully chosen wines, strong coffees and sugary sweets.

Hansa Hotel Restaurant (☎ 400311; www.hansahotel.com.na; 3 Hendrick Witbooi St; mains N$95-215) While there are a couple of worthy newcomers staking their territory within Swakopmund's ever-increasing gourmet restaurant scene, it's hard to top history, especially when the Hansa Hotel is steeped in it. In the main dining hall at this classic colonial spot, you can indulge in culinary excesses such as Kalahari-truffle topped ostrich steak, oryx medallions in wildberry sauce and bacon-wrapped monkfish filets drenched in herbed butter.

Drinking & Entertainment

After spending your day chasing down an adrenaline rush, there's nothing much left to do except get plastered. Swakopmund likes to party, and there a few bars to get your drink on. In addition to the places listed, the Tug and the Lighthouse (see opposite) have popular happy-hour spots to coincide with Swakop sunsets.

Fagin's Pub (Hendrick Witbooi St) This extremely popular, down-to-earth watering hole is reminiscent of a US truckies' stop, complete with a jocular staff, a faithful clientele and evening videos of your day's adrenaline activities.

Cool Bananas (14 Nathaniel Maxuilili St) Housed inside the Swakop Lodge, this bar-club is packed when the overland trucks roll into town, which means you can be assured of plenty of drunken revelry well into the morning hours.

Rafter's Action Pub (cnr Tobias Hainyeko & Woermann Sts) At Rafter's, it's a safe bet that the music is always pounding, the strobes are always flashing and everyone is strutting their stuff on the dance floor, regardless of the time of night.

Captain's Tavern Pub (2 Bahnhof St) This upmarket tavern attracts highbrow clientele from the Swakopmund Hotel & Entertainment Centre, and sometimes features live music.

Shopping

Street stalls sell Zimbabwean crafts on the waterfront by the steps below Cafe Anton on Bismarck St.

Karakulia Craft Centre (☎ 461415; www.karakulia.com.na; 3 Knobloch St) This local carpet factory produces original and beautiful African rugs, carpets and wall hangings in karakul wool and offers tours of the spinning, dyeing and weaving processes.

Cobwebs (☎ 404024; brigadon@iafrica.com.na; 10 Tobias Hainyeko St) This arts shop sells African masks, crafts and other traditional artefacts.

Peter's Antiques (☎ /fax 405624; 24 Tobias Hainyeko St) This place is an Ali Baba's cave of treasures, specialising in colonial relics, historic literature, West African art, politically incorrect German paraphernalia, and genuine West African fetishes and other artefacts from around the continent.

Getting There & Away

AIR

Air Namibia (☎ 405123; www.airnamibia.com.na) has several flights a week between Windhoek's Eros Airport and Walvis Bay (see p330), from where you can easily catch a bus or taxi to Swakopmund.

BUS

There are several weekly buses between Windhoek and Swakopmund (N$180, five hours) on the **Intercape Mainliner** (www.intercape.co.za). You can easily book your tickets in advance online.

Also consider **Town Hopper** (www.namibiashuttle.com), which runs private shuttle buses between Windhoek and Swakopmund (N$220), and also offers door-to-door pick-up and drop-off service.

Finally, combis (minibuses) run this route fairly regular frequency, and a ride between Windhoek and Swakopmund shouldn't cost more than N$100. Swakopmund is also a minor public transport hub, serving various regional destinations including Walvis Bay by combi, with fares averaging between N$15 and N$30.

CAR

Swakopmund is about 400km west of Windhoek on the B2, the country's main east–west highway.

HITCHING

Hitching isn't difficult between Swakopmund and Windhoek or Walvis Bay, but conditions can be rough if heading for Namib-Naukluft Park or the Skeleton Coast; hitchers risk heatstroke, sandblasting and hypothermia – sometimes in the same day.

TRAIN

Trans-Namib (☎ 061-2982175) trains operate throughout the day and night (from N$75), though they're not very convenient or popular, especially given the ease of bus travel.

See p386 for information on the plush *Desert Express* 'rail cruise' to and from Windhoek.

WALVIS BAY
☎ 064 / pop 65,000
Walvis Bay (vahl-fis bay) is situated 30km south of Swakopmund, and is the only real port between Lüderitz and Luanda (Angola).

The natural harbour at Walvis Bay is the result of the sand spit Pelican Point, which forms a natural breakwater and shelters the city from the strong ocean surge.

Due to the city's strategic location, Walvis Bay has a long and storied history of British and South African occupation. Since 1992 the city has rested firmly in Namibian hands, and is the country's second-largest city after Windhoek. Today, Walvis Bay boasts a tanker berth, a dry dock and container facilities, as well as a lucrative salt works and fish-processing industry.

Unlike Swakopmund, Walvis Bay was snatched by the British years before the German colonists could get their hands on it. As a result, Walvis Bay is architecturally uninspiring, and lacks the Old World ambience of its northerly neighbour. In marked contrast, the area around Walvis Bay is home to a number of unique natural attractions, including one of the largest flocks of flamingos in the whole of Southern Africa.

History
Although Walvis Bay was claimed by the British Cape Colony in 1795, it was not formally annexed by Britain until 1878 when it was realised that the Germans were eyeing the harbour. In 1910, Britain relinquished its hold on Walvis Bay, and it became part of the newly formed Union of South Africa.

When the Germans were defeated after WWI, South Africa was given the UN mandate to administer all of German South West Africa as well as the Walvis Bay enclave. This stood until 1977, when South Africa unilaterally decided to return it to the Cape Province. The UN was not impressed by this unauthorised act, and insisted that the enclave be returned to the mandate immediately. In response, South Africa steadfastly refused to bow.

When Namibia achieved its independence in 1990, Namibians laid claim to Walvis Bay. Given the strategic value of the natural harbour, plus the salt works (which produced 40,000 tonnes annually – some 90% of South Africa's salt), the offshore guano platforms and the rich fishery, gaining control over Walvis Bay became a matter of great importance for Namibia.

In 1992, after it had become apparent that white rule in South Africa was ending, the two countries agreed that South Africa would re-

move its border posts, and that both countries would jointly administer the enclave. Finally, facing growing domestic troubles and its first democratic elections, South Africa gave in, and at midnight on 28 February 1994, the Namibian flag was raised over Walvis Bay for the first time.

Orientation
Walvis Bay is laid out in a grid pattern. Although some streets have been renamed after South-West African People's Organisation (Swapo) luminaries, Walvis Bay streets, from 1st to 15th Sts, run northeast to southwest. The roads, from 1st to 18th Rds, run northwest to southeast. North of town along the coast are the small holiday settlements of Dolfynpark and Langstrand.

Information
Computerland I-café (Sam Nujoma Ave; per hr N$20) Internet access.
Police (☎ 10111; cnr 11th St & 13th Rd)
Post office (Sam Nujoma Ave) Provides public telephones and fax services.
Viggo-Lund Bookseller (Sam Nujoma Ave) Has a modest selection of popular fiction.
Walvis-i (☎ 209170; Shop 6, Hickory Creek Spur Bldg, Nangolo Mbumba Dr; ☽ 9am-5pm Mon-Fri, 9am-1pm Sat) Provides visitor information.
Welwitschia Medical Centre (13th Rd; ☽ 24hr)

Sights
DUNE 7
In the bleak expanse just off the C14, 6km by road from town, Dune 7 (Map p331) is popular with locals as a slope for sandboarding and skiing. The picnic site, which is now being engulfed by sand, has several shady palm trees tucked away in the lee of the dune.

If you want to do as the locals do, then head to a petrol station and buy a 'dune board' for about N$30 (a flexible piece of masonite board) and a jar of polish. This is a much cheaper alternative than organising a sandboarding trip in Swakopmund, and has some do-it-yourself appeal.

RHENISH MISSION CHURCH
Walvis Bay's oldest remaining building, the **Rhenish Mission Church** (5th Rd) was prefabricated in Hamburg, Germany, reconstructed beside the harbour in 1880 and consecrated the following year. Because of machinery sprawl in the harbour area, it was relocated to its present

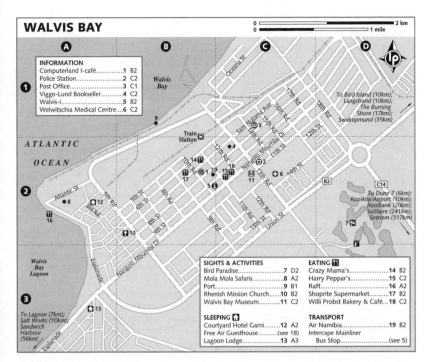

WALVIS BAY

INFORMATION
Computerland I-café.............1 B2
Police Station.......................2 C2
Post Office..........................3 C1
Viggo-Lund Bookseller..........4 C2
Walvis-i..............................5 B2
Welwitschia Medical Centre...6 C2

SIGHTS & ACTIVITIES
Bird Paradise........................7 D2
Mola Mola Safaris................8 A2
Port....................................9 B1
Rhenish Mission Church......10 B2
Walvis Bay Museum.............11 C2

SLEEPING
Courtyard Hotel Garni.........12 A2
Free Air Guesthouse..........(see 18)
Lagoon Lodge.....................13 A3

EATING
Crazy Mama's......................14 B2
Harry Peppar's....................15 C2
Raft...................................16 A2
Shoprite Supermarket..........17 B2
Willi Probst Bakery & Café...18 C2

TRANSPORT
Air Namibia........................19 B2
Intercape Mainliner
    Bus Stop.......................(see 5)

site in the mid-20th century, and functioned as a church until 1966.

ROOIBANK
Rooibank, located 20km from town at the southeastern corner of the former Walvis Bay enclave, is named for a cluster of red granite outcrops on the northern bank of the Kuiseb River. This area is best known as the site of one of Namibia's few Topnaar Khoikhoi settlements. Notice the unusual vegetation, which includes the fleshy succulent dollar bush and the !nara bush, a leafless plant that bears the spiky !nara melons (see boxed text, p335), which are still a staple for the Topnaar.

THE RAILWAY
During the winter, rail services between Swakopmund and Walvis Bay are often plagued by windblown sand, which covers the tracks and undermines the track bed and sleepers. This isn't a new problem – 5km east of town on the C14, notice the embankment which has buried a section of narrow-gauge track from the last century. In front of the train station are the remains of

the *Hope,* an old locomotive that once ran on the original narrow-gauge railway. Both were abandoned after the line was repeatedly buried beneath 10m sand drifts. The *Hope* is now a national monument, and stands on 6th St in front of the train station.

WALVIS BAY MUSEUM
The town **museum** (Nangolo Mbumba Dr; admission free; 9am-12.30pm & 3-4.30pm Mon-Fri) is located in the library. It concentrates on the history and maritime background of Walvis Bay, but also has archaeological exhibits, a mineral collection and natural history displays on the Namib Desert and the Atlantic Coast.

BIRD ISLAND
Along the Swakopmund road, 10km north of Walvis Bay, take a look at the offshore wooden platform known as Bird Island (Map p331). It was built to provide a roost and nesting site for sea birds and a source of guano for use as fertiliser. The annual yield is around 1000 tonnes, and the smell from the island is truly unforgettable.

CENTRAL NAMIBIA

FLAMINGOS AT WALVIS

Lesser and greater flamingos flock in large numbers to pools along the Namib Desert coast, particularly around Walvis Bay and Lüderitz. They're excellent fliers, and have been known to migrate up to 500km overnight in search of proliferations of algae and crustaceans.

The lesser flamingo filters algae and diatoms (microscopic organisms) from the water by sucking in, and vigorously expelling water from its bill. The minute particles are caught on fine hairlike protrusions, which line the inside of the mandibles. The suction is created by the thick fleshy tongue, which rests in a groove in the lower mandible and pumps back and forth like a piston. It has been estimated that a million lesser flamingos can consume over 180 tonnes of algae and diatoms daily.

While lesser flamingos obtain food by filtration, the greater flamingo supplements its algae diet with small molluscs, crustaceans and other organic particles from the mud. When feeding, it will rotate in a circle while stamping its feet in an effort to scare up a tasty potential meal.

The greater and lesser flamingos are best distinguished by their colouration. Greater flamingos are white to light pink, and their beaks are whitish with a black tip. Lesser flamingos are a deeper pink – often reddish – colour, with dark-red beaks.

Located near Walvis Bay are three diverse wetland areas, namely the lagoon, the salt works and the Bird Paradise at the sewage works. Together they form Southern Africa's single most important coastal wetland for migratory birds, with up to 150,000 transient avian visitors stopping by annually, including massive flocks of both lesser and greater flamingos. The three wetland areas are as follows:

- **The Lagoon** This shallow and sheltered 45,000-hectare lagoon, southwest of Walvis Bay and west of the Kuiseb River mouth, attracts a range of coastal water birds in addition to enormous flocks of lesser and greater flamingos. It also supports chestnut banded plovers and curlew sandpipers, as well as the rare Damara tern (see the boxed text, p321).

- **The Salt Works** Southwest of the lagoon is this 3500-hectare saltpan complex, which currently supplies over 90% of South Africa's salt. As with the one in Swakopmund, these pans concentrate salt from seawater with the aid of evaporation. They also act as a rich feeding ground for prawns and larval fish.

- **Bird Paradise** Immediately east of town along the C14 at the municipal sewage purification works is this nature sanctuary, which consists of a series of shallow artificial pools, fringed by reeds. An observation tower and a short nature walk afford excellent bird-watching.

THE PORT

With permission from the public relations officer of the **Portnet** (☎ 208320) or from the Railway Police, beside the train station near the end of 13th Rd, you can visit the fishing harbour and commercial port, and see the heavy machinery that keeps Namibia's import-export business ticking. Don't forget to bring your passport!

AROUND WALVIS BAY
Sandwich Harbour

Sandwich Harbour (Map p331), located 56km south of Walvis Bay, historically served as a commercial fishing and trading port. Some historians suggest that the name may be derived from an English whaler, the *Sandwich*, whose captain produced the first map of this coastline. Still, others contend that the name

may also be a corruption of the German word *sandfische*, a type of shark often found here. History aside, at present the harbour is a total wilderness devoid of any human settlement.

While few people would think of visiting such a remote destination, 4WD enthusiasts regard an excursion to Sandwich Bay as a true test of their off-road mettle. If you think you have what it takes, the **Topnaar 4WD Trail** extends from Walvis Bay through the sand sea to Sandwich Harbour, Conception Bay and the fabulous *Edward Bolen* shipwreck.

Assuming you have a sturdy high-clearance 4WD vehicle, follow the left fork 5km south of Walvis Bay. When the road splits at the salt works, bear left again and continue across the marshy Kuiseb Delta. After 15km, you will be entering the Namib-Naukluft Park, and must purchase a permit at the gate.

For the final 20km into Sandwich Harbour you can either continue straight along the sandy beach (time your journey for low tide) or bear left past the control post and follow the tracks further inland. However, dune shifts may present tedious stretches of deep sand or alter the route entirely. Bring a shovel, a towrope and a couple of planks in case you get stuck.

One last thing: even if you've logged a good number of hours in Namibia's back country, don't underestimate the difficulty of this route. A good number of hardened 4WD veterans in Swakop and Walvis won't tackle this route unless they are part of a convoy, so you should probably heed their advice and find safety in number.s

For the less adventurous, tour operators in Swakopmund (p313) and Mola Mola in Walvis Bay (see below) can arrange day-trips.

Activities
KAYAKING
Run by the very amenable Jeanne Mientjes, **Eco-Marine Kayak Tours** (☎ 203144; www.emkayak .iway.na; 3hr tour from N$495) offers sea-kayaking trips around the beautiful Walvis Bay wetlands. Note that there is no central office, though bookings can be made over the phone or through your accommodation.

MARINE SAFARI
Mola Mola Safaris (☎ 205511; www.mola-namibia.com; cnr Esplanade & Atlantic St; prices variable) This marine safari company offers fully customisable boating trips around the Walvis Bay and Swakopmund coastal areas, where you can expect to see dolphins, seals and countless birds. Prices are dependent on your group size and length of voyage. Mola Mola also offers a variety of land safaris, including guided 4WD trips to Sandwich Harbour and sights beyond.

Sleeping
Accommodation options are located either in the city centre, or at Langstrand (Long Beach), which is 10km north of Walvis Bay on the road to Swakopmund. While there are plenty of recommendable places to stay in Walvis, most travellers prefer to bed down in Swakopmund and simply visit Walvis Bay on a day trip.

The Courtyard Hotel Garni (☎ 206252; 16 3rd Rd; s/d from N$600/680; ▨ ▯) Owing to regular renovations, the Courtyard is one of the better hotels

in Walvis Bay, yet still occupies an affordable price bracket. Elegant rooms with polished hardwood floors surround two manicured courtyards, and guests can access the indoor heated pool and sauna.

Free Air Guesthouse (☎ 202247; www.namibia-walvis bay-guesthouse.com; cnr 12th Rd & 9th St; s/d N$655/919; ▯) A welcome new addition to the Walvis Bay accommodation market, Free Air occupies a visually arresting building with sharp lines and smooth surfaces. Minimalist rooms with carefully selected design flourishes are comfortable and soothing, as is the screened patio where you can sip a cappuccino and watch the waves roll in.

Lagoon Lodge (☎ 200850; www.lagoonlodge.com.na; 2 Nangolo Mbumba Dr; s/d N$710/1060; ▨) This French-run lodge commands a magnificent location next to the lagoon, and features individually decorated rooms with private terraces facing out towards the sand and sea. The interior courtyard is awash in rich pastels, which lend a positively Caribbean look and feel to the poolside verandah.

The Burning Shore (☎ 207568; www.burningshore.na; s/d from N$895/1380; ▨ ▨) This once little known resort, located south of Walvis Bay along the Langstrand (Long Beach), received a huge publicity boost in 2006 following Angelina Jolie's and Brad Pitt's surprise trip to Namibia. While much of the hype has since dissipated, the Burning Shore remains a secluded retreat where you can soak up the beauty and the serenity of the dunes and the ocean. Rooms are luxurious without being pretentious, which lends a relaxed elegance and cool sophistication to the entire property.

Eating
In addition to the listings below, you can also dine out in nearby Swakopmund, which has a much wider and more diverse selection of restaurants.

Willi Probst Bakery & Café (☎ 202744; cnr 12th Rd & 9th St; light meals N$15-35) If you're feeling nostalgic for Swakopmund (or Deutschland for that matter), take comfort in knowing that Probst specialises in stodgy German fare: pork, meatballs, schnitzel and the like.

Harry Peppar's (☎ 203131; cnr 11th Rd & Nangolo Mbumba Dr; pizzas N$40-55) Harry comes up with all sorts of creative thick-crust pizzas, and if you're feeling lazy and don't want to stop by and say hi, he'll deliver his mad creations right to your hotel.

Crazy Mama's (☎ 207364; cnr Sam Nujoma Ave & 11th Rd; mains N$45-65) This funky little bistro, which is centred on an enormous hewn tree, gets rave reviews for its warm vibes, friendly service and ever-changing menu offering varied food items that span the culinary globe.

The Raft (☎ 204877; Esplanade; mains N$75-125) This Walvis Bay landmark sits on stilts off-shore, and has a great front-row view of the ducks, pelicans and flamingos. The partner restaurant to the Tug in Swakopmund, you can expect a similar offering of high-quality meats and seafood in addition to spectacular sunsets and ocean views.

Getting There & Away

AIR
Air Namibia (☎ 203102; www.airnamibia.com.na) has several flights a week between Windhoek's Eros Airport and Walvis Bay's Rooikop Airport, located 10km southeast of town on the C14.

BUS & COMBI
All buses and combis to Walvis Bay run via Swakopmund – for more information, see p325.

HITCHING
Hitching isn't difficult between Walvis Bay and Swakopmund, but weather conditions can be rough if heading for Namib-Naukluft Park or the Skeleton Coast. For more on hitching, see p386.

NAMIB-NAUKLUFT PARK

The present boundaries of Namib-Naukluft Park, one of the world's largest national parks, were established in 1978 by merging the Namib Desert Park and the Naukluft Mountain Zebra Park with parts of Diamond Area 1 and bits of surrounding government land. Today, it takes in over 23,000 sq km of arid and semi-arid land, and protects various areas of vast ecological importance in the Namib and the Naukluft, including Sossusvlei, Sandwich Harbour and Welwitschia Drive. The Namib-Naukluft Park also abuts the NamibRand Nature Reserve, the largest privately owned property in Southern Africa, forming a massive wildlife corridor that promotes migratory movement.

For coverage of Welwitschia Drive and Sandwich Harbour, see p316 and p328, respectively.

NAMIB SECTION

While most people associates the Namib solely with Sossusvlei, the desert sweeps across most of Central Namibia, and is characterised by a large array of geological formations. Given the extremes of temperature and environment, you will need a 4WD vehicle in addition to good navigation skills in order to properly explore the Namib. However, a surprisingly comprehensive network of bush campsites provides a reliable safety net, and truly this is one place where the journey itself is worth much more than the destination.

Sights

KUISEB CANYON
Located on the Gamsberg Pass route west of the Khomas Hochland, Kuiseb Canyon contains the ephemeral Kuiseb River, which is no more than a broad sandy riverbed for most of the year. Although it may flow for two or three weeks during the rainy season, it only gets as far as Gobabeb before seeping into the sand. At Rooibank (p327), drinking water for Walvis Bay is pumped from this subterranean supply.

It was in Kuiseb Canyon that the famous geologists Henno Martin and Hermann Korn went into hiding for three years during WWII, as recounted in Martin's book *The Sheltering Desert*. Today, the canyon's upper reaches remain uninhabited, though there are scattered Topnaar Khoikhoi villages where the valley broadens out near the north river bank.

HAMILTON HILLS
The range of limestone hills known as the Hamilton Hills, south of Vogelfederberg campsite, rises 600m above the surrounding desert plains. It provides lovely desert hikes, and the fog-borne moisture supports an amazing range of succulents and other botanical wonders.

Sleeping

The Namib-Naukluft Park has eight exclusive camps, some of which have multiple but widely spaced campsites. Sites have tables, toilets and braai pits, but no washing facili-

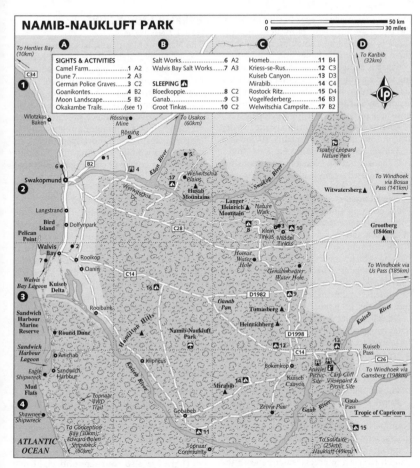

NAMIB-NAUKLUFT PARK

SIGHTS & ACTIVITIES
Camel Farm.......................1 A2
Dune 7..............................2 A3
German Police Graves......3 C2
Goanikontes....................4 B2
Moon Landscape.............5 B2
Okakambe Trails............(see 1)
Salt Works........................6 A2
Walvis Bay Salt Works......7 A3

SLEEPING
Bloedkoppie.....................8 C2
Ganab...............................9 C3
Groot Tinkas..................10 C2
Homeb.............................11 B4
Kriess-se-Rus...................12 C3
Kuiseb Canyon...............13 D3
Mirabib...........................14 C4
Rostock Ritz....................15 D4
Vogelfederberg...............16 B3
Welwitschia Campsite.....17 B2

ties. Brackish water is available for cooking and washing but not drinking – be sure that you bring enough water. All sites must be prebooked through Namibia Wildlife Resorts (NWR) in Windhoek (p234) or Swakopmund (p313). Camping costs US$100 per site plus N$50 per person, and fees are payable when the park permit is issued.

Bloedkoppie (Blood Hill) has among the most beautiful and popular sites in the park. If you're coming from Swakopmund, they lie 55km northeast of the C28, along a signposted track. The northern sites may be accessed with 2WD, but they tend to be more crowded. The southern sites are quieter and more secluded, but can be reached only by 4WD. The surrounding area offers some pleasant walking,

and at Klein Tinkas, 5km east of Bloedkoppie, you'll see the ruins of a colonial police station (basically a ruined hut) and the graves of two German police officers dating back to 1895.

Groot Tinkas must be accessed with 4WD, and rarely sees much traffic. It enjoys a lovely setting beneath shady rocks and the surroundings are super for nature walks. During rainy periods, the brackish water in the nearby dam attracts a variety of birdlife.

Vogelfederberg is a small facility, 2km south of the C14, and makes a convenient overnight camp. Located just 51km from Walvis Bay, it's more popular for picnics or short walks. It's worth looking at the intermittent pools on the summit, which shelter a species

CENTRAL NAMIBIA

of brine prawn whose eggs hatch only when the pools are filled with rainwater. The only shade is provided by a small overhang where there are two picnic tables and braai pits.

Ganab is a dusty, exposed facility, translating to 'Camelthorn Acacia', that sits beside a shallow stream bed on the gravel plains. It's shaded by hardy acacia trees, and a nearby bore hole provides water for antelopes.

Kriess-se-Rus is a rather ordinary site in a dry stream bank on the gravel plains, 107km east of Walvis Bay on the Gamsberg Pass Route. It is shaded, but isn't terribly prepossessing, and is best used simply as a convenient stop en route between Windhoek and Walvis Bay.

Kuiseb Canyon is a shady site at the Kuiseb River crossing along the C14 and is also a convenient place to break up a trip between Windhoek and Walvis Bay. The location is scenic enough, but the dust and noise from passing vehicles makes it less appealing than other campsites. There are pleasant short canyon walks, but during heavy rains in the mountains the site can be flooded; in the summer months, keep tabs on the weather.

Mirabib is a pleasant facility that accommodates two parties at separate sites, and is comfortably placed beneath rock overhangs along a large granite escarpment. There's evidence that these shelters were used by nomadic peoples as early as 9000 years ago, and also by nomadic shepherds in the 4th or 5th century.

Homeb is located in a scenic spot upstream from the most accessible set of dunes in the Namib-Naukluft Park, and can accommodate several groups. Residents of the nearby Topnaar Khoikhoi village dig wells in the Kuiseb riverbed to access water beneath the surface, and one of their dietary staples is the !nara melon (see boxed text, p335), which obtains moisture from the water table through a long taproot. This hidden water also supports a good stand of trees, including camelthorn acacia and ebony.

Getting There & Away

The main park transit routes, the C28, C14, D1982 and D1998, are all open to 2WD traffic. However, the use of minor roads requires a park permit (N\$40 per day plus N\$10 per vehicle), which can either be picked up at any of the park gates or arranged in advance through NWR. While some minor roads in the park are accessible to high-clearance 2WD vehicles, a 4WD is highly recommended.

NAUKLUFT MOUNTAINS

☎ 063 / elev 1973m

The Naukluft Mountains, which rise steeply from the gravel plains of the central Namib, are characterised by a high plateau bounded by gorges, caves and springs cut deeply from dolomite formations. The Tsondab, Tsams and Tsauchab Rivers all rise in the massif, and the relative abundance of water creates an ideal habitat for mountain zebras, kudus, leopards, springboks and klipspringers. In addition to wildlife watching, the Naukluft is home to a couple of challenging treks that open up this largely inaccessible terrain.

History

In the early 1890s the Naukluft was the site of heated battle between the German colonial forces and the Nama. In January 1893 a contingent of Schutztruppe soldiers estimated that they could force the Nama to flee their settlement at Hoornkrans in three days. However, due to their unfamiliarity with the terrain, and their lack of experience in guerrilla warfare, the battle waged for months, resulting in heavy losses on both sides. Eventually, the Nama offered to accept German sovereignty if they could retain their lands and weapons. The Germans accepted, thus ending the Battle of the Naukluft.

Information

Most Naukluft visitors come to hike either the Waterkloof or Olive Trails. These hikes are open to day visitors, but most hikers want to camp at Naukluft (Koedoesrus), which must be prebooked.

There are also four-day and eight-day loops, which have more restrictions attached. Thanks to stifling summer temperatures and potentially heavy rains, these two are only open from 1 March to the third Friday in October. Officially, you can only begin these hikes on the Tuesday, Thursday and Saturday of the first three weeks of each month. The price of N\$100 per person includes accommodation at the Hikers' Haven hut on the night before and after the hike, as well as camping at trailside shelters and the Ubusis Canyon Hut. In addition, you'll have to pay N\$50 per person per day and another N\$10 per day for each vehicle you leave parked. Groups must comprise three to 12 people.

Due to the typically hot, dry conditions and lack of reliable natural water sources, you must

NAUKLUFT MOUNTAINS

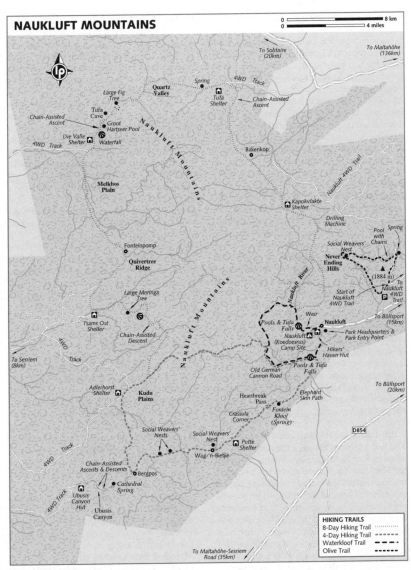

carry at least 3L to 4L of water per person per day, as well as food and emergency supplies.

Sights & Activities

WATERKLOOF TRAIL

This lovely 17km anticlockwise loop takes a total of about seven hours to complete, and begins at the Naukluft (Koedoesrus) campsite,

located 2km west of the park headquarters. It climbs the Naukluft River and past a frog-infested weir (don't miss the amazing reed tunnel!) and a series of pools, which offer cool and refreshing drinking and swimming. About 1km beyond the last pool, the trail then turns west, away from the Naukluft River and up a kloof (ravine). From there to the halfway point, the route traverses an increasingly open plateau.

Shortly after the halfway mark, the trail climbs steeply to a broad 1910m ridge, which is the highest point on the route. Here you'll have fabulous desert views before you begin a long, steep descent into the Gororosib Valley. Along the way, you'll pass several inviting pools full of reeds and tadpoles, and climb down an especially impressive waterfall before meeting up with the Naukluft River. Here, the route turns left and follows the 4WD track back to the park headquarters.

OLIVE TRAIL

The 11km Olive Trail, named for the wild olives that grow alongside it, begins at the car park 4km northeast of the park headquarters. The walk runs clockwise around the triangular loop and takes four to five hours.

The route begins with a steep climb onto the plateau, affording good views of the Naukluft Valley. It then turns sharply east and descends a constricted river valley, which becomes deeper and steeper and makes a couple of perfect U-turns before it reaches a point where hikers must traverse a canyon wall – past a pool – using anchored chains. In several places along this stretch, the dramatic geology presents an astonishing gallery of natural artwork. Near the end of the route, the trail strikes the Naukluft 4WD route and swings sharply south, where it makes a beeline back to the car park.

FOUR-DAY & EIGHT-DAY LOOPS

The two big loops through the massif can be hiked in four and eight days. For many people the Naukluft is a magical place, but its charm is more subtle than that of Fish River Canyon in southern Namibia. For example, some parts are undeniably spectacular, such as the Zebra Highway, Ubusis Canyon and Die Valle (look for the fantastic stallion profile on the rock beside the falls). However, a couple of days involve walking in relatively open country or along some maddeningly rocky riverbeds.

The four-day 60km loop is actually just the first third of the eight-day 120km loop, combined with a 22km cross-country jaunt across the plateau back to park headquarters. It joins up with the Waterkloof Trail at its halfway point, and follows it the rest of the way back to park headquarters. Alternatively, you can finish the four-day route at Tsams Ost

Shelter, midway through the eight-day loop, where a road leads out to the Sesriem-Solitaire Rd. However, you must prearrange to leave a vehicle there before setting off from park headquarters. Note that hikers may not begin from Tsams Ost without special permission from the rangers at Naukluft.

These straightforward hikes are marked by white footprints (except those sections that coincide with the Waterkloof Trail, which is marked with yellow footprints). Conditions are typically hot and dry, and water is only reliably available at overnight stops (at Putte, it's 400m from the shelter).

To shorten the eight-day hike to seven days, it's possible to skip Ubusis Canyon by turning north at Bergpos and staying the second night at Adlerhorst. Alternatively, very fit hikers combine the seventh and eighth days.

In four places – Ubusis Canyon, above Tsams Ost, Die Valle and just beyond Tufa Shelter – hikers must negotiate dry waterfalls, boulder-blocked kloofs and steep tufa formations with the aid of chains. Some people find this off-putting, so be sure you're up to it.

NAUKLUFT 4WD TRAIL

Off-road enthusiasts can now exercise their machines on the national park's 73km Naukluft 4WD Trail. It begins near the start of the Olive Trail and follows a loop near the northeastern corner of the Naukluft area. The route costs N$220 per vehicle plus an additional US$50 per person per day, including accommodation in one of the four stone-walled A-frames at the 28km point. Facilities include shared toilets, showers and braai pits. Up to four vehicles/16 people are permitted here at a time. Book through the NWR office in Windhoek (p234).

Sleeping

In addition to the unofficial campsites along the trails, there are several accommodation options outside the park.

Tsauchab River Camping (Map p310; ☎ 293416; www.natron.net/tsauchab, camping per site N$100 plus per person N$70, s/d chalet N$640/1060) If you're an avid hiker (or just love excellent settings!), you're in for a treat. The scattered campsites here sit beside the Tsauchab riverbed – one occupies a huge hollow tree – and each has a private shower block, a sink and braai area. From the main site, an 11km day hike climbs to the summit of Aloekop. Beside a spring 11km

!NARA MELONS

Historically, human existence in the Namib Desert has been made possible by an unusual spiny plant, the !nara melon. It was first described taxonomically by the same Friedrich Welwitsch who gave his name to the welwitschia plant.

Although the !nara bush lives and grows in the desert, it is not a desert plant since it lacks the ability to prevent water loss through transpiration. So it must take in moisture from the groundwater table via a long taproot. As a result, !nara melons are an effective way of monitoring underground water tables: when the plants are healthy, so is the water supply! Its lack of leaves also protects it from grazing animals, although ostriches do nip off its tender growing shoots.

As with the welwitschia, the male and female sex organs in the !nara melon exist in separate plants. Male plants flower throughout the year, but it's the female plant that produces the 15cm melon each summer, providing a favourite meal for jackals, insects and humans. In fact, it remains a primary food of the Topnaar Khoi-Khoi people, and has also become a local commercial enterprise. Each year at harvest time, the Topnaar erect camps around the Kuiseb Delta to collect the fruits. Although melons can be eaten raw, most people prefer to dry them for later use, or prepare, package and ship them to urban markets.

away from the main site is the 4WD exclusive site, which is the starting point for the wonderful 21km Mountain Zebra Hiking Trail.

Büllsport Guest Farm (Map p310; ☎ 693371; www.natron.net/tour/buellspt; s/d incl half board N$660/990) This scenic farm, owned by Ernst and Johanna Sauber, occupies a lovely, austere setting below the Naukluft Massif, and features a ruined colonial police station, the Bogenfels arch and several resident mountain zebras. A highlight is the 4WD excursion up to the plateau and the hike back down the gorge, past several idyllic natural swimming pools.

Zebra River Lodge (Map p310; ☎ 693265; www.zebrariver.com; s/d incl full board N$850/1580) Occupying a magical setting in the Tsaris Mountains, this is Rob and Marianne Field's private Grand Canyon. The surrounding wonderland of desert mountains, plateaus, valleys and natural springs is accessible on a network of hiking trails and 4WD tracks. If you take it very slowly, the lodge road is accessible by 2WD vehicles.

Getting There & Away

The Naukluft is best reached via the C24 from Rehoboth and the D1206 from Rietoog; petrol is available at Büllsport and Rietoog. From Sesriem, 103km away, the nearest access is via the dip-ridden D854.

SESRIEM & SOSSUSVLEI

☎ 063

Despite being Namibia's number one tourist attraction, Sossusvlei still manages to feel isolated. Hiking through the dunes, which are

part of the 32,000 sq km sand sea that covers much of the region, is a sombre experience. The dunes reach as high as 325m, and are part of one of the oldest and driest ecosystems on earth. However, the landscape here is constantly changing – wind forever alters the shape of the dunes, while colours shift with the changing light, reaching the peak of their brilliance just after sunrise.

The gateway to Sossusvlei is Sesriem (Six Thongs), which was the number of joined leather ox-wagon thongs necessary to draw water from the bottom of the nearby gorge. Although it's currently experiencing a bit of a growth spurt, Sesriem remains a lonely and far-flung outpost, home to little more than a petrol station and a handful of tourist hotels and lodges.

Information

Sesriem Canyon and Sossusvlei are open year-round between sunrise and sunset. If you want to see the sunrise over Sossusvlei, you must stay inside the park, either at the Sesriem Camp Site or the Sossus Dune Lodge. From both places, you are allowed to start driving to Sossusvlei about 15 minutes before the general public is allowed through the main gates. If you're content with simply enjoying the morning light, however, you can stay in Sesriem or Solitaire and simply pass through the park gate once the sun rises above the horizon.

All visitors headed for Sossusvlei must check in at the park office and secure a park entry permit (see p28).

CENTRAL NAMIBIA

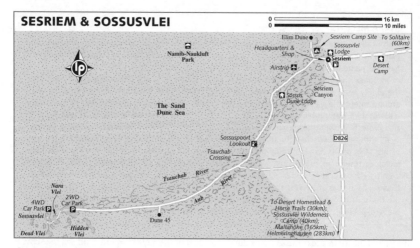

Sights & Activities

SOSSUSVLEI

Sossusvlei, a large ephemeral pan, is set amid red sand dunes that tower up to 200m above the valley floor and more than 300m over the underlying strata. It rarely contains any water, but when the Tsauchab River has gathered enough volume and momentum to push beyond the thirsty plains to the sand sea, it's completely transformed. The normally cracked dry mud gives way to an ethereal blue-green lake, surrounded by greenery and attended by aquatic birdlife, as well as the usual sand-loving gemsbok and ostriches.

This sand probably originated in the Kalahari between three and five million years ago. It was washed down the Orange River and out to sea, where it was swept northwards with the Benguela Current to be deposited along the coast. The best way to get the measure of this sandy sprawl is to climb a dune, as most people do. And of course, if you experience a sense of *déjà vu* here, don't be surprised – Sossusvlei has appeared in many films and advertisements worldwide, and every story ever written about Namibia features a photo of it.

At the end of the 65km 2WD road from Sesriem is the 2WD Car Park, and only 4WDs can drive the last 4km into the Sossusvlei Pan itself. Visitors with lesser vehicles park at the 2WD Car Park and walk, hitch or catch the shuttle (N$150 round trip) to cover the remaining distance. If you choose to walk, which really is the best way to take in all the desert scenery, allot about 90 minutes, and carry enough water for a hot sandy slog in the sun

SESRIEM CANYON

The 1km-long, 30m-deep Sesriem Canyon, 4km south of the Sesriem headquarters, was carved by the Tsauchab River through the 15-million-year-old deposits of sand and gravel conglomerate. There are two pleasant walks: you can hike upstream to the brackish pool at its head or 2.5km downstream to its lower end. Check out the natural sphinxlike formation on the northern flank near the canyon mouth.

DUNE 45

The most accessible of the large red dunes along the Sossusvlei road is Dune 45, so-called because it's 45km from Sesriem. It rises over 150m above the surrounding plains, and is flanked by several scraggly and often photographed trees.

ELIM DUNE

This often visited red dune, 5km north from the Sesriem Camp Site, can be reached with 2WD vehicles, but also makes a pleasant morning or afternoon walk.

HIDDEN VLEI

The rewarding 4km return hike from the 2WD Car Park to Hidden Vlei, an unearthly dry vlei (low, open landscape) amid lonely dunes, makes a rewarding excursion. The route is marked by white-painted posts. It's

THE NAMIB DUNES

The Namib dunes stretch from the Orange to the Kuiseb Rivers in the south, and from Torra Bay in Skeleton Coast Park to Angola's Curoca River in the north. They're composed of colourful quartz sand and come in varying hues – from cream to orange and red to violet.

Unlike the ancient Kalahari dunes, those of the Namib are dynamic, which means that they shift with wind, and are continuously sculpted into a variety of distinctive shapes. The top portion of the dune, which faces the direction of migrations, is known as the slipface, and is formed as the sand spills from the crest and slips down. Various bits of plant and animal detritus also collect here and provide a meagre food source for dune-dwelling creatures, and it's here that most dune life is concentrated.

The following is a list of the major types of dunes found in the Namib:

■ **Parabolic Dunes** Along the eastern area of the dune sea (including those around Sossusvlei), the dunes are classified as parabolic or multicyclic, and are the result of variable wind patterns. These are the most stable dunes in the Namib, and therefore the most vegetated.

■ **Transverse Dunes** The long, linear dunes along the coast south of Walvis Bay (p325) are transverse dunes, which lie perpendicular to the prevailing southwesterly winds. As a result, their slipfaces are oriented towards the north and northeast.

■ **Seif Dunes** Around the Homeb campsite in the Namib-Naukluft Park (p330) are the prominent linear or seif dunes, which are enormous all-direction oriented sand ripples. With heights of up to 100m, they're spaced about 1km apart and show up plainly on satellite photographs. They're formed by seasonal winds; during the prevailing southerly winds of summer, the slipfaces lie on the northeastern face. In the winter, the wind blows in the opposite direction, which causes slipfaces to build up on the southern-western faces.

■ **Star Dunes** In areas where individual dunes are exposed to winds from all directions, a formation known as a star dune appears. These dunes have multiple ridges, and when seen from above may appear to have a star shape.

■ **Barchan Dunes** These dunes prevail around the northern end of the Skeleton Coast (p304) and south of Lüderitz (p348), and are the most mobile as they are created by unidirectional winds. When shifting, barchan dunes take on a crescent shape, with the horns of the crescent aimed in the direction of migration. In fact, it is barchan dunes that are slowly devouring the ghost town of Kolmanskop near Lüderitz.

■ **Hump Dunes** Typically forming in clusters near water sources, hump dunes are considerably smaller than other dune types. They are formed when sand builds up around vegetation (such as a tuft of grass), and held in place by the roots of the plant, forming a sandy tussock. Generally, hump dunes rise less than 3m from the surface.

most intriguing in the afternoon, when you're unlikely to see another person.

DEAD VLEI
The rugged 6km return walk from Sossusvlei to Dead Vlei is popular with those who think the former is becoming overly touristy. Despite the name, it's a lovely spot and is just as impressive as its more popular neighbour.

Sleeping
Advanced reservations are essential at all of the places listed below, especially during the high season, school holidays and busy weekends.

Sesriem Camp Site (Map p336; campsite N$300 plus per person N$150) With the exception of the upmarket Sossus Dune Lodge, this is the only accommodation inside the park gates – staying here guarantees that you will be able to arrive at Sossusvlei in time for sunrise. Given its popularity, you must book in advance at the NWR office in Windhoek (p234), and arrive by sunset or the camp staff will reassign your site on a stand-by basis; anyone who was unable to book a site in Windhoek may get in on this nightly lottery. A small shop at the office here sells snacks and cold drinks, and the campsite bar provides music and alcohol nightly.

CENTRAL NAMIBIA

Desert Camp (Map p336; ☎ 683205; www.desertcamp .com; s/d N$730/900; ☒) The sister property of the Sossusvlei lodge, located 3km outside the park gate, targets midrange travellers who want the comforts of a lodge without having to part with too much cash. Desert Camp consists of 20 East African style canvas tents, complete with en suite bathrooms, kitchenettes and braai (BBQ) pits, which fan out from the central communal area. Here's the best part: if you place your dinner order with reception, in the evening you will be hand delivered game steaks, mixed salads and other tasty treats.

The Desert Homestead & Horse Trails (Map p310; ☎ 293243; www.deserthomestead-namibia.com; s/d N$825/1325; ☒) This reader-recommended lodge, located about 30km southeast of Sesriem, specialises in horse riding through the Namib-Naukluft Park. Whether you're keen for a sundowner or an overnight desert 'sleep-out' ride, the professional staff and exceptional horses will make your experience a memorable one. Even if you're not a riding enthusiast, the lodge itself is reminiscent of a traditional Namibian homestead, and the country cooking, which utilises locally grown produce, is not to be missed.

Sossusvlei Lodge (Map p336; ☎ 293223; www.sossu svleilodge.com; s/d from N$1915/2550; ☒) This curious place bears a strong resemblance to what happens when squabbling children topple a stack of coloured blocks. People either love it or hate it, but it does make a statement. Accommodation is in self-contained chalets with private verandahs, and guests can mingle with one another in the swimming pool, bar-restaurant and observatory. Despite the high price tag, this lodge is outside the park gate, so arriving at Sossusvlei in time for sunrise is not possible.

Sossus Dune Lodge (Map p336; ☎ 061-2857200; www .nwr.com.na/sossus_dune_lodge.html; s/d US$600/835 incl full board from N$2300/3600; ☒) If money is no object, then splash out at this brand-new and ultra-exclusive lodge, which is administered by NWR, and is one of only two properties located inside the park gates. Constructed entirely of local materials, the lodge consists of elevated bungalows that run alongside a curving promenade, and face out towards the silent desert plains. In the morning, you can roll out of your plush queen-sized bed, take a hot and steamy shower, sit down to a light breakfast of filter coffee and fresh fruits, and

then be one of the first people to watch the morning light wash over Sossusvlei.

Getting There & Away

Sesriem is reached via a signposted turn-off from the C14, and petrol is available in town. There is no public transport leading into the park, though hotels can arrange tours if you don't have your own vehicle.

In 2006, the road leading from the park gate to the 2WD park was paved, though the speed limit remains 60km/h. Although the road is conducive to higher speeds, there are oryx and springbok dashing about, so drive with extreme care.

SOLITAIRE & AROUND

Solitaire is a lonely and aptly named settlement of just a few buildings about 80km north of Sesriem along the A46. Although the town is nothing more than an open spot in the desert, the surrounding area is home to several guest farms and lodges, any of which serve as an alternative base for exploring Sossusvlei.

Sleeping & Eating

Solitaire Guest Farm (Map p310; ☎ 062-572024; www .solitaireguestfarm.com; camping per person N$70, r per person N$430; ☒) This inviting guest farm, located 6km east of Solitaire on the C14, is a peaceful oasis situated between the Namib plains and the Naukluft Massif. Bright rooms, home-cooked meals and relaxing surroundings make this guest farm a good choice.

Solitaire Country Lodge (Map p310; ☎ 061-256598; www.namibialodges.com; camping per person N$100, s/d N$465/665; ☒ ☒) Tiny little Solitaire is back on the tourist map, thanks to this swish property administered by the Country Lodge group. Despite being only a few years old, the property was designed to evoke images of a colonial-era farmhouse, albeit one with a large swimming pool in the backyard!

Swartfontein Mountain and Desert Guest Lodge (Map p310; ☎ 062-572004; s/d incl half board N$650/1150; ☒) This Italian-run guest farm lies at the top of the 1850m Spreetshoogte Pass, on the 8100-hectare Namib-Spreetshoogte Private Nature Reserve. The lodge occupies a farmhouse constructed by a German colonial soldier in 1900, though the stylish decor is Italian all the way. In addition to the dramatic location, perks include pasta dinners, guided hikes and wildlife drives through the reserve.

CENTRAL NAMIBIA

Rostock Ritz (Map p331; ☎ 064-403622; kuecki@mweb .com.na; s/d chalets N$1069/1669; 🏊) Established by the owner of Kücki's Pub in Swakopmund, this unique accommodation is known for its bizarre water gardens and cool and cave-like cement-domed chalets. The staff can arrange a number of activities, including hiking, a visit to the nearby hot springs and the obligatory trip to Sossusvlei. The Ritz lies east of the C14, just south of the C26 junction.

Getting There & Away
Solitaire is connected to Sesriem by the unpaved C19, and petrol is available in town.

NAMIBRAND NATURE RESERVE
Bordering the Namib-Naukluft Park, this reserve is essentially a collection of private farms that together protect over 200,000 hectares of dunes, desert grasslands and wild, isolated mountain ranges. Currently, several concessionaires operate on the reserve, offering a range of experiences amid one of Namibia's most stunning and colourful landscapes. A surprising amount of wildlife can be seen here, including large herds of gemsbok, springbok and zebras, as well as kudu, klipspringers, spotted hyenas, jackals, and Cape and bat-eared foxes.

Access by private vehicle is restricted in order to maintain the delicate balance of the reserve. Accommodation prices are also extremely high, which seeks to limit the tourist footprint. As a result, you must book in advance through any of the lodges listed below, and then arrange either a 4WD transfer or a chartered fly-in.

Sleeping
Wolwedans Dune Lodge (Map p310; ☎ 061-230616; www.wolwedans.com; chalet per person incl full board & activities from N$2855; 🍴 🏊) One of the more affordable lodges in the NamibRand (at this price bracket, affordable is a relative term), Wolwedans features an architecturally arresting collection of raised wooden chalets that are scattered amid towering red sand dunes. Service is impeccable, and the atmosphere is overwhelmingly elegant, yet you can indulge in your wild side at anytime with chauffeured 4WD dune drives and guided safaris.

Sossusvlei Wilderness Camp (Map p310; ☎ 061-274500; www.wilderness-safaris.com; chalet per person incl full board & activities from N$4600; 🏊) This fine instalment in the Wilderness Camp collection is situated on a mountainous 7000-hectare private reserve that fosters large game herds and their predators. Guests stay in exquisite stone, timber and thatched bungalows nestled between rock outcroppings for maximum privacy – each bungalow features a private plunge pool far that lies far from wandering eyes.

Sossusvlei Mountain Lodge (Map p310; ☎ in Johannesburg 27-11-809 4300; www.andbeyond.com; chalet per person incl full board & activities from N$4995; 🍴 🏊) This fashionable accommodation frequently appears in *Condé Nast* as one of the top lodges in the world. The property contains 10 chalets, which are constructed from locally quarried stone, and appear to blend effortlessly into the surrounding landscape. The interiors are nothing short of regal, and feature personal fireplaces, marble baths and linen-covered patios. Of special interest is the on-site observatory, which boasts a high-powered telescope and local star charts.

Southern Namibia

Although the tourist trail in Namibia firmly swings north towards Etosha National Park, the deserts of Southern Namibia sparkle beneath the sun – quite literally – as they're filled with millions of carats of diamonds. Since the Germans first unearthed vast treasure troves resting beneath the sands, much of the region has been dubbed the Sperrgebeit (Forbidden Area). Following the very recent declaration of Namibia's newest national park, this virtually pristine biodiversity hotspot is now open to the general public for the first time in more than a century.

While Sperrgebeit National Park has been grabbing all the headlines recently, the nearby port of Lüderitz has long been a traveller's favourite. A surreal colonial relic that has largely disregarded the 21st century, Lüderitz clings fiercely to its European roots, astounding travellers with traditional German architecture set against a backdrop of fiery sand dunes and deep blue seas. Heading inland into the parched interior, the incongruous Old World grandeur of Duwisib Castle provides further evidence of past European conquest and occupation.

Southern Namibia is also a veritable paradise for outdoor enthusiasts and lovers of adventure sports alike. Regarded as one of the largest canyons in the world, as well as one of the most spectacular sights in the whole of Africa, Fish River Canyon poses a monumental challenge to hikers and trekkers. The region is also home to the Orange River, which forms the border between Namibia and South Africa, and is famous for its raging white-water rapids and stark surrounds.

HIGHLIGHTS

- Watching the dunes slowly retake the ghost town of Kolmanskop in **Sperrgebiet National Park** (p354)

- Dining on fresh crayfish and authentic sauerkraut served with frothy pints of Hansa draught beer in the seaside town of **Lüderitz** (p348)

- Hiking through **Fish River Canyon National Park** (p358), one of Africa's greatest natural wonders

- Marvelling at the impossibly remote German anachronism that is **Duwisib Castle** (p346)

- Exploring the winding bends of the **Orange River** (p362) by canoe, kayak or raft

★ Duwisib Castle

★ Lüderitz

★ Sperrgebiet National Park

★ Fish River Canyon National Park

★ Orange River

SOUTHERN NAMIBIA

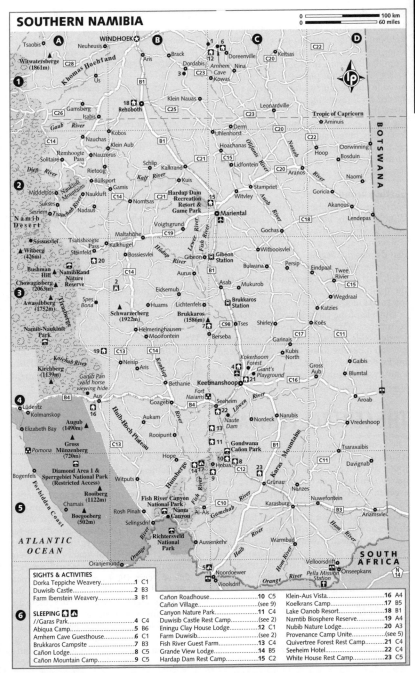

0 ───── 100 km
0 ───── 60 miles

SIGHTS & ACTIVITIES
Dorka Teppiche Weavery.................................1 C1
Duwisib Castle...2 B3
Farm Ibenstein Weavery.................................3 B1

SLEEPING
//Garas Park...4 C4
Abiqua Camp..5 B6
Arnhem Cave Guesthouse..............................6 C1
Brukkaros Campsite..7 B3
Cañon Camp...8 C5
Cañon Mountain Camp....................................9 C5

Cañon Roadhouse..10 C5
Cañon Village...(see 9)
Canyon Nature Park......................................11 C4
Duwisib Castle Rest Camp...........................(see 2)
Eningu Clay House Lodge.............................12 C1
Farm Duwisib...(see 2)
Fish River Guest Farm..................................13 C4
Grande View Lodge.......................................14 B5
Hardap Dam Rest Camp.................................15 C2

Klein-Aus Vista..16 A4
Koelkrans Camp...17 B5
Lake Oanob Resort..18 B1
Namtib Nature Lodge....................................19 A4
Nubib Nature Lodge......................................20 A3
Provenance Camp Unite..............................(see 5)
Quivertree Forest Rest Camp.......................21 C4
Seeheim Hotel..22 C4
White House Rest Camp................................23 C5

Geography

Southern Namibia takes in everything from Rehoboth in the north to the Orange River along the South African border, and westward from the Botswana border to the Forbidden Coast. The central plateau is characterised by wide open country, and the area's widely spaced rural towns function mainly as commercial and market centres. Further south, the landscape opens up into seemingly endless plains, ranges and far horizons. In the far south of the region, the Fish River Canyon forms a spectacular gash across the otherwise flat landscape.

Getting Around

While sparse public transport connects Windhoek to the border, and Keetmahshoop out to Lüderitz, a private vehicle is necessary if you want to access any of the stunning nature that defines this region. A 2WD vehicle can tackle the vast majority of the roads down south, and you'll have no problems accessing the trailheads for Fish River Canyon or the long and lonely road out to Lüderitz.

Outside of the rainy season, a 2WD with reasonable clearance will survive most of the coastal roads around the Lüderitz peninsula, but you'd be wise to avoid the off-road sand tracks. For any excursion into the Sperrgebiet, a sturdy 4WD with full support equipment is absolutely essential.

THE CENTRAL PLATEAU

The central plateau is bisected by the B1, which is the country's main north–south route, stretching from the South African border to Otjiwarongo. For most drivers, this excellent road is little more than a mesmerising broken white line stretching towards a receding horizon – a paradise for lead-foot drivers and cruise-control potatoes. Most of the central plateau's towns are situated off the main B1 route, and serve either as good bases for exploring the region's natural attractions, or, at the very least, obligatory fuel stops en route to destinations further south.

DORDABIS

☎ 062

The lonely ranching area around Dordabis is the heart of Namibia's karakul country, and supports several sheep farms and weaveries. At the **Farm Ibenstein Weavery** (Map p341; ☎ 573524; ⏰ 8am-12.30pm & 2.30-5.30pm Mon-Fri, 8am-noon Sat), located 4km down the C15 from Dordabis, you can learn about spinning, dyeing and weaving, as well as purchase handwoven rugs and carpets.

You can also try the **Dorka Teppiche Weavery** (Map p341), which produces some of the finest original rugs and weavings in the country as well as progressive marble and soapstone sculpture. The weavery is located on the grounds of the Eningu Clay House Lodge (see below).

Yes, the name **Eningu Clay House Lodge** (Map p341; ☎ 226979; www.eningulodge.com; Peperkorrel Farm; s/d incl half board N$960/1680) sounds a lot like the title of a children's book, but appropriately enough, this place is a bit of a fantasy. It was painstakingly designed and constructed by Volker and Stephanie Hümmer, whose efforts with sun-dried adobe have resulted in an appealing African-Amerindian architectural cross. It really is visually arresting, and activities here include wonderful hiking trails (with a mountain hut en route), wildlifeviewing, archery, star-gazing through their telescope, and tours to the adjoining Dorka Teppiche Weavery and sculpture studio. To get there, follow the D1458 for 63km southeast of Chief Hosea Kutako International Airport and then turn west on the D1471; travel for 1km to the Eningu gate.

To reach Dordabis, head east from Windhoek on the B6 and turn right onto the C23, 20km east of town; the town centre is 66km down this road.

ARNHEM CAVE

With a subterranean length of 4.5km, Arnhem Cave is the longest cave system in Namibia. Formed in a layer of limestone and dolomite, Arnhem was sandwiched between folds of stratified quartzite and shale, and discovered in 1930 by farmer DN Bekker. Shortly thereafter, mining operations began extracting the deposits of lucrative bat guano, which were commonly used at the time as fertiliser.

Guided tours (1/2hr tours incl equipment rental N$120/145) dive into darkness, beyond the reach of sunlight. Because it's dry, there are few stalagmites or stalactites, but it's possible you could see up to six bat species: the giant leaf-nosed bat, the leaf-nosed bat, the long-fingered bat, Geoffroy's horseshoe bat, Denti's horseshoe bat and the Egyptian slit-faced bat. It's also inhabited by a variety of insects, worms, shrews and prawns. The grand finale is the indescribable first view of the blue-cast natural light as you emerge from the depths.

The **Arnhem Cave Guesthouse** (Map p341; ☎ 581885; arnhem@mweb.com.na; camping per person N$105, 2-person chalet N$690) lies within an hour's walk of Arnhem Cave, and is located on the same farm. Dayvisitors can arrange guided tours here, while overnight visitors are treated to a bucolic retreat lying just beyond the lights of the capital.

To get to the guesthouse, turn south 3km east of Chief Hosea Kutako International Airport on the D1458. After 66km, turn northeast on the D1506 and continue for 11km to the T-junction, where you turn south on the D180. The guesthouse is 6km down this road.

REHOBOTH
☎ 062

Rehoboth lies 85km south of Windhoek and just a stone's throw north of the Tropic of Capricorn. A particularly photo-worthy sign marks this latitudinal line, so be sure to pull over to the side of the road and snap a quick pic.

Originally founded in 1844 as a German mission, Rehoboth was abandoned in 1864, but was revived a decade later by the Basters, an ethnic group of mixed Khoikhoi/Afrikaner origin, who migrated north from the Cape under Hermanus van Wyk. The **town museum** (☎ 522954; admission N$5; ☿ 10am-noon & 2-4pm Mon-Fri, 10am-noon Sat), housed in the 1903 residence of the settlement's first colonial postmaster, recounts this history.

If you're looking to rehabilitate your travel-worn body and mind, a surprisingly relaxing retreat is the **Lake Oanob Resort** (Map p341; ☎ 522370; www.oanob.com.na; campsites N$85-95, s/d N$640/840, 6-bed chalets N$1750; ▨), located alongside the Oanob Dam, just west of town. The resort is seemingly incongruous with the rest of the dry and arid central plateau as it's centred on a stunningly calm and tranquil blue lake home to leaping fish and cooing water birds. Amenities include a shaded camping area, a thatched bar and restaurant, and beautiful stone self-catering bungalows on the lake's shores.

Both the **Intercape Mainliner** (www.intercape .co.za) bus and the train between Windhoek and Keetmanshoop pass through Rehoboth.

There are a few weekly services, with fares from Windhoek starting at N$270 and a duration of one hour.

HOACHANAS
☎ 063

If you have your own vehicle, it's worth a short side trip to the tiny settlement of Hoachanas, on the C21, 50km east of Kalkrand. The town is home to **Farm Jena**, which hosts the Anin Women's Project ('Jena' is Nama for 'many birds'). This project enables Nama women to create lovely colourful embroidered textiles – cotton and linen clothing, bedding, pillow slips, tablecloths and other items – for distribution to shops all over Namibia. Contact **Anin** (☎ 061-235509) in Windhoek to arrange a tour.

MARIENTAL
☎ 063

The small administrative and commercial centre of Mariental is home to the large-scale Hardap irrigation scheme, which allows citrus-growing and ostrich farming. For most travellers, however, Mariental is little more than a petrol stop before heading out west to Sesriem and Sossusvlei (p335).

If you get stuck for the night, the well-established **Mariental Hotel** (☎ 242466; Marie Brandt St; s/d N$300/400; ▨) has plush rooms with modern amenities as well as an attractive dining room serving Namibian standards.

Both the **Intercape Mainliner** (www.intercape .co.za) bus and the train between Windhoek and Keetmanshoop pass through Mariental. There are a few weekly services, with fares from Windhoek starting at N$270 and a duration of one hour.

HARDAP DAM RECREATION RESORT & GAME RESERVE
☎ 063

This **recreation resort** (per person N$40, plus per vehicle N$10; ☿ sunrise-6pm), 15km northwest of Mariental, is a 25,000-hectare wildlife park with 80km of gravel roads and a 15km hiking loop. Hardap is Nama for 'nipple'; it was named after the conical hills topped by dolerite knobs that dot the area.

Admission entitles you to use the pool and the several picnic sites east of the lake. Between sunrise and sunset you can walk anywhere in the reserve, but camping is allowed only at the rest camp. Note that swimming isn't permitted in the dam.

BEWARE OF FALLING ROCKS

A meteorite is an extraterrestrial body that survives its impact with the earth's surface without being destroyed. Although it's estimated that about 500 meteorites land each year, only a handful are typically recovered. However, in a single meteor shower sometime in the dim and distant past, more than 21 tonnes of 90% ferrous extraterrestrial boulders crashed to earth in southern Namibia. It's rare for so many meteorites to fall at once, and these are thought to have been remnants of an explosion in space, which were held together as they were drawn in by the earth's gravitational field.

Thus far, at least 77 meteorite chunks have been found within a 2500-sq-km area around the former Rhenish mission station of Gibeon, 60km south of Mariental. The largest chunk, which weighs 650kg, is housed in Cape Town Museum, South Africa while other bits have wound up as far away as Anchorage, Alaska. Between 1911 and 1913, soon after their discovery, 33 chunks were brought to Windhoek for safekeeping. Over the years, they've been displayed in Zoo Park and at Alte Feste in Windhoek, but have now found a home on Post Street Mall (see p234).

Most travellers come for the **blue lake**, which breaks up the arid plateau landscape and provides anglers with carp, barbel, mudfish and blue karpers. The lake also supports countless species of water birds, including flamingos, fish eagles, pelicans, spoonbills and Goliath herons.

The **Hardap Dam Rest Camp** (Map p341; campsite N$50, s/d/q/chalet N$450/600/1200/1600; 🏊) offers varied accommodation, a shop, restaurant, kiosk and swimming pool. The restaurant and cliff-top pool afford a great vista over the lake. Book through Namibia Wildlife Resorts (NWR) office in Windhoek (p234).

To get to the resort, you will need your own vehicle – take the signposted turning off the B1, 15km north of Mariental, and continue 6km to the entrance gate.

BRUKKAROS

With a 2km-wide crater, this extinct volcano (1586m) dominates the skyline between Mariental and Keetmanshoop. It was formed some 80 million years ago when a magma pipe encountered ground water about 1km below the earth's surface and caused a series of violent volcanic explosions.

From the car park, it's a 3.5km hike to the crater's southern entrance; along the way, watch for the remarkable **quartz formations** embedded in the rock. From here, you can head for the otherworldly **crater floor**, or turn left and follow the southern rim up to the abandoned sunspot research centre, which was established by the US Smithsonian Institute in the 1930s.

The basic **Brukkaros Campsite** (Map p341; 🕿 in Windhoek 061-255977; www.nacobta.com.na; camping per person N$35), which is administered by Namibia Community Based Tourism Association (Nacobta) has sites with toilets and a bush shower, but you must supply your own drinking water. Half of the campsites are literally carved out of the volcano and offer some truly stunning views across the valley.

Brukkaros rises 35km west of Tses on the B1. Follow the C98 west for 40km and then turn north on to the D3904 about 1km east of Berseba. It's then 8km to the car park. Note that a 4WD is required to access some of the higher campsites at Brukkaros Campsite.

KEETMANSHOOP
🕿 063

Keetmanshoop (*kayt*-mahns-*hoo*-up) sits at the main crossroads of Southern Namibia, but it's the surrounding countryside that draws most traveller's attention. The area is home to a large concentration of *kokerboom* (quiver trees), which belong to the aloe family, and can grow to heights of 8m. The name is derived from their lightweight branches, which were formerly used as quivers by the San hunters; they would remove the fibrous heart of the branch, leaving a strong, hollow tube.

In the town itself, there are a few examples of German colonial architecture, including the 1910 **Kaiserliches Postampt** (Imperial Post Office; cnr 5th Ave & Fenschel St), and the **town museum** (🕿 221256; cnr Kaiser St & 7th Ave; admission free; ⏰ 7.30am-12.30pm & 2.30-4.30pm Mon-Fri), which is housed in the 1895 Rhenish Mission Church, and outlines the history of Keetmanshoop with old photos, early farming implements, an old wagon and a model of a traditional Nama home.

About 25km north of town, //**Garas Park** (Map p341; ☎ 223217; morkel@namibnet.com; camping per person N$35 plus per vehicle N$5, day admission per person N$10 plus per vehicle N$5) has stands of *kokerboom*, lots of hiking tracks and drives through a fantasy landscape of stacked boulders, as well as some zany sculptures made from spare junk.

About 14km east of town, the **Quivertree Forest Rest Camp** (Map p341; ☎ 222835; www.quiver treeforest.com; camping per person N$80, s/d/tr/q bunga-lows N$330/465/555/800, day admission per person N$50) proudly boasts Namibia's largest stand of *kokerboom*. Rates include use of picnic facilities and entry to the Giant's Playground, a bizarre natural rock garden 5km away.

In the quiet Westdene neighbourhood of the town itself, **Pension Gessert** (☎ 223892; www .natron.net/gessert/main.html; 138 13th St; s/d N$250/350; 🖭) offers quaint and homey rooms, a beauti-ful garden and swimming pool, in addition to country-style cooking for the weary traveller.

Getting There & Away
BUS
There are several weekly buses between Windhoek and Keetmanshoop (from N$288; 7 hours) on the **Intercape Mainliner** (www.intercape .co.za). Book your tickets in advance online as this service continues on to Cape Town, South Africa and fills up quickly.

Combis (minibuses) also run up and down the B1 with fairly regular frequency, and a ride between Windhoek to Keetmanshoop shouldn't cost more than N$100. Less regular combis connect Keetmanshoop to the black township in Lüderitz, with fares averaging around N$175.

TRAIN
Trans-Namib (☎ 061-2982175) also operates a daily night train between Windhoek and Keetmanshoop (from N$90).

NAUTE DAM
This large dam on the Löwen River has been mooted as a new recreation area, though little to no investment has taken place yet. Regardless, the Naute Dam is an attractive spot that is surrounded by low truncated hills, and attracts large numbers of water birds. Camping is permitted, though there are no official facilities, and you must be self-suf-ficient. To get to the dam, drive 30km west of Keetmanshoop on the B4 and turn south on the D545.

SEEHEIM
It's a long and lonely drive southwest to Lüderitz, which is why you might want to consider stopping for the night at the Seeheim rail halt, 48km southwest of Keetmanshoop. Although the tiny town is home to little more than petrol stations and small shops, about 13km west on the B4 is the Naiams farm, where a signpost indicates a 15-minute walk to the remains of a 1906 **German fort**. The fort was raised to prevent Nama attacks on German travellers and Lüderitz-bound freight.

Accommodation of all varieties is avail-able at the historic **Seeheim Hotel** (Map p341; ☎ 250503; camping per person N$60, standard/luxury r per person N$200/400), which features an atmos-pheric old bar as well as several rooms full of period furniture.

The tarred B4 highway connects Keetman-shoop with Lüderitz, though you're going to need your own vehicle if you want to access this stretch of highway.

BETHANIE
☎ 063
One of Namibia's oldest settlements, Bethanie was founded in 1814 by the London Missionary Society, though oddly enough, the first missionary, Reverend Heinrich Schmelen, wasn't English but German (London was experiencing a staffing crisis). After seven years the mission was abandoned due to tribal squabbling, and although Schmelen attempted to revive it several times, he was thwarted by drought.

Schmelen's original 1814 mission station, **Schmelenhaus**, occupied a one-storey cottage. It was burnt to the ground when he left Bethanie in 1828, and later rebuilt in 1842 by the first Rhenish missionary, Reverend Hans Knudsen. The building now sits on the grounds of the Evangelical Lutheran Church and houses a museum full of old photos of the mission. If it's locked, a notice on the door will tell you where to pick up a key.

Also worth a look is the 1883 **home** of Captain Joseph Fredericks, the Nama chief who signed a treaty with the representa-tives of Adolf Lüderitz on 1 May 1883 for the transfer of Angra Pequena (present-day Lüderitz). It was here in October 1884 that Captain Fredericks and the German Consul General, Dr Friedrich Nachtigal, signed a treaty of German protection over the entire territory.

The sole accommodation in town is the **Bethanie Hotel** (☎ 283071; camping per person N$25, s/d N$300/500), a personality-steeped building centred on an intimate dining hall with more than a century of history on display.

The Bethanie turn-off is signposted on the B4, 140km west of Keetmanshoop.

DUWISIB CASTLE
☎ 063

A curious neo-baroque structure located about 70km south of Maltahöhe smack dab in the middle of the barren desert, this full-on European **castle** (Map p341; admission N$60; ☺ 8am-1pm & 2-5pm) was built in 1909 by Baron Captain Hans Heinrich von Wolf. After the German-Nama wars, the loyal Baron commissioned architect Willie Sander to design a castle that would reflect his commitment to the German military cause. He also married the stepdaughter of the US consul to Dresden, Miss Jayta Humphreys, and planned on ruling over his personal corner of German South West Africa.

Although the stone for the castle was quarried nearby, much of the raw material was imported from Germany, and required 20 ox wagons to transport it across the 330km of desert from Lüderitz. Artisans and masons were hired from as far away as Ireland, Denmark, Sweden and Italy. The result was a U-shaped castle with 22 rooms, all suitably fortified and decorated with family portraits and military paraphernalia. Rather than windows, most rooms have embrasures, which emphasise Von Wolf's apparent obsession with security.

As history would have it, WWI broke out, and the Baron reenlisted in the Schutzruppe (German Imperial Army), only to be killed two weeks later at the Battle of Somme. The Baroness never returned to Namibia, though some people claim that the descendants of her thoroughbred horses still roam the desert (see p348). In the late 1970s, ownership of the Duwisib Castle and its surrounding 50 hectares was transferred to the state, and is now administered by NWR.

Sleeping

Duwisib Castle Rest Camp (Map p341; campsites N$50) This very amenable camp occupies one corner of the castle grounds; the adjoining kiosk sells snacks, coffee and cool drinks. Book through the NWR office in Windhoek (p234).

Farm Duwisib (Map p341; ☎ 223994; www.farmduwisib.com; r per person without/with 2 meals N$390/440) Located 300m from the castle, this pleasant guest farm has rustic, self-catering rooms for two to four people, though you can also pay a bit extra for hearty dinners and proper breakfasts. While you're there, be sure to check out the historic blacksmith shop up the hill.

Getting There & Away

There isn't any public transport to Duwisib Castle. If you're coming from Helmeringhausen, head north on the C14 for 62km and turn northwest on to the D831. Continue for 27km, then turn west onto the D826 and travel a further 15km to the castle.

MALTAHÖHE
☎ 063

Maltahöhe, lying at the heart of a commercial ranching area, is a convenient stopover along the back route between Namib-Naukluft Park and Lüderitz. The area supports a growing number of guest farms and private rest camps.

In town, you can bed down for the night at the **Hotel Maltahöhe** (☎ 293013; dm N$60, s/d N$400/450), which has won several national awards for its amenable accommodation. It also operates a spic-and-span bunkhouse for budget travellers, and has a restaurant and bar offering Continental cuisine.

More or less midway between Maltahöhe and Sesriem, you'll find the **Nubib Nature Lodge** (Map p341; ☎ 683007; www.nublodge.iway.na; s/d N$520/910), a splendidly remote bush camp run by a very welcoming couple. Country-style Afrikaans cooking is on the menu here, though you can quickly burn off the calories on nature walks through the reserve.

HELMERINGHAUSEN
☎ 063

Helmeringhausen is little more than a homestead, hotel and petrol station, and has been the property of the Hester family since 1919. The highlight is the idiosyncratic **Agricultural Museum** (☎ 283083; Main St; admission free; ☺ on request), established in 1984 by the Helmeringhausen Farming Association. It displays all sorts of interesting old furniture and farming implements collected from local properties, as well as an antique fire engine.

Helmeringhausen Hotel (☎ 233083; s/d N$450/760; 💧) is a surprisingly swish hotel with classically elegant rooms in addition to a very popular restaurant and bar. The food is excellent, the beer is cold and it has a well-stocked wine cellar. However, those who like eating game meat may feel uncomfortable being watched by all those accusing trophies.

Helmeringhausen is 130km south of Maltahöhe on the C14.

THE SOUTH COAST

The south coast of Namibia is dominated by Sperrgebiet (Forbidden Area), which plays host to the country's highly lucrative and highly secure diamond mining efforts. In years past, this region wouldn't have featured high on your itinerary unless you were looking for trouble, though the recently declared Sperrgebiet National Park may yet prove to be a tremendous tourist drawcard. Although much of the park has yet to open up, the town of Lüderitz, which is rich in German colonial architecture, and occupies an otherworldly setting between the dunes and sea, is a pleasant place to spend a few days.

AUS
☎ 063
After the Germans surrendered to the South African forces in 1915, Aus became one of two internment camps for German military personnel – military police and officers were sent to Okahandja in the north while noncommissioned officers went to Aus. Since the camp quickly grew to 1500 prisoners and 600 South African guards, residents were forced to seek shelter in flimsy tents. However, the resourceful inmates turned to brick-making and constructed houses for themselves – they even sold the excess bricks to the guards for 10 shillings per 1000. The houses weren't opulent – roofs were tiled with unrolled food tins – but they did provide protection from the elements. The prisoners also built several wood stoves and even sank boreholes.

After the Treaty of Versailles the camp was dismantled, and by May 1919 it was closed. Virtually nothing remains, though several of the brick houses have been reconstructed. The former camp is 4km east of the village, down a gravel road, then to the right; there's now a national plaque commemorating it.

Aside from the prison camp, Aus is home to two highly recommendable guest farms where you can slow down and spend some time soaking up the desolate beauty of the shifting sands.

Sleeping
Klein-Aus Vista (Map p341; ☎ 258021; www.namibhorses .com; camping N$75, hut N$125, r/chalet per person incl meals N$495/725; 🍴 💧) This 10,000-hectare ranch, 3km west of Aus, is a hiker's paradise – the highlight of the ranch is a magical four-day trekking route, which traverses fabulous wild landscapes. Meals are available at the main lodge, and accommodation is in the main lodge or one of the two wonderful hikers' huts: the dormitory hut Geister Schlucht, in a Shangri-la–like valley, or the opulent Eagle's Nest complex, with several chalets built right into the boulders. Beyond the wonderful hiking, activities include horse riding and 4WD tours through the ranch's vast desert concession.

Namib Biosphere Reserve (Map p341; ☎ 683055; www.namtib.net; s/d incl full board N$600/1030) In the beautiful Tirasberge, this private reserve is run by ecologically conscious owners who've created a self-sustaining farm in a narrow valley, with distant views of the Namib plains and dune sea. There is an incredible wealth of nature on display here, and it's certainly worth spending a night or two out here getting acquainted with all the empty space. To reach the reserve, take the C13 north of Aus for 55km, then turn west on the D707; after 48km turn east onto the 12km farm road to the lodge.

Getting There & Away
Aus is 125km east of Lüderitz on the B4. Travel in this region typically requires a private vehicle.

THE AUS–LÜDERITZ ROAD
If you've come to Aus, chances are you're heading for Lüderitz. Between Aus and the coast, the road crosses the desolate southern Namib, which is distinct from the gravel plains to the north. The area is distinguished by the pastel-coloured Awasib and Uri-Hauchab ranges, which rise from the plains through a mist of windblown sand and dust – the effect is mesmerising and ethereal.

About 10km from Aus, start watching out for feral desert horses (see the boxed text, p348). About 20km west of Aus, turn north

WILD HORSES

On the desert plains west of Aus live some of the world's only wild desert-dwelling horses. The origin of these eccentric equines is unclear, though several theories abound. One theory suggests that the horses descended from Schutztruppe (German Imperial Army) cavalry horses abandoned during the South African invasion in 1915, while others claim they were brought in by Nama raiders moving north from beyond the Orange River. Yet another theory asserts that they descended from a load of shipwrecked horses en route from Europe to Australia. Still others maintain that the horses descended from the stud stock of Baron Captain Hans-Heinrich von Wolf, the original owner of the Duwisib Castle (see p346).

These horses, whose bony and scruffy appearance belies their probable high-bred ancestry and apparent adaptation to the harsh conditions, are protected inside the Diamond Area 1. In years of good rain, they grow fat and their numbers increase to several hundred. Their only source of water is Garub Pan, which is fed by an artificial borehole.

If not for the efforts of a few concerned individuals, the horses would probably have been wiped out long ago. These individuals, led by security officer Jan Coetzer of Consolidated Diamond Mines (CDM), recognised that the horses were unique, and managed to secure funding to install the borehole at Garub Pan. At one stage, the Ministry of Environment & Tourism (MET) considered taming the horses for use on patrols in Etosha National Park, though the proposal fell through. There have also been calls to exterminate the horses by individuals citing possible damage to the desert environment and gemsbok herds. So far, however, the tourism value of the horses has swept aside all counter-arguments.

The horses may also be valuable for scientific purposes. For instance, they urinate less than domestic horses, and are smaller than their supposed ancestors. The horses are also able to go without water for up to five days at a time. These adaptations may be valuable in helping scientists understand how animals cope with changing climatic conditions.

at the sign 'Feral Horses' and follow the track for 1.5km to Garub Pan, which is home to an artificial water hole.

When the wind blows – which is most of the time – the final 10km into Lüderitz may be blocked by a barchan dune field that seems bent upon crossing the road. Conditions do get hazardous, especially if it's foggy, and the drifts pile quite high before road crews clean them off. Obey local speed limits, and avoid driving at night if possible.

LÜDERITZ
☎ 063

Before travelling to Lüderitz, pause for a moment to study the country map, and appreciate the fact that the town is sandwiched between the barren Namib Desert and the windswept South Atlantic coast. As if Lüderitz's wholly unique geographical setting wasn't impressive enough, its surreal German art nouveau architecture will seal the deal. Something of a colonial relic scarcely touched by the 21st century, Lüderitz might recall a Bavarian *dorfchen* (small village), with churches, bakeries and cafes. Indeed, the local community is proud of the town's unique heritage, and travellers

often find they're greeted in Lüderitz with a warm smile and a cold pint.

Unlike its more well-heeled Teutonic rival Swakopmund on the central coast (p311), relative isolation, poor transport links and a struggling economy have worn heavy on Lüderitz over the decades. The town itself feels a bit like it's stuck in a time warp, but it's this very lack of modernity and ever-so-slow pace that gives Lüderitz its captivating Old World charm. And of course, it's the natural environment surrounding the town where Southern Namibia really comes to life. The rocky coastline of the Lüderitz peninsula harbours flamingo flocks and penguin colonies, while the adjacent Sperrgebiet National Park is arguably the country's wildest and most pristine landscape.

History

In April 1883 Heinrich Vogelsang, under orders from Bremen merchant Adolf Lüderitz, entered into a treaty with Nama chief Joseph Fredericks and secured lands within an 8km radius of Angra Pequeña (Little Bay). Later that year Lüderitz made an appearance in Little Bay, and following his recommendation, the German chancellor Otto von Bismarck designated South Western Africa a protectorate of the German empire. Following the discovery of diamonds in the Sperrgebiet in 1908, the town of Lüderitz was officially founded, and quickly prospered from the gem trade.

Indeed, the history of diamond mining in Namibia parallels the history of Lüderitz. Although diamonds were discovered along the Orange River in South Africa, and among the guano workings on the offshore islands as early as 1866, it apparently didn't occur to anyone that the desert sands might also harbour a bit of crystal carbon. In 1908, however, railway worker Zacharias Lewala found a shiny stone along the railway line near Grasplatz and gave it to his employer, August Stauch. Stauch took immediate interest and, to his elation, the state geologist confirmed that it was indeed a diamond. Stauch applied for a prospecting licence from the Deutsche Koloniale Gesellschaft (German Colonial Society) and set up his own mining company, the Deutsche Diamanten Gesellschaft (German Diamond Company), to begin exploiting the presumed windfall.

In the years that followed, hordes of prospectors descended upon the town of Lüderitz with dreams of finding wealth buried in the sands. Lüderitz became a boomtown as service facilities sprang up to accommodate the growing population. By September 1908, however, diamond dementia was threatening to escalate out of control, which influenced

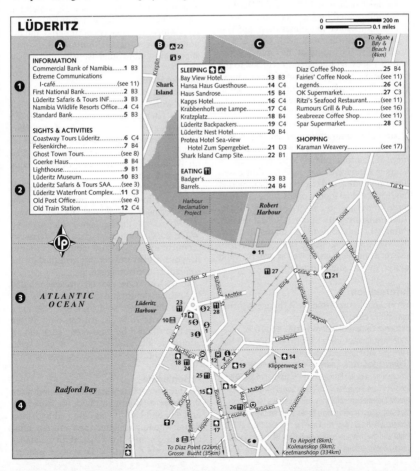

LÜDERITZ

0 — 200 m
0 — 0.1 miles

INFORMATION
Commercial Bank of Namibia......**1** B3
Extreme Communications
I-café....................................(see 11)
First National Bank......................**2** B3
Lüderitz Safaris & Tours INF......**3** B3
Namibia Wildlife Resorts Office...**4** C4
Standard Bank.............................**5** B3

SIGHTS & ACTIVITIES
Coastway Tours Lüderitz.............**6** C4
Felsenkirche...............................**7** B4
Ghost Town Tours....................(see 8)
Goerke Haus...............................**8** B4
Lighthouse..................................**9** B1
Lüderitz Museum.......................**10** B3
Lüderitz Safaris & Tours SAA....(see 3)
Lüderitz Waterfront Complex....**11** C3
Old Post Office..........................(see 4)
Old Train Station.......................**12** C4

SLEEPING
Bay View Hotel.........................**13** B3
Hansa Haus Guesthouse...........**14** C4
Haus Sandrose..........................**15** B4
Kapps Hotel...............................**16** C4
Krabbenhoft une Lampe...........**17** C4
Kratzplatz..................................**18** B4
Lüderitz Backpackers.................**19** C4
Lüderitz Nest Hotel...................**20** B4
Protea Hotel Sea-view
    Hotel Zum Sperrgebiet.........**21** D3
Shark Island Camp Site.............**22** B1

EATING
Badger's....................................**23** B3
Barrels......................................**24** B4

Diaz Coffee Shop......................**25** B4
Fairies' Coffee Nook................(see 11)
Legends.....................................**26** C4
OK Supermarket.......................**27** C3
Ritzi's Seafood Restaurant......(see 11)
Rumours Grill & Pub..............(see 16)
Seabreeze Coffee Shop...........(see 11)
Spar Supermarket....................**28** C3

SHOPPING
Karaman Weavery...................(see 17)

Shark Island

Harbour Reclamation Project

Robert Harbour

ATLANTIC OCEAN

Lüderitz Harbour

Radford Bay

To Agate Bay & Beach (4km)

To Diaz Point (22km); Grosse Bucht (35km)

To Airport (8km); Kolmanskop (8km); Keetmanshoop (334km)

the German government to intervene by establishing the Sperrgebiet. This 'Forbidden Zone' extended from 26°S latitude southward to the Orange River mouth, and stretched inland for 100km. Independent prospecting was henceforth *verboten*, and those who'd already staked their claims were forced to form mining companies.

In February 1909 a diamond board was created to broker all diamond sales and thereby control prices. However, after WWI ended, the world diamond market was so depressed that in 1920, Ernst Oppenheimer of the Anglo-American Corporation was able to purchase Stauch's company, along with eight other diamond-producing companies. This ambitious move led to the formation of Consolidated Diamond Mines (CDM), which was administered by De Beers South Africa and headquartered in Kolmanskop (p355).

In 1928 rich diamond fields were discovered around the mouth of the Orange River, and in 1944 CDM decided to relocate to the purpose-built company town of Oranjemund (p356). Kolmanskop's last inhabitants left in 1956, and the sand dunes have been encroaching on the town ever since.

In 1994, CDM gave way to Namdeb Diamond Corporation Limited (Namdeb), which is owned in equal shares by the government of Namibia and the De Beers Group. De Beers is a Johannesburg- and London-based diamond mining and trading corporation that has held a virtual monopoly over the diamond trade for much of its corporate history. Today, diamonds are still Lüderitz's best friend, though it's also home to several maritime industries, including the harvesting of crayfish, seaweed and seagrass, as well as experimental oyster, mussel and prawn farms.

Information

Several banks on Bismarck St change cash and travellers cheques.

Extreme Communications I-café (☎ 204256; Waterfront Complex; per hr N$20; ⏰ 8am-5pm Mon-Fri, 9am-1pm Sat) Provides reliable internet access.

Lüderitz Safaris & Tours (☎ 202719; ludsaf@ africaonline.com.na; Bismarck St; ⏰ 8am-1pm & 2-5pm Mon-Fri, 8am-noon Sat, 8.30-10am Sun) Provides reliable tourist information, organises visitor permits for the Kolmanskop ghost town (p355), books seats on the schooner *Sedina*, which sails past the Cape fur seal sanctuary at Diaz Point and the penguin colony on Halifax Island, and sells curios, books, stamps and phonecards.

Namibia Wildlife Resorts office (NWR; ☎ 202752; Schinz St; ⏰ 7.30am-1pm & 2-4pm Mon-Fri) This local office can help with national park information.

Dangers & Annoyances

Stay well clear of the Sperrgebiet unless you're part of an organised tour as much of the area remains strictly off-limits despite its recent declaration as a national park. The northern boundary is formed by the B4 and extends almost as far east as Aus. The boundary is patrolled by some fairly ruthless characters, and trespassers will be prosecuted (or worse).

Sights
LÜDERITZ TOWN

Lüderitz is chock-a-block with colonial buildings, and every view reveals something interesting. The curiously intriguing architecture, which mixes German imperial and art nouveau styles, makes this bizarre little town appear even more other-worldly.

Goerke Haus

Lieutenant Hans Goerke came to Swakopmund with the Schutztruppe in 1904, though he was later posted to Lüderitz, where he served as a diamond company manager. His **home** (Diamantberg St; admission N$16), designed by architect Otto Ertl and constructed in 1910 on Diamond Hill, was one of the town's most extravagant.

Goerke left for Germany in 1912 and eight years later his home was purchased by the newly formed Consolidated Diamond Mines (CDM) to house the company's chief engineer. When the CDM headquarters transferred to Oranjemund in 1944, the house was sold to the government and became occupied by the resident Lüderitz magistrate.

In 1981, however, the magistrate was shifted to Keetmanshoop, and the house (which was in dire shape) was sold back to CDM for a token sum of 10 South African rand on the condition that it be renovated. They did an admirable job, and the house is now open to the public.

Felsenkirche

The prominent **Evangelical Lutheran church** (Kirche St; admission free) dominates Lüderitz from high on Diamond Hill. It was designed by Albert Bause, who implemented the Victorian influences he'd seen in the Cape. With assistance from private donors in Germany, constrution of the church began in late 1911 and was completed the following year. The brilliant stained-glass panel situated over the altar was donated by Kaiser Wilhelm II, while the Bible was a gift from his wife.

Lüderitz Museum

This **museum** (☎ 202582; Diaz St; admission N$10; ☺ 3.30-5pm Mon-Fri) contains information on the town's history, including displays on natural history, local indigenous groups and the diamond-mining industry. Phone to arrange a visit outside standard opening hours.

Old Train Station

Lüderitz's first **train station** (cnr Bahnhof St & Bismarck St) was finished in 1907 along with the railway line itself. However, following the discovery of diamonds the facilities became swamped, and a new station was commissioned in 1912 to handle the increased traffic.

Old Post Office

The **old post office** (Schinz St) was originally designed by railway commissioner Oswald Reinhardt in 1908, though it now serves as the NWR office.

LÜDERITZ PENINSULA

The Lüderitz Peninsula, much of which lies outside the Sperrgebiet, makes an interesting half-day excursion from town.

Agate Bay, just north of Lüderitz, is made of tailings from the diamond workings. There aren't many agates these days, but you'll find fine sand partially consisting of tiny grey mica chips.

The picturesque and relatively calm bay, **Sturmvogelbucht**, is a pleasant place for a braai (barbecue), though the water temperature would be amenable only to a penguin or polar bear. The rusty ruin in the bay is the remains of a 1914 Norwegian whaling station; the salty pan just inland attracts flamingos and merits a quick stop.

At **Diaz Point**, 22km by road from Lüderitz, is a classic lighthouse and a replica of the cross erected in July 1488 by Portuguese navigator Bartolomeu Dias on his return from the Cape of Good Hope. Portions of the original have been dispersed as far as Lisbon, Berlin and Cape Town. From the point, there's a view of a nearby seal colony and you can also see cormorants, flamingos, wading birds and even the occasional pod of dolphins.

Halifax Island, a short distance offshore south of Diaz Point, is home to Namibia's best-known jackass penguin colony. Jackass or Cape penguins live in colonies on rocky offshore islets off the Atlantic Coast. With binoculars, you can often see them gathering on the sandy beach opposite the car park.

Grosse Bucht (Big Bay), at the southern end of Lüderitz peninsula, is a wild and scenic beach favoured by flocks of flamingos, which feed in the tidal pools. It's also the site of a small but picturesque shipwreck on the beach.

Just a few kilometres up the coast is **Klein Bogenfels**, a small rock arch beside the sea. When the wind isn't blowing a gale, it makes a pleasant picnic spot.

Activities

A rewarding activity is to dig for the lovely crystals of calcium sulphate and gypsum known as sand roses, which develop when moisture seeps into the sand and causes it to crystallise into flowery shapes. The NWR office in town issues digging permits, which are valid for a two-hour dig, and up to three sand roses or a total weight of 1.5kg. Diggers must be accompanied by a Ministry of Environment & Tourism (MET) official, and have to use their hands or other light tools to extract the sand roses (hard tools would damage other buried specimens).

Tours

With the exception of the Kolmanskop ghost town, allow at least five days to plan any excursion into the Sperrgebiet as tour companies need time to fill out all of the paperwork and acquire all of the necessary permits.

Coastway Tours Lüderitz (☎ 202002; www.coast ways.com.na) This highly reputable company runs multiday self-catering 4WD trips deep into the Sperrgebiet.

Lüderitz Safaris & Tours (☎ 202719; ludsaf@ africaonline.com.na; Bismarck St; ☺ 8am-1pm & 2-5pm Mon-Fri, 8am-noon Sat, 8.30-10am Sun) A popular booking agency for tours to the Kolmanskop ghost town as well as other local destinations.

Ghost Town Tours (☎ 204033; www.ghosttowntours .com; Goerke Haus) This company operates day trips to Kolmanskop, Elizabeth Bay and other sights in the Sperrgebiet.

Sleeping

BUDGET

Shark Island Camp Site (day entry N$40, campsite N$50 plus per person N$20, 6-person bungalow N$450, lighthouse N$850) This is a beautifully situated but aggravatingly

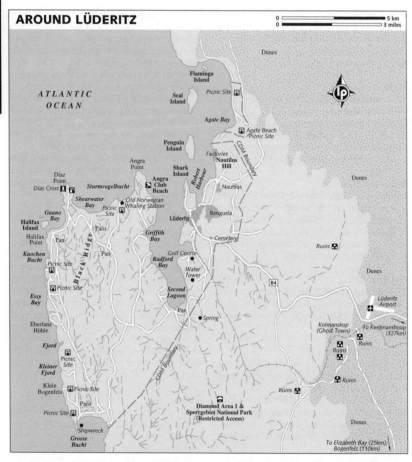

AROUND LÜDERITZ

windy locale. Shark Island is connected to the town by a causeway but is no longer an island, thanks to the harbour reclamation project that attached it to the mainland. The centrepiece of the island is a historic lighthouse that caps the central rock, and features two bedrooms, a living room and a kitchen – perfect for self-caterers! Book accommodation through the NWR office in Windhoek (p234) or in Lüderitz (p350) – if space is available, bookings can also be made at the entrance.

Lüderitz Backpackers (☎ 202000; www.namibweb .com/backpackers.htm; 7 Schinz St; camping N$115, dm/d N$145/365) Housed in a historic colonial mansion, this friendly place is the only true backpackers spot in town. The vibe is congenial and low-key, and the friendly management

is helpful in sorting out your onward travels. And of course, the usual backpacker amenities are on offer here, including a communal kitchen, braai pit, TV lounge and laundry facilities.

Krabbenhoft une Lampe (☎ 202674; info@klguest house.com; 25 Bismarck St; s from N$150/250) One of the more unusual sleeping options in town, the Krabbenhoft is a converted carpet factory that now offers a number of basic rooms and self-catering flats upstairs from a weaver (see opposite). Accommodation is very basic, but the novelty factor can't be beat.

Hansa Haus Guesthouse (☎ 203581; mcloud@ africaonline.com.na; Klippenweg St; s/d from N$200/400) This imposing hilltop home, which dates back to 1909 and is presently splashed out in regal blues and rich woods, boasts dramatic sea views and quiet surroundings. Rooms feature high ceilings and picture windows that perfectly complement this authentic colonial offering.

MIDRANGE

Kapps Hotel (☎ 202345; pmk@mweb.com.na; Bay Rd; r per person from N$225) This is the town's oldest hotel, dating back to 1907, though a recent renovation has managed to retain the historical ambience while adding a touch of modernity. The attached Rumour's Grill is a great place to drop into for either a cold beer at the end of a long drive or a strong nightcap on the way up to bed.

Bay View Hotel (☎ 202288; www.luderitzhotels.com; Diaz St; r per person from N$340; 🏊) This historic complex, owned by the Lüderitz family, is one of the most established hotels in town, yet offers surprisingly well-priced accommodation. Airy rooms surround a courtyard and a swimming pool, and there's also an onsite bar and seafood restaurant specialising in local oysters.

Kratzplatz (☎ 202458; kratzmr@iway.na; 5 Nachtigal St; s/d from N$350/450) Housed in a converted church complete with vaulted ceilings, this centrally located B&B offers a variety of different rooms to choose from. The attached Barrels restaurant has a lively beer garden and a wonderful German kitchen that draws both guests and outside diners.

Haus Sandrose (☎ 202630; www.haussandrose.com; 15 Bismarck St; s/d from N$350/480, f from N$900) The Sandrose is solely comprised of three uniquely decorated rooms surrounding a sheltered garden, ensuring a personalised level of service not found elsewhere in town. This is a lovely option for anyone who would rather be a house guest as opposed to an anonymous face at a hotel reception desk.

TOP END

Lüderitz Nest Hotel (☎ 204000; www.nesthotel.com; 820 Diaz St; r per person from N$580; 🖳 🏊) Lüderitz's oldest upmarket hotel occupies a jutting peninsula in the southwest corner of town complete with its own private beach. Each room is stylishly appointed with modern furnishings and faces out towards the sea. Amenities include a pool, sauna, terraced bar and a collection of gourmet restaurants.

Protea Hotel Sea-view Hotel Zum Sperrgebiet (☎ 203411; www.seaview-luederitz.com; cnr Woermann & Göring Sts; s/d from N$705/1123; 🖳 🏊) In a town defined by its colonial heritage, the Protea bucks the trend with a modern offering of polished steel and sparkling glass. There are only 22 rooms here, each accented by a sweeping terrace facing out towards the sea.

Eating & Drinking

If the sea has been bountiful, various hotels serve the catch of the day, though you can always count on a long list of German specialities. If you're self-catering, there are a number of supermarkets as well as small seafood merchants in town. And finally, if you're a drinker, any of the restaurants listed below double as watering holes, though Lüderitz tends to be fairly subdued once the sun drops.

Diaz Coffee Shop (☎ 203147; cnr Bismarck & Nachtigal Sts; snacks & meals N$10-30) The cappuccinos are strong and the pastries are sweet, and the ambience wouldn't at all look out of place in Munich.

Seabreeze Coffee Shop (☎ 245615; Waterfront Complex; snacks & meals N$10-30) This waterfront cafe offers attractive sea views, so make it a double espresso and linger a bit longer than you normally would.

Badger's (☎ 202855; Diaz St; meals N$20-45) An excellent choice for a cold lager and some hot pub grub, Badger's is a lively spot where you can count on finding good company.

Rumours Grill & Pub (☎ 202655; Bismarck St; meals $25-55; 🕙 lunch & dinner) Part bustling sports bar, part German-style beer garden, Rumours is something of a Lüderitz institution that has been in business for decades.

Barrels (☎ 202458; 5 Natchtigal St; mains N$35-75) A wonderfully festive restaurant accented by occasional live music, Barrels offers rotating daily specials highlighting fresh seafood and German staples.

Legends (☎ 203110; Bay Rd; mains N$45-85) This understated restaurant has a relaxed atmosphere and serves up a healthy mix of seafood, grilled meats, pizzas and burgers, as well as the odd vegetarian option or two.

Ritzi's Seafood Restaurant (☎ 202818; Waterfront; mains N$85-215) Occupying a choice location in the new waterfront complex, Ritzi's is the town's top spot for amazing seafood matched with equally amazing sunset views.

Shopping

Karaman Weavery (☎ 202272; 25 Bismarck St) This shop specialises in locally woven high-quality rugs and garments in pastel desert colours,

WHAT'S FOR DINNER IN LÜDERITZ

Can you recommend a good beer to start things off right? Of course I can! Namibia has some of the best beers in Africa, and you really can't leave here without having a Windhoek Lager. Have you ever heard of *Reinheitsgebot*? (Translation: the German beer purity law of 1516, which states that beer can only be made from water, barley and hops.) Windhoek is still brewed according to this traditional law, which means that you don't have to worry about getting a hangover if you drink too many!

I'll have a Windhoek then! Any special appetisers to go with it? Today we have raw oysters on the menu, which were pulled right from the bay here in Lüderitz. If you don't like oysters, might I recommend the crayfish cocktail? There was a crayfish festival in town last weekend, so I can guarantee that they're in season. We also get good prawns from all along the coast, and we can serve them either grilled in white wine or boiled and served on a bed of garden salad.

The crayfish cocktail sounds delicious. And for the main course? We have a large selection of uniquely Namibian dishes, though we're also proud to celebrate our German heritage here in Lüderitz. If you want to try something local, our catch of the day is kingklip (pink cusk eel), which is pan-fried in butter and lemon, and dressed up with ground peppercorns and fresh parsley. If you want to try something German, you can't go wrong with the *Eisbein* (an entire roasted pig leg, joint and all!), which is served with sauerkraut and mashed potatoes. If you have a big appetite, the *Eisbein* will take you a good hour or so to work all the meat and fat from the bone!

I think I'll have a go at the Eisbein then! And, if I still have room for dessert? If you manage to finish the *Eisbein*, bone marrow and all, then you're going to need a shot of Underberg (a traditional German digestive bitter made from aromatic herbs). We also have some lovely *Apfelstrudel* (apple strudel), but we'll see how you do with the *Eisbein* first!

Author's Note: While I was able to strip all the meat from the bone, the surrounding layer of 'crackling' or braised pig fat proved to be way too much for one person of normal appetite to stomach! The apple strudel was completely out of the question, though the Underberg managed to stave off the indigestion, at least until the next morning…

Sue, a life-long resident of Lüderitz, works as a waitress at a couple of spots around the town. While perusing the list of daily specials, she explains what's for dinner.

with Namibian flora and fauna the favoured designs. It accepts special orders and can post them worldwide.

Getting There & Away

AIR
Air Namibia travels several times a week between Windhoek and Lüderitz, at least once weekly to/from Swakopmund and at least twice weekly to/from Walvis Bay. The airport is 8km southeast of town.

BUS
Somewhat irregular combis connect Lüderitz to Keetmanshoop, with fares averaging around N$175. Buses depart from the southern edge of town at informal bus stops along Bismarck St.

CAR & MOTORCYCLE
Lüderitz and the scenery en route (see p347) are worth the 334km trip from Keetmanshoop via the tarred B4.

SPERRGEBIET NATIONAL PARK

Although it's been off-limits to the public for most of the last century, in 2008 the Namibian government inaugurated its newest national park, the Sperrgebiet. Known worldwide as the source of Namibia's exclusive diamonds, the Sperrgebiet (Forbidden area) is set to become the gem of Namibia's protected spaces. Geographically speaking, the park encompasses the northern tip of the Succulent Karoo Biorne, an area of 26,000 sq km of dunes and mountains that appear dramatically stark, but represent one of 25 outstanding global 'hotspots' of unique biodiversity.

The Sperggebiet originally consisted of two private concessions: Diamond Area 1 and Diamond Area 2. The latter, home to the Kolmanskop ghost town and Elizabeth Bay, has been open to the public for some time now. Since 2004, parts of the former have also been opened up to specialist conservation groups, though given the diamond industry's security concerns, access has been carefully controlled.

At the time of research, the Namibian Ministry of Environment & Tourism (MET) announced its intent to open up further tourism concessions within Area 1. While it will most likely be at least another couple of years before travel restrictions are fully eased, the chance to be one of the first civilians to step foot in this zone is an enticing prospect.

Orientation & Information

The 'Forbidden Zone' was established in 1908 following the discovery of diamonds near Lüderitz. Although mining operations were localised along the coast, a huge swathe of Southern Namibia was sectioned off in the interest of security.

As a diamond mining concession, the Sperrgebiet has been off-limits to the public and scientists for most of the last century, and the tight restrictions on access have helped to keep much of the area pristine. De Beers Centenary, a partner in De Beers Consolidated Diamond Mines, continues to control the entire area until the MET establishes a management plan for the park.

Forty percent of the park is desert, and 30% is grassland; the rest is rocks, granite mountains and moonscape. Though the area has yet to be fully explored, initial scientific assessments have discovered 776 plant species, 230 of which are thought to be unique to the park. There are also populations of gemsbok, brown hyenas and rare, threatened reptile species, including the desert rain frog. Bird species are extremely varied, and include the dune lark, black-headed canary and the African oystercatcher.

The area has been identified as a priority area for conservation in the **Succulent Karoo Ecosystem Plan** (SKEP; www.skep.org). SKEP is a joint Namibian and South African initiative that brings together all the stakeholders in the region from government ministries to local populations. The program is supported by the **Critical Ecosystem Partnership Fund** (CEPF; www.cepf.net), which acts as its locally based coordination team.

Also involved is the **Namibian Nature Foundation** (NNF; www.nnf.org.na), which will eventually take over the planning for the park and will focus on community-based initiatives to ensure that locals benefit. The development of tourism in the Sperrgebiet is expected to stimulate the economy of Lüderitz, which will serve as the main gateway to the park.

Tours

Until the park loosens its tight restrictions on public access, it's in your own best interest to have a healthy respect for the boundaries. Armed guards in the Sperrgebiet have a lot of time on their hands – don't make their day. Select sights in the national park are open to visitors on private tours – for listings of approved operators, see p351.

Sights

KOLMANSKOP GHOST TOWN

Given that permits can be arranged from Namdeb with relative ease, the most popular excursion from Lüderitz is the ghost town of Kolmanskop. Named after an early Afrikaner trekker Jani Kolman, whose ox-wagon became bogged in the sand here, Kolmanskop was originally constructed as the CDM headquarters. Although Kolmanskop once boasted a casino, bowling alley and a theatre with fine acoustics, the slump in diamond sales after WWI and the discovery of richer pickings at Oranjemund ended its heyday. By 1956, the town was totally deserted, and left to the mercy of the shifting desert sands. Today, Kolmanskop has been partially restored as a tourist attraction, and the sight of decrepit buildings being invaded by dunes is simply too surreal to describe.

You can turn up at any time, and you're not required to arrive as part of an organised tour, though you do need to purchase a permit (N$40) in advance through either the NWR office in Lüderitz (p350) or a local tour operator. To photograph Kolmanskop you have to purchase an additional permit for N$125. Guided tours (in English and German), which are included in the price of the permit, depart from the museum in Kolmanskop at 9.30am and 11am Monday to Saturday, and at 10am Sunday and public holidays. After the tour, you can return to the museum, which contains relics and information on the history of Namibian diamond mining.

ELIZABETH BAY

In 1986, CDM again began prospecting in the northern Sperrgebiet, and found bountiful

DIAMOND DEMENTIA
Geology & the 4 Cs

Diamonds are the best known allotrope (form) of carbon, and are characterised by their extreme hardness (they are the hardest naturally occurring mineral) and high dispersion of light (diamonds are prismatic when exposed to white light). As a result, they are valued for industrial purposes as abrasives since they can only be scratched by other diamonds, and for ornamental purposes since they retain lustre when polished. It's estimated that 130 million carats (or 26,000kg) of diamonds is mined annually, yielding a market value of over US$9 billion.

Diamonds are formed when carbon-bearing materials are exposed to high pressures and temperatures for prolonged periods of time. With the exception of synthetically produced diamonds, favourable conditions only occur beneath the continental crust, starting at depths of about 150km. Once carbon crystallises, a diamond will then continue to grow in size so long as it is exposed to both sufficiently high temperatures and pressures. However, size is limited by the fact that diamond-bearing rock is eventually expelled towards the surface through deep-origin volcanic eruptions. Eventually, they are forced to the surface by magma, and are expelled from a volcanic pipe.

Since the early 20th century the quality of a diamond has been determined by four properties, now commonly used as basic descriptors of a stone – carat, clarity, colour and cut. The carat weight measures the mass of a diamond, with one carat equal to 200mg. Assuming all other properties are equal, the value of a diamond increases exponentially in relation to carat weight since larger diamonds are rarer.

Clarity is a measure of internal defects known as inclusions, which are foreign materials or structural imperfections present in the stone. Higher clarity is associated with value, and it's estimated that only about 20% of all diamonds mined have a high enough clarity rating to be sold as gemstones.

Although a perfect diamond is transparent with a total absence of hue, virtually all diamonds have a discernable colour due to chemical impurities and structural defects. Depending on the hue and intensity, a diamond's colour can either detract from or enhance its value (yellow diamonds are discounted, while pink and blue diamonds are more valuable).

---

diamond deposits around Elizabeth Bay, 30km south of Kolmanskop. The estimated 2.5 million carats weren't expected to last more than 10 years, but CDM installed a full-scale operation, and rather than duplicate their Lüderitz facilities here, they provided their workers with daily transport from the town. Half-day tours to Elizabeth Bay, which must be booked through tour operators in Lüderitz, also take in Kolmanskop and the Atlas Bay Cape fur seal colony.

BOGENFELS SEA ARCH
One-third of the way down the Forbidden Coast between Lüderitz and Oranjemund is the 55m natural sea arch known as Bogenfels (Bow Rock). Bogenfels has only been opened to private tours for a few years, which also take in the mining ghost town of Pomona, the Maerchental Valley, the Bogenfels ghost town and a large cave near the arch itself. Again, you must book this trip through tour operators in Lüderitz.

Sleeping
There are no tourist lodges within the national park, and bush camping is strictly forbidden. While it is likely that some form of accommodation will be constructed in the years to come, in the meantime your best option is to base yourself in Lüderitz (see p351).

Getting There & Away
Do not attempt to access the Sperrgebiet in a private vehicle as you will be inviting a whole mess of trouble. The only exception to this statement is Kolmanskop, which can be accessed if you have a sturdy 4WD along with the necessary permits.

ORANJEMUND
☎ 063
Oranjemund, at the mouth of the Orange River, owes its existence to diamonds. So great was its wealth that in 1944 it supplanted Kolmanskop as the CDM headquarters. With a population of less than 10,000, Oranjemund

Finally, the cut of a diamond describes the quality of workmanship and the angles to which a diamond is cut.

International Trade

The international trade in diamonds as gemstones is unique in comparison to precious metals like gold and platinum since diamonds are not traded as a commodity. As a result, the price of diamonds is artificially inflated by a few key players, and there exists virtually no secondary market. For example, wholesale trade and diamond cutting was historically limited to a few locations, including New York, Antwerp, London, Tel Aviv and Amsterdam, though recently centres have been established in China, India and Thailand.

Since its establishment in 1888, De Beers has maintained a virtual monopoly on the world's diamond mines and distribution channels for gem-quality stones. At one time it was estimated that over 80% of the world's uncut diamonds were controlled by the subsidiaries of De Beers, though this percentage has dropped below 50% in more recent years. However, De Beers continues to take advantage of its market position by establishing strict price controls, and marketing diamonds directly to preferential consumers (known as sight holders) in world markets.

Once purchased by sight holders, diamonds are then cut and polished to sell as gemstones, though these activities are limited to the select locations mentioned earlier. Once they have been prepared, diamonds are then sold on one of 24 diamond exchanges known as bourses. This is the final tightly controlled step in the diamond supply chain, as retailers are only permitted to buy relatively small amounts of diamonds before preparing them for final sale to the consumer.

In recent years the diamond industry has come under increasing criticism regarding the buying and selling of conflict or 'blood' diamonds. In response to increasing public concern, the Kimberley Process was instituted in 2002, which was aimed at preventing the trade of conflict diamonds on the international market. The main mechanism by which the Kimberley Process operates is by documenting and certifying diamond exports from producing countries in order to ensure that proceeds are not being used to fund criminal or revolutionary activities.

is now an archetypal company town, with 100% employment and subsidised housing and medical care for its workers and their families. Despite its desert location, Namdeb Diamond Corporation Limited (Namdeb) maintains a golf course and large areas of green parkland.

All Oranjemund visitors must have a permit from **Namdeb** (☎ in Windhoek 061-2043333; www .debeersgroup.com/namdeb) and, as yet, there's no real tourism in the town. Applications for a permit must be made at least one month in advance and should be accompanied by a police affidavit stating that you've never been convicted of a serious crime. Normally, permits are issued only to those who have business in the town.

Security is so strict in Oranjemund that even broken equipment used in the mining operations may never leave the site, lest it be used to smuggle diamonds outside of the fence. Despite this, a fair number of stolen diamonds manages to reach the illicit mar-

ket. Thieves come up with some ingenious methods, including carrier pigeons, discarded rubbish and tunnels.

Road access to the town is via Alexander Bay, across the border in South Africa.

THE FAR SOUTH

Situated within the angle between Southern Africa's two most remote quarters, Namaqualand and the Kalahari, Namibia's bleak southern tip exudes a sense of isolation from whichever direction you approach it. Travelling along the highway, the seemingly endless desert plains stretch to the horizon in all directions, only to suddenly tear asunder at the mighty Fish River Canyon. This gash across the desert landscape is one of Namibia's most stunning geological formations, luring in each winter determined bands of trekkers bent on traipsing across its vast expanse.

GRÜNAU
☎ 063

For most travellers, Grünau is either the first petrol station north of the South African border, or a logical overnight stop for weary drivers between Cape Town and Windhoek.

An excellent spot to lie down for the night is the **White House Rest Camp** (Map p341; ☎ 262061; campsites N$30, r per person N$150). Dolf and Kinna de Wet's wonderful and popular B&B – yes, it is a white house – has well-priced, self-catering accommodation. This renovated farmhouse, which dates from 1912, is architecturally stunning. Kitchen facilities are available, though the hosts will also provide set meals and braai packs on request. To get there, head 11km towards Keetmanshoop on the B1 and turn west at the White House signpost; it's 4km off the road.

Grünau is 144km northwest of the Velloorsdrift border crossing along the C10, and 142km north of the Noordoewer border crossing along the B1.

FISH RIVER CANYON NATIONAL PARK
☎ 063

Nowhere else in Africa will you find anything quite like Fish River Canyon. Despite the seeming enormity of this statement, the numbers don't lie: the canyon measures 160km in length and up to 27km in width, and the dramatic inner canyon reaches a depth of 550m. Although these figures by themselves are impressive, it's difficult to get a sense of perspective without actually witnessing the enormous scope of the canyon. In order to do this, you will need to embark on a monumental five-day hike that traverses half the length of the canyon, and ultimately tests the limits of your physical and mental endurance. Your reward, however, will be the chance to tackle one Namibia's, and indeed, one of Africa's, greatest natural wonders.

History

The San have a legend that the wildly twisting Fish River Canyon was gouged out by a frantically scrambling snake *Koutein Kooru*, as he was pursued into the desert by hunters. However, the geological story is a bit different…

Fish River, which joins the Orange River 110km south of the canyon, has been gouging

out this gorge for aeons. Surprisingly, Fish River Canyon is actually two canyons, one inside the other, which were formed in entirely different ways. It's thought that the original sedimentary layers of shale, sandstone and loose igneous material around Fish River Canyon were laid down nearly two billion years ago, and were later metamorphosed by

FISH RIVER CANYON NP

0 — 8 km
0 — 4 miles

SIGHTS & ACTIVITIES

Bushy Corner	1	B4
Dolerite Dyke	2	A3
Dolerite Dyke	3	B3
Fool's Gold Corner	4	A5
Four Finger Rock	5	B4
Hell's Corner	6	A3
Hikers' Viewpoint	7	B3
Kanebis Bend	8	B4
Kooigoedhoogte Pass	9	B4
Main Viewpoint	10	B3
Rock Pinnacle	11	B4
Rockies Point	12	B3
South (Eagle's Rock) Viewpoint	13	B4
Sulphur (Palm) Springs	14	B3
Sulphur Springs Viewpoint	15	B3
Sunset Point	16	B3
Thilo von Trotha's Grave	17	A4
Three Sisters Rocks	18	B4

SLEEPING

Ai-Ais Hot Springs Resort	19	A5
Hobas Camp Site & Information Centre	20	B3

heat and pressure into more solid materials, such as gneiss. Just under a billion years ago, cracks in the formation admitted intrusions of igneous material, which cooled to form the dolerite dykes (which are now exposed in the inner canyon).

The surface was then eroded into a basin and covered by a shallow sea, which eventually filled with sediment – sandstone, conglomerate, quartzite, limestone and shale – washed down from the surrounding exposed lands. Around 500 million years ago, a period of tectonic activity along crustal faults caused these layers to rift and to tilt at a 45° angle. These forces opened a wide gap in the earth's crust and formed a large canyon.

This was what we now regard as the outer canyon, the bottom of which was the first level of terraces that are visible approximately 170m below the eastern rim and 380m below the western rim. This newly created valley naturally became a watercourse (the Fish River, oddly enough), which began eroding a meandering path along the valley floor and eventually gouged out what is now the 270m-deep inner canyon.

Information

The main access points for Fish River Canyon are at Hobas, near the northern end of the park, and Ai-Ais, near the southern end. Both are administered by the NWR. Accommodation must be booked in advance through the Windhoek office (p234). Daily park permits, N$80 per person and N$10 per vehicle, are valid for both Hobas and Ai-Ais.

The **Hobas Information Centre** (Map p358; 7.30am-noon & 2-5pm) at the northern end of the park is also the check-in point for the five-day canyon hike. Packaged snacks and cool drinks are available here, but little else.

The Fish River typically flows between March and April. Early in the tourist season, from April to June, it may diminish to a trickle, and by mid-winter, to just a chain of remnant pools along the canyon floor.

Following the death of an ill-prepared hiker in 2001, the NWR decided to prohibit day hikes into Fish River Canyon. During the cooler months, however, you may be able to get special permission at Hobas to hike down from Hikers' Viewpoint. Shorter hikes are possible in the Canyon Nature Park private concession.

Sights
HOBAS

From Hobas, it's 10km on a gravel road to the **Hikers' Viewpoint** (Map p358; at the start of the hiking route), which has picnic tables, braai pits and toilets. Just around the corner is a good overview of the northern part of the canyon. The **Main Viewpoint** (Map p358), a few kilometres south, has probably the best – and most photographed – overall canyon view. Both these vistas take in the sharp river bend known as Hell's Corner.

AI-AIS

The **hot springs** (Map p358; per person N$15; 9am-9pm) at Ai-Ais (Nama for 'Scalding Hot') are beneath the towering peaks at the southern end of Fish River Canyon National Park. Although the 60°C springs have probably been known to the San for thousands of years, the legend goes that they were 'discovered' by a nomadic Nama shepherd rounding up stray sheep. They're rich in chloride, fluoride and sulphur, and are reputedly therapeutic for sufferers of rheumatism or nervous disorders. The hot water is piped to a series of baths and Jacuzzis as well as an outdoor swimming pool.

A pleasant diversion is the short scramble to the peak, which rises above the opposite bank (note that the trail is not marked). It affords a superb view of Ai-Ais, and you will even see the four pinnacles of Four Finger Rock rising far to the north. The return trip takes approximately two hours.

Amenities include a shop, restaurant, petrol station, tennis courts, post office and, of course, a swimming pool, spa and mineral bath facilities.

Be advised that during the summertime, there's a serious risk of flooding – Ai-Ais was destroyed by floods in both 1972 and 2000.

CANYON NATURE PARK

Technically outside Fish River Canyon National Park, this **nature park** (Map p341; 683005; www.canyonnaturepark.com) is a private concession situated in the confluence of the Löwen and Fish River Canyons amid some of the most amazing geology imaginable. The best part of visiting is that the area falls outside the jurisdiction of NWR, which means you don't need to book through Windhoek if you want to trek here.

From April to October, you can tackle the five-day 85km **Löwenfish hiking trail**, which takes in the Löwen Canyon and several days along Fish River Canyon, interrupted by several ascents to the plateau and descents down scenic cliffs

Campsites (with no facilities) are situated at water sources, and the last night you can stay at the **Koelkrans Camp** (Map p341; camping per person N$80) on the floor of the canyon, with cooking facilities and hot showers. On the last day, hikers climb out of the canyon for the last time and follow a scenic route back to the base camp at Grande View Lodge (see Sleeping, p361).

Stages may also be done as one- to four-day hikes. Prebooking is essential, and prices vary depending on the size of your group and the length of your intended hike.

Activities
FISH RIVER HIKING TRAIL

The five-day **hike** (per person N$100) from Hobas to Ai-Ais is Namibia's most popular long-distance walk – and with good reason. The magical 85km route, which follows the sandy riverbed past a series of ephemeral pools,

---

FISH RIVER CANYON HIKING ROUTE

From Hobas, it's 10km to **Hikers' Viewpoint**, which is the start of the trail – hikers must find their own transport to this point. The steep and scenic section at the beginning takes you from the canyon rim to the river, where you'll have a choice of fabulous sandy campsites beside cool, green river pools.

Although the map in this book shows the route following the river quite closely, it's important to note that the best route changes from year to year. This is largely due to sand and vegetation deposited by the previous year's floods. In general, the easiest hiking will be along the inside of the river bends, where you're likely to find wildlife trails and dry, non-sandy terrain that's free of vegetation tangles, slippery stones or large boulders.

After an exhausting 13km hike through the rough sand and boulders along the east bank, the **Sulphur Springs Viewpoint** track joins the main route. If you're completely exhausted at this stage and can't handle the conditions, this route can be used as an emergency exit from the canyon. If it's any encouragement however, the going gets easier as you move downstream, so why not head a further 2km to **Sulphur Springs**, set up camp and see how you feel in the morning?

Sulphur Springs – more commonly called **Palm Springs** – is an excellent campsite with thermal sulphur pools (a touch of paradise) to soothe your aching muscles. The springs, which have a stable temperature of 57°C, gush up from the underworld at an amazing 30L per second and contain not only sulphur, but also chloride and fluoride.

Legend has it that during WWI, two German prisoners of war hid out at Sulphur Springs to escape internment. One was apparently suffering from asthma, and the other from skin cancer, but thanks to the spring's healing powers, both were cured. It's also said that the palm trees growing here sprang up from date pips discarded by these two Germans.

The next section of the hike consists mostly of deep sand, pebbles and gravel. The most direct route through the inside river bends requires hikers to cross the river several times. The **Table Mountain** formation lies 15km beyond Sulphur Springs, and a further 15km on is the first short cut, which avoids an area of dense thorn scrub known as **Bushy Corner**. Around the next river bend, just upstream from the **Three Sisters** rock formation, is a longer short cut past **Kanebis Bend** up to **Kooigoedhoogte Pass**. At the top, you'll have a superb view of **Four Finger Rock**, an impressive rock tower consisting of four thick pinnacles (though they more closely resemble a cow's udder than fingers).

After descending to the river, you'll cross to the west bank and start climbing over yet another short cut (although you can also follow the river bend). At the southern end of this pass, on the west bank of the river, lies the **grave** of Lieutenant Thilo von Trotha, who was killed here after a 1905 confrontation between the Germans and the Nama.

The final 25km into Ai-Ais, which can be completed in one long day, follows an easy but sandy and rocky route. South of von Trotha's grave, the canyon widens out and becomes drier. Be advised that during the end of winter, the final 15km are normally completely dry, so you will need to carry sufficient water.

begins at Hikers' Viewpoint, and ends at the hot spring resort of Ai-Ais.

Due to flash flooding and heat in summer months, the route is open only from 1 May to 30 September. Groups of three to 30 people may begin the hike every day of the season, though you will have to book in advance as the trail is extremely popular. Reservations can be made at the NWR office in Windhoek (p234).

Officials may need a doctor's certificate of fitness, issued less than 40 days before your hike, though if you look young and fit, they may not ask. Hikers must arrange their own transport to and from the start and finish as well as accommodation in Hobas and Ai-Ais.

Thanks to the typically warm, clear weather, you probably won't need a tent, but you must carry a sleeping bag and food. In Hobas, check on water availability in the canyon. In August and September, the last 15km of the walk can be completely dry and hikers will need several 2L water bottles to manage this hot, sandy stretch. Large plastic soft-drink bottles normally work just fine.

For detailed information on the route, see the boxed text, opposite.

Sleeping

Accommodation inside the national park must be prebooked through the NWR office in Windhoek (p234).

Hobas Camp Site (Map p358; campsite N$50 & N$20 per person; 🛉) Administered by NWR, this pleasant and well-shaded camping ground near the park's northern end is about 10km from the main viewpoints. Facilities are clean, and there's a kiosk and swimming pool, but no restaurant or petrol station.

Ai-Ais Hot Springs Resort (Map p358; campsite N$50 & N$20 per person, flats from N$600; 🛉) Also administered by NWR, amenities include washing blocks, braai pits and use of the resort facilities, including the hot springs. All flats have private baths and basic self-catering facilities, and there is also an on-site restaurant and small grocery store.

Fish River Guest Farm (Map p341; ☎ 683005; http://www.canyonnaturepark.com/accommeast.htm; r per person with shared bathroom from N$250) Located near the eastern rim in the Canyon Nature Park concession off the C12, this historic farmhouse serves self-catering hikers of all skill levels. Private hiking trails lead from the farm

down to the rim where you can partake in self-guided hikes of varying skill levels.

Grande View Lodge (Map p341; ☎ 683005; www .canyonnaturepark.com/accommwest.htm; r per person from N$1550; 🛉 🛉) Perched on the western rim in the Canyon Nature Park concession along the D463, the Grande View is by far the most luxurious lodge in the region. Unwind in your private stone chalet before congregating in the dining room for a sophisticated sundowner.

Getting There & Away

There's no public transport to Hobas or Ai-Ais, and you'll really need a private vehicle to get around.

GONDWANA CAÑON PARK

Founded in 1996, the 100,000-hectare Gondwana Cañon Park was created by amalgamating several former sheep farms and removing the fences to restore the wilderness country immediately northeast of Fish River Canyon National Park. Water holes have been established and wildlife is now returning to this wonderful, remote corner of Namibia. In the process, the park absorbed the former Aurauries-Steenbok Nature Reserve, which had been created earlier to protect not only steenboks, but also Hartmann's mountain zebras, gemsboks and klipspringers.

Information

Funding for the park is derived from a 5% bed levy applied to all four Cañon lodges. Any and all of these properties can be booked through the **reservation centre** (☎ 061-230066; www.gondwana-canyon-park.com). A wide range of activities from 4WD excursions and guided hikes to horseback riding and scenic flights are available at all of the lodges.

Sleeping

Cañon Roadhouse (Map p341; ☎ 061-230066; www.gondwana-canyon-park.com/cr.htm; s/d from N$620/990, camping per person N$85; 🛉) This wonderfully unique place attempts to re-create a roadhouse out on the wildest stretches of Route 66 – at least as it exists in the collective imagination. Buffets are served on an antique motorcycle, the stunning window shades are made from used air filters and the bar stools are air filters from heavy-duty vehicles.

Cañon Mountain Camp (Map p341; ☎ 061-230066; www.gondwana-canyon-park.com/c_m_c.htm; r per person from N$295) One of the more budget orientated properties in the Cañon collection, this remote mountain camp occupies a high altitude setting amid dolerite hills. Self-caterers can take advantage of the fully equipped kitchen, braai pits and communal lounges.

Cañon Village (Map p341; ☎ 061-230066; www .gondwana-canyon-park.com/c_v.htm; s/d from N$995/1590; 🆒 🐾) Drawing inspiration from the Cape-Dutch villages of yesteryear, this wonderfully bucolic spot hugs a rock face on the outskirts of Fish River Canyon National Park. The centrepiece is a thatched restaurant serving traditional Afrikaner specialities featuring fresh local produce and delicious game meats.

Cañon Lodge (Map p341; ☎ 061-230066; www .gondwana-canyon-park.com/cl.htm; s/d from N$995/1590; 🆒 🐾) This mountain retreat is one of Namibia's most stunning accommodation options, consisting of red stone bungalows perfectly integrated into its boulder-strewn backdrop. The restaurant, housed in a 1908 farmhouse, is decorated with historic farming implements and rambling gardens.

Getting There & Away
Gondwana Cañon Park can be accessed via private vehicle along the C37.

NOORDOEWER
☎ 063

Noordoewer sits astride the Orange River, which has its headwaters in the Drakensberg Mountains of Natal (South Africa) and forms much of the boundary between Namibia and South Africa. The river was named not for its muddy colour, but for Prince William V of Orange, the Dutch monarch in the late 1770s. Although the town primarily serves as a border post and a centre for viticulture, it serves as a good base for organising a canoeing or rafting adventure on the Orange River.

Activities
RIVER TRIPS
Canoe and rafting trips are normally done in stages and last three to six days. The popular trips from Noordoewer north to Aussenkehr aren't treacherous by any stretch – the white-

water never exceeds Class II – but they do provide access to some wonderfully wild canyon country. Other possible stages include Aussenkehr to the Fish River mouth; Fish River mouth to Nama Canyon (which has a few more serious rapids); and Nama Canyon to Selingsdrif.

Amanzi Trails (☎ in South Africa 27-21-559 1573; www.amanzitrails.co.za) This well-established South African company is based in Abiqua Camp (see below), and specialises in four-/five-day guided canoe trips down the Orange River costing N$1950/2250 per person. It also arranges shorter self-guided trips and longer excursions up Fish River for more experienced clients.

Felix Unite (☎ in South Africa 27-21-670-1300; www.felixunite.com) Another highly reputable South African operator, Felix Unite is based in Provenance Camp, and specialises in four-/six-day guided canoe and rafting trips down the Orange River costing N$2200/2450 per person. It can also combine these excursions with lengthier trips around the Western Cape of South Africa.

Sleeping
Abiqua Camp (Map p341; ☎ 297255; www.amanzitrails .co.za/abiqua_river_camp/abiqua_camp.html; camping per person N$55, s/d/tr chalet N$300/355/410) This friendly and well-situated camp, 15km down Orange River Rd, sits on the riverbank opposite some interesting sedimentary formations. This is the launch point for Amanzi Trails, so you can stock up on supplies, indulge in a hot meal and get a good night's rest before embarking on your canoe trip.

Camp Provenance (Map p341; ☎ in South Africa 27-21-670-1300; www.felixunite.com; camping per person N$70, permanent tw tent N$350, tw cabana N$650) Approximately 10km west of Noordoewer is this safari chic river camp and launch point for Felix Unite. Purists can pitch their own tent on the grassy field, while lovers of creature comforts can bed down in a permanent tent or chalet, and stockpile their reserves for the paddling ahead.

Getting There & Away
Noordoewer is located just off the B1 near the South African border, and is only accessible by private transport.

Namibia Directory

CONTENTS

ACCOMMODATION

Accommodation in Namibia is some of the most well-priced and well-kept in Southern Africa, and covers a huge range of options from hotels, rest camps, campsites, caravan parks, guest farms, backpacker hostels, B&Bs, guesthouses and luxury safari lodges. Most establishments are graded using a star system based on regular inspections carried out by the Hospitality Association of Namibia (HAN).

Hotels with restaurants also get a Y rating: YY means it only has a restaurant licence, while YYY indicates full alcohol licensing. For a full list of accommodation pick up the comprehensive booklets *Southern Africa: Where to Stay, Welcome to Namibia – Tourist Accommodation & Info Guide* and

the *Namibia B&B Guide,* free from the tourist office (see p234). HAN also publishes a map showing the locations of most lodges and guest farms.

Many of the lower-budget and backpacker places do not include breakfast in the price. In B&Bs, guesthouses, farmstays and safari lodges, breakfast is usually included in the cost of the room along with either half-board or full-board options. The former would include breakfast and a set dinner, while the latter also provides lunch (either a set lunch or a buffet-style spread).

In this book, where appropriate, accommodation options are split into budget, midrange and top-end categories for ease of reference. In general, a budget double room is anything under US$65, although you can pay as little as US$12 for a dorm bed. Midrange options are priced anywhere from US$65 to US$130, and above this you'll be well on your way to all the comforts of home. Many B&Bs are priced between US$65 and US$130, and are comfortable and welcoming places to stay.

In major tourist centres like Windhoek and Swakopmund, as well as at the top-notch safari lodges and camps, you'll be paying upwards of N$1350 a night, and sometimes much, much more. Although most top-end places quote their prices in US dollars, payment can be made in local currency. Note that most places have a separate rate for Namibian residents. Discounted rates for children are rare although a number of lodges do offer special family rooms.

Whilst most budget and midrange options tend to have a standard room price, many top-end places change their prices according to high/low season. High season is from May to

BOOK ACCOMMODATION ONLINE

For more accommodation reviews and recommendations by Lonely Planet authors, check out the online booking service at www.lonelyplanet.com. You'll find the true, insider lowdown on the best places to stay. Reviews are thorough and independent. Best of all, you can book online.

NAMIBIA DIRECTORY

October, while low season corresponds with the rains (January to April). Where appropriate, we have listed high/low rates for lodges.

If you are booking one of the high-end lodges you will usually have to confirm your booking with a credit card; this is not necessary, however, for the bulk of accommodation.

B&Bs

Bed & breakfast (B&B) establishments are mushrooming all around the country. As private homes, the standard, atmosphere and welcome tends to vary a great deal. And in some places in Swakopmund and Windhoek, readers have complained of unpleasant racism. On top of this some places don't actually provide breakfast (!), so it pays to ask when booking. Generally speaking, however, B&Bs are a pleasure to frequent, and can be one of the highlights of any trip to Namibia.

For listings, pick up the *Namibia B&B Guide* or contact the **B&B Association of Namibia** (www .accommodation-association.com), which also lists a number of self-catering flats and guest farms.

Camping

Namibia is campers' heaven, and wherever you go in the country you'll find a campsite nearby. These can vary from a patch of scrubland with basic facilities to well-kitted-out sites with concrete ablution blocks with hot and cold running water.

In many of the national parks, campsites are administered by the **Namibia Wildlife Resorts** (NWR; www.nwr.com.na), and need to be booked beforehand through its offices in Windhoek, Swakopmund and Khorixas. For more details, see p28. These sites are all well maintained, and many of them also offer accommodation in bungalows.

The non-profit organisation **NACOBTA** (Namibia Community Based Tourism Association; ☎ 061-250558; www .nacobta.com.na; PO Box 86099, Windhoek) has also established many well-kept and affordable camps throughout the country.

To camp on private land, you'll need to secure permission from the landowner. On communal land – unless you're well away from human habitation – it's a courtesy to make your presence known to the leaders in the nearest community.

Most towns also have caravan parks with bungalows or rondavels (round huts), as well as a pool, restaurant and shop. Prices are normally per site, with a maximum of eight people and two vehicles per site; there's normally an additional charge per vehicle. In addition, a growing number of private rest camps with well-appointed facilities are springing up in rural areas and along major tourist routes.

PRACTICALITIES

- Namibia uses the metric system for weights and measures.

- Plugs have three round pins; the current is 220/240V, 50Hz. If you don't have the right adaptor, you can always buy a plug locally and connect it yourself. Note that a voltage adaptor is needed for US appliances.

- While Namibia ostensibly enjoys freedom of the press, no Namibian newspaper is known for its coverage of international events, and none takes a controversial stance on political issues. There are a decent number of commercial newspapers, of which the *Namibian* and the *Windhoek Advertiser* are probably the best. The *Windhoek Observer,* published on Saturday, is also good. The two main German-language newspapers are *Allgemeine Zeitung* and *Namibia Nachrichten.*

- The Namibian Broadcasting Corporation (NBC) operates a dozen or so radio stations broadcasting on different wavebands in nine languages. The two main stations in Windhoek are Radio Energy (100 FM) and Radio Kudu (103.5 FM); the best pop station is Radio Wave, at 96.7FM in Windhoek.

- The NBC broadcasts government-vetted TV programs in English and Afrikaans. News is broadcast at 10pm nightly. Most top-end hotels and lodges with televisions provide access to satellite-supported DSTV, which broadcasts NBC and a cocktail of cable channels: MNET (a South African-based movie and entertainment package), CNN, ESPN, MTV, BBC World, Sky, Supersport, SABC, SATV, NatGeo, Disney and Discovery, among other channels.

Guest Farms

Farmstays are a peculiarly Namibian phenomenon, whereby tourists can spend the night on one of the country's huge private farms. They give an intriguing insight into the rural white lifestyle although, as with B&Bs, the level of hospitality and the standard of rooms and facilities can vary enormously. Again, generally speaking, the emphasis is on personal service, and quaint rural luxury, and bedding down on a huge rural estate in the middle of the bush can be a uniquely Namibian experience.

As an added bonus, many of these farms have designated blocks of land as wildlife reserves, and offer excellent wildlife viewing and photographic opportunities. With that said, many also serve as hunting reserves, so bear this in mind when booking if you don't relish the thought of trading trophy stories over dinner.

For all farmstays, advance bookings are essential.

Hostels

In Windhoek, Swakopmund, Lüderitz and other places, you'll find private backpacker hostels, which provide inexpensive dorm accommodation, shared ablutions and cooking facilities. Most offer a very agreeable atmosphere, and are extremely popular with budget travellers. On average, you can expect to pay around N$85 per person per night. Some also offer private doubles, which cost around N$200 to N$350.

Hotels

Hotels in Namibia are much like hotels anywhere else, ranging from tired old has-beens to palaces of luxury and indulgence. Rarely, though, will you find a dirty or unsafe hotel in Namibia given the relatively strict classification system, which rates everything from small guesthouses to four-star hotels.

One-star hotels must have a specific ratio of rooms with private and shared facilities. They tend to be quite simple, but most are locally owned and managed, and do provide clean, comfortable accommodation with adequate beds and towels. Rates range from around N$300 to N$400 for a double room, including breakfast. They always have a small dining room and bar, but few offer frills such as air-conditioning.

Hotels with two- and three-star ratings are generally more comfortable, and are often used by local businesspeople. Rates start at around N$450 for a double, and climb to N$900 for the more elegant places.

There aren't really many four-star hotels in the way that we know them, though most high-end lodges could qualify for a four-star rating. To qualify for such a rating, a hotel needs to be an air-conditioned palace with a salon, valet service and a range of ancillary services for business and diplomatic travellers.

Safari Lodges

Over the last five years the Namibian luxury safari lodge has come along in leaps and bounds, offering the kind of colonial luxury that one always associated with Botswana. The **Gondwana Desert Collection** (www.gondwana-desert-collection.com) is a prime example.

Most of the lodges are set on large private ranches or in concession areas. Some are quite affordable family-run places with standard meals or self-catering options. In general they are still more affordable than comparable places in Botswana or the Victoria Falls area, yet more expensive than those in South Africa.

ACTIVITIES

Given its stunning landscapes, Namibia provides a photogenic arena for the multitude of outdoor activities that are on offer. These range from the more conventional hiking and 4WD trails to sandboarding down mountainous dunes, quadbiking, paragliding, ballooning and camel riding. Most of these activities can be arranged very easily locally, and are relatively well priced. Throughout this book, information on activities is listed in regional chapters.

4WD Trails

Traditionally, 4WD trips were limited to rugged wilderness tracks through the Kaokoveld, Damaraland and Bushmanland, but recently an increasing number of 4WD trails have been established for 4WD enthusiasts. Participants must pay a daily fee, and are obligated to travel a certain distance each day, and stay at pre-specified campsites. You'll need to book at least a few weeks in advance through the **Namibian Wildlife Resorts** (NWR; www.nwr.com.na). For details, see p234.

Among the most popular routes are Isabis 4WD Trail in the Namib Desert Park (p334), Naukluft 4WD Trail in the Naukluft

Mountains (p334) and the Topnaar 4WD Trail (p328). Major routes are found in the relevant chapters.

Canoeing & Rafting

Along the Orange River, in the south of the country, canoeing and rafting trips are growing in popularity. Several operators in Noordoewer (p362) offer good-value descents through the spectacular canyons of the Orange River, along the South African border. White-water rafting on the Kunene River is available through the inexpensive Kunene River Lodge at Swartbooi's Drift (p301), and also through several more upmarket operators.

Fishing

Namibia draws anglers from all over Southern Africa, and rightfully so. The Benguela Current along the Skeleton Coast brings kabel-jou, steenbras, galjoen, blacktails and copper sharks close to shore. Favoured spots include the various beaches north of Swakopmund, as well as more isolated spots further north.

In the dams, especially Hardap (p343) and Von Bach (p252), you can expect to catch tila-pia, carp, yellowfish, mullet and barbel. Fly-fishing is possible in the Chobe and Zambezi Rivers in the Caprivi region; here you'll find barbel, bream, pike and Africa's famed fight-ing tiger fish, which can grow up to 9kg.

Hiking

Hiking is a highlight in Namibia, and a grow-ing number of private ranches have established wonderful hiking routes for their guests.

You'll also find superb routes in several na-tional parks. Multiday walks are available at Waterberg Plateau (p257), the four- or eight-day Naukluft loops (p334), the Ugab River (p307), Daan Viljoen Game Park (p238) or Fish River Canyon (p360), but departures are limited, so book as far in advance as possible.

Hiking groups on national park routes must consist of at least three but no more than 10 people, and each hiker needs a doc-tor's certificate of fitness (forms are available from the Windhoek NWR office, p234) issued no more than 40 days before the start of the hike. If you're young and you look fit, this requirement might be waived on most trails, with the exception of the demanding 85km hike in Fish River Canyon. The NWR can recommend doctors, but again, in most cases, this requirement is waived.

While this might seem restrictive to some folk who are accustomed to strapping on a pack and taking off, it does protect the envi-ronment from unrestrained tourism, and it ensures that you'll have the trail to yourself – you'll certainly never see another group.

Rock Climbing

Rock climbing is popular on the red rocks of Damaraland, particularly the Spitzkoppe and the Brandberg, but participants need their own gear and transport. For less experienced climbers it's a dangerous endeavour in the desert heat, so seek local advice beforehand, and never attempt a climb on your own. For more information on these sites, see p292.

Sandboarding

A growing craze is sandboarding, which is commercially available in Swakopmund and Walvis Bay. You can choose between sled-style sandboarding, in which you lay on a masonite board and slide down the dunes at very high speeds, or the stand-up version, in which you schuss down on a snowboard. See p319.

BUSINESS HOURS

Normal business hours are 8am or 9am to 1pm, and 3pm to 5pm Monday to Friday. In the winter, when it gets dark early, some shops open at 8am, and close around 4pm. Lunch-time closing is almost universal. Most city and town shops open from 9am to 12.30pm on Saturday.

Banks, government departments and tourist offices also keep these hours. Post offices on the other hand are open 8am to 4.30pm Monday to Friday, and 8.30am to 11am on Saturday. Only a few petrol stations, mostly along highways, are open 24 hours. In outlying areas, it may be hard to find fuel after hours or on Sunday.

Restaurant opening hours vary accord-ing to the type of establishment – as a rule, cafes and cheap eats will be open all day long, closing in the early evening. More expensive restaurants will be open from around 10.30am to 11pm Monday to Saturday, usually with a break between lunch and dinner. Run-of-the-mill bars open around 5pm until late, while nightclubs and late-night drinking spots open their doors around 9pm (or 10pm) and keep going until 5am.

In this book we have only listed opening hours where they differ significantly from these broad guidelines.

CHILDREN

Many parents regard Africa as just too dangerous for travel with children, but in reality, Namibia presents few problems to families travelling with children. As a destination it's relatively safe healthwise, largely due to its dry climate and good medical services; there's a good network of affordable accommodation, and an excellent infrastructure of well-maintained roads. In addition, foreigners who visit Namibia with children are usually treated with great kindness, and a widespread local affection for the younger set opens up all sorts of social interaction.

Still, it has to be said that travelling around Namibia with very small children (underfives) will present some problems, not least because it's hot and distances can be vast. It's also difficult to see what very small children will take away from the experience, and parents will probably spend most of their time fretting over safety.

For invaluable general advice on taking the family abroad, see Lonely Planet's *Travel with Children* by Brigitte Barta et al. Also have a read of the boxed text 'Travelling with Children' (p274) written by Ian Ketcheson, who spent two years living in Namibia with his partner and young daughter.

Practicalities

While there are few attractions or facilities designed specifically for children, Namibian food and lodgings are mostly quite familiar and manageable. Family rooms and chalets are normally available for only slightly more than double rooms; these normally consist of one double bed and two single beds. Otherwise, it's usually easy to arrange more beds in a standard adult double room for a minimal extra charge.

Camping can be exciting, but you'll need to be extra vigilant so your kids don't just wander off unsupervised, and you'll also need to be alert to potential hazards such as mosquitoes and campfires. Remember that most mosquito repellents with high levels of DEET may be unsuitable for young children. You should also keep sturdy enclosed shoes on their feet to protect them from thorns, bees and scorpion stings.

If you're travelling with kids, you should always invest in a hire car, unless you want to be stuck for hours on public transport. Functional seatbelts are rare even in taxis, and

accidents are common – a child seat brought from home is a good idea if you're hiring a car or going on safari. Even with your own car, distances between towns and parks can be long, so parents will need to provide essential supplemental entertainment (toys, books, games, a Nintendo DS, etc).

Canned baby foods, powdered milk, disposable nappies and the like are available in most large supermarkets.

Sights & Activities

Travelling by campervan and camping, or faking it in luxury tented lodges, are thrilling experiences for young and old alike, while attractions such as the wildlife of Etosha National Park (p264) or the world's biggest sandbox at Sossusvlei (p335) provide ample family entertainment.

Full-scale safaris are generally suited to older children. Remember that endless hours of driving and animal viewing can be an eternity for small children, so you'll need to break up your trip with lots of pit stops and picnics, and plenty of time spent poolside where possible. In Windhoek, a visit to the zoo (p235) also provides a good break.

Older children are well catered for with a whole host of exciting activities. Swakopmund (p311) is an excellent base for these. They include everything from horse riding and sandboarding to ballooning and paragliding. Less demanding activities might include looking for interesting rocks (and Namibia has some truly incredible rocks!); beachcombing along the Skeleton Coast; or running and rolling in the dunes at Lüderitz, Sossusvlei, Swakopmund and elsewhere along the coast.

CLIMATE CHARTS

Namibia's climatic variations correspond roughly to its geographical subdivisions. Generally, the mountainous and semi-arid central plateau (including Windhoek) is a bit cooler than the rest of the country. In the winter 'dry season' (May to October), you can expect clear and sunny days, averaging around 25°C, and cold nights. At this time the Kalahari region of eastern Namibia is usually hotter than the central plateau. In summer (November to April), daytime temperatures in Windhoek may climb to over 40°C, but can fall to below freezing during the night.

Rainfall is heaviest in the northeast, which enjoys a subtropical climate, and along the

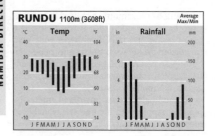

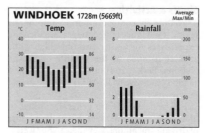

Okavango River rainfall reaches over 600mm annually. As a result, Owamboland, Kavango and Caprivi are more humid. From January to March, the northeastern rivers may flood, making some roads either impassable or hard to negotiate. Also note that the northern and interior regions experience the 'little rains' between October and December, while the main stormy period occurs from January to April.

Further south, the climate is hot and dry as you move from the semi-arid central plateau to the arid Namib Desert. Here, rainfall dwindles to barely 15mm a year, and surface temperatures can reach a staggering 70°C.

CUSTOMS REGULATIONS

Most items from elsewhere in the Southern African Customs Union – Botswana, South Africa, Lesotho and Swaziland – may be imported duty free. From elsewhere, visitors can import duty free 400 cigarettes or 250g of tobacco, 2L of wine, 1L of spirits and 250ml of eau de Cologne. Those aged under 18 do not qualify for the tobacco or the drinks allowances. There are no limits on currency import, but entry and departure forms ask how much you intend to spend or have spent in the country.

Firearms require a temporary import permit, and must be declared at the time of entry; automobiles may not be sold in Namibia without payment of duty. For pets, you need a health certificate and full veterinary documentation; note that pets aren't permitted in national parks or reserves.

DANGERS & ANNOYANCES

Namibia is one of the safest countries in Africa. It's also a huge country with a very sparse population, and even the capital Windhoek smacks more of a provincial town than an urban jungle. Unfortunately however, crime is on the rise in the larger cities, in particular Windhoek, but a little street sense will go a long way here.

Insect Bites & Stings

Most hazardous insects are confined to the far northwest of the country in the watery environs of the Kunene, Okavango and Kwando river systems. As you'd expect, malaria is rife here, so it's important to take antimalarial precautions. Another waterborne disease is bilharzia, which is usually present in stagnant or slow-moving water.

Most nasty of all is the prevalence of tsetse flies in eastern Caprivi, which are especially active at dusk (see p392).

Snake bites and scorpion stings are another potential hazard. Both snakes and scorpions love rocky hidey-holes. If you're camping or trekking through any canyons or rocky areas, always pack away your sleeping bag when it's not in use, and tap out your boots to ensure that nothing has crept inside them during the night. Don't walk around barefoot or stick your hand in holes in the ground or in rocks. Another sensible precaution is to shake out your clothes before you put them on. Remember, snakes don't bite unless threatened or stepped on.

For more information on these and other health risks see the Health chapter, p387.

Scams

Just about the worst scam you'll encounter in Namibia is the pretty innocuous palm-ivory nut sellers scam practiced at various petrol stations. It starts with a friendly approach from a couple of young men, who ask your name. Without you seeing it they then carve your name onto a palm-ivory nut and then offer it to you for sale for anything up to N$70, hoping that you'll then feel obligated to buy the personalised item. You can obtain the same sort of thing at any curio shop for around N$20. It's hardly the crime of the century but it pays to be aware.

A more serious, but far from common, trick is for one guy to distract a parked motorist while a friend grabs your bags from the back seat. So always keep the doors of your vehicle locked, and be aware of distractions.

The Sperrgebiet

En route to Lüderitz from the east, keep well clear of the Sperrgebiet (Forbidden Zone), the prohibited diamond area. Well-armed patrols can be overly zealous. The area begins immediately south of the A4 Lüderitz–Keetmanshoop road and continues to just west of Aus, where the off-limits boundary turns south towards the Orange River. While restrictions are likely ease in the near future as the area transitions to a national park, for the time being it's best to have a healthy respect for the boundaries.

Theft

Theft isn't rife in Namibia, but Windhoek, Swakopmund, Tsumeb and Grootfontein have increasing problems with petty theft and muggings, so it's sensible to conceal your valuables, not leave anything in your car, and avoid walking alone at night. It's also prudent – and sensitive – to avoid walking around cities and towns bedecked in expensive jewellery, watches and cameras. Most hotels provide a safe or secure place for valuables, although you should be cautious of the security at some budget places.

Certainly you should never leave a safari-packed vehicle anywhere in Windhoek or Swakopmund, other than in a guarded car park or private parking lot.

Theft from campsites can also be a problem, particularly near urban areas. Locking up your tent may help, but anything left unattended is still at risk.

Vegetation

Another unusual natural hazard is the euphorbia plant. Its dried branches should never be used in fires as they release a deadly toxin when burnt. It can be fatal to inhale the smoke or eat food cooked on a fire containing it. If you're in doubt about any wood you've collected, leave it out of the fire. Caretakers at campsites do a good job of removing these plants from around pitches and fire pits, so you needn't worry excessively. As a precaution, try to only use bundles of wood that you've purchased in a store to start fires. If you're bush camping, best to familiarise yourself with the plant's appearance. There are several members of the family, and you can check out their pictures either online or at the tourist information centres in Windhoek.

DISCOUNT CARDS

There is no uniformly accepted discount card scheme in Namibia, but a residence permit entitles you to claim favourable residents rates at hotels. Hostel cards are also of little use, but student cards score a 15% discount on Intercape Mainliner buses, and occasionally receive discounts on museum admissions. Seniors over 60, with proof of age, also receive a 15% discount on Intercape Mainliner buses, and good discounts on domestic Air Namibia fares.

EMBASSIES & CONSULATES
Namibian Embassies & High Commissions

Namibia has diplomatic representation in many countries, including China. As a rule you should approach the consulate rather than the embassy (where both are present) on visa matters. That said, the majority of travellers to Namibia will not need a visa (see p375).

Angola (☎ 02-227535; 95 Rua dos Coqueiros No 37, Luanda)

Austria (☎ 431-402 9370; Strozzigasse 1014, Vienna)

Botswana (☎ 267-390 2181; Debswana House, Gaborone)

China (☎ 8610-653 2 2211; Diplomatic Office Bldg, 2-9-2 Ta Yuan, Beijing)

France (☎ 01 44 17 32 65; 80 Ave Foch; Square de l'Ave Foch, Paris)

Germany (☎ 49-30 254 0950; Wichmannstrasse 5, Berlin)

India (☎ 91-11 614 0389; D-6/24 Vasant Vihar, New Delhi)

South Africa (☎ 012-481 9100; 702 Church St, Arcadia, Pretoria)

UK (☎ 020-7636 6244; 6 Chandos St, London)

USA (☎ 202-986-0540; www.namibianembassyusa.org; 1605 New Hampshire Ave NW, Washington, DC)

Zambia (☎ 01-26 04 07; 30A Mutenda Rd, Lusaka)

Zimbabwe (☎ 04-88 58 41; Lot 1 of 7A, Borrowdale Estates, 69 Borrowdale Rd, Harare)

Embassies & Consulates in Namibia

Since Namibian independence, numerous countries have established diplomatic missions here. All the following addresses are in

Windhoek (☎ area code 061) and opening hours are weekdays only.

It's important to realise what your own embassy – the embassy of the country of which you are a citizen – can and can't do to help you if you get into trouble. Generally speaking, it won't be much help in emergencies if the trouble you're in is remotely your own fault. Remember that you are bound by the laws of the country you are in. Your embassy will not be sympathetic if you end up in jail after committing a crime locally, even if such actions are legal in your own country.

Angola (Map p236; ☎ 227535; 3 Dr. Agostino Neto St; ☷ 9am-1pm)

Botswana (off Map p233; ☎ 221941; 101 Klein Windhoek; ☷ 8am-12.30pm)

Canada (Map p236; ☎ 251254; Suite 1118, Sanlam Centre, 154 Independence Ave; ☷ 8am-12.30pm)

Finland (Map p236; ☎ 221355; 5th fl, Sanlam Centre, 154 Independence Ave; ☷ 9am-noon Mon, Wed & Thu)

France (Map p236; ☎ 229021; 1 Goethe St; ☷ 8.30am-12.30pm & 2-5pm Mon-Thu, 8.30am-12.30pm Fri)

Germany (Map p236; ☎ 273100; 6th fl, Sanlam Centre, 154 Independence Ave; ☷ 9am-noon)

Italy (off Map p233; ☎ 228602; Anna St & Gevers St, Ludwigsdorf; ☷ 8.30am-12.30pm & 2-5pm Mon-Thu, 8.30am-12.30pm Fri)

Kenya (Map p236; ☎ 226836; 5th fl, Kenya House, 134 Robert Mugabe Ave; ☷ 9am-12.30pm & 2-5pm)

Malawi (Map p236; ☎ 221391; 56 Bismarck St, Windhoek West; ☷ 8am-noon & 2-5pm)

South Africa (Map p233; ☎ 205 7111; RSA House, cnr Jan Jonker St & Nelson Mandela Dr, Klein Windhoek; ☷ 8.15am-12.15pm)

UK (Map p236; ☎ 223022; 116A Robert Mugabe Ave; ☷ 8am-1pm & 2-4pm Mon-Thu, 8am-noon Fri)

USA (Map p236; ☎ 221601; 14 Jan Jonker St; ☷ 8.30am-noon Mon, Wed & Fri)

Zambia (Map p236; ☎ 237610; cnr Sam Nujoma Dr & Mandume Ndemufeyo Ave; ☷ 8am-1pm & 2-4pm)

Zimbabwe (Map p236; ☎ 228134; Gamsberg Bldg, cnr Independence Ave & Grimm St; ☷ 9am-12.30pm & 2-3pm)

FESTIVALS & EVENTS

Surprisingly, Namibia has relatively few local festivals and events.

Mbapira/Enjando Street Festival The capital's biggest street party occurs in March. It's also a good excuse for people to dress in extravagant ethnic clothes that bring the streets to life.

Windhoek Karnival (WIKA) Established in 1953 by a small group of German immigrants, Windhoek's April Karnival is now one of the highlights of the cultural calendar, culminating in the Royal Ball.

Wild Cinema Festival (www.wildcinema.org) Relatively new to the festival scene is this film festival held in May. It showcases the work of local and South African talent at cinemas throughout the city.

Maherero Day This is one of Namibia's largest festivals, and it falls on the weekend nearest 26 August. Dressed in traditional garb, the Red Flag Herero people gather in Okahandja for a memorial service to commemorate their chiefs killed in the Khoikhoi and German wars. Similar events are staged by the Green Flag Herero (weekend nearest 11 June) at Okahandja, and the White Flag Herero (weekend nearest 10 October) at Omaruru.

Küska (Küste) Karnival Another Teutonic carnival held in late August/early September in Swakopmund. This festival hasn't been recommended in this guide as non-white travellers have often complained about the racist atmosphere of the event.

/AE//Gams Arts Festival Windhoek's main arts festival is held in October, and includes troupes of dancers, musicians, poets and performers all competing for various prizes.

Oktoberfest Windhoek stages its own Oktoberfest – an orgy of food, drink and merrymaking.

FOOD

In general you should be able to snack to your heart's content for under US$10. A standard meal in a Western-style restaurant will usually cost between US$10 and US$20; while a real splurge will hardly break the bank at around US$20 to US$35.

Drinks

Alcohol isn't sold in supermarkets, and must be purchased from a *drankwinkel* (bottle store); standard opening hours are 8am to 6pm Monday to Friday and 8.30am to 1pm Saturday.

GAY & LESBIAN TRAVELLERS

Like many African countries, homosexuality is illegal in Namibia, based on the common law offence of committing 'an unnatural sex crime'. Namibia is also very conservative in its attitudes, given the strongly-held Christian beliefs of the majority. In view of this, discretion is certainly the better part of valour as treatment of gays can range from simple social ostracism to physical attack.

In 1996 Namibia's president Sam Nujoma initiated a very public campaign against homosexuals, recommending that all foreign gays and lesbians be deported or excluded from the country. One minister called homosexuality a 'behavioural disorder which is alien to African culture'.

In response, the **Rainbow Project** (☎ 061-230710; trp@mweb.com.na; PO Box 26122, Windhoek) was formed to tackle the escalating violence against the gay community. Its work has engendered passionate debate but overall its efforts have been rewarded with considerable success and the organisation can now operate openly in Windhoek. Namibian lesbians (and other women's interests) are represented by **Sister Namibia** (☎ 061-230618; sister@iafrica.com.na; 163 Nelson Mandela Ave, Eros, PO Box 40092, Windhoek).

HOLIDAYS

Banks, government offices and most shops are closed on the following public holidays; when a public holiday falls on a Sunday, the following day also becomes a holiday.

New Year's Day 1 January
Good Friday March or April
Easter Sunday March or April
Easter Monday March or April
Independence Day 21 March
Ascension Day April or May
Workers' Day 1 May
Cassinga Day 4 May
Africa Day 25 May
Heroes' Day 26 August
Human Rights Day 10 December
Christmas 25 December
Family/Boxing Day 26 December

INSURANCE

A travel insurance policy to cover theft, loss and medical problems is a good idea. Some policies offer lower and higher medical-expense options; the higher ones are chiefly for countries that have extremely high medical costs, such as the USA. Some policies specifically exclude 'dangerous activities', which can include scuba diving, motorcycling and even trekking. If 'risky' activities are on your agenda, as they may well be, you'll need the most comprehensive policy.

You may prefer to have an insurance policy that pays doctors or hospitals directly rather than you having to pay on the spot and claim later. If you have to claim later, make sure you keep all documentation. Some policies ask you to call back (reverse charges) to a centre in your home country, where an immediate assessment of your problem is made. Check that the policy covers ambulances or an emergency flight home.

For details of health insurance see the Health chapter (p387), and for more details on car insurance see the Transport chapter (p385).

Worldwide travel insurance is available at www.lonelyplanet.com/travel_services. You can buy, extend and claim online anytime – even if you're already on the road.

INTERNET ACCESS

Internet access is firmly established and widespread in Namibia, and connection speeds are fairly stable. Most towns have at least one internet cafe where you can access Hotmail, Yahoo! and any other webmail accounts. Plan on spending N$15 to N$20 per hour online. An increasing number of backpacker hostels, hotels in larger towns and some top-end lodges also offer internet access. Still, the relatively high cost of accessing the internet – on average one year of internet access costs more than the average annual income – is still a major constraint in rural areas.

If you're travelling with a notebook or hand-held computer, some top-end hotels have ethernet connections or dataports in the rooms, and wi-fi hot spots are becoming more and more common with each passing year. Be advised however that carrying a laptop around can be more trouble than it's worth, especially given Namibia's sandy environment.

LEGAL MATTERS

All drugs are illegal in Namibia, penalties are stiff and prisons deeply unpleasant. So don't think about bringing anything over the borders or buying it while you're here. The police are also allowed to use entrapment techniques, such as posing as pushers, to catch criminals, so don't be tempted.

The legal age of sexual consent is 12 for girls and just seven for boys, although sex with a girl under 16 can still be prosecuted under the Sexual Offence Act. The age of consent for marriage, however, is 15 for girls and 18 for boys, and in both cases parental consent is also required.

Police, military and veterinary officials are generally polite, and on their best behaviour. In your dealings with officialdom, you should always make every effort to be patient and polite in return.

The national emergency number for the police is ☎ 10111.

NAMIBIA DIRECTORY

MAPS

A good all-round map of the region is the Michelin map *Central and South Africa* (series number 746) at a scale of 1:4,000,000, although it's not sufficiently detailed for Namibia. For more detail you might pick up the Namibia map produced by Reise-Know-How-Verlag (1:250,000) or the Freytag & Berndt map (1:200,000).

Shell Roadmap – Namibia is the best reference for remote routes, and includes a good Windhoek city map, but the Caprivi Strip is only a small-scale inset. Shell publishes *Kaokoland-Kunene Region Tourist Map,* which depicts most major routes and tracks in northwestern Namibia. It's sold at bookshops and tourist offices at a minimal cost. Another petrol company, BP Namibia, produces a 1:2,500,000 map, with insets for most towns, including Oshakati, Ondangwa and Otjiwarongo.

For the average tourist (ie if you're not planning your own self-drive safari), these satellite maps with GPS coordinates are far too detailed. Much better is the *Republic of Namibia Tourist Road Map* produced by the Ministry of Environment & Tourism (MET), which shows major routes and sites of interest. It's distributed free at tourist offices, hotels and travel agencies. The reverse side has detailed maps of Windhoek, Swakopmund and Walvis Bay.

The best place to purchase maps in Namibia is at petrol stations, although you can get your hands on more general maps at local bookshops.

In the USA, **Maplink** (www.maplink.com) is an excellent and exhaustive source for maps of Namibia. A similarly extensive selection of maps is available in the UK from **Stanfords** (www.stanfords.co.uk) and in Australia from **Map Land** (www.mapland.com.au).

MONEY

The currency of Namibia is the Namibian dollar (N$). It's divided into 100 cents, and is linked to the South African rand. The rand is also legal tender in Namibia at a rate of 1:1. This can be confusing, given that there are three sets of coins and notes in use: old South African, new South African and Namibian. We quote prices in Namibian and occasionally US dollars in this book.

Namibian dollar notes, which all bear portraits of Nama leader Hendrik Witbooi, come in denominations of N$10, N$20, N$50, N$100 and N$200, and coins in values of 5, 10, 20 and 50 cents, and N$1 and N$5.

Money can be exchanged in banks and exchange offices. Banks generally offer the best rates, and travellers cheques normally fetch a better rate than cash. When changing money, you may be given either South African rand or Namibian dollars; if you'll need to change any leftover currency outside Namibia, the rand is a better choice.

Travellers cheques may also be exchanged for US dollars cash – if the cash is available – but banks charge a hefty commission. There is no currency black market, so beware of street changers offering unrealistic rates.

See the inside front cover for a table of exchange rates or log on to www.xe.com. The Getting Started chapter has information on costs (p17).

ATMs

Credit cards can be used in ATMs displaying the appropriate sign or to obtain cash advances over the counter in many banks – Visa and MasterCard are among the most widely recognised. You'll find ATMs at all the main bank branches throughout Namibia, and this is undoubtedly the simplest (and safest) way to handle your money while travelling.

Cash

While most major currencies are accepted in Windhoek and Swakopmund, once away from these two centres you'll run into problems with currencies other than US dollars, euro, UK pounds and South African rand (you may even struggle with pounds). Play it safe and carry US dollars – it makes life much simpler.

Credit/Debit Cards

Credit cards are accepted in most shops, restaurants and hotels, and credit-card cash advances are available from ATMs. Check charges with your bank.

Credit-card cash advances are available at foreign-exchange desks in most major banks, but set aside at least an hour or two to complete the rather tedious transaction.

You should check the procedure on what to do if you experience problems or if your card is stolen. Most card suppliers will give you an emergency number you can call free of charge for help and advice.

Tipping

Tipping is welcomed everywhere, but is expected only in upmarket tourist restaurants where it's normal to leave a tip of 10% to 15% of the bill. Some restaurants add a service charge as a matter of course. As a rule, taxi drivers aren't tipped, but it is customary to give N$2 or so to petrol-station attendants who clean your windows and/or check the oil and water. Note that tipping is officially prohibited in national parks and reserves.

At safari lodges, it's customary to tip any personal guides directly (assuming they merit a tip), and also to leave a tip with the proprietor, to be divided among all the staff.

Travellers Cheques

Travellers cheques can be cashed at most banks and exchange offices. American Express (Amex), Thomas Cook and Visa are the most widely accepted brands.

It's preferable to buy travellers cheques in US dollars, UK pounds or euros rather than another currency, as these are most widely accepted. Get most of the cheques in largish denominations to save on per-cheque rates.

You must take your passport with you when cashing cheques.

PHOTOGRAPHY & VIDEO

While many Namibians enjoy being photographed, others do not; the main point is that you should always respect the wishes of the person in question, and don't snap a picture if permission is denied.

Officials in Namibia aren't as sensitive about photography as in some other African countries, but it still isn't a good idea to photograph borders, airports, communications equipment or military installations without first asking permission from any uniformed personnel that might be present.

The world has gone digital, so if you're still shooting print and slide film, it's best to bring extra rolls from home. On the flip side, memory cards for digital cameras are widely available in Windhoek and Swakopmund, and most internet cafes can burn your photos onto CD. Prices are generally very cheap for these services, and shouldn't cost more than a few US dollars.

For pointers on taking pictures in Africa, look out for Lonely Planet's *Travel Photography* book.

POST

Domestic post generally moves slowly; it can take weeks for a letter to travel from Lüderitz to Katima Mulilo, for example. Overseas airmail post is normally more efficient.

Postcards to Europe and the US cost around N$2.50. An airmail letter to the US and Europe costs slightly more depending on the destination. It can take up to two weeks for mail to arrive in Europe and US, while a letter to Australia may take up to three weeks.

Poste restante works best in Windhoek (mail to: Poste Restante, GPO, Windhoek, Namibia). Photo identification is required to collect mail.

All post offices sell current issues of Namibia's commemorative stamps, which are collectable.

SHOPPING

Namibia's range of inexpensive souvenirs includes all sorts of things, from kitsch African curios and batik paintings to superb Owambo basketry and Kavango woodcarvings. Most of the items sold along Post Street Mall in Windhoek are cheap curios imported from Zimbabwe. Along the highway between Rundu and Grootfontein, roadside stalls sell locally produced items, from baskets and simple pottery jars to the appealing woven mats and wooden aeroplanes that are a Kavango speciality. In Rundu, and other areas of the northeast, you'll find distinctive San material arts – bows and arrows, ostrich-egg beads and leather pouches. An excellent place to browse a whole range of craft work is the Namibia Crafts Centre (p245) in Windhoek.

The pastel colours of the Namib provide inspiration for a number of local artists, and lots of galleries in Windhoek and Swakopmund feature local paintings and sculpture. Also, some lovely items are produced in conjunction with the karakul wool industry, such as rugs, wall hangings and textiles. The better weaving outlets are found in Dordabis, Swakopmund and Lüderitz.

Windhoek is the centre of the upmarket leather industry, and there you'll find high-quality products, from belts and handbags to made-to-measure leather jackets. Beware, however, of items made from crocodile or other protected species, and note that those comfortable shoes known as *Swakopmunders* are made from kudu leather. Several shops have now stopped selling them.

Minerals and gemstones are popular purchases, either in raw form or cut and polished as jewellery, sculptures or carvings. Malachite, amethyst, chalcedony, aquamarine, tourmaline, jasper and rose quartz are among the most beautiful. You'll find the best jewellery shops in Windhoek and Swakopmund and the most reputable of these is House of Gems in Windhoek (p245).

If you're interested in something that appears to be exotic or resembles an artefact, ask about its provenance. Any antiquity must have an export/import permit and the dealer must have a licence to sell antiquities.

Buying souvenirs derived from protected wild species – cheetahs, leopards, elephants or (heaven forbid) rhinos – is forbidden. In Windhoek and other places, you'll see lots of ivory pieces and jewellery for sale. The only legitimate stuff is clearly marked as culled ivory from Namibian national parks.

Bargaining

Bargaining is only acceptable when purchasing handicrafts and arts directly from the producer or artist, but in remote areas, prices asked normally represent close to the market value. The exception is crafts imported from Zimbabwe, which are generally sold at large craft markets for inflated prices that are always negotiable.

SOLO TRAVELLERS

Compared with Botswana, Namibia is a great destination for solo travellers, given its network of excellent hostels and range of budget accommodation. Places like the Cardboard Box Backpackers (p240), Chameleon Backpackers Lodge & Guesthouse (p240) and Desert Sky Backpackers (p321) don't just provide a good bed for the night, but operate as mini social centres, where you can meet up with other travellers. Unlike some destinations, most hotels and lodges in Namibia offer a fair single rate, although accommodation may become more pricey during busy times of the year – such as the school holiday period.

The drawbacks of travelling alone are the general loneliness when covering huge distances without someone to chat to or argue with. Nor will you have anyone to watch your bags or your back, and the price of safaris and organised activities can be high. If you want to hire a car, you'll be paying top dollar

unless you can join a group to make things more affordable.

TELEPHONE

The Namibian fixed-line phone system, run by **Telecom Namibia** (www.telecom.na) is very efficient, and getting through to fixed-line numbers, all beginning with a three-digit area code, is extremely easy. However, like the rest of Africa, the fixed-line system is rapidly being overtaken by the massive popularity of prepaid mobile phones.

International call rates are relatively expensive. For example calls to the UK/US and Europe cost upwards of N$20 per minute, and N$25 per minute to the rest of the world at peak times. But charges drop dramatically to neighbouring countries.

Given the increasing number of wi-fi hot spots in the country, using Skype is also becoming a more common (and much cheaper) alternative.

Domestic call rates are very reasonable, and as elsewhere it's more expensive to call a mobile phone (in fact double the rate).

There's only one slim telephone directory for the entire country, listing private and business addresses. The Yellow Pages also covers the whole country.

Mobile Phones

MTC (www.mtc.com.na) is the only mobile service provider in Namibia, operating on the GSM 900/1800 frequency, which is compatible with Europe and Australia but not with North America (GSM 1900) or Japan. There is supposedly coverage from Ariamsvlei at the southern border to Oshikango and Ruacana in the far north, although in reality it's hard to get a signal outside the major towns.

MTC offers a prepaid service called Tango, which since its introduction has become the package of choice in Namibia. After paying a one-off SIM-card fee, subscribers can buy prepaid vouchers at most stores across Namibia.

You can easily buy a handset in any major town in Namibia, which will set you back from N$750 to N$900.

Most Namibian mobile phone numbers begin with 081, which is followed by a seven-digit number.

Phone Codes

When phoning Namibia from abroad, dial the international access code (usually 00, but 011 from the USA), followed by the country code ☎ 264, the area code without the leading zero, and finally, the required number. To phone out of Namibia, dial ☎ 00 followed by the desired country code, area code (if applicable) and the number.

When phoning long-distance within Namibia, dial the three-digit regional area code, including the leading zero, followed by the six- or seven-digit number.

To phone some rural areas, you must dial the code and ask the exchange operator for the desired number.

Phonecards

Telecom Namibia phonecards are sold at post offices to the value of N$20, N$50 and N$100. They are also available at most shops and a number of hotels. Public telephone boxes are available at most post offices and can also be found scattered around town.

TIME

In the summer months (October to April), Namibia is two hours ahead of GMT/UTC. Therefore, if it's noon in Southern Africa, it's 10am in London, 5am in New York, 2am in Los Angeles and 8pm in Sydney. In the winter (April to October), Namibia turns its clocks back one hour, making it only one hour ahead of GMT/UTC and one hour behind South African time.

TOURIST INFORMATION
Local Tourist Offices

The level of service in Namibia's tourist offices is generally high, and everyone speaks impeccable English, German and Afrikaans.

Namibia's national tourist office, **Namibia Tourism** (☎ 061-220640, 284 2360; www.namibiatourism.com.na; Independence Ave, Private Bag 13346) is in in Windhoek, where you'll also find the local **Windhoek Information & Publicity Office** (☎ 061-290 2058; Post St Mall), for more city-specific information.

Also in Windhoek is the office of **Namibia Wildlife Resorts** (Map p236; ☎ 061-285 7200; www.nwr.com.na; Erkrath Bldg, Independence Ave) where you can pick up information on the national parks and make reservations at any NWR campsite. For more information on NWR see the National Parks and Reserves chapter, p29.

Other useful tourist offices include **Lüderitzbucht Safaris & Tours** (p350) in Lüderitz, **Namib-i** (p313) in Swakopmund and **Travel North** (p262) in Tsumeb.

Tourist Offices Abroad

The Ministry of the Environment and Tourism maintains a number of tourist offices abroad. The staff are friendly and professional and are eager to promote Namibia as a tourist destination.

France (☎ 01 40 50 88 363; 20 Ave Recteur Poincar, Paris)
Germany (☎ 069-133 7360; 42-44 Schillerstrasse, Frankfurt)
South Africa Johannesburg (☎ 011-785 4626; 1 Orchard Lane, Rivonia, Johannesburg); Cape Town (☎ 021-422 3298; Ground fl, The Pinnacle, Burg St, Cape Town)
UK (☎ 0870 330 9333; Suite 200, Parkway House, Sheen Lane, London)

TRAVELLERS WITH DISABILITIES

There are very few special facilities, and people with limited mobility will not have an easy time in Namibia. All is not lost, however, and with an able-bodied travelling companion, wheelchair travellers will manage here. This is mainly because Namibia has some advantages over other parts of the developing world: footpaths and public areas are often surfaced with tar or concrete; many buildings (including safari lodges and national park cabins) are single-storey; car hire is easy and hire cars can be taken into neighbouring countries; and assistance is usually available on internal and regional flights. In addition, most safari companies in Namibia – including budget operators – are happy to 'make a plan' to accommodate travellers with special needs.

VISAS

All visitors require a passport from their home country that is valid for at least six months after their intended departure date from Namibia. You may also be asked for an onward plane, bus or rail ticket, although checks are rarely made. Nationals of the following countries do not need visas to visit Namibia: Angola, Australia, Botswana, Brazil, Canada, EU countries, Iceland, Japan, Kenya, Mozambique, New Zealand, Norway, Russia, Singapore, South Africa, Switzerland, Tanzania, the USA, Zambia, Zimbabwe and most Commonwealth countries. Citizens of most Eastern European countries do require visas.

Tourists are granted an initial 90 days, which may be extended at the **Ministry of Home Affairs** (☎ 061-292 2111; info@mha.gov.na; cnr Kasino St & Independence Ave, Private Bag 13200, Windhoek). For the best results, be there when the office opens at 8am, and submit your application at the

3rd-floor offices (as opposed to the desk on the ground floor).

VOLUNTEERING

Namibia has a good track record for grassroots projects and community-based tourism. The largest organisation in the country is **NACOBTA** (Namibia Community Based Tourism Association; ☎ 061-250558; www.nacobta.com.na), which runs various campsites.

But, it's seldom possible to find any volunteering work in-country due to visa restrictions and restricted budgets. Any organisations that do offer volunteer positions will need to be approached well in advance of your departure date. It also has to be said that many conservation outfits look for volunteers with specific skills that might be useful in the field.

The most well-known organisations offering volunteer positions are Save the Rhino Trust, the AfriCat foundation and the Cheetah Conservation Fund. Projects like the Integrated Rural Development and Nature Conservation may also offer the occasional post. Details of these organisations can be found on p73.

Other international organisations which offer volunteering in Namibia include the youth development charity **Raleigh International** (www.raleighinternational.org) and **Project Trust** (www.projecttrust.org.uk) in the UK and **World Teach** (www.worldteach.org) in the US. Another very worthwhile organisation which you can support from the comfort of your own home is the **Namibian Connection Youth Network** (www.namibia connection.org). You can register with them as a professional affiliate and offer your mentorship and advice to young Namibians via email.

WOMEN TRAVELLERS

On the whole Namibia is a safe destination for women travellers, and we receive few complaints from women travellers about any sort of harassment. Having said that, Namibia is still a conservative society. Many bars are men only (by either policy or convention), but even in places that welcome women, you may be more comfortable in a group or with a male companion. Note that accepting a drink from a local man is usually construed as a come-on.

The threat of sexual assault isn't any greater in Namibia than in Europe, but women should still avoid walking alone in parks and back streets, especially at night. Hitching alone is not recommended. Also, never hitch at night and, if possible, find a companion for trips through sparsely populated areas. Use common sense and things should go well.

In Windhoek and other urban areas, wearing shorts and sleeveless dresses or shirts is fine. However, if you're visiting rural areas, wear knee-length skirts or loose trousers and shirts with sleeves. If you're poolside in a resort or lodge where the clientele is largely foreign, then somewhat revealing swimwear is acceptable, though it's best to err on the side of caution at locally owned hotels.

Namibia Transport

CONTENTS

GETTING THERE & AWAY

Unless you are travelling overland, most likely from Botswana or South Africa, flying is by far the most convenient way to get to Namibia. But, Namibia isn't exactly a hub of international travel, nor is it an obvious transit point along the major international routes.

At the time of research, Air Namibia announced that they were suspending their direct flights from London Gatwick to Windhoek. For the foreseeable future, flights between Frankfurt and Windhoek however will most likely continue. Johannesburg and Cape Town, in South Africa, also serve as major transit points for Namibia, with several airlines including British Airways and South African Airways offering competitive fares.

A few adventurous and resourceful souls with their own vehicles still travel overland to Namibia from Europe, but most routes pass through several war zones and should only be considered after some serious planning and preparation.

ENTERING THE COUNTRY

Entering Namibia is straightforward and hassle-free. Most nationalities (including nationals from the UK, USA, Australia, Japan and all the western European countries) don't even require a visa (see p375). If you are entering Namibia across one of its land borders, the process is painless. You will, however, need to have all the necessary documentation and insurance for your vehicle (see p382).

Passport

All visitors entering Namibia must hold a passport that is valid for at least six months. Also, allow a few empty pages for stamp-happy immigration officials, especially if you're crossing over to Zimbabwe and/or Zambia to see Victoria Falls. In theory, although seldom in practice, you should also hold proof of departure either in the form of a return or onward ticket.

AIR

Most international flights into Namibia arrive at Windhoek's **Chief Hosea Kutako International Airport** (WDH; ☎ 061-299 6602; www.airports.com.na),

---

WARNING – THINGS CHANGE

The information contained in this chapter is particularly vulnerable to change: prices for international travel are volatile, routes are introduced and cancelled, schedules change, special deals come and go, and rules and visa requirements are amended. Airlines and governments seem to take pleasure in making price structures and regulations as complicated as possible. You should check directly with the airline or your travel agency to make sure you understand how a fare (and ticket you may buy) works. In addition, the travel industry is highly competitive, and there are many lurks and perks.

The upshot of this is that you should get opinions, quotes and advice from as many airlines and travel agencies as possible before parting with your hard-earned cash. The details given in this chapter should be regarded as pointers and are not a substitute for your own careful, up-to-date research.

42km east of the capital. Shorter-haul international flights may also use Windhoek's in-town **Eros Airport** (ERS; ☎ 061-299 6500), although this airport mainly serves internal flights and light aircraft.

The main carrier is Air Namibia, which flies routes to within Southern Africa as well as long-haul flights to Frankfurt. Reservations are best handled via the internet or telephone.

Airports & Airlines

The main airport in Windhoek is fairly well served by international flights from Germany, South Africa, Zimbabwe and Zambia. Many travellers also connect through Johannesburg or Cape Town in South Africa, both of which are served by an array of international and domestic carriers.

AIRLINES FLYING TO & FROM NAMIBIA

Air Namibia (☎ 299 6000; www.airnamibia.com.na)
British Airways (☎ 248528; www.ba.com)
Lufthansa (☎ 238205; www.lufthansa.com)
South African Airways (☎ 237670; www.flysaa.com)
TAAG Angola (☎ 226625; www.taag.com.br)

Tickets

As Namibia is served by relatively few international airlines, tickets for direct flights can be expensive. Because of this, many travellers choose to fly to Johannesburg on a cheap ticket, and then pick up a connection to Windhoek. Return flights from Jo'burg to Windhoek are generally a few hundred dollars, although if you book your internal flight at the same time as your main flight, you'll always get a better deal. Note that the airport departure tax for international flights is included in the cost of your plane ticket.

INTERCONTINENTAL (RTW) TICKETS

Discount round-the-world (RTW) tickets are a tempting option if you want to include Namibia on a longer journey, but note that the most common African stop is Johannesburg. The following are online agents for RTW tickets:

Air Treks (www.airtreks.com)
Bootsnall (www.bootsnall.com)
Round the World Flights (www.roundtheworldflights.com)
Travel Bag (www.travelbag.co.uk)
The Traveller UK (www.thetraveleruk.com)

Africa

Rennies Travel (www.renniestravel.com) and **STA Travel** (www.statravel.co.za) have offices throughout Southern Africa. Check their websites for branch locations.

BOTSWANA

Air Namibia runs several flights a week between Windhoek and Maun. This is a very popular route and the small planes that operate it are often filled well in advance, so you'll need some forward planning.

SOUTH AFRICA

South African Airways has daily flights connecting Cape Town and Johannesburg to Windhoek. Johannesburg is also the main hub for connecting flights to other African cities.

ZIMBABWE & ZAMBIA

Air Namibia no longer flies to Harare, although it continues to run a few flights a week to Victoria Falls (Zimbabwe). Again, this is a very popular route, and the small planes that operate it are often filled well in advance, so you'll need some forward planning. For Zambia you will need to transit through Jo'burg for flights to Lusaka or Livingstone.

Asia

Coming from Southeast Asia, the best possible departure point is Bangkok, which has bucket shops (discount agents) galore. South African Airways services a plethora of routes to Asia, including Bangkok and Hong Kong. You might also consider flying **Kenya Airways** (www.kenya-airways.com) or **Qantas** (www.qantas.com.au), both of which offer similar routes at competitive prices.

STA Travel proliferates in Asia, with branches in **Bangkok** (☎ 02-236 0262; www.statravel.co.th), **Singapore** (☎ 6737 7188; www.statravel.com.sg), **Hong Kong** (☎ 2736 1618; www.statravel.com.hk) and **Japan** (☎ 03 5391 2922; www.statravel.co.jp). Another resource in Japan is **No 1 Travel** (☎ 03 3205 6073; www.no1-travel.com).

Australia

Flying to Southern Africa from Australia and New Zealand is surprisingly awkward and expensive. The cheapest options normally include routings via Jo'burg. Both Qantas and British Airways fly from Perth and Sydney to Johannesburg (and back) several times a week.

Note that it can sometimes work out cheaper to keep going right around the world on a round-the-world (RTW) ticket than to do a U-turn on a return ticket.

For the location of STA Travel branches call ☎ 1300 733 035 or visit www.statravel.com.au. **Flight Centre** (☎ 133 133; www.flightcentre.com.au) has offices throughout Australia. For online bookings, try www.travel.com.au.

Canada

Canadians will typically find the best deals starting with a hop to New York or Washington, as fares from Toronto and Vancouver are generally higher than from the USA. Alternatively, you can fly with Air Namibia through Frankfurt. **Travel Cuts** (☎ 800-667-2887; www.travelcuts.com) is Canada's national student travel agency. For online bookings try www.expedia.ca and www.travelocity.ca.

Continental Europe

From continental Europe, the easiest options are Air Namibia's nonstop flights between Windhoek and Frankfurt.

STA Travel (Austria www.statravel.at; Denmark www.statravel.dk; Finland www.statravel.fi; Germany www.statravel.de; Sweden www.statravel.se; Switzerland www.statravel.ch), the international student and young person's travel giant, has branches in many European nations. There are also many STA-affiliated travel agencies (www.statravelgroup.com) across Europe. Visit the website to find an STA partner close to you.

Other recommended travel agencies across Europe include:

BELGIUM
Acotra Student Travel Agency (☎ 02 51 286 07)
Holland International (☎ 070-307 6307)

FRANCE
Anyway (☎ 08 92 30 23 01; www.anyway.fr)
Lastminute (☎ 08 99 78 50 00; www.lastminute.fr)
Nouvelles Frontières (☎ 08 25 00 08 25; www.nouvelles-frontieres.fr)
OTU Voyages (www.otu.fr)
Voyageurs du Monde (www.vdm.com)

GERMANY
Expedia (www.expedia.de)
Kilroy Travel Group (www.kilroygroups.com)
Lastminute (☎ 01805 284 366; www.lastminute.de)

ITALY
CTS Viaggi (www.cts.it)

NETHERLANDS
Airfair (☎ 0900-77 17 717; www.airfair.nl)
NBBS Reizen (☎ 0900-10 20 300; www.nbbs.nl)

SCANDINAVIA
Kilroy Travel Group (www.kilroygroups.com)

SPAIN
Barcelo Viajes (☎ 902 200 400; www.barceloviajes.com)
Viajes Zeppelin (☎ 915 425 154; www.viajeszeppelin.com)

India

Flights between South Africa and Mumbai (Bombay) or Delhi are common, given the large Indian population in South Africa; South African Airways and Kenya Airways are the main carriers. **STIC Travels** (www.stictravel.com) has offices in dozens of Indian cities.

Middle East

Al-Rais Travels (www.alrais.com) In Dubai
Egypt Panorama Tours (☎ 2-359 0200; www.eptours.com) In Cairo
The Israel Student Travel Association (ISTA; ☎ 02-625 7257) In Jerusalem

New Zealand

Inevitably, Kiwis will need a connection through Australia. RTW fares for travel to or from New Zealand are worth checking out as they are often good value, especially in high season. Both **Flight Centre** (☎ 0800 243 544; www.flightcentre.co.nz) and **STA Travel** (☎ 0508 782 872; www.statravel.co.nz) have branches throughout the country. The site www.travel.co.nz is recommended for online bookings.

UK & Ireland

Both British Airways and South African Airways fly nonstop between London and Johannesburg (and Cape Town) at least once a day. **Virgin Atlantic** (www.virgin-atlantic.com), which also flies several times a week between London and Jo'burg, usually offers the cheapest fares.

Advertisements for many travel agencies appear in the travel pages of the weekend broadsheet newspapers, in *Time Out,* the *Evening Standard* and in the free magazine *TNT* (www.tntmagazine.com).

NAMIBIA TRANSPORT

CLIMATE CHANGE & TRAVEL

Climate change is a serious threat to the ecosystems that humans rely upon, and air travel is the fastest-growing contributor to the problem. Lonely Planet regards travel, overall, as a global benefit, but believes we all have a responsibility to limit our personal impact on global warming.

Flying & Climate Change

Pretty much every form of motorised travel generates CO_2 (the main cause of human-induced climate change) but planes are far and away the worst offenders, not just because of the sheer distances they allow us to travel, but because they release greenhouse gases high into the atmosphere. The statistics are frightening: two people taking a return flight between Europe and the US will contribute as much to climate change as an average household's gas and electricity consumption over a whole year.

Carbon Offset Schemes

Climatecare.org and other websites use 'carbon calculators' that allow travellers to offset the level of greenhouse gases they are responsible for with financial contributions to sustainable travel schemes that reduce global warming – including projects in India, Honduras, Kazakhstan and Uganda.

Lonely Planet, together with Rough Guides and other concerned partners in the travel industry, support the carbon offset scheme run by climatecare.org. Lonely Planet offsets all of its staff and author travel.

For more information check out our website: www.lonelyplanet.com.

For students or travellers under 26 years, popular travel agencies include **STA Travel** (☎ 0870 163 0026; www.statravel.co.uk), which has branches across the country; and **Trailfinders** (☎ 0845 058 5858; www.trailfinders.co.uk), which has branches throughout the UK.

Other recommended travel agencies include:

Flight Centre (☎ 0870 499 0040; www.flightcentre .co.uk)

Flightbookers (☎ 0800 082 3000; www.ebookers.com)

North-South Travel (☎ 01245-608291; www.north southtravel.co.uk) Donates part of its profit to projects in the developing world.

Quest Travel (☎ 0871 423 0135; www.questtravel.com)

Travel Bag (☎ 0870 607 0620; www.travelbag.co.uk)

USA

Delta Air Lines (www.delta.com) and **United Airlines** (www.united.com) offer weekly flights from Chicago and/or Atlanta to Jo'burg, and then a connection to Windhoek. Sometimes however, it may actually be cheaper to buy a US–Frankfurt return fare, and then buy a new ticket for the Frankfurt–Windhoek section of your journey.

Discount travel agents in the USA are known as consolidators (although you won't see a sign on the door saying 'Consolidator'). San Francisco is the ticket consolidator capital of America, although some good deals can be found in Los Angeles, New York and other big cities.

The following agencies are recommended for online bookings:

Cheap Tickets (www.cheaptickets.com)

Expedia (www.expedia.com)

Kayak (www.kayak.com)

Lowest Fare (www.lowestfare.com)

Orbitz (www.orbitz.com)

STA Travel (www.sta.com) For travellers under the age of 26

Travelocity (www.travelocity.com)

LAND

Thanks to the Southern African Customs Union, you can drive through Namibia, Botswana, South Africa and Swaziland with a minimum of ado. To travel further north requires a *carnet de passage*, which can amount to heavy expenditure.

If you're driving a hire car into Namibia you will need to present a letter of permission from the rental company saying the car is allowed to cross the border. For more information on taking a vehicle into Namibia see p382.

Border Crossings

Namibia has a well-developed road network with easy access from neighbouring countries.

The main border crossings into Namibia are as follows:

- From Angola – Oshikango, Ruacana, Rundu
- From Botswana – Buitepos, Mahango and Mpalila Island
- From South Africa – Noordoewer, Ariamsvlei
- From Zambia – Katima Mulilo

All borders are open daily, and the main crossings from South Africa (Noordoewer and Ariamsvlei) are open 24 hours. Otherwise, border posts are generally open between 9am and 5pm. Immigration posts at some smaller border crossings close for lunch between 12.30pm and 1.45pm. It is always advisable to reach the crossings as early in the day as possible to allow time for any potential delays. There's no public access between Alexander Bay and Oranjemund (6am to 10pm) without permission from the diamond company CDM. For more information on opening hours check out the website www.namibweb.com/border.htm.

ANGOLA
To enter Namibia overland, you'll need an Angolan visa permitting overland entry. At Ruacana Falls, you can enter the border area temporarily without a visa to visit the falls by signing the immigration register (see p275).

BOTSWANA
The most commonly used crossing is at Buitepos/Mamuno, between Windhoek and Ghanzi, although the border post at Mohembo/Mahango is also popular. The only other real option is the crossing at Ngoma Bridge across the Chobe River. The Mpalila Island/Kasane border is only available to guests who have pre-booked accommodation at upmarket lodges on the island.

Drivers crossing the border at Mahango must secure an entry permit for Mahango Game Reserve at Popa Falls. This is free if you're transiting, or US$3 per person per day plus US$3 per vehicle per day if you want to drive around the reserve (which is possible in a 2WD).

ZAMBIA
A new kilometre-long **bridge** (☼ 7am-6pm) spans the Zambezi between Katima Mulilo and Wenela, providing easy access to Livingstone

and other destinations in Zambia. If you're heading to the Victoria Falls, the road is now tarred all the way to Livingstone, and is accessible by 2WD vehicle, even in the rainy season.

ZIMBABWE
There's no direct border crossing between Namibia and Zimbabwe. To get there you must take the Chobe National Park transit route from Ngoma Bridge through northern Botswana to Kasane/Kazungula, and from there to Victoria Falls.

Bus
There's only really one main inter-regional bus service connecting cities in Namibia with Botswana and South Africa. Intercape Mainliner has services between Windhoek and Johannesburg and Cape Town (South Africa). They also travel northeast to Victoria Falls, and between larger towns within Namibia.

BOTSWANA
On Monday and Friday you can catch a very useful shuttle-bus service from Windhoek to Maun, via Ghanzi, with Audi Camp (see p126). Other than this, the public transport options between the two countries are few and far between. The Trans-Kalahari Hwy from Windhoek to Botswana, via Gobabis, crosses the border at Buitepos/Mamuno. Unfortunately, passengers on the Intercape Mainliner between Windhoek and Victoria Falls may not disembark in Botswana.

SOUTH AFRICA
The **Intercape Mainliner** (☎ in South Africa 27-21 380 4400; www.intercape.co.za) service runs between Windhoek and Cape Town. Students and seniors receive a 15% discount. Bus tickets can be easily booked by phone or via the internet.

ZAMBIA
The **Intercape Mainliner** (☎ in South Africa 27-21 380 4400; www.intercape.co.za) service also runs between Windhoek and Livingstone.

ZIMBABWE
At the time of research, the only public transport between Namibia and Zimbabwe is the weekly **Intercape Mainliner** (☎ in South Africa 27-21 380 4400; www.intercape.co.za), which travels between Windhoek and Victoria Falls.

NAMIBIA TRANSPORT

Car & Motorcycle

Crossing land borders with your own vehicle or a hire car is generally straightforward as long as you have the necessary paperwork – the vehicle registration documents if you own the car, or a letter from the hire company stating that you have permission to take the car over the border, and proof of insurance.

Note that Namibia implements a road tax, known as the Cross-Border Charge (CBC) for foreign-registered vehicles entering the country (motorcycles don't have to pay). Passenger vehicles carrying fewer than 25 passengers are charged N$70 per entry. It is very important that you keep this receipt as you may be asked to produce it at police roadblocks, and fines will ensue if you can't produce it.

See opposite for information about driving around Namibia. Before departure you should always contact your local automobile association to double-check that you have all the necessary documents for driving around Namibia.

SOUTH AFRICA

You can drive to Namibia along good, sealed roads from South Africa, either from Cape Town (1490km) in the south, crossing the border at Noordoewer, or from Jo'burg (1970km) in the east, in which case the border crossing is at Nakop.

Hiring a Car in South Africa

Renting a car in South Africa will probably work out cheaper than renting one in Namibia. All major international car-rental companies have offices all over South Africa. Also recommended are the competitive local agencies **Around About Cars** (☎ 0860 422 4022; www.aroundabout cars.com), **Britz** (☎ 27-011 396 1860; www.britz.co.za) and **Buffalo Campers** (☎ 27-11 704 1300; www.buffalo .co.za), which offers a 4WD for about US$100 per day, including insurance, free kilometres and also cooking/camping equipment.

The cheapest 2WD will end up costing the rand equivalent of about US$40 per day, and a 4WD will cost in the region of US$85 per day.

Purchasing a Car in South Africa

If you are planning an extended trip (three months or more) in Namibia, it may be worth considering purchasing a second-hand car in South Africa.

It's worth noting that cars bought in Cape Town will be viewed less favourably at sale time than those purchased in Johannesburg. This is because Cape Town cars are considered to be at risk of rust given the city's seaside location. On the flipside, cars with a Jo'burg registration tend to fetch a higher premium when re-sold in Cape Town.

If you're buying, newspapers in Jo'burg are obviously one place to start looking. Used-car dealers won't advertise the fact, but they may be willing to buy back a car bought from them after about three months for about 60% of the purchase price – if the car is returned in good condition.

Naturally, check the vehicle documents from the previous owner. A roadworthy certificate (usually included when a car is bought from a used-car dealer) is required; as is a certificate from the police (also provided by most car dealers) to prove that the car isn't stolen. Once bought, re-register the vehicle at a Motor Vehicle Registration Division in a major city. Also recommended is a roadworthiness test by the Automobile Association (R100 to R300, membership not required) before you buy anything.

For a *very* rough idea of prices, don't expect a vehicle for less than the rand equivalent of US$4000 to US$6000. A 4WD Land Rover or equivalent model will cost around US$8000 to US$10,000.

Train

The only rail service still operating connects Keetmanshoop with Upington, South Africa (from N$90, 12½ hours, twice weekly). It departs Keetmanshoop at 9am Wednesday and Saturday, and Upington at 5am Sunday and Thursday. In Namibia, these trains connect with services to/from Windhoek (from N$75, 11 hours, daily Sunday to Friday). In South Africa, they connect with services to/ from Jo'burg and Cape Town.

GETTING AROUND

Namibia is a sparsely populated country, and distances between towns can be vast. However, there is an excellent infrastructure of sealed roads, and to more remote locations, there are well-maintained gravel and even salt roads. With such a low population density, it's hardly surprising that the public transport network is limited. Public buses do serve the main towns, but they won't take you to the country's major sights. By far the best way to experience Namibia is in the comfort of your own hire car.

AIR

Air Namibia has an extensive network of local flights operating out of Eros Airport (see p377). There are regular flights to Tsumeb; Rundu and Katima Mulilo; Lüderitz and Alexander Bay (South Africa); and Swakopmund and Oshakati/Ondangwa. Passengers are allowed a baggage limit of 20kg; additional weight will set you back around N\$20 per kilogram. For details of Air Namibia's local offices, log on to the website www.airnamibia.com.na.

Charter Flights

Charter flights are often the best – and sometimes the only – way to reach remote lodges. In the past it was possible to 'hitch a ride' on charter flights around the country, but in recent years the industry has become more regulated, and it is now virtually impossible to book a flight only, without also booking a safari package.

Some companies, however, do offer 'scenic' flights that enable you to enjoy the heady sensation of flying over Namibia's dramatic dunescapes. Pleasure Flights (see p320) in Swakopmund is just such an operation, offering flight-seeing tours along the Skeleton Coast and over Fish River Canyon. To get the best price you'll need a group of five people.

BICYCLE

Namibia is a desert country, and totally unsuitable for a biking holiday. Distances are great and horizons are vast; the climate and landscapes are hot and very dry; and, even along major routes, water is scarce and villages are widely spaced. What's more, the sun is intense and prolonged exposure to the burning ultraviolet rays is hazardous to your health. As if all of this wasn't enough of a deterrent, also bear in mind that bicycles are not permitted in any national parks.

Of course, loads of Namibians do get around by bicycle, and cycling around small cities and large towns is much easier than a cross-country excursion. With that said, be wary of cycling on dirt roads as punctures from thorn trees are a major problem.

Fortunately however, many local people operate small repair shops, which are fairly common along populated roadsides.

BUS

Namibia's bus services aren't extensive. Luxury services are limited to the **Intercape Mainliner** (☎ 061-227847; www.intercape.co.za), which has scheduled services from Windhoek to Swakopmund, Walvis Bay, Grootfontein, Rundu and Katima Mulilo. You're allowed only two items of baggage, which must not exceed a total of 30kg. Fares include meals on the bus. For details of prices see the relevant regional chapters.

There are also local combis (minibuses), which depart when full and follow main routes around the country. From Windhoek's Rhino Park petrol station they depart for dozens of destinations. For more details on local routes see the Getting There and Away section in regional chapters.

In Windhoek, a few cheap local buses connect the city centre with outlying townships, but they're rapidly being phased out in favour of the more convenient shared taxis.

CAR

The easiest way to get around Namibia is in your own car, and an excellent system of sealed roads runs the length of the country from the South African border at Noordoewer to Ngoma Bridge on the Botswana border and Ruacana in the northwest. Similarly, sealed spur roads connect the main north–south routes to Buitepos, Lüderitz, Swakopmund and Walvis Bay. Elsewhere, towns and most sites of interest are accessible on good gravel roads. Most C-numbered highways are well maintained and passable to all vehicles, and D-numbered roads, although a bit rougher, are mostly (but not always) passable to 2WD vehicles. In the Kaokoveld, however, most D-numbered roads can only be negotiated with a 4WD.

Nearly all the main car-rental agencies have offices at the airport. Ideally, you'll want to hire a car for the duration of your holiday, but if cost is an issue, you might consider a shorter hire from either Windhoek or Swakopmund. If you can muster a group of four, hiring a car will undoubtedly work out cheaper than an organised tour. For more information, see boxed text p176.

Automobile Associations

The **Automobile Association of Namibia** (Map p236; AAN; ☎ 061-224201; fax 222446; 15 Carl List House, Independence Ave, PO Box 61, Windhoek) is part of the international AA. It provides highway information and you can also acquire maps from them if you produce your membership card from your home country.

Driving Licence

Foreigners can drive in Namibia on their home driving licence for up to 90 days, and most (if not all) car-rental companies will accept foreign driving licences for car hire. If your home licence isn't written in English then you'd be better off getting yourself an International Driving Permit (IDP) before you arrive in Namibia.

Fuel & Spare Parts

The network of petrol stations in Namibia is good, and most small towns have a station. Mostly diesel, 95 unleaded and 97 super (leaded) are available, and one litre costs around N$10, although prices do vary according to the remoteness of the petrol station. Although the odd petrol station is open 24 hours, most are open 7am to 7pm.

All stations are fully serviced (there is no self-service), and a small tip of a couple of Namibian dollars is appropriate, especially if the attendant has washed your windscreen.

As a general road safety rule, you should never pass a service station without filling up, and it is advisable to carry an additional 100 litres of fuel (either in long-range tanks or jerry cans) if you're planning on driving in more remote areas. Petrol stations do run out of petrol in Namibia, so you can't always drain the tank and expect a fill-up at the next station.

Spare parts are readily available in most major towns, but not elsewhere. If you are planning on some 4WD touring, it is advisable to carry the following: two spare tyres, jump leads, tow rope and cable, a few litres of oil, wheel spanner and a complete tool kit. A sturdy roll of duct tape will also do in a pinch.

If you're renting a hire car make sure you check you have a working jack (and know how to use it!) and a spare tyre. As an extra precaution, double check that your spare tyre is fully pressurised as you don't want to get stuck out in the desert with only three good wheels.

Hire

For a compact car, the least expensive companies charge US$40 to US$60 per day (the longer the hire period, the lower the daily rate) with unlimited kilometres. Hiring a 4WD vehicle opens up remote parts of the country, but it can get expensive at US$85 to US$100 per day.

Most companies include insurance and unlimited kilometres in their standard rates, but some require a minimum rental period before they allow unlimited kilometres. Note that some internationally known companies, such as Avis and Budget, charge amenable daily rates, but sometimes only allow 200 free kilometres per day. Most companies also require a N$1000 deposit, and won't hire to anyone under the age of 23 (although some go as low as 21).

It's cheaper to hire a car in South Africa and drive it into Namibia, but you need permission from the rental agency, as well as the appropriate paperwork to cross the borders. Drivers entering Namibia in a foreign-registered vehicle with less than 25 passengers must pay a N$70 road tax at the border. Most major international car-rental companies will allow you to take a vehicle to neighbouring South Africa, Botswana and Zimbabwe, but only if you clear it with the company beforehand so they can sort out the paperwork. Rental companies are less happy about drivers going to Zambia, and will not allow you to go anywhere else in Africa.

Naturally, you should always check the paperwork carefully, and thoroughly examine the vehicle before accepting it. Car-rental agencies in Namibia have some very high excesses due to the general risks involved in driving on the country's gravel roads (for driving tips see p176). You should also carefully check the condition of your car and never *ever* compromise if you don't feel totally happy with its state of repair.

It is probably best to deal with one of the major car-rental companies listed below. For information about hiring a car in South Africa and then driving it to Namibia, see p382.

Avis (www.avis.com) Offices in Windhoek, Swakopmund, Tsumeb and Walvis Bay as well as at the airport.

Budget (www.budget.co.za) Another big agency with offices in Windhoek and Walvis Bay as well as at the airport.

Imperial (www.imperialcarrental.co.za) Offices in Windhoek, Swakopmund, Tsumeb, Lüderitz, Walvis Bay and at both Hosea Kutako and Eros airports.

Triple Three Car Hire (www.333.com.na) A competitive local car-rental firm with offices in Swakopmund and Walvis Bay.

Additional charges will be levied for the following: dropping off or picking up the car at your hotel (rather than the car-rental office); each additional driver; a 'cleaning fee' (which can amount to US$50!) may be incurred – at the discretion of the rental company; and a 'service fee' may be added.

Always give yourself plenty of time when dropping off your hire car to ensure that the vehicle can be checked over properly for damage etc. The car-rental firm should then issue you with your final invoice before you leave the office.

It is nearly always advisable to pay with a 'gold level' credit card which will offer you some protection should anything go wrong, and will possibly cover you for collision as well. American Express cards have a good reputation among travellers for providing comprehensive insurance for rental vehicles.

Insurance

Although insurance is not compulsory it is *strongly* recommended. No matter who you hire your car from, make sure you understand what is included in the price (unlimited kilometres, tax, insurance, collision-waiver and so on), and what your liabilities are. Most local insurance policies do not include cover damage to windshields and tyres.

Third-party motor insurance is a minimum requirement in Namibia. However, it is also advisable to take Damage (Collision) Waiver, which costs around US$20 extra per day for a 2WD; and about US$40 per day for a 4WD. Loss (Theft) Waiver is also an extra worth having.

For both types of insurance, the excess liability is about US$1500 for a 2WD and US$3000 for a 4WD. If you're only going for a short period of time, it may be worth taking out the Super Collision Waiver, which covers absolutely everything, albeit at a price.

Purchase

Unless you're going to be staying in Namibia for several years, it's not worth purchasing a vehicle in-country. The best place to buy a vehicle is across the border in South Africa (see p382).

Road Hazards

In addition to its fantastic system of sealed roads, Namibia has everything from high-speed gravel roads to badly maintained main routes, farm roads, bush tracks, sand tracks, salt roads and challenging 4WD routes. Driving under these conditions requires special techniques, appropriate vehicle preparation, a bit of practice and a heavy dose of caution. For in-depth tips on how to drive in the toughest conditions, see p176.

Around Swakopmund and Lüderitz you should also watch out for sand on the road. It's very slippery, and can easily cause a car to flip over if you're driving too fast. Early-morning fog along the Skeleton Coast roads is also a hazard so keep within the prescribed speed limits.

Road Rules

To drive a car in Namibia, you must be at least 21 years old. Like most other Southern African countries, traffic keeps to the left side of the road. The national speed limit is 120km/h on sealed roads out of habitation, 80km/h on gravel roads and 40km/h in all national parks and reserves. When passing through towns and villages, assume a speed limit of 60km/h, even in the absence of any signs.

Highway police use radar, and love to fine motorists (about N$70, plus an additional N$10 for every 10km you exceed the limit) for speeding. Sitting on the roof of a moving vehicle is illegal, and wearing seat belts (where installed) is compulsory in the front (but not back) seats. Drunk driving is also against the law, and your insurance policy will be invalid if you have an accident while drunk. Driving without a licence is also a serious offence. The legal blood-alcohol limit in Namibia is 0.05%.

If you have an accident causing injury, it must be reported to the authorities within 48 hours. If vehicles have sustained only minor damage, and there are no injuries – and all parties agree – you can exchange names and addresses and sort it out later through your insurance companies.

In theory, owners are responsible for keeping their livestock off the road, but in practice animals wander wherever they want. If you hit a domestic animal, your distress (and possible vehicle damage) will be compounded by the effort involved in finding the owner and the red tape involved when filing a claim. Wild animals can also be a hazard, even along the highways. The chances of hitting a wild or domestic animal is far, far greater after dark, so driving at night is definitely not recommended.

HITCHING

Although hitching is possible in Namibia, it's illegal in national parks, and even main highways receive relatively little traffic. On a positive note, it isn't unusual to get a lift of 1000km in the same car. Truck drivers generally expect to be paid, so agree on a price beforehand; the standard charge is N$15 per 100km.

Lifts wanted and offered are advertised daily at Cardboard Box Backpackers (p240) and Chameleon City Lodge (see p240) in Windhoek. At the Namibia Wildlife Resorts office, also in Windhoek (p234), there's a notice board with shared car hire and lifts offered and wanted.

Hitching is never entirely safe in any country; if you decide to hitch, understand that you are taking a small but potentially serious risk. Travel in pairs and let someone know where you're planning to go if possible.

MOTORCYCLE

Biking holidays in Namibia are popular due to the exciting off-road riding on offer. Unfortunately, however, it's difficult to rent a bike in Namibia, though the car companies listed in this section generally have a couple in their fleet. Note that motorcycles aren't permitted in the national parks, with the exception of the main highway routes through Namib-Naukluft Park.

LOCAL TRANSPORT

Public transport in Namibia is geared towards the needs of the local populace, and is confined to main roads between major population centres. Although cheap and reliable, it is of little use to the traveller as most of Namibia's tourist attractions lie off the beaten track.

Taxi

The standard shared taxi fare within Windhoek is approximately N$10, including to Khomasdal and Katutura. Note, however, that they operate like buses, and follow standard routes, so you have to know which ones are going your way.

Individual taxis, especially if you order one by phone, may charge anywhere from US$20 to US$50.

Only in Windhoek are taxis common – no other place is big enough to warrant extensive services. For more information see p247.

TRAIN

Trans-Namib Railways (☎ 061-2982032; www.transnamib .com.na) connects some major towns, but trains are extremely slow – as one reader remarked, moving 'at the pace of an energetic donkey cart'. In addition, passenger and freight cars are mixed on the same train, and trains tend to stop at every post, which means that rail travel isn't popular and services are rarely fully booked.

Windhoek is Namibia's rail hub, with services south to Keetmanshoop and Upington (South Africa); north to Tsumeb; west to Swakopmund; and east to Gobabis. Trains carry economy and business-class seats but, although most services operate overnight, sleepers are not available. Book at train stations or through the Windhoek booking office (p247); tickets must be collected before 4pm on the day of departure.

Tourist Trains

There are also two tourist trains, which are upmarket private charters that aim to recreate the wondrous yesteryear of rail travel. The relatively plush 'rail cruise' aboard the **Desert Express** (☎ 061-298 2600; www.desertexpress. na) offers a popular overnight trip between Windhoek and Swakopmund (single/double from N$2700/5100) twice weekly in either direction. En-suite cabins with proper beds and furniture are fully heated and air-conditioned, and have large picture windows for gazing out at the passing terrain. It also offers a special seven-day package (single/double from N$19,500/25,000) combining Swakopmund and Etosha National Park, complete with game drives, picnic bush lunches and plenty of long and glorious rail journeys to savour.

The **Shongololo Dune Express** (☎ in South Africa 27-21-556 0372; www.shongololo.com), which journeys between Cape Town and Tsumeb via Aus, Mariental, Swakopmund and Otjiwarongo, does 16-day trips taking in Namibia's main sites. All-inclusive fares range from N$37,000 to N$46,500 depending on the type of cabin. Regardless of which level you choose, the Shongololo is one of the world's most luxurious trains, and is something akin to a 5-star hotel on wheels. Guests are wined and dined to their stomach's content, and you can expect fine linens, hot showers, ample lounge space and a permeating sense of railway nostalgia.

Health

CONTENTS

As long as you stay up-to-date with your vaccinations and take basic preventive measures, you're unlikely to succumb to most of the health hazards covered in this chapter. While Botswana and Namibia have an impressive selection of tropical diseases on offer, it's more likely you'll get a bout of diarrhoea or a cold than an exotic malady. The main exception to this is malaria, which is a real risk in lower-lying areas.

BEFORE YOU GO

A little predeparture planning will save you trouble later. Get a check-up from your dentist and from your doctor if you have any regular medication or chronic illness, eg high blood-pressure and asthma. You should also organise spare contact lenses and glasses (and take your optical prescription with you); get a first-aid and medical kit together; and arrange necessary vaccinations.

Travellers can register with the **International Association for Medical Advice to Travellers** (IAMAT; www.iamat.org), which provides directories of certified doctors. If you'll be spending much time in more remote areas, consider doing a first-aid course (contact the Red Cross or St John's Ambulance), or attending a remote medicine first-aid course, such as that offered by **Wilderness Medical Training** (WMT; www.wildernessmedicaltraining.co.uk).

If you are bringing medications with you, carry them in their original containers, clearly labelled. A signed and dated letter from your physician describing all medical conditions and medications, including generic names, is also a good idea. If carrying syringes or needles, be sure to have a physician's letter documenting their medical necessity.

INSURANCE

Find out in advance whether your insurance plan will make payments directly to providers, or will reimburse you later for overseas health expenditures. In Botswana and Namibia, most doctors expect payment in cash. It's vital to ensure that your travel insurance will cover any emergency transport required to get you to a hospital in a major city, or all the way home, by air and with a medical attendant if necessary. Not all insurance covers this, so check the contract carefully. If you need medical assistance, your insurance company might be able to help locate the nearest hospital or clinic, or you can ask at your hotel. In an emergency, contact your embassy or consulate.

RECOMMENDED VACCINATIONS

The **World Health Organization** (www.who.int/en/) recommends that all travellers be covered for diphtheria, tetanus, measles, mumps, rubella and polio, as well as for hepatitis B, regardless of their destination. The consequences of these diseases can be severe, and outbreaks do occur.

According to the **Centers for Disease Control & Prevention** (www.cdc.gov), the following vaccinations are recommended for Botswana and Namibia: hepatitis A, hepatitis B, rabies and typhoid, and boosters for tetanus, diphtheria and measles. Yellow fever is not a risk in the region, but the certificate is an entry requirement if you're travelling from an infected region.

MEDICAL CHECKLIST

It's a very good idea to carry a medical and first-aid kit with you, to help yourself in the case of minor illness or injury. Following is a list of items to consider packing.

- antibiotics (prescription only), eg ciprofloxacin (Ciproxin) or norfloxacin (Utinor)
- antidiarrhoeal drugs (eg loperamide)
- acetaminophen (paracetamol) or aspirin
- anti-inflammatory drugs (eg ibuprofen)
- antihistamines (for hay fever and allergic reactions)
- antibacterial ointment (eg Bactroban) for cuts and abrasions (prescription only)
- antimalaria pills, if you'll be in malarial areas
- bandages, gauze
- scissors, safety pins, tweezers, pocket knife
- DEET-containing insect repellent
- permethrin-containing insect spray for clothing, tents and bed nets
- prickly-heat powder for heat rashes
- sun block
- oral rehydration salts
- iodine tablets (for water purification)
- sterile needles, syringes and fluids if travelling to remote areas

INTERNET RESOURCES
There is a wealth of travel health advice on the internet. The Lonely Planet website at www.lonelyplanet.com is a good place to start. The World Health Organization publishes the helpful *International Travel and Health,* available free at www.who.int/ith/. Other useful websites include **MD Travel Health** (www.mdtravelhealth.com) and **Fit for Travel** (www.fitfortravel.scot.nhs.uk).

Official government travel health websites include:

Australia (www.smarttraveller.gov.au/tips/travelwell.html)
Canada (www.hc-sc.gc.ca/index_e.html)
UK (www.dh.gov.uk/PolicyAndGuidance/HealthAdviceFor Travellers/fs/en)
USA (www.cdc.gov/travel/)

FURTHER READING
- *A Comprehensive Guide to Wilderness and Travel Medicine* (1998) Eric A Weiss
- *Healthy Travel* (1999) Jane Wilson-Howarth
- *Healthy Travel Africa* (2000) Isabelle Young
- *How to Stay Healthy Abroad* (2002) Richard Dawood

- *Travel in Health* (1994) Graham Fry
- *Travel with Children* (2009) Brigitte Barta et al

IN TRANSIT

DEEP VEIN THROMBOSIS (DVT)
Prolonged immobility during flights can cause DVT – the formation of blood clots in the legs. The longer the flight, the greater the risk. Although most blood clots are reabsorbed uneventfully, some might break off and travel through the blood vessels to the lungs, where they could cause life-threatening complications.

The chief symptom is swelling or pain of the foot, ankle or calf, usually but not always on just one side. When a blood clot travels to the lungs, it may cause chest pain as well as breathing difficulties. Travellers with any of these symptoms should immediately seek medical attention. Ways to prevent DVT include the following: walk about the cabin, perform isometric compressions of the leg muscles (ie contract the leg muscles while sitting), drink plenty of fluids and avoid alcohol.

JET LAG & MOTION SICKNESS
If you're crossing more than five time zones you could suffer jet lag, resulting in insomnia, fatigue, malaise or nausea. To avoid jet lag try drinking plenty of fluids (nonalcoholic) and eating light meals. Upon arrival, get exposure to natural sunlight and re-adjust your schedule (for meals, sleep etc) as soon as possible.

Antihistamines such as dimenhydrinate (Dramamine) and meclizine (Antivert, Bonine) are usually the first choice for treating motion sickness. The main side effect of these drugs is drowsiness. A herbal alternative is ginger (in the form of ginger tea, biscuits or crystallised ginger), which works like a charm for some people.

IN BOTSWANA & NAMIBIA

AVAILABILITY & COST OF HEALTH CARE
Good quality health care is available in all of Botswana and Namibia's major urban areas, and private hospitals are generally of excel-

lent standard. Public hospitals by contrast are often underfunded and overcrowded, and in off-the-beaten-track areas, reliable medical facilities are rare.

Prescriptions are generally required in Botswana and Namibia. Drugs for chronic diseases should be brought from home. There is a high risk of contracting HIV from infected blood transfusions if you need to receive a blood transfusion. To minimise this, seek out treatment in reputable clinics, such as those recommended in the country chapters of this book. The **BloodCare Foundation** (www.bloodcare.org. uk) is a useful source of safe, screened blood, which can be transported to any part of the world within 24 hours.

INFECTIOUS DISEASES

Following are some of the diseases that are found in Botswana and Namibia, though with a few basic preventative measures, it's unlikely that you'll succumb to any of these.

Cholera

Cholera is caused by a bacteria and spread via contaminated drinking water. You should avoid tap water and unpeeled or uncooked fruits and vegetables. The main symptom is profuse watery diarrhoea, which causes debilitation if fluids are not replaced quickly. An oral cholera vaccine is available in the USA, but it is not particularly effective. Most cases of cholera can be avoided by close attention to drinking water and by avoiding potentially contaminated food. Treatment is by fluid replacement (orally or via a drip), but sometimes antibiotics are needed. Self-treatment is not advised.

Dengue Fever (Break-bone Fever)

Dengue fever, spread through the bite of the mosquito, causes a feverish illness with headaches and muscle pains similar to those experienced with a bad, prolonged attack of influenza. There might be a rash. Mosquito bites should be avoided whenever possible. Self-treatment: paracetamol and rest.

Filariasis

Filariasis is caused by tiny worms migrating in the lymphatic system, and is spread by the bite from an infected mosquito. Symptoms include localised itching and swelling of the legs and/or genitalia. Treatment is available. Self-treatment: none.

Hepatitis A

Hepatitis A, which occurs in both countries, is spread through contaminated food (particularly shellfish) and water. It causes jaundice and, although it is rarely fatal, it can cause prolonged lethargy and delayed recovery. If you've had hepatitis A, you shouldn't drink alcohol for up to six months afterwards, but once you've recovered, there won't be any long-term problems. The first symptoms include dark urine and a yellow colour to the whites of the eyes. Sometimes a fever and abdominal pain might be present. Hepatitis A vaccine (Avaxim, VAQTA, Havrix) is given as an injection: a single dose will give protection for up to a year, and a booster after a year gives 10-year protection. Hepatitis A and typhoid vaccines can also be given as a single dose vaccine, hepatyrix or viatim. Self-treatment: none.

Hepatitis B

Hepatitis B, found in both countries, is spread through infected blood, contaminated needles and sexual intercourse. It can also be spread from an infected mother to the baby during childbirth. It affects the liver, causing jaundice and occasionally liver failure. Most people recover completely, but some people might be chronic carriers of the virus, which could lead eventually to cirrhosis or liver cancer. Those visiting high-risk areas for long periods or those with increased social or occupational risk should be immunised. Many countries now routinely give hepatitis B as part of the childhood vaccination program. It is given singly or can be given at the same time as hepatitis A (hepatyrix). A course will give protection for at least five years. It can be given over four weeks or six months. Self-treatment: none.

HIV

HIV, the virus that causes AIDS, is an enormous problem in Botswana and Namibia, with a devastating impact on local health systems and community structures. Botswana in particular has one of the highest rates of infection on the continent, with an HIV-positive incidence of more than 20% in Namibia and 40% in Botswana, second only to nearby Swaziland. The virus is spread through infected blood and blood products, by sexual intercourse with an infected partner, and from an infected mother to her baby during childbirth and breastfeeding.

HEALTH

It can be spread through 'blood to blood' contacts, such as with contaminated instruments during medical, dental, acupuncture and other body-piercing procedures, and through sharing used intravenous needles.

At present there is no cure; but medication that might keep the disease under control is available. In 2002 the Botswana government elected to make antiretroviral drugs available to all Batswana citizens free of charge, becoming the first country in the world to offer this treatment for free. Still, for people living in remote areas of the country access to such treatment is a problem, as is the continuing stigma attached to 'owning up' to having the infection. In Namibia, antiretroviral drugs are still largely unavailable, or too expensive for the majority of Namibians.

If you think you might have been infected with HIV, a blood test is necessary; a three-month gap after exposure and before testing is required to allow antibodies to appear in the blood. Self-treatment: none.

Malaria

Apart from road accidents, Malaria is probably the only major health risk that you face while travelling in this area, and precautions should be taken. The disease is caused by a parasite in the bloodstream spread via the bite of the female Anopheles mosquito. There are several types of malaria; falciparum malaria is the most dangerous type and the predominant form in Botswana and Namibia. Infection rates vary with season and climate, so check out the situation before departure. Several different drugs are used to prevent malaria, and new ones are in the pipeline. Up-to-date advice from a travel health clinic is essential as some medication is more suitable for some travellers than others (eg people with epilepsy should avoid mefloquine, and doxycycline should not be taken by pregnant women or children aged under 12).

The early stages of malaria include headaches, fevers, generalised aches and pains, and malaise, which could be mistaken for flu. Other symptoms can include abdominal pain, diarrhoea and a cough. Anyone who develops a fever in a malarial area should assume malarial infection until a blood test proves negative, even if you have been taking antimalarial medication. If not treated, the next stage could develop within 24 hours, particularly if falciparum malaria is the parasite: jaundice, then reduced consciousness and coma (also known as cerebral malaria) followed by death. Treatment in hospital is essential, and the death rate might still be as high as 10% even in the best intensive-care facilities.

Many travellers think that malaria is a mild illness, and that taking antimalarial drugs causes more illness through side effects than actually getting malaria. This is unfortunately not true. If you decide against antimalarial drugs, you must understand the risks, and be obsessive about avoiding mosquito bites. Use nets and insect repellent, and report any fever or flu-like symptoms to a doctor as soon as possible. Some people advocate homeopathic preparations against malaria, such as Demal200, but as yet there is no conclusive evidence that this is effective, and many homeopaths do not recommend their use.

Malaria in pregnancy frequently results in miscarriage or premature labour, and the

---

ANTIMALARIAL A TO D

■ A – Awareness of the risk. No medication is totally effective, but protection of up to 95% is achievable with most drugs, as long as other measures have been taken.

■ B – Bites, to be avoided at all costs. Sleep in a screened room, use a mosquito spray or coils, sleep under a permethrin-impregnated net at night. Cover up at night with long trousers and long sleeves, preferably with permethrin-treated clothing. Apply appropriate repellent to all areas of exposed skin in the evenings.

■ C – Chemical prevention (ie antimalarial drugs) is usually needed in malarial areas. Expert advice is needed as resistance patterns can change, and new drugs are in development. Not all antimalarial drugs are suitable for everyone. Most antimalarial drugs need to be started at least a week before and continued for four weeks after the last possible exposure to malaria.

■ D – Diagnosis. If you have a fever or flu-like illness within a year of travel to a malarial area, malaria is a possibility, and immediate medical attention is necessary.

risks to both mother and foetus during pregnancy are considerable. Travel throughout the region when pregnant should be carefully considered. Adults who have survived childhood malaria have developed immunity and usually only develop mild cases of malaria; most Western travellers have no immunity at all. Immunity wanes after 18 months of nonexposure, so even if you have had malaria in the past and used to live in a malaria-prone area, you may no longer be immune.

Rabies

Rabies is spread by receiving bites, or licks from an infected animal on broken skin. Few human cases are reported in Botswana and Namibia, with the risks highest in rural areas. It is always fatal once the clinical symptoms start (which might be up to several months after an infected bite), so post-bite vaccination should be given as soon as possible. Post-bite vaccination (whether or not you've been vaccinated before the bite) prevents the virus from spreading to the central nervous system. Animal handlers should be vaccinated, as should those travelling to remote areas where a reliable source of post-bite vaccine is not available within 24 hours. Three preventive injections are needed over a month. If you have not been vaccinated, you'll need a course of five injections starting 24 hours or as soon as possible after the injury. If you have been vaccinated, you'll need fewer post-bite injections, and have more time to seek medical help. Self-treatment: none.

Schistosomiasis (Bilharzia)

This disease is a risk in parts of Botswana and Namibia. It's spread by flukes (minute worms) that are carried by a species of freshwater snail, which then sheds them into slow-moving or still water. The parasites penetrate human skin during swimming and then migrate to the bladder or bowel. They are excreted via stool or urine and could contaminate fresh water, where the cycle starts again. Swimming in suspect freshwater lakes or slow-running rivers should be avoided. Symptoms range from none, to transient fever and rash, and advanced cases might have blood in the stool or in the urine. A blood test can detect antibodies if you might have been exposed, and treatment is readily available. If not treated the infection can cause kidney failure or permanent bowel damage. It's not possible for you to infect others. Self-treatment: none.

Tuberculosis (TB)

Tuberculosis is spread through close respiratory contact and occasionally through infected milk or milk products. BCG vaccination is recommended if you'll be mixing closely with the local population, especially on long-term stays, although it gives only moderate protection against the disease. TB can be asymptomatic, only being picked up on a routine chest X-ray. Alternatively, it can cause a cough, weight loss or fever, sometimes months or even years after exposure. Self- treatment: none.

Typhoid

This is spread through food or water contaminated by infected human faeces. The first symptom is usually a fever or a pink rash on the abdomen. Sometimes septicaemia (blood poisoning) can occur. A typhoid vaccine (typhim Vi, typherix) will give protection for three years. In some countries, the oral vaccine Vivotif is also available. Antibiotics are usually given as treatment, and death is rare unless septicaemia occurs. Self-treatment: none.

Yellow Fever

Although not a problem within Botswana and Namibia, you'll need to carry a certificate of vaccination if you'll be arriving from an infected country. For a list of countries with a high rate of infection, see the websites of the **World Health Organization** (www.who.int/wer/) or the **Centers for Disease Control & Prevention** (www.cdc.gov/travel/blusheet.htm).

TRAVELLERS' DIARRHOEA

This is a common travel-related illness, sometimes simply due to dietary changes. It's possible that you'll succumb, especially if you're spending a lot of time in rural areas or eating at inexpensive local food stalls. Sometimes dietary changes, such as increased spices or oils, are the cause. To help prevent diarrhoea, avoid tap water unless you're sure it's safe to drink (see p393). To avoid diarrhoea, only eat fresh fruits or vegetables that have been cooked or peeled, and be wary of dairy products that might contain unpasteurised milk. Although freshly cooked food can often be a safe option, plates or serving utensils might be dirty, so be selective when eating food from street vendors (make sure that cooked food is piping hot all the way through). If you develop diarrhoea, be sure to drink plenty of fluids, preferably an oral rehydration solution containing lots of water and some salt and sugar. A few loose stools don't require treatment but, if you start having more than four or five stools a day, you should start taking an antibiotic (usually a quinoline drug, such as ciprofloxacin or norfloxacin) and an antidiarrhoeal agent (such as loperamide) if you're not within easy reach of a toilet. If diarrhoea is bloody, persists for more than 72 hours or is accompanied by fever, shaking chills or severe abdominal pain, you should seek medical attention.

Amoebic Dysentery

Contracted by eating contaminated food and water, amoebic dysentery causes blood and mucus in the faeces. It can be relatively mild and tends to come on gradually, but seek medical advice if you think you have the illness as it won't clear up without treatment (which is with specific antibiotics).

Giardiasis

This, like amoebic dysentery, is also caused by ingesting contaminated food or water. The illness usually appears a week or more after you have been exposed to the offending parasite. Giardiasis might cause only a short-lived bout of typical travellers' diarrhoea, but it can also cause persistent diarrhoea. Ideally, seek medical advice if you suspect you have giardiasis, but if you are in a remote area you could start a course of antibiotics.

ENVIRONMENTAL HAZARDS
Heat Exhaustion

This condition occurs following heavy sweating and excessive fluid loss with inadequate replacement of fluids and salt, and is primarily a risk in hot climates when taking unaccustomed exercise before full acclimatisation. Symptoms include headaches, dizziness and tiredness. Dehydration is already happening by the time you feel thirsty – aim to drink sufficient water to produce pale, diluted urine. Self-treatment: fluid replacement with water and/or fruit juice, and cooling by cold water and fans. The treatment of the salt-loss component consists of consuming salty fluids as in soup, and adding a little more table salt to foods than usual.

Heatstroke

Heat exhaustion is a precursor to the much more serious condition of heatstroke. In this case there is damage to the sweating mechanism, with an excessive rise in body tempera-

ture, irrational and hyperactive behaviour, and eventually loss of consciousness and death. Rapid cooling by spraying the body with water and fanning is ideal. Emergency fluid and electrolyte replacement is usually also required by intravenous drip.

Insect Bites & Stings

Mosquitoes might not always carry malaria or dengue fever, but they (and other insects) can cause irritation and infected bites. To avoid these, take the same precautions as you would for avoiding malaria (see p390). Use DEET-based insect repellents. Excellent clothing treatments are also available; mosquitos that land on treated clothing will die. Bee and wasp stings cause real problems only to those who have a severe allergy to the stings (anaphylaxis). If you are one of these people, carry an EpiPen – an adrenaline (epinephrine) injection, which you can give yourself. This could save your life.

Scorpions are found in arid areas. They can cause a painful bite that is sometimes life-threatening. If bitten by a scorpion, seek immediate medical assistance. Medical treatment should be sought if collapse occurs.

Ticks are always a risk away from urban areas. If you do get bitten, press down around the tick's head with tweezers, grab the head and gently pull upwards. Avoid pulling the rear of the body as this may squeeze the tick's gut contents through the attached mouth parts into the skin, increasing the risk of both infection and disease. Smearing chemicals on the tick will not make it let go and is not recommended.

Bed bugs are found in hostels and cheap hotels and lead to itchy, lumpy bites. Spraying the mattress with crawling-insect killer after changing bedding will get rid of them. Scabies are also found in cheap accommodation. These tiny mites live in the skin, often between the fingers, and they cause an intensely itchy rash. The itch is easily treated with malathion and permethrin lotion from a pharmacy; other members of the household also need treating to avoid spreading scabies, even if they do not show any symptoms.

Snake Bites

Basically, avoid getting bitten! Don't walk barefoot, or stick your hand into holes or cracks. Boomslangs tend to hang out in trees, especially on overhanging limbs, so also exercise caution when walking in forests. However, about half of those bitten by venomous snakes are not actually injected with poison (envenomed). If bitten by a snake, do not panic. Note precisely what the snake looked like (if you can). Immobilise the bitten limb with a splint (such as a stick) and apply a bandage over the site with firm pressure, similar to bandaging a sprain. Do not apply a tourniquet, or cut or suck the bite. Get medical help as soon as possible. It will help get you the correct antivenin if you can identify the snake, so try to take note of its appearance.

Water

Stick to bottled water while travelling in Botswana and Namibia, and purify stream water before drinking it.

TRADITIONAL MEDICINE

According to estimates, as many as 85% of residents of Botswana and Namibia rely in part, or wholly, on traditional medicine. Given the high costs and unavailability of Western medicine in many rural areas, traditional healers are the first contact for many when falling ill. The *sangoma* (traditional healer) and *inyanga* (herbalist) hold revered positions in many communities, and traditional medicinal products are widely available in local markets. Unfortunately, some traditional medicines are made from endangered or threatened species like aardvarks, cheetahs and leopards.

HEALTH

Language

CONTENTS

WHO SPEAKS WHAT WHERE

Botswana

English is the official language of Botswana and is used extensively in most government departments and major businesses. It is the medium of instruction in all schools and universities from the fifth year of primary school and is understood by anyone who has had more than a basic education.

The most common language, however, is Tswana (p400), which is also commonly known as Setswana. Tswana is a Bantu language in the Sotho-Tswana language group that is understood by around 90% of the population. It is the language of the dominant population group, the Batswana, and is used as a medium of instruction in early primary school. The second most common Bantu language is Sekalanga, which is a derivative of the Shona language spoken by the Bakalanga people who are centred around Francistown.

The book *First Steps in Spoken Setswana* is a useful resource. It's available from book stores in Gaborone and Francistown. The *Setswana-English Phrasebook* is based on an original that was written many moons ago by Molepolole missionary AJ Wookey. It's a little confusing but is still the best phrasebook around.

Namibia

As a first language, most Namibians speak either a Bantu dialect or one of several Khoisan languages.

The Bantu language group includes the Owambo, Kavango, Herero and Caprivian languages. There are eight dialects from Owambo (p400); Kwanyama and Ndonga are the official Owambo languages. The Kavango has four separate dialects: Kwangali, Mbunza, Sambiyu and Geiriku, of which Kwangali is the most widely used. Herero (p398) is a rolling, melodious language, rich in colourful words. Most Namibian place names that begin with 'O' – eg Okahandja, Omaruru and Otjiwarongo – are derived from the Herero language. In the Caprivi, the most widely spoken language is Lozi (or Rotsi, p399), which originally came from Barotseland in Zambia.

Khoisan dialects include Khoikhoi (Nama), Damara (p396) and San dialects like !Kung San (p398). They are characterised by 'click' elements, which can be difficult to learn – but don't let that stop you from having a go. Names that include an exclamation mark are of Khoisan origin and should be rendered as a sideways click sound, similar to the sound one would make when encouraging a horse, but with a hollow tone (like the sound made when pulling a cork from a bottle). Many native Khoisan speakers also speak at least one Bantu and one European language, normally Afrikaans. The language of the Damara people, who are actually of Bantu origin, is also a Khoisan dialect.

The new constitution drawn up at the time of Namibian independence designated English as the official language, even though it was the native tongue of only about 2% of the population. It was decided that, with English, all ethnic groups would be at equal disadvantage, and it was recognised that adopting the language of international business would appeal to both tourists and investors. Since independence, Namibia has used an English-language curriculum for its educational system, but the most common lingua franca is Afrikaans (p395), which is the first language of more than 150,000 Namibians of diverse ethnic backgrounds. Most Namibian coloureds and Rehoboth Basters speak it as a first language and only in the Caprivi is English actually preferred over Afrikaans as a lingua franca.

Thanks to Namibia's colonial past, German is also widely spoken (p397), but is the first language of only about 2% of people. In the far north, around Rundu and Katima Mulilo, you'll also hear a lot of Portuguese.

AFRIKAANS
Pronunciation

a	as the 'u' in 'pup'
e	when word stress falls on **e**, it's as in 'net'; when unstressed, it's as the 'a' in 'ago'
i	when word stress falls on **i**, it's as in 'hit'; when unstressed, it's as the 'a' in 'ago'
o	as the 'o' in 'fort', but very short
u	as the 'e' in 'angel' with lips pouted
r	a rolled 'rr' sound
aai	as the 'y' sound in 'why'
ae	as 'ah'
ee	as in 'deer'
ei	as the 'ay' in 'play'
oe	as the 'u' in 'put'
oë	as the 'oe' in 'doer'
ooi/oei	as the 'ooey' in 'phooey'
tj	as the 'ch' in 'chunk'

Conversation & Essentials

Hello.	Hallo.
Goodbye.	Totsiens.
Good morning.	Goeiemôre.
Good afternoon.	Goeiemiddag.
Good evening.	Goeienaand.
Good night.	Goeienag.
Yes./No.	Ja./ Nee.
Please.	Asseblief.
Thank you.	Dankie.
Do you speak English/Afrikaans?	Praat u Engels/Afrikaans?
I only understand a little Afrikaans.	Ek verstaan net 'n bietjie Afrikaans.
How are you?	Hoe gaan dit?
Well, thank you.	Goed dankie.
Pardon.	Ekskuus.
How?	Hoe?
How many/much?	Hoeveel?
When?	Wanneer?
Where?	Waar?

Food & Drink

beer	bier
bread	brood
cheese	kaas

cup of coffee	koppie koffie
dried and salted meat	biltong
farm sausage	boerewors
fish	vis
fruit	vrugte
glass of milk	glas melk
meat	vleis
vegetables	groente
wine	wyn

In the Country

bay	baai
beach	strand
caravan park	woonwapark/karavaanpark
field/plain	veld
ford	drif
game reserve	wildtuin
hiking trail (short)	wandelpad
hiking trail (long)	staproete
lake	meer
marsh	vlei
mountain	berg
river	rivier

Numbers

1	een
2	twee
3	drie
4	vier
5	vyf
6	ses
7	sewe
8	ag
9	nege
10	tien
11	elf
12	twaalf
13	dertien
14	veertien
15	vyftien
16	sestien
17	sewentien
18	agtien
19	negentien
20	twintig
21	een en twintig
30	dertig

40	veertig
50	vyftig
60	sestig
70	sewentig
80	tagtig
90	negentig
100	honderd
1000	duisend

Shopping & Services

bank	bank
city	stad
city centre	middestad
pharmacy/chemist	apteek
police	polisie
post office	poskantoor
rooms	kamers
tourist bureau	toeristeburo
town	dorp

Time & Days

When?	Wanneer?
am/pm	vm/nm
today	vandag
tomorrow	môre
yesterday	gister
daily/weekly	daagliks/weekblad

Monday	Maandag (Ma)
Tuesday	Dinsdag (Di)
Wednesday	Woensdag (Wo)
Thursday	Donderdag (Do)
Friday	Vrydag (Vr)
Saturday	Saterdag (Sa)
Sunday	Sondag (So)

Transport & Directions

avenue	laan
car	kar
highway	snelweg
road	pad, weg
station	stasie
street	straat
track	spoor
traffic light	verkeerslig
utility/pick-up	bakkie

arrival	aankoms
departure	vertrek
one-way ticket	enkel kaartjie
return ticket	retoer kaartjie
to	na
from	van
left	links

right	regs
at the corner	op die hoek

DAMARA/NAMA

The very similar dialects of the Damara and Nama peoples, whose traditional lands take in most of Namibia's wildest desert regions, belong to the Khoisan group of languages.

As with the San dialects (see !Kung San on p398), they feature several 'click' elements, which are created by slapping the tongue against the teeth, palate or side of the mouth. These are normally represented by exclamation points (!), single or double slashes (/, //) and a vertical line crossed by two horizontal lines (‡).

Conversation & Essentials

Hello.	!Gâi tses.
Good morning.	!Gâi-//oas.
Good evening.	!Gâi-!oes.
Goodbye.	!Gâise hâre.
	(to a person staying)
Goodbye.	!Gâise !gûre.
	(to a person leaving)
Yes.	Î.
No.	Hâ-â.
Please.	Toxoba.
Thank you.	Aio.
Excuse me.	‡Anba tere.
Sorry/Pardon.	Mati.
How are you?	Matisa?
I'm well.	!Gâi a.
Do you speak English?	Engels !khoa idu ra?
What is your name?	Mati du /onhâ?
My name is ...	Ti /ons ge a ...
Where is the ...?	Mapa ... hâ?
Go straight.	‡Khanuse ire.
Turn left.	//Are /khab ai ire.
Turn right.	//Am /khab ai ire.
far	!nu a
near	/gu a
I'd like ...	Tage ra ‡khaba ...
How much?	Mati ko?
market	‡kharugu
shop	!khaib
small	‡khariro
large	kai
What time is it?	Mati ko /laexa i?
today	nets
tomorrow	//ari

Animals

baboon	//arub
dog	arib

EMERGENCIES – DAMARA/NAMA

Help!	Huitere!
Call a doctor!	Laedi aoba ‡gaire!
Call the police!	Lapa !nama ‡gaire!
Leave me alone.	//Naxu te.
I'm lost.	Ka tage hâi.

---

elephant	‡khoab
giraffe	!naib
goat	piri
horse	hab
hyena	‡khira
leopard	/garub
lion	xami
monkey	/norab
rabbit	!oâs
rhino	!nabas
warthog	gairib
zebra	!goreb

Numbers

1	/gui
2	/gam
3	!nona
4	haka
5	kore
6	!nani
7	hû
8	//khaisa
9	khoese
10	disi
50	koro disi
100	/oa disi
1000	/gui /oa disi

GERMAN

Owing to Namibia's colonial legacy, many Namibians speak German as a first or second language. It serves as the lingua franca in Swakopmund and is also widely used in Windhoek and Lüderitz.

Conversation & Essentials

Good day.	Guten Tag.
Goodbye.	Auf Wiedersehen.
Yes.	Ja.
No.	Nein.
Please.	Bitte.
Thank you.	Danke.
You're welcome.	Bitte sehr/Bitte schön.
Sorry. (excuse me, forgive me)	Entschuldigung.
Do you speak English?	Sprechen Sie Englisch?
How much is it?	Wieviel kostet es?

Shopping & Services

a bank	eine Bank
the ... embassy	die ... Botschaft
the market	der Markt
the newsagent	der Zeitungshändler
the pharmacy	die Apotheke
the post office	das Postamt
the tourist office	das Verkehrsamt

What time does it open/close?	Um wieviel Uhr macht es auf/zu?

EMERGENCIES – GERMAN

Help!	Hilfe!
Call a doctor!	Holen Sie einen Arzt!
Call the police!	Rufen Sie die Polizei!
I'm lost.	Ich habe mich verirrt.

Time, Days & Numbers

What time is it?	Wie spät ist es?
today	heute
tomorrow	morgen
yesterday	gestern
in the morning	morgens
in the afternoon	nachmittags

Monday	Montag
Tuesday	Dienstag
Wednesday	Mittwoch
Thursday	Donnerstag
Friday	Freitag
Saturday	Samstag/Sonnabend
Sunday	Sonntag

0	null
1	eins
2	zwei/zwo
3	drei
4	vier
5	fünf
6	sechs
7	sieben
8	acht
9	neun
10	zehn
11	elf
12	zwölf
13	dreizehn
100	hundert
1000	tausend

Transport & Directions

Where is the ...?	Wo ist die ...?
Go straight ahead.	Gehen Sie geradeaus.

Turn left.	Biegen Sie links ab.
Turn right.	Biegen Sie rechts ab.
near	nahe
far	weit
timetable	Fahrplan
bus stop	Bushaltestelle
train station	Bahnhof

HERERO/HIMBA

The Herero and Himba languages are quite similar, and will be especially useful when travelling around remote areas of North-Central Namibia and particularly the Kaokoveld, where Afrikaans remains a lingua franca and few people speak English.

Conversation & Essentials

Hello.	Tjike.
Good morning.	Wa penduka.
Good afternoon.	Wa uhara.
Good evening.	Wa tokerua.
Good night.	Ongurova ombua.
Yes.	Ii.
No.	Kako.
Please.	Arikana.
Thank you.	Okuhepa.
How are you?	Kora?
Well, thank you.	Mbiri naua, okuhepa.
Pardon.	Makuvi.
How many?	Vi ngapi?
When?	Rune?
Where?	Pi?

Do you speak ...?	U hungira ...?
Afrikaans	Otjimburu
English	Otjingirisa
Herero	Otjiherero
Himba	Otjihimba
Owambo	Otjiwambo

EMERGENCIES – HERERO/HIMBA

Help!	Vatera!
Call a doctor!	Isana onganga!
Call the police!	Isana oporise!
I'm lost.	Ami mba pandjara.

In the Country

caravan park	omasuviro uo zo karavana
game reserve	orumbo ro vipuka
(short) hiking trail	okaira komakaendro uo pehi (okasupi)
(long) hiking trail	okaira ko makaendero uo pehi (okare)

marsh	eheke
mountain	ondundu
point	onde
river (channel)	omuramba

Time, Days & Numbers

today	ndinondi
tomorrow	muhuka
yesterday	erero

Monday	Omandaha
Tuesday	Oritjaveri
Wednesday	Oritjatatu
Thursday	Oritjaine
Friday	Oritjatano
Saturday	Oroviungura
Sunday	Osondaha

1	iimue
2	imbari
3	indatu
4	iine
5	indano
6	hamboumue
7	hambomabari
8	hambondatu
9	imuvyu
10	omurongo

Transport

travel	ouyenda
arrival	omeero
departure	omairo
to	ko
from	okuza
one way (single)	ourike
return	omakotokero
ticket	okatekete

!KUNG SAN

The click-ridden languages of Namibia's several San groups are surely among the world's most difficult for the uninitiated to learn. Clicks are made by compressing the tongue against different parts of the mouth to produce different sounds. Perhaps the most useful dialect for the average traveller is that of the !Kung people, who are concentrated in Northern Namibia.

In normal speech, the language features four different clicks (lateral, palatal, dental and labial), which in Namibia are usually represented by //, ‡, /, and !, respectively. However, a host of other orthographies are in use around the region, and clicks may be represented as 'nx', 'ny', 'c', 'q', 'x', '!x', '!q', 'k', 'zh', and so on. To simplify matters, in the very rudimentary phrase list that follows, all clicks are represented by **!k** (locals will usually forgive you for ignoring the clicks and using a 'k' sound instead).

The first English-Ju/hoansi dictionary (Ju/hoansi is the dialect spoken by most Namibian San) was compiled in 1992 by the late Patrick Dickens, and published by Florida State University in the USA.

Greetings & Conversation

Hello.	*!Kao.*
Good morning.	*Tuwa.*
Goodbye, go well.	*!King se !kau.*
How are you?	*!Ka tseya/tsiya?* (to m/f)
Thank you (very much).	*(!Kin)!Ka.*
What is your name?	*!Kang ya tsedia/tsidia?* (to m/f)
My name is ...	*!Kang ya tse/tsi ...* (m/f)

LOZI

Lozi (also known as Rotsi) is the most common Caprivian dialect, and is spoken through much of the Caprivi region, especially around Katima Mulilo. As you can see from the list of options in the words and phrases below, social status is strongly reflected in spoken Lozi.

Conversation & Essentials

Hello.	*Eeni, sha.* (to anybody)
	Lumela. (to a peer)
	Mu lumeleng' sha. (to one or more persons of higher social standing)
Goodbye.	*Siala foo/Siala hande/Siala sinde.* (to a peer)
	Musiale foo/Musiale hande/Musiale sinde. (to more than one peer or one or more persons of higher social standing)
Good morning.	*U zuhile.* (to a peer)
	Mu zuhile. (to more than one peer or one or more persons of higher social standing)
Good afternoon/evening.	*Ki manzibuana.* (to anybody)
	U tozi. (to a peer)
	Mu tozi. (to one or more persons of higher social standing)
Good night.	*Ki busihu.* (to anybody)
Please.	*Sha.* (only used to people of higher social standing)

Thank you.	*N'itumezi.*
Thank you very much.	*N'i tumezi hahulu.*
Excuse me.	*Ni swalele.* (informal)
	Mu ni swalele. (polite)
Yes.	*Ee.* (to a peer)
	Eeni. (to more than one peer or one or more persons of higher social standing) Add *sha* at the end to mean 'sir/madam'.
No.	*Awa.* (to a peer or peers)
	Batili. (to one or more persons of higher social standing)
Do you speak English?	*Wa bulela sikuwa?* (to peers)
	W'a utwa sikuwa? (to more than one peer or one or more persons of higher standing)
	Mw'a bulela sikuwa?
	Mw'a utwa sikuwa?
I don't understand.	*Ha ni utwi.*
What is your name?	*Libizo la hao ki wena mang'?* (to peer)
	Libizo la mina ki mina bo mang'? (to a person of higher social standing)
What is this?	*Se king'?*
What is that?	*S'ale king'?/Ki sika mang' s'ale?* (near/far)
Where?	*Kai?*
Here.	*Fa/Kafa/Kwanu*
(Over) there.	*F'ale/Kw'ale*
Why?	*Ka baka lang'/Kauli?*
How much?	*Ki bukai?*
enough/finish	*Ku felile*

Time & Numbers

What time is it?	*Ki nako mang'?*
today	*kachenu*
tomorrow	*kamuso kakusasasa* (early morning) or *ka mamiso*
tomorrow	*kamuso*
yesterday	*mabani*

1	*il'ingw'i*
2	*z'e peli or bubeli*
3	*z'e t'alu or bulalu*
4	*z'e ne or bune*
5	*z'e keta-lizoho*
6	*z'e keta-lizoho ka ka li kang'wi*
7	*supile*
10	*lishumi*
20	*mashumi a mabeli*
1000	*likiti*

OWAMBO

Owambo (Oshiwambo) – and specifically the Kwanyama dialect – is the first language of more Namibians than any other and also the language of the ruling Swapo party. As a result, it's spoken as a second or third language by many non-Owambo Namibians of both Bantu and Khoisan origin.

Conversation & Essentials

Good morning.	Wa lalapo.
Good evening.	Wa tokelwapo.
How are you?	Owu li po ngiini?
I'm fine.	Ondi li nawa.
Yes.	Eeno.
No.	Aawe.
Please.	Ombili.
Thank you.	Tangi.
Do you speak English?	Oho popi Oshiingilisa?
How much is this?	Ingapi tashi kotha?
Excuse me.	Ombili manga.
I'm sorry.	Onde shi panda.
I'm lost.	Ombili, onda puka.
Can you please help me?	Eto vuluwu pukulule ndje?

Directions

Where is the ...?	Openi pu na ...?
here	mpaka
there	hwii
near	popepi
far	kokule
this way	no onkondo
that way	ondjila
Turn right.	Uka kohulyo.
Turn left.	Uka kolumoho.

Time, Days & Numbers

today	nena
yesterday	ohela
tomorrow	ungula

Monday	Omaandaha
Tuesday	Etiyali
Wednesday	Etitatu
Thursday	Etine
Friday	Etitano
Saturday	Olyomakaya
Sunday	Osoondaha

1	yimwe
2	mbali
3	ndatu
4	ne
5	ntano
6	hamano
7	heyali
8	hetatu
9	omugoyi
10	omulongo

TSWANA

Tswana, also commonly known as Setswana, is the language of the Tswana people.

Pronunciation

Tswana can be pronounced more or less as it is written. There are two exceptions to this: **g**, which is pronounced as English 'h' or, more accurately, as a strongly aspirated 'g'; and **th**, which is pronounced as a slightly aspirated 't'.

Accommodation

camping ground	lefelo la go robala mo tenteng
guesthouse	matlo a baeng
hotel	hotele
youth hostel	matlo a banana

Where is a ... hotel?	Hotele e e ... ko gae?
cheap	go tlase ka di tlotlwa
good	siame

Could you write the address?	Nkwalele aterese?
Do you have any rooms available?	A go na le matlo?

I'd like ...	Ke batla ...
a single room	kamore e le mongwe
a double room	kamore tse pedi
a room with a bathroom	kamore e e nang le ntlwana ya go tlhapela
to share a dorm	go tlhakanela kamore

How much is it ...?	Ke bokae ...?
for one night	bosigo bo le bongwe
for two nights	masego a mated
per person	motho a le mongwe

Conversation & Essentials

Hello.	Dumêla mma/rra. (to a woman/man) Dumêlang. (to a group)
Hello!	Ko ko! (announcing your arrival outside a yard or house)

Goodbye.	Tsamaya sentle. (to person leaving)
Goodbye.	Sala sentle. (to person staying)
Yes.	Ee.
No.	Nnyaa.
Please.	Tsweetswee.
Thank you.	Kea leboga.
Excuse me/Sorry.	Intshwarele.
Pardon me.	Ke kopa tsela.
OK/No problem.	Go siame.
How's it going?	O kae?
I'm fine.	Ke tlhotse sentle. (polite)
	Ke teng. (informal)
How are you?	A o tsogile?
	(lit: 'how did you wake up?'; asked in the morning)
	O tlhotse jang? (asked in the afternoon/evening)
Are you well?	A o sa tsogile sentle?
Yes, I'm well.	Ee, ke tsogile sentle.
Come on in!	Tsena!
What's your name?	Leina la gago ke mang?
My name is ...	Leina la me ke ...
Where are you from?	O tswa kae?
I'm from (Australia).	Ke tswa kwa (Australia).
Where do you live?	O nna kae?
I live in (Maun).	Ke nna kwa (Maun).
Where are you going?	O ya kae?

Directions

Which way is ...?	Tsela ... e kae?
Where is the station/hotel?	Seteseine/hotele se kae?
Can you show me on the map ...?	A o mpotshe mo mepeng?
Is it far?	A go kgala?
Go straight ahead.	Thlamalala.
Turn left.	Chikela mo molemong.
Turn right.	Chikela mo mojeng.
near	gaufi
far	kgakala

Food & Drink

What would you like?	O batla eng?
I'd like ...	Ke batla ...
I'm vegetarian.	Ke ja merogo fela.
Cheers!	Pula!
breakfast	sefitlholo
lunch	dijo tsa motshegare
dinner	selaelo

meals	dijo
menu	karate tsa dijo
beef	nama ya kgomo
bread	borotho
butter	mafura
chicken	koko
egg	mai
fish	tlhapi
food	dijo
fruit	leungo
goat	pudi
meat	nama
milk	mashi
mutton	nku
rice	raese
sugar	sukiri
vegetables	merogo
coffee	kofi
soft drink	sene tsididi
tea	tee
water	metsi
boiled water	metsi a a bedileng

Health

Where is the ...?	E ko kae ...?
chemist/ pharmacy	khemesiti
dentist	ngaka ya meno
doctor	ngaka
hospital	sepatela
I'm ill.	Ke a lwala.
My friend is ill.	Tsala yame e a lwala.
I need tampons	Ke mose tswalong.
I need pads.	Ke kopa go itshireletsa.
I'm suffering from thrush.	Ke na le bogwata mo bosading.
aspirin	pilisi
condoms	dikausu
diarrhoea	letshololo
medicine	molemo
nausea	go feroga sebete
stomachache	mala a a botlhoko
syringe	mokento

Language Difficulties

Do you speak (English)?	A o bua (Sekgoa)?
Does anyone here speak English?	A go na le o o bua Sekgoa?
I don't understand.	Ga ke tlhaloganye.
Could you speak more slowly, please?	A o ka bua ka bonya tswee-tswee?

Shopping & Services

I'm looking for a/the ...	Ke batla ...
bank	ntlo ya polokelo
city centre	toropo
market	mmaraka
museum	ntlo ya ditso
post office	poso
public toilet	matlwana a boitiketso
tourist office	ntlo ya bajanala
What time does it open/close?	Ke nako mang bula/tswala?
How much is it?	Ke bokae?
It's too expensive.	E a dura.
Can you lower the price?	Fokotsa tlhwatlhwa?

Time, Days & Numbers

What time is it?	Ke nako mang?
today	gompieno
tomorrow	ka moso
tonight	bosigong jono
yesterday	maabane
next week	beke e e tlang
afternoon	tshogololo
night	bosigo
Monday	mosupologo
Tuesday	labobedi
Wednesday	laboraro
Thursday	labone
Friday	latlhano

Saturday	matlhatso
Sunday	tshipi
0	lefela
1	bongwe
2	bobedi
3	borara
4	bone
5	botlhano
6	borataro
7	bosupa
8	borobabobedi
9	boroba bongwe
10	lesome
20	masome a mabedi
30	masome a mararo
40	masome a mane
50	masome a matlhano
60	masome amarataro
70	masome a supa
80	masome a a robang bobedi
90	masome a a robang bongwe
100	lekgolo
1000	sekete

Transport

Where is the ...?	E ko kae ...?
bus stop	maemelo a di bese
train station	maemelo a terena
What time does the ... leave/arrive?	E ... goroga nako mung?
boat	sekepe
bus	bese
canoe	mokoro
train	terena
I'd like ...	Ke batla ...
a one-way ticket	karata ya go tsamaya fela
a return ticket	karata ya go boa
first class	ya ntlha
second class	ya bobedi

Also available from Lonely Planet:
Africa Phrasebook

Glossary

ablutions block – camping-ground building with toilets, showers and a washing-up area
Afrikaans – language spoken in South Africa, which is a derivative of Dutch
ANC – African National Congress; ruling party in South Africa
apartheid – literally 'separate development of the races'; a political system in which people are officially segregated according to their race
ATVs – all-terrain vehicles

bakkie – Afrikaans term for a pick-up truck
Bantu – the name used to describe over 400 ethnic groups in Africa united by a common language
barchans dunes – migrating crescent-shaped sand dunes
Basarwa – Batswana term for the San people; it means 'people of the sticks' and is considered pejorative
Batswana – Tswana name for the people of Botswana; adjective referring to anything of or from Botswana; also (confusingly) refers to people from the Batswana tribe; plural of Motswana
BDF – Botswana Defence Force; the Botswanan army
BDP – Botswana Democratic Party
Bechuanaland – the name given by the British to describe the Crown Colony they established in Botswana in 1885
Benguela Current – the frigid current that flows northwards along the west African coast as far as Angola from Antarctica
biltong – dried meat that can be anything from beef to kudu or ostrich
biodiversity hotspot – the term used to describe an area that has a rich biological diversity that is also threatened with destruction
BNF – Botswana National Front
boerewors – Afrikaner farmer's sausage
Boers – the Dutch word for 'farmer' which came to denote Afrikaans-speaking people
bogobe – sorghum porridge; a staple food
bojalwa – a popular and inexpensive sprouted-sorghum beer
bojazz – Botswana jazz
boomslang – dangerous and venomous tree-dwelling 2m-long snake
borankana – Tswana word meaning traditional entertainment
borehole – a deep well shaft in the ground used for the abstraction of water, oil or gas
braai – Afrikaans term for a barbecue featuring lots of meat grilled on a special stand called a *braaivleis*

BSAC – British South Africa Company; late 19th-century company led by Cecil Rhodes
bushveld – flat grassy plain covered in thorn scrub

CDM – Consolidated Diamond Mines
Chibuku – *bojalwa* that is brewed commercially; the 'beer of good cheer' drunk in Zimbabwe and also in Botswana
chilli bites – spicy *biltong*, seasoned with *peri-peri*
CKGR – Central Kalahari Game Reserve
combi – usual term for 'minibus'
conflict diamonds – diamonds mined in conflict areas which are then sold illicitly
cuca shops – small bush shops of Northern Namibia; named for an Angolan beer that was once sold there

dagga – marijuana; pronounced 'dakha'
Debswana – De Beers Botswana Mining Company Ltd, partly owned by the Botswanan government, which mines, sorts and markets diamonds from Botswana
difaqane – forced migration or exodus by several Southern African tribes in the face of Zulu aggression in the 19th century
dikgotla – traditional Batswana council of village elders
Ditshwanelo – the Botswana Centre for Human Rights
donkey boiler – a water tank positioned over a fire and used to heat water
drankwinkel – literally 'drink shop', an off-licence or bottle store
drift – river ford, mostly dry
DTA – Democratic Turnhalle Alliance
dumpi – a 375ml bottle of beer
DWNP – Department of Wildlife and National Parks, which runs the Botswana government-owned national parks/reserves

efundja – period of heavy rainfall in Northern Namibia
ekipa – traditional medallion historically worn by Owambo women as a sign of wealth and status
elenga – village headman
eumbo – immaculate Owambo kraal; very much like a small village enclosed within a pale fence
euphorbia – several species of cactuslike succulents

FPK – First People of the Kalahari, a local advocacy organisation working for the right of San who have been forcibly resettled from the Central Kalahari Game Reserve in the town of New Xade

game scout camp – a term loosely referring to a park/reserve office; could be (but is not necessarily) a campsite

Gcawama – supernatural San being who represents evil
Gemütlichkeit – a distinctively German atmosphere of comfort and hospitality
Gondwanaland – the prehistoric supercontinent which included most of the land masses in today's southern hemisphere
GPS – Global Positioning System
Great Zimbabwe – an ancient Southern African city located in modern Zimbabwe that was once the centre of a vast empire known as Monomotapa
guano – droppings from seabirds or bats which is harvested as a fertiliser

inselberg – isolated range or hill typical of the pro-Namib and Damaraland plains

jarata – tiny yards of a traditional Batswana house
jesse – dense, thorny scrub, normally impenetrable to humans
jol – party, both verb and noun
Jugendstil – German art nouveau architecture prevalent in Swakopmund and parts of Windhoek and Lüderitz

karakul – variety of central Asian sheep, which produces high-grade wool and pelts
karata – phonecard; also ticket
KCS – Kalahari Conservation Society
KDT – Kuru Development Trust, based in D'kar near Ghanzi
kgadi – alcohol made from distilled brown sugar and berries or fungus
kgalagadi – Tswana word meaning 'the Kalahari Desert'
kgosi – Tswana word for 'chief'
kgotla – traditionally constructed Batswana community affairs hall or open area used for meetings of the *dikgotla*
Khoisan – language grouping taking in all Southern African indigenous languages
kimberlite pipe – geological term for a type of igneous intrusion, in which extreme heat and pressure have turned coal into diamonds
kloof – ravine or small valley
koeksesters – small, gooey Afrikaner doughnuts, dripping in honey or sugar syrup
kokerboom – quiver tree; grows mainly in Southern Namibia
konditorei – German pastry shop; found in larger Namibian towns
kopje – also *kopie;* small hill
kraal – Afrikaans version of the Portuguese word *'curral'*; an enclosure for livestock

lapa – circular area with a firepit, used for socialising
lediba – Tswana word for 'lagoon'; the singular of *madiba*
lekgapho – a unique Batswana design used to decorate *ntlo*

lekker – pronounced 'lakker'; anything that's good, nice or tasty
location – Namibian and South African name for township

mabele – Tswana word for sorghum, used to make *bogobe*
mabelebele – millet
madiba – Tswana word for 'lagoons', plural of *lediba*
magapu – melons
mahango – millet; a staple of the Owambo diet and used for brewing a favourite alcoholic beverage
maize mielies – imported food rapidly replacing *bogobe* and maybe *mabele* as a staple food in Botswana; sometimes known by the Afrikaans name, *mealie pap* or just *pap*
marimba – African xylophone, made from strips of resonant wood with various-sized gourds for sound boxes
mbira – see *thumb piano*
mealie pap – Afrikaans name for maize-meal porridge; a staple food for most Namibians
MET – Namibia's Ministry of Environment & Tourism
miombo – dry open woodland, comprised mostly of acacia and/or mopane or similar bushveld vegetation
Modimo – supreme being and creator of early Batswana tribal religion
mokolane – Tswana name for the palm *Hyphaene petersiana*
mokoro – traditional dugout canoe used in the Okavango Delta; plural *mekoro*
monoko – ground nuts or peanuts
morama – an immense tuber, the pulp of which contains large quantities of water and serves as a source of liquid for desert dwellers
Motswana – one Tswana person, ie the singular of Batswana
Mukuru – San first ancestor

Nacobta – Namibian Community-Based Tourism Association group, which organises community-based amenities for tourists, such as rest camps and tours of traditional areas
!nara – type of melon that grows in the Namib Desert
nartjie – tasty local tangerine; pronounced 'narkie'
NDF – Namibian Defence Forces, the Namibian military
ngashi – a pole made from the mogonono tree and used on a *mokoro*
NGO – nongovernmental organisation
N!odima – supernatural San being who represents good
n!oresi – traditional San lands; 'lands where one's heart is'
ntlo – round hut found in Batswana villages
NWR – Namibian Wildlife Resorts; semiprivate overseer of visitor facilities in Namibia's national parks
nxum – the 'life force' of the San people's tradition

GLOSSARY

omaeru – soured milk; a dietary staple of the Herero people
omiramba – fossil river channels in north and west Botswana; singular *omuramba*
omulilo gwoshilongo – 'sacred fire' that serves as a shrine in each Owambo *eumbo;* a log of mopane that is kept burning around the clock
oshana – dry river channel in Northern Namibia and Northwestern Botswana
oshikundu – alcoholic beverage made from *mahango;* popular throughout areas of Northern Namibia

pan – dry flat area of grassland or salt deposits, often a seasonal lake bed
panhandle – an informal geographic term used to describe an elongated protrusion of a geopolitical entity similar in shape to a peninsula and usually created by arbitrarily drawn international boundaries; in the case of Botswana and Namibia, this refers to the area of the Caprivi Strip
panveld – area containing many pans
pap – see *maize mielies*
participation safari – an inexpensive safari in which clients pitch their own tents, pack the vehicle and share cooking duties
peri-peri – chilli sauce of Portuguese origin often used on chicken meals
potjie – pronounced 'poy-kee', a three-legged pot used to make stew over an open fire; the word also refers to the stew itself, as well as a gathering in which a *potjie* forms the main dish
pronking – four-legged leaping, as done by some antelopes (particularly springboks)
pula – the Botswana currency; 100 thebe; also Tswana word for 'rain'

quadbike – four-wheeled motorcycle often called an ATV (all-terrain vehicle)

robot – a traffic light
rondavel – a round hut which is often thatched
rooibos – literally 'red bush' in Afrikaans; an insipid herbal tea that reputedly has therapeutic qualities
rusks – solid bits of biscuitlike bread made edible by immersion in tea or coffee

SACU – Southern African Customs Union, comprised of Botswana, South Africa, Lesotho, Namibia and Swaziland
San – a tribal group, which has inhabited Botswana for at least 30,000 years
sangoma – traditional Batswana doctor who believes that he/she is inhabited by spirits
savannah – grasslands with widely spaced trees
sefala huts – traditional granaries of the Batswana

segaba – a traditional musical instrument consisting of a bow made from one piece of long wood, a tin, nylon fishing line and fly whisk
seif dunes – prominent linear sand dunes, as found in the Central Namib Desert
Setswana – another word for Batswana or Tswana
shebeen – illegal drinking establishment
shongololo – ubiquitous giant millipede
Sperrgebiet – 'forbidden area'; alluvial diamond region of Southwestern Namibia
strandwolf – the Afrikaans name given to the Namib Desert brown hyena
Swapo – South-West Africa People's Organization; Namibia's liberation army and the ruling political party

thebe – one-hundredth of a pula; Tswana word for 'shield'
thumb piano – consists of narrow iron keys mounted in rows on a wooden sound board; the player plucks the ends of the keys with the thumbs; known as *mbira* in Tswana.
toktokkie – Afrikaans for the fog-basking tenebrionid beetle
township – indigenous suburb; generally a high-density black residential area
tsama – a desert melon historically eaten by the San people, and by livestock
Tswana – 'language of the Batswana; the predominant language of Botswana

Unita – National Union for the Total Independence of Angola
Uri – desert-adapted vehicle that is produced in Namibia

veld – open grassland, normally in plateau regions
veldskoens – comfortable bush shoes of soft leather, similar to moccasins; sometimes called *vellies*
Veterinary Cordon Fence – a series of 1.5m-high, wire fences aimed at segregating wild and domestic animals
vetoes – literally 'fat cake'; an Afrikaner doughnut
vile – pronounced 'flay'; any low open landscape, sometimes marshy
vlei – low-lying, marshy ground, covered with water during the rainy season

watt – Kavango dugout canoe
welwitschia – cone-bearing shrub native to the northern Namib plains
wildlife drive – a trip to spot wildlife, also known as a 'game drive'
WIMSA – Working Group for Indigenous Minorities of Southern Africa; an umbrella organisation representing a number of southern African minority groups
WMA – Wildlife Management Area

GLOSSARY

The Authors

MATTHEW D FIRESTONE
Coordinating Author, Namibia

Matt is a trained biological anthropologist and epidemiologist who is particularly interested in the health and nutrition of indigenous populations. His first visit to Botswana and Namibia in 2001 brought him deep into the Kalahari, where he performed a field study on the traditional diet of the San. Unfortunately, Matt's promising academic career was postponed due to a severe case of wanderlust, though he has relentlessly travelled to more than 50 different countries in search of a cure. Matt is hoping that this book will help ease the pain of other individuals bitten by the travel bug, though he fears that there is a growing epidemic on the horizon.

ADAM KARLIN
Botswana

On this trip, his third Africa expedition for Lonely Planet, Adam was charged by elephants, watched hippos dance to Credence Clearwater Revival, got drunk with a mad South African lion chaser, was lost in the desert where he almost froze to death until a dog fell asleep on him, and went on a road trip with Botswana's only licensed hypnotherapist. All in a day's work. Botswana, like everywhere else in Africa, shocked Adam with its beauty. He can't wait to go back.

CONTRIBUTING AUTHORS

David Lukas teaches and writes about the natural world from his home on the edge of Yosemite National Park. He has contributed Environment and Wildlife chapters to more than 25 Lonely Planet guides, including *Tanzania, East Africa, South Africa, Botswana & Namibia*, and *Ethiopia & Eritrea*.

Nicola Simmonds has worked in and backpacked around Indonesia, India, Sri Lanka, Europe, Japan, and Central and South America. Having then lived in Angola and Zimbabwe for seven years (with her husband and, eventually, three kids), mastering water shortages, African bureaucracy and out-of-control economies, covering Zimbabwe post 'dollarisation' was nothing but joy. She has just spent a year in Sri Lanka and is currently figuring out where to go next.

LONELY PLANET AUTHORS

Why is our travel information the best in the world? It's simple: our authors are passionate, dedicated travellers. They don't take freebies in exchange for positive coverage so you can be sure the advice you're given is impartial. They travel widely to all the popular spots, and off the beaten track. They don't research using just the internet or phone. They discover new places not included in any other guidebook. They personally visit thousands of hotels, restaurants, palaces, trails, galleries, temples and more. They speak with dozens of locals every day to make sure you get the kind of insider knowledge only a local could tell you. They take pride in getting all the details right, and in telling it how it is. Think you can do it? Find out how at **lonelyplanet.com**.

Behind the Scenes

THIS BOOK

The 1st edition of *Botswana & Namibia* was written by Paula Hardy and Matthew D Firestone, with contributions from Dr Caroline Evans (Health chapter), Ian Ketcheson, Fiona Watson and Elizabeth Bovair. This 2nd edition was written by Matthew D Firestone, Adam Karlin and Nicola Simmonds (Victoria Falls) with contributions from David Lukas and Mara Vorhees. This guidebook was commissioned in Lonely Planet's Melbourne office, and produced by the following:

Commissioning Editors Stefanie Di Trocchio, Holly Alexander, Shawn Low
Coordinating Editor Jeanette Wall
Coordinating Cartographer Birgit Jordan
Coordinating Layout Designer Vicki Beale
Managing Editor Brigitte Ellemor
Managing Cartographer Shahara Ahmed
Managing Layout Designer Sally Darmody
Assisting Editors Sarah Bailey, Carly Hall, Kristin Odijk
Cover Research Naomi Parker, lonelyplanetimages.com
Internal Image Research Jane Hart, lonelyplanetimages.com
Project Manager Chris Girdler
Language Content Laura Crawford

Thanks to Imogen Bannister, Lucy Birchley, Ross Butler, Melanie Dankel, Diana Duggan, Lisa Knights, Ross Macaw, Annelies Mertens, Wayne Murphy, Adrian Persoglia, Averil Robertson, Amanda Sierp, John Taufa, Tashi Wheeler, Juan Winata

THANKS
MATTHEW D FIRESTONE

To my wonderfully supportive parents, thank you so much for always sticking by my side, through both the highs and the lows. To Kim and Aki, thank you both for finally taking the trip out to Namibia and experiencing the country that I love so much. To my editor Stef, thank you for all the guidance and support you've shown me throughout this project. And last but not least, thank you to Adam for braving the Botswanan wilds – let's hope your survival skills serve you well on our next assignment, 2JG2 Chad.

ADAM KARLIN

Ke a leboga to Matt and Gordon, my South African buddies, JP, Tarryn, Celia and Marylin in Gaborone, Leslee Hall in the USA, Mma George at Botswana tourism, Lorraine, Karen, Dani and Kay in Maun, Sally, Sean, Heloise and Adrian (my adopted Motswana family) and KT, KB and the rest of the bar staff at the Bridge who successfully calculated my tab. And thanks to Matthew Firestone for his patience on producing 2JG2 Southern Africa. *Tsamaya sentle.*

THE LONELY PLANET STORY

Fresh from an epic journey across Europe, Asia and Australia in 1972, Tony and Maureen Wheeler sat at their kitchen table stapling together notes. The first Lonely Planet guidebook, *Across Asia on the Cheap,* was born.

Travellers snapped up the guides. Inspired by their success, the Wheelers began publishing books to Southeast Asia, India and beyond. Demand was prodigious, and the Wheelers expanded the business rapidly to keep up. Over the years, Lonely Planet extended its coverage to every country and into the virtual world via lonelyplanet.com and the Thorn Tree message board.

As Lonely Planet became a globally loved brand, Tony and Maureen received several offers for the company. But it wasn't until 2007 that they found a partner whom they trusted to remain true to the company's principles of travelling widely, treading lightly and giving sustainably. In October of that year, BBC Worldwide acquired a 75% share in the company, pledging to uphold Lonely Planet's commitment to independent travel, trustworthy advice and editorial independence.

Today, Lonely Planet has offices in Melbourne, London and Oakland, with over 500 staff members and 300 authors. Tony and Maureen are still actively involved with Lonely Planet. They're travelling more often than ever, and they're devoting their spare time to charitable projects. And the company is still driven by the philosophy of *Across Asia on the Cheap*: 'All you've got to do is decide to go and the hardest part is over. So go!'

408

BEHIND THE SCENES

NICOLA SIMMONDS

There are four people I want to thank: James, my husband, for covering for me while I was gone; Justine Smith for donning her backpack and joining me on the road – and off the Falls; the world's best travel agent: Belinda at Experience Africa Safaris in Harare; and finally, Richard of Fawlty Towers, Livingstone, who's on a passionate crusade to bring back budget travel so more and more people will come to Africa for 'the experience of their lifetime' – his words.

OUR READERS

Many thanks to the travellers who used the last edition and wrote to us with helpful hints, useful advice and interesting anecdotes:

Celia Alfie, Peter Birkert, Julian Blackshaw, Johannes Blaschegg, Bernhard Bouzek, Birgit Braun, Phileem Calder-Potts, Bonnie Carol, Catherine Couturier, Ray Cranston, Jeanie Davison, Niels, Ellenbroek, Frans Ewals, Birte Gernhardt, Cees Geuzebroek, Helle Goldman, Helen Gourley, Cecilia Harlitz, Melanie Henschel, Annette Hilton, Myriam Kamminga, Pauline Karelse, Aleksander Kedzior, Annelies Kolk, Klaus-Peter Kownatzki, Audun Lem, Roger Litton, Francesca Longhi, Erich Looser, Kersten Mangado, Gary Malinek, Claire Mcquillam, Krzysztof Miduch, Gretchen Miller, John Mole, Paul Nugteren, Corinne Parnell, Michael Poesen, Charlie Radclyffe, James Rodgers, Milena Sardella, Valeska Schaudy, Patrick Schmidt, Alex Schulte, Jeremy Stokes, Samantha Sutherland, Severine Thomas, Fabio Tosetti, Eddy Veraghtert, Angeline Veraghtert, Susanne Viebahn, Alan Whitworth, Virginia Winstanley.

ACKNOWLEDGMENTS
Many thanks to the following for the use of their content:

Globe on title page ©Mountain High Maps 1993 Digital Wisdom, Inc.

Internal photographs by Lonely Planet Images, and by Adrian Bailey p34 (#1), p36 (#1), p37 (#2), p39 (#2), p43 (#2), p44 (#1), p45 (#4); Pascale Beroujon p48 (#1, #2); Manfred Gottschalk p46 (#4); Dave Hamman p34 (#4), p35 (#3), p38 (#1), p42 (#1); Luke Hunter p44 (#5); Dennis Jones p38 (#4), p47 (#2), p48 (#3); Frans Lemmens p46 (#1); Andrew Parkinson p33, p35 (#2), p36 (#3), p37 (#3), p41 (#2, #3), p45 (#3); Carol Polich p40 (#4), p47 (#3); Mitch Reardon p40 (#1); David Wall p39 (#3), p42 (#4), p45 (#2); Ariadne Van Zandbergen p43 (#3).

All images are the copyright of the photographers unless otherwise indicated. Many of the images in this guide are available for licensing from Lonely Planet Images: www.lonelyplanetimages.com.

SEND US YOUR FEEDBACK

We love to hear from travellers – your comments keep us on our toes and help make our books better. Our well-travelled team reads every word on what you loved or loathed about this book. Although we cannot reply individually to postal submissions, we always guarantee that your feedback goes straight to the appropriate authors, in time for the next edition. Each person who sends us information is thanked in the next edition and the most useful submissions are rewarded with a free book.

To send us your updates – and find out about Lonely Planet events, newsletters and travel news – visit our award-winning website: **lonelyplanet.com/contact.**

Note: we may edit, reproduce and incorporate your comments in Lonely Planet products such as guidebooks, websites and digital products, so let us know if you don't want your comments reproduced or your name acknowledged. For a copy of our privacy policy visit lonelyplanet.com/privacy.

Index

000 Map pages
000 Photograph pages

GreenDex

It seems like everyone's going 'green' these days, but how can you know which businesses are actually ecofriendly and which are simply jumping on the sustainable bandwagon? The following listings have all been selected by Lonely Planet authors because they demonstrate an active sustainable-tourism policy. Some are involved in conservation or environmental education, and many are owned and operated by local and indigenous operators, thereby maintaining and preserving regional identity and culture.

We want to keep developing our sustainable-tourism content. If you think we've omitted someone who should be listed here, or if you disagree with our choices, email us at talk2us@lonelyplanet.com.au. For more information about sustainable tourism and Lonely Planet, see www.lonelyplanet.com/responsibletravel.

424

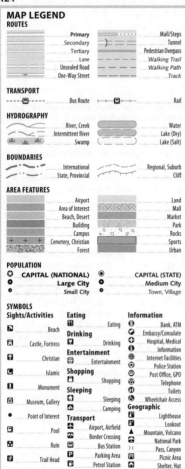

MAP LEGEND

ROUTES
- Primary
- Secondary
- Tertiary
- Lane
- Unsealed Road
- One-Way Street
- Mall/Steps
- Tunnel
- Pedestrian Overpass
- Walking Trail
- Walking Path
- Track

TRANSPORT
- Bus Route
- Rail

HYDROGRAPHY
- River, Creek
- Intermittent River
- Swamp
- Water
- Lake (Dry)
- Lake (Salt)

BOUNDARIES
- International
- State, Provincial
- Regional, Suburb
- Cliff

AREA FEATURES
- Airport
- Area of Interest
- Beach, Desert
- Building
- Campus
- Cemetery, Christian
- Forest
- Land
- Mall
- Market
- Park
- Rocks
- Sports
- Urban

POPULATION
- ⊕ CAPITAL (NATIONAL)
- ● Large City
- ○ Small City
- ◉ CAPITAL (STATE)
- ● Medium City
- ○ Town, Village

SYMBOLS

Sights/Activities
- 🏊 Beach
- 🏰 Castle, Fortress
- ✝ Christian
- ☪ Islamic
- 🏛 Monument
- 🏛 Museum, Gallery
- ● Point of Interest
- 🏊 Pool
- 💠 Ruin
- 🥾 Trail Head
- 🐦 Zoo, Bird Sanctuary

Eating
- 🍴 Eating

Drinking
- ☕ Drinking

Entertainment
- 🎭 Entertainment

Shopping
- 🛍 Shopping

Sleeping
- 🛏 Sleeping
- ⛺ Camping

Transport
- ✈ Airport, Airfield
- Border Crossing
- 🚌 Bus Station
- 🅿 Parking Area
- ⛽ Petrol Station
- 🚕 Taxi Rank

Information
- 💲 Bank, ATM
- Embassy/Consulate
- ✚ Hospital, Medical
- Information
- @ Internet Facilities
- Police Station
- Post Office, GPO
- ☎ Telephone
- Toilets
- ♿ Wheelchair Access

Geographic
- 🗼 Lighthouse
- Lookout
- ▲ Mountain, Volcano
- National Park
-)(Pass, Canyon
- 🏕 Picnic Area
- Shelter, Hut
- Waterfall

LONELY PLANET OFFICES

Australia (Head Office)
Locked Bag 1, Footscray, Victoria 3011
☎ 03 8379 8000, fax 03 8379 8111
talk2us@lonelyplanet.com.au

USA
150 Linden St, Oakland, CA 94607
☎ 510 250 6400, toll free 800 275 8555
fax 510 893 8572
info@lonelyplanet.com

UK
2nd fl, 186 City Rd,
London EC1V 2NT
☎ 020 7106 2100, fax 020 7106 2101
go@lonelyplanet.co.uk

Published by Lonely Planet Publications Pty Ltd
ABN 36 005 607 983

Printed by Gopsons Papers Ltd.
Printed in India.